Economic Prospects for the Northeast

Economic Prospects for the Northeast

---

edited by HARRY W. RICHARDSON

JOSEPH H. TUREK

 Temple University Press · *Philadelphia*

Temple University Press, Philadelphia 19122
© 1985 by Temple University. All rights reserved
Published 1985

Printed in the United States of America

Library of Congress Cataloging in Publication Data
Main entry under title:

Economic prospects for the Northeast.

 Includes bibliographical references and index.
 1. Northeastern States—Economic conditions—Addresses,
essays, lectures.   2. Northeastern States—Economic
policy—Addresses, essays, lectures.   I. Richardson, Harry
Ward.   II. Turek, Joseph H.
HC107.A115E26   1984   338.974   84-2617
ISBN 0-87722-360-2

Contents

Tables

Figures

Preface and Acknowledgments

With the exceptions of Chapters 1, 2, and 12, earlier versions of each chapter were presented at a conference on "Economic Prospects of the Northeast" held at the State University of New York (SUNY) at Albany, April 16–17, 1982, under the SUNY Research Foundation's Conversations within the Disciplines Program. The idea behind the conference was to bring together a variety of viewpoints on diagnosis and interpretation of economic trends, assessment of future prospects, and evaluation of policy options relating to the economic development of the northeastern United States. The contributors were selected not only for their specific areas of experience but also to represent a wide spectrum of opinions. As a result, the book reflects intellectual diversity rather than monolithic judgments. The participants in the conference included not only academics and researchers but also state officials, practicing planners, businessmen, and interested citizens. Their contributions helped to enliven the discussion on the papers and assisted in their revision.

We are very grateful for financial support to: the SUNY Research Foundation; Dr. Warren Ilchman, Vice President of Research, and Dean of the Graduate School at SUNY–Albany; and Dr. John Webb, Dean of the College of Social and Behavioral Sciences, SUNY–Albany. Without their help the conference could not have taken place and the book could not have been produced. We also thank Mrs. June Kennedy for efficiently typing the manuscript.

HARRY W. RICHARDSON
JOSEPH H. TUREK

DECEMBER 1983

xiii

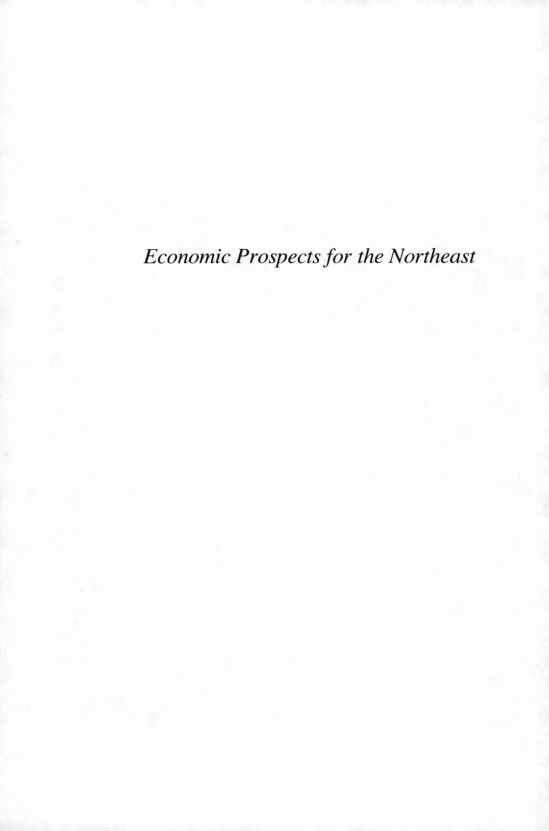

Economic Prospects for the Northeast

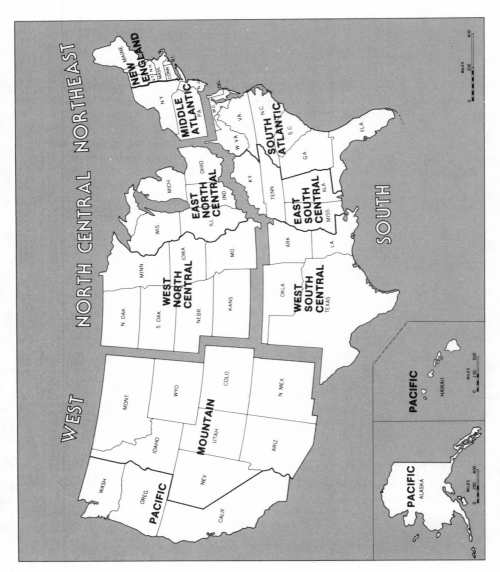

Regions of the United States. *Source:* U.S. Department of Commerce, Bureau of the Census.

HARRY W. RICHARDSON

JOSEPH H. TUREK

1 *Introduction*

This book diagnoses economic problems of the Northeast[1] in the context of national economic development, assesses its future prospects, and discusses what, if anything, might be done in terms of policy to enhance these prospects. Because the book consists of chapters written by several authors, it does not speak with one voice. Instead, there is a diversity of views on diagnosis, prediction, and prescription. We regard this diversity as a benefit since the purpose of the book is to illuminate the debate, not to offer pat solutions to very complex problems.

In spite of their different perspectives, some of which reflect alternative ideologies, the authors agree that the last decade has been an era of much slower national (and indeed world) economic growth and that the Northeast has—with the exception of a few bright spots—performed much below the national average. Although this slower growth is worrisome to residents and policymakers in the region, it is not necessarily a problem for the country as a whole because the Northeast is traditionally a high-income region; so its slower growth compared with other regions (especially those in the South and the West—apart from California) could be reconciled with interregional convergence in per capita incomes.

[1]The Northeast encompasses the New England (Connecticut, Maine, Massachusetts, New Hampshire, Rhode Island, and Vermont) and the Middle Atlantic census regions (New York, New Jersey, and Pennsylvania). Some of the analysis could also be extended to the industrial states of the Midwest such as Ohio, Illinois, and Michigan.

There are difficulties with this sanguine view. In many areas of the North-east, unusually high living costs erode much of the region's apparent income advantage. It is unclear whether or not proper deflation of the region's above-average money income per capita would pull real income below the United States average. If current trends continue, however, a drop below average would occur in the relatively near future. Although no region has any right to a standard of living above the national average, and some regions must fall below average unless living standards are uniform everywhere, dropping be-low the national average is especially painful to residents of a region that has been one of the wealthiest in the country for much of its history.

Much depends, of course, on the region's prospective income path in the medium-term future. There are at least three alternative scenarios. One is based on the hypothesis that interregional factor movements are equilibrating so that all regions will converge to a stable equilibrium in which regional per capita incomes are more or less all at the same level, except for minor perturbations.

The second scenario assumes that both capital and labor are shifting from the Frostbelt to the Sunbelt in response to agglomeration economies in Sun-belt cities and that this process will not be reversed easily. The result is a persistent rise in per capita incomes in the Sunbelt regions relative to the Northeast and the Midwest. The prognosis is that the per capita income time paths will cross over and subsequently diverge.

A third hypothesis accepts the cross-over thesis but argues that powerful equilibrating mechanisms, specifically changes in relative costs, prices, and wages among regions, will eventually reverse the process. The Sunbelt will then become relatively unattractive to both migrants and mobile industry be-cause of rising housing and other living costs and production (especially wage and land) costs respectively. Moreover, the favorable resource endow-ments of some parts of the Sunbelt (e.g., plentiful energy supplies) are offset by supply problems in others, such as the potentially severe water shortage that afflicts much of the West as its population and economic base continue to expand.[2] According to these views, any tendency for regional income paths to diverge in favor of the West and the South will not last for more than a decade or two but will boomerang back. The long-run time paths of regional per capita incomes might then be described in terms of secular cycles, ac-cording to which regional incomes rise above or fall below the national aver-age depending on their relative cost and price advantages or disadvantages.

Optimism about the long-run prospects for the Northeast rests heavily on which of these alternative scenarios is preferred. The stable-equilibrium sce-

[2] Furthermore, a faster rate of exploitation of the West's energy resources will exacerbate its water supply problems (Ballard and Devine, 1982).

nario is the most optimistic because it implies an end to the net shifts out of the region that have been dominant in recent decades. The cyclical scenario is also relatively optimistic since the situation will be self-correcting, and at some point in the future the region will again become attractive to mobile population and economic activities. The troubling features of this scenario are uncertainty about when the turning point will occur and concern about the length and amplitude of the cycles. The cross-over scenario offers the most pessimistic outlook because it implies, at least in the absence of strong intervention, a downward path for the region that will not be reversed easily. According to this scenario, the Northeast (the New England and Middle Atlantic states) might become the poorest of the census regions by the year 2000. Those who subscribe to this view of the future are unlikely to favor standing idly by and allowing it to happen.

Prospects for the region are substantially affected by what happens to the national economy. Regional economic development depends considerably on national economic development. As argued in Chapter 12, there is a growing belief that national (and world) economic growth is slowing down, more or less permanently. If this is so, it will be increasingly difficult for currently slow-growing regions to grow at all. A slowing down in national growth does not necessarily moderate interregional differentials in economic performance. Moreover, "slowth" (slow growth) impedes the formation of a national consensus in support of intervention to help lagging regions. When the economy grows at a healthy rate, the residents of rapidly growing and prosperous regions may be willing to share an increment of their growth with those in less-fortunate regions. As "slowth" sets in, on the other hand, interregional development tends toward a zero-sum game in which gains to some regions imply *absolute* losses to others. Under such conditions, inhabitants of relatively well-off regions will be less tolerant of a decline in absolute incomes to compensate less-favored regions.

Future prospects for the Northeast will vary from one part of the region to another. A region made up of nine states with heterogeneous economic structures cannot be treated as a uniform entity. Most of the chapters in this book recognize these interstate differences, but it should also be emphasized that the heterogeneity continues down to the intrastate level. The most striking example of local spatial diversity is within New York City where the economic buoyancy of Manhattan associated with the strength of the quaternary sector contrasts vividly with the stagnation of the surrounding boroughs (see Chapter 9). There are many other illlustrations of local differentials in current economic performance and future prospects throughout the region. For example, the much-vaunted injection into the region's aging industrial structure of a dynamic "high-tech" sector is limited to a few geographical areas such as parts of Massachusetts, Connecticut, and a few counties within New

York State (e.g., Westchester, Nassau, and Suffolk).[3] A detailed evaluation of the region's economic future would need to be undertaken at a high degree of spatial disaggregation, such as subregions within each state. Although many chapters in this book discriminate among different parts of the region (especially at the state level), microspatial studies remain a target for future research.

One of the most striking findings of this study (demonstrated in detail in Chapter 3) is that the economic deceleration of the Northeast is not a recent phenomenon, as implied in popular debate on Frostbelt–Sunbelt shifts, but goes back at least fifty years, to 1930 and probably earlier. The future of the region must be analyzed in the context of its long-run past rather than in terms of what has happened in the last decade or so. However, many economic indicators suggest that the *relative* decline in the 1970s was more precipitous than in preceding decades. The conundrum is whether the intensification of the last decade marks the beginning of a new era or whether the future will be more like the relatively smooth readjustments of the last fifty years. Of course, the answer to this question may depend heavily on what happens to the national economy over the next twenty years (i.e., will the "slowth" hypothesis turn out to be correct?). Also, there are other speculations. For instance, the secular-cycles scenario raises the possibility of a turnaround in the region, whereby growth performance will be much less sluggish than in the past (see Chapter 5). How we assess these prospects will determine whether or not public policy intervention is needed and, if so, what types of policy are most appropriate.

Among the authors, there is no clear consensus about what policy actions may be appropriate. Vaughan, for example, favors the creation of incentives at the state level to promote the development and growth of new, small, and innovative firms (Chapter 10), while both Harrison and Savitch (Chapters 7 and 9 respectively) argue that there is a major role in regional and local development for "creative" public enterprise (a position rejected by Vaughan on the ground that governments cannot afford to hire high-quality venture capitalists). This is just one example of disagreement, or at least varying shades of opinion, among analysts of the regional problem. Others (not among the authors represented here) have proposed a massive capital investment and infrastructure program to revitalize the aging urban and industrial capital stock of the Northeast (e.g., the Reconstruction Finance Corporation proposal of Felix Rohatyn[4]). However, the role of public infrastructure in inducing private investment, particularly in cases of long-established industrial regions as opposed to newly developing regions, is not known. Another

[3]In discussing the reinvigorating role of "high-tech" industries, their potential negative effects on income distribution have to be considered in any balanced assessment (see Chapter 7).

[4]A summary of this proposal is given in F. G. Rohatyn's "Alternatives to Reaganomics," *New York Times Magazine*, 5 December 1982, pp. 72–90.

choice may be between economic revitalization and social amelioration. In another context, Miernyk (1982) has suggested that the latter course may be more appropriate for Frostbelt states.

There may be more scope for state and local government intervention than for the federal spatial policies that were dominant in the 1960s. Federal spatial intervention was never very successful because the political process inhibited discrimination in favor of severely depressed states. Moreover, pressures for reduction in the size (or at least moderation in the expansion) of the federal government have now spread beyond the Republican party. To the extent that place-oriented policies are feasible, they are probably most effective if they are targeted at specific problem areas within states rather than applied to broad regions. Of course, there are sound and unsound state policies. If state and local governments were to engage in competitive bidding to attract outside industry (a common practice in the past), business firms would gain and taxpayers would lose. A more reasonable strategy would emphasize aid to firms that are viable in the long run but are suffering from temporary difficulties (i.e., avoiding plant closures without giving permanent subsidies) and policies for managing the decline of communities that are heavily dependent on "sunset" industries, overcoming bottlenecks to economic development by key public investments, and setting up incentive mechanisms to promote the entry and expansion of small, indigenous firms. Such a broadly based strategy would have to be described as pragmatic rather than being neatly labeled as liberal or conservative.

References

Ballard, S. C., and M. D. Devine. 1982. *Water and Western Energy: Impacts, Issues, and Choices.* Boulder, Col.: Westview Press.

Miernyk, W. H. 1982. *Regional Analysis and Regional Policy.* Cambridge, Mass.: Oelgeschlager, Gunn and Hain.

HARRY W. RICHARDSON

2 Regional
Development Theories

This chapter briefly reviews some of the major regional development theories that may be useful in improving understanding of long-term interregional development trends in mixed-market economies such as the United States. It provides a theoretical setting for the mainly empirical analyses that follow in later chapters of the book.

The Neoclassical Model

Given the dominance of neoclassical ideology in Western economies, it is hardly surprising that neoclassical models of regional development have received most attention in the literature on regional growth theory. A major appeal of the neoclassical model is that its simplest and most naive version predicts interregional per capita income convergence. If the following assumptions are made (full employment, perfect competition, a single homogeneous commodity, zero transport costs, identical production functions exhibiting constant returns to scale in all regions, a fixed labor supply, and zero technical progress), this model shows that the marginal product of labor (wage rate) and the marginal product of capital (rate of return to capital) are direct and inverse functions respectively of the capital-labor ratio. Labor will flow from low- to high-wage regions, and capital will flow in the opposite direction (since low [high] wages are associated with high [low] returns to capital) until factor returns are equalized in each region. Thus, the regional growth process is associated with a convergence in regional per capita incomes (Smith, 1975).

A more flexible variant of the model would allow for regional differences in production functions. From a regional production function of the type

$$Y_i = K_i^{a_i} L_i^{1-a_i} T_i \tag{1}$$

where Y = output, K = capital, L = labor, T is a residual reflecting technical progress and similar considerations, a is a parameter ($0 < a < 1$) representing capital's output share, and subscript i denotes region i, it is possible to derive the growth equation

$$y_i = a_i k_i + (1 - a_i) l_i + t_i \tag{2}$$

where y, k, l, and t are the growth rates in output, capital, labor, and technical progress respectively. Furthermore, since investment is the sum of local savings and net capital inflow minus depreciation,

$$k_i = s_i v_i^{-1} + \sum_j b_{ji} (a_i v_i^{-1} - a_j v_j^{-1}) - d_i \tag{3}$$

where s is the savings-output ratio, v is the capital-output ratio, b_{ji} is a parameter for converting the differential in the marginal product of capital (a/v) between region i and region j into a net capital import rate (k_{ji}), and d is the annual depreciation rate. Similarly, labor supply growth is the sum of natural increase plus net inmigration,

$$l_i = n_i + \sum_j c_{ji} (W_i - W_j) \tag{4}$$

where n is the rate of natural increase and c_{ji} is a parameter for converting the differential in the regional wage (W) into a net migration rate.

To achieve equilibrium growth in the interregional system a mechanism is needed for equating investment with full-employment savings. The national rate of interest (r) is such a mechanism if a perfect capital market is assumed. Thus, an equilibrium condition is that $r = a_i/v_i$ in each region. Hence steady growth requires

$$r = a_i v_i^{-1} = a_i Y_i / K_i \tag{5}$$

If r is given, output and capital must grow at the same rate if a_i is to remain constant. Thus, $y_i = k_i$. Substituting for k_i in equation (2),

$$y_i = k_i = t_i / (1 - a_i) + l_i \tag{6}$$

In the special case of zero technical progress ($t_i = 0$), output, capital, and labor must all grow at the same rate to achieve steady growth. However, the equilibrium growth rate does *not* have to be the same in *all* regions. Borts and Stein (1964, pp. 167–69) showed that equilibrium growth rates in output could vary among regions because of differential growth rates in labor supply if the demand for labor is perfectly elastic. This result is compatible with equalized rates of return to capital and labor in all regions because demand adjustment to a faster rate of increase in labor supply implies that a faster rate of growth in output will not lead to higher wages. Growth is clearly supply determined in this model. The requirements for equilibrium growth become more complicated if the zero technical progress assumption is dropped. Moreover, y_i and k_i may be permitted to diverge if the capital-output ratio (v_i) varies across regions. It is also possible to introduce variable returns to scale (Lande and Gordon, 1977). These refinements, however, need not be considered here.

A Cumulative Causation Model

The main rival to the neoclassical model is the class of theories known as cumulative causation (CC) models; their simplest versions predict regional income divergence, but this prediction is by no means an inevitable consequence of adopting this model (see pp. 11, 19). The major difference between the "naive" versions of the CC and neoclassical models is that the CC approach allows for increasing returns to scale rather than assuming constant returns. As a result, both capital and labor flow in the same direction rather than in opposite directions. Growth rate differentials not only may persist over time, but also *may* become wider as long as the increasing returns-to-scale effect continues. The attraction of CC models is not so much their predictions as their compatibility with the existence of agglomeration economies, which many regional economists consider an important determinant of regional growth performance.

There are many variants of the CC model. The first, but loose, conception was by Myrdal (1957) who argued that regional inequality will tend to increase over time as a few leading regions exploit initial advantages that become self-sustaining. Linkages between growing and lagging regions will be both favorable ("spread effects") and unfavorable ("backwash effects"), but the latter will tend to predominate. Dixon and Thirlwall (1975) developed a CC model in which growth was export-led so that regional growth is a function of demand for its exports. Although this is consistent with another mainstream regional development model, the so-called export base model, other growth triggers besides exports could be allowed in a more general CC model.

Perhaps the simplest version of a CC model is based on the idea that the rate of productivity growth (t) is a function of the growth rate in regional output (y), the so-called Verdoorn effect. This relationship could reflect the importance of agglomeration economies and increasing returns to scale in regional development. Ignoring subscripts, we may write

$$t = e + fy \tag{7}$$

where f is the Verdoorn coefficient. Efficiency wages are obtained by deflating an index of money wages with an index of productivity. The rate of growth in efficiency wages (w) will therefore be inversely related to the rate of productivity growth:

$$w = g - ht \tag{8}$$

Low efficiency wages will stimulate output growth if markets are competitive. Hence, the lower the growth rate of efficiency wages, the faster output grows:

$$y = m - pw \tag{9}$$

Substituting (7) and (8) into (9), and introducing a time term, yields

$$y_{t+1} = m + p\,(eh-g) + fhpy_t \tag{10}$$

or

$$y_{t+1} = x + zy_t$$

where $x = m + p\,(eh-g)$ and $z = fhp$. To find the equilibrium growth rate (y^*), we set

$$y^* = y_t = y_{t+1} \tag{11}$$

and solve for y^* to obtain

$$y^* = x/(1-z) = [m+p\,(eh-g)]\,(1-fhp)^{-1} \tag{12}$$

The general solution to the first-order linear equation (11) is

$$y_t = (y^0 - y^*)z^t + y^0 \tag{13}$$

where y^0 is the initial output growth rate. It is important to note that this model generates cumulative growth *only* if the parameters are of particular values.

The conditions for cumulative growth are that $z > 1$, $x < 0$, and that $y^0 > y^*$. Interestingly, the only test of this particular model (Kumar-Misir, 1974) showed that in Canada $z < 1$ so that the interregional growth process was convergent rather than cumulative. On the other hand, the signs on the regression coefficients of equations (7) through (9) were all correct (i.e., $f > 0$, $h < 0$, and $p < 0$). Moreover, since the values of the f coefficient varied widely among Canadian provinces, the test suggested that interregional growth differentials might persist even in equilibrium.

A Post-Keynesian Model

A version of a post-Keynesian demand model[1] of interregional growth may start with the concept of a probabilistic interregional savings-flow matrix

---

[1] There are many post-Keynesian regional growth models, all of them relatively similar (e.g., Hartman and Seckler, 1967; Richardson, 1969, pp. 323–31; Bolton, 1966; Guccione and Gillen, 1974). A particularly interesting version (Thirlwall, 1980) derives a simple growth rule

$$P = \sum_i \sum_j S_{ij} \tag{14}$$

where S_{ij} = flow of savings from region i to region j. Dividing each element of this matrix by its corresponding sum we obtain a transitional probability matrix $P*$ with elements $p_{ij} = S_{ij}/S_i$. This matrix $P*$ can be partitioned into

$$P* = \left(\begin{array}{c|c} Q & R \\ \hline 0 & I \end{array} \right) \tag{15}$$

where the Q matrix represents transient states, R is a matrix of absorbing states, I is an identity matrix, and 0 is a null matrix. There is a matrix T with the same dimensions as R such that

$$T = (I - Q)^{-1}R \tag{16}$$

This matrix contains the probabilities of inputs to the system (i.e., savings), getting from each transient state (e.g., a short-term savings institution in one of the regions) to each absorbing state (fixed investment in one of the regions). Eventually an equilibrium will be reached where all savings are absorbed into investment in one or another of the regions of the system.

Given an initial vector of regional savings (S^0) and a diagonal matrix ($\hat{R}$) of intraregional absorption coefficients, we can derive an equilibrium distribution vector of capital stock increments (ΔK^*), assuming that total system savings = total investment,

$$\Delta K^* = (I-Q)^{-1}\hat{R}S^0 \tag{17}$$

The system of regions can grow endogenously if a savings-income and an output-capital stock relation are introduced on Harrodian lines.

$$S = \hat{S}Y \tag{18}$$

$$y = \chi / \pi$$

where y = growth rate of income, χ = growth rate of exports and π = income elasticity of demand for imports, as a dynamic version of the Harrod foreign trade multiplier. This is very similar to the export base model where regional growth depends on regional export performance. It can also be combined with the Verdoorn effect to obtain a CC model where regions producing goods with a high income elasticity of demand in export markets will be persistently favored because output (export) growth boosts productivity growth.

Thirlwall's discussion of the model's policy implications is illuminating. Policymakers should aim at raising the rate of growth of regional exports and reducing the income elasticity of demand for imports. It has been pointed out elsewhere (Kaldor, 1970) that regional labor subsidies can be regarded as a regional equivalent to currency devaluation. But imposing such subsidies to make a region's exports cheaper will not be effective in raising the growth rate of exports. Instead, policymakers should introduce measures to stimulate industries producing goods for which the demand is income elastic outside the region. Obviously, it is very difficult for *regional* policymakers to intervene to reduce the income elasticity of demand for imports.

and

$$Y = \hat{V}^{-1}K \qquad (19)$$

where Y = a vector of regional incomes, $\hat{S}$ = diagonal matrix of regional propensities to save, and $\hat{V}$ = diagonal matrix of regional capital-output ratios. Combining equations (18) and (19) and substituting $\hat{S}\hat{V}^{-1}K^0$ for S^0 and ΔK^1 for ΔK^* in equation (17)

$$\Delta K^1 = (I-Q)^{-1}\hat{R}\hat{S}\hat{V}^{-1}K^0 \qquad (20)$$

Since

$$K^1 = K^0 + \Delta K^1 \qquad (21)$$

$$K^1 = K^0 + (I-Q)^{-1}\hat{R}\hat{S}\hat{V}^{-1}K^0 \qquad (22)$$

By matrix multiplication, let

$$Z = (I-Q)^{-1}\hat{R}\hat{S}\hat{V}^{-1} \qquad (23)$$

$$\therefore K^1 = K^0 + ZK^0 \qquad (24)$$

$$= (I + Z)K^0 \qquad (25)$$

and by expansion

$$K^n = (I + Z)^n K^0 \qquad (26)$$

where K^n is the terminal vector of regional capital stocks.

Therefore, regional growth depends on capital investment, and the future interregional distribution of capital stock depends on its initial distribution and on the structural parameters of the system: propensities to save, capital-output ratios, the interregional savings-flow matrix, and intraregional invest-ment (absorbing) coefficients. The model allows the comparative static con-ditions of savings-investment equilibrium (i.e., total system savings = total system investment at the end of each period) to be satisfied within a frame-work of continuous growth (capital → income → savings → additions to capital).

The important feature of this model is that there is no steady-state growth path (except as a result of flukes in parameter values). Each region will grow at a different rate from its closed-economy growth path. Whether the growth paths converge or not depends on the parameters of the interregional savings-flow matrix. However, if there are built-in polarization flows in favor of the higher-income regions (Richardson, 1973a), regional incomes will diverge over time. Also, by changing the coefficients the model can accommodate divergence in some phases of development and convergence in others; for example, it could be made compatible with Williamson's inverted-U-curve measuring changes in an index of regional disparities over time (Williamson, 1965).

Uneven Regional Development

This approach, which differs from more formal models, involves the application of neo-Marxist or other radical analyses to interpretations of interregional economic trends (*Review of Radical Political Economics*, 1978; Massey and Batey, 1977; Carney, Hudson, and Lewis, 1980). Although the work tends to be theoretical or at least conceptual, it pays much more attention to institutional forces. Some of the research has an empirical component, usually in the form of case studies illustrating the theory rather than in the form of hypothesis testing.

These theories are difficult to summarize in a few paragraphs because the literature reflects wide variations in viewpoints. For example, there is a debate as to whether analogues to imperialism, such as the internal colonialism model, are useful for explaining the persistent backwardness of lagging regions. The current tendency is to discredit this type of model because it ignores, or at best underestimates, the significance of the class struggle. For instance, Lovering (1978) argues that it is wrong to treat the Welsh experience as the subordination of a distinct society to a central elite (the English ruling class) with separatism seen as the solution. Instead, economic development in Wales is best understood as an example of capitalist uneven development.

A central proposition of the uneven regional development theorists is that regional growth differentials do not reflect the net result of the operation of abstract and impersonal market forces, but the purposive actions of the capitalist class. Moreover, as long as capitalism survives, intervention to correct regional inequalities will be ineffectual because the state is merely the coercive instrument of capitalist-class interests. In the spatial context capitalism manifests itself in several ways. First, antagonism between city and countryside results from exploitation; the surplus of the rural sector is extracted for the benefit of urban capitalists. Cheap food allows the capitalists to keep down industrial wages while rural savings are diverted to the cities to fuel urban capital accumulation. Second, the spatial concentration of production is not the result of market orientation (i.e., minimization of transport costs) or the uneven spatial distribution of raw materials but is explained by the centralization of capital into large production units, especially in manufacturing. Third, and related to the preceding point, the spatial penetration of capital is very uneven. Since capitalist decisions are motivated only by the pursuit of private profit rather than social benefit, there may be vast areas of a country that are chronically deprived of investment (a "permanent reserve of stagnant places"; Walker, 1978, p. 34). These areas may be found at all spatial levels—interregionally (core-periphery), intraregionally (growth pole-hinterland), and within cities (ghetto-suburb). Fourth, capital is highly mobile, and this mobility offers many opportunities for exploitation. Examples include the shift of industry to the southern United States to exploit non-unionized labor (Malizia, 1978) and the development of ephemeral boom-towns as a response to the world energy crisis (Markusen, 1978). Fifth, regional policies will have only marginal impacts in improving welfare because "the 'regional' element of policy is completely subsidiary" and a smoke screen for giving "a large subsidy to industrial capital to enable it to survive the profits squeeze" (Pickvance, 1978, p. 241). In summary, uneven regional development is an inevitable manifestation of the built-in crises and instability of capitalism, and "capitalist expansion and change produce regional inequality insofar as it is necessarily a by-product of personal inequality, the basis of capital accumulation" (Goldsmith, 1978, p. 15).

Of these influences, the mobility of capital is probably the most important, since sudden and dramatic shifts in the location of capital accumulation can have devastating impacts on area economic development (e.g., plant shutdowns in company towns). The extent of these shifts is intensified by the increasing internationalization of capital and the associated behavior of multinational corporations. Advances in communications technologies have facilitated spatial separation between corporate headquarters and production plants. As a result, head offices are heavily concentrated in a few world metropolises (Manhattan, London, Frankfurt, Zurich, Tokyo) while production operations are becoming more dispersed. According to Goldsmith (1978), this is the overwhelmingly predominant trend in Western Europe. However, the decentralization of production plants into peripheral regions is not primarily to achieve real productivity gains, but to raise profits by direct reductions in wage bills permitted by the social conditions (unemployment, weak unions) found in labor reserve regions (Läpple and Hoogstraten, 1980). At the same time, in certain sectors (e.g., marine-related industries, petrochemical complexes) locational concentration into large "territorial production complexes" is necessary for survival. It is unclear whether or not the centralization forces dominate the dispersal tendencies.

Even where dispersal of economic activity and apparent convergence occur, the benefits are negligible. First, the penetration of peripheral regions in the developed countries is very unstable because capital may easily relocate if it becomes more profitable to exploit lower wages in the developing countries. Second, the rapidity of the shifts from the heartland to the periphery (especially in the United States) have exacerbated the problems of regional decline and stagnation in the heartland (Northeast and Midwest); capital has been scrapped sooner than necessary, a tendency aggravated by investment and tax policies. Third, the spatial penetration of lagging regions has been very uneven, creating wide gaps in the rate of development *within* regions. Finally, the dispersal in economic activity has not been accompanied by improvements in the distribution of income because dispersal has taken place to raise profits and hold down wages rather than to raise general levels of welfare. Hence, interregional convergence in average incomes per capita has been associated with a worsening income distribution in leading and lagging regions alike.

Regional Imbalance and Mesoeconomic Power

Holland (1976) has developed a theory of regional development that shares some affinity with the uneven regional development school in its emphasis on regional imbalance and the role of the capitalist industrial sector in generating and maintaining this imbalance. Holland also directly acknowledges the contributions of Marx: "There is a wealth of virtually unmined regional source material in Marx whose relevance to regional problems in contemporary capitalist economies is compelling" (Holland, 1976, p. 36). However, the uneven regional development theorists repudiate Holland as an apologist for state capitalism.

Holland's text is, nevertheless, "an extension of imbalance or disequilibrium theory, and an attempt to demonstrate that the trend to regional inequality is intrinsic to capitalist economic growth" (Holland, 1976. p. 54). He combines Marx's analysis of the concentration of capital (and long-term substitution of capital for labor) with Myrdal's principle of cumulative causation (Myrdal, 1957) and Perroux's emphasis on unbalanced growth and polarization (Perroux, 1955).[2] His own specific contribution is to analyze the role in this process of two major trends in modern capitalism: the rise of mesoeconomic power in national economies and the spread of multinational operations by very large firms. Holland argues the need for a new branch of economics, mesoeconomics, *intermediate* between macroeconomic theory and policy and the micro level of the small competitive firm. Mesoeconomics analyzes the behavior of very large firms in the economy, the mesoeconomic sector. They dominate the economy (in Britain the top 100 manufacturing firms' control of net output rose from one-fifth in 1950 to one-half in 1970; it may reach two-thirds by 1985), eliminating many of the small firms competing with their products but spawning a host of small dependent satellites that provide them with inputs. These large firms and their satellites tend overwhelmingly to locate in the more developed regions, and thus to exacerbate the problem of spatial inequality. The result is a pattern of spatial dualism with the modern mesoeconomic firms concentrated in the developed regions and the small-scale, low-productivity microeconomic firms concentrated in the lagging regions.

The situation has been aggravated by the rapid expansion of mesoeconomic firms into multinational operations. The regional incentives available

---

[2]Holland (1976, pp. 49–50) overemphasizes the spatial aspects of polarization in Perroux's work. It should be recalled that Perroux considered geographical space as "banal."

for locating in the problem regions of developed countries are swamped by the profitability of using cheap labor in developing countries and the greater ease of extracting profits from these locations to tax havens abroad. As a result, when multinational mesoeconomic firms decentralize out of the core regions or establish branch plants they are likely to leapfrog the peripheral regions of the developed countries and choose profitable sites in developing countries.

In other words, regional mesoeconomics is concerned with the analysis of how the locational strategies and tactics pursued by large corporations distort the pattern of development by reinforcing regional imbalances and counteracting the spatial redistribution policies of national governments. The policy implications of this theory are the harnessing of mesoeconomic power by direct controls, large but conditional subsidies to priority growth sectors in lagging regions, "planning agreements" on location between the state and monopoly corporations, and above all, by direct state participation in production in growth industries through new public enterprises.

Autonomous Growth Centers and the Life-Cycle Theory of Agglomeration Economies

A feature of interregional development trends in the United States has been a redistribution of population from the metropolitan areas of the older industrial regions of the Northeast and Midwest to those of more recently developed regions of the South and West.

Spatial development is more comprehensible in terms of the differential growth of nodal regions than of homogeneous regions. The expansion of urban (later metropolitan) areas has been the hub of regional growth, and these areas have grown because cities offered agglomeration economies to both firms and households. The spatial unevenness of development within regions suggests the relevance of growth-pole (or growth-center) analysis.

The concept of the growth pole was originally aspatial (i.e., limited to economic space). The basic idea focused on a propulsive industry and its linked industries that grow faster than the rest of the economy because of modern technology and high rates of innovation, income-elastic demand for their output in national and/or international markets, and large multiplier effects. Subsequently, the concept was applied to geographical space by spatially clustering this set of dynamic industries in an urban area and by concentrating the spillover and multiplier effects not over the economy as a whole but in the surrounding hinterland. In even later versions the growth pole was generalized to mean the geographical clustering of economic activity as a whole rather than interdependent sectors. The policy implication of this broadened concept is that the spatial concentration of economic activity induces faster regional development than dispersal.

However, even in this diluted form the growth-pole concept is not very helpful to explanations of interregional trends in regional development. There are two problems. First, the growth pole is almost invariably an intra-regional phenomenon examining the pole in the context of its hinterland. Second, the growth pole or growth center is a link between theory and regional policy much more than an obvious component of regional development theory. However, these problems can be resolved by conceptualizing a nationally dispersed system of autonomous growth centers (AGCs) rather than a planned growth pole within a single region.[3]

These AGCs will grow at different rates at varying points of time depending on the strength of their agglomeration economies and other locational advantages, and there will be a high correlation between the growth rate of an AGC and that of its surrounding region.[4] An interesting hypothesis to explain the southward and westward shifts in the United States in the pace of metropolitan (and hence regional) growth is that agglomeration economies follow an inverted U-shape over the life cycle of the city (Fogarty and Garofalo, 1981). The older cities suffer from weakened agglomeration economies that reduce their attractiveness for mobile economic activities (and dampen growth rates of existing industries) while in the newer cities opposite forces are at work.[5] The hypothesis remains theoretical because agglomeration economies are notoriously difficult to measure.[6]

This hypothesis can be made compatible with cumulative causation models if the shift in the locus of cumulative advantages from the Northeast and Midwest to the South and West can be explained satisfactorily. The realiza-

[3]The concept of an autonomous growth center is very similar to that of a "spontaneous growth center [SGC]." "Spontaneous growth centers are those that are growing without benefit of special assistance, or at least without benefit of conscious or explicit policy. In a lively socio-economic system, there will always be a number of these centers, whose growth derives from the dynamics of the system" (Alonso and Medrich, 1972, p. 230). The term AGC is used in preference to SGC merely to avoid commitment to the size class ranges and operational definitions used in Alonso and Medrich's paper.

[4]For example, in the United States if the large standard metropolitan statistical areas (SMSAs) with above-average growth rates and their state are treated as proxies for the AGCs and their regions, inspection of their population growth rates over the decade 1970–80 confirms this correlation. In many cases (e.g., Dallas, Phoenix, San Jose, New Orleans, Denver, Nashville, El Paso) the two growth rates were very similar.

[5]Vining (Vining and Kontuly, 1977; Vining, Pallone, and Plane, 1981) subscribes to the first part of this hypothesis ("the disappearance of the agglomeration advantages of the core regions"), but prefers to explain the growth of cities in the periphery in terms of "the site-specific natural endowments of the periphery."

[6]Carlino (1981), using a returns-to-scale (RTS) parameter in manufacturing as a measure of agglomeration economies, found no significant difference between core and periphery cities. Fogarty and Garofalo (1981) suggest that the type of RTS measure used by Carlino and others is seriously biased. Their results provide evidence of the declining efficiency of capital in older cities. They also point out that the benefits of productivity growth may easily be swamped by rising labor, energy, and other resource costs.

tion that shifts in economic activity and population have been gradual (and go back more than fifty years) makes the life-cycle theory of agglomeration economies a more convincing explanation, since they imply a relatively smooth movement up (in the periphery) and down (in the core) the slopes of the agglomeration economy function. At some point, however, what begins as a gradual diffusion process quickens and cumulative causation gets under way at the new locations (the so-called turnaround or clean break of the 1970s in the United States?).

Evaluation

The most obvious way of evaluating the alternative theories of regional development is to test them with data drawn from individual countries. However, there are two main objections to this approach. First, each of the theories has several variants and by changing a few assumptions and some of the parameter values the different models can generate the same predictions. In principle, the way around this problem would be to test subhypotheses embodied in each theory, but this runs into the second problem, which is the scarcity of data on some of the key variables, especially those on interregional capital flows and yields. In view of these constraints, the following discussion will be restricted to general comments on the alternative theories and to a very broad evaluation of their merits.

A naive approach to evaluation would be to determine whether or not regional development trends were convergent and then to determine which of the alternative theories best explains the observed trends. Unfortunately, this approach will not work. First, although there appears to be a tendency toward interregional per capita income convergence in many countries, this tendency is far from universal, varies in intensity over time, and has failed to equalize regional income disparities by a wide margin. Second, although the neoclassical model is widely regarded as the convergence model par excellence, several other regional development theories (the post-Keynesian and life-cycle theory of agglomeration economies models and, in some circumstances, the cumulative causation model) can lead to convergence given certain parameter values, while a multisector neoclassical model (or one with increasing returns to scale or with heterogeneous regional production functions) can generate divergence. Third, the spatial dispersion of population (labor) and economic activity (capital) is not identical with interregional per capita income convergence; both may be important aspects of subnational development, yet both may not be predicted by the same model. Certainly, the simple neoclassical model described above would not predict population dispersal *unless* the low-income regions also had the highest population densities.

If there were better data on interregional factor flows (especially elusive capital), a sounder test of the robustness of the alternative theories might be whether their predictions of the direction of capital and labor flows were correct. The models previously discussed separate into two main groups on this point. The exception is the post-Keynesian model; whether capital flows in the same direction as labor depends on the parameters of the interregional savings-flow matrix (but other post-Keynesian models such as a two-region Harrod-Domar model [Richardson, 1969, pp. 323–31; Holland, 1976, pp. 70–81] are more specific in their predictions). Neoclassical, neo-Marxist (uneven regional development), and Holland's regional imbalance theory [7] all predict that capital flows from high- to low-wage regions with the inference that profits and wages are inversely related.[8] Conversely, both the cumulative-causation and life-cycle theory predict that capital and labor flow in the same direction because of increasing returns and agglomeration economies. However, the only way of testing the directional hypotheses about factor flows is to assume that capital flows are embodied in fixed capital, and to use data on the establishment of new firms and on plant relocations as proxies for capital flows. This is far from satisfactory. Evidence from the United States suggests that capital and labor flow in the same direction. The Western European experience is mixed, even within the same country, partly because there are housing and other constraints on interregional labor mobility, partly because regional policy impacts may intervene. The internationalization of capital has undoubtedly resulted in the flow of capital from high- to low-wage countries with labor flowing in the other direction, to the limited extent permitted by national immigration laws. On the whole, a confusing picture.

The two main rivals in regional development theory remain the neoclassical model and the cumulative causation model. Notwithstanding the versatility of both models with respect to convergence-divergence, the emergence of an interregional equilibrium in per capita incomes would powerfully strengthen support for the neoclassical position.

In the relatively near future, an opportunity will develop to test the appropriateness of the neoclassical compared with the cumulative causation model. The key question is whether regional per capita income curves will stabilize

[7] However, in Holland's theory mesoeconomic firms bypass the low wages of lagging regions of developed countries to benefit from the far lower wages prevailing in the developing countries (see especially Holland, 1976, p. 57).

[8] These theories may appear strange bedfellows until it is remembered that Marx's economic theory drew heavily upon the principles of the classical economists. The process of spatial development is essentially similar in both the neoclassical and the neo-Marxist models, even in their contemporary versions. What differs is the language ("profit maximization" becomes the "werewolf hunger for surplus value") and intent (are capitalists callously indifferent to the social effects of capital shifts on regions of origin as the neo-Marxists suggest?). However, the outcomes of the spatial development process are also perceived differently, equilibrating in the one case and crisis-ridden and unstable in the other.

close to equality (i.e., an approximation to neoclassical equilibrium) or whether they will cross over, with the four lower-income regions (South Atlantic, East South Central, West South Central, and Mountain) then becoming progressively richer than the four regions of the Northeast and the Midwest.[9] The latter development would be more consistent with the cumulative causation model. The competing hypotheses of interregional income equilibrium and the "crossover" is the most intriguing question in contemporary regional economics.

An important criterion for evaluating alternative regional development theories is the usefulness of their policy implications. The theories discussed in this chapter imply quite different policy prescriptions. The neoclassical models suggest the need to eliminate barriers to the mobility of both labor and capital and the use of taxes and subsidies to change the relative prices of inputs among regions, especially in the presence of externalities.[10] The cumulative causation theories are consistent with strategies to promote agglomeration economies in lagging regions (e.g., growth-center policies), measures to reduce efficiency wages (e.g., wage subsidies to labor in backward regions), and capital incentives to boost productivity growth—by raising the Verdoorn coefficient, f, in equation (7). The policy implications of post-Keynesian regional growth models vary with the specifications of each model. In the model discussed in the text, much depends on the structure of the interregional savings-flow matrix. This could be changed to favor low-income regions via the provision of incentives to place savings in development banks or other institutions that invest in lagging regions. The growth-rule model (see note 1), on the other hand, implies the promotion of regional export growth, particularly by measures to shift the region's economic structure in favor of export products with a high income elasticity of demand.

The policy implications of the uneven regional development theories are no different from those of other neo-Marxist models. State intervention is useless as long as control of the means of production remains in the hands of the capitalist class. Social democratic versions of regional imbalance theories, on the other hand, could imply a wide range of policies from controls on the internationalization of capital and taxes, and/or direct controls on the sudden relocation of capital, to measures to equalize levels of investment within and between regions (perhaps by using state enterprises to compen-

[9]This question was also raised by Alonso (1980, p. 12): "Regional equalization of per capita incomes in the United States has proceeded rapidly among the nation's geographic regions and between metropolitan and non-metropolitan areas. Indeed, it is not unreasonable to consider the possibility that the per capita income curves of the Sunbelt and the Frostbelt will not merely stop at convergence, but may in fact cross over. . . . Will the curve of regional inequality rise once more?"

[10]For example, the imposition of pollution taxes equal to marginal damages would accelerate convergence by depressing wages and profits in the high-density, high-income regions where marginal damages are greater (Siebert, 1973).

sate for the unevenness of private-sector investment), to support unionization, and to design regional policy incentives that maximize benefits to target
groups. Holland's version of these models calls for harnessing mesoeconomic power by direct controls and public sector participation in production.
Finally, the life-cycle theory of agglomeration economies model is, like
some versions of the cumulative causation model, compatible with growth-
center strategies, at least in the sense that it implies reinforcing the advantages of spontaneously growing urban centers by helping them to move up
the agglomeration function more rapidly. The policy problem may be acute,
however, if the lagging regions lack AGCs or if the city size distribution is
heavily primate. In such situations regional policies will probably fail. The
least damage will be done by avoiding "worst-first" regional strategies at all
costs.

Questions for Future Research

Deductive economic theories are not produced in a vacuum. They implicitly assume a specific environment that is usually based on stylized facts.
The regional development theories reviewed here not only assume a particular place (Western market economies) but also a particular time and background (the growth and technology of the present and recent past). There
may be emerging trends and changes in the future environment that will
make current theories obsolete and require new theories. A state-of-the-art
review cannot be expected to resolve this problem, but it may be helpful for
future research to point to some of these changes.

One of the more interesting ideas of recent years is that there are complex
interactions among five bell-shaped curves, relating to economic growth, income inequality, regional inequality, geographic concentration and dispersion, and demographic change (Alonso, 1980). Although much is known
about what happens on the left-hand side and inflection point of these curves,
at least with respect to first-order interactions, "the right-hand side has been
left largely dangling and unexamined" (Alonso, 1980, p. 5). Obviously, the
industrialized countries are well on the right-hand side of most of these
curves. Better understanding of the interactions among the curves in this
range might demand revision of regional development theory. For instance,
what are the implications of the slowing down in national economic growth
for regional development? It is well known that concern for national growth
has diverted attention from regional policies. But slower growth may affect
regional development trends. In such an environment interregional factor
flows will tend to be dampened. Conceivably, the main source of interregional economic change might be differential rates of decline (in terms of
plant closures and layoffs) rather than of growth. Would this phenomenon
lead to a new process of regional income divergence or would it be spatially

random? Although there have been a few case studies of economic stagnation and decline in individual regions, there is no general theory of regional economic decline. Yet there is no sound reason for expecting economic growth and decline to be symmetric. Similar questions are raised by the possibility that the demographic curve might become negative in the near future. What are the implications of such a development for interurban and interregional migration? The impact of the decline in the population of urban areas on regional development has barely been examined at the theoretical level.

Another problem posed for regional development theory is the current significance of agglomeration economies. These have played a critical role in many models of regional development. Many observers believe that agglomeration economies are becoming less important.[11] A major reason is that rapid changes in telecommunications and computer technology are reducing the need for face-to-face contacts and eroding the benefits gained from minimizing communication costs. If spatial proximity is no longer a major efficiency factor for firms in interdependent industries and for departments within the same company, agglomeration economies are weakened and locational constraints are substantially relaxed. When this is combined with the fact that in most Western European countries almost all regions are sufficiently well endowed with infrastructure and skilled labor pools to be considered feasible locations for all economic activities other than resource-based industries, existing location theories contribute little to the theory of regional development. Perhaps the determinants of location and of regional growth differentials in developed countries are becoming increasingly noneconomic (e.g., the pull of amenities on migrants and the locational preferences of managers). An earlier work (Richardson, 1973b) identifying agglomeration economies and locational preferences as key variables in regional growth theory suggested that the former was more important. Perhaps it should be the other way around.

Another important consideration revolves around the importance of natural resource constraints on regional development, a problem of growing concern since the oil embargo of 1973–74 and its aftermath. This problem has several dimensions, some of which have theoretical significance (Richardson, 1977; Miernyk, 1979). The gap between energy-rich and energy-poor regions adds a new twist to the convergence-divergence debate, especially since in many countries energy and other natural resources are concentrated in the periphery. Energy-poor regions suffer in at least two ways: production costs are increased for energy-intensive industries and the internal terms of trade shift unfavorably against them. The theory of regional development

[11]There is some evidence to the contrary, though it is not fully convincing. Carlino (1981) found that agglomeration economies in manufacturing were still increasing even into the late 1970s, but there is some doubt that the returns to scale measure is an appropriate proxy for agglomeration economies (see n. 6).

needs modification when applied to resource frontier regions because rates of economic development pick up much faster than when regional growth is based on industrialization, a much more gradual process. Furthermore, natural resource exploitation may generate fast rates of development only for a relatively short time. This creates a need for relatively disposable infrastructure, which raises not only critical technological and policy issues, but also interesting theoretical questions such as those posed by the theory of boom-towns (Cummings and Schulze, 1978). The debate on agglomeration economies leaves an unresolved question as to whether or not lower communication costs will be offset by rising transport (energy) costs. A more general question must be considered: how important is access to cheap energy resources as a determinant of regional development? It is not coincidental that the six fastest-growing states in the 1970s in terms of per capita income were Wyoming, Louisiana, Oklahoma, North Dakota, Alaska, and Texas or that the population of West Virginia grew faster than the national average after two decades of population decline.

Changes in general economic conditions may demand major revisions in regional development theory, perhaps even new theories. For example, the slowing down of national economic growth rates may require the formulation of theories of regional economic decline, while the implications of zero or negative population growth for regional development have scarcely been explored, Moreover, the importance of locational preferences and amenities in regional development may surpass that of agglomeration economies, which have been weakened by technological advances in communications. Finally, natural resource constraints may be a serious retarding influence on regional growth, especially in core regions. On the other hand, some peripheral regions are being stimulated by access to abundant and lower-cost energy resources. These changes boost the revival of supply-led models of regional development.

References

Alonso, W. 1980. Five bell shapes in development. *Papers of the Regional Science Association* 45: 5–16.

Alonso, W., and E. Medrich. 1972. "Spontaneous growth centers in twentieth-century America urbanization." In *Growth Centers in Regional Economic Development*, edited by N. M. Hansen, 229–65. New York: The Free Press.

Bolton, R. E. 1966. *Defense Purchases and Regional Growth*. Washington, D.C.: Brookings Institution.

Borts, G. H., and J. L. Stein. 1964. *Economic Growth in a Free Market*. New York: Columbia University Press.

Bourne, L. S., and M. I. Logan. 1976. "Changing urbanization processes at the margin: the examples of Australia and Canada." In *Urbanization and Counter-Urbanization*, edited by B. J. L. Berry, 111–43. Beverly Hills: Sage.

Carlino, G. A. 1981. The role of agglomeration economies in metropolitan decline. Paper presented at the Eastern Economics Association meeting, Philadelphia, April 9–11.

Carney, J., R. Hudson, and J. Lewis, eds. 1980. *Regions in Crisis: New Perspectives in European Regional Theory*. London: Croom Helm.

Cummings, R. G., and W. D. Schulze. 1978. Optimal investment strategies for boomtowns: a theoretical analysis. *American Economic Review* 68: 374–85.

Dixon, R., and A. P. Thirlwall. 1975. A model of regional growth rate differences on Kaldorian lines. *Oxford Economic Papers* 27: 201–14.

Fogarty, M. S., and G. Garofalo. 1981. The urban capital stock and the life-cycle of cities. Paper presented at the Eastern Economics Association meeting, Philadelphia, April 9–11.

Glickman, N. J. 1978. *The Growth and Management of the Japanese Urban System*. New York: Academic Press.

Goldsmith, W. W. 1978. Marxism and regional policy: an introduction. *Review of Radical Political Economics* 10 (3): 13–17.

Guccione, A., and W. J. Gillen. 1974. A Metzler-type model for the Canadian regions. *Journal of Regional Science* 14: 173–89.

Hall, P., and D. Hay. 1980. *Growth Centers in the European Urban System*. Berkeley: University of California Press.

Hartman, L. M., and D. Seckler. 1967. Towards the application of dynamic growth theory to regions. *Journal of Regional Science* 7: 167–73.

Holland, S. 1976. *Capital versus the Regions*. London: Macmillan.

Kaldor, N. 1970. The case for regional policies. *Scottish Journal of Political Economy* 17: 337–47.

Kawashima, T. 1977. *Changes in the Spatial Population Structure of Japan*. Laxenburg, Austria: International Institute for Applied Systems Analysis, Research Memo RM-77-25.

Kumar-Misir, L. M. 1974. Regional economic growth in Canada: an urban-rural functional area analysis. Master's thesis, University of Ottawa.

Lande, P. S., and P. Gordon. 1977. Regional growth in the United States: a re-examination of the neoclassical model. *Journal of Regional Science* 17: 61–69.

Läpple, D., and P. van Hoogstraten. 1980. "Remarks on the spatial structure of capitalist development: the case of the Netherlands." In *Regions in Crisis. See* Carney et al., 1980, 117–66.

Lovering, J. 1978. The theory of the "internal colony" and the political economy of Wales. *Review of Radical Political Economics* 10 (3): 55–67.

Malizia, E. 1978. Organizing to overcome uneven development: the case of the U.S. South. *Review of Radical Political Economics* 10 (3): 87–94.

Markusen, A. R. 1978. Class, rent and sectoral conflict: uneven development in Western U.S. boomtowns. *Review of Radical Political Economics* 10 (3): 117–29.

Massey, D. B., and P.W.J. Batey, eds. 1977. *Alternative Frameworks for Analysis.* London: Pion, London Papers in Regional Science (7).

Miernyk, W. H. 1979. A note on recent regional growth theories. *Journal of Regional Science* 19: 303–8.

Molle, W., B. van Holst, and H. Smit. 1980. *Regional Disparity and Economic Development in the European Community.* Farnborough: Saxon House.

Myrdal, G. 1957. *Rich Lands and Poor.* New York: Harper and Row.

Perroux, F. 1955. Note sur la notion de 'pole de croissance' (Note on the concept of 'Growth Poles'). *Economie appliquée* 7: 307–20.

Pickvance, C. G. 1981. "Policies as chameleons: an interpretation of regional policy and office policy in Britain." In *Urbanization and Urban Planning in Capitalist Society,* edited by M. Dear and A. J. Scott, 231–65. New York: Methuen.

Review of Radical Political Economics 10, no. 3 (Fall 1978). Special issue on Uneven Regional Development.

Richardson, H. W. 1969. *Regional Economics: Location Theory, Urban Structure and Regional Change.* New York: Praeger.

Richardson, H. W. 1973a. A Markov chain model of interregional savings and capital growth. *Journal of Regional Science* 13: 17–27.

Richardson, H. W. 1973b. *Regional Growth Theory.* London: Macmillan.

Richardson, H. W. 1977. "Natural resources, factor mobility and regional economics." In *The International Allocation of Economic Activity,* edited by B. Ohlin, 115–23. London: Macmillan.

Siebert, H. 1973. Environment and regional growth. *Zietschrift fur Nationalökonomie* 33: 79–85.

Smith, D. M. 1975. Neoclassical growth models and regional growth in the United States. *Journal of Regional Science* 15: 165–81.

Stöhr, W., and F. Tödtling. 1978. "An evaluation of regional policies–experiences in market and mixed economics." In *Human Settlement Systems: International Perspectives on Structure, Change and Public Policy,* edited by N. M. Hansen, 85–119. Cambridge: Ballinger.

Thirlwall, A. P. 1980. Regional problems are "balance-of-payments" problems. *Regional Studies* 14: 419–25.

Vanhove, N., and L. H. Klaassen. 1980. *Regional Policy: A European Approach.* Farnborough: Saxon House.

Vining, D. R., Jr., and T. Kontuly. 1977. Increasing returns to city size in the face of an impending decline in the size of large cities: which is the bogus fact? *Environment and Planning A* 9: 59–62.

Vining, D., R. Pallone, and D. Plane. 1981. Recent migration patterns in the developed world: a clarification of some differences between our and IIASA's findings. *Environment and Planning A* 13: 243–50.

Walker, R. A. 1978. Two sources of uneven development under advanced capitalism: spatial differentiation and capital mobility. *Review of Radical Political Economics* 10 (3): 28–37.

Williamson, J. G. 1965. Regional inequalities and the process of national development. *Economic Development and Cultural Change* 13: 3–45.

World Bank. 1980. *World Development Report, 1980*. New York: Oxford University Press.

Yuill, D., K. Allen, and C. Hull, eds. 1980. *Regional Policy in the European Community: the Role of Regional Incentives*. New York: St. Martin's Press.

JOSEPH H. TUREK

3 The Northeast in a National Context: Background Trends in Population, Income, and Employment

The Northeast[1] has been in a state of unambiguous relative decline for many years. At the same time, the regions of the South and West have experienced dynamic growth in population and employment. The purpose of this chapter is to quantify this phenomenon, popularly known as the "Frostbelt-Sunbelt shift." The following trends provide a contextual framework for the remainder of the book.

The importance of studying national trends as a first step toward understanding the geographical redistribution of economic activity away from the Frostbelt cannot be overemphasized. No single region grows (or declines) in a vacuum. The economic prospects of the Northeast depend, to a great extent, on what happens in the national system as a whole and, to a slightly lesser degree, in the international economy. To ignore this fact is tantamount to assuming that regional economies are closed and hence, that interregional linkages are insignificant.

The slower the rate of real economic growth in the United States, the closer the parallel between regional growth and a zero-sum game. At the "zero national growth" extreme, it is clear that expansion in some regions is possible only at the expense of decline in others. Even when the national

[1]The delimitation of regions adopted here conforms to the classification scheme established by the Bureau of the Census. A complete listing of these regions, their constituent states, and the abbreviations used throughout the chapter may be found in Table 3.2. The Northeast (NE and MA) and North Central (ENC and WNC) macroregions make up the Frostbelt; the South (SA, ESC, and WSC) and West (MT and PAC) macroregions, the Sunbelt.

growth rate is positive, the notion of competitive growth is still highly relevant. Capital and labor move across space in response to interregional price differentials;[2] thus stimulating growth in the receiving region and inhibiting growth in the sending region. The interdependence of regions is also illustrated by the concept of generative growth, in which the growth of one region (or group of regions) is transmitted to others through supply linkages and commodity trade (Richardson, 1973, pp. 86–88). Accordingly, any speculation on the fate of the Northeast must necessarily involve an assessment of the economic prospects of the national system and its constituent regions.

It will be shown that the Northeast—and the entire Frostbelt—has been declining relative to the Sunbelt for at least five decades. Since it cannot be argued that the Northeast is *suddenly in trouble*, why has attention only recently turned to the economic problems of this region? It is because the slowing of national economic growth has forced the realization that the size of the "economic pie" will no longer expand as rapidly as it did in the past. What was once relative decline has now turned, in many areas of the Frostbelt, to absolute decline. This new awareness was further underscored by the advent of "stagflation," the OPEC oil embargo, recurring state and local fiscal crises, and more recently, the Reagan administration's budget cuts. In response to this slowdown in growth, regions began to pursue more aggressive policies designed to foster their own economic expansion. In particular, the conflict between the Frostbelt and the Sunbelt has taken the form of increased competition for federal budgetary outlays, tax paying population, and private-sector employment.

The first writer to stress the idea that Sunbelt expansion impeded Frostbelt growth was Sale (1975), whose research inspired a series of articles in the popular press on this theme.[3] Was it a coincidence that the economic climate at that time satisfied the conditions of a zero-sum game? Real gross national product (GNP) had declined for the second consecutive year, and the national unemployment rate had reached a post–World War II high of 8.5 percent. On top of this, the OPEC oil embargo focused attention on the importance of energy, and, perhaps for the first time, the implications of interregional differences in resource endowments were recognized (see Chapter 6). However, there is little reason to assume that interest in the subject of regional conflict

---

[2]Factor flows—both direction and magnitude—do not depend exclusively on spatial price differentials. Furthermore, growth in the receiving (sending) region is not necessarily stimulated (inhibited) by these flows. Parts of the Sunbelt are already suffering the consequences of rapid and unanticipated population growth: rising crime rates, inadequate infrastructure, increasingly severe water shortages, traffic congestion, pollution, and housing shortages.

[3]Among these are included "The Second War Between the States," *Business Week*, 17 May 1976, 92–98; "Federal Spending: The North's Loss is the Sunbelt's Gain," *National Journal* (see Havemann, 1976); "The Pork-Barrel War Between the States," *U.S. News and World Report*, 5 December 1977, 39–41; and "Sunbelt vs. Frostbelt: A Second Civil War," *Saturday Review* (see Sutton, 1978).

will rise and fall with fluctuations in the business cycle. Through the imposition of severance taxes on fossil fuels, energy-producing states of the Sunbelt have been able to shift at least part of their tax burden onto the energy-
consuming states of the Frostbelt. Even as the nation recovers from the
1981–82 recession, the present administration has renewed its pledge to balance the federal budget. Given the findings reported in Chapter 11, it is clear
that a program of increased taxation coupled with nondefense spending cuts
will lead to a significant transfer of funds from the Frostbelt to the Sunbelt.
While only time will tell, it seems unlikely that the problems of the Northeast
will wane with the resurgence of national economic growth.

Population

The 1970–80 decade marked the first time in American history that a region experienced a drop in resident population *between* censuses (Table 3.1).
This event was not a portent of some dramatic change about to take place in
the spatial distribution of economic activity. Rather, it was the manifestation
of a structural transformation whose roots have long since been established.
On the basis of 1970–80 population growth rates, the nine census regions
are easily characterized as fast-growing (SA, ESC, WSC, MT, and PAC) or
slow-growing/declining (NE, MA, ENC, and WNC). The growth rates of the
former group range from 126.3 to 326.3 percent of the national growth rate
while those of the latter range from −9.6 to 45.6 percent. In fact, since the
1930s, the SA, MT, and PAC regions have consistently grown more rapidly
than the nation as a whole, while the NE, MA, ENC (except during 1950-
60), and WNC regions all had population growth rates that were consistently
below the United States average. These trends in the relationship between
regional and national growth rates are directly reflected in the changing distribution of population across regions. Since 1930, the share of national
population living in the fast-growing regions has increased and the share re-
siding in the slow-growing regions has decreased (see below, p. 38).
After achieving a post-Depression peak of 18.5 percent during the 1950s,
the national population growth rate assumed a path of steady decline (Table
3.1). During this period, every region experienced a decline in the rate of
natural population increase, and total population growth slowed in six of the
nine regions (the MA region suffered the greatest percentage reduction and
the SA region the smallest). The three exceptions (ESC, WSC, and MT) all
exhibited accelerating growth as a result of net in-migration. Between 1970
and 1980, every region of the Sunbelt had a positive net migration rate (i.e.,
in-migration exceeded out-migration), while the regions of the Frostbelt *all*
had net migration rates that were either negative or close to zero. While interregional differences in net migration rates have been prominent in vir-

TABLE 3.1
Population Growth Rates by Region, 1930–1980 (in percent)

Region	1930–40† Population	1930–40† Natural Increase	1930–40† Net Migration	1940–50 Population	1940–50 Natural Increase	1940–50 Net Migration	1950–60 Population	1950–60 Natural Increase	1950–60 Net Migration	1960–70 Population	1960–70 Natural Increase	1960–70 Net Migration	1970–80 Population	1970–80 Natural Increase	1970–80 Net Migration
New England	3.3	3.8	−0.5	10.4	8.5	1.9	12.8	12.5	0.3	12.7	9.7	3.0	4.2	4.0	0.2
Middle Atlantic	4.9	4.6	0.3	9.5	7.9	1.6	13.3	12.3	1.0	8.9	8.9	*	−1.1	3.8	−4.9
East North Central	5.3	5.7	−0.4	14.2	10.8	3.4	19.2	16.9	2.3	11.1	11.5	−0.4	3.5	6.7	−3.2
West North Central	1.7	−2.6	4.3	4.0	10.6	−6.6	9.5	15.3	−5.8	6.1	10.0	−3.9	5.2	5.9	−0.7
South Atlantic	12.9	12.0	0.9	18.8	19.6	−0.8	22.6	19.6	3.0	18.1	13.0	5.1	20.5	6.8	13.7
East South Central	9.0	12.7	−3.7	6.5	18.8	−12.3	5.0	17.8	−12.8	6.3	12.1	−5.8	14.5	8.0	6.5
West South Central	7.3	11.1	−3.8	11.3	18.9	−7.6	16.6	20.6	−4.0	14.0	14.3	−0.3	22.9	10.1	12.8
Mountain	12.1	12.1	*	22.3	18.1	4.2	35.1	24.1	11.0	20.9	16.4	4.5	37.2	12.1	25.1
Pacific	18.6	4.9	13.7	47.8	14.0	33.8	40.2	18.4	21.8	25.2	13.2	12.0	19.8	7.9	11.9
United States	7.3	—	—	14.5	—	—	18.5	—	—	13.4	—	—	11.4	—	—

†1930–1940 net intercensal migration calculated by survival rate method; remainder by components of change method. Natural increase is population growth rate less net migration rate.

*Rounds to less than 0.1 percent.

Sources: Population: U.S. Department of Commerce, Bureau of the Census, 1980 Census of Population, vol. 1, Ch. A, pt. 1 (Washington, D.C.: Government Printing Office, April 1983). Net Migration: for 1930–1940, U.S. Department of Commerce, Bureau of the Census, Historical Statistics of the United States: Colonial Times to 1970, p. 93 (Washington, D.C.: Government Printing Office, 1976); for 1940–1950, 1950–1960, 1960–1970: U.S. Department of Commerce, Bureau of the Census, Statistical Abstract of the United States (Washington, D.C.: Government Printing Office, various issues); for 1970–1980, Jackson et al. (1981, table 3.2, p. 60).

tually every decade, not until the 1970s did an unambiguous spatial pattern emerge.

Since 1930, the MT and PAC regions have consistently registered population gains because of positive net migration. Until 1970 the same could be said for the MA region and, since 1940, for the NE region as well. The chronic tendency for the ESC and WSC regions to lose population via out-migration appears to have been reversed during the 1970s. Over the last two decades, the ENC and WNC regions have lost population as a result of migration flows while the SA region has gained. Not all the growth resulting from positive net migration, however, is at the expense of the "declining" regions: because of substantial net immigration from abroad, the total number of regional in-migrants exceeds the total number of regional out-migrants.

From the perspective of the regional policymaker, it is important to know how much of the variation in regional population growth rates is attributable to interregional disparities in net migration rates. Any variation in the overall growth rate of a region that is not accounted for by migration must be due to natural increase.[4] While the spread in the rates of natural increase (8.3 percentage points during the period from 1970 to 1980) is substantially smaller than that for population growth rates (38.3 percentage points) and net migration rates (30.0 percentage points), the variation across regions remains striking. The rate of natural increase in the MA region, for example, was less than a third of that in the MT region.

At least part of the interregional variation in the rate of natural increase is due to differences in the age distribution of the resident population across regions. In 1970, 34.4 percent of the MA population was between the ages of eighteen and forty-four; the corresponding figure for the MT region was 35.9 percent (U.S. Department of Commerce, 1971, p. 25). By 1979, this same age group made up 39.0 percent and 40.9 percent of the populations of the MA and MT regions, respectively (U.S. Department of Commerce, 1980, p. 32). In 1970, the marriage rate—a proxy measure for the rate of family formation— was 8.4 (per 1,000 population) in the MA region and 22.6 in the MT region (U.S. Department of Commerce, 1980, p. 86). The trend toward divergence of regional fertility rates is documented in a recent study of regional growth patterns (Jackson et al., 1981, pp. 73–77).

In general, slow-growing regions tended to have low, and fast-growing regions, high, rates of both natural increase and net migration. However, since 78.5 percent of the point spread between population growth rates is accounted for by net migration rates, interregional variations in population growth are more the result of differences in migration patterns than of differences in fertil-

---

[4]In fact, it is the net migration rate and not the rate of natural increase that is calculated as the residual.

ity. Nevertheless, the role of net migration as a determinant of population growth in any *single* region varies among regions. For example, during the last decade, net migration accounted for 4.8 percent of the population growth in the NE region and 67.5 percent of that in the MT region. Between 1970 and 1980, the rate of natural increase exceeded the net migration rate in the NE, ENC, WNC, and ESC regions. This suggests that the growth experiences of these regions were influenced more by natural increase than by migration (the reverse would hold true for the MA, SA, WSC, MT, and PAC regions). On this point, both the ESC and MA regions desert their usual regional groups (fast- and slow-growing, respectively).

The relocation decision of individuals and households are a function of economic conditions in both the sending and receiving regions. The greater the perceived disparity in economic well-being between any two regions, the greater will be the population flow from the low-welfare region to the high-welfare region. Hence, regions where migration figures prominently in population growth tend to be those in which economic well-being has increased *or* decreased most dramatically. (This conclusion is supported by the income and employment data presented below.) Few would quarrel with the argument that migration into the South and West reflects a relative improvement in employment opportunities and living conditions in those regions.

Population redistribution has also been taking place within regions. Between 1970 and 1980, every region except the WNC and WSC experienced more rapid growth in nonmetropolitan than in metropolitan areas. Nonmetropolitan areas grew at a rate of 13.5 percent in NE and 21.9 percent in MA; the corresponding figures for metropolitan areas are 8.0 percent and −2.1 percent (Jackson et al., 1981, p. 165). On the basis of the 1980 census data, 35 new Standard Metropolitan Statistical Areas (SMSAs) have been designated: 7 in the Northeast, 5 in the North Central (the net gain here is 4 since WNC lost 1), 14 in the South, and 9 in the West (*New York Times*, 30 November 1981, p. B17). Interestingly, despite a regional growth rate of −1.1 percent and a metropolitan area growth rate of −2.1 percent, the MA region gained two SMSAs (both in New York).

During the 1970–80 decade, the ten most rapidly growing states were located in the fast-growing regions of the Sunbelt (Table 3.2); seven of these ten were in the MT region. Of the ten slowest growing states, nine are in the Northeast and North Central (i.e., the Frostbelt) regions. The paradox of the slowest-growing area, the District of Columbia, in the fast-growing SA region is easily explained by urban decentralization from the nation's most urbanized area. Out-migrants from the District of Columbia have been absorbed in Maryland and Virginia, thus joining the nonresident commuting workforce.

The concentration of fast-growing states in one regional group and slow-

TABLE 3.2
State Population Growth Rates, 1970–1980 (in percent)

New England (NE) SD = 10.5*		*South Atlantic (SA) SD = 15.9*	
Maine	13.2	Delaware	8.6
New Hampshire	24.8	Maryland	7.5
Vermont	15.0	Dist. of Columbia	−15.7
Massachusetts	0.8	Virginia	14.9
Rhode Island	−0.3	West Virginia	11.8
Connecticut	2.5	North Carolina	15.5
		South Carolina	20.4
Middle Atlantic (MA) SD = 2.9		Georgia	19.1
New York	−3.8	Florida	43.4
New Jersey	2.7		
Pennsylvania	0.6	*East South Central (ESC) SD = 1.5*	
		Kentucky	13.7
East North Central (ENC) SD = 2.0		Tennessee	16.9
Ohio	1.3	Alabama	12.9
Indiana	5.7	Mississippi	13.7
Illinois	2.8		
Michigan	4.2	*West South Central (WSC) SD = 5.3*	
Wisconsin	6.5	Arkansas	18.8
		Louisiana	15.3
West North Central (WNC) SD = 1.3		Oklahoma	18.2
Minnesota	7.1	Texas	27.1
Iowa	3.1		
Missouri	5.1	*Mountain (MT) SD = 14.5*	
North Dakota	5.6	Montana	13.3
South Dakota	3.6	Idaho	32.4
Nebraska	5.7	Wyoming	41.6
Kansas	5.1	Colorado	30.7
		New Mexico	27.8
Pacific (PAC) SD = 6.8		Arizona	53.1
Washington	21.0	Utah	37.9
Oregon	25.9	Nevada	63.5
California	18.5		
Alaska	32.4		
Hawaii	25.3		

*The standard deviation (SD) measures the relative intraregional dispersion of state population growth rates around the regional mean. The regional growth rate (a weighted average of state growth rates) was used in place of the arithmetic mean in computing the standard deviations.

Sources: Population: U.S. Department of Commerce, Bureau of the Census, *1980 Census of Population*, vol. 1, Ch. A, pt. 1 (Washington, D.C.: Government Printing Office, April 1983). Net Migration: for 1930–1940, U.S. Department of Commerce, Bureau of the Census, *Historical Statistics of the United States: Colonial Times to 1970*, p. 93 (Washington, D.C.: Government Printing Office, 1976); for 1940–1950, 1950–1960, 1960–1970: U.S. Department of Commerce, Bureau of the Census, *Statistical Abstract of the United States* (Washington, D.C.: Government Printing Office, various issues); for 1970–1980, Jackson et al. (1981, table 3.2, p. 60).

growing states in another suggests a degree of uniformity in regional demographic performance. Intraregional dispersion measures, however, paint a somewhat different picture. The greatest intraregional variation occurs in the SA, MT, and NE regions, and the smallest in the WNC, ESC, and ENC regions (see Table 3.2). There is a positive correlation between regional growth rates and absolute intraregional variations in population growth; thus rapidly growing regions are less homogeneous in this respect than regions that are growing slowly.[5] While demographic stagnation appears widespread in the Frostbelt regions, growth in the Sunbelt regions is much more centralized (see below, p. 46).

Income

Unless otherwise specified, all calculations are based on personal income data deflated by the *national* consumer price index for urban wage earners and clerical workers. Admittedly, this procedure introduces some distortion because there are substantial interregional variations in the cost of living.[6] The few available examples of regional price deflators suggest that the cost of living is higher in the Frostbelt than in the Sunbelt, so the use of national deflators will overstate real income in the former and understate it in the latter.

Not surprisingly, the regions with the largest populations also have the highest levels of personal income (the rank correlation between these two variables is .933, significant at the 99 percent level[7]). The growth rates of total personal income (Table 3.3) show that the geographical distribution of fast-growing and slow-growing regions parallels the classification by population growth rates, though the differentials are less dramatic—possibly because of a cost-of-living bias.[8]

[5]One possible explanation of this finding is that the dispersion within regions is due to disparities in base period state populations. This is because the smaller (larger) the initial population level, the greater (lesser) will be the percentage change associated with any given increment. Using the coefficient of variation of 1970 state populations for each region as a measure of the intraregional base period disparity, the *partial* correlation coefficient between regional growth rates and intraregional variations in growth rates was computed. The relationship was found to be little affected by the introduction of state sizes into the analysis. In only two instances does the distribution of 1970 populations appear to make much difference: in the NE region where the disparity is very high and in the ESC region where it is very low.

[6]Unfortunately, regional price indices are not available. Some measures of regional price levels have been calculated, e.g., Williamson (1980), but the time periods covered do not coincide with those examined here.

[7]The rank correlation coefficient (Spearman's Rho) is calculated as

$$\rho = 1 - \frac{6 \sum_{i=1}^{n} D_i^2}{n \, (n^2 - 1)}$$

where D_i is the difference between rankings of the variables for the ith observation and n is the sample size. To test the significance of the coefficient, calculate $z = \rho \sqrt{n - 1}$ and find the corresponding probability level from the cumulative normal distribution.

[8]The reduction in differences across regions becomes quite apparent when the coefficients

TABLE 3.3

Real Personal Income Growth Rates by Region, 1930–1980*

Region	1930–40		1940–50		1950–60		1960–70		1970–80	
	Total	Per Capita	Total	Per Capita	Total	Per Capita	Total	Per Capita	Total	Per Capita
New England	13.5%	10.4%	71.8	48.9	47.9	28.5	66.8	46.5	34.0	24.1
Middle Atlantic	7.9	3.7	78.2	56.4	41.9	22.6	56.2	43.3	14.1	16.5
East North Central	21.0	15.8	125.8	88.9	45.9	18.7	59.0	41.2	37.4	28.8
West North Central	10.9	9.3	144.1	131.7	31.9	18.5	60.6	53.3	52.7	39.4
South Atlantic	45.9	31.2	157.5	105.1	63.4	28.9	97.7	64.2	82.4	32.5
East South Central	34.7	25.0	177.0	198.0	48.1	21.1	79.6	66.7	77.9	41.4
West South Central	30.8	23.0	194.0	198.3	49.2	8.2	82.2	55.4	123.1	61.3
Mountain	28.8	16.6	176.6	113.0	73.3	22.3	81.2	43.2	129.4	38.5
Pacific	31.0	13.0	186.0	70.3	89.1	28.2	78.9	36.1	81.7	33.4
United States	19.5	12.5	128.3	90.0	51.3	24.1	71.9	47.6	58.4	30.8

*Percent change in constant 1967 dollars.

Sources: for 1930, 1940: U.S. Department of Commerce, Office of Business Economics, *Regional Trends in the United States Economy: A Supplement to the Survey of Current Business* (Washington, D.C.: Government Printing Office, 1951); for 1950: U.S. Department of Commerce, Bureau of Economic Analysis, *Survey of Current Business* (Washington, D.C.: Department of Commerce, August 1971), vol. 51, no. 8; for 1960: *Survey of Current Business*, August 1979, vol. 59, no. 8; for 1970, 1980: *Survey of Current Business*, July 1981, vol. 61, no. 7.

With very few exceptions, the growth rates of personal income in the NE, MA, ENC, and WNC regions have been consistently below the national average, while those of the SA, ESC, WSC, MT, and PAC regions have been uniformly above. There is no perceptible trend toward convergence of regional income *growth rates* over time.[9] During the 1960s, the MA region grew at a rate that was 78.2 percent of the United States average while the SA region grew 35.9 percent faster than the nation. Between 1970 and 1980, the MA growth rate fell to a mere 24.1 percent of the national mean, and the MT region skyrocketed to 221.6 percent.

The lower-than-average growth rates in the Northeast and the North Central regions imply, of course, a steady decline in their shares of personal income (Table 3.4). In 1930, 71.5 percent of all income went to residents of the Frostbelt and 28.6 percent went to those of the Sunbelt; by 1980 the corresponding shares were 49.4 percent and 50.6 percent. Over this same period, the share of income going to the Northeast fell from 40.1 percent to 23.1 percent. The relationship between income shares and population shares is immediately obvious from Table 3.4. The distribution of total income among the regions, however, is more than a reflection of the population distribution. It also depends critically on the volume of economic activity located in each region, the composition of output and the extent of interregional wage (and other factor payment) differentials.

The residents of the NE, MA, and PAC regions have enjoyed the highest levels of per capita income since 1930 while those of the ESC, WSC, and SA have historically received the lowest. It is interesting to note that the WNC, a slow-growing Frostbelt region, is relatively poor, and the PAC, a fast-growing Sunbelt region, is relatively rich. During the 1970s, per capita income grew fastest in the WSC, ESC, and WNC regions and slowest in the MA, NE, and ENC regions (Table 3.3). The fact that the coefficient of variation of per capita incomes fell from 12.7 percent in 1970 to 9.7 percent in 1980 indicates a general tendency toward income convergence. This trend is reflected in the widening of the percentage point spread between (relative) regional per capita income growth rates: from 64.2 between 1960 and 1970 to 145.5 between 1970 and 1980.

Figure 3.1 classifies each state and region by its 1970 per capita income level and by its per capita income growth rate during the 1970–80 period. If per capita incomes have converged over time, these two variables will be

of variation of the two data sets are compared: 1.01 for population growth rates and 0.64 for real personal income growth rates.

[9] During the 1970s, income growth rates actually diverged. Over time, the spread in income growth rates (as measured by the standard deviation) is best described by a pattern of explosive oscillations. If this trend continues, one might expect to observe the "crossover" of high-income and low-income regions some time in the future.

TABLE 3.4
Regional Distribution of Personal Income and Population, 1930–1980*

Region	1930			1940			1950			1960			1970			1980		
	Per Capita Income Index	Regional Share of Total U.S. Income	Population (%) of Total U.S.	Per Capita Income Index	Regional Share of Total U.S. Income	Population (%) of Total U.S.	Per Capita Income Index	Regional Share of Total U.S. Income	Population (%) of Total U.S.	Per Capita Income Index	Regional Share of Total U.S. Income	Population (%) of Total U.S.	Per Capita Income Index	Regional Share of Total U.S. Income	Population (%) of Total U.S.	Per Capita Income Index	Regional Share of Total U.S. Income	Population (%) of Total U.S.
New England	129.2	8.6	6.6	126.5	8.1	6.4	106.6	6.6	6.2	109.8	6.4	5.9	109.2	6.4	5.8	106.1	5.8	5.5
Middle Atlantic	147.6	31.5	21.3	134.1	27.9	20.8	116.9	23.3	19.9	115.8	22.1	19.1	113.1	20.7	18.3	106.4	17.3	16.2
East North Central	108.1	22.2	20.5	111.8	22.5	20.2	111.4	22.4	20.1	107.3	21.7	20.2	103.5	20.5	19.8	102.7	18.9	18.4
West North Central	85.0	9.2	10.8	82.2	8.4	10.2	95.3	8.9	9.3	91.7	7.9	8.6	94.7	7.6	8.0	98.1	7.4	7.6
South Atlantic	64.0	8.2	12.8	76.5	10.3	13.5	80.9	11.3	14.0	83.6	12.1	14.5	91.4	13.8	15.1	92.0	15.0	16.3
East South Central	43.2	3.5	8.0	48.8	4.0	8.2	68.9	4.6	7.6	67.5	4.5	6.7	74.8	4.7	6.3	78.1	5.1	6.5
West South Central	58.0	5.7	9.9	64.3	6.4	9.9	90.9	7.8	9.6	81.1	7.7	9.5	84.7	8.1	9.5	95.4	10.0	10.5
Mountain	83.7	2.5	3.0	87.3	2.7	3.1	94.9	3.2	3.4	93.8	3.6	3.8	91.5	3.8	4.1	94.5	4.7	5.0
Pacific	124.4	8.7	7.0	125.1	9.7	7.7	115.6	11.6	10.0	118.9	14.1	11.8	111.4	14.5	13.1	112.6	15.8	14.0
United States	100	100	100	100	100	100	100	100	100	100	100	100	100	100	100	100	100	100

*Regional percentages may not total 100 because of rounding.

Sources: Population shares: U.S. Department of Commerce, Bureau of the Census, *1980 Census of Population*, vol. 1, Ch. A, pt. 1 (Washington, D.C.: Government Printing Office, April 1983). Per capita income and regional income shares, for 1930, 1940: U.S. Department of Commerce, Office of Business Economics, *Regional Trends in the United States Economy: A Supplement to the Survey of Current Business* (Washington, D.C.: Government Printing Office, 1951); for 1950: U.S. Department of Commerce, Bureau of Economic Analysis, *Survey of Current Business* (Washington, D.C.: Department of Commerce, August 1971), vol. 51, no. 8; for 1960: *Survey of Current Business*, August 1979, vol. 59, no. 8; for 1970, 1980: *Survey of Current Business*, July 1981, vol. 61, no. 7.

38

1970 Per Capita Income
(data includes the
50 states plus D.C.)   Per Capita Income Growth Rate (1970–1980)

	Above Average	Below Average
Above Average	6*	9
Below Average	29	7†

1970 Per Capita Income
(for the 9 census regions)   Per Capita Income Growth Rate (1970–1980)

	Above Average	Below Average
Above Average	1‡	3
Below Average	5	0

FIGURE 3.1. Relationship between income levels and growth rates, 1970–1980.

*Illinois, Maryland, California, D.C., Washington, Alaska, ordered by growth rate, lowest to highest.
†Arizona, Vermont, Utah, Indiana, Maine, Pennsylvania, Rhode Island, ordered by growth rate, lowest to highest.
‡Pacific.

inversely related and most of the observations should appear in the lower left and upper right cells of the associated contingency tables.

In the case of the states, 38 of the 51 observations provide evidence that convergence has taken place (the chi square statistic is 13.67, which is significant at the 99 percent level). This result, however, merely indicates that the two variables being examined are not independent. A single observation in either the upper left or the lower right cell might be sufficient to result in a widening of the per capita income differential. In fact, this is exactly what happened. In 1970, the lowest per capita income state was 64.8 percent of the national average while the highest was 124.5 percent (a spread of 59.7 percentage points). By 1980, the corresponding figures were 69.1 percent and 134.3 percent (a 65.2 point spread). This increase is explained solely by the fact that Alaska, which ranked fourth in the nation in 1970 per capita income, had a per capita income growth rate almost twice the national average in the 1970s.[10] The other states in the upper left cell either had lower income ranks and/or lower growth rates. Without Alaska, convergence would have occurred.

The case for a narrowing of the per capita income differential at the regional level is much stronger. The pattern in the lower contingency table indicates that eight of the nine regions conform to the convergence hypothesis (the chi square statistic is 5.63, which is significant at the 95 percent level).[11] PAC's location in the upper left cell reflects higher-than-average per capita income growth rates in Alaska, California, and Washington. With the poorest region's income level rising from 74.8 percent of the national average to 78.1 percent while the richest fell from 113.1 percent to 112.6 percent, interregional convergence is unambiguously evident (see Figure 3.2).

Furthermore, to the extent that regional incomes are converging over time, this is more the result of stronger growth in the low-income regions than of significant reductions in the (relative) per capita income of the richer regions. That the NE, MA, and ENC regions have been able to maintain above-average per capita incomes in the face of declining relative employment levels is largely the result of net out-migration and lower rates of natural increase. This finding differs from the earlier conclusion of Perloff Dunn, Lampard, and Muth (1960, p. 51): the "pulling down" of high income levels is much stronger than the "upward push" of low incomes.

The relationship between population growth and income growth is illustrated in Table 3.5. With the exception of Louisiana, the ten fastest-growing states in total income are also the states with the most rapidly increasing populations. As with population growth rates, the MT region is disproportionately represented in this group. Similarly, the ten slowest-growing states in total income also had the slowest-growing populations (except for Delaware).

If per capita income growth is analyzed, the pattern of relative growth and decline changes considerably. Of the ten states enjoying rapid total income growth, only five (Wyoming, Alaska, Texas, Colorado, and Louisiana) are also placed in the top ten with respect to per capita income growth. In these states, above-average population growth is more than outweighed by above-average increases in total income. In four of the remaining five states, population growth rates were so high that they liquidated much of the improvement in the standard of living resulting from a rise in the volume of economic

---

[10]The increase in Alaska's per capita personal income may be highly overstated due to distortions arising from the use of the national price deflator. According to Miernyk's calculations (see Table 6.1), Alaska ranks 39 in *real* per capita personal income when a state deflator is used. A part of the very substantial increase in Alaska's income is undoubtedly due to shifts in the relative price of energy, an area in which the state is highly specialized.

[11]The lower significance level is attributable to the reduction in sample size that accompanies the switch from states to regions.

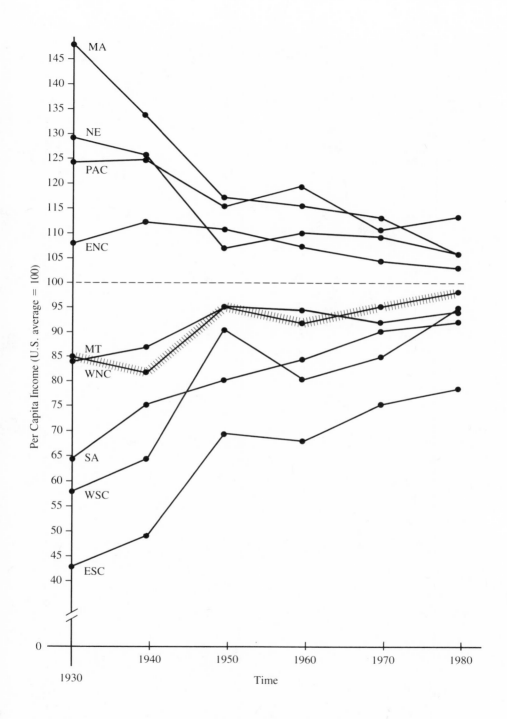

FIGURE 3.2. Relative regional per capita income convergence, 1930–1980.

TABLE 3.5
Fastest and Slowest Growing States, 1970–1980

Total Personal Income*

State	1980 Income (millions $)	% Change 1970–80	Income Rank 1970	Income Rank 1980
Fastest Growing:				
1. Wyoming	5,152	208.3	51	49
2. Nevada	8,597	161.1	46	41
3. Arizona	23,951	151.2	31	29
4. Alaska	5,136	146.6	50	50
5. Florida	88,675	132.2	9	8
6. Texas	136,146	132.1	6	3
7. Colorado	29,029	125.2	26	24
8. Utah	11,203	115.8	39	36
9. New Mexico	10,219	114.5	41	37
10. Louisiana	35,645	110.9	22	21
Slowest Growing:				
1. New York	180,646	0.1	2	2
2. Dist. of Columbia	7,699	3.0	37	43
3. Massachusetts	58,232	24.1	10	10
4. New Jersey	80,724	26.0	8	9
5. Illinois	120,434	29.2	3	4
6. Rhode Island	8,975	30.0	36	39
7. Ohio	102,410	31.1	5	6
8. Pennsylvania	112,220	31.3	4	5
9. Connecticut	36,510	33.9	18	19
10. Delaware	6,172	38.4	43	46

Per Capita Personal Income*

State	1980 Income (millions $)	% Change 1970–80	Income Rank 1970	Income Rank 1980
Fastest Growing:				
1. Wyoming	10,898	85.1	31	6
2. Louisiana	8,458	67.5	47	36
3. Oklahoma	9,116	62.6	35	29
4. North Dakota	8,747	61.4	41	34
5. Alaska	12,790	60.0	4	1
6. Texas	9,545	59.3	32	19
7. Kansas	9,983	53.7	23	16
8. Arkansas	7,268	51.5	50	49
9. Alabama	7,488	47.3	49	48
10. Colorado	10,025	47.3	19	15
Slowest Growing:				
1. Hawaii	10,101	5.5	7	14
2. New York	10,260	8.1	5	12
3. Vermont	7,827	11.1	33	41
4. Nevada	10,727	18.1	6	7
5. Delaware	10,339	18.9	10	10
6. New Jersey	10,924	19.6	3	5
7. Massachusetts	10,125	22.2	11	13
8. Illinois	10,521	22.4	8	8
9. Utah	7,649	26.9	40	46
10. Ohio	9,462	27.7	15	20

*Income figures expressed in current dollars.
Source: Based on data from U.S. Department of Commerce, Bureau of Economic Analysis, *Survey of Current Business*, vol. 61, no. 7 (Washington, D.C.: Department of Commerce, July 1981).

activity. With respect to rapid per capita income growth, the MT states are less prominent than those of the South and Central regions (WSC, WNC, and ESC).

Six of the states with the slowest total income growth (New York, Massachusetts, New Jersey, Illinois, Ohio, and Delaware) also experienced very slow per capita income growth. Their very slow population growth rates were unable to compensate for lower-than-average growth in total income. Of these six, however, all but Delaware ranked higher in per capita income growth than total income growth, which suggests that below-average increases in population helped to mitigate declines in per capita income. Somewhat unexpectedly, Nevada and Utah, both of which were among the top ten states in terms of *total* income growth, had population growth rates that were high enough to place them among the states with the slowest *per capita* income growth.

At this level of analysis, it is not possible to determine the extent to which population "causes" income, or vice versa. A rise in population may spur income growth either through induced investment in the region or through higher levels of local consumption. Conversely, an increase in income levels could result in higher population growth rates either because families feel better able to bear the financial burden of children or because higher income signals the availability of job opportunities to potential in-migrants. It is most likely that causality is bidirectional, with both population and income being determined simultaneously by a set of interdependent variables.

Conceptually, the distinction between population growth resulting from natural increase and that from in-migration is critical. In-migration tends to have a far greater expansionary effect on the regional economy than does natural increase because it leads to more housing (and public infrastructure) development and it has a more immediate impact on the supply of labor. Also, to the extent that selective migration occurs (e.g., if migrants have higher income levels and educational attainments than nonmigrants) these effects are amplified.

As already observed, population and total income are highly correlated in terms of both size and growth rates. The relationship between population and per capita income, on the other hand, is much less exact: the correlation between 1980 regional levels is .259 and between 1970–80 regional growth rates, .571 (the correlation coefficients are even lower when the data are disaggregated to the state level). This is because interregional differences in per capita income levels and growth rates also depend on the manner in which industry mix, participation rates, labor force composition, and wage rates vary across regions.

It is well known that the economic welfare of a region is strongly influenced by its economic structure. This argument has taken many forms, but almost all are based on the hypothesis that some occupational (industrial) structures are more conducive to growth than others.[12] In order to determine whether differences in industry mix can account for some of the interregional variation in per capita incomes, the technique of shift-share analysis is applied to regional earnings.[13] Changes in earned income are decomposed into three categories: (1) the national growth effect—changes that reflect overall national growth; (2) the industry mix effect—changes attributable to the industrial composition of the region's economic base; and (3) the shift effect— changes that reflect shifts in the distribution of industry among the various regions, ostensibly representing changes in relative locational advantages. Table 3.6 presents the breakdown of regional income growth by category totals.[14] In view of the controversy surrounding the use of shift-share, considerable caution should be exercised when interpreting its results.[15]

Surprisingly, the slow-growing MA region has the most advantageous industry mix in the nation, followed next by the WSC and MT regions. At the same time, the MA region also has the greatest negative shift effect, overwhelming its favorable mix effect. The two effects are complementary and positive in the WSC and MT regions. The most striking finding, however, is that the shift effect is negative for *all* the Frostbelt and positive for *all* the Sunbelt. This is consistent with the trend of population and income shifts from the Northeast and North Central regions to those of the South and the West. This redistribution of population and economic activity reflects inter alia changes in interregional competitiveness.

In the NE, MA, and ENC regions, the shift effect is negative for almost every industry group (not shown). Conversely, this effect is positive for almost all industry groups in the Sunbelt regions. As a result, the evidence

---

[12]The export base theory, the theory of growth poles, and the Clark-Fisher hypothesis stress, respectively, the importance of exports, "motor" or driving industries, and the secondary and tertiary production sectors.

[13]The industrial categories were (1) agriculture, fishing, and forestry; (2) mining; (3) contract construction; (4) manufacturing; (5) transportation, communication, and public utilities; (6) retail and wholesale trade; (7) finance, insurance, and real estate; (8) services; and (9) government.

[14]To conserve space, the breakdown by industry for each region is not shown in the table. A complete copy of the results is available from the author, upon request.

[15]Perhaps the most damning criticism of shift-share analysis is that its results are highly sensitive to the level of industrial disaggregation as well as the duration of the time period examined; both weaknesses were observed in this study. On the other hand, useful insights can be gained by observing how the results change as the level of aggregation is varied. There is some evidence to indicate that the shift component (sometimes known as the differential component) may be unstable over time (Thirlwall, 1967). Finally, the procedure implicitly assumes that industries are independent and that no intersectoral supply linkages exist. So long as the structural relationship between industries remains the same, this problem is not too serious. However, once the region experiences a shift in structure, the predictive power of the technique is severely impaired. For a more detailed discussion of shift-share analysis, see Richardson (1979) and Fothergill and Gudgin (1979).

TABLE 3.6
Shift-Share Analysis of Regional Income, 1970–1980

Region	Actual Change* in Regional Income	Decomposition of Change*		
		National Growth	Industry Mix	Shift
New England	51,660.0	59,570.0	−15.8	−7,894.2
Middle Atlantic	141,582.0	199,503.5	2,711.4	−60,632.9
East North Central	173,285.0	203,520.5	−2,798.1	−27,437.4
West North Central	69,646.0	73,365.4	−2,008.5	−1,710.9
South Atlantic	152,605.0	135,992.5	−565.0	17,177.5
East South Central	51,809.0	46,398.1	−371.4	5,782.3
West South Central	115,028.0	78,314.8	2,440.8	34,272.4
Mountain	53,958.0	36,464.5	1,103.9	16,389.6
Pacific	164,324.0	140,625.7	−359.8	24,058.1

*In millions of dollars.
Source: Based on data from U.S. Department of Commerce, Bureau of Economic Analysis, *Survey of Current Business* vol. 61, no. 7 (Washington, D.C.: Department of Commerce, July 1981).

does not support the hypothesis that income *growth* is largely determined by regional industrial composition. Redistribution between the Sunbelt and the Frostbelt is more satisfactorily explained by the fact that production costs in *all* industries are rising in the Frostbelt relative to the Sunbelt (see Chapter 5).

While industry mix explains little of the interregional variation in growth rates, there is some evidence for a relationship between industrial composition and the *level* of regional income. Even if migration occurred at a rate sufficient to equalize industry wages across regions (an unlikely event because of informational constraints and barriers to mobility), interregional income differentials could result from wage differentials across industries. A region with a disproportionate concentration of high-wage industries will, *ceteris paribus*, have a higher level of per capita income than a region whose employment structure is weighted toward low-wage industries.

As noted earlier, regions with fast-growing populations experienced greater intraregional variations in population growth rates than slow-growing ones. There is a similar correlation between regional income growth and intraregional variations in income growth rates. Although the strength of this relationship is slightly reduced when base period income disparities (within regions) are taken into account, the sign of the correlation coefficient is unchanged. This implies that state income growth is less homogeneous in the regions of the Sunbelt than in those of the Frostbelt. In the NE, MA, and ENC regions, states with the highest income levels have the slowest growth rates. States with the highest income levels in the Sunbelt, on the other hand, tend to enjoy the fastest rates of growth. Florida and Texas are the most striking examples.

One possible explanation of Sunbelt heterogeneity is that particular states are "driving" the rest of their region. This would account for the tendency of growth to be more spatially concentrated in fast-growing regions. By creating a favorable growth environment, the dynamic performance of these growth centers—or, more accurately, growth states—stimulates the neighboring states in the same region. Such stimulus may take the form of increased demand for both intermediate inputs and final goods and services. Additionally, rising wages in the growth states may lead to higher wages in other states as a result of intraregional population redistribution, via its effects on local labor supply.

Employment

With minor exceptions, the employment data in Table 3.7 tell the same story as the population and income statistics.[16] Employment growth in the Frostbelt has been slower than the national average since the 1940–50 period while the reverse is true for the majority of the Sunbelt. Only the ESC and WSC regions deviate significantly from general trends. Prior to 1970, these two regions had more in common with the Frostbelt than with the Sunbelt. Net out-migration from the ESC and WSC regions between 1930 and 1970 closely matches the decline in employment shares that resulted from below-average job growth.

Table 3.8 allocates regional employment by industry for 1940 and 1980. Only four industries show substantial variation in employment shares across regions: agriculture, mining, manufacturing, and government. Generally speaking, the WNC and the ESC regions have had the largest employment shares in agriculture; the MT and WSC in mining; the NE, ENC, and MA in manufacturing; and the SA, PAC, and MT in government. This distribution largely reflects the locational advantages of the different geographical regions. The relatively small variation across regions in the remaining industries is explained by the fact that these sectors produce market-oriented goods and services for which proximity to the consumer is essential.

[16]Since the primary goal of this section is to highlight general trends in employment over time and across regions, it was felt that the data set ought to be as comprehensive and internally consistent as possible. The *Census of Population* data base was selected because (1) it covers *all* workers; (2) it includes employment in agriculture, the significance of which varies substantially from one region to the next; (3) it is organized by place of residence, thus eliminating problems associated with interstate (and interregional) labor commuting; and (4) it has been adjusted to ensure intercensal comparability. Because of changes in the standard industrial classification (SIC) code over time, however, some incomparability is inevitable. The PAC region totals include Alaska and Hawaii back to 1940. The government sector includes all employment in uniquely governmental functions; that is, legislative, executive, and judicial (federal, state, and local) as well as active-duty personnel in the federal military. To the extent that government employees also work in other sectors, these persons are allocated to the appropriate industrial classifications (see U.S. Department of Commerce, n.d.).

TABLE 3.7
Employment Growth by Region, 1930–1980

Region	Growth Rates (% change)				Employment (millions)	
	1940–50	*1950–60*	*1960–70*	*1970–80*	*1930*	*1980*
New England	19.6	13.0	18.2	17.6	3.060	5.751
Middle Atlantic	21.9	10.6	11.8	6.6	9.774	15.702
East North Central	28.9	12.3	17.4	13.5	9.257	17.847
West North Central	19.2	5.7	12.4	21.7	4.514	7.779
South Atlantic	28.0	19.6	28.0	34.4	6.215	16.360
East South Central	14.4	2.9	15.0	26.5	3.411	5.839
West South Central	23.6	15.0	21.9	43.8	4.152	10.343
Mountain	42.3	35.7	28.3	60.6	1.261	5.017
Pacific	55.5	39.7	29.1	38.8	3.732	14.527
United States	26.7	15.5	19.5	25.0	45.376	99.166

Sources: for 1940, 1950, 1960, 1970: U.S. Department of Commerce, *Regional Employment by Industry, 1940–1970: Decennial Series for United States, Regions, States, Counties* (Washington, D.C.: Government Printing Office, n.d.); for 1980: U.S. Department of Commerce, Bureau of the Census, *Provisional Estimates of Social, Economic, and Housing Characteristics*, Supplementary Report, 1980 Census of Population and Housing (Washington, D.C.: Government Printing Office, March 1982).

Since 1940, most regions have had a consistent reduction in the share of employment in agriculture and mining. On the other hand, the share of employment in finance, insurance, and real estate (FIRE) and services has risen continuously since 1950. For the remaining industries, employment shares have fluctuated considerably both over time and across regions. For example, while the percentage of total workers employed in the governmental sector nationally has consistently risen since 1940, corresponding employment shares in the NE and PAC regions fell after 1960. Similarly, the reduction in the share of national manufacturing employment between 1960 and 1970 was foreshadowed in the NE region as early as 1950.

If an industry grows at a rapid pace nationally, one might expect that a region containing a large share of that industry will also grow rapidly. Between 1970 and 1980, the fastest-growing industries nationally were mining, FIRE and services (Table 3.9).[17] The slowest-growing sectors were agriculture, manufacturing, and government. Of course, since these growth rates refer to highly aggregated industrial groupings, growth rates for individual

[17] Because agricultural and mining employment were not reported separately in the provisional estimates of the 1980 census, the *Employment and Earnings* data (compiled by the Bureau of Labor Statistics) were used to compare 1970–80 industry growth rates. Using the census figures on employment in agricultural occupations as a proxy for agricultural employment, census data were disaggregated to provide estimates of mining employment. Since the rank ordering of results generated by this procedure—in terms of both employment levels and employment growth rates—was highly consistent with the *Employment and Earnings* data, there is sufficient confidence in the estimates to justify reporting them in Tables 3.8 and 3.9.

TABLE 3.8

Regional Employment Allocated by Industry, 1940 and 1980 (in percent)*

Region	Agriculture, Forestry, & Fisheries		Mining		Contract Construction		Manufacturing		Public Utilities, Transportation, & Communication		Wholesale & Retail Trade		Finance, Insurance, & Real Estate		Services		Government	
	1940	1980	1940	1980	1940	1980	1940	1980	1940	1980	1940	1980	1940	1980	1940	1980	1940	1980
New England	5.4	1.3	0.2	0.1	4.7	4.6	38.8	27.9	6.0	5.7	17.3	18.9	3.7	6.4	20.0	29.6	4.0	5.5
Middle Atlantic	4.8	1.4	2.5	0.5	4.9	4.2	31.3	24.3	8.2	7.7	18.6	19.4	5.0	6.8	20.9	30.2	3.9	5.5
East North Central	13.7	2.3	1.2	0.6	4.2	4.5	31.9	28.7	7.3	6.6	17.7	20.3	3.1	5.3	17.6	26.6	3.2	4.8
West North Central	32.6	6.9	1.0	1.0	4.1	5.6	12.5	18.6	7.2	7.5	17.7	21.3	2.9	5.5	18.5	28.2	3.4	5.4
South Atlantic	25.9	2.5	2.5	0.9	4.7	6.9	20.7	19.8	5.7	7.1	13.4	19.6	2.1	5.5	19.6	26.5	5.3	10.2
East South Central	41.6	3.3	3.2	1.8	3.9	6.4	14.7	24.6	4.9	7.1	11.3	19.5	1.5	4.6	16.5	25.8	2.4	6.9
West South Central	34.5	3.4	2.8	3.5	4.6	8.5	10.2	17.1	6.1	7.6	16.4	20.7	2.3	5.6	19.6	27.1	3.4	6.5
Mountain	26.7	3.7	6.5	3.7	5.4	7.7	8.5	11.9	8.4	7.3	17.7	21.0	2.3	6.0	19.5	29.7	5.0	8.8
Pacific	13.6	2.7	1.6	0.7	6.0	5.7	17.6	19.0	7.9	7.0	20.8	20.8	4.2	6.7	21.9	29.3	6.4	7.9
United States	19.1	2.8	2.0	1.2	4.7	5.8	23.7	22.0	7.0	7.1	16.9	20.2	3.3	5.9	19.4	28.2	4.0	6.9

*Because of rounding, rows may not total 100%.

Sources: for 1940, 1950, 1960, 1970: U.S. Department of Commerce, *Regional Employment by Industry, 1940–1970: Decennial Series for United States, Regions, States, Counties* (Washington, D.C.: Government Printing Office, n.d.); for 1980: U.S. Department of Commerce, Bureau of the Census, *Provisional Estimates of Social, Economic, and Housing Characteristics*, Supplementary Report, 1980 Census of Population and Housing (Washington, D.C.: Government Printing Office, March 1982).

TABLE 3.9
Industry Growth Rates, 1940–1980*

Industry	1940–1950	1950–1960	1960–1970	1970–1980
Total	26.7%	15.5	19.5	25.0
Agriculture, Forestry, & Fisheries	−17.1	−37.1	−35.5	−5.4
Mining	1.4	−28.8	−5.7	85.0
Contract Construction	67.0	14.2	13.9	25.7
Manufacturing	37.7	23.1	10.0	8.9
Public Utilities, Transportation, & Communication	42.3	2.7	12.4	35.8
Wholesale & Retail Trade	39.8	14.6	26.8	28.4
Finance, Insurance, & Real Estate	30.5	43.7	37.9	51.3
Services	17.1	38.2	42.8	37.7
Total Government	97.5	40.8	23.8	9.6

*Percentage change in U.S. employment, by industry.

Sources: Regional Employment by Industry, 1940–70: Decennial Series for United States, Regions, States, Counties, U.S. Department of Commerce (Washington, D.C.: Government Printing Office, no date). For 1940, 1950, 1960, 1970: U.S. Department of Commerce, *Regional Employment by Industry, 1940–1970: Decennial Series for United States, Regions, States, Counties* (Washington, D.C.: Government Printing Office, n.d.); for 1980: U.S. Department of Commerce, Bureau of the Census *Provisional Estimates of Social, Economic, and Housing Characteristics,* Supplementary Report, 1980 Census of Population and Housing (Washington, D.C.: Government Printing Office, March 1982).

subsectors may diverge from industry averages. Compared with the 1960–70 period, major changes include the acceleration of mining and the slowing down of the governmental sector. These changes are easily explained by the repercussions of the energy crisis and the wave of fiscal conservatism, respectively (on the latter, see Chapter 8).

It is noteworthy that the service sector, long regarded as the driving force of postindustrial economies, experienced a decline in the rate of employment growth during the 1970s—the first time in four decades. Given that the service industry accounted for 28.2 percent of all jobs nationally in 1980 (up from 25.6 percent in 1970) and given that service employment growth throughout the 1970s was surpassed only by FIRE and mining (5.9 and 1.2 percent, respectively, of total employment), it would be premature to predict the demise of this industry. Nevertheless, there is a strong feeling that high technology has replaced services as the growth sector of the future. The transition from services to high technology is, in fact, seen by many as a natural progression, an indication of our ascent up the hierarchy of economic structure.

The fastest-growing regions (in terms of employment) in the 1970s were the MT, WSC, PAC, and SA; the slowest-growing were the MA, ENC, and

NE. This is the first decade in which the WNC and ESC regions pulled themselves up from the bottom ranks, and the first time since the 1940s that NE is among the three slowest-growing regions. Consistent with the trends in population and income, employment stagnation is becoming increasingly concentrated in the industrial heartland of the Frostbelt.

The strong performance of the regions in the Sunbelt reflects not only their high share of rapid-growth industries, but also their relatively low share of slow-growth industries, particularly manufacturing. For example, in 1970 the MT region had the highest mining employment share, followed closely by the WSC. In addition, FIRE and services figured prominently in the employment profiles of the MT and PAC regions, and only the ESC region had a manufacturing share that exceeded the national average. Despite very respectable FIRE and service shares, growth in the NE and MA regions has been hampered by the preponderance of manufacturing. With the loss of over 300,000 manufacturing jobs between 1970 and 1980, the service industry became the dominant employment sector in the Northeast. Given the dismal performance of manufacturing during the last two decades, the value of state and local policy initiatives designed specifically to forestall further manufacturing losses appears rather dubious.[18] These losses, while clearly painful in the short run, may actually help to enhance the prospects for economic growth in the long run. The ENC region, the only region in the nation whose employment base is still dominated by manufacturing, is in much the same position as the NE and MA regions. (In spite of smaller FIRE and service shares, the ENC region grew at a faster rate than the MA.) The evidence indicates a high correlation between the industrial composition of a region and its overall employment growth rate.

By applying shift-share analysis to regional employment data,[19] industry mix can be analyzed more systematically. Table 3.10 presents the results of this analysis by category totals for the period from 1970 to 1980. As before, the shift effect is negative for *all* regions in the Frostbelt and positive for *all*

---

[18] In the late 1970s, the Temporary Commission on [New York] City Finances (1978, p. 279) noted that: "While the commission recognizes that the transformation from a manufacturing-oriented to a service-oriented economy is both inevitable and desirable, it concludes that an attempt must be made to retain, and possibly even expand, the city's manufacturing base." In light of the present discussion, the conclusion (1978, p. 292) of the commission that "the future of manufacturing in New York City is like the future of the city itself" is almost certainly wrong.

[19] The *Employment and Earnings* data were used in the shift-share analysis. In order to calculate average regional earnings by industry, comparability between income data and employment data was essential. Since only earned income is reported by both industry and region, use of the broader-based census data would have understated average earnings in those industries having a relatively large number of nonwage earners. Furthermore, due to the manner in which government employment is treated in the census compilation, its use would have caused average earnings to be overstated in the government sector and understated in most of the remaining industries.

TABLE 3.10
Shift-Share Analysis of Regional Employment, 1970–1980

Region	Actual Change* in Regional Employment	Decomposition of Change*		
		National Growth	Industry Mix	Shift
New England	949	1,276	−37	−290
Middle Atlantic	882	3,985	−64	−3,039
East North Central	2,248	4,111	−360	−1,503
West North Central	1,562	1,506	57	−1
South Atlantic	4,158	2,952	4	1,202
East South Central	1,308	1,079	−72	301
West South Central	3,324	1,689	142	1,493
Mountain	1,835	747	127	961
Pacific	3,942	2,571	144	1,227

*In thousands of persons.
Source: Calculations based on U.S. Department of Labor, Bureau of Labor Statistics, *Employment and Earnings*, monthly (Washington, D.C.: Department of Labor).

those in the Sunbelt.[20] The most interesting finding, however, is the negative (positive) mix effect for the MA (SA and PAC) region(s). Because industry mix was favorable in the MA region when earned income was the reference base, the economic structure of that region may be heavily weighted toward high-wage-growth, slow-employment-growth industries. The converse, of course, is true for the SA and PAC regions.

These results support the conclusion that relatively high employment shares in manufacturing are the greatest impediment to job growth in the Frostbelt. In both the NE and MA regions, the negative mix effect for manufacturing more than offset the combined positive shifts in the FIRE and service sectors. Furthermore, while the shift effect was negative for all industries in the MA region, it was positive (though small) for manufacturing and government in the NE region. This positive shift in manufacturing may be a consequence of the growth of high-technology production, an area in which NE appears to be developing a comparative advantage (see Chapter 7).

Table 3.11 computes average earnings for each region in eight nonagricultural industries in 1970 and 1980. In 1970, overall earnings were highest in the PAC, MA, ENC, and NE regions and lowest in the ESC, WNC, and WSC regions. Over the 1970–80 period, average earnings grew fastest in the WSC, ESC, and ENC regions and slowest in the NE, PAC, and SA regions. By 1980, NE had fallen from fourth to sixth place (in terms of average earnings), SA had dropped from sixth to seventh, and WSC had risen from seventh to fourth.

[20]The lessening of the relative disadvantage of the WNC region is almost certainly due to the absence of the agricultural sector from the *Employment and Earnings* data set.

TABLE 3.11
Average Regional Earnings by Industry (in dollars)

Region	Total	Mining	Contract Construction	Manu- facturing	Public Utili- ties, Trans- portation, & Communi- cation	Wholesale & Retail Trade	Finance, In- surance, & Real Estate	Services	Government
Earnings in 1970									
New England	8,585	*	12,820	8,650	9,722	6,900	9,116	8,341	8,933
Middle Atlantic	9,213	11,843	12,587	9,301	11,069	7,744	9,832	9,319	8,658
East North Central	8,991	11,030	13,992	9,937	10,639	7,300	9,380	8,369	7,501
West North Central	8,198	9,419	12,167	8,973	10,032	6,945	8,922	7,478	7,360
South Atlantic	8,322	10,591	9,458	7,383	9,489	6,735	8,609	8,622	9,831
East South Central	7,608	11,082	9,345	7,157	9,269	6,649	8,142	7,975	7,586
West South Central	8,232	10,150	10,058	8,376	9,488	6,732	8,614	8,035	8,376
Mountain	8,531	10,121	12,014	8,774	10,033	6,775	9,184	8,243	8,517
Pacific	9,879	11,658	13,381	10,199	11,057	7,735	9,922	9,508	10,351
United States	8,803	10,677	11,990	9,015	10,304	7,196	9,211	8,531	8,859
Earnings in 1980									
New England	16,509	*	21,810	19,153	22,492	12,337	18,255	15,198	15,194
Middle Atlantic	18,061	30,345	22,370	21,095	25,941	13,896	20,842	16,794	15,317
East North Central	17,948	27,978	24,577	23,190	24,831	12,938	18,715	15,418	14,140
West North Central	16,206	26,830	23,356	20,096	24,239	12,528	18,461	13,779	13,646
South Atlantic	16,250	27,087	17,444	16,803	23,091	12,381	17,329	15,675	17,050
East South Central	15,630	28,587	18,724	16,834	22,843	12,144	17,253	14,321	14,316
West South Central	17,453	27,758	20,381	20,004	23,146	13,634	18,110	16,145	14,893
Mountain	16,934	28,310	22,014	19,738	23,718	12,344	18,198	15,325	15,847
Pacific	19,172	31,759	26,224	21,858	25,543	14,168	20,490	17,842	18,871
United States	17,470	28,350	21,320	20,482	24,207	13,115	18,952	15,936	16,096

*Employment data not available at a sufficient level of disaggregation to permit computation of average earnings.

Sources: Based on data from U.S. Department of Commerce, Bureau of Economic Analysis, *Survey of Current Business*, vol. 61, no.7 (Washington, D.C.: Department of Commerce, July 1981); U.S. Department of Labor, Bureau of Labor Statistics, *Employment and Earnings* (Washington, D.C.: Department of Labor, monthly).

It has been suggested that the level of per capita income in a region is inversely related to the proportion of the regional labor force employed in the primary sector (i.e., agriculture, forestry, and fisheries). The rank correlation coefficient between primary-sector employment shares in 1970 and per capita income in 1970 was −.683, not quite significant at the 95 percent level. The same correlation for 1950 was −.800, which is statistically significant. Thus, the drag imposed on a regional economy as a result of specializing in primary activities has diminished. The probable explanation of this change is that such industries have become increasingly capital intensive, embodying technological advances that spur productivity growth.

To what extent are the average earnings of a region a function of its economic structure? In 1970, the highest-earnings region (PAC) did not rank first in employment shares in any of the four highest-paying industries. Similarly, the region with the lowest average earnings (ESC) did not have the largest employment shares in any of the four lowest-paying industries. The argument that industry mix is the sole determinant of interregional earnings differentials implicitly assumes that industry earnings (or wage rates) are equalized across regions. However, the data indicate that average earnings tended to be high in *all* industries in the PAC region and low in most industries in the ESC region.

This phenomenon can be explained in a variety of ways. The first possibility is that industry employment and income data are too highly aggregated. Intrasectoral differences in productivity may give rise to earnings differentials across industry subcategories. For example, in 1970 the average hourly wage in manufacturing was $3.36, but wages ranged from $4.49 an hour in petroleum refining to $2.10 an hour in men's and boys' apparel (U.S. Department of Commerce, 1971, pp. 219–21). But it is most unlikely that *every* industry in a region would be heavily weighted toward either high- or low-paying subsectors.

A second explanation is that the capital-labor ratio is higher (lower) in regions with high (low) average earnings. Because of the paucity of regional capital stock data, it is impossible to test this hypothesis. In the *manufacturing* sector in 1970, the correlation between capital-labor ratios and average earnings was −.066. Not only is the relationship between labor productivity and factor intensity extremely weak, but the sign is wrong as well. Whether similar results would be obtained for the other sectors is uncertain, although Browne (1979) has argued that investment in manufacturing is a fairly reliable indicator of regional investment in general.

A third explanation is that high-earnings (low-earnings) regions are labor-shortage (surplus) regions. In this case, one would expect the PAC region to have had a low unemployment rate in 1970 and the ESC region to have had a high unemployment rate. However, the correlation between average earnings and regional unemployment rates in 1970 was .567, implying that high-wage regions tend to experience above-average unemployment.

Finally, higher regional earnings may merely reflect higher living costs. This would account for the fact that all industries in high-wage regions tend to pay more than the same industries in low-wage regions. This possibility underscores the need to develop a consistent set of regional price deflators. It is likely that once regional earnings are deflated by the appropriate price indices, the pattern of relative regional incomes will change significantly (see Table 6.1).

Wages, Migration, and Growth

The data indicate that low regional wages impart a competitive advantage to producers located within such regions and, in general, are associated with rapid employment growth.[21] The major exception occurs in the NE region, with both low earnings and low job growth. The NE experience might be explained in terms of interregional differences in the pattern of firm closures and starts. Garn and Ledebur (1982) indicate that closure (start) rates are higher (lower) in the Northeast than in the nation as a whole.[22] These above-average closure rates are due to the geographical shift in population and markets away from the Northeast, and a below-average ability to sustain production in the face of temporary downturns in demand. To the extent that older industrial plants are less efficient (and more costly to operate) than new facilities, the regions in which such plants are located should have an above-average number of business failures—particularly during recessions—and a slower rate of employment growth (Engerman, 1965). In the case of NE, it would seem that low wages are insufficient to completely counter the adverse effects of Frostbelt out-migration and a possibly technologically obsolete capital infrastructure.[23]

Rapid employment growth tends to stimulate overall income growth as well as wage rate growth (this is true for both regions and industries). As output and employment growth rates increase and labor needs become more urgent, rising wages play a critical role in bringing about the requisite

---

[21] As above, the observations that follow are based on the analysis of simple correlation coefficients and general regional trends. For the purposes here, this approach is quite satisfactory. However, it is realized that the wage-adjustment mechanism should be studied in the context of a general equilibrium regional growth framework. Clearly, such an endeavor is beyond the scope of this chapter.

[22] Closure and start rates are reported only for the Northeast, West, South, and North Central regions. These statistics are not provided for the individual subregions. It is assumed that the rates for the Northeast are representative of both the NE *and* MA regions.

[23] Low wages and slow wage growth in the NE region may, in fact, be the consequence of an obsolete capital stock and a below-average rate of investment. An alternative explanation is offered by Harrison in Chapter 7.

interregional and interindustry resource transfers. On the demand side of the labor market, the most important determinants of wage growth are the capital stock growth rate and the growth in demand for regional outputs. On the supply side, the relevant factors include the labor force growth rate and the unemployment rate.[24] Labor force growth is conveniently broken down into changes in labor force participation rates, rates of natural population increase and net migration rates. Interregional variations in the elasticities of labor supply and demand will be partly responsible for wage rate growth differences across regions.

Since 1951, the ESC and WSC regions have experienced the greatest rates of (manufacturing) capital formation, and the MA and ENC, the lowest (Table 3.12). While the MA region has consistently been below the national average, the NE region enjoyed above-average growth during the 1960s. In general, capital stock growth has been most rapid in the South and West, and slowest in the Northeast and North Central regions. It is interesting that when the data are disaggregated to smaller regional groupings, investment patterns no longer neatly follow Frostbelt/Sunbelt lines. Between 1970 and 1975, for example, the WNC region grew at a rate above the national average while the capital stock of the PAC region expanded at a rate that was only 88.6 percent of the national mean. Over the five time intervals examined, there are six (seven) instances of above (below) average growth rates in the Frostbelt (Sunbelt).

Virtually all economists agree that capital accumulation is a critical factor in the growth process. Investment not only adds to local demand (provided that the capital goods are produced within the region), but also serves to expand productive capacity. Since much technological progress is capital embodied, the importance of this last point should not be underestimated. As might be expected, the correlation between capital stock growth and income growth is both positive and highly significant. The data support the earlier contention that in the NE region the advantages associated with relatively low wage rates are partially offset by a high-cost, technologically inferior capital stock. The economic climate of the South, on the other hand, is enhanced by low wages and rapid capital accumulation.

It has already been seen that regional capital-labor ratios (k) do not adequately explain interregional variations in average earnings. While economic theory predicts a positive relationshhip between these two variables, the data

[24]The role of the unemployment rate as a determinant of wage growth is a controversial topic. Hanham and Chang (1981) suggest that "labor hoarding by employers seriously undermines the value of using unemployment as an indication of excess demand for labor." Martin (1981) states that "the rank-order correlation between wage levels and unemployment rates across regions is positive (though not statistically significant)." In the present study, the correlation between earnings growth and unemployment rates is negative, though not statistically significant.

TABLE 3.12
Manufacturing Capital Stock Growth Rates, 1951–1976 (in percent)

Region	1951–55	1955–60	1960–65	1965–70	1970–75	1951–76
New England	15.5	17.7	15.3	31.7	13.1	141.1
Middle Atlantic	14.1	12.7	8.6	22.1	9.4	88.2
East North Central	21.1	16.5	12.5	24.9	11.2	125.7
West North Central	13.7	12.7	17.7	25.4	22.0	153.1
South Atlantic	19.3	23.5	22.4	33.8	26.7	217.0
East South Central	22.7	28.0	25.3	41.6	25.4	264.4
West South Central	24.1	17.3	13.9	38.3	28.9	223.6
Mountain	17.5	22.1	16.7	28.0	41.5	218.9
Pacific	15.1	19.8	17.4	28.1	15.6	146.7
United States	18.3	17.7	14.6	28.5	17.6	148.7
Northeast	14.3	13.7	9.9	24.1	10.2	98.4
North Central	20.0	16.8	13.3	25.0	13.7	129.8
South	21.7	22.0	19.8	36.8	27.3	228.1
West	15.5	20.2	17.2	28.1	19.9	158.2

Source: Lynn E. Browne, Vice President, Federal Reserve Bank of Boston (unpublished data).

indicate a negative—albeit very weak—correlation. The values of k are low (high) relative to earnings in the PAC and MA (WSC and ESC) regions. However, if price levels are higher in the PAC and MA regions, the discrepancy is explained by distortions arising from the use of *money* earnings in the computations.

Consistent with theoretical expectations, a positive correlation between wage growth and k growth is observed. As k growth increases, the marginal productivity of labor and the demand for labor inputs grow faster, and wage growth accelerates. This should result in the eventual convergence of regional earnings and the equalization of k growth rates. The presence of agglomerative forces, however, may cause this process to be unstable, and divergent growth may be the ultimate result.

Thus far, the discussion of wage dynamics has focused entirely on the demand side of the market. To what extent are interregional variations in wages and wage growth explained by supply factors? *Ceteris paribus*, an increase in the labor force participation rate, the net migration rate, or the rate of natural population increase should cause wages and wage growth to decline. If wages are inflexible downward, as is generally argued, it is likely that an increase in the supply of labor will result in slower wage growth rather than reduced earnings. Complications also arise from the fact that labor supply and labor demand are, to some degree, interdependent. For example, in-migration increases not only the supply of labor but also the demand for output—and, hence, the *derived* demand for labor. The unemployment rate, which may be viewed as a measure of the short-run absorptive capacity of a region, should be inversely related to wage growth.

Nationally, labor force participation rates have been rising over time. This is largely due to the growing number of women who have entered the work force, up from 27.4 percent in 1940 to 52.0 percent in 1981. The most dramatic change in the pattern of female participation is the rapidly expanding role played by married women. As a result of liberalized attitudes concerning sex-role stereotypes and the fact that wage growth in many sectors of the economy has failed to keep pace with inflation, households with two or more workers are no longer exceptional. Of all married women (with husband present), 14.7 percent participated in 1940 compared with 51.0 percent in 1981 (U.S. Department of Commerce, 1982). In 1980, the highest labor force participation rates were observed in the PAC, MT, and NE regions, the lowest in the ESC, MA, and SA regions. From 1970 to 1980, the expected negative correlation between participation rate growth and regional wage growth was found.

The rate of natural population increase might reasonably be expected to affect the labor market only in the long run. It is possible, however, that natural increase may affect labor supply in the short run by influencing the participation rate of existing workers. Higher birth rates may cause secondary workers to enter the labor force if family income is insufficient to meet all the additional expenses associated with larger family size. On the other hand, many women leave the workforce for a period of time for the purpose of childrearing. From 1970 to 1980, the correlation between the rate of natural population increase and wage growth was positive.

Between 1970 and 1980, net migration rates and wage growth were found to be positively related. In order to understand this result, it is necessary to discuss the directional causality of the relationship between the two variables. The above finding reflects the fact that the rational individual will respond to the economic incentives created by rising wages and growing employment opportunities. The correlation between 1970–80 wage growth and 1960–70 net migration rates is negative, which is consistent with the argument that a growing labor force will have a depressive effect on wage growth. The tendency for migrants to flow from the Frostbelt to the Sunbelt works against income convergence (unless, of course, *real* incomes in the Sunbelt are higher than in the Frostbelt) and should extend the time needed for equalization to occur.

It is very difficult to generalize about unemployment rates because they are so highly volatile. To correct for cyclical variability, changes in unemployment rates are usually evaluated at similar phases of the cycle (i.e., from peak to peak and trough to trough). Even so, intertemporal comparisons are complicated by (1) the changing demographic configuration of the labor force, (2) definitional and computational changes in statistical methodology, (3) institutional and social changes that affect labor supply, and (4) legislative initiatives that affect the demand for labor.[25]

The latest surge in unemployment rates (1980–82) coincides with the high interest rates brought on by the Federal Reserve Board's anti-inflationary monetary strategy. Interestingly, the 1981–82 recession is the first since the 1948–49 downturn in which interest rates increased rather than decreased. Because the producers of durable goods tend to be highly concentrated in only a few geographical areas, a strong spatial bias in the distribution of burdens associated with this latest downturn may be expected.

Not surprisingly, industry unemployment rates vary considerably over the business cycle. The agricultural sector exhibits high rates of joblessness when times are good, and the mining industry appears especially susceptible to high unemployment rates when times are bad. It is worth noting that the mining industry—in a radical departure from past experience—had one of the lowest unemployment rates during the 1973–75 recession, probably a consequence of intensified exploration for mineral resources following the 1973 oil embargo. In terms of extremes, however, there seems to be substantial consistency across the cycle. For example, from 1949 to 1980 the construction industry has had the highest rate of unemployment, and government and FIRE sectors, the lowest.

It is somewhat curious that durable goods manufacturing, commonly assumed the most cyclically sensitive industry, ranks among the hardest hit in only one recession since 1949 (and even then, its rate of unemployment was a full 6.8 percentage points below that of the construction industry). Undoubtedly, the reason manufacturing has been singled out in this respect is because it constitutes such a large part of the employment base. Despite inordinately high unemployment rates, the construction industry has never accounted for more than 12.5 percent of national unemployment (U.S. Department of Labor, 1980, pp. 78–79). Manufacturing, on the other hand, has been responsible for as much as 34.9 percent of the nation's joblessness. Because of the relative decline in manufacturing employment shares over time, the manufacturing share of unemployment has diminished. In fact, by 1970 the wholesale and retail trade sector comprised a larger percentage of those unemployed than did durable goods manufacturing.

The spatial distribution of unemployment will depend on general economic conditions (i.e., the cyclical phase) and the labor market characteris-

---

[25] Among the institutional and social changes that affect labor supply, Flaim (1979) includes changes in the unemployment insurance program, the effect of multiworker families on job search, and the work-seeking requirements of many welfare programs. The legislative initiatives that may affect labor demand include the minimum wage and various government-sponsored job programs.

tics of the different geographical areas. Since the industrial composition of regions is becoming increasingly similar over time (as shown in Table 3.8), there is reason to believe that interregional variations in cyclical sensitivity will gradually become less important. In the long run, then, the supply side of the market in general and net interregional migration in particular may be the key determinants of unemployment rate differentials.

It is no easy matter to classify regions on the basis of unemployment rates (Table 3.13).[26] Except for a very brief period in the late 1960s, the Frostbelt/ Sunbelt dichotomy is entirely meaningless. Each of the broad regional groupings (Northeast, North Central, South, and West) has one or more subregions that are prone to high unemployment.

In 1960 the Northeast and the West had the highest rates of unemployment. By the end of the decade, unemployment was concentrated in the Sunbelt—primarily in the West. As the nation began its recovery from the 1973–75 recession, the pattern of the early 1960s reemerged. While the South and West enjoyed relatively low levels of joblessness in 1980, the Northeast hovered around the mean, and the North Central region experienced unemployment rates far in excess of the national average. As previously suggested, the phenomenon of rising interest rates in a recession led to a strong bias in the geographical incidence of unemployment.

The WNC region consistently shows the lowest unemployment rates. This may be due to the fact that a relatively large share of its labor force is employed in agriculture, a sector in which "disguised" unemployment tends to be quite high. Of the remaining regions, the WSC and the SA also exhibit a marked tendency toward low jobless rates. Incidentally, the WNC region and the South have the lowest levels of unionization in the nation, and the greatest preponderance of "open-shop" jobs. To the extent that unions limit entry into the various occupations, a direct relationship between percentage unionized and unemployment rates may be expected. In the Northeast (West), the NE (MT) region is less prone to joblessness than the MA (PAC) region.

From 1960 to 1975, the PAC region had the highest unemployment rate in the nation. Not until 1980, however, did its jobless rate fall below the national average. During the latter half of the 1970s, the highest rates of unemployment were concentrated in the Northeast—principally in the MA region.

[26]Reliable regional unemployment data are almost as sparse as data on regional capital stocks. In 1960 the Department of Labor developed a seventy-step formula in order to estimate total unemployment for states. When these estimates were compared with those of the 1960 census, a regional bias in the "handbook method" was discovered. The method tended to overestimate during recessions and underestimate during recoveries; furthermore, the procedure did not adequately standardize unemployment insurance data for interarea differences in legal definitions of unemployment (Ziegler, 1977, p. 15). This estimation formula was used until 1974 when the Bureau of Labor Statistics modified the handbook method by using a benchmarking procedure.

TABLE 3.13
Relative Unemployment Rates*

Region	1960	1962	1967	1969	1971	1973	1975	1977	1979	1980
New England	90.2	80.0	76.3	85.7	116.9	112.2	120.0	110.0	93.1	84.5
Middle Atlantic	105.9	116.4	94.7	91.4	101.7	108.2	109.4	124.3	120.7	105.6
East North Central	102.0	105.5	92.1	91.4	101.7	91.8	104.7	92.9	105.2	131.0
West North Central	78.4	65.5	68.4	68.6	72.9	79.6	61.2	68.6	69.0	80.3
South Atlantic	92.2	101.8	100.0	97.1	76.3	81.6	100.0	97.1	94.8	90.1
East South Central	109.8	103.6	110.5	105.7	88.1	85.7	92.9	91.4	105.2	111.3
West South Central	94.1	96.4	97.4	105.7	89.8	87.8	75.3	81.4	81.0	80.3
Mountain	98.0	90.9	128.9	120.0	103.4	106.1	88.2	94.3	86.2	88.7
Pacific	119.6	114.5	150.0	145.7	147.5	142.9	115.3	117.1	110.3	98.6
United States (%)	5.1	5.5	3.8	3.5	5.9	4.9	8.5	7.0	5.8	7.1

*United States rate = 100.
Sources: L. E. Browne, Regional unemployment rates—why are they so different? New England Economic Review (July/August 1978): 5–26; Schwab (1970); U.S. Department of Commerce (1982).

By 1980, the ENC region—with a jobless rate more than 30.0 percent greater than the national average—clearly dominated the unemployment statistics, followed next by the ESC region.

In 1980 the distribution of unemployment by duration exhibited a strong spatial pattern. Of the eight states having the greatest percentages of short-term unemployment (less than five weeks), seven were located in the Sunbelt (U.S. Department of Labor, 1980, p. 46). Job leavers and reentrants constituted an above-average share of the unemployed in the MT region and the South (U.S. Department of Labor, 1980, p. 8). Apparently, dynamic job growth in the Sunbelt and the associated expanded employment opportunities have increased the relative incidence of frictional unemployment. Six of the eight states having the largest shares of long-term unemployment (fifty-two weeks or more) were located in the Frostbelt. A large share of the unemployed in the Northeast and North Central regions consisted of persons who had lost their jobs: above-average firm closure rates and layoffs in industries ravaged by competition from abroad (e.g., automobile manufacturing and steel) have led to pervasive structural unemployment in the Frostbelt.

During the 1970s, the Frostbelt lost population through net out-migration while the Sunbelt gained from net in-migration. These migration flows make little sense because average earnings (and per capita incomes) were higher in the Frostbelt. The anomaly may be explained in a number of ways.

1. Interregional differences in the cost of living are such that *real* per capita incomes are higher in the Sunbelt than in the Frostbelt. Migrants, of course, are assumed not to suffer from money illusion.
2. As a determinant of migration, the probability of finding a job may be just as important as the prospect of higher income. *Ceteris paribus*, an individual will be more likely to move to a region with a low unemployment rate than to one with a high jobless rate (Todaro, 1969; Greenwood, 1981, p. 158).[27] The fact that unemployment rates in the Frostbelt rose relative to those in the Sunbelt during the period in question lends support to this hypothesis.
3. The data are too highly aggregated. *Individual* migrants may increase their incomes even if they move from high-wage to low-wage regions. The use of average earnings masks the wide range of intraregional incomes, and the use of aggregate flow data obscures the fact that many

[27] A similar argument can be made with respect to employment growth. Consider the PAC region, for example, which had the greatest migration rate *and* the highest unemployment rates during the 1960s. In this case, above-average job growth attracted migrants, not all of whom were able to find work (as evidenced by the high jobless rate). Unemployment rates and job growth can also work in the same direction (e.g., in the SA, WSC, and MT regions during the 1970s). "Greater rates of employment growth obviously provide a significant inducement to in-migration," concluded Greenwood (1981, p. 175) from the results obtained using a simultaneous-equation urban growth model.

migrants are highly educated and among the most productive workers in the labor force of the sending region.
4. Some migration is motivated by noneconomic considerations. For example, people retire, enter/leave the armed forces, and attend school, all of which may result in interregional shifts (Long and Hansen, 1979). A migrant who is currently employed may be willing to sacrifice money income for nonpecuniary benefits. The desire to live closer to relatives, climatic conditions, and cultural or social amenities are just a few of the factors that may influence the migration decision.

Any of the above explanations is sufficient to reconcile the paradox of net in-migration to low-income regions and net out-migration from high-income regions.

According to Rones (1980, p. 17), the single most important determinant of migration is unemployment status. In the 1950s and the 1960s, interregional migration tended to raise unemployment rates at the destination and lower them at the origin. This logically follows from the assumption that many migrants are out of work and seeking employment.[28] During the 1970s, however, the relationship between migration and unemployment rates was reversed. Among the factors that may have played a role in this reversal are interregional differences in the type of unemployment, and the employment status and occupational/industrial affiliation of the migrant population. The migration of persons not participating in the labor force (e.g., retirees and students) may cause unemployment rates to increase (decrease) in the sending (receiving) region if demand shifts are sufficiently strong. The same result may occur if the unemployment rate of the migrant population is especially low. Over the period 1974–76, Long and Hansen (1979) found that 27 percent of migrants were motivated by job transfers while 23 percent relocated for the purpose of seeking work.

Conclusion

Population, income, and employment have been declining in the Frostbelt relative to the Sunbelt since 1930. While the factors contributing to this transformation are numerous, a single underlying cause may be identified: the erosion of the Frostbelt's comparative cost advantages in production. High wages, a technologically obsolete capital stock, extensive unionization, an industrial mix disproportionately weighted toward sectoral outputs for which demand is waning, and relatively low levels of new investment impair

---

[28] If the majority of migrants are unemployed, the unemployment rate of the migrant population should be greater than that of either the sending or receiving region. Under these conditions, interregional migration should lower the unemployment rate at the origin and raise it at the destination.

the Frostbelt's ability to compete with the Sunbelt and with foreign producers.

Because of differential growth rates, regions have become increasingly similar over time. If present trends continue, the eventual equalization of regional per capita incomes will probably occur. Ironically, the out-migration of population from the Frostbelt has been the single most important factor in muting the rate of relative per capita income decline. Whether per capita income growth paths will stabilize after convergence is an unanswered question.

If the geographical dispersion of persons and jobs represents the private market's response to a changing economic climate and if externalities are moderate, the transformation is consistent with the goals of economic efficiency.[29] If the shift toward the Sunbelt serves spatial equity objectives (i.e., results in a more equal interregional distribution of income), it is probably also consistent with macroeconomic redistributive policies. Under these conditions, intervention in the process is difficult to justify so long as convergence continues.

Whether the tendency for the Northeast to decline in terms of income is undesirable is a value judgement that depends on the perspective (and region of residence) of the observer. To argue that the transformation should be stopped through government intervention, even if this were possible, is equivalent to arguing that the Frostbelt is somehow more deserving than the Sunbelt. Since such a stance is not likely to be taken by the federal government, most attempts to "stem the tide" will be made at the state level. If these attempts are to succeed, state and local governments in declining regions must appreciate that their problems are only a single facet of a larger, multidimensional evolutionary process and gear their policies accordingly. Efforts to resist change will fail unless they focus on the root cause of the transformation—the inability to compete. For the Frostbelt, the key to prosperity lies not in the solicitation of federal aid or in the proliferation of tax havens, but in the willingness and ability to *adapt* itself to the exigencies of a changing economic environment.

References

Brown, A. A., and E. Neuberger, eds. 1977. *Internal Migration: A Comparative Perspective*. New York: Academic Press.

Browne, L. E. 1979. Regional capital formation. *New England Economic Indicators* (June): 3–8.

[29]The argument that market outcomes are efficient depends critically on the assumption that there are no distortions in the price signals to which producers and consumers respond. It would, of course, be wrong to suggest that this condition is actually satisfied. Environmental externalities, government regulation, agricultural price supports, rent controls, minimum wage legislation, and taxation are just a few of the more obvious sources of distortion found in modern economies.

Browne, L. E., P. Mieszkowski, and R. F. Syron. 1980. Regional investment patterns. *New England Economic Review* (July/August): 5–23.

Engerman, S. 1965. "Regional aspects of stabilization policy." In *Essays in Fiscal Federalism*, edited by R. A. Musgrave, 7–62. Washington, D.C.: The Brookings Institution.

Flaim, P. O. 1979. The effect of demographic changes on the Nation's unemployment rate. *Monthly Labor Review* 102, no. 3 (March): 13–23.

Fothergill, S., and G. Gudgin. 1979. In defence of shift-share. *Urban Studies* 16: 309–19.

Garn, H. A., and L. C. Ledebur. 1982. "Congruencies and conflicts in regional and industrial policies." In *Regional Dimensions of Industrial Policy*, edited by M. E. Bell and P. S. Lande, 47–80. Lexington, Mass.: Lexington Books.

Greenwood, M. J. 1981. *Migration and Economic Growth in the United States: National, Regional, and Metropolitan Perspectives*. New York: Academic Press.

Hanham, R. Q., and H. Chang. 1981. "Wage inflation in a growth region: the American Sun Belt." In *Regional Wage Inflation and Unemployment*, edited by R. L. Martin, 75–95. London: Pion Limited.

Havemann, J., R. L. Stanfield, and N. R. Peirce. 1976. Federal spending: the North's loss is the Sunbelt's gain. *National Journal* 8, no. 26 (June 26): 878–91.

House, P. W., and R. G. Ryan. 1979. *The Future Indefinite: Decision-Making in a Transition Economy*. Lexington, Mass.: Lexington Books.

Jackson, G. et al. 1981. *Regional Diversity: Growth in the United States, 1960–1990*. Boston: Auburn House Publishing Company.

Kneese, A. V., and F. L. Brown. 1981. *The Southwest Under Stress: National Resource Development Issues in a Regional Setting*. Baltimore: Johns Hopkins University Press.

Long, L. H., and K. A. Hansen. 1979. Reasons for interstate migration. *Current Population Reports*. Special Studies, ser. P-23, no. 81, 5–6. U.S. Department of Commerce, Bureau of the Census. Washington, D.C.: Government Printing Office.

Martin, R. L. 1981. "Wage-change interdependence amongst regional labour markets: conceptual issues and some empirical evidence for the United States." In *Regional Wage Inflation and Unemployment* edited by R. L. Martin, 96–135. London: Pion Limited.

Perloff, H. S., E. S. Dunn, Jr., E. E. Lampard, and R. F. Muth. 1960. *Regions, Resources, and Economic Growth*. Lincoln: University of Nebraska Press.

Richardson, H. W. 1973. *Regional Growth Theory*. London: The Macmillan Press Ltd.

Richardson, H. W. 1979. *Regional Economics*. Urbana: University of Illinois Press.

Rones, P. L. 1980. Moving to the sun: regional job growth, 1968 to 1978. *Monthly Labor Review* 103, no. 3 (March): 12–19.

Rosen, R. 1980. Identifying States and areas prone to high and low unemployment. *Monthly Labor Review* 103, no. 3 (March): 20–24.

Sale, K. 1975. *Power Shift: The Rise of the Southern Rim and Its Challenge to the Eastern Establishment*. New York: Random House.

Sawers, L., and W. K. Tabb, eds. 1984. *Sunbelt/Snowbelt: Urban Development and Regional Restructuring.* New York: Oxford University Press.

Schwab, P. M. 1970. Unemployment by region and in 10 largest States. *Monthly Labor Review* 93, no. 1 (January): 3–12.

Sutton, H. 1978. Sunbelt vs. Frostbelt: a second civil war. *Saturday Review* (April 15): 28–37.

Temporary Commission on City Finances. 1978. "Taxation and manufacturing in New York City." In *Revitalizing the Northeast: Prelude to an agenda,* edited by G. Sternlieb and J. W. Hughes, 279–308. New Brunswick, N.J.: Center for Urban Policy Research.

Thirlwall, A. P. 1967. A measure of the proper distribution of industry. *Oxford Economic Papers* 19: 46–58.

Todaro, M. P. 1969. A model of labor migration and urban unemployment in less developed countries. *American Economic Review* 59: 138–148.

U.S. Department of Commerce. (n.d.) *Regional Employment by Industry, 1940–70: Decennial Series for United States, Regions, States, Counties.* Washington, D.C.: Government Printing Office.

U.S. Department of Commerce, Bureau of the Census. 1971. *Statistical Abstract of the United States.* Washington, D.C.: Government Printing Office.

U.S. Department of Commerce. July 1979. *State Quarterly Economic Developments.* Washington, D.C.: Government Printing Office.

U.S. Department of Commerce, Bureau of the Census. 1980. *Statistical Abstract of the United States.* Washington, D.C.: Government Printing Office.

U.S. Department of Commerce, Bureau of the Census. 1982. *Statistical Abstract of the United States.* Washington, D.C.: Government Printing Office.

U.S. Department of Labor. 1980. *Handbook of Labor Statistics.* Washington, D.C.: Government Printing Office.

U.S. Department of Labor. 1982. *Geographic Profile of Employment and Unemployment, 1980.* Washington, D.C.: Government Printing Office.

Williamson, J. G. 1980. "Unbalanced growth, inequality, and regional development: some lessons from U.S. history." In *Alternatives to Confrontation: A National Policy toward Regional Change,* edited by V. A. Arnold, 3–61. Lexington, Mass.: Lexington Books.

Ziegler, M. 1977. Efforts to improve estimates of State and local unemployment. *Monthly Labor Review* 100, no. 11 (November): 12–18.

GEORGE STERNLIEB

JAMES W. HUGHES

4 *The National Economy and the Northeast: A Context for Discussion*

Increasing concerns about the future of the United States economy, as well as regional variations within it, have generated explosive growth in the literature of economic development and in public awareness. Indeed, to the cynic, part of the problem may well be the reinforcement of trends by public hysteria in response to the release of the latest economic indicators. To a nation rapidly becoming addicted to the weekly report of the Federal Reserve's vagaries, viewing them as a forecasting tool, it is difficult to provide appropriate longer-term contexts within which to gauge the sweep of development.

Gross National Product

Table 4.1 presents data, both in current and in constant 1972 dollars, for the gross national product (GNP) from 1960 to 1981, together with equivalent annual percentage changes. From 1965 through 1973, the GNP of the United States increased by one-third, measured in constant dollars. The magnitude of this accomplishment has sometimes been underestimated. It was the equivalent of adding all of Japan's (1965) economy to ours, and roughly equal to adding half that of the total USSR.

But the annual data in Table 4.1 indicate the abrupt discontinuity generated by the energy revolution of 1973, with a disastrous downturn in the subsequent two years. A rapid recovery ensued in 1976, clearly stimulated by an

TABLE 4.1
Gross National Product, 1960–1980*

| Year | Current Dollars | | Constant 1972 Dollars | |
	GNP	Average Annual Percent Change[†]	GNP	Average Annual Percent Change[†]
1960	506	4.0	737	2.4
1965	688	6.3	926	4.7
1970	982	7.4	1,075	3.0
1971	1,063	8.2	1,107	3.0
1972	1,171	10.2	1,171	5.8
1973	1,307	11.6	1,235	5.5
1974	1,413	8.1	1,218	−1.4
1975	1,529	8.2	1,202	−1.3
1976	1,718	12.4	1,300	8.2
1977	1,918	11.6	1,372	5.5
1978	2,156	12.4	1,437	4.7
1979	2,414	12.0	1,483	3.2
1980	2,626	8.8	1,481	−0.1
1981	2,922	11.3	1,510	2.0

*In billions of dollars.
†Change from prior year; for 1960, 1965, and 1970, average annual change for preceding five years.
Sources: U.S. Department of Commerce, Bureau of Economic Analysis, *The National Income and Products Accounts of the United States, 1929–74* (Washington, D.C.: Government Printing Office, 1976); *Survey of Current Business*, Bureau of Economic Analysis, U.S. Department of Commerce (Washington, D.C.: Department of Commerce, July issues and February 1982).

inflationary economy; the results—and the costs—of the latter remain with us today. In contrast to the one-third growth of the economy between 1965 and 1973, growth in the next eight years (1973 to 1981) was only at the 22 percent level, and to achieve this involved a high price in terms of inflation.

The pattern of "stagflation" (i.e., a relatively slow-growth economy), despite the nominally stimulative effects of inflation, is reflected in Table 4.2, which shows quarterly data from 1979 to 1981 illustrating the start-stop nature of the nation's economic performance. Despite an abrupt downturn in GNP during the first half of 1982 (extending the doleful performance of 1981's fourth quarter), real interest rates remained close to all-time high levels. The failure to exercise both fiscal and monetary restraint had come home to roost. Significant and permanent reductions in the rate of inflation were overridden by the erosion of public confidence in the government's capacity to adopt long-run programs of fiscal stability, which was mirrored in the reality of punitive real interest rates. The repeated shocks endured by the aggregate economy need little elaboration and should not be underestimated. However, it is important to be aware of the accomplishments of the economy during this relatively slow-growth era.

TABLE 4.2
Gross National Product by Quarter, 1979–1981*

Year and Quarter	GNP	Percent Change from Previous Quarter
1979		
I	$1,479.9	1.0
II	1,473.4	−0.4
III	1,488.2	1.0
IV	1,490.6	0.2
1980		
I	1,501.9	0.8
II	1,463.3	−2.6
III	1,471.9	0.6
IV	1,485.6	0.9
1981		
I	1,516.4	2.1
II	1,510.4	−0.4
III	1,515.8	0.4
IV	1,495.6	−1.3

*In billions of constant 1972 dollars.
Source: U.S. Department of Commerce, Bureau of Economic Analysis, *Survey of Current Business* (Washington, D.C.: Department of Commerce, monthly).

Labor Force and Employment Patterns

Table 4.3 presents data on GNP per person in the labor force. While gross national product per labor force participant increased by 12 percent in the eight years from 1965 to 1973, it was little more than stable (1.6 percent) in the subsequent period from 1973 through 1980. This is explained less by the slowdown in GNP growth than by the absolute increase in the size of the labor force. The decline in GNP growth over the two time periods was not matched by a comparable decline in labor-force growth. On the contrary, the rate of labor-force growth remained more or less constant, and absolute growth even increased (16 million in the period 1973–80 compared with 14.2 million in 1965–73).

This change is reflected in the nation's employment growth patterns (Table 4.4). In the years from 1960 to 1975, one of the most rapid growth eras in American history, the annual average increments in total employment were under 1.6 million. From 1975 to 1981, on the other hand, they averaged 50 percent higher (about 2.4 million). In the six years from 1975 to 1981, the American economy generated nearly 80 percent as many new jobs as in the decade of the 1960s.

With an economy at best maturing, at worst suffering from a chronic decline in its competitive edge, the United States has managed to absorb the "baby boom." The impact of this phenomenon has been the subject of much debate. Has the economy slowed down because of changes in consumption and savings patterns associated with the baby boom? Or have attitudes toward work and leisure been significantly affected by this demographic shock, thereby creating an undisciplined—and therefore uncompetitive—labor force in the United States? Have levels of productivity fallen because productive investment has failed to keep pace with the demands of the increment of population? These and many more theses have been advanced, linking the fertility patterns of a generation ago with the economic events of today.

Employment Profiles

The meaning of these dynamics still lacks clarification. Some explanations are no more than rationalizations of alternative political philosophies. What is far from uncertain, however, is the changing profile of United States employment. Table 4.4 provides information on the broad sweep of changes in manufacturing, private nonmanufacturing, and government employment from 1960 to 1981.

The relative decline in manufacturing employment is a familiar phenomenon and is clearly mirrored in the data of the table. The private nonmanufacturing sector grew seven times as rapidly as manufacturing from 1960 to 1975, and two-and-a-half times as rapidly between 1975 and 1981.

In the earlier period, however, it is striking that government employment experienced the highest rate of growth, with nearly nine jobs in that sector in

TABLE 4.3
Gross National Product per Person in Labor Force (Labor Force Participant)

Year	GNP (billions of 1972 $)	Civilian Labor Force (millions of persons)	GNP per Person in Labor Force
1965	926	74.5	$12,430
1970	1,075	82.7	12,998
1973	1,235	88.7	13,923
1980	1,481	104.7	14,145
Percent Change			
1965–73	33.3	19.1	12.0
1973–80	19.9	18.0	1.6

Sources: U.S. Department of Commerce, Bureau of Economic Analysis, *Survey of Current Business* (Washington, D.C.: Department of Commerce, monthly); U.S. Department of Labor, Bureau of Labor Statistics, *Employment and Earnings* (Washington, D.C.: Department of Labor, monthly).

TABLE 4.4
United States Employment Change by Sector, 1960–1981*

Sector	Total Employment			Change: 1960–1975			Change: 1975–1981		
	1960	1975	1981	Number	Percent	Ave. Annual Change	Number	Percent	Ave. Annual Change
Total	52,073.6	75,952.8	90,209.0	23,879.2	46.6	1,591.9	14,256.2	18.8	2,376.0
Manufacturing	16,725.6	18,194.9	20,133.4	1,469.3	8.8	98.0	1,938.5	10.7	323.1
Private non-manufacturing	27,058.6	42,990.6	53,344.1	15,932.0	58.9	1,062.1	10,353.5	24.1	1,725.6
Government	8,289.4	14,767.3	16,731.5	6,477.9	78.1	431.9	1,964.2	13.3	327.4

*Employees on nonagriculture payrolls as of March of the respective years; excludes Hawaii and Alaska. Numbers are in thousands.
Source: U.S. Department of Labor, Bureau of Labor Statistics, *Employment and Earnings* (Washington, D.C.: Department of Labor, monthly).

1975 for every five in 1960. The years since 1975 have been marked by much slower growth, as the magic (or poison, take your choice) of Proposition 13, Proposition 2½, generalized caps, and federal cutbacks began to work. Nevertheless, despite these strictures, there was an increase of nearly two million government jobs between 1975 and 1981.

As we move into the 1980s, the private nonmanufacturing sector dominates the employment structure, with a labor force in 1981 two-and-a-half times that of manufacturing. Again, many hypotheses have been suggested, several implying that the relative decline of manufacturing employment reflects the increasing noncompetitiveness of the United States.

International Comparisons

West Germany and Japan are typically regarded as the success stories in this discussion. Tables 4.5 and 4.6 provide background data on this comparison. Changes in total employment in the United States relative to her two major economic rivals reveal the scale of the American accomplishment. From 1969 to 1979, total employment in the United States increased by nearly a quarter, while West Germany's growth declined and Japan's was only a third of that in the United States. Some interpreters may view this growth as a burden rather than an asset, but the United States—in contrast to her competitors—has developed an unparalleled pattern of broad labor-force participation in a nonagricultural economy, one which increasingly merits the description "postindustrial." When placed in a relatively slow-growth context, the implicit character of a share-the-work economy becomes obvious if unintended.

A focus on the broad employment sectors, in terms of both absolute and incremental growth, between 1969 and 1979 shows a surprising degree of comparability in the employment pattern of the three countries (Tables 4.6 and 4.7). While there are variations in the scale and importance of some service sectors, such as finance, the proportion of the total workforce in manufacturing is remarkably similar. The data suggest that the broad sectoral allocation of America's labor force is not a major variable in explanations of her slow GNP growth.

Alternative Employment Partitions

The aggregate employment picture obscures changes at the margin that may be crucial for future prospects. A different employment perspective is presented in Table 4.8, showing increases from 1976 to 1981 according to a different partitioning approach. This groups the economy into five distinct sectors: high technology, energy, old-line industry, services, and govern-

TABLE 4.5
Total Employment: United States, West Germany, and Japan, 1969–1979*

| Nation | 1969 | 1974 | 1979 | Change: 1969–79 | |
				Number	Percent
United States	77,902	85,936	96,945	19,043	24.4
West Germany	25,871	25,688	25,041	−830	−3.2
Japan	50,400	52,370	54,790	4,390	8.7

*Annual averages; totals include wage and salary employees, self-employed persons, and unpaid family workers. Numbers are in thousands.

Source: Organization for Economic Cooperation and Development, (OECD), Labor Force Statistics, 1968–1979 (Paris: OECD, 1981).

ment. These may offer a preliminary insight into the growth areas of the 1980s, and a basis for questioning the Northeast's participation within them.

Casual extrapolation of the growth trends of Table 4.7 clearly has severe limitations, not only in terms of the future of the nation as a whole but also of the Northeast in particular. For example, in April 1982, twelve million square feet of office space were under construction in Denver, most of it related to hydrocarbon extraction industries. The projects, planned in an era when a barrel of oil cost thirty-four dollars or more, may come on-stream with real prices much below this level. The recent halt in exploitation of such areas as oil shale and oil sand deposits is evident. This is merely one example of the possible dangers of treating the immediate past as a firm guide to the immediate future.

Similarly, high-technology sectors are beginning to follow the maturation path of the more traditional manufacturing industries. Texas Instruments and Data General, hailed as high-technology leaders in the economy, are now laying off personnel, with the spectre of Japanese dominance in very large-scale integrated circuits on the horizon.

Service sectors, whose growth seemed inexorable, are now showing signs of vulnerability because of rising costs. Production services are tending to have their functions internalized within companies. The human services sector depends heavily on public expenditures and private-sector fringe benefits, and the flagging of commitment in these spheres hardly requires elaboration.

The Changing Distribution of Regional Employment

The increasing contribution of the South and West to national population growth, revealed by the 1980 census, is closely paralleled by the changing regional distribution of job growth. While much of the economic trauma of the older regions surfaced during the national recession of 1974–1975, the basic phenomenon, in less severe form, persisted both before and after.

TABLE 4.6

Comparative Employment Change by Industrial Sector: United States, West Germany, and Japan, 1969–1979*

Sector	United States				West Germany				Japan			
			Change: 1969–79				Change: 1969–79				Change: 1969–79	
	1969	1979	Number	Percent	1969	1979	Number	Percent	1969	1979	Number	Percent
Total	77,902	96,945	19,043	24.4	25,871	25,041	−830	−3.2	50,400	54,790	4,390	8.7
Agriculture, hunting, forestry, and fishing	3,698	3,455	−243	−6.6	2,395	1,558	−837	−34.9	9,460	6,130	−3,330	−35.2
Manufacturing, mining, and quarrying	21,780	23,001	1,221	5.6	10,407	9,122	−1,285	−12.3	13,690	13,450	−240	−1.8
Utilities	933	1,101	168	18.0	193	220	27	14.0	270	330	60	22.2
Construction	4,820	6,299	1,479	30.7	2,066	1,891	−175	−8.5	3,710	5,360	1,650	44.5
Wholesale and retail trade, hotels and restaurants	15,418	20,769	5,351	34.7	3,831	3,617	−214	−5.6	10,010	12,280	2,270	22.7
Transportation, storage, and communications	4,713	5,576	863	18.3	1,476	1,493	17	1.2	3,110	3,490	380	12.2
Finance, insurance, real estate, and business services	5,093	7,979	2,886	56.7	1,060	1,369	309	29.2	1,320	1,850	530	40.2
Community, social, and personal services	21,447	28,764	7,317	34.1	4,443	5,771	1,328	29.9	8,780	11,810	3,030	34.5
Other	—	—	—	—	—	—	—	—	50	90	40	80.0

*Annual averages; totals include wage and salary employees, self-employed persons, and unpaid family workers. Numbers are in thousands.
Source: Organization for Economic Cooperation and Development (OECD), *Labor Force Statistics, 1968–1979* (Paris: OECD, 1981).

TABLE 4.7
Comparative Employment Structures: United States, West Germany, and Japan, 1969–1979*

Sector	United States		West Germany		Japan	
	1969	1979	1969	1979	1969	1979
Agriculture, hunting, forestry, and fishing	4.7%	3.6%	9.3%	6.2%	18.8%	11.2%
Manufacturing, mining, and quarrying	28.0	23.7	40.2	36.4	27.2	24.5
Utilities	1.2	1.1	0.7	0.9	0.5	0.6
Construction	6.2	6.5	8.0	7.6	7.4	9.8
Wholesale and retail trade, hotels and restaurants	19.8	21.4	14.8	14.4	19.9	22.4
Transportation, storage, and communications	6.0	5.8	5.7	6.0	6.2	6.4
Finance, insurance, real estate, and business services	6.5	8.2	4.1	5.5	2.6	3.4
Community, social, and personal services	27.5	29.7	17.2	23.0	17.4	21.6
Other	—	—	—	—	0.1	0.2
Total	100.0	100.0	100.0	100.0	100.0	100.0

*Percent distribution—percentages may not total 100 because of rounding.
Source: Organization for Economic Cooperation and Development (OECD), *Labor Force Statistics, 1968–1979* (Paris: OECD, 1981).

TABLE 4.8
Alternative Employment Partitions: 1976–1981 Change*

Sector	Percent Change
Old-line industry	9.5
High technology	32.6
Energy	43.2
Services	26.3
Government	7.1

*Excludes wholesale and retail trade, includes Hawaii and Alaska.
Source: G. Sternlieb and J. W. Hughes, *Demographic Trendlines and Economic Reality: Planning and Markets in the 1980s* (New Brunswick, New Jersey: Rutgers University Center for Urban Policy Research, 1982). Courtesy of the Center for Urban Policy Research, Publications Division.

However, it was during the recession that the long-term transformation in the nation's social and economic parameters came under scrutiny. The aging industrial heartland of America—stretching from New England to the upper Midwest—began to experience unique strains associated with economic contraction and population migration to the Sunbelt. The traditional bases of industrial America have become prisoners of their early history and are experiencing the dislocations caused by accelerating technological change, a maturing economy, and, at least in the past, a mobile and footloose population.

Total Employment

In 1960 the Northeast (15.2 million jobs) and the North Central region (15.3 million) were the major employing regions in the country. The South lagged well behind (13.8 million) while the West had just about half the Northeast total (7.7 million). By 1981 the balance sheet had changed drastically. The Northeast had fallen far behind the North Central region and had barely two-thirds of the jobs held in the South, while the West was moving much closer to parity. Thus, the general impression of a burgeoning Sunbelt and a lagging Northeast is fully confirmed in national employment data.

Table 4.9 displays regional growth shares of total employment change for five-year periods from 1960 through 1975 and for the six-year interval from 1975 to 1981. Each of the periods under scrutiny reflects very different growth characteristics. National economic cycles largely determine individual regional cycles, though the regions are also driven by their own internal growth dynamics.

The weakness of the Northeast and the growing strength of the South was clear from 1960 to 1965, a period of modest national performance. The former accounted for only 14.5 percent of the nation's employment gains while the latter obtained 38.5 percent. The boom period of 1965 to 1970 obscured the differences in performance by dampening the interregional spread. Yet the South still obtained more than a third of the nation's employment growth.

Many economic problems of the Northeast and the Middle Atlantic states have been attributed to sluggish national performance between 1970 and 1975, when total employment gains of the nation (5.9 million jobs) dropped to half the level (11.9 million) of the preceding quinquennium. The Northeast region had gained 2.5 million jobs in the first period but actually lost jobs (35,700) between 1970 and 1975. When the national economy stagnates, the older regions' (Northeast and North Central) growth shares plummet and those of the South and West surge.

The reverse phenomenon occurred in the national job boom (14.3 million) of 1975 to 1981. But the recaptured shares of the Northeast and North Central states failed to return to the levels of the preceding high-growth era (1965–1970). The strength of the national economy moderated the trauma of the older regions but did not fully eliminate it.

Viewing the period as a whole (1960–1981), the high costs of the 1974-75 recession to the Northeast region and Middle Atlantic division become evident. Whether this phenomenon will be repeated during national economic recessions of the 1980s remains to be seen.

Manufacturing Employment

Despite the rise of the postindustrial or service economy, manufacturing remains a key factor, both directly and indirectly because of its multiplier

TABLE 4.9
Regional Growth Shares of Total Employment Change, 1960–1981*

Region and Division	Absolute Growth Increment				Percentage Share of National Growth			
	1960–1965	1965–1970	1970–1975	1975–1981	1960–1965	1965–1970	1970–1975	1975–1981
Northeast Region	875.7	2,465.9	−35.7	1,819.4	14.5	20.7	−0.6	12.8
Middle Atlantic Division	594.2	1,818.2	−223.9	1,019.2	9.8	15.3	−3.8	7.1
New England Division	281.5	647.7	188.2	800.2	4.7	5.4	3.2	5.6
North Central Region	1,422.2	3,240.6	872.1	2,548.5	23.6	27.2	14.7	17.9
East Central Division	989.7	2,332.6	317.6	1,621.2	16.4	19.6	5.4	11.4
West North Central Division	432.5	980.5	554.5	927.3	7.2	7.6	9.4	6.5
South Region	2,323.6	4,033.6	3,305.1	5,973.5	38.5	33.9	55.8	41.9
South Atlantic Division	1,182.8	2,146.6	1,695.2	2,712.0	19.6	18.0	28.6	19.0
East South Central Division	509.4	668.5	569.1	733.9	8.4	5.6	9.6	5.1
West South Central Division	631.4	1,218.5	1,040.8	2,527.6	10.5	10.2	17.6	17.7
West Region	1,420.4	2,171.3	1,784.4	3,914.8	23.5	18.2	30.1	27.5
Mountain Division	322.8	493.7	771.5	1,155.1	5.3	4.1	13.0	8.1
Pacific Division	1,097.6	1,677.6	1,012.9	2,759.7	18.2	14.1	17.1	19.4
United States†	6,041.9‡	11,911.4	5,925.9	14,256.2	100.0	100.0	100.0	100.0

*Employees on nonagricultural payrolls as of March of respective periods. Numbers are in thousands.
†Excludes Hawaii and Alaska.
‡Numbers and percentages may not sum to national totals because of rounding.
Source: U.S. Department of Labor, Bureau of Labor Statistics. *Employment and Earnings* (Washington, D.C.: Department of Labor, monthly).

impacts on other activities. Also, changes in manufacturing employment shed light on shifts in the pattern of industrialization and service employment for the nation and its regions.

Slow growth in national totals shows movement away from an economy dominated by manufacturing employment. Total employment in this sector grew by less than 9 percent from 1960 to 1975 and less than 11 percent from 1975 to 1981 (see Table 4.4).

The period from 1960 to 1975 was marked by very abrupt manufacturing declines within the Northeast region, with a job loss of nearly 14 percent. Between 1975 and 1981, on the other hand, the vigor of the national economy helped the region to bottom out, and manufacturing employment increased modestly. Nevertheless, in both periods the South and West secured the bulk of new manufacturing activity.

It is important to draw attention in this context to the significant turnaround of the New England division's manufacturing sector. From 1960 to 1975 this area lost more than 10 percent of its manufacturing jobs. Between 1975 and 1981 this trend was reversed by an increase of slightly more than 17 percent, reflecting the emergence of new growth elements—particularly in electronics and computers. Much of this was gestated, either physically or intellectually, in the research and development facilities of Route 128, the Boston metropolitan circumferential freeway. From 1975 to 1981 this apparently moribund region expanded manufacturing jobs more than one-and-a-half times the national rate and at a rate comparable with that of the South (the nation's most rapidly growing manufacturing region).

Table 4.10 shows that the New England division accounted for more than 11 percent of the total national growth in manufacturing employment from 1975 to 1981 after having been a substantial net loser in the preceding two decades. The Middle Atlantic division, tied to older forms of manufacturing, began to resemble the New England of several decades ago, when it was losing its dominance in labor-intensive industries (especially textiles) to the South and elsewhere.

However, much of the stability of the older regions (Northeast and North Central) between 1975 and 1981 may be a consequence of the improvement in the national economy. In all four periods, manufacturing employment in the Northeast and North Central regions fluctuated between slow growth and absolute decline in concert with national growth performance. The pattern of the South and West, on the other hand, fluctuated between slow and fast growth.

Private Nonmanufacturing Employment

Nonmanufacturing activity increasingly creates most of the new employment opportunities for Americans. In 1960 the manufacturing sector ac-

TABLE 4.10
Regional Growth Shares of Manufacturing Employment Change, 1960–1981 *

Region and Division	Absolute Growth Increment				Percentage Share of National Growth			
	1960–1965	1965–1970	1970–1975	1975–1981	1960–1965	1965–1970	1970–1975	1975–1981
Northeast Region	−110.1	264.9	−936.2	177.0	−15.2	12.0	−63.8	9.1
New England Division	−20.7	77.1	−212.1	220.2	−2.8	3.5	−14.4	11.4
Middle Atlantic Division	−89.4	187.8	−724.1	−43.2	−12.4	8.5	−49.4	−2.2
North Central Region	189.7	624.5	−579.8	177.5	26.2	28.2	−39.5	9.2
East Central Division	148.0	428.0	−585.4	66.8	20.5	19.3	39.9	3.4
West North Central Division	41.7	195.7	5.6	110.7	5.8	8.8	0.4	5.7
South Region	520.6	951.6	23.9	935.9	72.0	43.0	1.6	48.3
South Atlantic Division	250.4	424.3	−73.6	426.2	34.6	19.2	−5.0	21.9
East South Central Division	157.1	233.3	31.4	105.9	21.7	10.5	2.1	5.5
West South Central Division	113.1	293.9	66.1	403.8	15.6	13.3	4.5	20.8
West Region	122.7	372.5	25.1	648.1	17.0	16.8	1.7	33.4
Mountain Division	25.4	82.9	54.0	153.7	3.5	3.7	3.7	7.9
Pacific Division	97.3	289.6	−28.9	494.7	13.5	13.1	−2.0	25.5
United States †	722.9‡	2,213.4	−1,467.0	1,938.5	100.0	100.0	−100.0	100.0

*Employees on nonagriculture payrolls as of March of respective periods. Numbers are in thousands.
† Excludes Hawaii and Alaska.
‡ Numbers and percentages may not sum to national totals due to rounding.
Source: U.S. Department of Labor, Bureau of Labor Statistics, *Employment and Earnings* (Washington, D.C.: Department of Labor, monthly).

counted for slightly more than 16.7 million jobs while private nonmanufacturing employed 27 million (Table 4.4). By 1981 the gap had widened substantially. Manufacturing had increased only to 20 million jobs while private nonmanufacturing employment nearly doubled, to 53 million. Thus the United States, as an advanced, highly developed technological society, has rapidly moved from an economy dominated by manufacturing to a postindustrial era of services and allied activities.

Even though there are no absolute job declines in any of the four time periods detailed in Table 4.11, the private nonmanufacturing sector was also subject to the waves of national economic tides. Again, these were much more apparent in growth rates of older regions. In both the South and West, on the other hand, each succeeding time period between 1960–1965 and 1975–1981 resulted in larger absolute increases than in preceding periods. This reflects not only the economic attractiveness of Sunbelt territories but also the stimulus of their more rapid population growth to the growth of service activities. While employment growth in this sector has barely offset manufacturing stagnation in the Northeast and North Central regions, it has reinforced the growth dynamics of the South and West.

Total Government Employment

The period from 1960 to 1975 was an era characterized by marked increases in government employment. Stimulated by the need to cope with the baby boom and by the emergence of a variety of publicly financed social programs, total national employment in this sector increased by more than 6.4 million jobs, or 78 percent (Table 4.4). While there was some evidence of a slowdown after 1975, the net national gain between 1975 and 1981 nevertheless amounted to 2 million jobs (13.3 percent).

Government employment is increasing most rapidly in the Sunbelt regions (Table 4.12). Between 1960 and 1965 the South captured 32.9 percent of government employment growth; this share surged to 52.1 percent over the 1975–81 period. In contrast, the Northeast's share in the corresponding time periods declined from 20.5 percent to 9.9 percent. While there have been criticisms of the regional allocation of federal government jobs, these disparities substantially reflect interregional differences in the growth of both employment and population. The field offices of the Federal Housing Administration, the Veterans Administration, and the Social Security Administration are all in the business of servicing local activity and will increase or decrease in line with local employment and population changes. To that degree, government employment, rather than being independent of other forms of growth, is in large part its corollary. Thus, government employment mirrors demographic shifts and the geographic movement of other economic sectors.

TABLE 4.11
Regional Growth Shares of Private Nonmanufacturing Employment Change, 1960–1981*

Region and Division	Absolute Growth Increment				Percentage Share of National Growth			
	1960–1965	1965–1970	1970–1975	1975–1981	1960–1965	1965–1970	1970–1975	1975–1981
Northeast Region	661.7	1,628.7	507.7	1,447.2	17.6	23.9	9.4	13.9
New England Division	235.9	454.7	285.7	499.1	6.2	6.6	5.3	4.8
Middle Atlantic Division	425.8	1,174.0	222.0	948.1	11.3	17.2	4.1	9.2
North Central Region	585.6	1,813.9	1,126.6	1,999.2	22.9	26.6	20.9	19.3
East Central Division	589.0	1,327.5	706.9	1,289.6	15.7	19.5	13.1	12.5
West North Central Division	269.0	486.8	419.6	709.6	7.1	7.1	7.8	6.9
South Region	1,283.1	2,151.6	2,433.6	4,015.1	34.2	31.6	45.2	38.8
South Atlantic Division	655.7	1,188.3	1,264.4	1,819.7	17.4	17.4	23.5	17.6
East South Central Division	249.1	297.5	411.3	435.2	6.6	4.3	7.6	4.2
West South Central Division	378.3	665.8	757.9	1,760.2	10.0	9.7	14.0	17.0
West Region	945.4	1,209.8	1,311.3	2,892.0	25.2	17.7	24.3	27.9
Mountain Division	209.8	253.9	558.9	851.3	5.5	3.7	10.3	8.2
Pacific Division	735.6	955.9	752.4	2,040.7	19.1	14.0	13.9	19.7
United States†	3,748.8‡	6,804.0	5,379.2	10,353.5	100.0	100.0	100.0	100.0

*Employees on nonagriculture payrolls as of March of respective periods. Numbers are in thousands.
†Excludes Hawaii and Alaska.
‡Numbers and percentages may not sum to national totals due to rounding.
Source: U.S. Department of Labor, Bureau of Labor Statistics. *Employment and Earnings* (Washington, D.C.: Department of Labor, monthly).

TABLE 4.12
Regional Growth Shares of Government Employment Change, 1960–1981*

Region and Division	Absolute Growth Increment				Percentage Share of National Growth			
	1960–1965	1965–1970	1970–1975	1975–1981	1960–1965	1965–1970	1970–1975	1975–1981
Northeast Region	323.2	565.3	400.7	195.2	20.5	19.5	19.8	9.9
New England Division	66.3	108.3	122.2	80.9	4.2	3.7	6.0	4.1
Middle Atlantic Division	256.9	457.0	278.5	114.3	16.3	15.8	13.7	5.8
North Central Region	377.5	800.8	323.1	371.8	24.0	27.7	15.9	18.9
East Central Division	256.0	574.7	193.7	264.8	16.2	19.9	9.5	13.5
West North Central Division	121.5	226.1	129.4	107.0	7.7	7.8	6.4	5.4
South Region	517.3	932.7	848.0	1,022.5	32.9	32.3	41.9	52.1
South Atlantic Division	277.4	533.4	504.3	466.1	17.6	18.4	24.9	23.7
East South Central Division	101.6	138.1	127.6	192.8	6.4	4.7	6.3	9.8
West South Central Division	138.3	261.2	216.1	363.6	8.8	9.0	10.7	18.5
West Region	353.2	588.5	447.6	374.7	22.4	20.3	22.1	19.1
Mountain Division	88.0	157.0	158.1	150.1	5.6	5.4	7.8	7.6
Pacific Division	265.2	431.5	289.5	224.6	16.8	14.9	14.3	11.4
United States†	1,571.2‡	2,887.3	2,019.4	1,964.2	100.0	100.0	100.0	100.0

*Employees on nonagriculture payrolls as of March of respective periods. Numbers are in thousands.
†Excludes Hawaii and Alaska.
‡Numbers and percentages may not sum to national totals due to rounding.
Source: U.S. Department of Labor, Bureau of Labor Statistics. *Employment and Earnings* (Washington, D.C.: Department of Labor, monthly).

Parameters of the 1980s

Over the next decade the growth trends of the last half dozen years will continue to dominate the situation. The energy requirements of our society will reassert themselves. The future cutting edge of United States competitiveness will certainly lie in the high-technology arena. There will undoubtedly be continued loss of many old-line industries in a world whose labor force has grown more and more homogenized. It is imperative to maintain our cutting edge in new sectors, and there is a strong national consensus on this point. However, the human-service sectors will probably decline. This is especially true in the Northeast, because of a relatively mature balance between the secondary and tertiary industries, in contrast to rapidly growing, later-developing areas that are still playing service catch-up.

It is evident that the Northeast is particularly vulnerable to the national business cycle. It suffers more severely in recessions and fails to share fully in national peaks. Yet the central precondition of a bright future for the Northeast is a vigorous performance by the national economy.

There are signs, however, that the performance of the northern tier of the Northeast states offers some insight into the region's potential. This is mirrored in the shift from industries that have moved out of the region (and probably out of the United States) to an increased focus on both hi-tech production and the creation of hi-tech brains and entrepreneurs.

Within the regional context, four parameters are likely to dominate the reshuffling of market shares over the next decade. The first of these is the decline in birth rates, the so-called baby bust. This in turn implies a much lower growth rate in the labor force, reducing the labor-absorption problems of the last decade. Will this reverse the trend toward less capital input per worker? What will its impact be on the mobility of firms? Will there be the same fluidity of location and assumptions that a labor force is readily available?

Second, the degree of individual mobility is strongly shaped by inflationary expectations. While mobility has many unexplored mysteries, it does appear to decline in parallel with downturns in the economy. In the current era, the deflation taking place in collectibles, particularly housing, is probably not a transient phenomenon but one of great potency. It will lead to substantial reduction in personal mobility over the short to intermediate runs. This could stabilize the Northeast, but its permanence depends on the economic vitality and opportunities generated in the area.

A third parameter is the homogenization of production costs in the United States. This has resulted in a substantial reduction of the housing-buying power of Northeasterners, who seek homeownership in alternate areas of the country (one exception would be the North Central states, which have been hit even harder). This is particularly true of shifts to the West but is also becoming apparent in shifts to the South. Labor costs, and many other costs of doing business, are moving toward approximate equilibrium. Over recent decades the lagging performance of the Northeast economy compared with the dynamism of the Sunbelt high-growth sectors has resulted in unexpected stabilizing elements. For example, current data on wage levels in the Houston area suggest that they are substantially higher than those of the Northeast region as a whole, perhaps even higher than in New York City.

The significance of labor costs is in turn a function of associated capital investment (i.e., nonlabor productivity multipliers). These vary from industry to industry, but are particularly important in a few key sectors. The Northeast region lags behind in this respect, as the flow of capital investment over the last two generations has moved away.

In a more positive vein, however, the potential of large-scale automation—of robotics and computer-aided manufacturing—may not be spatially bound since the structure of costs is independent of international labor cost differentials. The Northeast has an opportunity to be competitive in tapping this potential reservoir of new capital investment *if* there is enough flexibility on the part of organized labor.

A fourth major element is the effort to provide a political economy within the Northeast that is competitive with the rest of the nation. While the issue of appropriate tax legislation is discussed elsewhere in this volume (Chapter 10), obviously changing the fiscal environment plays an important signaling role. This is especially significant in light of the ascendancy of supply-side economics, which receives more bipartisan support than often appreciated. With some diffidence we suggest that New Hampshire heralded; New York City, under Mayor Koch, endorsed; and Massachusetts, suddenly grown conservative, confirmed the new economic necessities of regional development.

Summary

1. Analysis of long-term employment patterns provides statistical evidence of a secular relative decline in the economic strength of the Northeast and North Central regions and substantial relative and absolute growth in the South and West.

2. National economic cycles have exacerbated regional growth differentials. When national employment growth slows down, the Northeast and North Central regions bear the brunt of the recession. When the economy advances more rapidly, the major benefits accrue to the South and West.

3. The sharpest variations are evident in the manufacturing sector. The aging industrial belt is afflicted with a large but shrinking volume of old-line manufacturing activity. Most new manufacturing jobs have been created in the Sunbelt.

4. Population growth and general economic expansion have stimulated job growth in the private nonmanufacturing and government sectors. These rapidly growing activities (especially nonmanufacturing) are becoming increasingly concentrated in the regions of the South and the West.

5. Demographic mobility in the 1970s facilitated the spatial redistribution of the nation's economic activity; people were able to follow jobs (or conversely, population movements stimulated employment growth). In the 1980s, however, housing and economic constraints may impede demographic mobility, exacerbating the strains caused by interregional job growth variations.

6. The employment boom of the late 1970s partially obscures the underlying trends in the national economy. A return to stagnation of the national economy in the mid-1980s may revive the regional traumas that surfaced during the 1974–1975 recession. The capacity of the national economy to adapt to changing world economic conditions will be mirrored in interregional employment differentials.

BENJAMIN H. STEVENS

5 Regional Cost Equalization and the Potential for Manufacturing Recovery in the Industrial North

Background on Southern Economic Growth

The industrial decline of the Northeast, Middle Atlantic, and East North Central states (the industrial belt), during the last twenty years, has been of substantial public and private concern. Its most obvious effect has been a general decline in the economies of northern states, adversely affecting unemployment rates, incomes, public costs and revenues, and other measures of economic health.

To some extent this decline has been viewed as something that requires federal intervention in what is described as the "new war between the states." The industrial growth of the Sunbelt has been assumed to be at the cost of the Frostbelt, and many suggestions have been made for federal policies to mitigate the relative shift of industry from North to South. Some underlying hypotheses in these calls for federal intervention have been that the South has traditionally "stolen" industry from the North; that federal policy has favored southern development relative to northern industrial growth; and that the entire process is irreversible and will lead ultimately to the North's becoming the "poor region," as the South once was.

Although there may be some truth in these hypotheses, the recent relative shift in manufacturing employment from the Frostbelt to the Sunbelt can be explained mainly by basic economic factors that influence the location deci-

Acknowledgment: Some of the research reported here received support from NSF Grant #SES-8025378 to the Regional Science Research Institute.

85

sions of industrialists. The South has had the advantages of lower labor and energy costs, lower tax costs, a more amenable climate, and a lower level of "interference" in business operations from both government and unions. Furthermore, there has been a cumulative growth process. As Wheat (1973) notes, industries are becoming increasingly market oriented; and it has been the southern markets that have been growing, partly because of the earlier migration of national market industry.

It is true that federal intervention helped to start this process. An implicit goal of the New Deal in the 1930s and 1940s was to help the South move more rapidly through the final phase of post–Civil War reconstruction. The Tennessee Valley Authority, rural electrification, road building, agricultural extension and soil conservation, improvements in rivers and harbors, and the concentration in the South of federal construction of military bases and ordnance production facilities (and the sale of the latter at "surplus" prices to private producers after World War II) were designed partly to alleviate poverty and stagnation in the South. The construction of the interstate highway system inadvertently continued this process of infrastructure improvements, opened new low-wage labor markets for exploitation, and provided better access to national and regional markets.

Many of the southern states have, for their part, tried to attract (or "steal") industry through "right to work" laws and other restrictions on unions; through tax abatements and other incentives (including the innovative use of public bond financing for industrial land and buildings); and by providing generally a probusiness "climate." These efforts appear to have been successful, although it is very difficult to determine the contribution of any particular program or policy to the industrial growth of the South.

Whatever the specific causes, the effects are clear. The South and Southwest have been enjoying growth rates in industrial activity, employment, population, and income that have been substantially higher than those of the North.

Countervailing Forces and the Slowing of Growth

The establishment of preconditions for the growth process would not have led to such rapid rates of relative growth if, in fact, production costs had not been lower in the South. And to believe that this process will continue inexorably requires that one reject accepted theories of interregional equalization.

For example, Borts and Stein (1964) would argue that the increase in demand for labor and other factors in the South and the decrease in demand for these factors in the North would have the expected effects on the relative costs of these factors. Thus, one would expect southern wages to rise toward the national average and northern wages to decline toward the same level, as indeed they have been doing. Furthermore one would expect increased demand for public services and the increasing costs associated with rapid urbanization in the South to push up tax rates. Growth, particularly when poorly planned and controlled, has indeed led to higher levels of environmental pollution in the South (although it has not made the climate colder). At least part of the attraction of the South is its less formal, more easy going, "small town" way of life, which has been disappearing in some areas, while at the same time smaller towns in the North have become more attractive destinations for migrants from congested metropolitan areas.

In other words, as an oversimplification, industrial decline of the North and industrial growth of the South have made the two regions similar in a number of ways. Unless one rejects basic comparative cost location theory, one would expect this process of relative industrial shift to slow down.

Evidence, however, does not suggest that the process has slowed significantly. Yet one would expect a lag, both in information about what is happening to relative costs and to other relative attractions in the South, and also in changing decision patterns, given the expected life of fixed capital. A decision to build a plant in an area is made well in advance of construction, which in turn leads full utilization of capacity by a measurable amount of time.

Thus, southern growth in the very recent past is partly the result of location decisions made as long ago as a decade. It may also consist preponderantly of growth in region-serving, market-oriented industries, as already suggested by Wheat (1973).

It would, of course, be interesting to know what location decisions are being made currently and how they are being affected by relative changes in both the North and the South. Failing this, it is certainly worth considering the potential effects of relative cost changes on future industrial growth in both regions.

Trends in Relative Production Costs

As part of a National Science Foundation (NSF) sponsored research project at the Regional Science Research Institute (RSRI), it has been possible to put together a time series of relative wage, capital, energy, and total costs for two-digit manufacturing industries in selected states for the period 1967–1980. Wage costs were obtained from the regional economic information system of the Bureau of Economic Analysis (BEA) of the United States Department of Commerce. Capital costs were estimated by using a modified version of the calculation outlined in Treyz, Friedlaender, and Stevens (1980), based on corporate income and property tax rates in each state. Relative energy costs were calculated from the data provided in a report from the United States Department of Energy (1979; updates through 1980). For each cost element, relative cost is defined as the cost for the input to the industry in the state divided by the United States average for the same input and industry.

In combining individual relative energy costs by type of fuel into an overall energy cost measure, relative production costs for each material input into an overall relative material cost measure, and relative total material, energy, labor, and capital costs into a relative total cost measure, a Cobb-Douglas production function with constant returns to scale and factor neutral technical change is used.[1] The exponents in this production function are the proportions of each factor specified by the corresponding input coefficients for each industry from an appropriate aggregation of data in the 1972 national input-output study by the BEA (U.S. Department of Commerce, 1979).

Export employment is defined here as the number of employees producing goods for shipment out of the region rather than for local consumption or use as inputs. The number of export employees is calculated as a residual by subtracting local from total employment. Local employment is calculated by multiplying the regional purchase coefficient (RPC) for a sector times total local demand for the sector's output.

The RPC for each sector in each state is available from the state input-output forecasting and policy simulation models constructed by RSRI and reported in Stevens et al. (1983) and Treyz, Stevens, and Ehrlich (1982). The estimation of RPCs and the calculation of total in-state demand are discussed in Stevens et al. (1980).

The argument for examining export employment is that this part of total employment is most subject to competition from producers in other states. Firms producing for local use are assumed to have a distinct locational advantage due to proximity. On the other hand, one could argue that imports, especially of manufactured goods, will be freely substituted for local production if their delivered costs are lower than those of the same sector within the state. Research is being conducted to determine whether the elasticity of such substitution is the same as, or less than, the elasticity of substitution between imports of the same good from two or more states.

The main question is whether relative costs are falling in declining states, and vice versa, as the theory would predict. A secondary question, to be explored in only a preliminary way, is whether such declines lead to increases in the state's share of export or total employment.

---

[1]The appropriateness of using the same production function for all states is discussed in Treyz, Friedlaender, and Stevens (1980). In contrast to that presentation, however, the cost calculation here assumes that the labor intensity of production is also the same in all states. This assumption is probably not justified and will be changed in later analyses of these data.

Cost and Employment Trends

Table 5.1 summarizes selected cost and employment measures for all two-digit standard industrial classification (SIC) manufacturing industries for major regions for selected years. The regional data and the employment totals include only those states for which BEA data are available. Thus the eight regions presented are comprised of only the thirty-one major manufacturing states specified in the note to Table 5.1. The cost measures are weighted averages, with state employment in each industry used to weight the industry's relative costs.

In Table 5.1, several measures of employment accompany the cost data for each regional grouping. These include total employment, employment as a proportion of the United States total for the same sector, export employment, export employment as a proportion of export employment summed across all states, and export employment as a share of total regional employment.

Table 5.2 presents cost and employment data for selected two-digit SIC manufacturing industries for selected states and years. Note that the employment share calculations are based on total United States employment, not just total employment in the thirty-one states in Table 5.1. Table 5.2 is included to demonstrate the substantial variations in cost and employment behavior among industrial states and industries in several regions over the period.

Turning first to Table 5.1, one notes a tendency toward regional equalization of wage costs. Regions that have been declining absolutely and/or relatively in manufacturing employment have also had declining relative wage levels and vice versa. This is as expected from the neoclassical theory.

However, the East North Central (ENC) and West regions are notable exceptions. It could be argued that wage adjustment in the ENC region is impeded by the disproportionate number of jobs in that region for which wages are set by union contracts (e.g., in the steel and automobile industry). This is true for transportation equipment (SIC 37) for the ENC states of Ohio and Illinois.

The labor market of the West region, whose data here are overwhelmingly dominated by California, may be responding to excess supply even in the face of rising employment. This could be explained by the high level of migration into California, at least part of which apparently takes place even when immigrants are not certain that jobs will be available. Mexican immigrants, especially, may serve to prevent tightness in the overall California labor market.

Relative wage costs are notably below the national average for growing regions, and vice versa, with the exceptions of New England (NE) and the West. If past trends in relative regional wages continue, it would appear that

TABLE 5.1

Regional Trends in Manufacturing Employment and Relative Costs, 1967–1980*

Region	1967	1970	1973	1976	1978	1980	Overall % Change
New England							
Employment (000)	**1224.28**	**1131.47**	**1089.26**	**1032.48**	**1119.44**	**1170.46**	−4.40
Share total employment	.0687%	.0639%	.0597%	.0600%	.0600%	.0638%	−7.15
Export employment (000)	**962.46**	**874.79**	**842.55**	**810.22**	**883.53**	**925.19**	−3.87
Share total exports	.0774%	.0710%	.0660%	.0675%	.0680%	.0721%	−6.89
Share state employment†	.7861	.7731	.7735	.7847	.7893	.7905	.55
Relative total costs	1.006	1.015	1.027	1.023	1.015	1.013	.612
Relative wage costs	.988	1.001	1.009	.994	.984	.984	−.449
Relative capital costs	.999	1.012	1.022	1.017	1.013	1.009	.983
Relative energy costs	1.332	1.339	1.495	1.560	1.408	1.428	7.213
Middle Atlantic							
Employment (000)	**4334.75**	**4159.56**	**3938.90**	**3537.88**	**3645.46**	**3572.19**	−17.59
Share total employment	.2433%	.2349%	.2157%	.2056%	.1962%	.1948%	−19.97
Export employment (000)	**3163.51**	**3012.90**	**2843.63**	**2563.57**	**2654.32**	**2602.49**	−17.73
Share total exports	.2546%	.2445%	.2228%	.2136%	.2042%	.2028%	−20.32
Share state employment	.7298	.7243	.7219	.7246	.7281	.7285	−.17
Relative total costs	1.023	1.037	1.046	1.048	1.044	1.038	1.491
Relative wage costs	1.055	1.063	1.071	1.064	1.058	1.054	−.121
Relative capital costs	1.005	1.019	1.024	1.022	1.019	1.017	1.175
Relative energy costs	1.143	1.158	1.171	1.279	1.245	1.218	6.601
East North Central							
Employment (000)	**5160.06**	**5045.38**	**5233.80**	**4781.56**	**5160.02**	**4673.37**	−9.43
Share total employment	.2897%	.2849%	.2867%	.2779%	.2777%	.2548%	−12.04
Export employment (000)	**3669.92**	**3590.12**	**3752.35**	**3401.08**	**3675.35**	**3314.92**	−9.67
Share total exports	.2953%	.2913%	.2940%	.2833%	.2828%	.2584%	−12.51
Share state employment	.7112	.7116	.7169	.7113	.7123	.7093	−.27
Relative total costs	1.016	1.024	1.034	1.031	1.037	1.031	1.438
Relative wage costs	1.038	1.040	1.070	1.069	1.082	1.071	3.233
Relative capital costs	.996	1.015	1.017	1.013	1.016	1.018	2.166
Relative energy costs	1.156	1.167	1.137	1.095	1.138	1.052	−9.006

West North Central

Employment (000)	1210.62	1202.99	1280.07	1238.29	1353.04	1348.45	11.39
Share total employment	.0680%	.0679%	.0701%	.0720%	.0728%	.0735%	8.17
Export employment (000)	958.53	950.24	1020.61	985.74	1078.19	1079.48	12.62
Share total exports	.0771%	.0771%	.0800%	.0821%	.0830%	.0841%	9.08
Share state employment	.7918	.7899	.7973	.7960	.7969	.8005	1.11
Relative total costs	.994	.993	.986	.984	.985	.984	−1.003
Relative wage costs	.963	.977	.964	.974	.974	.980	1.793
Relative capital costs	.999	.992	.994	.991	.992	.995	−.343
Relative energy costs	1.255	1.219	1.131	1.059	1.060	.989	−21.227

South Atlantic

Employment (000)	2344.69	2483.59	2701.38	2568.69	2783.55	2844.66	21.32
Share total employment	.1316%	.1403%	.1480%	.1493%	.1498%	.1551%	17.83
Export employment (000)	1609.91	1706.24	1844.19	1773.87	1939.38	1994.18	23.87
Share total exports	.1295%	.1385%	.1445%	.1478%	.1492%	.1554%	19.97
Share state employment	.6866	.6870	.6827	.6906	.6967	.7010	2.10
Relative total costs	.967	.947	.948	.957	.958	.956	−1.151
Relative wage costs	.878	.886	.888	.894	.894	.895	1.985
Relative capital costs	.997	.962	.963	.968	.968	.967	−2.931
Relative energy costs	.967	.965	.971	1.100	1.064	1.026	6.107

East South Central

Employment (000)	834.35	898.36	1029.14	978.88	1051.43	998.50	19.67
Share total employment	.0468%	.0507%	.0564%	.0569%	.0566%	.0544%	16.22
Export employment (000)	639.21	700.89	812.78	770.64	826.53	786.00	22.96
Share total exports	.0514%	.0569%	.0637%	.0642%	.0636%	.0613%	19.10
Share state employment	.7661	.7802	.7898	.7873	.7861	.7872	2.75
Relative total costs	.944	.923	.922	.930	.935	.939	−.497
Relative wage costs	.840	.848	.847	.858	.865	.872	3.774
Relative capital costs	.992	.956	.954	.958	.960	.965	−2.764
Relative energy costs	.724	.779	.791	.885	.909	.927	28.100

TABLE 5.1—*continued*

Region	1967	1970	1973	1976	1978	1980	Overall % Change
West South Central							
Employment (000)	**955.48**	**1052.66**	**1133.86**	**1204.38**	**1340.09**	**1450.08**	51.76
Share total employment	.0536%	.0594%	.0621%	.0700%	.0721%	.0791%	47.39
Export employment (000)	**559.13**	**642.65**	**705.83**	**736.99**	**824.85**	**906.00**	62.04
Share total exports	.0450%	.0522%	.0553%	.0614%	.0635%	.0706%	56.94
Share state employment	.5852	.6105	.6225	.6119	.6155	.6248	6.77
Relative total costs	.960	.934	.927	.946	.953	.966	.529
Relative wage costs	.915	.910	.891	.923	.934	.961	4.997
Relative capital costs	.999	.967	.965	.972	.980	.985	-1.356
Relative energy costs	.804	.778	.750	.857	.844	.859	6.886
West							
Employment (000)	**1748.67**	**1733.84**	**1851.87**	**1865.46**	**2131.06**	**2283.94**	30.61
Share total employment	.0982%	.0979%	.1014%	.1084%	.1147%	.1245%	26.84
Export employment (000)	**864.63**	**844.59**	**941.02**	**961.73**	**1113.54**	**1222.42**	41.38
Share total exports	.0696%	.0685%	.0737%	.0801%	.0857%	.0953%	36.94
Share state employment	.4944	.4871	.5081	.5155	.5225	.5352	8.25
Relative total costs	1.035	1.054	1.036	1.029	1.024	1.026	-.895
Relative wage costs	1.110	1.092	1.048	1.035	1.018	1.027	-7.410
Relative capital costs	1.014	1.041	1.038	1.036	1.034	1.030	1.575
Relative energy costs	1.122	1.100	1.085	1.046	1.084	1.088	-2.985

*The regional compositions are as follows:
New England (Vermont, Massachusetts, and Connecticut), Middle Atlantic (New York, New Jersey, and Pennsylvania), East North Central (Ohio, Michigan, Indiana, Illinois, and Wisconsin), West North Central (Minnesota, Iowa, Nebraska, and Missouri), South Atlantic (Maryland, Virginia, North Carolina, South Carolina, Georgia, and Florida), East South Central (Kentucky, Tennessee, and Mississippi), West South Central (Louisiana, Oklahoma, and Texas), and West (Utah, Colorado, and California). These were the only states for which a full set of data was available for all sectors in all years of the period under study.

†Weighted average across states within the region.

Source: Primary data provided by the U.S. Department of Commerce, Regional Economic Information Service of the Bureau of Economic Analysis (unpublished). Used with permission of the Regional Science Research Institute, Amherst, Mass.

TABLE 5.2
Employment Shares and Relative Costs in Selected Industries and States, 1967 and 1980

State		Apparel		Lumber		Printing		Stone, Clay, and Glass		Fabricated Metals		Nonelectrical Machinery		Transportation Equipment		Instruments	
		U.S. Employment Share (%)	Relative Costs	ES	RC	ES	RC	ES	RC	ES	RC	ES	RC	ES	RC	ES	RC
Connecticut	1967	1.13	1.01	0.35	1.03	1.77	1.00	1.29	1.05	4.29	1.00	3.55	1.01	5.15	1.01	4.69	0.99
	1980	0.83	1.03	0.33	1.01	1.94	1.01	1.13	1.03	4.14	1.02	2.57	1.02	4.69	1.01	3.82	1.00
Massachusetts	1967	3.98	1.00	0.88	1.02	4.18	0.99	1.91	1.07	3.17	0.99	4.02	1.00	2.09	0.99	6.89	1.00
	1980	3.14	1.02	0.74	0.99	3.48	1.01	1.99	1.05	3.29	1.00	4.39	0.99	1.86	1.00	8.03	1.04
New York	1967	20.24	1.10	2.55	1.03	17.07	1.05	7.62	1.07	6.60	1.01	9.29	1.03	5.23	1.01	27.60	1.05
	1980	13.36	1.11	2.06	1.00	12.41	1.10	5.78	1.08	5.05	1.01	6.95	1.05	3.88	1.03	18.37	1.10
Pennsylvania	1967	12.87	0.97	2.45	0.99	6.72	0.99	10.46	1.02	8.37	1.00	7.06	0.99	3.68	0.97	8.62	0.97
	1980	9.72	0.98	2.96	0.98	5.75	1.00	8.88	1.04	7.01	1.02	5.66	1.00	4.28	0.99	5.89	1.00
Illinois	1967	2.89	1.03	2.09	1.04	10.97	1.03	6.13	1.03	9.99	1.01	11.96	1.02	2.54	0.98	8.54	0.98
	1980	1.59	1.08	1.60	1.03	8.04	1.07	4.70	1.06	8.48	1.03	9.04	1.06	2.68	1.00	5.49	1.01
Ohio	1967	1.38	1.03	1.83	1.01	6.68	1.00	10.73	1.02	11.01	1.01	11.40	1.01	7.02	1.00	3.55	0.97
	1980	1.35	1.06	1.98	0.99	5.37	1.01	9.68	1.03	9.72	1.03	8.51	1.01	7.26	1.02	2.78	0.97
Minnesota	1967	0.59	0.99	1.04	1.03	2.11	0.99	1.15	1.02	1.96	1.01	2.96	0.99	0.31	0.97	4.00	1.02
	1980	0.46	1.04	1.67	1.03	2.68	1.00	1.37	0.99	2.31	1.02	3.54	0.99	0.41	0.94	3.97	1.00
Georgia	1967	4.86	0.95	4.31	0.93	1.28	0.98	2.19	0.94	1.00	0.93	0.68	0.91	2.20	0.99	0.53	0.88
	1980	5.72	0.94	4.19	0.93	1.87	0.94	2.70	0.93	1.30	0.93	0.88	0.90	1.80	0.98	0.68	0.90
Mississippi	1967	2.73	0.93	3.87	0.95	0.28	0.91	0.88	0.92	0.53	0.91	0.34	0.90	0.59	0.95	0.31	0.84
	1980	3.24	0.92	3.34	0.91	0.46	0.90	1.04	0.90	0.63	0.91	0.56	0.88	1.07	0.92	0.29	0.81
North Carolina	1967	4.76	0.93	4.84	0.93	1.23	0.94	2.12	0.93	0.82	0.93	1.28	0.92	0.28	0.91	0.68	0.91
	1980	6.95	0.93	5.04	0.90	1.64	0.91	2.70	0.90	1.69	0.93	1.95	0.93	0.77	0.89	1.42	0.95
Tennessee	1967	4.92	0.93	2.89	0.93	1.55	0.96	2.16	0.95	2.07	0.93	0.81	0.92	0.71	0.91	0.80	0.91
	1980	5.45	0.94	2.67	0.90	1.91	0.93	2.20	0.95	2.03	0.93	1.42	0.91	1.15	0.91	0.84	0.89
Texas	1967	3.88	0.96	3.47	0.96	3.51	0.96	4.39	0.95	3.86	0.96	3.05	0.96	3.73	0.99	2.21	0.93
	1980	5.90	0.98	5.17	0.96	4.97	0.95	6.64	0.95	6.02	0.96	6.39	0.98	4.27	0.97	2.89	0.94

Source: Primary data provided by the U.S. Department of Commerce, Regional Economic Information Service of the Bureau of Economic Analysis (unpublished). Used with permission of the Regional Science Research Institute, Amherst, Mass.

wages will not reach the national average for some time in the Middle Atlantic (MA) and West South Central (WSC) regions and for even longer in the South Atlantic (SA) and East South Central (ESC) regions. This is important because there are indications that industrial location decisions may be influenced by wage rates to an extent out of proportion to the relative contribution of wages to total costs.

However, it would be foolhardy to project the continuing growth or decline in wage costs at present rates of change. Changes in these rates may occur unless, as seems unlikely, rapid interregional migration eases labor market pressures.

The behavior of relative energy costs has, in most regions, an irregular trend pattern. Part of this irregularity was caused by the Arab oil boycott and the rapidly rising prices for imported oil during the mid and later 1970s.

After about 1975, however, one sees a downward trend in relative energy costs in most energy-poor regions and a rising trend in most energy-rich regions. This is presumably due to decontrol of domestic oil prices, which have been allowed to rise toward the price of the imported oil on which the Northeast is most dependent. This trend will probably continue as natural gas prices are also allowed to rise because the ENC, WNC, southern, and western regions are much more dependent on this energy source than the NE and MA regions.

Relative capital costs, which are based mainly on state and local tax rates on property and corporate income, have continued to rise in the industrial North and to fall elsewhere (again with the exception of the West). It was hypothesized earlier in this chapter that tax rates would tend to rise relatively in rapidly growing areas because of the demand for new public infrastructure and services. Apparently, however, continued industrial growth has increased the tax base in these areas at a rate sufficient to provide adequate tax revenues without disproportionate rate increases.

At the same time, both infrastructure and services must be maintained in the industrial North despite the declining tax base. More important, the dislocation in the employment structure of these areas has tended to increase welfare payments and the need for a variety of social services.

What will happen when growth rates decline in the South and West? One supposes that the growth in demands for public services will continue even after the growth rate of the tax base is insufficient to meet these demands without significant rate increases. Tax rate increases, coupled with wage, energy, and other cost rises that are likely to cause a slowing of growth, should tend to accelerate the approach to interregional equalization.

As already noted, data in Table 5.2 suggest the wide variety of trends in employment and costs among industries and areas. Perhaps most surprising is the extent of relative shifts (changes in the United States share) in, for example, paper (SIC 26); stone, clay, and glass (SIC 32); and transportation equipment (SIC 37). These are not ordinarily thought of as footloose industries; but they appear to be highly responsive to relative costs, at least for the selected states. The question of locational responsiveness will be explored further in the next section.

First, however, some interesting anomalies should be considered. For example, Massachusetts has shown a substantial growth in instruments (SIC 38) even though its relative costs have been higher than the national average and have grown more or less throughout the period. One might be tempted to explain this by agglomeration economies due to the concentration of high-technology industries in the Boston area, the availability of design and manufacturing workers with specialized skills, and other related factors. Actually it is probably better explained by the fact that photographic equipment is included in instruments (SIC 38), the Polaroid Corporation is the predominant employer in this industry in the state, and the founder and principal owner of the corporation wanted all his manufacturing plants in locations that would allow daily visits to each one.

Another example is provided by printing (SIC 27), which has enjoyed absolute and relative growth in Connecticut despite above-average and rising costs. This phenomenon is largely explained by the much-higher relative costs in neighboring New York. The dispersion of this industry out of New York into neighboring states is a process that has been going on much longer than the time period covered here.

Much of the printing industry is oriented to regional markets, of which New York is the largest. The close connections between composition, design, typography, and physical printing (and binding) make it difficult for distant printers to compete effectively in many aspects of the business. The question of market orientation, which has been studied intensively by authors such as Wheat (1973), cannot be covered adequately here.

However, it is worth noting (see Table 5.1) that substantial growth in the West has been taking place in the face of above-average and only slightly declining relative costs. One possible explanation is the relative isolation of the western market, which impedes competition by producers in other regions. The importance of this market is indicated by the fact that export employment is a much smaller share of total manufacturing employment in this region (the WSC region having the next smaller) than in any other. This also means that a smaller proportion of western production must compete in inter-regional markets, thereby reducing the comparative disadvantage associated with higher relative costs.

In any case, it would be a mistake to draw quick conclusions from apparent relationships between the growth and cost data given in these tables, which provide examples of every possible anomaly one might wish to find. Apparent inconsistencies in relationships between cost changes and employment growth are sufficient to make superficial analysis potentially misleading. Therefore, further discussion of these issues is continued in the next section of the chapter.

It is worth reiterating that there does appear to be a tendency toward inter-regional cost convergence. Table 5.1 suggests that the cost trends evident for most of the states and industries apply on average to all two-digit manufacturing industries and all regional groupings of states for which sufficient data are available.

However, the definition of convergence should perhaps be quite broad. Relative costs have, in a number of cases, fallen below or risen above national averages. How far such costs might diverge before once again converging would seem to depend on such factors as lags in decision making, mobility of labor and capital, operation of intrastate labor markets, vagaries of energy prices, and other issues.

Preliminary Analysis of Relative Costs and Employment Change

The data in Tables 5.1 and 5.2, and similar data for other two-digit manufacturing industries and a larger sample of states, require further analysis before conclusions can be drawn about relationshihps between relative costs and relative growth. As of this writing, much of this analysis has not been completed; a full-scale study of the effect of relative costs on industrial location is still in process. Nevertheless, preliminary results obtained in this analysis are worth reporting because of their implications for future industrial growth in both the North and the South.

In undertaking this analysis, a number of issues arise; one that has already been discussed is whether to focus on total or export employment. A second issue is whether to concentrate on cost levels, changes in cost levels, or both. One would expect more rapid decline in states with well-above-average costs, and more rapid growth in areas whose relative costs are well below national averages. In fact, there might exist a "threshold" level below which decision makers might be unable to recognize, or be relatively insensitive to, small deviations from national averages. Therefore, one might argue that the rate of change in employment share should be a nonlinear function of the deviation of a state's costs from the national average.

At the same time one would expect decision makers to be sensitive to the trend in costs. For any given relative cost level, a rising cost trend would make the area much less attractive than a tendency toward declining relative costs. Again there may be a nonlinearity in this relationship, given that the decision maker would be better able to recognize, and be more sensitive to, rapidly changing costs than to slow cost movements.

The foregoing considerations raise questions about the type of model to be used in the statistical estimation. Stevens, Treyz, and Ehrlich (1979) estimate an elasticity of response of export employment to changes in relative costs. But it is not clear that elasticity is the proper measure, especially if "elasticity" varies with the cost level and/or with the rate of change of costs. Therefore, although response elasticities are also measured here, one should understand that these results are preliminary and that further study may reveal a better measure of response.[2]

A third issue is the probable time lags between signals provided to the decision maker by levels and changes in levels of costs, the decision to reduce production and employment in an area or locate new facilities disproportionately in other areas, and the actual carrying out of these decisions. The length of the total time lag is hard to determine theoretically. One can argue that it should be related to the expected life of the physical capital that exists in a state, the present age of that capital, its mobility (perhaps more important for human than for physical capital), and related factors.

Previous analyses, such as that of Stevens, Treyz, and Ehrlich (1979), show that the full effects of a relative cost change are felt after approximately five years. But relative cost levels may persist either above or below national averages for varying periods of time before noticeable shifts take place. Employment shifts, according to theory, should begin as soon as relative costs exceed national averages by perceptible amounts, but this is clearly not the case.

There are numerous reasons why costs may deviate substantially from national averages for extended periods without significant relative growth or decline taking place. The most obvious is the effect of agglomeration economies or other factors that, for a variety of reasons, have not been included in the analysis. In any case, the space of a chapter does not permit an adequate answer to this question. Rather, the simplifying assumption is made that employment will respond to a weighted average of relative costs over the preceding five years. Additional analysis will be performed later in order to pin down the appropriate lag structure.

The first step in this preliminary analysis was to estimate an elasticity of response in export shares to changes in relative costs. This estimation was made industry by industry with a pooled time-series/cross-section sample of states and time periods. The time periods and states have already been specified.

[2]Elasticity of response, for the purpose of this discussion, can be most simply defined by reference to the following:

$$\Delta_t(e_i^k/E_i) = \alpha[\Delta_t(c_i^k/C_i)]^\beta$$

where e_i^k and E_i are employment in industry i in region k and in the United States, respectively; c_i^k and C_i are the corresponding total production costs; and β is the (hopefully negative) elasticity of response of the region's share of total national employment in i to a change in the region's relative production costs for i over the period t. This formulation assumes a constant elasticity of response over time and over all ranges of relative costs and cost changes. The elasticity can be interpreted as the percent change in k's employment share in industry i with a 1 percent change in k's relative costs.

The usual regression analysis was not used for a number of reasons, the most significant being that the states vary widely in their export shares of total employment. Therefore, the analysis was designed to avoid the dominance of large states with large shares as well as the influence of very small states for which a small change in export employment might be associated with a very large proportional change in share.

For this and related reasons, an iterative procedure was used first. In this procedure, the goal was to determine a best-fitting elasticity of response across all states and time periods. The method that was designed starts with an assumed elasticity and varies it systematically until the sum of the squared deviations of response from the estimated elasticity level is minimized. The greatest disadvantage of this method is that the usual statistical tests for the significance of the calculated elasticities are not readily available.

Nevertheless, the results are quite satisfactory (despite the fact that the residual sum of squares was very large in almost all cases). First, it is encouraging that the elasticities turned out to be appropriately negative for all manufacturing industries except textiles (SIC 22). The elasticities are, as one might hope, related to the "footlooseness" of the industries in question. Thus resource-based industries like lumber and wood products (SIC 24) have extremely low elasticities of response. Industries that are capital intensive and have heavy investments in fixed, immobile plant and equipment, such as petroleum refining (SIC 29) and chemicals (SIC 28), also appear to have very low elasticities of response.

At the other extreme, industries such as apparel (SIC 23), rubber and plastics (SIC 30), and instruments (SIC 38) all have large negative elasticities. These are industries in which, generally, the value/weight ratio of both inputs and outputs is fairly low so that they are not transportation dependent, capital intensity is low or capital equipment is movable, or both. Furthermore, these are relatively labor-intensive industries and therefore would be expected to be responsive to relative wage differentials. This unfortunately does not explain why the elasticity for textiles is of the wrong sign since this industry is, in many ways, quite similar to apparel and other footloose industries in its locational orientation.

The estimated elasticities range from very close to zero to as large as −13.45.[3] This range encompasses the overall elasticities previously measured by Treyz et al. (1977) and Stevens, Treyz, and Ehrlich (1979) for all industries in Massachusetts and the TVA service region, respectively. Although the calculation has not been made, it appears that the elasticities previously estimated for these two regions are something like the weighted average of the elasticities of the individual industries in those two regions, the

---

[3]For further discussion and detailed estimates of these elasticities, see Treyz and Stevens (1983).

weighting factors being the proportions of total regional manufacturing employment in each industrial sector.

Because of the potential errors in the indirect method used to calculate export employment, elasticity estimates were also made for total employment in each sector. The results are different but generally conform to the results obtained for export employment.

The second step in this preliminary analysis consisted of a log-linear regression with the logarithm of the ratio of the current-year's to previous-year's export share as the dependent variable. The independent variables are the logarithms, respectively, of the ratio of the moving average of relative total costs in the present year to that in the preceding year, the relative costs from the preceding year, and the export share from the preceding year.[4] The use of the moving average of relative costs in the preceding year is intended to take account of the fact that states in which the relative total costs for an industry are above the national average will tend to grow more slowly whether the costs are rising or falling, and vice versa. The previous year's share is included to take account of the fact that states already having a large export share in an industry will tend to have a lower percentage increase in that share for any given amount of export employment growth, other things being equal.

The log-linear regression has, of course, the advantage that the coefficient on the logarithm of the change in relative costs will be interpretable as an elasticity. At the same time, the use of the logarithms of the previous year's relative costs and export share allows, as previously suggested, the rate of growth in share to be an increasing function of the deviation of relative costs away from national averages. This is consistent with the idea that minor deviations from national averages may not be especially "noticeable" to decision makers.

The foregoing, however, is only a tentative formulation. As already noted, it is not clear that elasticity of response is indeed the proper measure, although it certainly is an intuitively (and theoretically) appealing one. Furthermore, it is not clear that the previous year's relative costs or export share will not behave as a proxy for other underlying variables, which are themselves important locational determinants. Clearly the effects of climate, market size and growth, and other factors must ultimately be accounted for in

[4]The estimated equation was of the form:

$$\log[(e_i^k/E_i)_t/(e_i^k/E_i)_{t-1}] = \alpha + \beta \ \log[c_i^k/C_i)_t/(c_i^k/C_i)_{t-1}]$$
$$+ \gamma \log[c_i^k/C_i]_{t-1} + \delta \log[e_i^k/E_i]_{t-1}$$

where e_i^k and E_i are industry i employment in region k and in the United States, respectively; c_i^k and C_i are the corresponding total production costs based on a five-year moving average; and β, γ, and δ are elasticities to be estimated.

order to get a clear picture of the specific effects of relative costs and changes in those costs.

The results of the log-linear regression are, unfortunately, less satisfactory (although perhaps more credible) than results from the direct estimation of elasticities. For many industries the variable that best explains the change in export share is the size of the share in the preceding period. In most cases, the sign of the coefficient on this variable is, as expected, negative. This indicates that the proportional increase in share is smaller for states that already have a large export share for the industry in question.

This may simply reflect the effects of absolute size on the measure of percent change. It may also reflect, however, the saturation of regional markets served by large-share states and a shift in location toward underserved regions.

After the share variable, the most significant of the other variables tested are generally the change in relative costs and the previous year's level of relative costs. The theory suggests that the coefficients on both of these variables should be negative. However, there are a number of cases where one is negative and the other is positive. Where the elasticity on change in relative costs is negative and the exponent on the previous year's level of relative costs is positive, this suggests that decision makers in the industry are responding to changes in costs irrespective of the level (where the coefficient on the latter is not significant) or responding more strongly where the level is higher. A possible explanation for the latter phenomenon would be differences in productivity associated with high cost areas that might be due to the high skill levels (associated with high wages in such areas). Furthermore, agglomeration economies could cause the production process in such areas to be different, with more of the lower-skilled (lower-wage) parts of the production process farmed out to other suppliers. This, of course, is not recognized in the calculation of relative total costs because the production function is assumed to be the same for all regions.

The opposite situation, where the export share responds positively to increases in costs and negatively to the cost level, is perhaps more difficult to explain. Evidence in Table 5.1 suggests that export shares often continue to increase in areas where costs are rising, as long as the cost levels are measurably below national averages. Nevertheless, one is tempted to conclude that this results from unexploited opportunities in growing regional (extrastate) markets, in the service of which the producing state has a comparative locational advantage. This would seem to be a better explanation than an appeal to the presumed "growth psychology" exhibited by businesses in certain parts of the South and West. Ultimately, however, one suspects that the effect of rising costs will turn negative if other underlying explanatory locational variables are included in the analysis.

In this regard, it should be noted that the percentage of total variation explained by most of these regression equations is very low. The highest R^2 for any of the industry-specific equations is less than .2, and many are in the range of .01 to .05. This clearly suggests that there are a number of other explanatory variables that should be taken into account if one hopes to explain relative shifts with a high degree of accuracy. It should also be noted that the comments on the signs of the variables have been made irrespective of whether the coefficients were in fact significant. In many cases the coefficients with "incorrect" signs are not statistically significant.

The question that arises from these two preliminary analyses is whether anything definitive can be concluded about the relative sizes of the elasticities of response of export shares to changes in relative costs. The elasticities determined in the regression analysis are generally not the same, and in many cases are quite different from those estimated by the first method. Further analysis was necessary to determine the sizes of the elasticities with greater certainty. These more recent results (Treyz and Stevens, 1983) confirm in general the accuracy of the relative sizes of these elasticities. Thus, it is clear that many industries do respond as expected to relative cost levels and changes in those levels.[5]

Prospects for Northern Industrial Recovery

The foregoing discussion may not make one very optimistic about a rapid change in the fortunes of the industrial North. However, evidence shows that the type of pessimism that has been endemic in public and private circles in recent years is probably not justified. The data certainly suggest that wage and energy costs are likely to decline in the North and rise in the South, although there is clearly stickiness in the downward direction in heavily industrialized states and unionized industries. Convergence of these costs should, on the basis of past behavior, reduce the rate of shift from the North to the South, unless tax rates in the North have to be raised so much that total costs fail to fall. The already substantial flow of migration from the North to the South and West may eventually include those in the North who need public assistance because of their jobless status.

The experience of New England suggests that the process of stemming decline is mainly a matter of time. New England manufacturing, on average, now has relative costs only slightly above the national average. For a number of industries, including some presented in Table 5.2, costs are already below the national average and in a few cases are continuing to fall.

---

[5] Detailed statistical results of the foregoing analyses will be available, on request, from the author.

The example of New England is emphasized simply because this area went through its heavy decline much earlier than the Middle Atlantic region, which suffered its heavy loss of manufacturing employment, in both absolute terms and as a share of the national total, during the 1970s. Although decline has started in the East North Central region, it may take most of the 1980s before costs in the region fall enough to encourage recovery. In this region, the problem of foreign competition in the automobile and steel industries may make recovery more difficult than it has been in New England and slower than it will probably be in the Middle Atlantic region.

The experience of the recent recession (1981–82) and recovery (1983–84) shows that while unemployment rates in New England have remained substantially less, and in the Middle Atlantic region somewhat less, than national rates, the East North Central region has continued to suffer unemployment rates well above those of the nation. One might expect this pattern to last a while longer. The recent evidence that even Texas is not recession-proof suggests that the nation is moving into a new era in which growth in the South and West at the expense of the North and East may no longer be as great an issue as in the recent past.

This is not to say that federal policy to alleviate problems associated with industrial decline in the North, particularly the fiscal problems associated with the declining tax base, would not be welcome and perhaps desirable. One might argue that such indirect interference in the equilibrating process would probably be less likely to create inefficiencies than would direct subsidies to save declining industries. At the moment, the federal government seems to prefer ignoring the problem of interregional readjustment entirely, except to the extent that federal policies may, perhaps inadvertently, continue to favor the South. Nevertheless, one can hope that, even without a shift in federal policy, the North will rise again.

References

Borts, G. H., and J. L. Stein. 1964. *Economic Growth in a Free Market*. New York: Columbia University Press.

Stevens, B. H., G. I. Treyz, and D. J. Ehrlich. 1979. On the estimation of regional purchase coefficients and elasticities of response for regional economic models. Discussion paper 114, Regional Science Research Institute, Amherst, Mass.

Stevens, B. H., G. I. Treyz, D. J. Ehrlich, and J. R. Bower. 1983. A new technique for the construction of nonsurvey regional input-output models. *International Regional Science Review* 8: 271–86.

Stevens, B. H. et al. 1982. *Basic Regional Input-Output for Transportation Impact Analysis: Handbook One of Regional Economic Analysis for Transportation Planning*. Amherst, Mass.: Regional Science Research Institute.

Treyz, G. I., A. F. Friedlaender, and B. H. Stevens. 1980. The employment sector of a regional policy simulation model. *Review of Economics and Statistics* 62: 63–73.

Treyz, G. I., et al. 1977. The Massachusetts economic policy analysis model. Department of Economics, University of Massachusetts, Amherst. Mimeo.

Treyz, G. I., B. H. Stevens, and D. J. Ehrlich. 1982. *A State Core Forecasting and Policy Simulation Model: Handbook Two of Regional Economic Analysis for Transportation Planning.* Amherst, Mass: Regional Science Research Institute.

Treyz, G. I., and B. H. Stevens. 1983. The TFS regional modeling methodology. Paper presented at the thirtieth annual North American meeting of the Regional Science Association, Chicago, November.

U.S. Department of Commerce, Bureau of Economic Analysis. 1979. *Input-Output Structure of the U.S. Economy, 1972* (public use computer tape).

U.S. Department of Energy, Energy Information Administration. 1981. *State Energy Data Report.* Washington, D.C.: Government Printing Office.

Wheat, L. F. 1973. *Regional Growth and Industrial Location.* Lexington, Mass.: D. C. Heath and Company.

WILLIAM H. MIERNYK

6 *Energy Constraints and Economic Development in the Northeast*

The Northeast in a Broader Setting

There has been a lively discussion among regional and interregional model builders about the direction of causation between the national economy and its constituent regions.[1] I agree with the position taken by Adams, Brooking, and Glickman (1975, p. 286) that causation runs "from national developments to the region but not from the region to the nation." In the present instance, this means that economic developments in the Northeast depend on economic developments in the United States. The latter, in turn, are influenced to a large extent by global developments.

Before turning to a discussion of specifically regional matters, a few words must be said about national economic problems and proposed remedies. The national economic situation is too well known to require elaboration or documentation. It is accurately summarized as one of "stagflation," a neologism whose unpleasant sound accurately describes an unpleasant state of economic affairs.

It is an unchallenged article of faith among conventional economists[2] that

Acknowledgment: I am indebted to Dee Knifong, James Cassell, and Churai Tapvong for research assistance; to Jean Stansberry for preparing Figure 6.1, and to Carla Uphold and Jean Gallaher for secretarial assistance.

[1]The highlights of this discussion are summarized in Miernyk (1982a), pp. 6–10 and 27–32.

[2]The term *conventional economist* is interpreted here to include neoclassical, Keynesian and neo-Keynesian, and Marxist economists, as well as intermediate shadings or combinations of these various schools of thought.

104

the "solution" to the economic problems of our age is growth and more growth. This chapter is based on an explicit rejection of the conventional solution. A basic premise of the following discussion is that the United States economy has become a nearly stationary state. This is defined as an economy in which the *rate* of output per employed worker is declining.[3] Furthermore, this decline is not transitory—it is a long-run trend. Evidence to support this assumption has been provided by Denison (1979) in a comprehensive study of national productivity.

Denison's measure of "national income per person employed" (NIPPE) is an excellent proxy for output per employed worker. He found that, between 1948 and 1973, NIPPE increased at an annual rate of 2.12 percent. Between 1973 and 1976, however, it declined at an annual rate of 0.22 percent (Denison 1979, pp. 104–8).

The conventional view, of course, is that the decline since 1973 is a temporary aberration—that once the right combination of policy levers is found, and appropriately manipulated, output per employed worker will increase, and the long-term growth trend will be resumed. That, of course, is consistent with the conventional view that growth is the "normal" state of affairs, so robust economic growth *must* return someday.

The conventional view of the future is strictly a matter of belief. All available evidence, however, is to the contrary. There has been a global decline in the rate of economic growth. While there might be brief periods of respite, that trend will continue. A logical consequence is that at some future time— again, on a global basis—there will be a tipping point, and the slow growth of recent years will be replaced by decline.

This, however, is not a forecast of catastrophe; the process of decline will be as gradual as the early stages of economic growth. In a future age more enlightened than ours, the rate of decline can be controlled, and the process stretched for a very long time. The point of this background—which might strike some as unduly gloomy, although that is far from the intent—is that, for practical purposes, future regional developments in the United States are likely to take place in the framework of a national zero-sum game. To conclude, as conventional economists do, that the answer to all economic problems is robust growth is simply to wish the problem away.

Energy Prices and Regional Shifts in Population, Income, and Employment

Chapter 3 demonstrated that population, income, and employment have declined in parts of the Northeast. What caused those shifts? Will they continue? Will the Northeast lose the economic preeminence it enjoyed from the

[3]The notion of a nearly stationary state is discussed more fully in Miernyk (1982a), pp. 67–71.

Colonial era until the late 1960s?[4] Finally, what role have energy prices played in those regional shifts?

The most dramatic economic event of the 1970s was the increase in crude oil prices from less than five dollars per barrel in 1970 to just under forty dollars per barrel in 1981. There can be little doubt that this upsurge in oil prices, which was accompanied by corresponding increases in other fossil-fuel prices, contributed significantly to rearrangement of the United States economic map.

There have always been fairly wide disparities in regional energy prices but, prior to 1970, these received little attention from scholars or popular writers. When energy prices were low, and falling with respect to other prices, they were not considered to be a significant variable in the analysis of regional development. This changed after the early 1970s, however, as energy costs became increasingly important in both business and household budgets. The impacts of rising energy prices were not limited to the direct costs of doing business and the cost of living. As recent events have dramatically demonstrated, rising energy prices were a major—if not *the* major—cause of inflation.

Most observers, particularly those writing for the popular and business press, appeared to take for granted that the major impact of rising energy prices was on the location of manufacturing industry.[5] There is little evidence to support the conclusion, however, that rising energy prices had a significant *direct* effect on the location of manufacturing industry. A paper by Schmenner (1984), presented to the Brookings Conference on Housing and Energy in the 1980s, provides convincing evidence to the contrary.

The attention paid to energy prices as a locational determinant by the popular and business press is not surprising, since few topics were more widely discussed during the 1970s than rising energy costs. Specialists in industrial location have long known, however, that location decisions are not based on a single component of cost, unless that component is clearly dominant.

In general, the decision to relocate a manufacturing plant is based on an analysis of all elements of spatially variable cost. Only in an unusual case would a firm realize savings on every element by moving a plant from one location to another. Savings might be realized on some components—for example, labor, transportation, and taxes. But the costs of other inputs—electric energy and raw materials, for instance—might be higher at the proposed new location. The plant will be relocated only if aggregate savings on some spatially variable costs are greater than increases in others.

---

[4]The "Northeast" is a flexible regional designation. In this chapter, it is defined as New England, New York, and New Jersey.

[5]For expressions of concern by business journalists, the Advisory Commission on Intergovernmental Relations, and others, see Miernyk (1981a).

If there is only one input with a lower cost at the new location, but if the saving on that input is greater than the added cost of all other inputs combined, that input would dominate the location decision. Those who believe differential energy prices have caused or will cause the relocation of manufacturing plants implicitly assume that the cost of energy is a dominant locational determinant. In the case of aluminum reduction plants, and a few other activities that are highly energy intensive, this might be true. But such activities have always been located in the Pacific Northwest and other areas where energy prices have been low. Such activities have never been an important part of the Northeast's economy.

Vulnerability to Rising Energy Costs

As part of a study conducted for the Small Business Administration, manufacturing establishments in New York and New Jersey were classified into three categories. The first two included establishments that were either directly or indirectly vulnerable to rising energy prices. The third consisted of establishments that were "sheltered" from such price increases (Miernyk, 1981b). The basis of this classification is an earlier study in which the location orientation of manufacturing industries was identified, using the national input-output model, at a fairly high level of industrial disaggregation (Miernyk, 1978, pp. 81–84). The criteria developed in the earlier study were applied to manufacturing industry in New York and New Jersey at the two-digit standard industrial classification (SIC) level. Aggregation probably overstated the number of workers employed in directly and indirectly vulnerable activities.

Directly vulnerable activities have two basic characteristics: (1) they are relatively energy intensive and (2) they have actual or potential competitors in other regions where energy prices are lower. Indirectly vulnerable activities are those that provide essential, localized inputs to directly vulnerable activities. "Sheltered" activities are in one sense a residual; they are those that are neither directly nor indirectly vulnerable to rising energy prices. Sheltered activities serve local markets or are tied to local resources. They do not compete with similar activities in other regions. Local transportation is one example; the manufacturer of a highly differentiated product is another. Clearly, the proportions of workers in these three categories are not fixed; they will be influenced by events that change over time. In 1976, however, an estimated 81 percent of all manufacturing workers in New York and New Jersey were employed in sheltered activities (Miernyk, 1981b, table 7, p. 19).

The classification of activities into directly or indirectly vulnerable, and sheltered, categories, with respect to changing energy prices, was extended to all regions in a paper prepared for a Resources for the Future (RFF)-Brookings Conference (Miernyk, 1980a). The study showed that, in 1970, about 22 percent of total employment in New England was in directly vulnerable activities, and that this region accounted for about 7 percent of national employment in the directly vulnerable category. In the same year, about 17 percent of total employment in New York and New Jersey was directly vulnerable to rising energy prices, and these states accounted for about 12 percent of the national total in this category.

By 1977, directly vulnerable employment had dropped to 19 percent of New England's total, and 15 percent of total employment in New York and New Jersey. Their shares of national employment in this category had been reduced to 6.5 percent and 9.7 percent, respectively, of the national total.

Total employment in New England had increased by about 156,000 jobs during this seven-year period. New York and New Jersey lost about 494,000 jobs at the same time. There was an absolute decline in directly vulnerable employment in the Northeast. This amounted to almost 80,000 jobs in New England, and about 289,000 jobs in New York and New Jersey.

At the same time that the Northeast experienced job losses, there were increases in directly vulnerable employment in the energy-surplus regions of the Southwest and the Rocky Mountain–Northern Plains. In the Southwest (which includes the energy-surplus states of Louisiana, New Mexico, Oklahoma, and Texas) there was a gain of about 210,000 jobs in the directly vulnerable category, and this region's share of the national total increased from 6.6 percent in 1970 to 8.5 percent in 1977. In the more sparsely populated Rocky Mountain–Northern Plains region, employment in directly vulnerable activities went up by about 40,000. The region's share of the national total increased from 1.2 percent in 1970 to 1.5 percent in 1977.

The same shifts are observed when employment data are examined on a state basis. All the large states in the Northeast—Connecticut, Massachusetts, New Jersey, and New York—registered declines in directly vulnerable employment between 1970 and 1977, ranging from 12 percent in Massachusetts to 21 percent in New York. These states, with the exception of Connecticut, also registered declines in the indirectly vulnerable category. The latter ranged from 4 percent in Massachusetts to 29 percent in New York. Connecticut reported an increase of 1 percent. New York, however, also reported a 6 percent decline in sheltered employment, the only state to do so. At the same time, while most energy-surplus states registered increases in directly vulnerable employment, there was a decline of almost 4 percent in this category in West Virginia, where there was an even larger decline of 12 percent in the indirectly vulnerable category.

These shifts might appear to contradict the assertion that there is little evidence to support the hypothesis that the major impact of differential increases in regional energy prices has been on the location of industry. The shifts described in the preceding paragraphs appear to be consistent with that hypothesis, but they do not insure that the hypothesis is a valid one. First, the data are highly aggregated and, as noted earlier, probably overstate the number of jobs that are directly vulnerable to increases in energy prices. Also, the relationship between changes in energy prices and changes in state employment is not entirely clear-cut. West Virginia is one example of an "unexplained" exception. Finally, while differential regional changes in energy costs might be among the factors behind these employment shifts, they are not necessarily the dominant ones.

Energy Prices and Changing Terms of Trade

If the major impact of rising energy prices has not been on the location of industry, how have regions been affected by these changes? One hypothesis states that the most important impact has been on changes in the terms of trade between energy-deficit and energy-surplus states. This, in turn, has affected the *relative* per capita income positions of the two sets of states. This does not, of course, shed any light on the employment shifts discussed in the preceding section. Another hypothesis to explain those shifts will be considered after discussing the terms-of-trade hypothesis and some of the evidence that supports it.

The hypothesis that the major regional impacts of rising energy prices would be on the terms of trade between energy-deficit and energy-surplus states was first advanced in a paper presented to a seminar on economic development, sponsored by the Economic Development Administration, in Washington, D.C., August 13–14, 1975 (Miernyk, 1976). That discussion was conducted in the future tense because the data available when the paper was written had only started to reflect the effects of the first round of OPEC price increases in 1974: "Since energy prices are likely to rise faster than the prices of other primary and intermediate inputs, the 'terms of trade' between EPs (energy producers) and ECs (energy consumers) will shift in favor of the former. Factors engaged in the production of energy will be rewarded more generously than they have in the past" (Miernyk, 1976, p. 22). Between 1974 and 1979 energy prices rose slowly, but exchange ratios calculated between selected commodities and fossil fuels showed that a substantial shift in the terms of trade had occurred between 1970 and 1978. The exchange ratios compared the "price" of selected commodities in terms of oil, natural gas, and coal. In 1970, for example, 4.9 million cubic feet of Texas natural gas would buy 1,000 pounds of New York butter. By 1978, 1.1 million cubic feet of Texas gas would buy 1,000 pounds of New York butter. A set of forty-five comparisons was included in the RFF-Brookings paper (Miernyk, 1980a).[6] The commodities compared with fossil fuels included basic agricultural prod-

---

[6]The ratios are also included in a summary of the conference (see Table A-2 in Landsberg and Dukert, 1981, p. 94).

ucts, such as corn, hogs, and soybeans; processed foods, such as butter and processed tomatoes; and sulfuric acid, representing an industrial commodity.

All but one of the comparisons showed substantial declines in exchange ratios during this period. The declines were particularly large when the selected commodities were compared with Texas natural gas. They ranged from a low of 50 percent, in the case of Illinois hogs, to 81 percent for New York eggs. Smaller, but still substantial, declines occurred when comparisons were made between the selected commodities and Oklahoma crude oil, as well as West Virginia coal. The only exchange ratio to register an increase was one between Illinois hogs and Oklahoma crude oil, where the ratio went up 5 percent between 1970 and 1978. Other declines ranged from a low of 31 percent for the exchange of Minnesota flaxseed and Oklahoma crude oil, to a high of 65 percent between New York eggs and Oklahoma oil. Similarly, declines in the ratio of selected commodities to West Virginia coal ranged from 54 percent for Minnesota flaxseed to a high of 72 percent for New York eggs (Landsberg and Dukert, 1981). A similar comparison of exchange ratios for the same commodities between 1970 and 1981 would show even sharper declines because the price of imported crude oil, which was about fifteen dollars per barrel in 1978, had increased to about thirty-eight dollars per barrel in 1981.

The terms of trade hypothesis has been approached from another angle by Manuel (1982a), who used conventional statistical methods to analyze changes in per capita income in energy-surplus and energy-deficit states. The purpose of the tests was "to determine whether the mean compound annual growth rate of real per capita personal income in energy producing states exceeded that of energy consuming states." The tests covered two time periods, 1967 to 1972 and 1973 to 1977 (Manuel, 1982a, pp. 4, 47).

Manuel found that "all groups of energy consuming and energy deficit states experienced real per capita personal income growth rates in the post-embargo years which were significantly below those of the pre-embargo period" (Manuel, 1982a, p. 34). He also found that "in the pre-embargo period sunbelt energy consuming and deficit states registered mean growth rates which were greater than those of the producing and surplus states. During post-embargo years the mean growth rates were reversed, producing and surplus states having outpaced the consuming and deficit counterparts" (Manuel, 1982a, pp. 33–34).

Manuel (1982b) also analyzed changes in per capita income in energy surplus and energy deficit states within a different analytical context. In this study, Manuel again compared state income growth rates in pre- and post-embargo periods. He observed what others have noted; namely, in the nation as a whole the growth of real income was "noticeably lower in the post-embargo years." He also found that "while energy deficit states experienced a slowdown of more than one percent on the average, energy surplus states registered a marginal acceleration in real income growth after the embargo" (Manuel, 1982b, p. 7).

Manuel was appropriately cautious about generalizing from his statistical tests. He noted:

> one cannot conclude with certainty that post-1973 energy prices were solely responsible for considerably slower growth rates in energy consuming and deficit states and for relative stability in producing and surplus counterparts. However, coupled with unequal energy resource endowments, higher energy prices after 1973 would appear to have buoyed producing state growth rates and detrimentally affected those of energy consuming and deficit states [Manuel, 1982b, p. 32].

In spite of Manuel's cautious caveat, which is certainly appropriate when evaluating regression results, his findings are consistent with the terms-of-trade hypothesis.

Energy Self-Sufficiency Quotients and Relative Per Capita Income Changes

A different approach has been used by this author to examine the relationship between state energy self-sufficiency and changes in *relative* per capita income. Energy self-sufficiency is expressed in per capita terms using an energy self-sufficiency quotient (ESSQ), which is a distant relative of the familiar location quotient (Miernyk, 1982b). A coefficient was calculated for each state using the formula:

$$ESSQ_i = \frac{EP_i - EC_i}{(POP_i \,/\, POP_{us}) \times 100}$$

where EP_i and EC_i are the percentage shares of domestic energy production and consumption in state i, and the denominator is each state's percentage share of United States population (Miernyk, 1982b). Relative per capita income is each state's per capita income expressed as a percent of the United States average.

ESSQs can only be computed for recent years since it was not until the Energy Information Administration was established in the United States Department of Energy that comprehensive data on state energy production and consumption were compiled and published.[7]

---

[7]Some of the valuable state information, which has greatly extended the analytical capabilities of those concerned with the questions discussed in this chapter, appears to be in danger. As a result of budget cuts and the lobbying efforts of some—but by no means all—energy trade associations, some state data published for the 1970s might not be available in the future.

A comparison of state ESSQs and changes in relative per capita income between 1960 and 1980 is given in Figure 6.1. The ESSQs cover a wide range; the positive quotients range from a low of 0.16 in Colorado to a high of 47.9 in Alaska. The range on the negative side is much narrower, going from −0.15 in Virginia to −1.3 in Delaware. The range of relative changes in per capita income between 1960 and 1980 is also wide, going from −13 percent in New York, Delaware, and Nevada, to an increase of 27 percent in Mississippi.

Figure 6.1 shows graphically that while there is a relationship between state energy self-sufficiency and movements up or down the per capita income ladder, it is not unambiguous. Colorado and Kansas are only marginally self-sufficient.[8] Both, however, registered gains in relative per capita income. Utah is also marginally self-sufficient, but during the period shown it registered a substantial decline in relative per capita income.

Two states, New Mexico and Montana, have high ESSQs, but both had small negative changes in relative per capita income between 1960 and 1980. Other factors clearly offset positive contributions to relative per capita income, which rising energy prices might have made in these two states.

In the remaining eight energy-surplus states there is a positive correspondence—although not a close statistical correlation—between energy self-sufficiency and increases in relative per capita income. As the lower right-hand quadrant shows, while a surplus of energy might be sufficient to explain improvement in a state's relative per capita income position, it clearly is not necessary. Indeed, the three states that registered the largest increases in relative per capita income during this period—Arkansas, Mississippi, and South Carolina—are energy-deficit states.

The states in this quadrant do not fall into a single, neat category. Some, such as Arkansas, Iowa, and Nebraska, are major agricultural states; others, such as Georgia and the Carolinas, experienced substantial industrial growth during the period. There is one reasonably clear-cut group of states, however, and this group is particularly relevant to the present discussion.

With the exception of Maine, where relative per capita income remained constant between 1960 and 1980, all the northeastern states moved down the per capita income ladder. The largest drop was in New York, but New Jersey, Connecticut, and Massachusetts also registered significant declines. And, of course, all the states in the Northeast are energy importers. Finally, while the range of interregional oil prices narrowed during the 1970s, as was true of gas utility prices, the spread in coal and electric energy prices widened between low- and high-cost regions (Miernyk 1981a).

One would be hard-pressed to deny that there has been a shift in income

---

[8]In the original study, these states and Utah were referred to as "break-even plus" states.

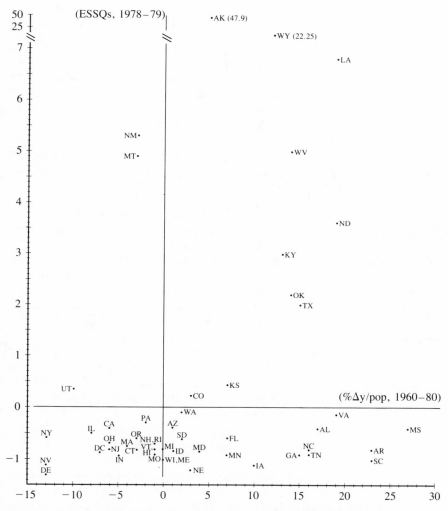

FIGURE 6.1.   State energy self-sufficiency quotients and percent changes in relative per capita income. *Source:* Compiled from data presented in Miernyk, 1982b.

from the Northeast to the energy-surplus states that export fossil fuels (or energy derived from fossil fuels) to the Northeast. While the evidence is far from conclusive, the major cause of this shift probably was the changing terms of trade between the two sets of states discussed in the preceding section.

Energy Prices and Changing Markets

A neglected aspect of the regional impact of rising energy prices has been investigated by Giarratani and Socher (1978). "High and rising energy prices," they say, "are likely to affect the national patterns of consumption and production to a significant extent. The impact of energy-induced price increases on individual consumer demand is already evident; however, the effect of these changes on the pattern of industrial location is likely to be more subtle" (Giarratani and Socher, 1978, p. 103).

Giarratani and Socher used a supply-constrained input-output model, and the concept of "income potential," to investigate the *induced* effects of differential increases in energy prices. An important consequence of increasing energy prices in the Northeast, according to their thesis, has been an increase in migration from this region to other areas where energy prices are lower. When heating costs, for example, were a relatively small part of family budgets, retirees and others on fixed incomes might not have been particularly concerned about them. But the spiraling increases in the cost of residential energy might well have been responsible for some of the shifts of population from parts of the Northeast to the South, and particularly to the Southwest. This, in turn, would be likely to cause a decline in market-oriented activities—even those that are not energy-intensive—in the Northeast, and a corresponding increase in such activities in low-cost energy areas.

Shifts in market-oriented activities would not be a *direct* result of higher energy costs in the Northeast, but would be induced by prior population shifts. Within the framework of traditional location theory, such "relocations" would not be attributed to rising energy prices. Market-oriented activities are attracted to concentrations of population, not sources of low-cost energy. But if population moves in response to lower energy prices, and if market-oriented activities follow population, the causal connection is quite clear. Although, as Giarratani and Socher have said, the connection is a subtle one, such relocations are an induced effect of differential increases in energy prices.

To test their hypothesis, Giarratani and Socher calculated income potential for each state in 1970 and 1974. Even during this period, which could not have been expected to significantly reflect the first round of OPEC oil price increases, they found that income potential increased more rapidly in energy-producing states than in those that produced no energy. The mean change in the former, they found, was 48.4 percent, while in the nonproducing states it was 45.9 percent.

> The same tendency is evident when comparing energy-surplus states to energy-deficit states. The mean increase in the former was 49.3 percent

compared to the latter's 47.2 percent. These conditions exhibit a reversal of those characterizing the 1965–70 period when the mean increase for energy-producing states was 50.3 percent versus 52.3 percent for non-producing states [Giarratani and Socher, 1978, p. 111].

The Weight of Evidence

Empirical tests of location theory are never as neat as those who make them might wish. It is a simple matter to define a set of theoretical boxes labeled "labor-oriented," "transport-oriented," "market-oriented," and "energy oriented" industries. But everyone who has spent a significant amount of time doing empirical regional work knows that a Procrustean effort is required to fit the imperfect data available into abstract theoretical boxes. Those boxes are not made of firm substance; they are very leaky.

Only in the extreme case where a single element of spatially variable cost is dominant—and that by a substantial margin—can we say with complete confidence that a business establishment (or a household) has a specific location orientation. What we are reduced to, ultimately, is the rather vague and not always satisfactory "on-balance" type of conclusion. Having issued this caveat, however, one can still say that differential increases in regional energy prices have had a significant impact on the migration of population and economic activity from high-cost, energy-deficit states to relatively low-cost, energy-surplus states. That, coupled with shifting terms of trade, has moved most of the northeastern states down the per capita income ladder, while the energy-surplus states have moved up. This is so even when income data are examined, as in Figure 6.1, without adjustments for regional differences in the cost of living. The impacts—both positive and negative—are even more evident when state per capita incomes are adjusted for differences in living costs.

There are no "official" state cost-of-living indexes measured from a common base. At irregular intervals the Bureau of Labor Statistics publishes figures showing different rates of increase in the cost of living in selected metropolitan areas. The geographical coverage of these indexes is far from complete, but more important, they tell us nothing about comparative costs of living among the states that include those areas. An attempt has been made by a private organization, the National Center for Economic Alternatives (NCEA), to estimate state per capita incomes adjusted for cost-of-living differences for a single year, 1977. The 1977 adjustment factors have been applied to 1980 per capita incomes in Table 6.1, which also gives percentage changes between unadjusted state per capita income and "adjusted" figures.

All the northeastern states have lower "real" than unadjusted per capita incomes. The differences range from a low of 2 percent in Vermont to 15

TABLE 6.1
Adjusted and Unadjusted Per Capita Income by State, 1980

Region and State	Per Capita Income		Percent Difference
	Adjusted	Unadjusted	
New England			
Connecticut	$10,665	$11,720	−9
Maine	7,687	7,925	−3
Massachusetts	8,606	10,125	−15
New Hampshire	8,766	9,131	−4
Rhode Island	8,594	9,444	−9
Vermont	7,670	7,827	−2
North Middle Atlantic			
New Jersey	9,722	10,924	−11
New York	9,131	10,260	−11
South Middle Atlantic			
Delaware	10,856	10,339	5
Maryland	10,774	10,460	3
Pennsylvania	9,245	9,434	−2
Virginia	9,768	9,392	4
West Virginia	8,658	7,800	11
Southeast			
Alabama	8,237	7,488	10
Florida	9,806	8,996	9
Georgia	8,880	8,073	10
Kentucky	8,298	7,613	9
Mississippi	7,304	6,580	11
North Carolina	8,757	7,819	12
South Carolina	7,993	7,266	10
Tennessee	8,415	7,720	9
Great Lakes			
Illinois	9,995	10,521	−5
Indiana	9,025	8,936	1
Michigan	9,552	9,950	−4
Minnesota	9,627	9,724	−1
Ohio	9,651	9,462	2
Wisconsin	8,881	9,348	−5
Southwest			
Arkansas	8.067	7,268	11
Louisiana	9.219	8,458	9
New Mexico	8,076	7,841	3
Oklahoma	10,119	9,116	11
Texas	10,309	9,545	8
Central Plains			
Iowa	9,545	9,358	2
Kansas	10,083	9,983	1
Missouri	8,982	8,982	0
Nebraska	9,459	9,365	1

116

TABLE 6.1—*continued*

| Region and State | Per Capita Income | | Percent |
	Adjusted	Unadjusted	Difference
Rocky Mountain–Northern Plains			
Colorado	$10,025	$10,025	0
Montana	8,877	8,536	4
North Dakota	9,009	8,747	3
South Dakota	8,040	7,806	3
Utah	7,955	7,649	4
Wyoming	11,552	10,898	6
Far West			
Arizona	9,143	8,791	4
California	10,282	10,938	−6
Hawaii	8,586	10,101	−15
Nevada	11,156	10,727	4
Northwest			
Alaska	8,314	12,790	−35
Idaho	8,298	8,056	3
Oregon	9,037	9,317	−3
Washington	9,794	10,309	−5

Sources: Unadjusted per capita income: Bureau of Economic Analysis, U.S. Department of Commerce, *Survey of Current Business* vol. 61, no. 7 (Washington, D.C.: Dept. of Commerce, July 1981), p. 31. Adjustment factors: News release of the National Center for Economic Alternatives, Washington, D.C., 7 January 1979.

percent in Massachusetts. On the other hand, all of the energy-surplus states, except Alaska, have higher "real" than unadjusted per capita incomes. Alaska's "real" per capita income, according to NCEA estimates, is 35 percent below its unadjusted counterpart. The pattern is not as clear as those who seek simple answers might wish. But even allowing for a reasonable margin of error in the NCEA estimates, the impacts of regional differences in rising energy prices are understated when per capita income differences are examined without adjustment for regional differences in living costs.

Price Effects and Tax Effects

All major energy-surplus states have levied severance taxes on fossil fuels. There is wide variation in the tax rates. The rates on oil vary from a low of 1.5 percent in Kentucky, which produces little oil, to 12.25 percent and 12.5 percent, respectively, in Alaska and Louisiana. The latter, of course, are major oil producers. The rate in Oklahoma is 7 percent, and Texas levies a tax of 4.6 percent. The highest rate on natural gas is the 10 percent tax levied by

Alaska. This is followed by a tax of 8.63 percent in West Virginia and 7.5 percent in Texas. The rate in Oklahoma is the same as that on oil, 7 percent. Tax rates on coal in Kentucky and West Virginia, which rank first and second in production, are 4.5 and 3.85, respectively. The highest rate is the 30.5 percent tax levied by Montana. This is followed by Wyoming's rate of 10.5 percent and New Mexico's levy of 8.4 percent (Cochran and Prestige, 1981).

As fossil fuel prices have increased, revenues from severance taxes have gone up substantially, even in states that levy modest taxes. In West Virginia, for example, the yield from the coal severance tax increased from $13 million in fiscal 1970–71 to an estimated $138 million in fiscal 1980–81, more than a ninefold increase. During this period the tax rate more than doubled, going from 1.89 percent to 3.85 percent. But at the same time the average price of West Virginia coal rose from $5.08 per ton to an estimated $40.00, an increase of 687 percent. Clearly, price increases have had much more to do with the increased tax revenue than rate increases. Data are not available to make similar comparisons for other fuels and other states. But with the possible exception of Montana, the effects of price increases probably outweigh those of tax increases in all energy-surplus states.

This point is of more than academic interest. State severance taxes have been challenged by utilities and by a group of United States representatives who formed the Northeast-Midwest Coalition (Miernyk, 1981a). The Supreme Court has ruled, however, that Montana has a constitutional right to levy a severance tax. It is not likely that the Northeast-Midwest Coalition will be able to accomplish by legislative means what the courts have already rejected: elimination or reduction of state severance taxes on fossil fuels. Even if this could be accomplished legislatively, however, it would have only a marginal effect on the comparative positions of energy-deficit and energy-surplus states. Price increases have had far more to do with changes in the terms of trade between them than have severance taxes.

The Northeast's Future Prospects

The authors of a major regional study wrote in 1960: "The most striking feature in the history of American manufacturing is the enduring strength of the Northeast. . . . Even today the great industrial belt in the Northeast continues to dominate the regional structure of American manufacturers much as it did at the beginning of this century" (Perloff et al. 1960, p. 151). But that era has ended; the Northeast is no longer the preeminent manufacturing region of the nation. And if NCEA estimates are reasonably accurate, real per capita income in the Northeast has dropped below the United States average (Miernyk, 1981a, p. 236). But the Northeast, and New England in particular, has experienced and overcome economic adversity in the past. When the textile industries migrated from the Northeast to the South, for example, they were replaced—at least in part—by electronics and other high-technology manufacturing activities. But the problem this time is not industrial relocation; instead, it is changes in the terms of trade that favor energy-exporting states over the energy-deficit Northeast.

What development could reverse this adverse shift to once again favor the Northeast? Lakshmanan (1981) has argued: "An older energy-importing industrial region like New England is increasingly specializing in high-value goods and services that have a high income 'elasticity' of demand (e.g., educational, medical, and high-technology services) leading the transition of the United States into a post-industrial services-oriented economy." This optimistic assessment is based implicitly on the Clark-Fisher hypothesis that changes in per capita income are a function of changes in economic structure. Essentially, Clark and Fisher postulated that as employment shifts from agriculture to industry, and subsequently to trade and service activities, per capita income will rise. Clark and Fisher worked with national data, but their thesis was extended to the regional level by Bean. (See Clark, 1940; Fisher, 1935; Bean, 1946; and Miernyk, 1979).

Implicitly or explicitly, all conventional development theories accept the Clark-Fisher hypothesis. The causes of economic progress and structural change are capital accumulation, technological progress, and increases in productivity engendered by the latter (Miernyk, 1979, p. 18).

Historically, the Clark-Fisher hypothesis held up well. Even to the casual observer it was clear that economies based heavily on the exploitation of resources—whether agricultural, mineral, or energy—had low per capita incomes. Those engaged in manufacturing had higher per capita incomes. Finally, economies producing sophisticated services—particularly business and financial services—had the highest per capita incomes of all. Before 1940 those relationships applied without exception to nations and to the regions of high-income, industrialized economies.

There is evidence, however, that in recent years the Clark-Fisher relationships are breaking down. This breakdown is one of the consequences of shifting terms of trade. If energy (and other resource) prices rise faster than the prices of manufactured goods and services, per capita incomes in resource-based economies will rise faster than those in manufacturing or service economies. In addition, as noted earlier, there will be some relocation of economic activity—if not directly in response to rising energy prices, then as a result of the migration of market-oriented industries from energy-deficit to energy-surplus states. The shifting terms of trade have affected not only manufacturing activities, but also services. Even activities such as higher education and insurance are not immune (Miernyk, 1982a, p. 105).

A study of thirteen southern states, comparing the relationship between economic structure and state per capita income, provided strong statistical support for the Clark-Fisher-Bean hypothesis in 1940. Not only was the statistical fit between relative per capita income and the proportion of agricultural employment a good one, it was nonlinear. As the percentage of agricultural employment declined, moving from state to state, there was a more than proportionate increase in state per capita income. By 1975, however, there was greater variability in the relationship between relative per capita income and agricultural employment, and the "best" statistical relationship was linear. Moreover, the slope of the line was fairly small. Differences between states with relatively little agricultural employment and those still heavily dependent on agriculture had been considerably narrowed during this thirty-five-year interval.

There was virtually no correlation between per capita income and manufacturing employment in the thirteen southern states in 1940. By 1975 there was a weak statistical relationship, but it was *negative*. Southern states with relatively large manufacturing sectors (such as the Carolinas) had lower per capita income than some (such as Florida, Maryland, and Virginia) with relatively small manufacturing sectors.

Finally, while there was a close statistical fit between per capita income and employment in the trades and services in both 1940 and 1975, the slope of the regression line had dropped sharply during this interval. By 1975 even relatively large movements across states were accompanied by only modest increases in per capita income (Miernyk, 1977).

A similar study for all regions in the United States used 1975 data and showed essentially the same breakdown in the Clark-Fisher-Bean relationships (Miernyk, 1980b). In view of the significant changes in relative per capita income after 1975, the relationship between economic structure and relative per capita income has probably been weakened further. States with the most rapid per capita income growth have been those producing energy, agricultural products, and minerals. Much of this improvement in income has been at the expense of older industrial regions, including the Northeast, in spite of the high proportion of service activities in some of the northeastern states.[9]

There could always be some radical development that would alter the trends of the 1970s, but nothing on the technological horizon suggests that this is likely in the immediate future. In the absence of such a development, the most likely projection is that the trends of the 1970s will continue through the 1980s and into the 1990s. Unlike earlier shifts, which resulted from industrial dislocation (such as the migration of textiles from the Northeast to the South) the shifts of the 1970s were gradual and orderly. The Northeast has demonstrated its capacity to adjust to moderate shifts in population and economic activity. Future adjustments probably will be no more traumatic than those of the immediate past.

[9] In an interesting study, Kader (1981) suggests that the Clark-Fisher relationship among nations is also much weaker now than in the past.

References

Adams, G. F., C. G. Brooking, and N. J. Glickman. 1975. On the specification and simulation of a regional econometric model: a model of Mississippi. *Review of Economics and Statistics* 57: 286–98.

Bean, L. H. 1946. "International industrialization and per capita income." In *Studies in Income and Wealth*, Vol. 8, pt. 5, 119–43. National Bureau of Economic Research. New York: National Bureau of Economic Research, Inc.

Clark, C. 1940. *The Conditions of Economic Progress.* London: Macmillan & Co., Ltd.

Cochran, T., and J. R. Prestige. 1981. *The United American Emirates.* Washington, D.C.: Northeast-Midwest Institute.

Denison, E. F. 1979. *Accounting for Slower Economic Growth.* Washington, D.C.: Brookings Institution.

Fisher, A.G.B. 1935. *The Clash of Progress and Security.* London: Macmillan & Co., Ltd.

Giarratani, F., and C. F. Socher. 1978. "The pattern of industrial location and rising energy prices." In *Regional Impacts of Rising Energy Prices*, W. H. Miernyk, F. Giarratani, and C. F. Socher, 103–16. Cambridge, Mass.: Ballinger.

Kader, A. A. 1981. Primary oriented countries and changes in economic structure. *Atlantic Economic Journal* 9: 90–91.

Lakshmanan, T. R. 1981. Regional growth and energy determinants: implications for the future. *The Energy Journal* 2: 1–24.

Landsberg, H. H., and J. M. Dukert. 1981. *High Energy Costs: Uneven, Unfair, Unavoidable?* Baltimore: Johns Hopkins University Press.

Manuel, D. P. 1982a. Tests of the effects of higher energy prices on State per capita income growth. *Growth and Change* 13, no. 3. July: 26–37.

Manuel, D. P. 1982b. Higher energy prices and resource endowments in an export base model context. *Review of Regional Studies,* forthcoming.

Miernyk, W. H. 1976. Regional economic consequences of high energy prices in the United States. *Journal of Energy and Development* 1: 213–39.

Miernyk, W. H. 1977. "Changing structure of the Southern economy." In *The Economics of Southern Growth*, edited by B. Liner and L. K. Lynch, 35–63. Research Triangle Park, N.C.: Southern Growth Policies Board.

Miernyk, W. H., et al. 1978. *Regional Impacts of Rising Energy Prices.* Cambridge, Mass.: Ballinger.

Miernyk, W. H. 1979. Resource constraints and regional development policy. *Atlantic Economic Journal* 8: 16–23.

Miernyk, W. H. 1980a. The differential effects of rising energy prices on regional income and employment. RFF-Brookings Conference on the Differential Impact of High and Rising Energy Costs, Oct. 9–10, Washington, D.C.

Miernyk, W. H. 1980b. "Regional shifts in economic base and structure in the United States since 1940." In *Alternatives to Confrontation*, edited by V. L. Arnold, 97–124. Lexington, Mass.: D. C. Heath.

Miernyk, W. H. 1981a. "Energy and regional development," in *Energy Costs, Urban Development and Housing*, edited by A. Downs and K. Bradbury, 226–86. Washington, D.C.: The Brookings Institution.

Miernyk, W. H. 1981b. *The Impact of Rising Energy Prices on Small Business in Region II*. Springfield, Va.: NTIS PB81 157604.

Miernyk, W. H. 1982a. *Regional Analysis and Regional Policy*. Cambridge, Mass.: Oelgeschlager, Gunn, and Hain.

Miernyk, W. H. 1982b. Energy availability and State economic development. *Journal of Energy and Development*. 7, no. 2. Spring 1982: 163–171.

Perloff, H.S., et al. 1960. *Regions, Resources and Economic Growth*. Baltimore: Johns Hopkins University Press.

Schmenner, R.W. 1984. "Energy and the location of industry." In *Energy Costs, Urban Development and Housing*, edited by A. Downs and K. Bradbury, 188–225. Washington, D.C.: The Brookings Institution.

U.S. Department of Commerce, Bureau of Economic Analysis. 1981. *Survey of Current Business*, Vol. 61, no. 7 (July). Washington, D.C.: U.S. Department of Commerce.

BENNETT HARRISON

7 Increasing Instability and Inequality in the "Revival" of the New England Economy

The economic base of the New England region has undergone a profound transformation over the last forty years. Indeed, the shift away from traditional mill-based manufacturing to services and so-called high-technology producers' equipment started earlier in New England than anywhere else in North America. Moreover, empirical evidence suggests that the transformation—or, as the business press likes to call it, the "shake-out of the older industries"—has proceeded farther in this region than in any other part of the subcontinent.

Every mature industrial region in North America (and probably throughout the capitalist world) is or soon will be going through some version of this economic transformation. In many places some of the most epoch-defining industries are involved, including steel and autos as well as textiles and shoes.

Acknowledgment: Of the dozens of people who worked directly on the research or who criticized various reports and manuscripts, special gratitude must be expressed to Ann Aubrey, Barry Bluestone, Gordon Clark, Denise DiPasquale, Norman Glickman, Maryellen Kelly, Doreen Massey, Alan Matthews, Charlotte Moore, Ed Soja, Glynnis Trainer, Suha Ulgen, Lynn Ware, and several anonymous reviewers. The research was funded by grants from the U.S. Economic Development Administration, the Employment and Training Administration of the U.S. Department of Labor, and the Work and Mental Health Center of the National Institute of Mental Health, and was based at the Massachusetts Institute of Technology–Harvard Joint Center for Urban Studies. None of these organizations is responsible for the particular statements or findings presented in this chapter. Reprinted with the kind permission of the Regional Science Association, University of Illinois at Urbana-Champaign, from *Papers of the Regional Science Association*, Vol. 50, 1982.

The reasons why, and the process by which, the transition is occurring are important subjects for study, and are dealt with at length elsewhere (Harrison, 1982; Bluestone and Harrison, 1982). This chapter is confined to an examination of certain *outcomes* of the process of regional economic base transformation, as they have been measured in a recently completed research project on the New England economy.

However profitable the so-called postindustrial revolution may have been for various elements in the business community (especially those engaged in high-tech production), the normative implications of the much-heralded "revival" of the England economy for the region's *workers* are much more ambiguous. Many new jobs clearly have been created, and more people are working than ever before. But the wages paid in a growing share of these jobs are declining, both in real terms and in relation to average wages in other areas in the United States. Jobs in unstable (e.g., part-year) industries are expanding, while employers are reorganizing work in ways that exacerbate that instability (e.g., by substituting part-time for full-time employees). The best-paying jobs (in the engineering industries and, more recently, in the production of computers) are becoming subject to sharp "boom-bust" cycles linked to rapidly changing technology and fluctuating foreign and domestic government military procurement. The distribution of earnings is becoming increasingly unequal, within and among industries, among year-round as well as part-year workers, between the races, and by gender. Finally, with increased "outsourcing" of parts and subassemblies to plants outside the region, along with the introduction of new types of labor-saving technology and the intensification of the labor process in many workplaces, sales and profit increases registered by companies operating in New England are translating into fewer new production jobs within the region.

The increasing instability of the region's economy can be traced largely to what is by now the conventional explanation among most regional and labor economists: a shift in industry mix toward those sectors exhibiting the most unstable demand for the product or service (Browne, 1978b; Piore, 1980, ch. 2). Unstable demand and managers' technological adaptations to it probably also explain, to some extent, the dramatically increasing inequality in the distribution of earnings.

Less conventionally, within as well as among industries, there is evidence of a gradual disappearance of the middle layer of jobs in the economy, leaving an increasingly bimodal distribution of "good" and "bad" jobs (defined as a function of wages, hours, and stability of employment). This middle layer of semiskilled good jobs has been disproportionately eliminated by the tendency of multiplant, multilocational, often multinational corporations to shift production and even light assembly operations out of the older, high-wage, highly unionized "mature" industrial regions, such as New England, into other parts of the subcontinent (or entirely beyond it), where the class consciousness of labor and the social wage won through past political struggles are less highly developed.

Even when neither relocation nor spatially differentiated branching are involved, there is still another force which tends to erode the skill-wage distribution at its "middle." This is the practice by many managers in both blue- and white-collar work settings of redesigning jobs in ways that effectively reduce (if not eliminate) the firm's need for semiskilled labor, whether or not a change in mechanization is involved. For management, the payoff to such "deskilling" of the labor process is the cheapening of the firm's wage bill, along with an increase in managerial control over the workplace. Both blessings are derived from managers' increased capacity to employ "marginalized" members of the local population—youth, housewives, elders ravaged by inflation, family heads moonlighting to pay the rent—because jobs no longer require the same degree of skill and training as in the past (Braverman, 1974; Zimbalist, 1979).

The New Economic Base

On the eve of the Second World War, New England's economy still resembled its nineteenth-century image. In 1940, two out of every five persons in the labor force were employed in the same industries that had dominated the economic base for a hundred years (e.g., textiles, shoes, and paper). Work was typically performed in old mills scattered throughout the countryside or concentrated in regional centers like Pawtucket, Rhode Island and Lynn, Massachusetts. The share of these industries' total employment in the region was more than twice as great as in the rest of the country. Because of this peculiar industry mix, almost 36 percent of New England's workers were employed as craftspersons or machine operators, whereas nationwide the proportion in these jobs was less than 30 percent (U.S. Bureau of the Census, 1940, tables 42, 43, 46).

By the late 1970s, mill-based employment had fallen to only a tenth of all jobs in the region (see Fig. 7.1). Even metalworking, aircraft, and electronics had declined in relative importance. Taken together, the private services (along with the trade sector) employed over half of all New Englanders. If government is included in this accounting, about two-thirds of all New England workers held jobs in the service sector (U.S. Bureau of the Census, 1977).[1] Typical of the services which have grown most rapidly are those

[1]The officially recorded growth of the service industries understates the magnitude of the true shift over this period. The Census Bureau classifies those service activities that take place *inside* firms according to the sector with which that firm's principal output is associated. For example, a steel company's real estate department is classified under manufacturing, and the data processing department of the telephone company is included in the count of employment in the communications industry.

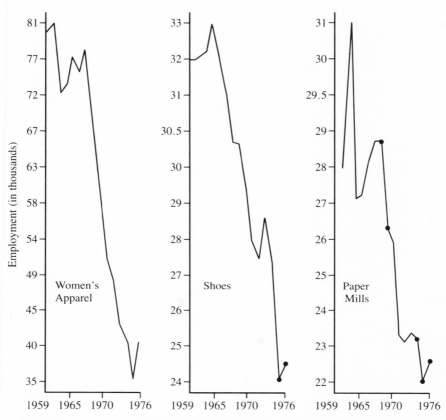

FIGURE 7.1   Annual employment in women's apparel, shoes, and paper mills in New England, 1959–1976. *Source*: Calculations by L. Ware, D. DiPasquale, and B. Bluestone, Social Welfare Research Institute, Boston College, using data from U.S. Department of Commerce, *County Business Patterns*. Black dots indicate that observations for some of the New England states were not available that year and had to be interpolated by a procedure, the details of which are available on request.

which distribute commodities, provide health care and offer lodging to tourists and business conventioneers (Fig. 7.2).

New England's economy was once based on the production of durable capital equipment and nondurable consumer goods, mostly bound for export to other parts of the country. It has now been transformed into one with a much smaller and far more highly specialized manufacturing base, many products of which are exported worldwide, alongside a very large service sector. This process has progressed so far that, of the twenty 3-digit standard industrial classification (SIC) industries that accounted for the largest shares

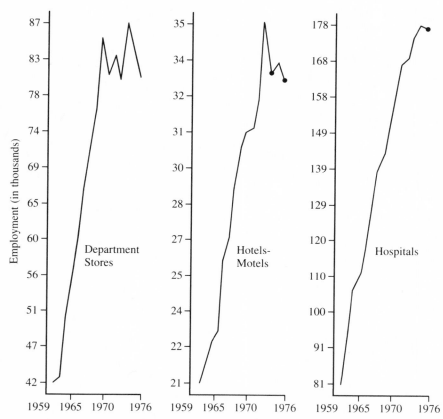

FIGURE 7.2 Annual employment in New England department stores, hotels-motels, and hospitals, 1959–1976. *Source*: Calculations by L. Ware, D. DiPasquale, and B. Bluestone, Social Welfare Research Institute, Boston College, using data from U.S. Department of Commerce, *County Business Patterns*. Black dots indicate that observations for some New England states were not available that year and had to be interpolated.

of private sector employment in New England between 1959 and 1976, only two had declining trends (Harrison, 1982, table 4).

The current fascination with so-called high technology in New England is appropriate; these companies constitute the region's most rapidly growing source of manufactured exports. There is no formal definition of "high-tech," but the term usually refers to small computers, semiconductors, microprocessors (computers on a chip), word processors, scientific and environmental sensing instruments, bioengineering and other medical and laboratory equipment, and all manner of electronic control systems for military use. Partly in response to such ambiguity and partly because of somewhat casual employment claims by trade associations, the Department of Manpower Development of the Commonwealth of Massachusetts has proposed an operational definition to permit systematic analyses over time. Their fifteen 3-digit manufacturing and six 3- and 4-digit service industries are listed in Table 7.1.

The growth of computer manufacturing employment has been extraordinary through the entire region, especially since 1970 (Figure 7.3). Four of

TABLE 7.1
Recent Employment Trends in Massachusetts High-Technology Industries

		Employment		
SIC	Industry	4th Quarter 1976	4th Quarter 1978	Percent Change
281	Industrial chemicals	1,213	1,272	4.9
282	Plastic materials	5,136	5,582	8.7
283	Drugs	2,199	2,463	12.0
351	Engines & turbines	6,783	5,817	−16.6
357	Office machines & computers	22,677	32,430	43.0
361	Electrical distribution	13,702	11,891	−13.2
362	Electronic industrial apparatus	2,767	3,112	12.5
366	Communication equipment	24,723	27,609	11.3
367	Electronic components	32,345	40,555	25.4
372	Aircraft & parts	7,785	9,229	18.5
376	Space vehicles & guided missiles	11,118	12,438	11.9
381	Engineering & scientific instruments	1,939	3,308	70.6
382	Measuring & control instruments	14,637	19,325	32.0
383	Optical instruments	4,786	6,435	34.5
386	Photographic equipment	12,391	17,866	44.2
737	Computer programming services	6,252	10,259	64.3
7391, 7397	Commercial research & development labs	8,163	8,677	6.3
7392	Business management & consulting services	8,470	9,003	6.3
891	Engineering and architectural services	18,695	24,688	32.1
892	Nonprofit educational, scientific, & research organizations	6,274	7,723	23.1
Total—High technology		212,055	259,582	22.4
Total—All Massachusetts private employment		1,929,150	2,132,695	10.6

Source: R. Vinson and P. Harrington, "Defining 'High Technology' Industries in Massachusetts," Policy and Evaluation Division, Department of Manpower Development, Commonwealth of Massachusetts, September 1979, p. 12; based on Employment Service ES-202 Reports.

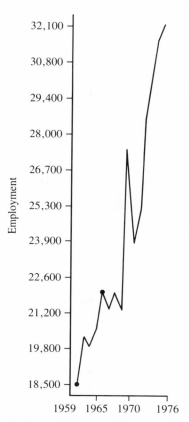

FIGURE 7.3. Annual employment in office machines and computer manufacturing in New England, 1959–1976. *Source*: Calculations by L. Ware, D. DiPasquale, and B. Bluestone, Social Welfare Research Institute, Boston College, using data from U.S. Department of Commerce, *County Business Patterns*. Black dots indicate that observations for some New England states were not available that year and had to be interpolated.

the industry's leading producers of minicomputers, aimed mainly at the small- and medium-sized business market, have their corporate headquarters in Massachusetts (Digital, Data General, Wang, and Prime). The Minneapolis-based Honeywell Corporation maintains major production facilities in and around Boston. And outside Burlington, Vermont, the New York–based IBM operates one of the world's largest and most highly automated micro-processor manufacturing plants.

What wages and working conditions do the people of the region confront in the "new" economy of New England? How has the transformation from the old mill– and electromechanical capital goods–based structure to the new mix, dominated by high technology and services, affected the ability of the region's workers to earn a living?

It is possible to draw five sets of conclusions about the effects of this economic transformation on New England's labor markets. These findings relate to: (1) the level, and (2) the distribution of earnings, (3) the (in)stability of employment, (4) barriers to upward mobility of certain groups of workers, and (5) deviations between the growth of business sales and the derived demand for New England labor. These conclusions are drawn from the findings of ten industry case studies based on corporate reports and primary in-depth interviews with managers in 223 companies doing business in the region; on the development of a new technique for manipulating standard census change data; and on an analysis of a sample from the United States Social Security Administration's Longitudinal Employer-Employee Analysis Data File (LEED). This LEED extract contains quarterly information on the intrafirm, interfirm, interindustry, and interstate mobility of 1 percent of all people covered by Social Security who worked anywhere in New England between 1957 and 1975.

Low and Declining Wage Levels

Throughout the postwar period, New England has consistently displayed the lowest relative manufacturing wages among the regions that make up the nation's old Frostbelt. By the mid-1970s, under pressure from above-average generation-long unemployment and expansion of the regional labor force (partly through employers' recruiting of unskilled workers from the Caribbean but mainly as a result of exceptional increases in female and teenage labor force participation rates), nominal manufacturing wages in New England fell below those of every other part of the country except the South Atlantic region (Table 7.2). Relative nominal earnings in *nonmanufacturing* jobs have also declined vis-a-vis other regions, including the South, especially since 1970 (Browne, 1978a; Harrison, 1982, table 7).

This transformation of New England into a relatively low wage area extends even to many of the "high-tech" occupations for which companies have long claimed to be experiencing critical labor shortages. According to United States Bureau of Labor Statistics area wage surveys and any number of private corporate salary surveys, Boston ranks among the lowest-paying areas in the country in such jobs as computer systems analyst and applications programmer (Harrison, 1982, table 10).

Because the cost of living is higher in New England than anywhere else in the continental United States, *real* wages in the region are now lower than those prevailing anywhere else in America—including the Deep South (see the penultimate column of Table 7.2). This reinforces the tendency toward high labor force participation, which in turn helps to hold wages down. Vicious cycles such as this have helped to re-create in New England the conditions supportive of a new wave of capital accumulation.

TABLE 7.2

Relative Hourly Earnings of Manufacturing Production Workers by Region, 1869–1976 (current dollars) *

Region/State	1869	1889	1909	1929	1947	1951	1960	1965	1970	1975 Unadjusted	1975 (Adjusted for Cost of Living)	1976
New England	105	99	98	94	97	94	92	93	95	92	(84)	87
Maine	78	75	91	81	87	87	—	—	—	—	—	81
New Hampshire	90	84	89	83	86	89	—	—	—	—	—	82
Vermont	91	88	100	94	87	89	—	—	—	—	—	85
Massachusetts	110	104	100	95	96	100	—	—	—	—	—	92
Rhode Island	102	93	95	88	92	93	—	—	—	—	—	80
Connecticut	115	108	102	100	105	105	—	—	—	—	—	99
Middle Atlantic	—	—	—	—	—	108	103	103	102	102	(98)	103
East North Central	—	—	—	—	—	116	113	114	113	116	(115)	117
West North Central	—	—	—	—	—	101	100	102	103	102	(105)	98
South Atlantic	—	—	—	—	—	88	80	81	83	82	(85)	89
East South Central	—	—	—	—	—	88	83	83	84	85	(93)	85
West South Central	—	—	—	—	—	90	92	92	92	93	(103)	92
Mountain	—	—	—	—	—	101	107	106	100	98	(103)	101
Pacific	—	—	—	—	—	124	116	116	114	110	(106)	117
Variation †	—	—	—	—	—	.13	.13	.13	.11	.11	—	.12

Sources: Data for 1869, 1889, 1909, 1929, and 1947: R. Eisenmenger, *The Dynamics of Growth in New England's Economy, 1870–1964* (Middletown, Conn.: Wesleyan University Press, 1967), pp. 24–26. Data for 1951 and 1976: B. Weinstein and R. Firestine, *Regional Growth and Decline in the United States: The Rise of the Sunbelt and the Decline of the Northeast* (New York: Praeger, 1978), pp. 54–56. "Pacific" excludes Hawaii and Alaska. Data for 1960, 1965, 1970, and 1975: L. Browne, "How Different Are Regional Wages?," *New England Economic Review* (Jan.–Feb. 1978): pp. 35, 43. Browne tabulated the nominal B.L.S. earnings data; B. Harrison constructed the ratios shown here. "Pacific" in 1960 does not include Alaska and Hawaii.

* Ratio of nominal average in the region to nominal average in the United States.

† Coefficient of variation (σ/x̄) across regions.

A strong case can be made that this relatively low wage status is the legacy of several factors: a generation of higher-than-average unemployment (in almost every year between 1950 and 1978, the unemployment rate in New England was above the national average); the successful re-creation of a large and disciplined labor force; and the generally supportive stance of key state and local government officials during the crucial years of transition to the new economic base (Harrison, 1982, pp. 32–52).

Increasing Inequality in the Distribution of Earnings

Between 1957 and 1975, many businesses in New England significantly increased their utilization of young workers and expanded the number of part-time and seasonal jobs. For example, by 1975, 35 percent of the wage-earners in the grocery store/supermarket industry were under age twenty, compared with the all-industry regional average of 12 percent (Cournoyer, 1980, p. 52). Local industry sources report that perhaps three-fourths of all department store employees in New England now work part-time (Bluestone et al., 1981b, p. 83). And fully two-thirds of those employed in the hotel-motel industry in 1975 worked during only one or two quarters of that year, usually during the summer months (Kurtz, 1980, p. 198). Each of these factors could, by itself, contribute to an increasing inequality in the distribution of earnings over time.

Our extract from the Social Security Administration's files measures the employment experience of about one million people who worked in New England between 1957 and 1975. It is possible to eliminate at least the effects of seasonality and of casual job attachment by youths by restricting the examination of the distribution of earnings to those who worked all four quarters (although not necessarily full-time) in the region in a year.[2] Gini coefficients (Table 7.3) were estimated for thirteen 3-digit SIC industries, and for the private sector as a whole, from 1957 to 1975 for all workers who spent at least part of all four quarters of each year in that industry. A rising Gini coefficient between years means that earnings among such workers became more unequally distributed over time. A declining Gini would indicate growing equality in the distribution of personal earnings.

[2] The LEED data file does not provide information on the weeks or hours of employment during each person's nineteen-year work history, but only on the number of quarters worked and the number of firms for which the person worked in each year. Since a number of jobs (including federal government employment) are not covered by Social Security, the condition usually known as "not in the labor force" can only be approximated in LEED by measuring those not in covered employment (this category will also capture those who are unemployed in any particular quarter). Finally, the earnings of those who receive more than the maximum taxable limit for the particular year are estimated by the Social Security Administration. The estimation procedure probably understates the variance among these high-earnings recipients, thereby biasing *downward* our estimates of inequality over the entire distribution.

TABLE 7.3

Level and Distribution of Nominal Annual Earnings of Four-Quarter Workers, 1957–1975

Industry and Sex	SIC	Year and Earnings Indicator					
		1957-1958*		1967		1975	
		Median	Gini	Median	Gini	Median	Gini
All covered employment		$3,640	.332	$5,230	.364	$8,270	.381
Manufacturing							
Women's outerwear	233						
All		2,170	.325	3,025	.286	5,135	.352
Women		2,065	.196	2,850	.218	4,970	.202
Men		5,175	.404	5,860	.311	9,920	.474
Paper mills	262						
All		4,425	.187	7,160	.195	11,430	.188
Women		3,260	.119	4,720	.173	8,210	.165
Men		4,610	.176	7,290	.181	11,690	.176
Commercial printing	275						
All		4,135	.315	6,485	.312	9,830	.279
Women		2,880	.221	3,305	.251	6,225	.236
Men		4,969	.297	7,320	.260	10,820	.254
Shoes	314						
All		2,720	.286	3,750	.305	5,600	.315
Women		2,380	.184	3,310	.191	4,910	.179
Men		3,540	.311	5,140	.332	7,140	.384
Metalworking machinery	354						
All		4,980	.270	7,315	.246	11,290	.294
Women		3,190	.164	4,975	.151	7,270	.235
Men		5,590	.258	7,820	.227	11,790	.280
Office machines & computers	357						
All		4,010	.184	7,710	.270	10,840	.287
Women		3,360	.138	4,770	.192	8,310	.196
Men		4,380	.173	8,980	.234	13,280	.270
Electronic components	367						
All		3,740	.293	4,800	.318	7,040	.328
Women		2,860	.175	3,790	.177	5,760	.179
Men		5,195	.245	7,630	.255	11,375	.301
Aircraft engines	372						
All		5,000	.197	7,810	.219	13,150	.217
Women		3,810	.081	5,320	.127	9,740	.104
Men		5,250	.191	8,290	.204	13,850	.208
Nonmanufacturing							
Department stores	531						
All		2,305	.386	3,246	.406	4,616	.443
Women		2,036	.294	2,794	.316	3,968	.325
Men		3,892	.380	6,124	.350	9,716	.432

TABLE 7.3—*continued*

| Industry and Sex | SIC | Year and Earnings Indicator | | | | | |
| | | 1957-1958* | | 1967 | | 1975 | |
		Median	Gini	Median	Gini	Median	Gini
Supermarkets	541						
All		2,860	.367	3,645	.399	4,680	.430
Women		1,960	.270	2,800	.285	3,700	.319
Men		3,630	.352	5,150	.392	6,975	.422
Commercial banks	602						
All		3,080	.296	4,760	.309	7,375	.302
Women		2,755	.133	4,100	.166	6,395	.206
Men		4,185	.327	6,740	.324	11,710	.301
Hotels-motels	701						
All		1,880	.364	2,470	.419	4,010	.398
Women		1,450	.344	1,895	.325	3,200	.344
Men		2,380	.315	3,410	.418	5,140	.401
Hospitals	806						
All		2,365	.323	3,995	.332	7,440	.310
Women		2,255	.271	3,850	.277	7,205	.252
Men		3,130	.400	4,890	.421	9,070	.401

*Because some of the first year (1957) data in our file were defective, we use 1957 if possible, otherwise 1958.

Source: Computations by A. Matthews, Social Welfare Research Institute, Boston College, using Social Security Administration's *Longitudinal Employer-Employee Data File*, containing a 1 percent sample of the social security records of all covered employees who ever worked inside New England between 1957 and 1975. Table includes only wages and salaries actually earned in New England.

Consider three industries that play a prominent role in the new economic structure in New England. The relative inequality in earnings of workers (both men and women) employed at some time in each quarter of the year in the production of office machines and computers increased over this time period by 60 percent. For women working four quarters in commercial banks, inequality worsened by the same percentage. And men working in all four quarters in the hotel-motel industry experienced a 17 percent increase in relative inequality of their earnings (this was the industry with the greatest *absolute* inequality of the three). There are a few industries in which inequality has not worsened. But for the aggregate of all private industries in the region (the first row of Table 7.3), earnings have definitely become more unequally distributed over time.

The Instability of Employment

Perhaps the most important contribution of the literature of the late 1960s and 1970s on "dual labor markets" (or, generally, labor market segmentation) was the discovery that unstable employment patterns are primarily related to the nature of the jobs themselves—that is, in the organization of the labor process rather than in "unstable behavior" by workers (Edwards, 1979, ch. 9–10). For example, many jobs in apparel and food processing are *explicitly* designed to be seasonal. Workers in these jobs experience periodic and predictable layoffs, with recall informally promised (although not always delivered) by their employers. Many jobs—indeed, an increasing number in industries such as hotels, department stores, and supermarkets—are built around the availability of cheap part-time labor. Full-time, year-round jobs in these industries are hard to find.

Apart from this growth in the incidence of part-time or part-year jobs in New England, there are three other aspects of job stability that are susceptible to measurement. The first is attachment of New England workers to particular employers. The second captures the volatility of regional employment over the business cycle. The third reflects the extreme year-to-year volatility of employment in the region's highest-paying blue-collar jobs: those in the engineering industries (especially those engaged in military production, for sale to the United States and foreign governments).

A worker's "attachment" to a particular employer or industry can be measured by data from the LEED file, which spans nineteen years. It is possible to measure (1) the percentage of persons who worked *only* in a particular industry during the year, and (2) the proportion of those *ever* employed in a particular industry, who worked for only one firm in that industry during the year. These annual percentages are then averaged over the whole period to obtain two indicators of "average job attachment" associated with each 3-digit industry. Low percentages mean "low average job attachment" (i.e., high interfirm or interindustry turnover in that industry). When these job attachment indicators were correlated with the long-run employment trend of each industry (growing, stable or declining) and with that industry's average annual earnings, it was discovered that *growing* industries in New England tend to display low average earnings and low average job attachment (high turnover), while *declining* industries tend to pay higher average wages and show lower turnover. In short, with the exception of high technology, the region's industry mix is becoming increasingly characterized by companies that provide *unstable* and *low-wage* jobs (Harrison, 1982, table 12).[3]

Another aspect of job instability is associated with the transmission of national and international business cycles to the regional economies of the ma-

---

[3]Of course, the variables "average earnings" and "average turnover" are not independent. Apart from the extent to which instability is built into a job (as in seasonal hotel work or in the manufacture of many types of apparel) or is the result of volatile swings in demand for the product or service, it is also to be expected that workers *leave* jobs that pay low wages more often than they leave jobs that do not. In other words, when they complain about their work-force being insufficiently committed to the job, employers are often bringing this on themselves by paying low wages.

jor trading countries. Researchers used to believe that regions containing the most cyclically volatile industries—automobiles and other durable goods, in particular—usually experienced the most severe local recessions and/or the slowest recoveries (Bretzfelder, 1978). In 1978, two economists at the Federal Reserve Bank of Boston published the findings of their own research on regional business cycles. In his paper, Syron first compared the extent of each region's decline into recession. He found that, in every post–World War II recession except 1960–61, firms in New England generally experienced a more severe decline than those elsewhere. Syron then statistically removed the long-run employment growth trend from each region's data, leaving a purely cyclical series to be examined. He concluded:

> It might be expected that over time regions would become more rather than less similar in their sensitivity to national economic fluctuations. . . . The trend over the last thirty years has been for a smaller proportion of the workforce to be employed in heavy industries that are tied to a particular locality because of the availability of raw materials. Advances in transportation and communications would also be expected to result in increased integration of regional economies. However, despite these developments there does not appear to be any trend toward a convergence in regional sensitivity to business cycles. If anything, regions seem to be becoming more dissimilar [Syron, 1978, p. 32].

In a companion study using the same data, Browne showed that industry mix is no longer a sufficient predictor of the probable severity of a region's response to the business cycle. She writes: "Recessions are not identical and while some industries may always be affected, others fare quite well on one occasion only to be severely impacted on another. Nonmanufacturing in general [was] more disrupted in 1975, relative to other sectors, than in earlier recessions" (Browne, 1978b, pp. 48–49). The implication for the New England region is that services are no longer "recession proof." Finally, Howland has discovered that a region's secular growth trend can no longer predict the severity of its recessions. She concludes that a period of significant employment growth does not improve the chances that the region's next recession will be a mild one (Howland, 1979).

There is yet another kind of cycle to which the New England economy seems especially sensitive: the boom-and-bust pattern of cyclical employment growth and decline in the engineering industries. Figure 7.4 dramatically illustrates this for the aircraft-metalworking complex. As rapid as was the Vietnam-induced buildup of employment in the first half of the sixties, the retrenchment that followed the cessation of war-related orders was precipitous. In fact, New England's extreme dependence on federal (and foreign) military procurement penetrates much of the industrial base through the derived demand for everything from instruments to new tools and dies to paper clips to various services. Another boom driven by military spending is forecast for the mid-1980s.

Barriers to Upward (or Intersectoral) Mobility

In New England, as elsewhere, workers move across locations, between employers, and even among different kinds of jobs. Whether that movement, however, leads to "upward" mobility in earnings and status can not be assumed.

One question of particular interest in assessing the normative implications of the transformation of the economic base concerns what has happened to those workers who eventually left (or were displaced from) old mill industries. How many were able to find jobs in the new "high-tech" companies or in the highly unionized, high-paying engineering industries—those industries that also show the greatest degree of job attachment, as measured by the indicators described earlier? Have shoe, apparel, and textile workers been forced to accept jobs in predominantly low-wage, less-stable services, where they probably have had to take wage cuts? And finally, how many displaced mill workers have moved out of New England altogether, either to look for similar jobs or to retire? The longitudinal character of the LEED file permits an analysis of these questions (Harrison, 1982, tables 14–15).

In 1958 there were about 833,000 people whose principal activity was to work in mill industries: food, textiles, apparel, lumber, leather goods and shoes, furniture, paper, and printing. Sometime after 1958, 674,000 of these workers left the New England mills, never to return. By 1975 only 18,000 of them—fewer than 3 percent—were employed in the "high-tech" industries of the region (defined for this purpose as electronics, instruments, and computers). Another 2,000 had migrated to "high-tech" jobs outside New England. Most went into the service sector (working for private service companies or for the federal government), dropped out of the labor force, or had no job at all. Only one-eighth of the group had retired by 1975.

The picture is no better for the youngest cohort. There were about 158,000 mill workers in 1958 under the age of twenty-five. Of these, 131,000 left the mill industries sometime after 1958. Where did they go? In 1975, eighteen years later, only 5,000 had been hired by the region's "high-tech" companies while another 1,000 had found "high-tech" jobs elsewhere. Like the older members of their cohort, the great majority took private service jobs, went to work for the federal government, dropped out, or were unemployed in 1975.

Therefore, few of those who leave the generally declining, older mill-based industries of the region are able to move into the relatively good jobs in growth sectors, such as high technology (or into the higher-paying jobs in the older,

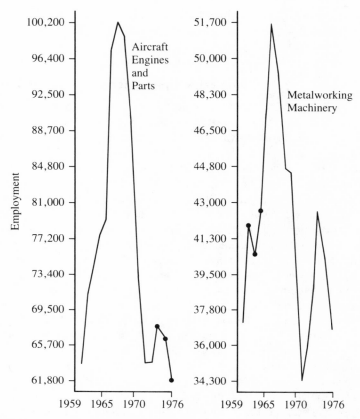

FIGURE 7.4.   Annual employment in aircraft engine and metalworking machinery manufacturing in New England, 1959–1976. *Source*: Calculations by L. Ware, D. DiPasquale, and B. Bluestone, Social Welfare Research Institute, Boston College, using data from U.S. Department of Commerce, *County Business Patterns*. Black dots indicate that observations for some New England states were not available that year and had to be interpolated.

established capital goods industries, such as aircraft and metalworking). Relatively few mill workers, even the youngest and presumably most mobile, move away from the region. But whether they move or not, they tend not to be hired by "high-tech" companies. The lesson seems clear: the region simply does not create enough new, well-paying jobs in its growth industries to absorb those displaced by industrial disinvestment, and the jobs created in sectors like high technology are going to other people, including many recruited from outside the region.

At the same time, the combination of deskilling and expansion of centralized management in industries such as department stores has thrown up major obstacles to the career advancement of another group of workers in New

England—women. Since 1957 the growth of department store management jobs (nearly all held by men) has greatly increased the incomes of older men, as indicated by a steepening over time of their age-earnings profiles (Fig. 7.5).

The situation is very different for women. Women used to hold most of the skilled buying and sales positions because they knew the products well and could discuss them intelligently with customers. The growth of television advertising, the huge one-story self-service store layout, and the introduction of

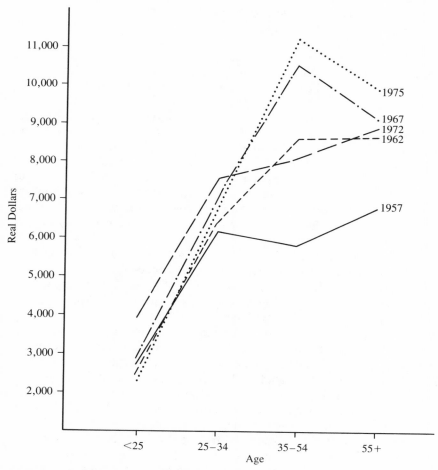

FIGURE 7.5. Age earnings profile for white males in New England department store industry, 1957–1975 (in real 1967 dollars). *Source*: Barry Bluestone, Patricia Hanna, Sarah Kuhn, and Laura J. Moore, *The Retail Revolution: Market Transformation, Investment, and Labor in the Modern Department Store* (Boston: Auburn House Pub. Co., 1981), fig. 6.1, p. 102. Reproduced with permission of the publisher.

automatic data processing point-of-sale computers have made it easier for managers to employ teenagers at the minimum wage. Consequently, the earnings opportunities of all but the most senior women employees have actually worsened over time. That is, *their* age-earnings profiles have become *flatter* since 1957 (Fig. 7.6).

This can be seen from another vantage point. Back in 1957 the personal earnings distributions of "year-round" (four-quarter) male and female employees in the department store industry were similar (Fig. 7.7). By 1975 they had diverged to an extraordinary degree. The male distribution had become bimodal, reflecting the presence of both part-time (but year-round) young men and full-time highly paid managers. The female distribution continues to exhibit its traditional shape: even the proportion of year-round women earning high salaries diminishes rapidly as the level of earnings increases. For example, in 1975 only 2 percent of the women working year-round in New England department stores earned more than $15,000, in contrast to more than 15 percent of the men (Fig. 7.8).

Even in such industries as nonprofit hospitals, where wages and opportunities for upward mobility have been somewhat better for New England women, the ratio of men's to women's earnings has not changed since the late 1950s. According to Barocci (1981, p. 145), this is because "the areas of greatest growth in employment are related to operation and maintenance of . . . management systems—traditionally male positions. . . . The doctors, if past is prologue, will resist relinquishing control to nurses while continuing to develop more and more subspecialties to enhance their control over hospital functions even further."

Among the nonmanagerial labor force, some people (especially middle-class youth) may find the proliferating part-time or seasonal service jobs attractive and helpful. But an important segment of the adult population—and many more young workers than is commonly supposed—find these jobs to be basically a dead end. The problem can be illustrated by the hotel-motel industry, one of New England's most rapidly growing industries since the late 1950s, but also the industry with the lowest average earnings (even for four-quarter workers) and among the most unequally distributed earnings. As a result, hotels exhibit extraordinarily high turnover. Part of the problem is the seasonality of the tourist-oriented segment of the industry. However, wages and working conditions are generally poor in *all* of the industry's segments, including those urban business-oriented hotels that in recent years have received much development aid from the federal government through the Urban Development Action Grant (UDAG) program.

The LEED file permits an analysis of how different groups in the labor force use hotel-motel jobs. The sample that was drawn for this particular investigation consists of everyone employed in the industry inside New England in 1969. The object was to trace their job histories in the succeeding six years: the number that moved out of hotels-motels into a "primary labor

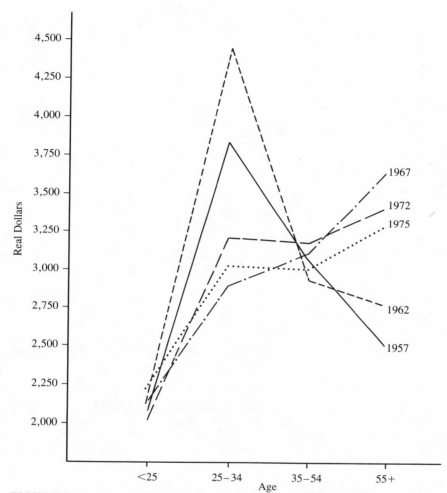

FIGURE 7.6. Age earnings profile for white females in New England department store industry, 1957–1975 (in real 1967 dollars). *Source*: Barry Bluestone, Patricia Hanna, Sarah Kuhn, and Laura J. Moore, *The Retail Revolution: Market Transformation, Investment, and Labor in the Modern Department Store* (Boston: Auburn House Pub. Co., 1981), fig. 6.2, p. 104. Reproduced with permission of the publisher.

market" job, and the number that remained in hotels-motels or moved into some other "secondary" (i.e., low-wage, high-turnover) job.[4]

Young white men proved to be far more successful than anyone else in using hotel-motel jobs as a stepping-stone to better jobs in the future. Men

[4]The definition we developed for operationalizing the "primary-secondary labor market" dichotomy is explained in Harrison and Hill (1979). This taxonomy is an extreme simplification of a highly complex structure (Edwards, 1979). For a general discussion of "good" and "bad" jobs in a *national* context, see Gordon (1980).

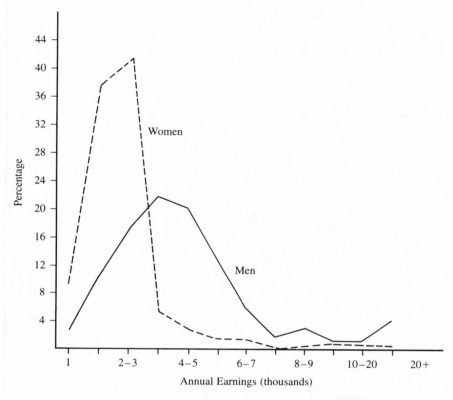

FIGURE 7.7. 1957 earnings distribution for New England's year-round department store workers, by sex. *Source*: Barry Bluestone, Patricia Hanna, Sarah Kuhn, and Laura J. Moore, *The Retail Revolution: Market Transformation, Investment, and Labor in the Modern Department Store* (Boston: Auburn House Pub. Co., 1981), fig. 6.4, p. 107. Reproduced with permission of the publisher.

who were under twenty-five years old in 1969 were twice as likely as women in the same age group to have moved, six years later, out of the low-wage sector. Both women and men who were still working in hotels or motels by age twenty-five faced odds of from two to one (men) to three to one (women) of remaining "stuck" in the secondary labor market (if not in hotels per se) six years later.

What changes in the organization of work in the hotel-motel industry might explain this growing divergence between upwardly mobile workers and people going nowhere? Changes in the *age structure* of the industry's work force cannot be the cause, since age-earnings profiles have, if anything, become flatter since the late 1950s (Harrison, 1982, pp. 100–104). On the other hand, the substitutions of coin-operated machines for personalized

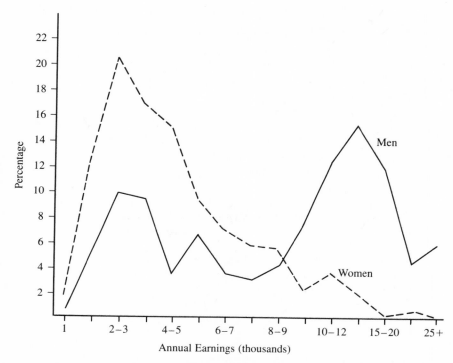

FIGURE 7.8. 1975 earnings distribution for New England's year-round department store workers, by sex. *Source*: Barry Bluestone, Patricia Hanna, Sarah Kuhn, and Laura J. Moore, *The Retail Revolution: Market Transformation, Investment, and Labor in the Modern Department Store* (Boston: Auburn House Pub. Co., 1981), fig. 6.3, p. 106. Reproduced with permission of the publisher.

room service and of the preparation of prefrozen foods in microwave ovens for versatile cooks in the hotel kitchen have reduced the utilization of skilled service workers. At the same time, the growth of franchising and of international corporate chains has led to the proliferation of jobs for highly paid managers, accountants, and other professionals.

Thus, although age, race, and sex are highly correlated with earnings in this industry (as in most others), they do not *cause* growing inequality in earnings. Rather, the structure of the jobs themselves is becoming more polarized. As this proceeds, minorities are allotted to maintenance/janitorial work, women are assigned to most of the "housework" jobs, and the vast majority of managerial and professional jobs involving finance and real estate functions are assigned to older white men (Kurtz, 1980, ch. 6).

The "Wedge" between the Growth of
Business Sales (and Profits) and the
Derived Demand for New England Labor

New England has clearly undergone a profound "restructuring" of its economic base in the years since World War II (Gibson et al., 1982; Massey and Meegan, 1982; Walker and Storper, 1981). For all the neoclassical imagery of the "adjustment" of regional economies to new "equilibria," the restructuring process continues unabated.

Most of us have observed the proclivity of the business press to declare "good news" for a region whenever—through some government contract or as a result of the development of new overseas markets—a local firm enjoys increasing sales and profits. The usual expectation is that a change in sales will lead to something like a proportional change in employment.[5] Is this actually occurring in New England?

Among seventy-six specific industries in New England for the years 1967 to 1972, the typical relationship between sales and employment could hardly be described as one of proportionality. Instead we find that:

rise in sales → proportional rise in employment in 3 industries
rise in sales → less than proportional rise in employment in 15 industries
rise in sales → fall in employment in 30 industries
fall in sales → proportional fall in employment in 0 industries
fall in sales → more than proportional fall in employment in 24 industries
fall in sales → less than proportional fall in employment in 4 industries.

Conventional wisdom held in only three of the seventy-six industries. In thirty industries, rising sales were accompanied by *declining* employment. What explains this substantial "wedge" between sales growth (or decline) and employment change occurring within the same set of plants?

At least three mediating forces can interfere with the translation of reported sales growth into jobs, income, and taxes for the region's workers and local governments. First, the introduction of labor-displacing machinery and

---

[5]The usual Keynesian multiplier assumption is that technology, the location, and the organization of work are all held constant for the purposes of forecasting—in other words, that the aggregate capital-output and capital-labor ratios (or schedules) are fixed for the period of analysis of the impact of new spending. The underlying microeconomics implicitly assume some kind of linear homogeneous aggregate production function. That is the logic that generates the deduction that an increase in output (or sales, assuming away inventory issues) will lead to a proportional derived demand for labor. Suppose, however, that we could account systematically for actual changes in production and organizational technologies, which are in reality far more complex than what is implied by neoclassical linear homogeneity. What might we find? That is what the model presented in the text is designed to accomplish.

equipment, or even a simple acceleration of the production pace, may mean that increases in output to meet expanding markets will not require proportional increases in labor time. Second, existing workers may be employed for longer hours to reduce the need for additional employees (this may also reflect a policy of taking up slack following a period of retrenchment in production). Finally, although sales and profits are attributed to a firm located in one place—in this case, New England—at least some part of the actual production may occur outside the region.

The magnitude of these factors can be estimated by decomposing census employment data over some period into the job change associated with changes in (1) the volume of sales (including exports) achieved by New England business; (2) the ratio of the actual volume of production undertaken in New England to sales, which varies with the extent to which the industry's firms record their sales (and profits) in New England while engaging in production (or purchasing inputs or components from) elsewhere; (3) labor productivity in the industry in this region; and (4) average hours per worker in the industry in the region.

At Boston College, Barry Bluestone, together with Peter Jordan and Alan Matthews, have developed a quantitative technique for sorting out these interacting tendencies as they relate to New England's manufacturing industries. They first applied the technique to census data on the aircraft industry for the period from 1967 to 1972, the most recent data available at the time. The analysis has been extended (by Matthews and this author) to all seventy-six 3-digit manufacturing industries in the region. It is not possible to analyze the restructuring of the service sector using this technique because it requires distinguishing between the sales registered by a business located in a particular place (in this case, New England) and the portion of final output actually produced at that location (value added)—a distinction which the Census Bureau does not make for service industries.

Taking the total discrete differential of the following identity:

$$PW \equiv VS \cdot \frac{VA}{VS} \cdot \frac{HR}{VA} \cdot \frac{PW}{HR}$$

where

PW = number of production workers
VA = real value added
VS = real value of shipments
HR = hours of work in production

yields the following expression:

$$dPW = \left(\frac{VA}{VS} \cdot \frac{HR}{VA} \cdot \frac{PW}{HR} \right) dVS + \left(VS \cdot \frac{HR}{VA} \cdot \frac{PW}{HR} \right) d\frac{VA}{VS}$$

change in employ-	change in employ-
ment due to change in	ment due to change
sales	in the proportion of
	sales actually pro-
	duced within New
	England

$$+ \left(VS \cdot \frac{VA}{VS} \cdot \frac{PW}{HR} \right) d\frac{HR}{VA} + \left(VS \cdot \frac{VA}{VS} \cdot \frac{HR}{VA} \right) d\frac{PW}{HR}$$

change in employ-	change in employ-
ment due to change in	ment due to change
productivity	in hours per worker

Interaction Terms

$$+ \left(VS \cdot d\frac{VA}{VS} \cdot d\frac{HR}{VA} \cdot d\frac{PW}{HR} \right) + \left(\frac{VA}{VS} \cdot dVS \cdot d\frac{HR}{VA} \cdot d\frac{PW}{HR} \right)$$

$$+ \left(\frac{HR}{VA} \cdot dVS \cdot d\frac{VA}{VS} \cdot d\frac{PW}{HR} \right) + \left(\frac{PW}{HR} \cdot d\frac{VA}{VS} \cdot d\frac{HR}{VS} \cdot dVS \right)$$

$$+ \left(dVS \cdot d\frac{VA}{VS} \cdot d\frac{HR}{VA} \cdot d\frac{PW}{HR} \right) + \left(VS \cdot \frac{VA}{VS} \cdot d\frac{HR}{VA} \cdot d\frac{PW}{HR} \right)$$

$$+ \left(VS \cdot \frac{HR}{VA} \cdot d\frac{VA}{VS} \cdot d\frac{PW}{HR} \right) + \left(VS \cdot \frac{PW}{HR} \cdot d\frac{VA}{VS} \cdot d\frac{HR}{VA} \right)$$

$$+ \left(\frac{VA}{VS} \cdot \frac{HR}{VA} \cdot dVS \cdot d\frac{PW}{HR} \right) + \left(\frac{HR}{VA} \cdot \frac{PW}{HR} \cdot dVS \cdot d\frac{VA}{VS} \right)$$

$$+ \left(\frac{PW}{HR} \cdot \frac{VA}{VS} \cdot dVS \cdot d\frac{HR}{VA} \right)$$

Because this is a nonprobabilistic procedure, its utility is an empirical question. That is, if the complex interaction term should dominate the total change in employment (dPW), there would be no practical way to decompose overall job change into flows that could be directly associated with changes in sales, local content, productivity, or work intensity. Obviously our chances for achieving a successful decomposition increase with the degree of informational disaggregation, which is why we chose to work at the 3- rather than the more familiar 2-digit level. Even then, there was no a priori guarantee that the technique would "work." In principle, the ratio of job change captured in interactions to overall job change (*dPW*) could vary between zero and one. The smaller that ratio, the more useful the technique.

Estimates of the inflation-adjusted components of the discrete differential were computed for all seventy-six 3-digit manufacturing industries in New England between 1967 and 1972. The interaction term accounted for an average of less than 5 percent of the variation in employment; its largest value in any single industry was only 23 percent. In this case, the technique clearly "worked" (Harrison, 1982, table 17). This exercise reveals the instability of the present economic base; that is, the continuing tendencies toward the restructuring and relocation of production and employment. In only three of the seventy-six industries (cleaning materials, building materials, and fabricated metal products) did sales increases produce proportionate increases in employment; these three together accounted for a miniscule share of the region's jobs. Forty-five other industries registered sales increases between 1967 and 1972. In fifteen of these, the job growth that rising sales would have otherwise created was partly offset by the shift of production or purchasing out of the region, by increased productivity, or by increased hours of work per employee. For example, the increased sales of engines and turbines might have been expected to generate a 35 percent increase in employment. However, a declining share of market value actually added within New England, and a substantial increase in productivity, held the actual employment increase to only 4 percent.

In the thirty other industries that enjoyed expanding sales, the expected employment was more than offset by some combination of production or purchasing dispersal, higher productivity, or increases in the average number of hours per worker. This was especially dramatic for the "office machines" segment of SIC 357. During the period under study (the late 1960s), New England companies manufacturing typewriters, scales, and traditional (non-electronic) cash registers went out of the country or were dramatically reorganized, especially in Connecticut. Had there been no changes in the location of production, in productivity, or in hours per worker, the employment of production workers in these activities might have been expected to increase by 66 percent. In fact, it declined by 1 percent.

The remaining twenty-eight industries in the sample suffered declining absolute sales during this period. In twenty-four, the predictably negative impact of falling sales on jobs was compounded by the shift of production or purchasing out of the region, by higher productivity, or by increased hours of work (in this category, shoes and electrical testing equipment displayed the greatest regional shift). In only four industries was the expected decline in employment mitigated somewhat by increases in the regional content of production or purchasing, by decreasing productivity, or by decreasing average hours per worker.

Conclusions

In developing scenarios of the future health of the region's economy, professional forecasters and the business media have focused most of their attention on what is likely to happen to the short- and medium-term demand for New England's principal exports. A particular issue that has attracted much interest is the extent to which the region has become "recession-proof" as a result of the transition to a "high-tech" *cum* services base (all evidence suggests that it has not).

Any *long-term* forecast of future economic conditions in New England will have to consider the possibility that the increasing instability of work and the polarization of jobs and income may spill over into regional politics, affecting the future investment climate. Low wages and weak (or nonexistent) unions created the current "good business climate" in the first place, within which "high-tech" and service expansion could occur. What political economists call crises in social reproduction could well give rise to resistance by different segments of the workforce to the perpetuation of "business as usual," leading to increased workplace and community disruption and creating upward pressure on both private wages and social welfare spending.

In an era of intensified capital mobility, this could endanger a new wave of corporate disinvestment. But it could also lead to widespread popular demand for an unprecedented measure of public economic planning to either regulate or replace "footloose" private capital (Bluestone and Harrison, 1982, ch. 8). In either event, the long-run growth of the regional economy as it is presently organized is by no means to be taken for granted.

References

Barocci, T. 1981. *Non-Profit Hospitals*. Boston: Auburn House.

Bluestone, B., et al. 1981a. *Aircraft Industry Dynamics*. Boston: Auburn House.

Bluestone, B., P. Hanna, S. Kuhn, and L. J. Moore. 1981b. *The Retail Revolution: Market Transformation, Investment, and Labor in the Modern Department Store.* Boston: Auburn House.

Bluestone, B., and B. Harrison. 1982. *The Deindustrialization of America.* New York: Basic Books.

Braverman, H. 1974. *Labor and Monopoly Capital.* New York: Monthly Review Press.

Bretzfelder, R. 1978. Regional patterns of change in non-farm income in recession and expansion. *Survey of Current Business* 58, no. 1 (January): 19–20.

Browne, L. 1978a. How different are regional wages? *New England Economic Review* (January-February): 33–43.

Browne, L. 1978b. Regional industry mix and the business cycle. *New England Economic Review* (November–December): 35-53.

Cournoyer, P. 1980. *The New England Retail Grocery Industry*. Springfield, Va.: National Technical Information Service, Access no. PB81-185761.

Edwards, R. 1979. *Contested Terrain*. New York: Basic Books.

Gibson, K., et al. 1982. "A theoretical approach to capital and labor restructuring." In *Regions in Crisis*, 2nd ed., edited by J. Carney. London: Croom Helm.

Gordon, D. M. 1980. *The Working Poor: Toward a State Agenda*. Washington, D.C.: Council of State Planning Agencies.

Harrison, B. 1982. Rationalization, restructuring, and industrial reorganization in older regions: the economic transformation of New England since World War II. Working Paper no. 72, MIT-Harvard Joint Center for Urban Studies.

Harrison, B., and E. Hill. 1979. The changing structure of jobs in older and younger cities. Working Paper no. 58, MIT-Harvard Joint Center for Urban Studies.

Howland, M. 1979. "The business cycle and long-run regional growth." In *Interregional Movements and Regional Growth*, edited by W. C. Wheaton, pp. 75–107. Washington, D.C.: The Urban Institute.

Kurtz, D. 1980. *The Lodging Business in New England*. Springfield, Va.: National Technical Information Service, Access no. PB81-188310.

Little, J. S. 1980. Foreign direct investment in the United States: recent locational choices of foreign manufacturers. *New England Economic Review* (November–December): 5–22.

Massey, D., and R. Meegan. 1982. *The Anatomy of Job Loss*. London: Methuen.

Piore, M. J. 1980. *Birds of Passage*. New York: Cambridge University Press.

Syron, R. 1978. Regional experience during business cycles—are we becoming more or less alike? *New England Economic Review* (November–December): 25–34.

U.S. Bureau of the Census. 1940. *1940 Census of Population*. U.S. Summary, Divisions and States. Washington, D.C.: Government Printing Office.

U.S. Bureau of the Census. 1977. *1977 County Business Patterns*. Washington, D.C.: Government Printing Office.

Walker, R., and M. Storper. 1981. Capital and locational change. *Progress in Human Geography* 5: 473–509.

Zimbalist, A., ed. 1979. *Case Studies in the Labor Process*. New York: Monthly Review Press.

ROY BAHL

8   *Fiscal Problems of Cities in the Northeast*

Looking out from 1975, nearly any observer of municipal finances would have offered a gloomy prognosis. New York was by no means the only city facing deep-seated economic problems and a taxable capacity growth too slow to accommodate the growth in expenditure requirements. Various analysts saw a real possibility for default in Buffalo, Detroit, Boston, Yonkers, Cleveland, and even New York State.

In fact, however, there have been relatively few cases of financial collapse since 1975. Cleveland, Wayne County, and the Chicago schools are notable exceptions, but there have not been many more New Yorks. Some have seen this absence of crisis as a sign of renewed fiscal and economic health in cities, while others are convinced that it reflects a postponement of crises yet to come. Which view is correct? Have overzealous analysts overstated the case? After all, the obsolete and crumbling central city infrastructure has not yet crumbled; ten more years of woefully deficient central city services have not produced more urban ghetto riots; "underpaid" public employees have not brought city operations to a standstill with a series of major strikes; public employee layoffs have been accomplished without noticeably severe declines in public servicing; and city governments have indeed been able to pay their bills. In light of this, is there still a fiscal crisis? If one is to argue a crisis outlook for northeastern cities, then one must explain the absence of severe financial distress since 1975—which is the purpose of this chapter.

150

Explaining the Financial Health of Cities[1]

New York City's financial collapse in 1975 changed nearly everyone's view of urban fiscal problems. The focus of interest shifted from concern with social problems and inadequate public services in inner cities to pre-occupation with financial strength and susceptibility to default. Public employee unions, local politicians and bureaucrats, federal and state government policymakers, the financial community, and even citizens' groups seem to accept the new priority. More than any other single factor, this change in public attitude may be responsible for maintaining the financial solvency of northeastern cities. In effect, it made possible the kinds of sacrifices from public employees and public service beneficiaries that were necessary.

Beyond this change in attitude, one might offer three hypotheses to explain why there were no more New Yorks.

1. *The Improving Economy Thesis*: The post–1975 economic recovery benefited cities, as has the 1983–1984 recovery; the most recent recession (1981–1982) did not harm them as badly as in 1975. A revitalization of central cities is occurring, and the demographic makeup of cities is changing in a way that lessens the pressure for increased public expenditures.

2. *The Increasing Resources Hypothesis*: Federal and State grant inflows were substantial enough to prop up the slow growth in state taxes in the immediate aftermath of the 1975 recession. Thereafter, inflation also bid up local tax revenues. The result was that resources were adequate to cover expenditure requirements. The more moderate effects of the latest (1981) recession on northeastern cities and the 1983 recovery have kept city revenues buoyant.

3. *The Deferral Hypothesis*: Because of the New York City scare, city governments were able to reduce employment rolls, dramatically slow the rate of increase in public employee wage rates, cut public service levels, and defer maintenance and additions to the capital stock.

Available evidence bears out some parts of each of these hypotheses as explanations of city financial health since 1975. Interestingly, each of these issues also highlights a relative disadvantage of northeast cities.

The fundamental issue here is whether the conditions and policies that have staved off default will continue into the 1980s; the specific concern is how cities in the declining region will fare.

[1] Some of this material is covered in more detail in Bahl (forthcoming), ch. 3.

The Improving Economy Thesis

A major factor that brought many central cities to the brink of financial disaster in 1975 was the decline in their economic base. The job and income loss shrunk available revenues, and the increased unemployment rate pressured social service expenditures. Some have hypothesized that the situation improved after 1975: (1) that city economies have recovered, thereby holding up revenue growth, and (2) that population size and composition have changed in ways that relieve public expenditure requirements.

EMPLOYMENT CHANGES

The competitive position of northeastern (and industrial midwestern) cities weakened in the decade of the 1970s. In a sense they were doubly damned, losing jobs to both the faster growing Sunbelt region and to their own suburbs. The litany of underlying causes is well known. The cost of doing business (labor, taxes, energy) is relatively high in the Northeast, and markets—population and income—are moving to the South and the West. Between 1950 and 1980, the Northeast regional share of national employment fell from 27.1 to 21.6 percent, that of personal income from 29.9 to 23.1 percent, and that of population from 26.1 to 21.7 percent.

Evidence suggests that central cities in the Northeast have received a declining share of this declining share and that employment suburbanization has occurred as industries have moved to newer, more modern, and campus-type facilities closer to their suburban employees. Unfortunately, this pattern cannot be documented as clearly as one would want. When one moves from a discussion of regional trends to analysis of individual cities, and to making city/suburban comparisons, a severe data constraint is encountered. There simply are not regular estimates of employment in city areas; analysts must be content with some form of extrapolation between population census years and retailing/manufacturing census years, or with analyzing a relatively small sample of coterminous city-counties. Both approaches are utilized in this chapter.

Seymour Sacks (1978) has adjusted census journey-to-work data to make intercensal estimates of employment in city areas. He finds a stereotype pattern: between 1970 and 1975, northeastern cities lost employment at an average annual rate of 1.6 percent; midwestern cities saw almost no change on average, but southern cities grew at 3.5 percent and western cities at 2.7 percent. Relative to their suburbs, cities in the Northeast fared badly. In only one of fifteen cases studied did central city employment increase as fast as suburban employment. Sacks's more recent work shows a continuation of this trend. Of sixteen large northeastern central cities for which there were data, only four showed any employment growth between 1975 and 1977.

By comparison, thirteen of twenty midwestern central cities, seventeen of twenty-four southern cities, and fourteen of seventeen western cities registered employment increases (U.S. Department of Housing and Urban Development, 1980, table 23). The average rates of change were −0.3 percent in the Northeast, 3.3 percent in the Midwest, 3.8 percent in the South, and 5.7 percent in the West. In only three of the northeastern standard metropolitan statistical areas (SMSAs) did city employment increase as fast as that in the suburbs.

The lack of regularly published data on central city employment severely limits the documentation of employment decline. One source of data, the Census Bureau's *County Business Patterns*, limits any comparisons of experiences across central cities to those ten cities that are coterminous with counties.[2] Though a very small sample, Baltimore, New York, Philadelphia, and St. Louis could represent the declining city type, and the remainder, the growing city type.

As seen in Table 8.1, Philadelphia and St. Louis experienced employment declines over the 1965–72 period, and there was virtually no growth in New York. Between 1973 and 1974, six of the ten central counties were losing employment with the four gaining counties—Indianapolis, Jacksonville, San Francisco, and Nashville—conspicuously outside the declining region. During the recession between 1974 and 1975, all ten counties lost employment.

During the post-1975 recovery period, the "declining" counties did not fare as well. None of the four experienced any employment increase until 1978, a full two years after the national recovery had begun. By 1979, when the national employment growth rate was 7.3 percent, the average growth rate for these four declining counties was 2.8 percent and for the six growing counties, 4.8 percent. In 1980 and 1981, the declining counties lost employment at a greater rate than the nation while the growing counties exceeded national economic performance.

These data also reveal a continuing trend toward suburbanization. The share of SMSA employment in the central city/county declined in all ten SMSAs studied (Table 8.2). It is interesting to note, however, that in 1979 in the four "declining" SMSAs the central city (county) employment share averaged 49.3 percent, while in the growing SMSAs it averaged 65.5 percent. In 1981, only in Jacksonville and San Francisco did the share increase.

DEMOGRAPHIC CHANGES

Another possibility is that some of the pressure is off central city budgets because of a changing population. The argument would go that local govern-

---

[2]These data also have the disadvantage that they exclude government and proprietorship employment. Furthermore, there is a substantial publication time lag in the data.

TABLE 8.1

Percent Increase in Employment in Ten Metropolitan Central Counties

County	1965–1972	1972–1973	1973–1974	1974–1975	1975–1976	1976–1977	1977–1978	1978–1979	1979–1980	1980–1981
Baltimore	4.0	1.7	-9.5	-6.7	-3.8	-1.2	2.2	1.8	0.8	-2.4
Denver	37.4	8.2	-7.4	-4.8	2.3	2.8	12.2	6.4	2.6	1.0
Indianapolis	15.9	6.4	2.1	-4.8	3.7	2.9	5.6	5.7	-2.2	-4.3
Jacksonville	37.6	8.0	5.8	-6.4	-0.9	-1.5	9.5	4.0	1.4	2.0
Nashville	32.3	8.1	4.4	-4.4	4.2	3.8	8.6	6.0	-2.1	1.3
New Orleans	10.8	2.0	-10.2	-4.0	1.2	1.0	9.1	4.2	-2.0	0.9
New York City	0.2	-3.0	-1.4	-6.2	-1.0	-2.7	3.1	4.3	-0.6	1.0
Philadelphia	-0.5	0.9	-3.2	-8.0	-1.3	-4.4	3.8	2.5	-2.8	-1.7
St. Louis	-1.8	1.7	-7.4	-11.5	-0.2	-3.9	4.8	2.5	-4.8	-4.8
San Francisco	10.3	2.2	15.2	-2.8	0.4	-5.3	10.9	2.3	1.2	4.9
United States	21.5	7.0	2.3	-4.7	3.4	3.9	8.1	7.3	-0.8	0.0

Source: U.S. Bureau of the Census, *County Business Patterns for 1965–81* (Washington, D.C.: Government Printing Office, 1966–1983).

TABLE 8.2
Percent of SMSA Employment in Central City/County*

County	1972	1975	1977	1979	1981
Baltimore	59.62	50.55	46.74	44.57	43.03
Denver	63.87	54.64	51.53	49.81	48.50
Indianapolis	87.13	86.18	85.43	84.31	83.75
Jacksonville	92.10	90.33	88.15	87.62	87.65
Nashville	78.70	78.03	76.40	75.48	75.15
New Orleans	72.33	63.28	58.45	59.44	55.10
New York City	84.10	81.78	80.50	79.97	79.75
Philadelphia	49.56	43.26	40.43	39.26	38.08
St. Louis	46.43	35.70	34.78	33.15	30.90
San Francisco	39.93	41.67	37.29	37.10	37.92

*1975 SMSA boundaries were used for all years.
Source: U.S. Bureau of the Census, *County Business Patterns for 1965–81* (Washington, D.C.: Government Printing Office, 1966–1983).

ment expenditure needs have been lessened because there is a smaller population to be served, fewer school-aged children, and fewer public assistance recipients. On the other side of the coin is the possibility that the composition of population has also changed in unfavorable ways (i.e., there is an increasing share of the elderly and the very poor, and a large backlog of unmet social needs to be dealt with).

In fact, the data bear out some of this argument. Between 1950 and 1980, population in the Northeast grew at a rate that was less than half that of the nation. Again, central cities have grown even slower than the rest of the region. Of the eighteen largest northeastern cities, only one had any population increase between 1970 and 1980. While compositional effects are less easily described, a few trends are evident; for example, population densities have declined and school enrollments have gone down.

The Increasing Resources Hypothesis

Another possible reason for the unexpected fiscal health of Northeastern cities is that their revenue systems have remained buoyant. The two elements of this strong revenue performance are the growth in federal grants and the favorable effects of inflation and economic growth on local tax revenues.

FEDERAL ASSISTANCE

A major reason why large central cities performed above expectations in the period immediately after the recession was the massive inflow of direct federal aid to cities. Much of the increase in federal assistance in the aftermath of the recession was the Carter administration's economic stimulus package.[3] Various analyses showed that the stimulus package was heavily targeted on large cities that were thought to be characterized by a high degree of fiscal strain (U.S. Department of the Treasury, 1978).

Growth in this aid, however, has tapered off since 1978 with the overall decline in federal assistance to state and local governments. Referring to Table 8.3, note that the ratio of federal aid to own-source revenue has declined in ten of the fifteen reported cases. But while distressed cities benefited more from federal aid increments, they may be most hurt by federal aid reductions. The admittedly limited comparison in Table 8.3 suggests that declining cities are more dependent on federal assistance.

What one may say from these data is that central cities did benefit substantially from direct federal assistance during the 1975–81 period. Indeed, this was a major force in supporting the budgets of northeastern cities during the fiscal crisis of the late 1970s. The pattern of increase in federal grants has been reversed since 1978, but the importance of such assistance in city budgets is much larger than it was ten years ago.

INFLATION, ECONOMIC GROWTH,
AND LOCAL TAXES

The post-1975 recovery and inflation had a stimulating effect on state and local government revenue, and the aftermath of the New York City scare helped local governments keep expenditure growth at a low level. As may be seen in Table 8.4, real per capita taxes increased in 1977 whereas real per capita expenditures actually fell. This, plus infusions of federal aid, gave state and local governments some much-needed breathing room. While local governments have been able to continue this pattern of real expenditure reduction, they have not been able to sustain real revenue increases. A combination of tax limitations, discretionary rate and base reductions, slow economic growth, and another recession led to real per capita tax revenue declines between 1977 and 1981. The revenue decline for state governments was less severe because income and sales tax revenues were more responsive to inflation and generated a growth that permitted discretionary reductions in 1979 and 1980.

Did northeastern cities fare any worse than the rest of the country? The data in Table 8.5 suggest that they did. When tax revenue grew at a high rate in these cities, the reason seemed to be a discretionary change (as suggested by a large difference in the growth rates between the two periods). Between

---

[3] Key elements of the stimulus package were antirecession fiscal assistance (ARFA), local public works (LPW), and public service employment under the Comprehensive Employment and Training Act (CETA).

TABLE 8.3

Direct Federal Aid to City Governments: Selected Cities and Fiscal Years

City	Federal Aid as Percent of Own Source General Revenue					Per Capita Federal Aid	
	1957	*1967*	*1976*	*1978*	*1981*	*1976*	*1981*
St. Louis	0.6	1.0	23.6	34.0	40.6	$ 86	$239
Newark	0.2	1.7	11.4	30.4	17.9	47	67
Buffalo	1.3	2.1	55.6	77.5	54.6	163	218
Cleveland	2.0	8.3	22.8	57.9	25.3	65	121
Boston	*	10.0	31.5	20.9	14.5	204	160
Unweighted averages	0.8	4.6	29.0	44.1	30.6	113	161
Baltimore	1.7	3.8	38.9	53.7	45.1	167	279
Philadelphia	0.4	8.8	37.7	29.7	16.1	129	103
Detroit	1.3	13.1	50.2	44.2	85.6	161	379
Chicago	1.4	10.9	19.2†	46.7	44.8	47	157
Atlanta	4.3	2.0	15.1	19.7	20.7	52	133
Unweighted averages	1.8	7.7	32.2	38.8	42.4	111	210
Denver	0.6	1.2	21.2	26.2	16.8	90	130
Los Angeles	0.7	0.7	19.3	31.2	21.1	54	90
Dallas	0.0	*	20.0	13.2	15.5	51	59
Houston	0.2	3.1	19.4	15.3	16.9	44	67
Phoenix	1.1	10.6	35.0	51.9	33.6	57	101
Unweighted averages	0.5	3.1	23.0	27.6	20.8	61	90
Unweighted averages of fifteen cities	1.1	5.2	28.1	36.8	31.3	95	154

*Less than 0.5 percent.

†Percentage based on federal aid excluding general revenue sharing: funds withheld pending judicial determination.

Source: U.S. Bureau of the Census, *City Government Finances in 1957,1967, 1976, 1978 and 1981* (Washington, D.C.: Government Printing Office, various years).

1975 and 1977, six of the ten cities in the declining regions had a real tax revenue increase, whereas between 1977 and 1981, only two of the ten had a real increase.

The Deferral Hypotheses

A third possible reason for the relatively strong performance of central cities since the 1974–75 recession has been their willingness and ability to hold the line on costs—even if it has meant reducing service levels. This retrenchment has taken a number of forms, including reductions in public employment, elimination of certain programs, and the deferral of capital facility maintenance and replacement. The data would seem to bear out these arguments and to suggest that northeast cities have led this retrenchment movement.

TABLE 8.4

Comparisons of State and Local Government Fiscal Activity, 1969–1981

Average Annual Percent Increase	1969–1974	1974–1975	1975–1976	1976–1977	1977–1978	1978–1979	1979–1980	1980–1981
*Real Per Capita Total Expenditures**								
State governments	4.6	7.1	9.2	-2.3	-2.0	-2.1	0.2	2.6
Local governments	3.6	4.8	5.0	-0.4	-0.3	-1.8	-2.4	0.6
Municipalities	3.9	4.7	4.9	-3.4	0.7	-3.9	-2.1	-0.5
Real Per Capita Current Expenditures								
State governments	5.7	8.5	5.1	3.4	4.5	-2.6	-0.1	2.7
Local governments	4.3	4.5	6.5	1.4	1.0	-2.2	-3.0	-0.3
Municipalities	4.7	3.8	5.6	0.1	1.2	-3.3	-3.4	-1.3
Real Long-Term Debt Outstanding								
State governments	4.4	0.3	9.7	4.5	6.2	-1.5	-3.5	0.3
Local governments	2.0	-4.3	0.9	3.2	0.3	-3.1	-2.3	-3.4
Municipalities	1.8	-4.3	5.3	1.2	4.1	-10.3	-3.2	-4.1
Employment								
State governments	4.0	3.4	2.0	3.7	2.2	3.6	1.1	-0.6
Local governments	3.8	2.2	0.7	3.8	0.9	1.5	0.9	-1.4
Municipalities	2.7	0.7	-1.6	2.9	-0.2	1.2	-1.2	-2.6
Real Per Employee Compensation								
State governments	0.6	-2.5	1.1	0.0	-0.8	-3.8	-3.5	-0.6
Local governments	0.6	-1.8	0.3	-0.3	-3.1	-3.2	-3.7	-0.6
Municipalities	1.5	-2.4	0.9	-1.5	-2.1	-4.6	-3.5	2.0
Real Per Capita Tax Revenues								
State governments	4.4	-2.1	4.4	5.3	3.0	-2.1	-4.2	-0.9
Local governments	2.7	-1.6	3.3	3.0	-1.2	-10.9	-6.4	-0.5
Municipalities	2.0	-1.4	3.5	3.9	-1.8	-8.2	-5.1	-1.0

*Amounts deflated by the consumer price index (CPI).

Sources: U.S. Bureau of the Census, *Governmental Finances in 1968–69, 1973–74, 1975–76, 1977–78, 1978–79, 1979–80, 1980–81* (Washington, D.C.: Government Printing Office, various years); U.S. Bureau of the Census, *Public Employment in 1981* (Washington, D.C.: Government Printing Office, various years); U.S. Bureau of the Census, *City Government Finances in 1968–69, 1973–74, 1974–75, 1975–76, 1976–77, 1977–78, 1978–79, 1979–80, 1980–81* (Washington, D.C.: Government Printing Office, various years).

TABLE 8.5

Indicators of Financial Performance: Twenty Largest Cities (average annual percent change), 1975–1980

City	Current Expenditures*		General Obligation Debt Outstanding		Employment		Payroll Per Employee		Taxes	
	1975–77	1977–81	1975–77	1977–81	1975–77	1977–81	1975–77	1977–81	1975–77	1977–81
Baltimore	7.1	0.1	0.2	9.2	-4.9	-2.2	-1.0	9.7	4.2	4.7
Boston	11.9	3.8	10.6	3.8	0.1	0.1	12.6	0.1	15.3	3.2
Cleveland	4.3	8.0	18.5	3.7	-7.6	-4.0	-1.9	5.3	3.0	12.9
Chicago	10.7	9.0	3.3	-2.0	-3.5	-1.7	5.8	6.7	4.9	4.9
Dallas	12.0	13.5	-1.4	7.7	2.5	-0.1	7.0	10.8	8.9	8.3
Detroit	5.2	12.3	-3.7	6.8	8.0	-3.9	12.8	14.1	7.0	2.3
Honolulu	19.1	1.6	7.8	4.5	7.3	-4.9	17.9	7.4	8.1	10.3
Houston	22.5	15.7	9.9	15.5	5.1	3.7	12.4	11.3	15.9	13.5
Indianapolis	13.4	8.9	2.8	2.4	-0.1	1.1	6.3	8.8	7.2	5.8
Los Angeles	8.8	9.5	8.0	1.6	-1.6	-2.8	2.3	10.9	10.9	6.4
Memphis	11.9	8.7	20.3	8.5	-13.8	-3.8	-6.1	9.5	8.9	8.7
Milwaukee	9.0	8.3	3.2	9.0	-1.9	-1.1	5.1	5.9	2.0	-1.1
New Orleans	12.2	13.4	-0.4	18.0	9.0	-6.6	26.0	8.1	7.3	13.1
New York	4.5	3.1	16.8	-8.9	-5.5	1.2	-0.7	7.5	11.5	5.4
Philadelphia	8.3	8.3	12.3	6.4	-0.3	-2.9	4.9	6.9	20.3	6.6
Phoenix	11.8	13.0	11.8	8.1	8.4	-0.1	15.2	10.3	12.6	9.6
San Antonio	19.6	10.9	25.6	20.3	1.7	-3.2	8.6	6.3	9.5	8.5
San Diego	8.5	10.3	-4.2	-2.0	1.4	-1.9	6.7	8.5	14.4	8.2
San Francisco	5.1	6.2	18.8	10.9	0.3	-1.1	3.2	10.9	15.6	1.2
Washington, D.C.	8.9	6.4	17.0	4.9	0.8	-3.8	7.1	8.1	16.6	11.2

*The average percent change in the CPI was 6.1 percent during 1975–1977 and 10.7 percent during 1977–1981.

Sources: U.S. Bureau of the Census, *City Government Finances in 1974–75, 1976–77, 1980–81* (Washington, D.C.: Government Printing Office); U.S. Bureau of the Census, *City Employment in 1975, 1977, 1981* (Washington, D.C.: Government Printing Office).

EMPLOYMENT REDUCTIONS

Examination of employment trends since 1975 reveals a slowdown in the number of employees added to state and local government payrolls. The pattern of state and local employment during recent years is in sharp contrast with most of the post–World War II period, when nonfederal public employment expanded at rates greatly above those for private industry and the federal government. For example, annual employment growth between 1962 and 1972 averaged 4.5 percent for the state/local sector as compared with a private industry growth rate of less than one-half that rate.

However, the reins appear to have been drawn on state and local government job expansion after 1974 (see Table 8.4). Average annual employment growth between 1974 and 1981 fell to about one-half the rate for the preceding ten years, and did not regain the level of the 1969–74 period.

Even more drastic than the curtailment of job growth for all nonfederal governments has been the abruptness with which municipalities have clamped down on their workforce growth. After growing at an average annual rate of 2.7 percent between 1969 and 1974, employment by municipalities grew very little from 1974 to 1975 and has actually declined since 1976.

Inspection of employment records for large cities shows that actual reductions in large city workforces are not uncommon and have not been for several years (Table 8.5). Nine of the twenty largest cities reduced employment between 1975 and 1977, and sixteen of the twenty largest cities reduced the number of employees on their payrolls between 1977 and 1981.

Have all municipalities continued to reduce employment since 1975? The answer from Table 8.5 is that it depends in part on the region and the growth/decline position of the local economy. Six of nine declining cities (and eight of eleven growing cities) had declines after 1975, or smaller rates of increase between 1977 and 1981 than between 1975 and 1977.

Finally, employment declines were made possible because of population decline. In fact, when the change in city employment per ten-thousand population is calculated for this sample of the twenty largest cities, only five of the nine declining cities have reduced employment in proportion to population decline.

COMPENSATION INCREASES

State and local governments may also have dealt with their fiscal problems by curbing the rate of increase in public employee compensation (i.e., by deferring compensation increases). One might ask whether the growth in public employee compensastion is out of line with the growth in private sector compensation, and whether governments are succeeding in slowing the growth in compensation.

The compensation restraint argument would seem borne out for the state and local government sector in general. Although average wage levels in state and local government have for some time exceeded private industry wage levels, the gap narrowed after 1977 and the state and local government sector has now fallen behind. The narrowing of the gap has come about because average wage growth in private industry accelerated after 1973, not because public employers succeeded in braking the rate at which their employees' wages grew. In fact, yearly growth in state and local government employee wages and salaries was greater in every year between 1972 and 1976 than it was throughout the period 1962 to 1972. After 1976, however, the growth in state and local government wages fell back to the rates of increase in the 1960s. Indeed state and local government employee salary rates have increased at a rate below the consumer price index (CPI) since 1977 (see Table 8.4).

The explanation for this slow growth in average compensation might be explained by factors other than deferral. First, some of the wage growth implied in the averages is an illusion. To the extent that governments add fewer new employees or even effect reductions in workforce size, this is likely to have a disproportionate impact on younger, lower-paid employees. By the nature of arithmetic averages, it is quite possible to reduce workforce size and to grant no wage increases to remaining employees and still end up with a higher average wage for the workforce. Second, the years 1972 to 1976 were marked by the most severe inflation encountered in twenty-five years, and it would not be surprising if government employers were unable to withstand employees' efforts to obtain some relief in the form of wage increments. Still, the growth of wages paid to the average state/local employee relative to advances in the CPI suggests that employees lost ground in terms of the purchasing power of their income.

If large cities generally were harder-pressed fiscally than were states or other local jurisdictions—as a reading of public employment trends seems to bear out—it might be expected that city employee wages could have grown at more modest rates than wages for other state/local employees. If the deferral hypothesis holds, one might expect compensation increases to fall short of CPI increases.

Of the cities compared in Table 8.5, five are in the Northeast region and another four are in the declining Midwest region. The remaining eleven are in the growing region. From 1975 to 1977, only three of the nine declining cities gave increments below the CPI (as compared to four of eleven growing cities). Between 1977 and 1981, however, one of the nine declining cities increased compensation above the rate of increase in the CPI, as compared to four of eleven growing cities.[4]

[4]To what extent these increases are the result of the preceding averaging effects is a matter

CAPITAL INVESTMENT

Capital investment is an easily deferred item of state and local government expenditure. New buildings can be postponed, cars and trucks can be used for another year, and major renovations can wait. Moreover, such deferrals are often politically expedient. Where are the political points for replacing obsolete underground water mains or increasing the efficiency of a sewage treatment plant?

In fact, capital expenditures of state and local governments have declined in real terms and as a share of the total budget. Peterson (1978) reports that gross capital investment fell from 27 percent of total state and local spending in 1965 to a low of 14 percent in 1977. As might be expected, there were real declines in state and local government debt outstanding through the late 1970s (Table 8.4).

While some of this decline might be attributed to the completion of the interstate highway system and to higher interest costs, much of it would appear to be due to the postponement of capital project investments and the deferral of maintenance and renovation. Such deferrals have made the financial position of state and local governments appear stronger than it is. What is the meaning of an annual budget surplus in a case where necessary capital expenditures have been put off? This question cannot be answered other than by relying on impressionistic evidence about the inadequacies of the existing capital stock.

One can, however, surmise that the postponement and deferral of capital renovation and maintenance does not have the same undesirable effects in every state and local area. Indeed, capital replacements can be put off and renovation cycles extended, apparently without causing cities to crumble. However, the older the capital stock the more likely are these effects to cut into public service levels and economic development efforts. One would suspect that the slowdown in capital spending would create particularly severe capital obsolescence problems for older cities. The implication of capital deterioration in these cities, which tend to be the more financially pressed in any case, is that the reported budgetary position overstates their financial health. In essence, a part of their budgetary balance is carried in the form of a gap between the "necessary" and actual condition of the local capital stock. Knowledge of fiscal distress could be supplemented if governments could be identified and ranked according to how much they have deferred capital expenditures and according to the condition of their capital stock.

---

for speculation—although the large size of some cities' increments to total payrolls would suggest that considerably more than the arithmetic of averaging has been at work. One explanation for some portion of the increases is that employees in large cities are more likely to be effectively organized to persuade employers to grant wage adjustments that offset a substantial part of cost-of-living increases. Although further pursuit of explanations for rapid growth in city wage expenditures would be beyond the scope of this chapter, the matter deserves careful study.

The Outlook

Can cities in a declining region continue their relatively strong fiscal performance? The answer depends on whether one expects continued help from a growing national economy, increasing federal grants, and a continued ability to defer wage rate increments and capital investment.

On the question of United States economic growth, it is interesting to speculate on how much of the national growth will actually benefit the declining region in any case. Federal grant reductions are a much more likely scenario than the increments of the 1970s. All of this suggests an outlook of very slow revenue growth for cities in the 1980s. The question then becomes whether continued deferrals are possible. Is the capital stock really obsolete, and will unions and central city residents continue to accept government retrenchment because of a fear of financial collapse?

Whatever the scenario of the 1980s, short of a dramatic turnaround in federal policy, northeastern cities are likely to feel more of a fiscal squeeze than is the rest of the country. The resource constraints will be most severe for the declining and distressed cities: all of the trends bend against them. They suffer most in recession and benefit least during recovery, their heavy reliance on the property tax makes them a sure fiscal loser during times of inflation, and their heavy dependence on federal aid makes them the biggest losers in the federal government expenditure retrenchment process.

References

Bahl, R. 1984. *State and Local Government Finances in a Changing National Economy.* New York: Oxford University Press.

Peterson, G. 1978. "Capital spending and capital obsolescence: the outlook for cities." In *The Fiscal Outlook for Cities: Implications of a National Urban Policy,* edited by R. Bahl. Syracuse: Syracuse University Press.

Sacks, S. 1978. Estimates of current employment trends and related information for large cities. Paper presented to the National Urban Roundtable, March. Mimeo.

U.S. Department of Housing and Urban Development. 1980. *Changing Conditions in Large Metropolitan Areas: Urban Data Report.* Washington, D.C.: Government Printing Office.

U.S. Department of the Treasury, Office of State and Local Finance. 1978. *Report on the Fiscal Impacts of the Economic Stimulus Package of 48 Large Urban Governments.* Washington, D.C.: U.S. Department of the Treasury.

H. V. SAVITCH

9 Boom and Bust in the New York Region: Implications for Government Policy

The older cities of the Northeast are considered to be in a serious decline, which began in the 1960s and was accompanied by a spate of popular and scholarly literature on the "urban crisis," a national debate about "saving our cities," and reams of legislation from Washington, D.C. In spite of these efforts the urban crisis continued with little abatement.[1] More recently, the demise of the city has been linked to the pattern of interregional shifts. The industrial and commercial heartland of America is shifting from the Frostbelt of the Northeast and Midwest to the Sunbelt of the South and Southwest. Evidence usually cited to support these claims consists of population shifts, migration of workers, and the movement of companies and jobs either to comfortable suburbs outside the urban core or to the open spaces of the Sunbelt.

The argument and supporting data for this transformation have been so compelling that the national debate has taken on the theme of "moving people to where the jobs are." Policymakers talk about "planned shrinkage" and the widespread evacuation from some urban cores. Some believe that urban decline is inexorable and that we cannot rescue the aging city "because deeply embedded in the culture is the feeling that it is an effluent, an inevitable dis-

---

[1] For a popular treatise on the subject, see Sale, 1974. For a more scholarly treatment, see Gorham and Glazer, 1976.

164

card with no enduring value."[2] Thus, we ought not salvage the city because we are not capable of that task. The best option is to leave the city and build anew.

The broad contours of economic and demographic movement out of aging cities toward the suburbs and the Sunbelt cannot be disputed. Although the policy implications arising out of this transformation are dubious, this is not an appropriate starting point. Rather, the best place to begin is to question whether the thesis of the declining Frostbelt city is overstated, misunderstood, or in need of crucial qualification.

Currents and countercurrents are operating simultaneously in many Frostbelt cities—bust may be accompanied by boom, and evacuation may be swiftly followed by replacement. As any good pollster knows, what questions we ask often shape the answer. Likewise, how we measure bust and boom can provide a profile of a metropolitan area, and it is important that we obtain as complete a profile as possible. Moreover, if we are to draw policy implications from statistical assessments, we must strive to understand these statistics—not simply to make naive interpretations but to understand the forces that are propelling social and economic change. In short, we must place these statistics in a broader historical and geopolitical context.

In the case of major Frostbelt cities, boom and bust are taking place along a particular historical and geographic configuration. Boom is more likely to be found in the very heart of the city—the central business district (CBD) and a large part of the urban core. On the other hand, bust takes place in the peripheral ring of the city. It is the inverse situation of the doughnut; the hole is filled with great wealth and dynamism while the ring decays. Beyond the urban core and peripheral ring is what we Americans call the suburb or exurb. Today it is an area of moderate growth and comfort sometimes mixed with pockets of decay.

The quality of this trifurcated development is perhaps even more important to understand than its quantity. Qualitatively, it is a result of the postindustrial revolution.[3] The postindustrial revolution, as some have asserted, has not bypassed the city. That revolution is very much alive in the CBD and a large section of the urban core. The infrastructure of a postindustrial society is in place within much of the urban core, and it is growing. In some areas this growth is so steady that it is flourishing in the wake of industrial evacuation and converting old neighborhoods into fashionable residential

---

[2]Berry, 1975, p. 175. A strategy of "moving people to jobs" was recommended by the Presidential Commission on a National Agenda for the 1980s (1980).

[3]The postindustrial society is generally defined in terms of a shift away from employment in the primary and secondary sectors to the tertiary and quaternary sectors emphasizing the management and diffusion of information; professional services in banking, finance, law, health and education, advertising, and so on; and recreational and entertainment services.

areas—hence, the growing popularity of "gentrification." [4] In other places, postindustrialism has created a boom in office construction; the building of hotels; and the provision of professional services in banking, law, advertising, and entertainment. In still others, it has stimulated real estate speculation, development, and brokerage services.

Postindustrialism, like many revolutions, has a seamy side. It has accentuated differences between rich and poor areas and has made parts of the urban core even less affordable for the middle class. It has pushed out middle-market businesses and thus may be partially responsible for the collapse of middle-class neighborhoods. Furthermore, it has prompted a real as well as a psychological polarization between luxury neighborhoods and slums.

In sum, there is a "mixed bag" of growth and decline, of affluence and poverty. Moreover, the boom and bust of the city are following opposite trajectories. Some locations grow richer and more desirable; others plummet to become sinkholes of the city.

The Problem

Research on the New York metropolitan region in the national context has generated several consistent results. First, the Northeast has declined relative to other regions in the Southeast, the Southwest, and the Far West (see Chapter 3), although the recent recession affected these regions severely in its later stages. Second, New York City lost population in the 1970s (a 10 percent decline), and its share in the region's population fell from 61 percent in 1950 to 46 percent in 1980. It also lost jobs up to 1977, after which it gained them. Third, demographic vitality improved with distance from the core, although Manhattan's decline was less (7.3 percent) than that of the outer boroughs (11.2 percent). The population of nearby suburbs remained stable, while that of outer suburbs (e.g., Suffolk County) increased. Fourth, the decline of New York City cannot be fully comprehended at either the aggregate or county level. At least one-fifth of the city's neighborhoods (including such diverse locations as lower Manhattan, the north shore of Staten Island, Coney Island, Far Rockaway, Corona, and Elmhurst) gained population in the 1970s.

The argument of this chapter is based on the hypothesis that the New York region can be divided into three rings: (1) Manhattan; (2) the other four boroughs plus Hudson, Essex, and Union counties in New Jersey; and (3) Nassau, Suffolk, Westchester, Rockland, and Putnam counties in New York; Bergen, Hudson, Passaic, Morris, Somerset, Middlesex, and Monmouth counties in New Jersey, and Fairfield county in Connecticut. Also, for some purposes, this third ring can be subdivided into an inner group (Westchester, Nassau, and Bergen) and an outer group consisting of the rest. This chapter will dem-

---

[4] See Laska and Spain, 1981, for an interesting analysis of gentrification.

onstrate that these rings display very different levels of economic performance. The core and the outer rings are doing very well, but the inner ring (especially the four outer boroughs) is doing poorly. The policy problem is, given the strength and resilience of Manhattan and the dynamism of the outer ring, how to devise a viable strategy for the other boroughs of New York City. New York City is experiencing a decline in population, but the employment decline has been turned around. However, the growth of employment in the city as a whole masks a major difference in performance between Manhattan and the other boroughs that is so striking as to deserve the description "boom and bust."

Employment Trends in New York City

Employment trends in New York City have to be interpreted cautiously because much depends on the period examined. For example, comparing the 1970 and 1980 census years suggests a rather gloomy picture. Between these two years blue-collar jobs in New York City declined from 911,100 to 676,800 while even white-collar jobs declined slightly (from 1,848,900 to 1,815,000). In individual sectors, manufacturing lost 150,000 jobs; retail trade, 69,800; construction, 32,200; and wholesale trade, 21,400. The only sectors to experience gains were health services (24,800) and the finance, insurance, and real estate (FIRE) sector (8,800). But these data are very misleading because a major shift occurred within the period. In fact, there was a sharp decline in employment between 1969 and 1977, but employment expanded year after year from 1977 through 1982 (the recession finally had an impact in 1983). Between 1977 and 1982, 162,000 new jobs were created in New York City, although only 45,000 of these went to existing New York City residents. One explanation of this is the changing composition of employment and the closer match between the skills needed in the quaternary sector and the capacities of suburban workers.

If manufacturing is regarded as the core of the city's old economic base and the FIRE sector as the core of the new, the New York City economy was transformed during this period, becoming one of the most striking examples of the postindustrial economy. The manufacturing sector of the city has long been in decline with employment falling from 1,072,900 in 1947 to 441,000 in 1983. The FIRE sector expanded in the late 1960s (jobs increased by 14 percent, 1964 to 1969) but declined in the early 1970s (employment fell by 7.5 percent, 1969 to 1974). However, this decline was temporary. Since 1977, FIRE employment has increased year by year, even through the recent recession. Moreover, in 1982 it surpassed manufacturing as the biggest generator of jobs and now employs half a million people. Its growth probably helps to explain why the incomes of New York City residents grew by 9 percent between 1977 and 1981 while income stagnated nationally. Local economic forecasters predict continued job expansion through the mid-1980s as CBD growth continues and as other employment-generating projects (the Convention Center, the Department of Defense port in Staten Island, and so forth) are completed. Although New York City weathered the last recession very well, the picture is not altogether rosy. First, unemployment remains serious—not so much because of the rate but because of its chronic nature and the mismatch problem; many new jobs are being created, but the unemployed lack the education or the skills to fill them. Second, the nature of the changes in economic structure is such that Manhattan gained almost all the benefits from the growth of the information-processing and other high-order services while the outer boroughs had no compensating development to offset their losses of blue-collar jobs. Also, they failed to benefit from the relocation of firms within the metropolitan region or from new entrants.

Businesses tend to locate either in the urban core or the second ring, shunning the first ring by "leapfrogging" over it.[5] Businesses choosing Manhattan are obviously not manufacturing establishments, but tend to be corporations with a national or international clientele that are not tied to a local market (Armstrong, 1972, p. 130). Professional services choosing the urban core tend to be the larger establishments hiring only white-collar workers. In the 1970s the number of professional firms (commodity and insurance brokers, realtors, lawyers) in the CBD with twenty or more employees increased while many of the smaller firms moved out (Savitch, 1981, p. 32).

The firms that leapfrogged over the first ring into the second tended to be engaged in manufacture (distant suburbs) or were smaller professional firms (both near and distant suburbs). In many cases these firms had a local or regional market rather than an international market.[6] Another aspect of this leapfrogging is that many firms split their activities between the CBD and the second ring. For example, publishing houses are known to keep their central offices in Manhattan while moving their technical and manual operations out to the distant suburbs of the second ring.

Why does leapfrogging occur? Why do the CBD and the second ring remain attractive while the first ring decays? These are complicated questions with no single answer. To begin with, massive private and public capital have always been invested in Manhattan's buildings, streets, piers, and infrastructure. Manhattan, the business hub of both the region and the nation, enjoys a continuous attraction for the business community. Private investment, and some public investment, continues to pour into Manhattan island, particularly its CBD. Investment in luxury brownstones, high rises, hotels, and office towers figures prominently. The architectural fabric of the urban core reflects the priorities that market forces assign to Manhattan.

---

[5]For an elaboration of leapfrogging from the urban core to the second ring, see Savitch, 1981.

[6]There are two exceptions to this generalization. Westchester and Fairfield counties contain a substantial number of large national and international corporate headquarters.

Moreover, Manhattan is the transportation center of the region. The railroad, the subway, bridges, postal services, and street patterns make Manhattan the hub of communications. A location in the urban core has considerable psychological value. It is the place that is most identifiable, easiest to reach, and most prestigious. A Manhattan business address continues to have substantial monetary worth. Architects and developers, for example, go to great lengths not only to locate in the CBD but to place the "right address" on their corporate letterhead.

Manhattan's agglomeration economies were self-reinforcing. Once infrastructure and businesses were concentrated in the urban core, other major investments were attracted: Lincoln Center, Rockefeller Center, the World Trade Center, and the Convention Center. The geography that created the urban core in the first instance—an island surrounded by navigable waters yet accessible to other land masses—was reinforced by the pull of the built environment.

The first ring, on the other hand, was built as an adjunct to Manhattan. Its design was the spokes—dispersed, separated, functional, but lacking in prestige—that could only be united through the hub. In general, its fabric and design lacked the expensive and durable quality of the urban core. Most neighborhoods in the Bronx and Kings were built for the working classes who commuted to Manhattan. Jersey City, which is in Hudson County, developed as the backyard of the urban core. The same could be said of Newark, located in Essex. At best, these were locations for heavy industry and for other businesses that could not afford to settle in the urban core. Many of the latter that succeeded subsequently moved to Manhattan.

As industrial and production needs changed after World War II, the first ring became even less desirable. Manhattan maintained its hold as the center of the region by attracting more white-collar firms. But the infrastructure of the first ring never had the same quality and appeal. Why stay in the aging and dilapidated periphery of the region when one could move to modern facilities in the open spaces of the second ring? The choice was clear. If a firm could afford it and did not require much land (e.g., for manufacturing operations), the best site would be in Manhattan. On the other hand, if land costs were an important factor or if large-scale production required more space, the second ring was the logical choice.

There were other considerations to favor leapfrogging. The construction of a major highway system made the second ring accessible. Thus, while rail trips to Grand Central or Penn Station remained acceptable, commuting to an outlying spoke in the Bronx was not, when the alternative was an easy drive to Westchester. Other well-known factors also contributed to the rise of the suburbs—lower taxes, low interest rates, federally subsidized mortgages, and income tax benefits.

The deterioration of the first ring also became self-reinforcing. Once poverty and depression hit the South Bronx and Jersey City, the outward trickle became an exodus. Manhattan could tolerate Harlem, because it had Park Avenue, Wall Street, and Greenwich Village.

Furthermore, large capital investments can, by creating positive neighborhood externalities, protect areas against intrusions of poverty and deterioration. If the West Side was in jeopardy of becoming another Harlem, Lincoln Center could be built to serve as a focal point for a new middle class. The dilapidation of Times Square could be offset by a midtown construction boom and the United Nations building. Real estate and other investments could be made profitably all over the urban core and CBD, but how many investors were willing to take a chance on the Bronx or Jersey City? The alternatives became obvious: remain in the urban core and contribute to its boom or leapfrog out to the second ring and take advantage of new land speculation. As a result, the economy of the first ring collapsed.

Boom and Bust: Manhattan and the First Ring

Although average household income in New York City increased by 69 percent between the two censuses of 1970 and 1980, in real terms it declined (perhaps by as much as 15 percent, possibly somewhat less if the unrecorded underground economy expanded vigorously during the decade). But the average disguised wide interborough differences. Out of 3,132 counties in the United States in 1980 Manhattan ranked 14 (down from 2 in 1970), Queens ranked 309, Staten Island 316, Brooklyn 1805, and the Bronx 2270. These ranks imply wide differentials in per capita income. As shown in Table 9.1, per capita income in Manhattan in 1980 was 3.7 times higher than in the Bronx and even 2.7 times higher than in Queens. On the other hand, Manhattan continues to house a significant number of poor households (the proportion on public assistance is double that in Queens, though lower than in the Bronx or Brooklyn; see Table 9.1).

However, as shown in Table 9.1, Manhattan's greater levels of prosperity did not prevent substantial population loss in the 1970s (112,000). Gentrification is probably a factor, as young professionals replace larger households in some of the island's marginal neighborhoods; more than 50 percent of Manhattan's rental housing stock is occupied by singles. The population of Queens has declined very little, largely as a result of the inflow of foreign-born and minority population. Staten Island grew rapidly from a small base, but the Bronx and Brooklyn lost a combined population of 675,000.

The past decades have seen major changes in the racial mix of New York City and its boroughs. In 1960, Manhattan had the highest share of blacks and Hispanics (36 percent of the total). This reflected the role of Manhattan up to 1960 as the manufacturing hub of the city. Immigrants from the South and the Caribbean came in search of jobs in apparel, trucking, small-scale factories, and services; they lived in Manhattan because of its relatively large

TABLE 9.1
Population and Income in New York City, 1970 and 1980

| Boroughs | Population in Thousands | | | Minorities | | | Percent Foreign Born | | Per Capita Income 1980 | Percent Households on Public Assistance, 1980 |
	1970	1980	Percent Change 1970–1980	Percent of Pop. 1980	Percent Increase 1970–1980	1970	1980			
Manhattan	1540	1428	−7.3	41.1	30.5	20.0	24.4	10,889	17.5
Brooklyn	2603	2231	−14.3	44.0	41.0	17.5	23.8	3,072	18.8
Queens	1987	1891	−4.8	29.4	90.8	21.0	28.6	4,046	8.8
Bronx	1472	1169	−20.6	52.6	57.4	15.6	18.4	2,943	26.1
Staten Island	295	352	19.2	11.0	116.9	9.0	9.8	3,745	6.8
New York City	7,898	7,071	−10.5	39.3	54.1	18.2	23.6	4,923	16.3

Source: U.S. Bureau of the Census, *Census of Population* (Washington, D.C.: Government Printing Office, 1970 and 1980).

low-income housing stock (old tenements and public housing). Brooklyn and the Bronx were mixed residential-industrial communities, while much of Queens and most of Staten Island were residential areas adjacent to open country.

The 1960–70 decade was a period of transition for the city. Manufacturing was moving out and the housing stock was aging. Manhattan held on because the departure of manufacturing had begun to be replaced by the construction of office towers, an inflow of professional and financial services, continued liveliness in theater and entertainment, and investment in the housing stock and neighborhood upgrading. For Bronx and Brooklyn, events took a different turn. There was little replacement for the departing manufacturing firms and the wholesale or retail businesses that moved elsewhere. Housing stock replacement took the form of new construction (in the North or East Bronx or along the eastern shore of Brooklyn) rather than rehabilitation.

These changes in economic structure were accompanied by major shifts in racial composition. Between 1960 and 1980 the minority population grew rapidly, and by 1980 accounted for almost two-fifths of the population of the city (Table 9.1). Although the most rapid increase in minority population in the 1970s occurred in Staten Island (from a very small base) and in Queens, the minority share in 1980 remained much higher in the Bronx and in Brooklyn. The minority share in Manhattan grew more slowly; its black population, in fact, declined by 18.2 percent. Although much of this differential growth might be interpreted as contributing to the income and skills gap between Manhattan and the other boroughs, some of the immigrants (especially foreign-born Asians, but also other groups) moved into specific neighborhoods (e.g., in Queens and Brooklyn) and enriched their new communities by providing skills and entrepreneurial talent.

Bust conditions in the first ring are reflected in land and housing prices and in tax assessments. Manhattan accounts for 53 percent of property tax assessments in New York City although its population share is only 20 percent, and these have risen almost six times as fast as the rest of the city since 1970. In the Bronx, tax assessments have declined absolutely. Residential housing prices in Manhattan are about four times the average for the other boroughs. These differentials are not surprising given the strength of the CBD boom in office building that has spilled over into other Manhattan neighborhoods and even parts of Brooklyn. The generator of this boom is an area of less than 9 square miles attracting two million workers each day. Its urban infrastructure is probably the most concentrated in the world. Within the metropolitan region's 4,000 square miles, this tiny area accounts for 50 percent of the region's office space. It also accounts for 8 percent of the nation's office space despite the growth of new international office centers, Houston and San Francisco.

In the 1960s, the best decade ever for midtown office construction, over 44

million square feet were built. The momentum continued during the 1970s
with the addition of another 33 million square feet, and projections for the
1980s are similar (New York Department of City Planning, 1981, p. 9).
Moreover, the demand for office space in Manhattan remains strong. Of the
4.9 million square feet completed in 1982, more than three million square
feet had been preleased at an average rental of $40.26 per square foot (Port
Authority of New York, 1982, p. 16). Manhattan is the second most expensive place to rent space in the world (after Tokyo). After a moderate slump in
the mid-1970s, the dollar value of office construction rose steadily between
1976 and 1980 in Manhattan, and the CBD regained its dominance in the
region. Although there has been some decline during the recent recession,
there are no grounds for believing that this is permanent.

The major firms locating in Manhattan's CBD are either corporate headquarters or professional and financial services establishments. By the year
2000, Manhattan is expected to retain more than one-half of the corporate
headquarters in the New York region, in spite of a trickle of relocations into
the second ring. It is not only national and regional corporate headquarters
and professional services that find the CBD appealing, but especially international and multinational corporations. In 1979 New York City contained 277
Japanese-owned businesses, 213 British enterprises, 175 French companies,
80 owned by the Swiss, 74 by Germans, 53 by Swedes, 43 by Italians, and
many other nations were represented in smaller numbers (*Le Monde*, 2 December 1980, p. 26). Before New York City obtained its international banking zone, there were 75 branches of foreign banks located there and 60 financial agencies; these numbers are now expected to double. A survey of 2,000
firms by New York City's Office of Economic Development reveals that 869
international firms occupied 12.8 million square feet of office space. Of all
disclosed commercial and residential purchases made by foreigners in the
United States, 40 percent of the value of these transactions involved real
property in the Manhattan CBD. Data on international communications and
transportation are an obvious index of the city's international role: 21 percent
of international telephone calls made in the United States were placed from
New York City, and in 1978 over 1.5 million visitors and businessmen arrived in the region's airports with New York City as their destination.[7]

Neighborhood Polarization

The interborough comparisons show a sharp contrast between Manhattan
and the other boroughs. These borough averages, however, mask wide differentials among communities, both within and among boroughs. Many indicators, such as household income or share of population with a college educa-

[7]For detailed statistics on New York as an international center, see Goldmark, 1979.

tion, can vary among communities by a factor of five or even ten. The performance of a neighborhood depends heavily on its proximity to the Manhattan core and on how it has been affected by the economic transformation of the last two decades. For example, Cobble Hill in Brooklyn has benefited from its accessibility to Manhattan's financial center. A former working-class community, it has been gentrified as young professionals moved into the neighborhood to refurbish brownstones and patronize specialty stores. Many of the poor have left the area, as indicated by a sharp decline in minority population and in the number of households on public assistance. At the other extreme, Bathgate in the Bronx is a fast-decaying, rubble-strewn neighborhood with more than a third of its population on welfare and a median income far below the poverty line. In general, the most striking finding from examination of neighborhood data is that the gaps in income disparities and social indicators between Manhattan neighborhoods and those elsewhere in the city have widened over the past two decades.

Policy Alternatives for the New York Region: Amenities and Resource Utilization

We should recognize that the boom and bust of New York is not solely the result of market forces. The city, the state, regional authorities, and public corporations have always been involved in urban development. Whether it was the establishment of mass transportation lines, the building of bridges and airports, the construction of the World Trade Center, or the development of luxury and moderate-income housing on Roosevelt Island, the public sector has played a leading role and thereby helped determine the settlement pattern of the New York region.

Both the city and state of New York have pursued policies designed to pump up the urban core and CBD of Manhattan. In the past, New York City established special offices to stimulate business growth and retention. Tax abatement, special zones, and other measures have been offered by the city to help corporations. For New York, bigger and higher is always deemed better, and the city has spared no effort to ensure that the Big Apple is the best. Zoning laws to ensure that a proper amount of sunlight reaches the sidewalks have been amended or flouted in order to suit building developers. The skyplane, for instance, is a method of calculating how much light and sky a tall building must not block from the streets or adjoining structures. To preserve this space, a builder is required to step the building's mass backward after it reaches a certain height. However, zoning variances, bonus zoning, and purchases and transfer of air rights have allowed office buildings to tower well above their intended heights at the expense of environmental protection. The strong gusts of wind that sweep down the office canyons of Manhattan during the winter are testimony to how far zoning laws are compromised in New York, as are the long shadows that darken the CBD in the early afternoon.

Despite this, the city and state of New York are adding yet more. A convention center is being built to the west of the CBD. An international banking zone, free of certain taxes and currency restrictions, has been declared in the heart of the downtown CBD. As if to pardon itself for not having enough space, the city has decided to fill in a section of the Hudson River in order to construct another huge complex, called Battery Park City.

More recently, the city has amended its zoning laws to stimulate office development on the West Side of Manhattan. Hitherto, most of Manhattan's development has centered around the East Side of the island. Now that this area is saturated with high-rise construction, the city has shifted its attention westward toward the vacant sites, battered taverns, and parking lots that skirt the waterfront. The plan calls for expanding the permitted volume of office space (by increasing the height of buildings), coupling these changes with tax abatements for developers. The vision is to extend Manhattan's CBD so that it embraces nearly the entire girth of mid-Manhattan. In the middle, close to Times Square, a new hotel and theater complex would be built. The project is huge, initiated under the auspices of city and state agencies such as the Urban Development Corporation and the New York City Public Development Corporation.

The issue here is not to critique the actions of New York City or State policymakers but to put public policy into a broader social welfare perspective. If government is going to reduce taxation and invest heavily in infrastructure and other public facilities for private enterprise, it should at least ensure that broader public purposes are also served. In the United States capitalist system, business lays the golden eggs and it would be dangerous to kill the goose. But it would be equally foolhardy to squander public resources without obtaining reciprocal benefits. For good or bad, government is the single institution that has a grasp of what is "public" and of what serves the general welfare. Only government has the capacity for coordinating activities and redistributing outputs so that a broad spectrum of interests is satisfied. All other institutions are "private" institutions, more or less atomistically oriented. It is a wild eighteenth-century hope that if we each pursue our individual needs to the exclusion of the interests of others, we will end up with what everybody wants. *Laissez-faire* economics has not existed in the United States for nearly a century, and with good reason.

Public intervention is concerned not only with equity but also with the efficient use of resources to promote full employment and to provide public amenities for all. It includes making the environment habitable and providing clean and cheap mass transportation, effective public education, parks, open space, and the full range of public goods. How to bring this about within the

New York region without jeopardizing the stronger sectors of the regional economy must involve compromise, balance, and nonideological flexibility.

Conventional thought has dominated public policy both in America and in the New York region. In the latter, we are accustomed to pursuing two lines of policy and dithering between one and the other. These policies can be represented by the following sets of choices: high taxation and expenditures versus low taxation and expenditures; increases versus reductions in government business regulation; and expansion versus decline of government assistance to business. In good times, taxes and expenditures tend to be increased. In bad times, business taxes are cut and public expenditures are retrenched. Similarly, good times are accompanied by increased efforts to regulate business (especially on environmental issues) while bad times augur a movement to eliminate bureaucratic intervention and "red tape." As for government assistance to business, in good times we are more magnanimous to needy areas; and offer incentives to locate in depressed neighborhoods. The tendency during bad times is to let businesses choose their locations freely to preserve jobs and investments.

A more creative approach might involve a mix of existing policies rather than cyclically switching between one policy and another. It implies that responses should not be fixed into ideological categories of doubtful validity (e.g., the belief that high taxes always discourage industry and that low taxes always encourage business investment). It calls for suspension of stereotypical judgments about the wisdom of unorthodox approaches (e.g., the belief that government activity always means waste and inefficiency while private enterprise is necessarily efficient). Instead, one should attempt to understand the propelling forces of society and to exploit its momentum to generate a better end result. For example, the analysis in this chapter indicates considerable strength in the New York CBD and a growth in its financial power. Why not then capitalize on the growing vitality of the CBD and carry its momentum elsewhere? To do this we must assure the continued prosperity of the CBD, while simultaneously adopting a strategy for transferring resources to needy areas of the New York region (i.e., we want to continue to feed the goose but we want to confiscate some of its eggs). Conventional policymaking assumes that both cannot be done at the same time (i.e., if we redistribute wealth we reduce incentives for production). Creative policymaking, on the other hand, may allow redistribution of wealth and increased productivity simultaneously. Higher taxation may not be counterproductive if coupled with improved facilities, amenities, and living conditions. Thus, we can tax and invest in the CBD simultaneously: taxation for purposes of redistribution and investment in amenities for purposes of retention. For this reason, the approach targeted at the CBD is called an "amenities approach."

The idea of urban amenity zones was promoted by Kenneth Orski, who argues that businesses are not attracted to an area because of its low taxes but because of its livability. He points out that low taxes are not a strong incentive for business because they account for only a small percentage of the cost of doing business. The fastest-growing cities in the United States are places with higher taxes, but which stand high on quality-of-life indices. Orski suggests that instead of reducing taxes, cities would do better to invest in landscaping, street furniture, better lighting and security, and improved public transportation (*New York Times*, 13 March 1982, p. 25).

The other side of an amenities approach for the CBD is a "resource utilization" approach for the first ring. This would implant resources directly into the most depressed areas of the first ring in order to revive them. In the past, conventional policy worked within the "givens" of private enterprise to revitalize abandoned areas. During the 1960s, government assumed that business could be lured into an area by tax incentives, accelerated depreciation allowances, and bonus tax reductions for hiring the unemployed. The Reagan administration's support of "urban enterprise zones" is consistent with this philosophy. Yet there is little reason to believe that this approach has worked in the past or will work in the future. Tax benefits may count for little when compared to the advantages of efficient transportation; a safe, clean environment; a talented labor pool; and cheap energy.

A more creative policy would sidestep the issue of operating within an existing framework to rejuvenate depressed areas. If the medicine failed to work in the past, why administer more doses in the future? An alternative is to build directly through public enterprise corporations in depressed areas with potential for development. Instead of propping up a faltering system of private enterprise with varying amounts of assistance, we could compete with it for greater productivity by using government resources in run-down sections of the first ring.

THE AMENITIES APPROACH: MORE PUBLIC
FACILITIES, NOT LESS

This approach would be concentrated in the CBD and urban core of Manhattan. It could also be extended to other areas of New York City, such as the gentrified neighborhoods close to Manhattan (Brooklyn Heights, Park Slope, and Cobble Hill in Kings County).

Increase Investment in Mass Transportation. Fixed lines of transportation, such as rail and subway facilities, are particularly crucial to the Manhattan CBD. Mass transportation ought not to be expected to pay the bulk of its own costs through commuter fares. Instead, public revenues should be raised to support subway and rail fares at a minimum subsidy of 85 percent. Fare reductions could be instituted for regular mass transit users through the introduction of special monthly subway passes. Subway and rail transportation should be well maintained and all facilities improved, especially those linking Manhattan with the first ring.

To raise revenues for improved mass transportation, heavier user taxes might be imposed on automobiles in the New York region, on gasoline and tire sales, and on bridge and tunnel tolls. Tolls for bridges and tunnels should be particularly heavy for single-driver automobiles with reductions for each additional passenger. The aim would be to discourage automobile usage in the CBD and urban core while at the same time providing cheap, efficient, safe, and comfortable mass transportation.

Manhattan's CBD and urban core can be conceived as a transportation grid with subway lines operating northward and southward on the island and bus lines operating eastward and westward. Subway stations should be better coordinated with special cross-town streets where surface transportation could take passengers along traffic-free routes. Free transfers from subway to bus or bus to subway could be established. Experiments could be initiated with smaller jitney-type electrically powered vehicles along traffic-free routes to improve the frequency of services.

Increase Investment in Safe, Secure, Clean Streets.   Safe and clean streets are tangible commodities, easily perceived and easily measured. They are critical determinants of whether middle-income individuals settle in the city or not. Local and state government should give a high priority to improving the condition of streets in the urban core. The particular methods for improvement might vary from increased sanitation services to a more efficient use of criminal deterrents, such as increased court loads, a firmer execution of the law, and more frequent police patrols.

Better street lighting has been associated with improved safety during evening hours. While well-lit streets may be an important factor in reducing crime, it is equally important to assure that streets are frequently used and attractive to pedestrians. Crowded streets are as important a deterrent as well-lit ones, and street lighting may be more valuable as a pedestrian magnet. One way to stimulate street use is to allow free space for kiosks and street vendors. Facilities might be built at strategic intersections or along certain cross-town streets. Vendors should be encouraged to operate these facilities during the evening, and might be induced to do so by low rental and maintenance rates.

One way of administering safe and clean streets more efficiently is to allow community boards to contract out for private services and to reimburse contractors for lower demands on city services. This has been suggested for such functions as sanitation pickups; it is well known that private carters are able to work faster and more cheaply than municipal sanitation services. To allow community boards to substitute private for municipal services would encourage healthy competition between public and private operations.

Increase Investment in the Creation of Small Parks, Promenades, Shopping Malls, and Cultural Exhibitions. Many of these facilities can be furnished by the city working with local community boards and units of neighborhood government. Federal, state, and local governments have for a long time given tax reductions to businesses and grants to nonprofit housing corporations. This idea could be extended to communities and individuals who wish to make capital investments in their own areas. Real estate or income taxes might be reduced according to the amounts and type of investment in public spaces.

The city could set aside as much available space as possible to establish squares and "vest pocket parks." Street furniture could be provided by the local community, via either community boards or private investment by residents. Underground shopping galleries and promenades might be established along certain major subway interchanges with tunnels leading from one side of the street to the other. These passageways could be lined with shopping facilities, cultural exhibits, and rest facilities to guard against vacant crime-prone corridors.

As America's leading international city (seat of the United Nations and headquarters for international finance and multinational corporations), New York City would benefit from having an American cultural center. The center might be jointly financed by the federal government, the business community, and the city and state government. It would help to promote American art, language, and literature and might include activities ranging from language instruction to plays, exhibits, and meeting facilities.

THE RESOURCE UTILIZATION APPROACH: JOIN
TAXATION TO PUBLIC INVESTMENT, AND
SUBSTITUTE GOVERNMENT PARTICIPATION FOR
GOVERNMENT REGULATION AND BUSINESS
ASSISTANCE

The primary aim of this approach is to restore and rejuvenate the first ring. Much of it involves a strategy of seed capital for new industry in depressed areas within the region and direct participation by public agencies in their future.

Increase taxation for corporations and individuals who choose to locate in the urban core, the CBD, and other areas that enjoy the improved amenities. Additional taxes should be introduced gradually and only after the amenities approach begins to show visible and tangible benefits. The taxes might take the form of a higher occupancy tax, varying in line with average incomes and property valuations in a particular area. Corporate headquarters in midtown would pay heavier taxes than residents in the East Village or new businesses on the lower East Side. A special tax rate could be established in urban amenity zones, and the zones could be expanded over time.

Allocate revenues from additional taxation to fund public enterprise corporations (PECs) in the first ring.   PECs could be started with private individuals or corporations eligible to own up to 49 percent of the stock. The controlling share would be owned by the public corporation. These would be managed like most autonomous public corporations, except that PEC boards would be required to reserve a number of seats for residents of the community in which the PEC operated.

PECs would be development corporations charged with initiating and operating businesses. They would be run with the objective of earning profits and would be subject to the same incentives as private enterprise. That is, after help with seed money and start-up costs, the PEC would be required to earn a return within a fixed period of time. Management and labor would be hired, fired, or promoted in a PEC on the same basis as the private sector.

PECs are intended to revive manufacturing operations in the first ring, though they are not limited to that sector. They could start housing and commercial construction, they could manage various trading or brokerage markets, or they could run professional facilities. One sector considered to have a high success potential in the South Bronx is the health industry. There is an available and experienced pool of health workers in the Bronx, the county contains major hospitals, and it is proximate to large pharmaceutical companies in Connecticut and New Jersey. One proposal calls for the establishment of specialist health centers (geriatric or psychiatric, for example) in the South Bronx and the creation of maintenance or service centers for sophisticated medical technology (Goodman and Aronowitz, 1981).[8]

PECs should be initiated with several tactical considerations in mind. First, a PEC should coordinate its activities with other projects, whether city, state, federal, or private. In doing so, PECs should take advantage of possibilities to combine complementary activities. They should conduct their operations in tandem with housing construction, hospital expansion, vocational training programs, and the award of federal contracts to private firms. Second, PECs, as public bodies, should plan their development in conjunction with infrastructure investments made by the city or state. For example, the construction of a new highway spur or the building of a sports stadium should make it possible for a PEC to establish vending or business concessions. The refurbishment of a subway system should make it possible for a PEC to exploit a variety of new opportunities. Third, PECs should take advantage of federal, state, or city inducements. The urban enterprise zone may fail if

---

[8]See Goodman, C., and S. Aronowitz, Why not create a health belt in the South Bronx? *New York Times*, 18 February 1981, p. A19.

conceived as a single initiative in an abandoned neighborhood of central Brooklyn. But in combination with the construction of subsidized housing, the building of a new subway station and an education program, the PEC might have some potential for success where ordinary businesses would founder. *The strategy of a PEC is based on injecting a concentrated, coordinated, and cumulative economic stimulus into a precise geographical location within a specific time frame.* A PEC operates on a principle of economic jujitsu—apply a lot of pressure on a small space within a short period of time and wait for the turnaround.

PECs should not work in isolation from one another. More than one PEC can begin activities in a neighborhood by engaging in complementary ventures. Nor should PECs be allowed to monopolize businesses within a neighborhood; a healthy mix of public and private enterprise is desirable. PECs are designed to invigorate an environment and to diversify its activities by creating positive externalities for all types of enterprise.

Undertake efforts to combat the tendency of private corporations to split headquarters and technical operations between the CBD and the second ring. As mentioned earlier, there is a tendency for large companies to retain their headquarters in the CBD and leapfrog their operations into the second ring. The city should pay particular attention to this development and make special efforts to attract appropriate manufacturing into the first ring (for example, via coordinating and administrative offices in the city and by a combination of information, cooperation, and persuasion). The advantages of proximity between the urban core and the first ring should be stressed. The city and the state should also invest in infrastructure in the first ring to make corporate location of technical operations there more attractive. This might include the provision of training programs, transportation systems, and other facilities. If city and state governments are going to continue to regulate and render assistance to business, they ought to divert their efforts toward restoring corporate enterprise in the first ring. Much of this can be accomplished through discretionary incentives that funnel assistance to first-ring enterprises and by modifying regulations to facilitate corporate location in depressed areas. The aim of this strategy is not the infeasible objective of the joint location of headquarter offices and production operations in the first ring; instead, firms should be encouraged to retain their headquarters in the CBD but choose a first-ring site for their production plant.

Why Choose an Amenities and Resource Utilization Approach?

A number of objections have been raised against an amenities and resource utilization approach, and these criticisms demand a response. Is it sensible to invest in public facilities in an urban core prone to vandalism and crime? Allowing public facilities to grow old and deteriorate without replacement only increases antisocial behavior and leaves areas even more vulnerable to crime. Dilapidation only invites further neglect and public demoralization. Administrators have made the mistake of converting our parks and public facilities into forbidden zones by closing them up, installing gates and security mechanisms, and withdrawing maintenance. An opposite course of action is justified; the best defense is a good offense. What is needed is more public use, more care and maintenance, and better facilities. Only then will acts of vandalism be seen as real and offensive violations of public resources. If we treat the citizenry as if they live in a cage, they will act in fear and live up to the worst of expectations. But if we invest in amenities, open up the environment, and demonstrate confidence in the future, citizens are more likely to act positively to protect these amenities. Investment increases the public stake in society. Disinvestment leads to withdrawal and resignation. Without increased amenities, the CBD and urban core run the risk of becoming urban ghost towns at the end of each working day. People who work in the CBD will continue to retreat into guarded apartment complexes or commute to suburban homes. With additional amenities we can link up the CBD with a larger and more vital residential urban core. If the city is more livable it will attract more business investment.

What reason is there to believe that PECs can succeed in areas that private enterprise has abandoned? Furthermore, if there are prospects for success, why not allow private enterprise to do the job? We should remember that there are areas of great potential within the first ring. It is proximate to a dynamic CBD and excellent port facilities, utilities and water lines are intact, and subway and elevated train lines still exist. The reasons why private enterprise left these areas are very complicated, but the first ring does have the potential for a comeback, provided it is carefully planned and supported.[9] The dynamics driving American private enterprise may not be suitable for such a regeneration because it stresses short-run profits. Many American firms (e.g., in the automobile industry) have been criticized for the lack of long-term planning. PECs can engage more easily in long-term planning and

---

[9]The reasons for the flight of private businesses include: the existence of a cheap nonunion labor pool in the South, especially in the 1950s; massive expenditures on a highway system that placed a premium on trucking and the automobile while devaluing the train; tax subsidies and loan guarantees for single-family housing; and the lack of investment in central city infrastructure. Not the least of these factors was the migration trends that brought a rural population from the South and the Caribbean to the city at a time when unskilled jobs in manufacturing were declining. However, the situation is changing. Labor is no longer as cheap in the South; energy costs may make some kinds of mass transit more competitive; housing tastes have changed and it is now possible for cooperative and condominium owners to reap tax benefits; and unskilled labor is now migrating from the city.

investment. As public corporations they would receive initial subsidies from government, enabling them to enjoy a reprieve from the pressure to earn immediate returns.

In addition, PECs would be able to work on lower profit margins than private enterprise. American private enterprise generally requires higher rates of return on investment than foreign—particularly Japanese—firms. Because the objective of the PEC is as much economic development as profit, it could adopt different priorities giving as much attention to community services and facilities as to profit rates. Also, the reinvestment patterns for PECs would be different than for private enterprise. While private enterprise responds to stockholders' demands for profits by seeking out the most lucrative opportunities in the Southwest or abroad, PECs could channel their investable resources back to communities in the first ring.

The nation's past experience with efforts to bring private enterprise into depressed areas with incentives has failed. Instead of offering tax abatements to private enterprise, we should try to retain lost tax dollars and channel these funds toward some form of public enterprise. Tax abatements, depreciation allowances, and concessions of free land are not free to the public. These "giveaways" represent lost opportunities that might be better undertaken by PECs with their higher degree of public responsibility.

Moreover, a critical advantage possessed by PECs is that they would be in a position to coordinate, plan, and concentrate their activities with other public agencies. As mentioned earlier, PECs might operate in tandem with other forms of public investment (health, hospitals, schools, transportation). This capacity for coordination may make the difference between the failure of an isolated private firm and the success of a planned public activity. There is no intent in these proposals that private firms should be "crowded out" from operating in the priority areas. On the contrary, public-private complementarity may be the recipe for success.

What will prevent PECs from behaving like private enterprises once they are established in a setting where profit signals determine success? There are no absolute safeguards against this; PECs must operate according to some stringent measure of performance, and profit-and-loss statements are very effective measures. However, PECs would contain some built-in checks against these risks. The major check would be the presence of community representatives on a PEC board. These representatives would be expected to pressure the PEC into acting on behalf of local interests. As public corporations, PECs would also be amenable to political pressure from the governor, mayor, or legislators.

In any event, it is not necessarily undesirable that PECs behave in some respects like private corporations. At worst, we would have a profit-making public enterprise that created jobs in a community and reinvested its profits back into the locality. Reinvestment is something declining neighborhoods sorely lack. They have suffered severely from disinvestment by banks that "red-line," landlords who "milk" buildings, and businessmen who spend earnings elsewhere.

Finally, is it politically naive to expect that voters and elected officials would accept the idea of a PEC? It is more naive to pursue our present policies in the belief that new approaches will not be accepted simply because they are new. The initiation of public policies is dependent upon control of a political agenda. Heterogeneous groups, lobbies, and special interests have been able to set the political agenda for America and determine what is and is not "realistic," and what is and is not appropriate for debate. Realism and political acceptability are artifacts created by politicians, interest groups, and opinion makers. At the turn of the century, how many individuals would have believed that a New Deal would be passed thirty years later? During the early 1950s, how many would have believed that public opinion would turn abruptly against the Vietnam War, force a president from office, and bring about the evacuation of American troops in a lost war? How many in the 1960s would have believed in the apparent power of the New Right in the 1980 election?

Political agendas can change and these changes often come about during periods of national crisis. The New Right and neoclassical economists are in the forefront of policy today. If their programs fail, in the new national crisis the body politic may be ready for change. Most ideas start at some end of the political spectrum and work their way to the middle. Now is the time to pave the path of public opinion with a different kind of political agenda. Neither public opinion nor the political agenda is immutable. The major obstacle to change is the belief that change is impossible or at least politically unacceptable.

References

Armstrong, R. B. 1972. *The Office Industry.* New York: Regional Plan Association.

Atelier Parisien d'Urbanisme. 1978. *Vingt ans d'evolution de Paris.* Paris: Atelier Parisien d'Urbanisme.

Berry, B. 1975. "The decline of the aging metropolis: cultural basis and social process." In *Post-Industrial America.* See Sternlieb and Hughes, 1975, 175–85.

Committee on the Future. 1979. *Regional and Economic Development Strategies for the 1980s.* New York: The Port Authority of New York and New Jersey.

De Bono, E. 1967. *New Think.* New York: Avon Books.

Glazer, N. 1975. "Social and political ramifications of metropolitan decline." In *Post-Industrial America.* See Sternlieb and Hughes, 1975, 235–44.

Goldmark, P. 1979. Foreign business in the economy of the New York–New Jersey Metropolitan Region. *City Almanac* 14, no. 2 (August): 1–14.

Gorham, W., and N. Glazer, eds. 1976. *The Urban Predicament*. Washington, D.C.: The Urban Institute.

Hall, P. 1977. *World Cities*. New York: McGraw-Hill.

Laska, D., and D. Spain. 1981. *Back to the City*. Elmsford, New York: Pergamon Press.

New York City Department of City Planning. 1981. *Environmental Impact Statement*. New York: Department of City Planning.

OECD. 1982. *Proceedings of the Tokyo Seminar on Urban Growth Policies in the 1980s*. Paris: Organization for Economic Cooperation and Development.

Peltier-Charier, M. C. 1979. *New York: La plus grande ville du tiers monde*. Paris: Institut d'Amenagement et d'Urbanisme de la Region d'Ile de France.

Pietri, J., and J. L. Husson. 1979. *Essai de comparison entre les trois grandes metropoles mondiales Paris, Londres, New York*. Paris: Institut d'Amenagement et d'Urbanisme de la Region d'Ile de France.

Port Authority of New York. 1982. *Regional Perspectives*. New York: Port Authority.

Presidential Commission on a National Agenda for the 1980s. 1980. *National Agenda for the 1980s*. New York: New American Library.

Sale, K. 1974. *Power Shift*. New York: Random House.

Savitch, H. V. 1981. Politics, planning and urban formation in London, New York, and Paris. Paper presented before the Greater London Group at the London School of Economics, January. Mimeo.

Sternlieb, G., and J. Hughes. 1975. "Prologue." In *Post-Industrial America: Metropolitan Decline and Inter-Regional Job Shifts*, edited by Sternlieb and Hughes, 1–25. New Brunswick: Center for Urban Policy Research.

Wynne, G., ed. 1979. *Survival Strategies: Paris and New York*. New Brunswick, N.J.: Transaction Books.

ROGER J. VAUGHAN

10 State Policies for Promoting Economic Development: The Case of New York State

During the last few years, economic development has become the pre-eminent public concern in all fifty states and for the nation as a whole. Economic issues dominated the presidential election and most of the gubernatorial elections in 1982. New York State, with the city's well-publicized brush with bankruptcy and a precipitous loss of jobs and population between 1969 and 1975, joined the battle early. Unfortunately, the public debate about the economy and the role of state policies in encouraging development is fraught with misunderstanding and hollow rhetoric. Political rivals advocate simplistic slogans and accuse each other of causing current distress. Few seem interested in exploring the causes of economic problems and in undertaking the serious task of building an effective strategy.

In the nineteenth century the American public was plagued by purveyors of snake oil. These salesmen persuaded their audiences to purchase a bottle of relatively harmless fluid by listing sufficient illnesses, real and imagined, that their medicine would cure. The more successful among them could induce mild hypochondria in even the most suspicious and healthy individuals and so make a sale. Economic policy is now being marketed by the same techniques.

Before we decide how to design a state economic development strategy at least three tasks must be undertaken: first, we must define the problems that the program is intended to address; second, we must identify the causes of these problems; and third, we must analyze the effectiveness of alternative policies to address these root causes. At present, state economic policy debates begin and end with a discussion of tax cuts. State taxes are regarded as the fiscal equivalent of the Mediterranean fruit fly—something to be eradicated so that the harvest of private-sector jobs is not jeopardized. Little attention is paid to the host of state regulatory and expenditure policies that, most empirical evidence suggests, are much more influential in shaping economic development than a host of special-interest provisions in the state tax code. The purpose of this chapter is to explore, using New York as a case study, the process of economic development and to show how a state economic strategy must be cast in a much broader framework than is traditionally used. We must regrettably conclude that much of what has passed as economic development policy has had little to do with economic development. It has had much more to do with income distribution in ways that have little to do with equity considerations.

In this chapter, four points will be argued:

1. The process of economic development necessarily involves the decline of some industries and the emergence of others. This process of "creative destruction" should not be blocked by state economic policies.
2. Many of the economic indicators that we use to measure our economic problems are inappropriate; they do not, in themselves, reflect a diagnosis of underlying problems.
3. The purpose of state economic policy is to lower the barriers that impede adjustment to economic change, not to preserve declining industries or bet the taxpayers' dollars on the roulette wheel of future growth prospects.
4. The true economic problems that we face, and that require state action, are the same we have always faced—how to extend the benefits of economic growth to as many people as possible. The real challenge to state economic policymakers is how to integrate a system for redistributing economic opportunity efficiently within an economy that allocates resources primarily through market systems.

Although New York State is the case study of this chapter, much of the discussion is applicable to the traditional thinking underlying economic policy debates at the federal, state, and local level.

What Is Economic Development?

Although "economic development" is the expressed goal of public policy, it is a concept that is poorly understood and ill defined when it is defined at all. Most state policy practitioners understand development in aggregate terms—an increase in the number of jobs and population, an increase in output and income, or a reduction in the unemployment rate. This is misleading because these aggregate measures mask dynamic shifts within the state economy—shifts whose speed creates many of the problems we must wrestle with, but are at the same time essential to sustain the process of development. "Economic development" has been confused with "economic growth." Growth is a *quantitative* change in the scale of the economy, usually measured with aggregate data.

Development is a *qualitative* change that involves structural changes in the economy, along with innovation and adaptation by firms, the labor force, and institutions (including state government). In New York, the rapid expansion of the finance industry, the much-publicized "communications revolution," the involvement of Rensselaer Institute of Technology with research for private corporations, and the disinvestment by Bethlehem Steel in the Lackawanna plant are examples of these types of structural change.

Development is prior to growth in the sense that growth cannot be sustained without the innovations and structural changes implicit in development. As with any other useful distinction, however, differences that appear sharp in concept are less sharp in reality. In some circumstances, growth might appear to "cause" development. In a dynamic economy, a host of minor developmental changes will accompany growth in output. Enterprises and households make incremental adaptations, such as minor reorganizations or migrations, in response to changing incomes, demands, prices, and other decision-determining parameters. As these incremental changes cumulate, the various economic actors find that the increasing scale and diversification of the economy cause problems that cannot be dealt with by minor adaptations. Major innovations or structural changes are called for. The economy may then enter a period of no growth, or slow growth, until those basic institutional adjustments occur. This developmental change sets the stage for another round of growth. However, "bailing out" declining industries through favorable state tax treatment, or even through direct grants, delays or prevents these necessary structural adjustments.

Development can also arise independently of the current rate of growth through exogenous forces or shocks, such as a recent increase in energy prices or major technological changes. These shocks and changes induce development by creating disequilibrium in the economy that necessitates major institutional and structural changes. The rapid growth of the "energy conservation" industry in New York and the expansion of electricity generation through "low-head" hydro power are two examples of disequilibrium-induced changes. The state's economic policies should not attempt to undo the impact of each shock simply because some firms or areas are harmed. These policies should be used to enhance the ability of the local economy to make the necessary adjustments. Those who bear a disproportionate share of the costs of adjustment should be *compensated*, not preserved to perform obsolete tasks. The goals of state economic development are not to return the economy to some defined equilibrium state, or even to steer the economy toward some anticipated or desired future equilibrium, but to facilitate the process of adjustment.

Schumpeter (1961) has pointed out that in a market economy this disequilibrium-dynamic process of development involves a process of "creative destruction" in which old resources are devalued while new resources are revalued. Contrary to economic textbooks, the disequilibrium nature of the process not only is endemic to a dynamic market economy, but also is necessary for the continual regeneration of the economy through entrepreneurship. This description differs from the traditional view of economic "progress," where the state economy and its component regions march inexorably along a growth path. Decline, devaluation, and disinvestment in some areas and industries are the counterparts of increases in values and growing investment in other areas and industries. For areas whose products were in demand during the last stage of development, the adjustments can be very painful indeed.

This points to the importance of *process* rather than *plan* in economic development policy. It is a waste of time to draw up elaborate development plans; it is far better to improve our understanding of the dynamics of the process and how we can best speed the adjustment.

In economic theory as taught in colleges and universities, adjustments are made instantaneously. Therefore, the problems that are central to state economic policy are removed by assumption. Yet, in the "real world," with its complex markets, risk-avoiding behavior, institutional inertia, and incessant shocks to the system, adjustments are not made instantly and are not always in the right direction. The failures of markets to adjust, whether because of government intervention or market structure, are of central concern to the design of public policy.

New York State's Economic Problems

New York State's economic policies, and those of most other states, have evolved in an ad hoc response to perceived problems. They have focused on symptoms rather than causes. If a plant threatens to move out, it is offered tax abatements and low-cost loans as inducement to stay. If a factory closes, development officials attempt to replace it by trying to steal another plant from another state. To encourage the growth of new industries, special tax credits are written into the tax code. For example, the state's investment tax credit was extended to certain types of vinegar equipment to stimulate wine growing. Yet these actions have little to do with development as it was defined in the preceding section. Discretionary responses to the problems of single firms or industries do not spur the types of broad institutional adjustments that are necessary to sustain development.

Each response has seemed like a reasonable and humane way of dealing with a problem. If there are unemployed people in Buffalo, then we should try to keep a factory from closing. This is a convenient viewpoint that gives policymakers the opportunity to debate ways of "helping" their constituents and special interest groups the chance to plead the causes of their dues-paying members. We are all familiar with the litany of problems—slow productivity growth, growing trade deficits, and rising unemployment—that are used to justify public intervention. But policymakers should not take remedial action until they have determined the causes of these problems, and a clear description of the symptoms, as with a medical diagnosis, is an important first step. Unfortunately, the frequently cited data used to verify symptoms of economic distress do not clearly establish either the extent or the type of economic problem; therefore, accurate diagnosis is almost impossible. Three measures—slow productivity growth, failure to compete with other nations, and high unemployment—have been used repeatedly in New York, as well as in the nation, to justify public action. They provide excellent examples of the misuse of data and "casual empiricism."

PRODUCTIVITY

Slow productivity growth has become one of the most important issues in the current economic policy debate. In 1979 and 1980, for the first time in United States economic history, national output rose and productivity (output per person-hour) fell. The measured rate of productivity growth in almost all sectors has been declining since World War II. The causes of slow productivity growth have been variously ascribed to loss of the work ethic, short-sighted management, the burden of regulation, or lack of competition.

This trend has been linked to the "failure of the American worker to compete in world markets," which, it is alleged, is a contributing factor to our balance of trade deficits. Falling productivity is also blamed for persistent inflation because, it is argued, if workers were more productive then increased demand would be absorbed by increased quantities of goods and services rather than by inflated prices. Neither of these arguments, however, is correct. Productivity and trade deficits are only tenuously connected, and inflation has contributed to, rather than resulted from, declining productivity by deterring investment. Furthermore, while admitting that the productivity numbers may be cause for concern, the case is far from proven; the data are misleading and the analyses have been confused.

It is often forgotten that "productivity" is *not* a measure of "efficiency." Labor productivity is the statistical relationship between the number of person-hours and the quantity of output. Efficiency is a measure of how well an enterprise uses its inputs—land, energy, capital, and materials, as well as labor—to produce its final output. While greater "efficiency" is invariably a goal to strive for, greater labor productivity is not. Consider a hypothetical example of a textile firm. If the firm cuts costs by replacing some equipment with extra workers while maintaining the level of production, it has improved its *efficiency*, even though labor productivity has fallen.

The idea of replacing machinery with labor may sound farfetched in an era characterized by machines replacing labor. However, the sudden increase in real energy prices in 1973 has led industry to reduce energy consumption per real unit of output. In the last few years, "energy productivity" has grown very rapidly, especially in the Northeast. Energy and capital equipment are complementary inputs, while energy and labor are substitutes. Therefore, rising energy prices have led to more labor-intensive methods of production and a more rapid expansion of labor-intensive industries relative to capital-intensive industries. This slows the growth of labor productivity. Had these changes not occurred, industry would not have been behaving efficiently. The "efficient" mix of inputs depends upon their relative price. That is what makes international comparisons misleading. Relative factor prices differ among nations according to wage rates, government subsidies, and resource endowments. Appropriate technology in one country—with its implicit labor productivity—is not necessarily appropriate technology in another. There are also wide variations in relative factor costs among states. In New York, with a relatively stagnant labor market, wage rates have been growing slowly relative to wages in southern states. The "effective" industrial response has resulted in relatively slow growth in labor productivity.

A second problem with the emphasis on productivity is that the data are of poor quality. Output, for example, is difficult to measure. An automobile in 1980 is more fuel efficient, safer, and better designed than an automobile in 1970. Production and installation of extra equipment require additional labor, which increases person-hours per vehicle, but does not mean that labor is less "productive." Adjusting output for quality is an elusive task.

Nowhere is measuring output more difficult than in the construction sector, second only to mining, nationwide, in the speed of productivity decline during the 1970s. Between 1954 and 1977, construction output, as measured by statisticians, increased by 58 percent while the use of construction materials increased by 133 percent. "Productivity" steadily declined. In large part, the decline can probably be explained by changes in the type of construction activity. Housing rehabilitation has increased relative to new housing construction, and rehabilitation is a more labor-intensive activity. Concern over energy prices led to much greater retrofitting of insulation, another labor-intensive activity.

The construction industry illustrates another problem with statistics. Not only are the data misleading, but in many instances they are completely missing (e.g., discounts for cash payments offered by general contractors—plumbers, painters, and electricians). The underground economy, spawned by escalating tax rates and expensive regulations, has grown rapidly during the 1970s—up to 20 percent of gross national product (GNP) by one measure. Yet its output is never neasured.

A reduction in productivity growth can even be economically sound. In mining and extraction, for example, the increased price of coal, oil, and natural gas has made many marginal resources economically viable. The increase from 1970 to 1980 in person-hours expended in mining a ton of coal is consistent with economic efficiency because the value of that coal has more than doubled.

Productivity measures do not include the quality of the workplace or the value of a cleaner environment. If a steel mill employs people to monitor work safety or to operate pollution abatement equipment, then person-hours per ton of steel increase. The value of increased worker satisfaction with the job or cleaner air is not measured.

Statistical error and confusion do not explain the entire slowdown in productivity growth. However, knowledge of the extent or even the existence of the productivity problem is insufficient for informed policy recommendations.

BALANCE OF TRADE

During 1978 and 1979, the United States imported more goods and services than it exported. Many states that are heavily dependent on trade, such as New York, have experienced severe local dislocation as import substitution industries have weakened while exports have failed to grow rapidly enough to absorb rising unemployment. A widening trade "deficit" also exists for certain products such as steel, electric appliances, and automobiles. A trade deficit is neither a result of declining labor productivity nor a presage of continued decline for major industrial states. The "competitiveness" of United States products abroad is determined by their price in terms of the local currency.

The declining share of United States industries in world markets is not necessarily a cause for public concern. As industrial and agricultural capacity in underdeveloped countries expand, their dependence on the United States for many basic goods, including steel, machinery, and automobiles, is reduced. Instead of buying manufactured goods, they purchase information processing services from the United States. Exports of financial services, computer software, and communications services are growing while manufacturing exports are declining.

This pattern reflects the basic gains from international trade. As trade expands, a country increasingly specializes in producing goods or services in which it enjoys a comparative advantage and reduces output of those in which it does not. Dependence on imports is not a deterrent to growth. Japan, which has grown more rapidly than the United States, is seven times more dependent on imports than the United States. The problems New York faces in declining, low-technology industries reflect the decline of the nation's comparative advantage in the production of low-technology goods. At the same time, some industries in New York have greatly expanded their exports including "high-technology" goods and financial and legal services. The inevitable decline in textile and apparel industries in the state is not a signal that they should be aided. It is a signal to shift resources into industries with stronger, long-run growth prospects.

UNEMPLOYMENT

The erratic secular increase in the unemployment rate is the third indicator that is most frequently cited as a symptom of a state's economic malaise. While the economic and social suffering resulting from high unemployment are undeniable and require public action, neither the number of unemployed nor the rate of unemployment are unambiguous indicators of the extent or the direction of change of the state's economic health. It is not known how many of the unemployed represent viable "targets" for state economic policy or how that share has changed over the last decade. Although space precludes a detailed discussion of the problems of measuring unemployment, the following observations can be made:

1. During the last decade, the extension of the level of benefits and the coverage of unemployment insurance have led to an increase in the average duration of frictional unemployment, thereby increasing the unemployment rate.
2. The increase in the number of two-worker households has allowed workers to search longer for a job once they become unemployed. Frictional unemployment has increased as secondary workers search for employment when the primary wage earner relocates.
3. The growing underground economy means that many individuals who appear either unemployed or not participating in the labor force are in fact working, albeit without the fringe benefits associated with more formal employment.
4. The rapid rate of structural change in the state's economy—a result of rapid technological progress and changing world trade patterns—has increased the unemployment rate as resources are shifted among firms, industries, and regions within the state.

Against these factors must be weighed the problems faced by underemployed and discouraged workers and by full-time employees who remain below the poverty level. The suffering is extensive, but in spite of decades of public employment and training problems, the extent of the "client" population is still unknown.

New York State is not without economic problems, but they are poorly defined and understood. To revive the medical analogy used in the opening of the chapter, we have behaved as doctors trying to diagnose a patient's illness by applying uncalibrated instruments to inappropriate parts of the anatomy. The complexity of the problems cannot be analyzed with the traditional and oversimplified measures that we use. Economic policy must be based on a much more detailed examination of the functioning of different parts of the economy. When plants close, we cannot simply blame imports, provide subsidized loans, and expect the problem to abate. In order to identify the true barriers to growth and development, we must examine why demand declined and how capital and labor markets operate.

Barriers to Economic Development in New York State

The wide gap between describing the state's economic problems and prescribing economic policies is usually spanned with only the most frail of analytic bridges. If the state's economic development strategy is to prove effective, we must provide a much sturdier means of transporting our concerns into action.

Loans, loan guarantees, and grants will have little long-run impact on an ailing industry or jurisdiction unless they also provide incentives for the recipients to adjust to change. Economic development strategies cannot stimulate growth if they are interpreted as an attempt to turn back the economic clock. They can only work if they are designed to remove the barriers to adjustment that were created by the failure of markets to operate efficiently and equitably.

Basically, states do not have problems with specific industries or communities. Instead, they have problems in the operation of the capital and labor markets that deter risk taking and impede the mobility of capital and labor between industries, regions, and occupations. Most of these barriers are the result of public policies—federal and state—that include the structure of taxes, regulations, and spending.

Land, labor, and capital—what economists call factors of production—are sold mainly through markets. For some factors, the markets are clearly defined. The price of labor is determined by negotiations between employers and workers—sometimes on an individual basis, sometimes for entire workforces. Land is sold through competitive bidding among purchasers. Other markets are less clearly defined. Amenities are rarely sold directly, but are reflected in the price a purchaser is willing to offer for a location with attractive features, such as clean air and ready access to recreational space. Publicly provided services are implicitly "sold," and the "price" is the local tax rate.

The purpose of the market is to send signals to the participants to indicate when they need to change their behavior and to indicate the direction of the appropriate change. The employer who fails to fill vacant slots needs to raise wages. A job seeker who cannot find employment must either look elsewhere or reduce the wages and conditions under which he or she hopes to work.

In fact, if there were no barriers to the operation of factor markets, there would be no unemployment. Anyone rendered jobless by industrial decline would move to another industry for which foresight had prepared him or her in advance. But markets do not operate perfectly. Uncertainty, less than perfect information, and relocation costs delay these moves and result in unemployment.

The theoretical economist defines one of the roles the public sector plays in economic development as that of helping improve the operation of markets by repairing the causes of their failures. These failures are:

Imperfect Information.   The unemployed worker does not know where job openings exist, or the investor does not have enough information to assess the viability of a project.

Transactions Costs.   The cost of relocation may prevent an unemployed worker from moving to a growing labor market, or the costs of a bond issue may make an investment nonviable.

Nonconstant Returns to Scale.   An economic activity, such as a job referral service, may be cheapest if performed nationwide, yet no single private company can capture these economies. Similarly, a very large venture capital corporation would undertake risky projects because its overall portfolio is diversified.

Externalities.   An activity that generates "spill-over" benefits that do not accrue to those paying for the activity will not be undertaken at an optimal level. For example, basic research will not be adequately funded privately because the sponsor will be able to capitalize on only part of the benefits. A firm will be reluctant to pay for non-job-specific training for an employee because that employee can leave for another company.

Second Best.   An imperfection in one market will lead to imperfections in related markets. If capital is denied to high-risk enterprises, then the level of employment in the high-risk sector will be below the socially optimal level.

Public Intervention.   Collecting taxes or regulating economic activity will distort the operation of markets. For example, taxing income discourages labor force participation. Regulating minimum wages reduces the number of low-wage jobs.

Monopolistic Power.   If a producer of a good or service, or the supplier of a factor of production, has a monopoly, then the good, service, or factor will be priced inefficiently high and its availability curtailed.

For many purposes this classification is useful. Yet, several relevant "failures" or barriers to development are missing or incompletely specified. The market failure concept is too static. Most "failures" are defined as deviations from the ideal (and totally unrealistic) model of perfect competition, which is a model of static, not dynamic efficiency. In a dynamic market economy, there will be a tendency for market imperfections to diminish since some entrepreneurs can profit from providing a good or service that remedies the fault. Overcoming barriers presumes that there is a supply of entrepreneurs to develop these new products and that these entrepreneurs do face incentives to bridge market gaps. If failures persist, either there is a lack of entrepreneurs or public intervention is acting as a barrier to development.

The second major weakness of the simple market failure analysis is its implicit suggestion that the best way to foster development is to remove all impediments to the "normal" functioning of a market economy. This assumes not only that all development resources are bought, sold, and produced in private markets, but also that the latter are self-organizing and self-perfectable. Rather than reflect further on the unreality of this viewpoint, note the following additional barriers to the dynamically efficient creation and utilization of resources for development:

Lack of Entrepreneurship.   New enterprises will not be set up without individuals who take risks, identify market gaps, have access to capital, and know business management. Many distressed communities lack a tradition of entrepreneurship.

Uncertainty.   State policy can either increase or decrease uncertainty and thereby have a significant adverse or positive effect on investment or other decisions by which the economy adjusts. Uncertainty has often been a significant deterrent in state and local economic development policy. Annual fluctuations in appropriations, quixotic changes in regulations, and bureaucratic politicking can deter long-term private sector investments.

Lack of integration or coordination among key parts of economic or political systems.   This is the gap and adversary relationship between public and private sectors.

This somewhat abstract discussion of barriers can be translated into an analysis of real barriers that identifies how public policies may be deterring rather than encouraging development. The Appendix to this chapter provides a more detailed discussion of barriers in labor and capital markets.

Because of these market failures, resources are not allocated efficiently. While inefficiency in the typical "static" model of the economy so beloved by economic theorists means only a slight reduction in real income, in a dynamic system it presents more serious problems. New sectors fail to emerge, and some communities and individuals bear a very large share of the costs of economic development.

Professor Alberto Shapero (1981, p. 20) of Ohio State University neatly summarized the appropriate role of state economic policy:

> Instead of trying to attract branch operations of older, established firms, economic development policies should be more concerned with new and developing firms. They should aim at diversity and reduced dependence in any community or region on one or a few sectors of economic activity. Rather than concentrating on specific firms, they should focus on creating the ecological conditions for new company formations.
>
> Economic development policies emphasizing new firm formations rather than relocations provide a relatively lower risk, lower cost, actuarial approach that is less subject to failure because it is not project oriented. It is concerned with establishing conditions propitious to company formations rather than with financing and servicing specific plants or industries.

This approach is necessarily entrepreneurial, emphasizing the development of new business. Governor Carey recognized this in his economic message in January 1981:

> The key to sustained economic progress is the continued development of new business enterprise. The range of new business is as broad and diverse as the economy itself. It includes the small young firms that pioneer in areas of high technology, and established corporate giants that invest hundreds of millions in the development of new products. It includes the farmer who seeks to market a new crop and the food processor who responds successfully to changing consumer demands.
>
> What all these have in common is a willingness to invest, to innovate, to take risks. The state by itself cannot create this entrepreneurial spirit—but it can create the conditions that allow it to flourish. It can do this by removing the barriers that currently inhibit growth and development. These barriers may be shortages of crucial factors—capital, energy, skilled labor—or more subtle barriers—the disincentives to investment or risk taking that are inherent in the tax codes or regulatory structure.

Correcting market failures and strengthening the environment for an entrepreneurial economy is only one part of the public sector role. It must also redistribute resources to those who, by accident of birth, location, or occupation are denied economic opportunities or who "lose" in the economic development process. Transfer payments, training programs, targeted procurement policies, and affirmative action initiatives are among the efforts that are used to redress the economic imbalance. However, the structure of many redistributive programs discourages rational economic behavior and therefore reduces market efficiency. Some trade-off between efficiency (speeding adjustment) and equity (compensating losers) is essential, but improved program design could greatly reduce the importance of the trade-off.

The principle of using public policies to remove barriers to economic adjustment provides basic guidelines for the design of an economic development strategy based on the concept of helping the economy function more effectively. This strategy goes beyond a zero-sum redistribution of resources from the successful regions and industries toward the unsuccessful. Instead, the removal of barriers to the efficient operation of factor markets can help productive resources flow where they are needed. The "ideal" adjustment process is that of innovative entrepreneurs, either within existing companies or through new enterprises, developing new products or new production techniques to meet the new demands posed by a constantly evolving economy. The purpose of public policy is to ensure that this evolutionary process does not slow or become mutated through market distortions, while at the same time preserving the power to protect individuals from environmental or economic abuse. The barriers that these entrepreneurs face may be financial—a tax system penalizing innovation or subsidizing the status quo—or institutional—regulations limiting competition or restricting input use or misdirected skills training programs starving new industries of needed manpower. The following section outlines policies that have been developed in New York State that do overcome market barriers.

Toward a State Economic Strategy

The conclusion from the preceding discussion is that the state's economic development policies must be aimed at removing the barriers to economic adjustment while, at the same time, compensating those harmed by the process. In a static economic framework, the achievement of equity and efficiency goals necessarily involves a trade-off. However, in a dynamic economy, policies that improve efficiency may also increase equity. Consider two hypothetical examples: first, a policy that encourages increased risk taking by private lending institutions may lead to increased investment in minority entrepreneurs, or in businesses in low-income communities; second, a student-aid program that provides access to education for qualified low-income individuals may increase the income of the participants as well as increasing overall economic growth. The trade-off may be more apparent than real.

In this section, the *process* of developing a state strategy is outlined, and specific policies adopted by New York are briefly described to illustrate the type of actions that can be taken within the conceptual framework defined in this paper.

DEVELOPING A STATE ECONOMIC STRATEGY

The first step in formulating an effective state economic development strategy is *not* to identify growth industries, to ask industry what it feels the state should do (the answer is inevitably to cut taxes), to respond to cries for help from ailing firms, or to develop a detailed multiyear plan. It is to analyze the ways in which capital, labor, land, and other markets work and to identify the ways in which they do not operate efficiently.

The second step is to evaluate alternative ways to overcome these inefficiencies. This process must be based on learning from past efforts. As a way of organizing this policy analysis process, we might begin by defining four broad objectives for a New York State development strategy:

1. Increasing the overall rate of growth.
2. Assisting severely distressed communities.
3. Assisting economically disadvantaged individuals.
4. Improving the quality of jobs (improved safety, stability, wages, etc.).

Having identified the barriers to the attainment of these objectives, we can identify sets of goals that correspond to each objective and the policy options that might be employed to reach them. Diagrammatically, the process can be seen as filling in the boxes in the matrix depicted in Figure 10.1. For each box, the causes of the problem must be defined and the policy options within each generic policy category (each row) identified.

Each matrix entry cannot be explored in this chapter. However, one row from the matrix can be used to illustrate the process through which the state government must proceed as it identifies the individual programs and policies to be incorporated into its overall strategy. Consider, for example, development finance policy options, and how they can meet the four basic development objectives (Table 10.1). The options defined are not necessarily effective or appropriate programs, but the process involves first identifying *all* possible options and then selecting those that best meet local needs and are most likely to overcome real factor market barriers.

The options listed in Table 10.1 represent only a sample of the possibilities that an imaginative state government can develop. The important steps are to define the generic issues within each broad objective and then to explore the powers of the state to influence public and private decisions to address each of these issues. This exercise necessarily involves many different state agen-

Policy Lever \ Objective	Increasing Overall Growth	Assisting Distressed Areas	Assisting Economically Disadvantaged Individuals	Improving Overall Job Quality
Labor Market				
Land Use				
Development Finance				
Energy Policy				
Taxation				
Transportation				
Infrastructure				
Regulation				

FIGURE 10.1.   Matrix for a state economic development strategy.

cies as well as the tax and budget departments. Policymakers must therefore define these issues and then coordinate the efforts of many departments in helping define options.

Having defined the options, the task is then to determine their probable effectiveness. This involves evaluating how effectively the program overcomes a genuine market barrier. Too little is known about the nature and extent of market barriers and the effectiveness of alternative programs to determine, on a rigorous basis, which program should be strenuously pursued. The state must therefore proceed with caution. As a body of knowledge is accumulated, the state will be able to develop policies with greater confidence. In order to learn from experience, it is important for the state to mandate a "policy analysis" group within each line agency whose tasks include ongoing evaluation of the effectiveness of the department's programs, analysis of alternative policies and programs, and assessment of barriers to the achievement of the programs' goals. Unfortunately, policy analysis is viewed as a luxury budget item and is rarely adequately funded.

TABLE 10.1
State Development Goals and Policy Options

Objectives	Goals	Options
1. Increasing macro growth rate.	a. Increasing the supply of risk capital.	Reduce state capital gains tax.
		Defer capital gains when reinvested in in-state businesses.
		Abolish corporate income tax for first two years for a new corporation.
		Set up state finance agency for new business/new product development.
		Direct public pensions to invest a certain percent of their resources in in-state business startups.
		Reduce state income tax on interest income earned by savers who deposit in "state enterprise fund."
	b. Increasing the supply of debt capital to small business.	Require all state-chartered banks to invest a certain percent of assets in small business.
		Reduce corporate tax rates for banks on the interest on loans to small business.
		Provide state loan guarantees.
		Encourage the development of a secondary market for the guaranteed portion of loans of small business.
	c. Increasing the availability of funds for research and development (R and D).	Allow the instant expensing of R and D spending for state tax purposes.
		Provide state matching grants for R and D investments.
		Offer state university for R and D activities.
2. Aiding distressed areas.	a. Stimulating risk capital in distressed areas.	Any of the above programs (1a) with a geographic eligibility.
		Extra investment tax credit or grants to investments in distressed areas.
		State grants to Small Business Investment Corporations (SBICs) with a distressed area focus.
		High-risk loan-loss reserve fund for investments in distressed areas.
	b. Aiding small business in distressed areas.	Require banks to make a certain portion of loans to business in distressed areas.
		Target state pension fund investments.
		Interest subsidies on investments in designated areas.

TABLE 10.1—*continued*

Objectives	Goals	Options
3. Aiding the disadvantaged.	a. Stimulating risk capital for minority entrepreneurs.	State grants to Minority Entrepreneur Small Business Investment Corporations (MESBICs). Technical assistance for minority entrepreneur development. Loan guarantees for minority business. Double deduction of losses from income against state corporate income tax for banks for investments in minority businesses. Targeted loan guarantee programs. Premiums to banks for loans to small minority businesses. High-risk, state loan agency for minority businesses. Loan subsidies for firms that purchase a large proportion of inputs from minority suppliers.
4. Improving job quality	a. Improving working conditions.	Tax-exempt loan or rapid depreciation for investments in equipment or facilities that improve health, safety, or recreational facilities. State matching grants to above investments.
	b. Increasing options for upward mobility.	Low-interest loans or tax credits for firms that provide training to disadvantaged workers. Technical assistance to aid firms implementing "upward mobility" programs.
	c. Reducing cyclical instability.	Low-interest-rate loans for firms with "work-sharing" programs. Interest subsidies based upon countercyclical level of firm inventories.

NEW YORK STATE
ECONOMIC DEVELOPMENT POLICIES

New York State provides some interesting case studies of what not to do and what to do in economic policy. Some policies and proposed initiatives have been consistent with the framework described in the preceding pages. Others are almost textbook examples of what not to do. Before discussing programs that do meet the broad criteria laid out above, it is worthwhile discussing one program that has not done so: the Job Incentive Program (JIP). Under JIP a company moving into the state, or one contemplating a move out, can receive generous abatements of its corporate franchise tax, coupled with local property tax abatement. The amount of the incentive is related to the number of jobs attracted or retained (whatever that really means) and to the amount of capital investment made. The incentive is "negotiated" between the Job Incentive Board that administers the program and the company. It is now costing the state about $50 million in foregone tax revenues. Most of the abatements have gone to large corporations, and have been negotiated by highly paid consultants who have data to prove that it would be cheaper to do business in locations outside the state. Tiffany's—the jewelry store on Fifth Avenue—was granted abatements of $5 million (over a ten-year period) for rehabilitation of two floors of its store because it had claimed that otherwise it would have to shift some of its "back-office" operations to New Jersey. A tax incentive to keep jobs at one of the prime locations in the world is not prudent use of the public fisc. The program has granted hundreds of millions of dollars worth of tax credits to over two thousand firms since 1968. Despite stiff opposition from the state's own Department of Commerce and the state legislature, the program was finally eliminated.[1]

The state has taken some creative steps through its tax code to stimulate new business development that, although experimental, are based on a conceptual approach to removing market barriers. In response to several research reports that have documented a shortage of equity capital for new business, in 1981 the state exempted from capital gains any investment made in a new productive enterprise (as distinct from investments in collectibles

---

[1]There were three reasons for this. First, a general sentiment among legislators that the program was inequitable (i.e., businesses that did not really "need" the credits were receiving them). Second, there was some question as to the efficacy of the program. Job retention, an extremely elusive concept, was very difficult to measure. It was impossible to tell whether, in the absence of the tax credit, a particular job would have been eliminated or a particular firm would have left the state. Furthermore, the tax credit was not directly related to the number of jobs *created*. The partial dependence of the credit on the amount of capital investment made resulted in benefits that were disproportionate to the number of new jobs created. Finally, and perhaps most compellingly, it was felt that the program was unaffordable during a period of fiscal austerity. In lieu of JIP, the legislature passed a Job Creation Credit. The high cost of the credit ($1,000 per job created, *not retained*) and a number of technical inadequacies were unacceptable to Governor Cuomo, and the bill was withdrawn before executive action was taken.

such as coins, works of art, and commodities).[2] At the same time, recognizing that the state's investment tax credit (ITC) did not benefit new businesses because they did not have a taxable income, the ITC was made refundable for businesses during the first three years of their life. This measure will substantially improve their cash flow during their rapid growth cycle, without rewarding older unprofitable companies. In addition, Governor Carey proposed in both 1981 and 1982 to replace the present legal list that defines eligible investments for public pension funds with a "prudent investor" guide used for private pension funds. This would have allowed some of the funds to be placed with private venture capital corporations to increase the availability of risk capital.[3]

The state has also begun the laborious process of reducing the burden of unnecessary and outmoded regulation. The Office of Business Permits offers a "one-stop" service to business, and is in the process of streamlining application procedures. Trucking regulation has also been simplified. An extensive program to deregulate large segments of the rapidly growing telecommunications business would create a more competitive and innovative environment. Again, either through the power of entrenched interests or through failure to understand the issue, the legislature has been very slow to act.[4]

Other programs also emphasize an entrepreneurial approach. New York has set up a Corporation for Innovation Development to provide small grants for the development of promising technological innovations. On a larger scale, the Rensselaer Polytechnic Institute's Center for Industrial Innovation is built with state funds but will be operated by grants from private corporations, an arrangement that promises to lead to the type of institutional change dictated by the changing technological and economic environment.

One final program is interesting because it provides an example of program innovation at the state level that can achieve both efficiency and equity goals at the same time. It also provides an example of state policy innovation that runs considerably ahead of policy innovation in Washington, D.C. In

[2]To avoid exempting speculative activities, the investments must be held by the investor for at least six years.

[3]The legislature has since enacted a bill that permits public pension funds to commit up to 5 percent of their total assets to any "eligible and prudent investment." In this context, an investment is said to be prudent if it earns a reasonable rate of return. The 5 percent "catch-all basket" currently involves approximately $600 million; of this amount, about $40 million is slated for venture capital ($25 million of which will remain in New York State). In 1983, a similar proposal was adopted for insurance companies.

[4]New York State appears to be making some progress in this direction. In 1981, Governor Carey deregulated telegraph services. Governor Cuomo, in 1982, deregulated radio telephone services. In his 1984 State of the State message, Cuomo proposed the leasing of state-owned property (primarily right-of-ways along the Thruway and commuter railways) for the purpose of laying broad-band capacity communication cables. These communication pathways (or "digital thruways") would provide low-cost data transmission capabilities to big businesses that want to establish their own networks.

1981, the governor proposed, and the legislature passed, the Temporary Employment Assistance Program (TEAP). TEAP allows general assistance welfare checks[5] to be used as a subsidy to private employers who hire and train the welfare recipient. The recipient receives full wages, while the employer receives the welfare grant as a subsidy for up to six months, and a trained and loyal employee at the end of it.[6] The individual receives training and a job. The program overcomes the cost barrier to hiring and training an unskilled individual, without incurring significant additional state expenditures. Within one year, the program had enrolled over five hundred people.[7]

These are only a few examples of the type of activity that states can undertake to achieve economic development objectives. They may not prove as successful as hoped and they may have to be modified over time, but they have been developed within a logical and consistent framework. This framework is essential if New York and other governments are to undertake successful economic policies and not repeat the mistakes of the past.

Appendix

LABOR MARKET BARRIERS

Economic development in an advanced economy is characterized by an increasing complementarity between human and physical capital. That is, with technological progress and a growing capital stock, jobs require trained and educated labor. There are fewer and fewer "unskilled" jobs through which the economically disadvantaged can gain a first step on the economic ladder. Furthermore, on-the-job learning is in several respects the most significant part of labor training. Yet access to education and training by low-income individuals is limited. While a company investing in a machine can secure a loan with the machine as collateral, an individual borrowing to finance postsecondary education can offer no such security. The result is that education and training are not as readily available to the poor as to those who can rely on well-off families for support. A prime concern of economic development strategy should be the removal of barriers to the mobility of the labor force—among occupations, industries, and areas. Let us briefly review

[5]General Assistance, or Home Relief as it is known in New York, is the only part of welfare under state control. Home Relief recipients tend to be single individuals. Poor households with children at home receive Aid to Families with Dependent Children (AFDC), a system that is federally controlled, although not fully federally funded.

[6]Unlike tax incentives, the program can be used by nonprofit firms and organizations, a rapidly growing sector in urban economies that is responsible for substantial job creation.

[7]TEAP, presently operating in only fifteen or twenty counties, has been quite successful. The Department of Social Services is now investigating the possibility of expanding the program to achieve statewide coverage.

some of the barriers to the efficient operation of the labor market, both with respect to the development and filling of job vacancies and to the acquisition of training.

Lack of Information.   Inadequate or inaccurate information is a chronic labor market problem. Programs to create job information banks and placement services attest to the depth of public concern. Labor markets include both the markets for skills (between labor and employers) and the markets for training (between labor and organizations that provide training, including employers). Thurow (1981) argues that the former markets work reasonably well while the latter operate poorly. An individual employee does not know which training will place him or her in the best competitive position. Yet, increasing the supply of some skills may take many years.

Transactions Costs.   Advertising, screening, and job-specific training are expensive activities. Regulations, such as affirmative action, have added to these costs. These costs are especially high when hiring the economically disadvantaged because the employer has little employment history or informal network information on which to base the decision. These costs are reflected in the tendency of employers to "hoard" labor during recessions and to employ those who have been screened through the recommendation of current employees, through certification by higher education, or through other employers. The combination of imperfect information and high transactions costs reduces the flexibility of the labor market to adjust to structural change and aggravates tendencies to exclude the disadvantaged from contention.

Legal Constraints.   Legislation such as the minimum wage, Occupational Safety and Health Act (OSHA), and affirmative action requirements may actively discourage employers from hiring the unskilled and encourage the substitution of capital for labor in order to reduce costs and the possibility of legal action.

On the other hand, the regulatory structure may inadequately define an employer's responsibility. For example, the incentives for the private sector to retain and retrain potentially "redundant" workers may be insufficiently strong. The longer a firm can expect to retain an employee, or the higher the costs of termination, the more likely the firm will provide more on-the-job training (OJT) and see the development of its human resources as an integral and important part of doing business. This means that a greater portion of the costs of adjustment can and should be internalized within the business sector.

Taxes.   There are many aspects of the tax structure that impede labor market adjustment, beyond the basic disincentive toward labor market participation inherent in the personal income tax. Human capital, unlike physical capital, cannot be depreciated, although the skills of a computer programmer become obsolete almost as rapidly as the machine he or she operates. Education or training costs that are not related to an employee's present job are not tax deductible. The failure to relate unemployment insurance (UI) premiums actuarially to the use of benefits penalizes low-turnover firms and subsidizes high-turnover firms. Volatile companies adjust labor forces rather than inventories. The fact that UI premiums and Social Security payments are not based on full salary or wages raises the cost to the employer of low-wage relative to high-wage workers. Of course, some of these barriers have been partially overcome. Some companies do subsidize education programs for their workforces and encourage "skill updating." But these benefits are not available everywhere.

Constraints on Mobility. The structure of transfer payments and other factors have created barriers to the effective redeployment of labor. Unemployment insurance and Trade Adjustment Assistance benefits have resulted in prolonged duration of unemployment. Individuals hold out longer and are less inclined to look extensively for alternative employment opportunities. Welfare payments are not geographically transferable.

In addition, laid-off workers may have heavy investments in their homes as well as accumulated skills, but these investments are illiquid. Relocation allowances, reverse mortgages, and other schemes need far more attention than they have yet received. Of course, policies that help to deal with transactions costs, other adjustment costs, and lack of information will be instrumental here, too.

Finally, labor market policies illustrate how poorly we recognize what is relevant from research knowledge and how poorly we use what we know. Although Theodore Shultz and Arthur Lewis were recently awarded the Nobel Prize in economics for specifying the importance of embodied human capital in the economic development of underdeveloped nations, the significance is only beginning to be recognized for local development policy in the United States. Manpower and "economic development" programs run along separate tracks, although they are truly joint products in an interactive, dynamic sense. *Any* economic enterprise creates two products: one is a product or service for sale and the other is trained labor. Investment in human resources is as much a form of investment and is as instrumental to economic development as investment in structures and equipment, so labor training can be used to build up business enterprise just as the expansion of business enterprise helps create trained labor. A strategy to link manpower and economic development programs should recognize this interaction.

CAPITAL MARKET BARRIERS

Physical investments in "bricks and mortar," equipment, inventories, and infrastructure have traditionally been a focal point of economic development policies. There is some evidence that the capital markets are less than perfect. However, the data are inadequate and the research results inconclusive. Yet, we do know enough to suggest several barriers to capital flows.

Lack of Information.   Collecting information to identify and evaluate investment opportunities in small business or distressed areas is expensive for potential lenders. The costs are highest for small projects and for projects in distressed areas where lenders have little comparable information on which to base their judgments. Because transactions costs do not rise proportionately with project size, banks naturally tend to seek large projects, where the costs will be spread over greater interest payments.

Transactions Costs.   Transactions costs constrain capital markets. While innovations in communications and institutions have significantly reduced these costs, the resulting growth in scale has increased the opportunity costs of investments in "distressed" communities, small business, old industrial plants, and other projects that have not experienced a reduction in transactions costs by proportionately as much as larger investments.

At the community level, the lack of institutional capacity to undertake loan packaging and servicing poses a constraint. A community, for instance, may lack a development corporation, or the requisite talents to plan and to identify and package investment opportunities. Preinvestment steps—information gathering and processing, risk reduction, and negotiation, among others—are costly. The question of who bears these transactions costs is one of the major issues in development finance.

Legal and Regulatory Constraints.   A variety of constraints impede flows of capital to uses that are very important developmentally, such as the financing of small business, business start-ups, and community development. This area requires a comprehensive and detailed analysis of the various laws and regulations affecting capital markets. We can do no more than point to some of the obvious constraints that exist at the state as well as the federal level.

The major constraints are banking laws, passed during the Depression, that have outlived their usefulness. The Glass-Steagal Act of 1933 has become an albatross impeding the evolution of financial institutions. It is a major impediment, for instance, to increasing the supply of venture capital for small business because it prevents commercial banks from assuming equity positions in enterprises. The McFadden Act limits competition by preventing interstate branching.

The financial institution regulatory framework, also a child of the New Deal, has not adapted to changing conditions. Arbitrary thresholds for underwriting and constraints on venture capitalists' liquidity impede the flow of capital to new enterprises. The regulatory framework goes beyond the reasonable objective of ensuring orderly markets and attempts, in addition, to protect people from themselves. Bank regulations are designed to ensure bank safety rather than the best use of capital resources for local and regional economic development.

Taxes. Our tax system significantly inhibits capital formation. A few of the major problems are:

1. The combination of corporate income tax and personal income tax on dividends favors earnings retention and debt financing over equity.
2. Depreciation allowances fail to account adequately for inflation or technological progress.
3. State and local business taxes are often not related to either profits or output.

The Results. The failure of capital markets to operate efficiently leads to a "rationing" of funds, which excludes, or at least limits, resources for certain types of projects. These include:

1. *Small Business.* Small businesses, and even some medium-sized businesses, face a persistent and serious problem of competing for capital, both debt and equity. Lack of equity capital is an especially acute problem. Venture capital is essential for the earliest stages of enterprise and new product development. There is also a lack of long-term "patient money" for established medium-sized enterprises that wish to expand.
2. *Old Industrial Plant.* There is a lack of buy-out money to finance the acquisition and renewal of old industrial plants in old industrial cities that are faced with acquisition or liquidation simply because the plants' rate of return may not be high enough for a large absentee-owner corporation.
3. *Projects in Distressed Areas.* There is a severe lack of front-end money to facilitate the initial stages of project development in distressed areas. Even more of a problem is the lack of talent and expertise (human resource capacity) to operate in "hostile economic environments" as well as risk capital.

By contrast, large corporations, in comparison to other economic units, have relatively easy and convenient access to capital for most any purpose.

What these studies suggest is that the structure of the capital market or other distortions impedes the allocation of capital to areas of investment that are critically important for economic development and that these distortions have persisted. One must distinguish between the real and the financial sides of capital markets. The latter adjust rapidly; the former—the key concern from the standpoint of development—do not. A major source of continuing disequilibrium is "imperfect competition"—the increasing concentration of assets and capital flows within large corporate networks and institutional networks restricted by regulation. Some of the observed gaps—for instance, the shortage of venture capital—may indeed be transient or cyclical. Innovations in communications networks and in financial intermediation provide a continuing impetus toward the "perfection" of financial markets, but do not remove basic sources of imperfection on the real side of the market. Government itself is a major source of distortion in capital markets.

References

Schumpeter, J. A. 1961. *The Theory of Economic Development*. New York: Oxford University Press.

Shapero, A. 1981. Entrepreneurship: Key to self-renewing economies. *Commentary* (April). Council for Urban Economic Development.

Thurow, L. C. 1981. *The Zero-Sum Society: Distribution and the Possibilities for Economic Change*. New York: Basic Books.

HARRY W. RICHARDSON

JOSEPH H. TUREK

11 *The Scope and Limits of Federal Intervention*

A Brief History of Federal Intervention

Compared with other mixed economies, *explicit*[1] regional policies in the United States have been extremely weak (some would even say nonexistent). There are obvious reasons for this: a dominant political ideology suspicious of government planning and favoring the allocation of resources by the free market; a high degree of individual mobility that enables people to respond to a lack of local opportunities by moving in search of new ones; constitutional limitations on actions benefiting some states and not others; and a political system ensuring that almost any federal program offers a share of its "goodies" to each state.

There have been only two periods in American history when explicit regional policies had any teeth. The first was in the 1930s, when the New Deal response to the Depression led to the creation of new institutions that permanently changed attitudes toward government intervention. Foremost among these institutions—from a regional policy viewpoint—was the Tennessee Valley Authority (TVA), established in 1933. The TVA, which was multisectoral in scope and multistate in areal coverage, built and operated hydroelectric plants, dams, and flood-control projects. Despite its apparent regional orientation, however, the TVA may be interpreted more as an instrument of sectoral than of spatial policy (House and Steger, 1982, p. 23). In addition to

[1] In this context, an explicit regional policy is defined as any policy or program designed to promote the economic growth and development of a specific region or group of regions.

211

promoting agricultural and industrial development in the valley, the TVA was also intended to further national defense, improve navigation, spur reforestation, provide for the proper use of marginal lands, and control flood waters (Schorr, 1975, p. 53). It is clear from this list of objectives that the TVA was not regarded solely as an instrument of regional development policy.[2]

In the 1950s the only regional policy instrument of any note was Defense Manpower Policy No. 4, intended to give preference in certain defense contracts to firms in high-unemployment areas. The impact of this program was probably not very substantial since relatively few contracts were involved, and "preferred" firms were required to match the lowest public bid (see Miernyk, 1982, p. 43). The program, which still exists, now focuses primarily on nondefense procurement by the Department of Defense and on facility location (Bolton, 1980, p. 163).

The 1960s were the second period of explicit regional development policies in the United States. The Area Redevelopment Act of 1961 established the Area Redevelopment Administration (ARA). In addition to manpower training, the ARA also provided infrastructure financing to eligible counties through loans and grants, as well as business loans. Counties with persistent unemployment could qualify for aid by preparing an Overall Economic Development Program (OEDP). These criteria were far from stringent since one-third of all the counties in the country—covering about one-fifth of the population—qualified.[3]

ARA policies had many defects. The sums available were so small that, in combination with the large number of qualifying areas, impacts were minimal. This same weakness remained under a new program also administered by the ARA, established by the Accelerated Public Works Act of 1962, which awarded public works grants of up to 75 percent of cost to high-unemployment areas. The manpower training programs of the ARA were undercut by the Manpower Development and Training Act of 1962, which made improved training programs available throughout the nation. The

[2]Historical records indicate that the regional planning function of the TVA was initially regarded as incidental. Congressional debate on the Tennessee Valley Authority Act, according to Hodge (1968, pp. 34–35), focused on the importance of power generation, fertilizer production, and flood control, almost completely ignoring the problems of regional development and planning.

[3]This extensive participation was far from accidental. In order to ensure that every state had its share of participating counties, the ARA stipulated that: "In any State where no area shall have otherwise qualified under the Act, an appropriate economic development area consisting of one or more counties may be designated (1) where the median annual income of families and unrelated individuals is lower than the median annual income in any other area with approximately the same population within the State, or (2) where the unemployment in the county or counties is most severe within the State, or (3) where the Federally-aided assistance rates are among the highest in the State" (*ARA Information Memo*, U.S. Department of Commerce, 20 July 1961).

ARA's policies failed to give special consideration to areas of high growth potential even in depressed regions and there was excessive emphasis on water and sewer systems. The ARA also failed to coordinate its projects with the states, in spite of the fact that state development programs were larger in scale.

The ARA was superseded in 1965 by two more ambitious initiatives: the Appalachian Regional Development Act (ARDA) and the Public Works and Economic Development Act (PWEDA). ARDA set up the Appalachian Regional Commission (ARC), a joint federal-state agency similar in scope and coverage to the TVA. The purpose of the ARC was to promote development in the Appalachian region, which covered all of West Virginia and parts of twelve other states from Mississippi to New York. Section two of ARDA required a concentration of public investment "in areas where there is a significant potential for future growth." Areas were classified into four levels according to the degree of development potential and, in the first five years of the commission's activities, 62 percent of investments were undertaken in level-one (i.e., highest potential) areas. There was some tendency to direct investments toward the smaller population centers, which was probably inefficient since level-one classification did not necessarily imply maximum growth potential. A high proportion of the ARC's initial allocation went into highway construction while four-fifths of supplemental funds were directed into human resource investments. Even though Appalachia received slightly more than its per capita share of federal resources in the post-ARC era (whereas before it had received considerably less), the economic impacts of ARC activities were marginal. Its political and institutional impacts were more important: strong state involvement and the demonstration that block grants could improve the effectiveness of a multisectoral planning institution.

Title V of PWEDA extended the idea of multistate regional authorities to other parts of the country. However, they were less independent than ARC and received only minor appropriations. The most important part of PWEDA was the creation of the Economic Development Administration (EDA) to assist distressed areas, defined in terms of three criteria: persistent unemployment, very low incomes, and unemployment resulting from plant closures. Eligible areas could take many forms (redevelopment area, development district, or economic development region), covering a wide range of population sizes. The criteria were so broad that eligible areas could be found in all parts of the country, an intentional result since wide congressional support was necessary for the legislation. By June 1966, eligible areas were designated in more than one-fourth of all the counties in the country; almost 70 percent of them had populations less than 25,000. Two-thirds of the areas qualified on unemployment rather than income grounds. The program included grants and loans for public works and infrastructure (three-fourths of expenditures), business loans, technical assistance, and planning support. Assistance was widely dispersed, but the Appalachian states were among the leaders in receipts. Nevertheless, California received more aid than any other state!

Because applications exceeded the financial resources available, it was necessary to develop project selection criteria. Initially, the best prepared applications tended to receive funding, which favored the relatively well-off communities. There followed an explicit shift to a "worst-first" strategy favoring the severely distressed areas. But this conflicted with efficiency and was incompatible with the growth-center concept implied by the development district. By 1968, therefore, EDA shifted its criteria to support growth centers. However, the designated growth centers were generally small and weak. Of 171 development centers designated by April 1970, only 30 had populations larger than 50,000. Three out of five were growing slower than the national average and almost two out of five suffered from population decline.

Although EDA limped on even into the life of the Reagan administration by emphasizing unemployment problems in central cities, its regional development programs withered away in the early 1970s. The Nixon administration supported the principle of federal decentralization and, as a result, a massive general revenue-sharing program was substituted for the area-specific aid programs. Since the 1960s there have been no new regional policy initiatives. The activist decade of the 1960s was a unique interlude. Moreover, even the intervention of the 1960s was weak compared with regional policies in Western Europe and Canada. The dominant strategy within the United States had been to use public funds to stimulate the private sector via infrastructure loans and grants and business loans. There had been no attempt to interfere with industrial location decisions.

Of course, intervention in regional development was less important than the other main area of explicit federal spatial policies, namely urban policy. The cities wield considerable political power in Congress, and over the years this has resulted in the adoption of a wide variety of programs to aid cities, especially central cities. There is no space here to review the full range of urban policies, so we will limit the discussion to some brief comments on a "representative" program of each recent administration.

In response to the Watts riots of 1965 and the subsequent infection of urban riots in many of the country's large cities, the Johnson administration developed a wide variety of urban programs summed up in the concepts of the "War on Poverty" and the "Great Society." The most typical of these was the Model Cities Program introduced in 1966. It aimed at harnessing public and (hopefully) private resources in a comprehensive plan to tackle the social, economic, and physical problems of ghetto areas, affecting housing, education, health and social services, income levels, employment, and job training. However, the program was largely a failure. It did not generate much construction for minority contractors; indeed, few of its resources went for economic development projects. The program was more successful in improving public services and in providing public-sector jobs, though many of these went to nonresidents of the target areas. It created a local bureaucracy that was not fully responsive to local needs and dampened local opposition by co-opting some of its more vocal and intelligent leaders. A number of these weaknesses were remedied in its successor institution, the Community Development Corporation (CDC). Some of the better-organized CDCs were more responsive to community needs and were successful in promoting a wide variety of activities and services, including job-creating private-sector productive activities. However, they vacillated between the pursuit of commercial profitability and the maximization of community benefits, and in the last analysis remained dependent on public subsidy for their viability.

The revenue-sharing program (1972) and the Community Development Block Grant (CDBG) system (1974) were the most representative programs of the Nixon and Ford administrations. Both encouraged greater local control over the allocation of resources granted by the federal government. An inevitable consequence of local autonomy, some recipient areas chose to use the grants to hold down taxes rather than to improve services or to finance programs to aid the poor. One study, for example, found that only 25.5 percent of all revenue-sharing funds went toward new spending while the remainder was used for substitutions of one form or another (Nathan et al., 1975, p. 199).[4] Despite assurances that revenue sharing was intended to supplement rather than replace existing categorical grants, its introduction was followed almost immediately by cutbacks in many of these grants. One of the more powerful arguments for revenue sharing was that it could be used as a redistributional device, helping the poor states more than the rich and core cities rather than suburbs. The use of partially offsetting allocation criteria (population, tax effort, and relative income) in combination with universal eligibility, however, tended to weaken redistributive impacts. Nevertheless, on a per capita basis, the allocation scheme did provide above-average aid to the regions of the Northeast and to central cities in general (Dommel, 1980). Redistribution between *areas*, of course, was no guarantee of a progressive redistribution between *persons*.

The CDBG system provided general purpose revenues to cities exhibiting signs of social and economic distress. CDBG consolidated a number of earlier single-purpose categorical programs administered by the Department of Housing and Urban Development. The enabling legislation allowed local officials to allocate funds in accordance with local priorities provided that benefits accrued "principally to persons of low and moderate incomes." Ini-

---

[4]These substitutions included restoration of federal aid, tax reduction, tax stabilization, program maintenance, avoidance of borrowing, and increased fund balance (Nathan et al., 1975, p. 199).

tially, the distribution formula included population, poverty, and over-crowded housing. A second formula was added in 1977, this one based on poverty, population change, and age of housing stock. Funding levels were calculated under both formulas, and the city received the larger of the two amounts. The dual formula allocation scheme, which increased CDBG sensitivity to the physical and fiscal dimensions of economic distress, shifted funding patterns in favor of the older declining cities of the Frostbelt. Relative to the displaced categorical grants, however, the share of funds going to metropolitan cities in the Northeast and North Central regions still declined by 6.5 percentage points (Bunce and Glickman, 1980, p. 520).

The most representative program of the Carter administration was the Urban Development Action Grant (UDAG) program introduced in 1977. The basic principle underlying UDAG was that of "leverage"; minimal public grants were used to stimulate private enterprise in urban areas that met certain criteria, primarily relating to poor economic performance. The program was focused on distressed central cities, but as usual the eligibility criteria had to be defined broadly enough for the program to be national in scope. As a result, there was no special geographical concentration on the older industrial cities of the Northeast and the Midwest. The sums available for the program were quite small, and best-prepared applications tended to be funded. In effect, the program offered rewards for "grantmanship." Little effort was made to evaluate the accuracy of the anticipated private sector investments and job creations specified in the grant applications. Moreover, there is a suspicion that many of the grants went to support projects that would have been undertaken in any event, and there was no attempt to direct funds toward key sectors. Nevertheless, the principle of "leverage" is potentially very important in an era of fiscal austerity.

Any review of the federal government's explicit spatial policies cannot avoid the conclusion that their impacts were minimal. Two main reasons account for this result. First, expenditures on explicit spatial policies have been dwarfed by expenditures on macro and sectoral policies that have much stronger implicit spatial impacts. Second, the nature of the political system in the United States weakens the geographical bias of explicit spatial policies since all regions and all states want their share of any new program that is introduced. This is an inevitable price to be paid for the benefits of a pluralist political system.

As a result of these considerations, we must conclude that the Northeast has not benefited substantially from federal regional and urban policies over the last two decades. Although parts of New York and Pennsylvania were within ARC's boundary, most of the expenditures were made in more distressed parts of the Appalachian region. The New England Regional Commission established under PWEDA had hardly begun business when the steam ran out of the regional policy initiatives. As for urban policies, the cities of the Northeast have not received much more assistance than the cities of other regions. The distress and need criteria were applied only *within* the boundaries of eligible areas, so that qualified central cities located in rapidly growing metropolitan areas in rapidly growing states were considered as eligible as cities in stagnating or declining metropolitan areas in slow-growing states. Thus, cities in states such as California and Texas were major beneficiaries of recent urban programs. Furthermore, deteriorating economic performance and population losses in the Northeast (and Midwest) during the 1970s were not fully reflected in the allocation of federal resources under the urban programs of that decade since the data available for measuring need, distress, and other eligibility criteria were outdated (often relating to the 1970 census). Although the "community and regional development" category in Table 11.2 below is a poor proxy for regional and urban policies, it may be noted that the concentration ratios for the two Northeast regions were lower (0.85 for New England and 0.87 for Middle Atlantic) than for any other region except the East North Central. The trouble is that the problems of the Northeast are related to slow growth (output, income, and population) rather than high unemployment and low incomes, but most of the explicit spatial programs rely heavily on unemployment, income, and other level indicators rather than measures of growth performance to determine eligibility criteria. In general, the Northeast is a nominally high-income region with unemployment rates close to the national average, and hence cannot be expected to benefit disproportionately from programs targeted to low-income and high-unemployment areas.

The Spatial Impacts of Federal Government Activities

As previously argued, explicit *spatial* policies have minimal impact in influencing the growth performance of different areas (regions, cities) because expenditures on such programs that exist are relatively small and because the political necessity to disperse expenditures among all the states dilutes their potential effects. There are explicit nonspatial policies that are targeted toward particular groups of people or to particular sectors. The former includes items such as social security payments, food stamps, housing subsidies, and welfare; the latter includes categories such as agricultural price supports, energy policies, and transport subsidies. These explicit policies may have implicit spatial impacts[5] that are very uneven because the target groups/sectors

---

[5] All policies have both explicit and implicit impacts, the former generally being intended and the latter unintended. The designation of a policy outcome as explicit or implicit depends, to a large extent, on one's point of view. An explicit regional policy, for example, may alter a region's distribution of income, and thus have an implicit impact that varies across income classes. Conversely, an explicit policy of income redistribution (e.g., a progressive personal income tax) may have an implicit impact on regions by diverting income from rich regions to poor ones.

are not uniformly distributed over space. Thus, the West North Central agricultural states gain most from agricultural subsidies; Florida's retirement population makes that state a massive recipient of social security payments; the energy-plus states such as Texas, Louisiana, Alaska, and Wyoming gain most from incentives to energy resource exploitation; and the nation's central cities receive the highest per capita inflows of welfare payments. These examples could be multiplied many times; Vaughan (1980) and Glickman (1980) present a comprehensive discussion.

In addition, there are many federal policies, most of them macroeconomic, that are intended to be applied uniformly over the country as a whole, but which result in strong implicit spatial impacts that are far from geographically neutral. For example, the regions with the most cyclically sensitive industrial structures—especially the East North Central region (Howland, 1979)—should derive the most benefit from macroeconomic stabilization policy.[6] However, the benefits of stabilization measures are not confined to cyclically unstable regions, since in their absence instability would be transmitted through the system via fluctuations in interregional trade and property income. Or to consider another illustration, monetary policy probably affects consumer durables production more than domestic business investment (because investment expenditures may be financed by retained earnings, transfers from foreign subsidiaries, and Euro-dollar borrowing) so that regions are affected differentially according to the weight of consumer durables production in their economic structures. The "crowding out" of private sector borrowing by federal government borrowing to finance budget deficits will have regionally discriminatory impacts if the interest elasticity of demand differs by industry and industry mix varies from one region to another. "Crowding out" could also affect borrowing by state and local governments, the degree of which may vary with the level of fiscal distress.

Another important point is that many of the implicit spatial impacts of macro and sectoral policies are not direct first-order effects but are second- or higher-order effects (induced impacts). These induced impacts may be the most important of all in some cases, yet they could easily be missed in a superficial analysis of the most immediate implicit spatial impacts. For example, the progressivity of the Federal Tax Code means that high-income and high-profit regions contribute more to federal tax revenues than their population share. But this effect may be swamped by the indirect effects of tax benefits that favor construction of new housing over rehabilitation and stimulate new investment in plant and equipment rather than refurbishing existing industrial capital (Peterson, 1980). There is widespread agreement that

---

[6]This argument applies best when fiscal policy is the dominant stabilization instrument. It is much less clear when monetary policy dominates. For example, during the 1981–82 recession, the high interest rates aimed at stabilizing prices had a devastating impact on the automobile industry and the East North Central region.

federal tax policies have had the unintended effects of promoting suburban development and undermining central cities, and of stimulating the growth of the Sunbelt and accelerating the industrial obsolescence of the Frostbelt. Similarly, with defense spending the regional allocation of prime contracts may be very different from the overall regional impact. Many federal defense dollars migrate across regional boundaries via interregional subcontracting. In addition, a heavy reliance on federal defense contracts may have significant impacts on a region's economy in the form of linkages between defense suppliers and other firms in the area's industrial structure, local multiplier effects, and cyclical sensitivity (Rees, 1981).

The analysis that follows is based on the direct regional impacts of federal spending and taxes. The above observations serve to remind us that these data will not capture the *total* spatial impact of federal activity.

The regional distribution of the overall activities of the federal government is summarized in Tables 11.1 and 11.2. These tables employ the concept of a "concentration ratio," which is calculated by dividing a region's share in federal taxes (total spending or individual expenditure category) by its share in the United States population. Thus, a tax concentration ratio greater than unity means that a region contributes more federal taxes than might be expected in terms of its population, while an expenditure concentration ratio greater than unity means that it receives more than its per capita share of that expenditure category.

The aggregate picture is presented in Table 11.1.[7] The tax column shows that the East North Central and Pacific regions contribute most to taxes, whereas the three regions of the South contribute least. The two Northeast regions also contribute more than their population share. These results are not surprising. Since the federal tax structure is progressive, high-income regions will contribute more to federal tax revenues than low-income regions.

Turning to total federal spending, the South Atlantic and the Pacific regions receive much more than might be expected on the basis of their populations, while the East North Central and West South Central regions receive significantly less. As for the Northeast, New England receives more than its population share while the Middle Atlantic receives less. There are many reasons for these differences, including the incidence of poverty, whether a region's industrial structure is biased in favor of subsidized industries, the willingness of states within a region to fulfill the matching requirements of federal grants, and many others. However, one of the largest federal expenditure categories, which is very unequally distributed geographically, is national defense. Regional concentration ratios for total nondefense spending

[7]Although the data of Tables 11.1 through 11.4 pertain to only one year (1980), construction of similar tables for other years showed that while year-to-year concentration ratios might change slightly, the overall ranking, dispersions around unity, and their interpretation remain the same.

TABLE 11.1
Regional Concentration Ratios* and Spending/Tax Shares for Federal Taxes and Spending, 1980

Region	Taxes	Total Spending	Nondefense Spending	Total Spending/Tax Share	Nondefense Spending/ Tax Share
New England	1.04	1.11	0.99	1.07	0.95
Middle Atlantic	1.09	0.95	1.04	0.87	0.95
East North Central	1.10	0.79	0.92	0.72	0.83
West North Central	0.99	0.99	1.03	1.00	1.04
South Atlantic	0.89	1.20	1.16	1.35	1.30
East South Central	0.75	0.97	1.05	1.29	1.40
West South Central	0.91	0.88	0.83	0.97	0.91
Mountain	0.89	1.04	1.01	1.17	1.13
Pacific	1.10	1.14	0.99	1.04	0.89

*Concentration ratios are measured by dividing the region's share of federal taxes (expenditures) by its share of national population.
Sources: Community Services Administration, *Geographic Distribution of Federal Funds in Summary: A Report of the Federal Government's Impact by State, County and Large City* (Washington, D.C.: Community Services Administration, 1980). Tax Foundation, *Facts and Figures on Government Finance* (Washington, D.C.: Tax Foundation, Inc., 1981), table 122.

are closer together than for total spending. Also, ranks change somewhat though the South Atlantic continues to lead the way in per capita receipts while the East North Central and the West South Central remain the chief laggards (though with bottom position reversed). However, an interesting result is that several regions cross over from above-average to below-average recipients (and vice versa) when defense spending is excluded. For instance, the New England and Pacific regions change from being leading beneficiaries to receiving slightly less than their population share. Conversely, the Middle Atlantic and East South Central regions (and much more modestly, the West North Central region) jump in the other direction.

The net effect of federal government activity is most easily seen by comparing a region's shares of spending and taxes. The final columns of Table 11.1 display the ratio of spending to tax share for total spending and for all nondefense spending. These ratios show that the South Atlantic and East South Central regions are the chief "gainers" from the net impact of the federal government, regardless of whether or not defense is excluded. The Mountain region is also a significant "gainer." The biggest "loser" is the East North Central region, especially because it benefits so little from defense allocations. The Middle Atlantic and West South Central regions are also net "losers." The West North Central region comes the closest to the case where the federal government's net impact is neutral. The New England and Pacific regions are particularly interesting in that they are net "gainers" only because of defense spending. Without defense, they contribute more in taxes than they receive in expenditures.

TABLE 11.2
Regional Concentration Ratios for Selected Federal Spending Categories, 1980

Region	Income Security	Defense	Health	Education, Employment, Training, & Social Services	Veterans' Benefits	Commerce & Housing Credits	Transportation	Natural Resources & Environment	Agriculture	Community & Regional Development	General Government	Energy	General Purpose Fiscal Assistance	Science & Technology
New England	1.01	1.49	1.20	1.04	1.09	1.04	1.02	0.56	0.18	0.85	0.71	0.38	1.04	0.75
Middle Atlantic	1.11	0.67	1.16	1.02	0.86	1.14	1.02	0.63	0.43	0.87	0.85	0.48	1.10	0.43
East North Central	0.95	0.44	1.12	0.84	0.79	1.10	0.61	0.52	0.57	0.69	0.59	0.73	0.90	0.36
West North Central	0.93	0.86	0.93	0.84	1.00	1.05	0.84	0.68	4.83	1.01	0.89	0.17	0.89	0.12
South Atlantic	1.11	1.33	1.06	1.17	1.22	1.08	1.55	1.05	0.69	0.99	2.01	0.88	0.85	1.31
East South Central	0.97	0.72	0.78	1.03	1.11	0.68	0.68	3.26	0.57	1.18	0.62	1.62	0.94	0.65
West South Central	0.82	1.02	0.73	0.83	1.10	0.79	0.83	0.50	1.26	1.14	0.57	0.64	0.80	1.00
Mountain	0.84	1.12	0.64	1.08	1.08	0.86	1.02	2.36	1.42	1.96	0.90	2.24	1.04	1.08
Pacific	0.91	1.63	0.95	0.97	0.92	0.89	1.05	1.05	0.64	0.91	0.86	1.63	1.01	2.76

Source: Community Services Administration, *Geographic Distribution of Federal Funds in Summary: A Report of the Federal Government's Impact by State, County and Large City* (Washington, D.C.: Community Services Administration, 1980).

The differential impacts according to whether or not defense is included suggests the possibility that regional concentration ratios may vary widely among federal spending categories. The experience with respect to defense can be generalized to all categories of spending as shown by the specific spending concentration ratios of Table 11.2. These data imply that the aggregate spending ratios even out much wider differentials within individual spending categories. All regions have a mix of above- and below-unity concentration ratios. Even the disfavored East North Central region receives an above-average allocation of health and commerce spending, while the South Atlantic region—the leading beneficiary of federal spending—receives little agricultural support and a below-average share of energy expenditures. The widest differentials are found in defense, and these are important since defense accounts for about one-fourth of total federal spending (the only larger spending category—income security, which accounts for one-third of the total—is more evenly distributed; see Table 11.3). The Pacific, New England, and South Atlantic regions receive most from defense spending while the East North Central, Middle Atlantic, and East South Central regions receive much smaller shares than might be expected on the basis of population size. Agriculture is also an unevenly distributed category with the West North Central region a massive gainer, and the Mountain and West South Central regions also having high concentration ratios. Its overall impact, however, is much smaller because its size in the total federal budget is much more modest than defense (Table 11.3). Energy, natural resources and environment, and science and technology are equally widely dispersed but are also small in volume (accounting for a total of 6 percent of federal spending; see Table 11.3). In all these sectors, the Northeast and North Central regions receive relatively little while the East South Central, Mountain, and Pacific regions are the major beneficiaries. The South Atlantic region receives a disproportionate share of federal spending on transportation (a temporary phenomenon resulting from subsidies to mass transit in Washington, D.C. and Atlanta) and general government (the burden of the Federal government administration itself). Other categories are more evenly distributed (though the Mountain region has a low concentration ratio for health and the East North Central region has a low ratio for community and regional development), probably because they tend to be allocated according to the distribution of population.

We decided to keep the analysis at the level of regional aggregates, largely for the sake of conciseness. However, as Table 11.4 suggests, regional averages mask wide variations among individual states. Within the Northeast region, Connecticut and Massachusetts receive the highest per capita shares in federal spending while New Jersey and Vermont receive the lowest. The interstate differentials are much wider for individual items of expenditure. For example, Connecticut receives a disproportionately high share of defense

TABLE 11.3
Functional Shares in Federal Spending, 1980

Function	Percent
Income security	33.2
Defense	24.6
Health	11.3
Education, training, employment, and social security	5.3
Veterans' benefits	4.2
Commerce and housing credit	4.1
Transportation	3.9
Natural resources and environment	3.4
Agriculture	2.0
Community and regional development	1.7
General government	1.4
Energy	1.4
General purpose fiscal assistance	1.4
Science, space, and technology	1.2
Administration of justice	0.5
International affairs	0.3
Interest	0.1
Total	100.0

Source: Community Services Administration, *Geographic Distribution of Federal Funds in Summary: A Report of the Federal Government's Impact by State, County and Large City* (Washington, D.C.: Community Services Administration, 1980).

spending while Vermont receives very little. Rhode Island is the chief beneficiary of federal spending on transportation while Massachusetts and New York are the primary recipients of health expenditures. None of the Northeast states fare well with respect to energy, natural resources and environment, and community and regional development outlays.

It is very important to stress that the use of terms such as *disproportionate*, *gainers*, and *losers* in the preceding discussion is not intended to have normative significance. The notion of a *fair share* in federal government activity does not make much sense. For example, if we accept the general principle of progressivity in the tax structure, it automatically follows that we should welcome the fact that high-income states (regions) will have above-average tax concentration ratios and hence are more likely to be net losers from federal government activity. Similarly, on the expenditure side it can hardly be expected that sector-specific categories such as defense and agricultural support could be distributed evenly over states or any other geographical areas. Although allocations in these sectors undoubtedly reflect a degree of political influence (e.g., senators protective of agricultural subsidy programs that benefit their states or of the continuity of defense contracts to local firms), the main reason for their geographical unevenness is simply that some areas

TABLE 11.4
Northeast States Concentration Ratios for Selected Federal Spending Categories

State	Total Spending	Income Security	Defense	Health	Education, Employment, Training, & Social Services	Veterans' Benefits	Commerce & Housing Credits	Transportation	Natural Resources & Environment	Agriculture	Community & Regional Development	General Government	Energy	General Purpose Fiscal Assistance	Science & Technology
Maine	1.01	1.01	1.01	1.01	1.21	1.41	1.01	0.81	0.60	0.20	1.01	0.40	0.00	1.21	0.00
New Hampshire	0.98	0.98	1.23	0.74	0.74	0.98	0.74	0.98	0.75	0.25	0.74	0.25	0.25	0.74	0.25
Vermont	0.89	0.89	0.44	0.89	1.33	1.33	1.33	0.89	0.88	0.44	0.89	0.44	0.00	1.33	0.00
Massachusetts	1.14	1.03	1.34	1.42	1.11	1.23	1.15	1.26	0.52	0.16	0.95	1.07	0.56	1.14	0.92
Rhode Island	0.96	1.20	0.96	1.20	1.20	1.20	0.96	1.72	0.48	0.00	0.72	0.48	0.24	0.96	0.48
Connecticut	1.24	0.95	2.40	1.02	0.80	0.73	0.95	0.80	0.59	0.22	0.73	0.44	0.37	0.87	1.10
New York	0.99	1.12	0.68	1.35	1.12	0.90	1.23	1.03	0.75	0.74	0.92	0.93	0.29	1.33	0.51
New Jersey	0.83	1.02	0.65	0.89	0.92	0.68	1.23	0.80	0.49	0.06	0.68	0.80	0.92	0.95	0.31
Pennsylvania	0.92	1.15	0.65	1.03	0.94	0.90	0.95	1.13	0.53	0.19	0.92	0.76	0.47	0.86	0.40

Source: Community Services Administration, *Geographic Distribution of Federal Funds in Summary: A Report of the Federal Government's Impact by State, County and Large City* (Washington, D.C.: Community Services Administration, 1980).

224

have comparative cost advantages in their production. Thus, there are no grounds for compensating states that receive few benefits from defense (or any other sector-specific) spending with above-average expenditures in other categories: "The difficulty with justifying transfers to states on the grounds that they are not receiving their fair share of defense expenditures is that there is no meaning to fair shares in defense spending any more than there is a meaning to fair share of automobile production or wheat production" (Mieszkowski, 1979, p. 33).

To sum up the above analysis from the point of view of the Northeast, New England is a modest net gainer from the *direct* effects of federal government activity while the Middle Atlantic region is a modest net loser. Both regions have above-average tax concentration ratios, reflecting their above-average per capita money income levels. New England is a net beneficiary only because it receives a high share of defense spending, while a low share of defense spending is the sole reason why the Middle Atlantic region receives a smaller proportion of total federal spending than its population share might suggest. Both regions receive very little agricultural support, have few federal government offices, and do not benefit much from federal spending on energy, natural resources, and science and technology. On the other hand, they rank highest in federal health expenditures. They benefit substantially from spending in the income security category but receive a low share of community and regional development outlays. In other spending categories, their shares are close to their population shares. As a whole, the Northeast is a modest "deficit" region in terms of federal government activity, because as a high-money-income region it contributes more to federal tax revenues (Table 11.5). It is not the result of the Northeast being discriminated against in federal spending.

Subsidies to Industry?

Almost all attempts to promote regional development—whether in the form of aid to businesses, individuals, or governments—have a substantial fiscal cost. Since there has been little interest in regional development policies over the last decade and a half, it would be surprising if interest was revived now in the current climate of fiscal austerity. There is little enthusiasm, even outside the Republican party, for embarking on major new federal programs. There is a technical solution available for resolving this dilemma, but it may not be practical in the United States context because of constitutional limitations. This is the adoption of a self-financing scheme where subsidies to some firms are financed out of taxes on other firms at zero fiscal cost. In countries without constitutional constraints the most obvious approach would be to tax firms in prosperous, rapidly growing areas to subsidize firms in lagging, stagnant regions. However, if this involved massive

TABLE 11.5
Regional Concentration Ratios for Federal Taxes and Spending

Region	Taxes	Total Spending	Non-Defense Spending	Health Spending	Spending/ Tax Share	Non-Defense Spending/ Tax Share
Northeast	1.08	0.99	1.04	1.17	0.92	0.96
North Central	1.07	0.85	0.97	1.06	0.79	0.91
South	0.87	1.05	1.03	0.90	1.21	1.18
West	1.05	1.12	1.00	0.87	1.07	0.95

Source: Community Services Administration, *Geographic Distribution of Federal Funds in Summary: A Report of the Federal Government's Impact by State, County and Large City* (Washington, D.C.: Community Services Administration, 1980).

transfers out of some states into others it is doubtful whether such a policy would be constitutional, and it certainly would not be politically feasible.[8] Transfers within states from prosperous to depressed areas would be more practicable, but these would do little to lift the economic performance of below-average states toward the national average. Another possibility might be to impose taxes on one sector to finance subsidies in another. For example, a windfall profits tax on oil and gas production, or some other major revenue source, might be used to build an industrial development fund to aid industrial expansion in depressed areas. This particular proposal has some appeal because it would involve net transfers from "energy-rich" to "energy-poor" areas, which might be appropriate if energy resource exploitation is considered to be a major reason why some parts of the country are growing much faster than others (see Chapter 6). On the other hand, such a step would raise expediency above Pareto efficiency, though perhaps policymakers can ill afford to be economic purists.

Migration Subsidies

An old idea, recently revived in the policy recommendations of the McGill Commission—an advisory commission for Carter's nonexistent second term—is to subsidize migration from stagnant to rapidly growing regions. These subsidies could be direct, such as monetary assistance to migrants to cover travel costs, initial housing expenses, and other "settling-in" costs, or indirect, such as education and retraining subsidies as a mechanism to increase the propensity and capacity to migrate or subsidies to firms that employ mi-

[8] Article I, Section 10 of the Constitution forbids states to enter into agreements with each other, though this could be relaxed with congressional approval. State taxes can be struck down if they conflict with Article IV, Section 2: "That Citizens of each State shall be entitled to all Privileges and Immunities of Citizens in the several States."

grant labor. The rationale for migration subsidies to overcome barriers to mobility is simple and obvious. The movement of labor from stagnant to growing regions will help to equilibrate local markets by creating better balance between regional labor supplies and employment opportunities. National output will be increased either as the result of a higher level of aggregate employment or because labor is transferred from low- to high-productivity industries. Wage growth will be dampened in destination regions while the major problems of stagnant regions, higher unemployment rates and low incomes, will be alleviated.

However, the real world is not as simple as the theoretical arguments suggest. Although some rapidly growing states (e.g., Texas) have unemployment rates well below the national average, the equation of stagnation with low incomes and very high unemployment is very blurred in Frostbelt areas. Much of the unemployment in the older manufacturing cities is cyclical, and unemployed workers—especially in highly paid skilled occupations—may prefer to wait around for the end of the recession rather than risk moving to join the less-skilled labor pools of southern and western cities. Also, it is not at all clear that current migration rates from the Frostbelt to the Sunbelt are suboptimal. Once again, we face the question of whether income paths will approach a stable equilibrium or cross over. If the latter hypothesis is valid, accelerating migration now might increase interregional inequities in the future.

Another set of problems relates to conditions in the destination regions. Several Sunbelt cities (Phoenix, Houston, San Diego, El Paso, and San Jose may be examples) are growing so fast that they are experiencing problems with absorption capacity. These difficulties show up in tight rental markets for housing, lags in public service provision, deteriorating environmental conditions, the growth of concentrated poverty pockets, symptoms of emerging fiscal stress, and even in rising unemployment. Many Sunbelt cities, in fact, rank as high on a "hardship scale" as the Frostbelt cities.[9] A recent evaluation of American cities listed many of the large Sunbelt cities as among the least desirable places to live because of such considerations as high housing costs, poor public services, and inferior environmental quality (Boyer and Savageau, 1981). Such conditions would only be exacerbated by a higher rate of in-migration.

Perhaps the most critical objection to a migration subsidy strategy is that it would be politically unacceptable to both the sending and the receiving regions. Politicians in the sending regions (e.g., New York State) are already concerned about population loss because it is translated directly into diminished political power through the consequent reduction in the number of congressional seats. At the more local level, a higher rate of out-migration could

[9]See J. A. Johnson's "The Sun Belt and the Frost Belt," *New York Times*, 29 Dec. 1981.

be translated into a smaller tax base and a rising per capita burden, downward multiplier effects on local service industries, and lost human capital investments, although out-migration streams may not be spatially concentrated enough for these effects to be noticeable. More in-migrants may not be welcome in the sending regions because of the above-mentioned social effects, strains on the capacity of the public service sector, risks of a greater welfare burden, and the spread of "growth-management" philosophies. At the national level, the appeal of this type of policy is much greater in conditions approximating full employment where migration subsidies could be targeted at scattered pockets of the unemployed. Under the economic conditions prevailing in recent years, such subsidies may merely be a device for reshuffling the unemployed.

The "New Federalism"

The "New Federalism" plan, as outlined in President Reagan's 1982 State of the Union address, proposed a dramatic restructuring of intergovernmental relations. Its underlying principle is the devolution of administrative discretion and political responsibility from the federal government to the various state governments. Reagan argued that shifting control of federal programs to the states would cut costs by reducing the paperwork associated with regulations and compliance monitoring, improve benefit targeting by increasing state flexibility to cater to particular local problems, and promote greater political accountability. Philosophically, this realignment of authority is justified by the belief that the federal government has become overly intrusive and bureaucratic, and that state governments are more responsive to voter demands and more likely to select programs that reflect voter preferences. This idea is implicit in Reagan's (1982) comment that ". . .a problem in one part of the country does not automatically mean that we need a new federal program in all fifty states."

The first phase of Reagan's federalism reform program was actually implemented prior to the formal public announcement of New Federalism. Tax relief, an integral part of the president's economic recovery package, was made possible by the 1981 Omnibus Budget Reconciliation Act, which slashed approximately $35.2 billion from projected fiscal year 1982 spending levels. The act established more restrictive income-eligibility standards for food stamps and public assistance, cut federal Medicaid payments to the states, reduced funding for subsidized housing, and consolidated fifty-seven categorical programs into nine block grants.[10] A better feel for the magnitude

[10]The nine block grants included: Maternal and Child Health Care Services, Preventive Health and Health Services, Alcohol and Drug Abuse and Mental Health Services, Primary Care, Social Services, Low-income Energy Assistance, Community Services, Community Development for Small Cities, and Elementary and Secondary Education.

of these cuts is provided by the following statistics: 687,000 households lost all or part of their Aid to Families with Dependent Children (AFDC) benefits, 1.1 million people were cut off from food stamps, 1.5 million people lost extended unemployment benefits, and 900,000 public service jobs were eliminated (Donnelly, 1981, pp. 461–62). Despite an administration promise to protect the "truly needy" by strengthening the "social safety net," there is ample evidence to suggest that the poor—and especially the working poor—bore the brunt of these cutbacks (Center for the Study of Social Policy, 1983). The purpose of federal income security outlays, as conceived by the Reagan administration, is to support *impoverished* individuals (those below the poverty level) and not to supplement the earnings of the employed with incomes above the poverty level.

The Reagan philosophy in general and the budget cuts in particular placed state and local officials in an uncomfortable position. The social welfare function of government had traditionally been performed at the federal level. Interstate differentials in fiscal capacity, a highly mobile population, the greater resources of the federal government, and the fact that poverty levels fluctuate directly with the level of aggregate economic activity provide the practical and theoretical justifications for this tradition. Reagan's reforms not only thrust part of this responsibility onto state governments, but also diminished the amount of monies provided to meet their needs. States had to choose between raising their own revenues through tax increases or accepting the program cuts. The fact that the nation was entering one of the deepest postwar recessions and that unemployment was on the rise served only to make matters worse. A recent study found that a large majority of states surveyed replaced less than 10 percent of lost federal revenues and concluded that, overall, ". . . most states were unable or unwilling to maintain service levels in the face of Federal cuts."[11] Reagan's budget cuts affected different regions differently. According to Muller (1982, p. 448), per capita reductions exceeded the national average in *every* Frostbelt region and were below it in *every* Sunbelt region. The West North Central and Middle Atlantic regions lost the most while the West South Central and South Atlantic regions lost the least.

Phase II, the centerpiece of New Federalism, consisted of two parts: a swap and a turnback. First, the federal government would take over the states' share of Medicaid costs beginning in fiscal year 1984 while the states would assume full financial responsibility for AFDC and food stamps. Second, the federal government would transfer to the states forty-three programs in education, transportation, social services, and community development, currently financed by categorical grants-in-aid. Using revenues from certain

[11]See J. Herber's "Study Tells How Fourteen States Responded to Aid Cuts," *New York Times*, 8 May 1983, p. 18.

excise taxes, the federal government would create a $28 billion trust fund for the states. During the turnback transition period, 1984 to 1987, these funds could be used to continue any or all of the transferred categorical programs or to finance new programs and forgo the old ones. The trust fund would be distributed to the states according to their 1979–81 funding shares in the forty-three displaced programs. Any state losing revenues as a result of the Medicaid–AFDC/food stamp swap would receive additional funds as compensation. The trust fund would be gradually phased out between 1988 and 1991, after which time the states would have to rely on their own resources to finance these programs.

The objections to New Federalism were numerous. In the past, federal control of programs ensured that minimum levels of provision were attained, especially for social programs targeted at low-income groups. Liberals feared that the plan would allow state governments to cut or eliminate some of these programs, either for ideological reasons or because maintenance would require tax increases. The experience of the 1981 block grants and funding cuts suggests that if states were free to choose, their responses would vary widely.[12] Where fiscal conservatives dominate the state legislature and the governor's mansion, program cuts are likely to be more popular. In states with a strong tradition of liberal social welfare policies, attempts would probably be made to maintain programs close to current levels and seek new—or increase existing—revenue sources.

The question of "replacement" was particularly important with respect to the categorical (turnback) programs because the size of the trust fund was smaller than the expected fiscal 1984 cost of providing these programs ($30.2 billion). Governors of less-wealthy states expressed concern over the absence of a mechanism to equalize interstate fiscal disparities after the trust fund expired. City officials felt that the "pass-through" provisions were insufficient to guarantee the continuation of existing spending patterns; this anxiety was probably heightened by the fact that states shifted money from large cities to smaller communities and rural areas after the federal budget cuts of 1981.

Having tightened the eligibility requirements for food stamps and AFDC in 1981, the Reagan administration in 1982 sought to divest itself of the programs completely. The swap, according to the administration, would be fiscally advantageous to the states because Medicaid was more expensive than the combined cost of AFDC and food stamps (in terms of state cost shares, $19.1 billion versus $16.5 billion) and also because Medicaid costs rise more rapidly than AFDC and food stamp costs. As a result of the com-

---

[12]One set of calculations suggests that New Federalism Phase II would require the states to raise taxes by 8.8 percent on average (the range is 3.1 percent in Alaska to 20.5 percent in New Hampshire), cut programs by about 30 percent, or some combination of both (Senator D. P. Moynihan, *New York Times*, 7 Feb. 1982).

pensating payments mechanism, the swap itself was redistributively neutral with respect to states—at least during the transition period. It did, however, discriminate against Medicaid recipients living in states with liberal program benefits. This is because a single national standard for Medicaid assistance would probably be lower (higher) than the pre-swap standards in liberal (restrictive) states, resulting in lower (higher) benefits or fewer (more) recipients. Most governors felt that all three programs should be administered by the federal government, once again raising the issue of jurisdictional responsibility for public welare and income redistribution. The complexity of the plan and wide-ranging criticism eventually compelled the administration to discontinue negotiations, and no legislation was ever sent to Congress.

In February of 1983, more than a year later, New Federalism was resurrected. The revised plan made no mention of a swap, but called for the consolidation of thirty-four programs into four "megablock" grants: an $11 billion grant to states, replacing twenty-two existing education, health, social services, and community development grants; a $2 billion grant to states, combining six previous ground transportation programs; an $850 million rural housing grant to states, replacing four categorical programs; and a $7 billion grant to cities and counties, merging general revenue sharing and the entitlement component of CDBGs (for details, see Granat, 1983). The federal government would fund these blocks through fiscal year 1988 at constant 1984 spending levels. Within blocks, states and localities would have virtually unlimited freedom to allocate the money among the supplanted programs. At the end of five years, states would assume full responsibility for both the administration and financing of these activities. Federal revenue sources—primarily excise taxes—would be turned over to the states at that time in order to help defray additional costs.

The major complaint came from mayors of large cities, who feared that if community development grants were merged with unrestricted revenue sharing funds, they would be diverted from their intended low-income clientele. Even with federal excise taxes at their disposal, states are likely to face revenue shortfalls. The closer proximity between voters and state officials may weaken the political resolve to raise taxes or even to maintain them at the levels previously set by the federal government. With federal funding for food stamps and AFDC scheduled to fall by 9 percent and 8.5 percent, respectively, in fiscal year 1984, states will again have to grapple with the question of replacement spending.

The capacity of the states to maintain the transferred programs may depend upon their current level of taxes. States with low taxes (measured either in per capita terms or as a percentage of personal income) would find it easier to finance the programs either by raising current tax rates or perhaps by introducing new taxes. For example, a large number of states have no income tax, while others have very high income tax rates.[13] The energy-surplus states obtain a substantial proportion of their revenues from severance taxes (Cochran and Prestidge 1981), giving them a revenue flexibility that other states lack. Table 11.6 presents state and local tax revenues in absolute amounts, as shares of personal income, and on a per capita basis. The data show wide variations among states. Excluding the special case of Alaska, New York and the District of Columbia have the highest per capita taxes, and three other states (Wyoming, Hawaii, and Massachusetts) have per capita taxes above $1,200. At the other extreme, four states (Mississippi, Alabama, Arkansas, and Tennessee) have per capita taxes below $700. However, low taxes in these states reflect low incomes as much as potential for raising taxes. New Hampshire, Florida, Indiana, Missouri, and Texas also have low per capita taxes but rank lowest on the more significant measure of share of taxes in personal income. Of course, there is a difference between capacity to raise taxes and willingness to raise them. Many of the low-tax states are fiscally conservative with a poor record for supporting social programs.

From the point of view of this book, the interesting question is: what would be the impact of New Federalism on the Northeast relative to the other regions? Parenthetically, we should point out that *if* and when New Federalism is implemented, its resemblance to the revised Phase II proposal may be quite distant.[14] The essence of Reagan's federalism reform plan is devolution: more state discretion and less federal intervention. Viewed in this light, it is easy to see that the relative distribution of regional impacts will depend on the nature of the spending cuts and the type of taxes that are reduced.

One very important point to keep in mind is that the Reagan program *as a whole* has moved the federal budget in the direction of defense spending and away from social spending. As seen in Table 11.5, per capita nondefense spending shares exceed per capita total spending shares in both the Northeast and North Central regions. The reverse is true for the regions of the South and West. Consequently, federal budgetary outlays have shifted from the Frostbelt to the Sunbelt. The benefits of tax reduction, on the other hand, tend to accrue primarily to the Frostbelt regions although the West follows very closely behind (see Tables 11.1 and 11.5). According to Muller (1982, p. 454), ". . . the Sunbelt will receive close to two-thirds of the total net flow resulting from policy shifts of the Reagan administration."[15]

---

[13]For instance, the maximum marginal rate of income tax in New York is 14 percent (the average rate on personal service income is 10 percent) while in California it is 11 percent.

[14]Significantly, President Reagan made no mention of New Federalism in his 1984 State of the Union address.

[15]Muller's data indicate that, even in the absence of defense expansion, the Sunbelt is favored over the Frostbelt. According to the data, this is the result of greater tax reductions in the Sunbelt rather than of larger spending cuts in the Frostbelt.

TABLE 11.6
State and Local Tax Revenues, 1980*

State	Taxes ($)	Percent of Personal Income	Per Capita $	State	Taxes ($)	Percent of Personal Income	Per Capita $
Alabama	2,528.4	8.7	649.97	Montana	786.8	11.7	999.69
Alaska	1,675.5	32.6	4,188.75	Nebraska	1,512.3	10.3	963.25
Arizona	2,738.2	11.4	1,007.42	Nevada	776.8	9.0	972.17
Arkansas	1,495.3	9.0	654.36	New Hampshire	681.5	8.1	739.98
California	27,745.5	10.7	1,172.23	New Jersey	8,376.5	10.4	1,137.49
Colorado	2,859.2	9.8	989.70	New Mexico	1,143.0	11.2	879.24
Connecticut	3,326.4	9.1	1,070.27	New York	26,245.5	14.5	1,494.87
Delaware	629.9	10.2	1,058.67	North Carolina	4,395.2	9.5	748.25
Dist. of Columbia	940.9	12.2	1,474.71	North Dakota	553.0	9.7	846.81
Florida	7,381.6	8.3	757.86	Ohio	8,747.7	8.5	810.20
Georgia	4,207.0	9.5	769.94	Oklahoma	2,500.7	9.0	826.66
Hawaii	1,232.8	12.6	1,277.52	Oregon	2,576.5	10.5	978.54
Idaho	712.0	9.3	754.28	Pennsylvania	11,605.9	10.3	978.00
Illinois	12,375.2	10.3	1,083.83	Rhode Island	939.9	10.5	992.46
Indiana	4,083.1	8.3	743.73	South Carolina	2,209.1	9.7	708.27
Iowa	2,817.6	10.3	967.24	South Dakota	544.1	10.1	788.55
Kansas	2,188.4	9.3	926.12	Tennessee	3,012.3	8.5	656.12
Kentucky	2,709.3	9.7	740.06	Texas	11,466.3	8.4	805.90
Louisiana	3,534.0	9.9	840.62	Utah	1,226.8	11.0	839.71
Maine	965.5	10.8	858.22	Vermont	459.9	11.5	900.02
Maryland	4,655.5	10.5	1,104.23	Virginia	4,574.1	9.1	855.61
Massachusetts	7,133.2	12.2	1,243.37	Washington	4,083.9	9.6	988.85
Michigan	9,956.4	10.8	1,075.44	West Virginia	1,551.7	10.2	795.75
Minnesota	4,585.5	11.5	1,124.73	Wisconsin	4,993.9	11.3	1,061.40
Mississippi	1,629.6	9.8	646.42	Wyoming	659.1	12.8	1,399.36
Missouri	3,734.3	8.4	759.46	United States	223,462.6	10.3	986.57

*In millions of dollars. Taxes are fiscal year; personal income is calendar year.

Source: Tax Foundation, Facts and Figures on Government Finance (Washington, D.C.: Tax Foundation, Inc., 1981); U.S. Department of Commerce, Bureau of Economic Analysis, Survey of Current Business, vol. 61, no. 7 (Washington, D.C.: Department of Commerce, July 1981).

New Federalism Phase I was implemented in fiscal year 1982 with the passage of the Omnibus Budget Reconciliation Act. Most of the spending cuts made at that time fell under the categories of income security, health, and social services. The data in Table 11.2 indicate that the major recipient of this type of spending is the Middle Atlantic region, followed next by the New England and South Atlantic regions. If the New Federalism Phase II revision is adopted, reduced federal outlays for education, health, community development, transportation, housing, and revenue sharing (general purpose fiscal assistance) are likely. Given the pervasiveness of these cuts, it is not too difficult to think of New Federalism as simply an across-the-board transfer of programs and financial responsibility from the national level to the state level. The following discussion of regional impacts is based on this interpretation.

Table 11.1 shows that the East North Central and Middle Atlantic regions contribute relatively more in taxes than they receive in expenditures. Conversely, the leading gainers from federal activities are the South Atlantic, East South Central, and Mountain regions. Total spending, however, is a poor indicator in a New Federalism context because it is inconceivable that national defense could be decentralized. Hence, nondefense spending is a more useful measure. Since the spatial incidence of defense spending is very unequal (see the defense column of Table 11.2), this adjustment changes the results. The East North Central region remains the chief loser while the leading gainers (the South Atlantic, East South Central, and Mountain regions) are also unchanged. But in this case the New England, Pacific, and West South Central regions join the Middle Atlantic region in contributing more in taxes than they receive in expenditures. When expressed in terms of broad regions, the North Central region is the chief loser from federal activities (excluding defense) while the South is the only gainer. The Northeast and the West are modest losers.

An explanation of why some regions gain and others lose is not difficult. There is a somewhat greater dispersion of concentration ratios for taxes than for nondefense spending. *Aggregate* nondefense spending is relatively equally distributed among regions; at the individual category level there are wider variations (Table 11.2), but these tend to cancel out overall. Differences in concentration ratios for taxes reflect regional income differentials so that the high-money-income regions tend to lose from federal activities while the low-money-income regions tend to gain. This is consistent with the liberals' emphasis on the redistributive impact of the federal government, but it should be noted that this is much more the result of the progressivity of the income and corporate tax structures than of overt attempts by the federal government to redistribute income and welfare via its spending powers.

The implication of this finding for New Federalism is that, in general, high-money-income regions (and states) would gain from its implementation while low-money-income regions (and states) would lose. The progressivity of the Federal Tax Code results in high-income regions subsidizing low-income regions. Major cutbacks in the scope of federal programs (presumably associated with or followed by federal tax cuts) would throw the states back on their own resources. The Northeast would benefit from such a change, although it would gain less than other high-income regions (i.e., the East North Central and Pacific regions). In short, regardless of political attitudes toward the concept of New Federalism, the Northeast would gain from its full implementation *provided that transferred federal programs were accompanied by equivalent tax cuts*. This gain would evaporate, on the other hand, if the federal government continued to finance the transferred programs through a permanent as opposed to a temporary Federalism Trust Fund.

A more general concern about New Federalism arises from the fact that most of the programs that would be transferred are targeted at either people or sectors in urban areas. Any cutbacks in these programs would have uneven spatial impacts, with the burden falling disproportionately on cities. Such programs might be more vulnerable in some state legislatures than in Congress because the political power of rural as opposed to urban areas is stronger in certain states. Many of the states in the East South Central, South Atlantic, and West North Central regions fall into this category, and in the first two cases at least, self-interest is reinforced by political conservatism. New Hampshire, Maine, and Vermont are the only northeastern states where this danger might be serious.

The Urban Enterprise Zone

The urban enterprise zone is the most recently touted policy instrument for reviving depressed areas in the United States. Although its immediate origins are in Britain (the 1977 "Freeport" proposal of the Reading and Berkeley geographer Peter Hall and the policy plan of the post-1979 Conservative government), the basic idea is very similar to the Free Trade Zone concept widely adopted in many developing countries. The Free Trade Zone concept involved the designation of a controlled area, typically the size of an industrial park, where foreign producers could produce goods usually for export without paying import duties and other taxes on raw materials or export duties on the finished products. The major benefit for the host country was the employment of local labor. The main attraction to the foreign producer was to obtain a supply of cheap, reliable workers without having to bear the tax costs usually associated with the establishment of a foreign plant. Since the Free Trade Zone variant is the only type of enterprise zone that has worked in practice, its key characteristics should be kept in mind in evaluating the scope for enterprise zone proposals in the United States.

We are concerned here with the principles behind the scheme rather than specific proposals such as outlined in the Kemp-Garcia Urban Jobs and Enterprise Zone Act of 1980. The bill proposed a range of tax incentives covering reductions in local property taxes, social security taxes, corporate taxes, and capital gains taxes as well as accelerated depreciation.[16] Of these benefits, the last was by far the most important because of a three-year write-off provision,[17] but its benefits have been largely eroded by the economy-wide depreciation incentives granted in the Economic Recovery Tax Act of 1981.

The March 1982 proposals of the administration suggested a new package of benefits: an investment tax credit of 3 to 5 percent for capital spending; a 10 percent property tax credit for industrial and residential construction projects; a 10 percent tax credit for wages paid to additions to the labor force and a 5 percent tax credit for wages earned in the zone; a tax credit for hiring disadvantaged groups, initially as high as 50 percent of wages; elimination of capital-gains taxes; extension of tax loss and credit carryover periods through the life of the zones; and guaranteed access to low-cost industrial revenue bonds. Significantly, some of the other original benefits, such as exemption from "burdensome" federal regulations, reductions in social security taxes and relaxation of the minimum wage laws, have been dropped. The administration has resisted all attempts to include cash grants in the package in order to keep direct costs at a minimum.

Obviously, the effectiveness of any scheme of this kind is likely to be directly related to the size of the incentives offered. But as the benefits rise so do the fiscal costs; hence, deriving the most cost-effective package in terms of net benefits is a very delicate calculation. Moreover, the probability of success is likely to be inversely related to the degree of blight and economic stagnation in the zone itself. On the other hand, the more depressed the zone the greater the benefits from revival. We like to think of a zone in an area such as the South Bronx as providing an effective test case of the concept. If the approach works in the South Bronx, it would have a good chance of success anywhere.

The designation of urban enterprise zones in terms of numbers, scale, and location is critically important. To be considered for enterprise zone status under the Kemp-Garcia Act, an area must contain at least four thousand persons and satisfy certain eligibility criteria defined in terms of unemployment and/or poverty.[18] It is doubtful whether the data are available to apply such

[16] Some of the more exotic incentives, such as exemption from minimum wage regulations or from building codes, have been dropped in recent discussions. A more recent proposal by Kemp-Garcia (H.R. 3824) proposed a somewhat different mix of tax incentives.

[17] See G. Sternlieb, "Kemp-Garcia Act: an initial evaluation," pp. 42–83, in Sternlieb and Listokin (1981).

[18] The alternative criteria were: (1) an average unemployment rate at least three times the national average, (2) 50 percent or more of families below the poverty level (defined as 85 percent of the average lower living standard determined by the Bureau of Labor Statistics), or (3) an average unemployment rate at least twice the national average *plus* at least 30 percent of families below the poverty level.

criteria unambiguously. In any event, the emphasis upon poverty and unemployment indicators suggests that the zones would be designated in ghetto areas. But such areas are primarily residential and have no experience in industrial activities. Typically the best chance of employing ghetto residents is by opening up jobs in nearby industrial and/or commercial neighborhoods, areas that are most unlikely to pass the criteria applied. In a program initiated by Congress, it is highly probable that too many zones would be created in too many areas, many of them hardly qualifying as depressed (the March 1982 proposals envisaged only twenty-five zones in each of the first three years). The administration bill, which is currently stalled in the House, has already been modified to require that one-third of the zones are located in rural areas. This balancing of geographical interests has weakened spatial policies repeatedly from the economic development districts designated by the ARA in the 1960s to the grants awarded under the UDAG program of the late 1970s. If too many zones are selected, the impact of the program will be diluted because the volume of mobile industry is limited; if some of the zones are in relatively prosperous regions (even in depressed pockets), their existence will undermine the prospects of the zones located in severely stagnant regions.

There is some doubt as to whether enterprise zones would work. Many studies have suggested that industrial location decisions are only marginally influenced by tax differentials.[19] The tax benefits would have to be massive to overcome the negative externalities and risks associated with entry into an area such as South Bronx. Since regional industrial growth differentials are largely explained in terms of differential rates of expansion rather than by interregional relocation, most of the potential candidates for enterprise zone entry would come from within the region. Any gains to one subarea would be offset by losses to another with very little net gain to the region as a whole other than output and employment growth induced by the tax savings.

The appeal of the enterprise zone concept to a Republican administration is primarily ideological (namely the appeal of a policy instrument based on tax *reductions*) rather than a sincere interest in economic intervention at the local level. Yet making the enterprise zone concept work would require much more than offering tax concessions. For example, the problem of industrial and commercial land assembly is difficult, even in areas such as South Bronx where derelict land is relatively abundant.

From the point of view of the future economic prospects of the Northeast, the enterprise zone idea is not very attractive in the context of interregional competition because it implies that the Northeast (and other older industrial regions) should compete against the Sunbelt regions by trying to revive its

---

[19] For example, see Wasylenko (1980), Meyer and Quigley (1977), Oakland (1978), the Advisory Commission on Intergovernmental Relations (1967), and Due (1961).

worst areas rather than capitalizing on its strengths. The case for enterprise zones is more convincing as a means of equalizing economic development *within regions* than as an instrument for combatting interregional shifts. Paradoxically, enterprise zones might be most effective in dealing with pockets of stagnation in very rapidly growing regions. The Northeast would benefit more from a policy instrument that narrows *interregional* cost differentials while giving the individual entrepreneur considerable leeway in deciding where, in terms of both subregion and specific site, to develop.

Returning to the Free Trade Zone analogy, it is most unlikely that designated enterprise zones would offer the pools of efficient, cheap labor that might attract outside industry. The proposed tax savings are quite small compared to the subsidies offered to firms entering lagging regions in other countries. The minimum wage laws are a major constraint on achievable labor cost economies (this explains why some enterprise zone proponents argued for relaxing minimum wage regulations within zones). Because of poor education, limited work experience, and lack of skills, *efficiency* wages are *higher* in ghetto areas than elsewhere. In any event, the most rapidly growing industries in the United States economy are not labor intensive. Because the United States labor force is highly mobile, firms can usually attract the workers they need wherever they are located and do not have to allow their locational choices to be unduly influenced by labor supply considerations. The most labor-intensive growth activities are found in the service sector (e.g., health and finance), but these activities would be difficult to attract to enterprise zones and, even if they could be attracted, would provide a dismal mismatch with the skills of the indigenous labor force.

Conclusions

The case for federal intervention in regional development rests heavily on hypotheses about the direction of long-term trends in regional per capita incomes in the United States. If regional income paths are converging toward a stable equilibrium, then we might argue that market forces reinforced by the implicit spatial impacts of macroeconomic and sectoral policies are doing an excellent job. If, on the other hand, regional income paths are about to cross over and subsequently diverge, with the Sunbelt regions soon surpassing the Frostbelt regions, the question of more federal intervention should be seriously considered. However, the difficulties in the way of effective intervention cannot be ignored. Historically, explicit federal regional development policies have been weak. Moreover, federal expenditures on place-oriented policies to favor particular regions and cities are very small compared to macro, sectoral, and people-oriented expenditures, all of which have significant implicit geographical impacts that are much stronger than explicit spatial policy impacts. The Northeast region is a modest net "loser" from federal government activities, largely because it contributes more than its population share to federal tax revenues—a consequence of its above-average money income. This finding is at odds with frequent reports in the media and by politicians that either the Northeast is heavily subsidized by the federal government or that the region is discriminated against. Neither of these assertions appears to be justified.

The current political climate (in 1984) is highly unfavorable to more federal intervention, but it would be wrong to allow the thinking and ideology of the present administration to taint all discussions on the scope for federal regional development policies in the next two decades. Nevertheless, there are grounds for the belief that a major sea-change is unlikely. First, even among liberals there are increasing doubts about the effectiveness of federal intervention and about the political obstacles in the way of generating financial resources to pay for major new initiatives. Second, regional development policies work best in a climate of rapid economic growth. If the era of secularly high growth rates is over, the problem becomes more that of easing the pain of regional adjustment in stagnant regions than of stimulating economic development in neglected geographical pockets. The adjustment process would be facilitated much more by people-oriented than by place-oriented measures.

Obvious strategies, such as strong industrial relocation policies, are probably ruled out by constitutional constraints. The alternative approach of migration subsidies to improve labor market adjustments may be politically unacceptable as well as involving social costs in both origin and destination cities. It is not clear that current interregional migration rates are suboptimal.

The Northeast region as a whole would have little to fear from the implementation of New Federalism proposals *if* program transfers were accompanied by equivalent federal tax cuts. This is because the Northeast currently subsidizes federal programs in low-money-income regions. This generalization may break down at the state level, since New York would certainly gain while Maine, for example, would lose.

The only explicit spatial initiative of the Reagan administration is the enterprise zone concept. It is doubtful whether enterprise zones would work: the tax benefits would probably be insufficient to compensate for the negative externalities and high risks involved in locating in distressed areas. Moreover, tax incentives alone have little influence on location decisions and would need reinforcement from other economic development programs, most of which are now being abandoned. Even if enterprise zones were successful, the most likely outcome would be intraregional relocation in what would be more or less a zero-sum game. It is difficult to believe that enterprise zones could affect interregional rates of growth. Moreover, the political process will probably result in their distribution among all states rather than being concentrated in the most distressed regions of the Northeast and the

Midwest. In any event, in the long history of regional development policies, not only in the United States but around the world, "worst-first" strategies have had a record of almost total failure.

These discouraging conclusions should not be construed as an argument against all public intervention to improve levels of living in the Northeast. But federal intervention would be more successful if directed to individuals rather than to places. If there is any scope for place-oriented policies, they should be implemented at state and local levels. The Northeast may gain higher returns from addressing the problems and needs of current economic activities than from dreaming about the prospects for attracting high-technology and other glamorous industries, which can probably find more attractive locations elsewhere.

References

Advisory Commission on Intergovernmental Relations. 1967. *State-Local Taxation and Industrial Location*. Washington, D.C.: Government Printing Office, Report A-30.

Alms, J., and J. Burkhead. 1982. "The future of fiscal federalism." In *Cities in the 21st Century*, edited by G. Gappert and R. V. Knight, 303–19. Beverly Hills: Sage Publications.

Bolton, R. 1980. "Impacts of defense spending on urban areas." In *The Urban Impacts of Federal Policies*, edited by N. J. Glickman, 151–74. Baltimore: Johns Hopkins University Press.

Boyer, R., and D. Savageau. 1981. *The Places Rated Almanac*. Chicago: Rand McNally.

Bunce, H. L., and N. J. Glickman. 1980. "The spatial dimensions of the Community Development Block Grant Program: targeting and urban impacts." In *The Urban Impacts of Federal Policies*, edited by N. J. Glickman, 515–41. Baltimore: Johns Hopkins University Press.

Center for the Study of Social Policy. 1983. Testimony submitted to the Joint Economic Committee Hearings. "Impacts of the new federalism." In *New Federalism: Its Impact to Date*, 304–40. Washington, D.C.: Government Printing Office.

Cochran, T., and J. R. Prestidge. 1981. "Growing disparity among States in revenue from nonrenewable energy resources." In *Financing State and Local Governments in the 1980s: Issues and Trends*, edited by N. Walzer and D. L. Chicoine, 247–62. Cambridge, Mass.: Oelgeschlager, Gunn, and Hain.

Committee on National Urban Policy. 1982. *Critical Issues for National Urban Policy: A Reconnaissance and Agenda for Further Study*. Washington, D.C.: National Academy Press.

Community Services Administration. 1980. *Geographic Distribution of Federal Funds in Summary: A Report of the Federal Government's Impact by State, County and Large City*. Washington, D.C.: Community Services Administration.

Dommel, P. R. 1980. "Distribution impacts of General Revenue Sharing." In *The Urban Impacts of Federal Policies*, edited by N. J. Glickman, 542–73. Baltimore: Johns Hopkins University Press.

Donnelly, H. 1981. "Health/Education/Welfare." In *Congressional Quarterly Almanac*, 461–62. Washington, D.C.: Congressional Quarterly, Inc.

Due, J. F. 1961. Studies of state and local tax influences on location of industry. *National Tax Journal* 14: 163–73.

Glickman, N. J., ed. 1980. *The Urban Impacts of Federal Policies*. Baltimore: Johns Hopkins University Press.

Granat, D. 1983. Low congressional priority given to "New Federalism." *Congressional Quarterly Weekly Report* 26 February, 422. Washington, D.C. Congressional Quarterly, Inc.

Hodge, C. L. 1968. *The Tennessee Valley Authority: A National Experiment in Regionalism*. New York: Russell and Russell.

House, P. W., and W. A. Steger. 1982. *Modern Federalism: An Analytic Approach*. Lexington, Mass.: Lexington Books.

Howland, M. 1979. "The business cycle and long-run regional growth." In *Interregional Movements and Regional Growth*, edited by W. C. Wheaton, 75–107. Washington, D.C.: The Urban Institute.

Joint Economic Committee. 1981. Hearings before the Subcommittee on Monetary and Fiscal Policy. *Enterprise Zones: The Concept*, Part 1, October 23. Washington, D.C.: Government Printing Office.

Meyer, J. R., and J. M. Quigley. 1977. "Fiscal influences upon location patterns." In *Local Public Finance and the Fiscal Squeeze: A Case Study*, edited by J. R. Meyer and J. M. Quigley, 1–18. Cambridge, Mass.: Ballinger.

Miernyk, W. 1982. *Regional Analysis and Regional Policy*. Cambridge, Mass.: Oelgeschlager, Gunn, and Hain.

Mieszkowski, P. 1979. "Trends in urban and regional development." In *Current Issues in Urban Economics*, edited by P. Mieszkowski and M. Straszheim, 3–39. Baltimore: Johns Hopkins University Press.

Muller, T. L. 1982. "Regional impacts." In *The Reagan Experiment*, edited by J. L. Palmer and I. V. Sawhill, 441–57. Washington, D.C.: Urban Institute.

Nathan, R., A. D. Manvel, S. E. Calkins, and associates. 1975. *Monitoring Revenue Sharing*. Washington, D.C.: The Brookings Institution.

Oakland, W. H. 1978. "Local taxes and intraurban industrial location: a survey." In *Metropolitan Financing and Growth Management Policies: Principles and Practice*, edited by G. F. Break, 13–30. Madison: University of Wisconsin Press.

Peterson, G. E. 1980. "Federal tax policy and the shaping of urban development." In *The Prospective City*, edited by A. P. Solomon, 399–425. Cambridge: MIT Press.

Pred, A. 1966. *The Spatial Dynamics of US Urban Industrial Growth, 1800–1914*. Cambridge: MIT Press.

Reagan, R. 1982. Budget Message of the President, 2 February. *Congressional Quarterly Almanac*, 6E-13E. Washington, D.C.: Congressional Quarterly, Inc.

Rees, J. 1981. "The impact of defense spending on regional industrial change in the United States." In *Federalism and Regional Development: Case Studies on the Experience in the United States and the Federal Republic of Germany*, edited by G. W. Hoffman, 193–220. Austin: University of Texas Press.

Schorr, P. 1975. *Planned Relocation*. Lexington, Mass.: Lexington Books.

Smith, S. 1983. Finance Committee revives enterprise zone proposal. *Congressional Quarterly Weekly Report*. 21 May, 1022. Washington, D.C.: Congressional Quarterly, Inc.

Sternlieb, G., and D. Listokin, eds. 1981. *New Tools for Economic Development: The Enterprise Zone, Development Bank and RFC*. New Brunswick, N.J.: Center for Urban Policy Research.

Tax Foundation. 1981. *Facts and Figures on Government Finance*. Washington, D.C.: Tax Foundation, Inc.

U.S. Department of Commerce, Bureau of the Census. 1979. *State and Metropolitan Area Data Book*. Washington, D.C.: Government Printing Office.

U.S. Department of Commerce, Bureau of the Census. 1981. *Statistical Abstract of the United States*. Washington, D.C.: Government Printing Office.

U.S. Department of the Treasury. 1980. *Federal Aid to States*. Washington, D.C.: Department of the Treasury.

Vaughan, R. J. 1980. "The impact of Federal policies on urban economic development." In *The Prospective City*, edited by A. P. Solomon, 348–98. Cambridge, Mass.: MIT Press.

Wasylenko, M. 1980. Evidence on fiscal differentials and intrametropolitan firm location, *Land Economics* 56: 339–49.

HARRY W. RICHARDSON

12 *Regional Policy in a "Slowth" Economy*

This chapter extends the argument advanced by Miernyk (1981)[1] and reflected in his contribution to this book that the slowing down in world economic growth (or "slowth"[2]) will require drastic rethinking of our ideas about regional policy. Although Miernyk himself emphasizes the short-fall of *long-run* energy supply below energy demand, there are many alternative explanations of slowth. These include the hypothesis of shrinking investment opportunities, built-in retardation forces in mature economies, the downswing of a Kondratieff long wave and the impact of exogenous shocks, while a United Nations report referred to "changing attitudes to work, the proliferation of government regulations, existing tax structures, accelerated inflation, shifts in relative prices, changes in the quality of the labor force, lack of adequate innovation and inadequate research and development" (United Nations Conference on Trade and Development, 1982, vol. 1, p. 3). At the time of writing (January 1984) the United States economy was performing rather well; because perceptions of long-term trends are colored by very recent experience, discussions of slowth are more muted than they were a few years ago. The problem of distinguishing between long-term trends and short-term cycles remains difficult, but there are no grounds to expect a reversal of the slowdown in secular growth.

---

[1] A version of this paper is reprinted as chapter 5 of his new book (Miernyk, 1982).

[2] "Slowth" is, of course, an abbreviation for slow growth. It is the title of a popular book by Rupferman and Levi (1980). They say that the term was first coined by an anonymous staff member of the Organization for Economic Cooperation and Development (OECD).

However, Miernyk's point is that even zero economic growth would not imply lack of change in the spatial distribution of population and economic activity. Instead, there would be "macro-stability and micro-flexibility" (Miernyk, 1981, p. 68) in which some regions gain and others lose. In particular, he suggests that interregional income convergence since the late 1960s has taken the form of upward shifts by net energy producers and downward shifts by net energy consumers (this reflects his explanation of slowth). This convergence does not, in his view, represent a steady movement toward a spatial equilibrium of interregional income paths. On the contrary, these income paths will "cross over" with the formerly low-income energy and resource-based regions rising above the national average. By the year 2000, Miernyk forecasts that the Rocky Mountain region would be the richest and New England the poorest in terms of per capita income.

The old economic development promotion strategies for lagging regions characteristic of the 1960s are inappropriate to the zero-sum game that prevails today. The two alternatives are to try to slow down (or stop) the interregional shifts from the Frostbelt to the Sunbelt or to accept the shifts and ameliorate the problems of those affected by them. The first alternative is inefficient and probably infeasible. The second alternative may be justified as long as the interregional shifts are from regions with above-average incomes to those with below-average incomes. It implies subsidies for the disadvantaged in the older industrial regions, but their costs may not be too high because these regions are not faced with sudden catastrophe. Instead, the demographic shifts have been quite moderate, and their economies have proven to be resilient.

Internationalization of Production, Slowth, and the Regional Problem

One specific explanation of slowth, especially in the mature capitalist economies, is found in radical critiques of capitalism, and more particularly in the role of multinational corporations (MNCs). The problems of slow growth in demand, endemic under late capitalism, are compounded by the actions of MNCs on the supply side. They have responded to declining rates of profit in parent countries (e.g., the United States, Western Europe, and Japan) by building plants in developing countries where the opportunities for exploiting labor (low wages equal high profits) are much greater. By leapfrogging in this way, they bypass the lagging regions in the parent country and take advantage of wage-cutting benefits in the developing countries (Holland, 1976). Thus, the increased internationalization of production has had dramatic effects on the lagging regions of developed countries. The rapid capital shifts by MNCs have resulted in regional and local policymakers having a much lower degree of leverage over them. Also, there are much greater risks that an individual region may lose its markets. Finally, the social costs of capital movements (both in and out) are given less attention than economic efficiency, cost-cutting, and profit maximization under conditions of slowth (Glickman and Petras, 1981).

The question arises as to whether these problems can be tackled by policy. Pickvance (1981) has argued that regional policy incentives in Britain are no longer intended to change the spatial distribution of industry but are merely a politically palatable means of giving massive subsidies to large-scale industry. The two pieces of evidence supporting this view are (1) that regional policy incentives have favored capital-intensive firms with little pretense at trying to generate employment and (2) that these incentives have been unselective in that they have been given to firms that would have moved to the assisted regions in any event. Thus, the "British government's strategy is to hold on to a share of . . . internationally mobile investment by offering increasing levels of restructuring aid" (Pickvance, 1981, p. 260). Holland (1976) suggested an alternative strategy for "harnessing mesoeconomic power"[3] including the selective use of public enterprise, public-private planning agreements for location decisions, strong location of industry controls, and threats of nationalization for MNCs that consider flight abroad.

In developing countries MNCs have tended to choose locations (except for resource industries) close to the primate city in the core region.[4] Governments have been reluctant to attempt to control their location decisions on the ground that the MNCs may flex their mesoeconomic muscles and choose to go elsewhere.[5] Thus, the MNCs have made little positive contribution to the attainment of regional policy objectives in developing countries. On the other hand, they have not contributed to slowth there, since the agglomeration economies of the core region remain strong enough that centralized locations are consistent with economic efficiency and growth maximization.

Zero-sum Game Implications of Slowth

There is widespread agreement that the end of the era of continued economic growth would have dramatic repercussions on society. Kenneth Bould-

---

[3]The mesoeconomic sector represents a middle layer between the macro level of national economic policy and the micro level of the small competitive firm. It consists of MNCs and other large-scale firms that wield almost independent power and are difficult to control by national governments.

[4]However, domestic firms are even more reluctant to decentralize.

[5]This argument may not be very strong. MNCs frequently operate plants in a particular developing country to supply the expanding domestic market behind high tariff walls rather than to export (Richardson, 1982).

ing suggested that slowth would demand major changes in ways of thinking, habits, and standards of decision making and in institutions.[6] Noam Chomsky (Oltmans, 1974, p. 285) argued that continued economic growth was a safety valve for redistribution demands:

> The idea that economic growth will continue without limit has been a very effective device for controlling and limiting demands for redistribution of wealth. . . . The notion of limitless growth could be employed to bring about consensus instead of conflict by overcoming the demands for redistribution of wealth, which would certainly be heard if one could not look forward to gaining more of life's benefits by some other method.

Similarly, Thurow (1980) has argued that distributional issues, being very contentious, are among the most difficult questions for democracies to solve.

In the context of developing countries, the redistribution-with-growth strategy (Chenery et al., 1974) was developed to tackle the problem that "trickle down" effects from uncontrolled growth were weak and appeared very late. The idea behind redistribution-with-growth was to redistribute the incremental output generated through growth by direct intervention by the government to redistribute productive assets to target groups (both the rural and urban poor). The argument was that the "haves" in developing countries might be persuaded by the political capital that could be created if at least part of the increment in growth were redistributed. But suppose the developing economies ceased to grow. The question of whether redistribution-*without*-growth is consistent with political stability is purely rhetorical.

The extension of these arguments to the regional policy sphere is rather obvious. Regional policy analysis has always assumed a growing economy in which redistribution of resources to lagging regions could be supported nationwide because it did not imply zero growth in the prosperous regions, only slower growth. But if the national economy ceases to grow,[7] interregional development becomes a zero-sum game in which gains to lagging regions require absolute (as well as relative) losses in the rich regions. In the zero-sum situation, support for regional policies is likely to evaporate. In the words of Shefrin (1980, p. 81), "Antagonism is built into the game." Miernyk (1980a, p. 18) warns that this situation "could lead to a virulent form of sectionalism," and it is not surprising that a chapter in a recent book is titled "Sunbelt versus Frostbelt: the war between the States" (House and Ryan, 1979). The recurrent debate in the United States about "fair shares" for regions in federal spending and the view of corporate executives who relocate

---

[6]This suggestion was made in a speech in May 1978 quoted by Hughes (1982, p. 3).

[7]Note that although zero economic growth is a fairly extreme case of slowth, it is not the limiting case since national economies can decline.

their plants out of the Northeast and Midwest to the South and West as traitors who should be charged an "exit" tax, if not hanged, are merely two signs that the war has already been declared.

Escape from the Zero-sum Dilemma?

Before discussing the regional policy implications of a slowth economy, it may be worthwhile to explore the question of whether there is any escape from the zero-sum interregional development game. The first point is that even if slowth is permanent, it does not mean that *zero* growth is imminent. If slowth is due to resource scarcity, this constraint is an ultimate boundary not a tight chain. It will be more difficult for regions and nations to grow, but not necessarily impossible. Even Miernyk recognizes this, suggesting that the change will be "slow and gradual" and at least mentioning the possibility of "positive economic growth for decades" (Miernyk, 1980a, p. 20). The drive to grow by firms, regions, and nations can, and will, continue. The real implication of slowth is that we can no longer look for automatic, sustained economic growth to solve all our problems, especially that of distribution. Furthermore, to the extent that slowth results from factors other than the law of diminishing returns (such as managerial failures, a declining innovation rate, or the substitution of a leisure for a work ethic) it is possible—though difficult and improbable—that the process could be reversed.

If slowth largely results from energy supply problems, it would be defeatist to accept that *nothing* could be done about them. Without joining the camp of "the perennial optimists who hope that some technological fix will come along" (Miernyk, 1980c, p. 51), there is *some* scope for further exploration, better recovery methods, the development of alternative fuels, and more conservation (Thompson, Karagonis, and Wilson, 1981; Yergin and Hillenbrand, 1982). Also, to the extent that the problems have been exacerbated by runaway growth in energy demand, slowth itself is part of the solution via its dampening effect on demand.

Moreover, the energy problem has widely differential effects from country to country. The worst sufferers are, and will be, those industrialized countries with fuel-hungry economies and negligible access to energy resources, such as many West European countries and Japan and the low-income countries with zero resources and a very limited capacity to pay world energy prices. The major oil-producing countries are the prime beneficiaries, of course, while several middle-income countries have recently discovered resources and begun to produce energy in sufficient quantities to meet their own needs. There is every reason to expect that the United States could weather the storm better than most. She remains a resource-rich country and her profligacy in the past means that there is more scope for fuel conservation than in most other countries. However, from the point of view of inter-regional development, the more successful the United States is in increasing energy supply the wider the gaps in economic performance between energy-producing regions and others.[8] Thus, ameliorating the national problem would only aggravate the regional problem.

Another argument, more common among planners in developing countries than in the United States, is that slowth is an opportunity to be grasped rather than a source of regret. Why? As long as growth was guaranteed, policymakers could rely on "trickle-down" hypotheses and redistribution-with-growth models to deliver higher living standards to lagging regions and the poor. That these mechanisms usually failed was casually ignored. But if aggregate growth ceases, these development-from-above mechanisms have to be abandoned. This creates a hospitable environment for experiments with novel strategies, variously labeled as "development-from-below," "self-reliance," basic needs development strategies, and selective spatial closure (Stöhr and Taylor, 1981). It would be another detour to begin to describe what these approaches mean. However, most of them share common characteristics. These include: an emphasis upon the mobilization of unexploited local resources (e.g., the use of unemployed labor in community projects); the substitution of the benefits of sharing in decision making for increases in material welfare; a focus on satisfying human needs through the provision of low-cost services rather than via the proliferation of consumer goods; rejection of high GNP growth rates for their own sake on the grounds that they are likely to be associated with an unequal distribution of income; and a variety of policy instruments for the protection of local industries, for guiding the structure of production toward labor-intensive basic goods, and for stopping leakages from local development impulses into other parts of the national economic system. Obviously, these strategies have more chance of being adopted in low-income countries not tainted by modernization or in very rich countries with nonconformists jaded by materialism (communes in Oregon or small villages in Maine and Vermont?).

The zero-sum game hypothesis in a regional policy context assumes that the benefits of policies to aid assisted regions will be at the expense of non-assisted regions. In an empirical analysis of West European experience, Ashcroft (1982) has suggested that this need not be the case. First, regional policy incentives have attracted foreign investment that might not otherwise have come to a particular country (e.g., in the United Kingdom, Belgium, Ireland). This is an extension to the world level of the argument that zero national growth is compatible with positive growth in some but not all regions. Zero world growth is equally compatible with positive national growth, especially

---

[8]To some extent, the output effect will be offset by a countervailing terms-of-trade effect as increasing supplies moderate any rise in prices.

for countries that are favored in international capital markets. Second, there is evidence that regional policy incentives have induced local assisted-area firms to expand, and only a fraction of this can be explained by substitution for growth elsewhere (e.g., income multiplier effects now retained locally that were formerly transmitted nationally). Third, and possibly most important, the spatial redistribution of national aggregate demand could raise the effective production potential of the economy (for example, by dampening inflation rates in the regions with the tighter labor markets; see Higgins, 1973). A British study suggested that the dispersal of one hundred government jobs would create twenty-nine additional jobs in the economy as a whole (Ashcroft and Swales, 1982), while the application of the REGINA model in France suggested that decentralization of industries from the Paris region would raise national output as well as contribute to interregional equity (Courbis, 1982). Ashcroft (1982, p. 28) concludes:

> The (regional) policies also need not have worked at the inevitable expense of the non-assisted areas: some net new jobs appear to be created in the assisted areas and some jobs replaced in the non-assisted areas due to regional-policy-induced indigenous expansions, the attraction of mobile foreign firms and improvements in the working of the interregional labor market.

Some economists believe that mature economies can combat slowth only by diversifying their industrial structures by promoting new innovations, new products and processes, and new industries. In the United States in recent years this argument has generated considerable pressure for a national industrial policy to encourage this process. Although it is possible that a national industrial policy could be directed toward shoring up declining industries, most economists would recommend the opposite—that national industrial policy should reinforce the private market by helping it to select and promote the "winners." Since the problems of lagging regions are very often the result of specialization in declining industries (national "losers"), this suggests a direct conflict between the aims of industrial policy and those of regional policy (Cameron, 1979). According to this view, policies to fight slowth in the aggregate economy would make regional problems worse and the implementation of regional policies more difficult (Bell and Lande, 1982).

However, there might be two possible escape routes from this dilemma. One is to promote the rapidly growing industries in the lagging regions. This is not as difficult as in, say, developing countries because lagging regions in mature economies usually have the necessary prerequisites in the form of infrastructure, services, and labor pools. However, in the United States at least, regional policy incentives have never had enough teeth to overcome corporate locational preferences. Moreover, West European experience suggests that such incentives have a high probability of being effective only when combined with controls on industrial development in the nonassisted regions, a weapon that may be both constitutionally impossible and ideologically repugnant in the United States.

The second solution might be to promote the small-scale business sector as a means of reconciling national regional policy and national industrial policy. In the United States, 60 percent of jobs are created in firms of less than twenty workers while perhaps one-half of all jobs are created by independent small entrepreneurs (Birch, 1979). Also, small firms account for a substantial proportion of all industrial inventions and innovations, and make a disproportionate contribution to new technological advances. This raises the possibility that promoting small businesses in lagging regions might stimulate job creation *and* promote productivity growth and innovations, thereby serving both regional and industrial policy goals. Unfortunately, this prescription has a major snag. The firms and industries that create many jobs are not the same firms and industries that are highly productive or innovative.

Since both escape routes seem closed in the United States, the trade-off between industrial growth policy and regional policy appears unavoidable.

> Recommendations for support of low-productivity industries do not mesh well with the primary aims of industrial policy—national efficiency, export expansion, import substitution, and GNP growth—even when justified by regional concentration of troubled industries. Similarly, recommendations for support of high-productivity activities (often very capital intensive, with limited employment opportunities concentrated in high-paying jobs) do not always support regional-policy objectives of employment growth, particularly among the low-skilled or long-term unemployed [Garn and Ledebur, 1982, p. 49].

Some years ago, I drew the distinction between "competitive" growth according to which "the growth of one region is always at the expense of another," clearly the zero-sum game case, and "generative" growth, whereby "the growth performance of an individual region can be raised . . . without necessarily adversely affecting the growth rate of its neighbors" (Richardson, 1973, pp. 86-88). Miernyk (1981, p. 10), perhaps a little unjustly, equates generative growth with the discredited growth-promoting regional policies of the 1960s and early 1970s. A somewhat different way of looking at generative growth is to be aware of its similarities with the self-reliant regional growth strategies. Even without the stimulus of outside aid, there may be some scope for local and regional policymakers to intervene to improve local prospects for development. True, these actions are not going to be of sufficient magnitude to have enough of a feedback effect on the national growth rate to eliminate slowth, but they offer some alternative to the defeatist alternative of lying down and allowing slowth to take its toll on lagging regions.

Actions might include improvements in intraregional spatial organization, eliminating bottlenecks in the transport or public service systems, and creating conditions favorable to local economic development (e.g., state policies to provide risk capital for small indigenous entrepreneurs). A striking example of the scope for generative-growth approaches is policies to promote small-scale industries in the secondary towns of peripheral regions in developing countries, where the major constraint on expansion is not the lack of effective demand but of credit and technical assistance. These and similar types of intervention are a much preferable strategy to the policy alternative implied by the competitive growth model, namely, interregional competitive bidding to attract the shrinking volume of mobile industry.

Do the considerations discussed in this section add up to the conclusion that slowth can be controlled and its zero-sum game implications for interregional development avoided? Unfortunately not. They suggest that the situation is not so bleak that recognition of slowth should be interpreted as approval of inaction, but they are, in the end, palliatives rather than solutions. The need for reassessing the appropriateness of regional policies under conditions of slowth remains as strong as ever.

Regional Policies in Recessions

There have been no observable experiences of how regional policies might work under conditions of slowth. The only possible period that might qualify as an era of secular stagnation is the 1930s (and even in this case a better description might be a very deep and long depression), but at that time regional policies were either in their infancy or, in some countries, did not exist. However, there are some experiences of the effectiveness of regional policies during cyclical recessions. Since it *may* be possible to extrapolate from the conditions of short-term recession to those of long-run slowth, examining regional policies in recession periods is a reasonable starting point.

For a variety of reasons regional policies do not work very well in recessions. There is a shift in the policymakers' preoccupations; they become much less concerned with the spatial distribution of output and employment than with their overall levels. Also, recessions lead to a sharp fall in government revenues, so that the resources available for regional expenditures, and the willingness to make these expenditures, decline. Firms become unresponsive to whatever incentives are offered, because the willingness to relocate is much stronger in conditions of rapid growth, especially since many firms move because they lack the space for expanding capacity at their existing site. As for individuals, the capacity of migrants to move out of areas with poor employment opportunities is reduced because both the monetary resources to finance a move are reduced and the incentives to move (e.g., expanding job opportunities) are weaker.

A more complex argument is that the rationale for regional policies is eroded during recessions. In countries where ratios of unemployment compensation to wages are high and where automatic stabilizers are powerful, the gap between recession and boom income levels is narrower in lagging than in prosperous regions. Furthermore, differentials in rates of unemployment between regions narrow because of influences such as the specialization of the more prosperous regions in rapidly growing but cyclically unstable industries. A more ambiguous point is the location of temporarily closed plants in multiplant firms: in some cases closures are spatially concentrated in the lagging regions because transport cost differentials make plants located there the high-cost establishments; in other situations, the peripherally located branch plants are the last to be shut down because, being more recent, they embody a superior (i.e, more efficient) technology. Higher absolute levels of unemployment are found everywhere and localized pockets of severe recession may be almost as frequent in the leading as in the lagging regions. In these circumstances, the government may (as the British government has in recent years) increase spatial selectivity in the distribution of its reduced regional policy expenditures, but over the country as a whole break away from the sole focus on lagging regions. Because the manufacturing sector is the most cyclically sensitive, in recession periods there may also be a shift of regional policy efforts toward promoting service industries and/or dispersing government employment.

During periods of high unemployment, the need to create jobs anywhere dominates the desirability of creating jobs at particular locations. Hence, regional policies have to compete on the same basis with other employment-creating measures. Can they compete? There is a dearth of research on this question, but one study of British experience (Marquand, 1980) suggested that per capita job creation costs from regional incentives were "of the same order of magnitude" as from other fiscal measures. If this were generally true, it would imply that there is no justification for deserting regional policies during cyclical recessions.

This brief review suggests that implementation of regional policies is more difficult during recessions. Also, the most favored strategy of inducing industry to relocate to lagging regions or, as is more common, of setting up new firms and branch plants there is particularly ineffective. There has not been a serious concern with this problem among policymakers because recessions turn around and the policies begin to work again. Of course, this solution—evaporation of the problem—cannot be expected under condition of slowth.

Regional Policy Options under Slowth

Slowth does not suggest a single unambiguous policy prescription. Instead, it points to a range of different regional policy options, which might be used singly or in combination. Many of the policy approaches that were followed in the 1960s and 1970s, both in the United States and around the world, are inappropriate for economies suffering from slowth. This is because most of them were aimed at promoting economic growth in lagging regions under the assumptions that aggregate economic growth would continue at a healthy rate and that the policy problem merely consisted of diverting a higher share of this growth to the less developed and/or depressed regions.

These obsolete policy measures include locational fiscal incentives to persuade firms to relocate from leading to lagging regions. Such measures work only when the volume of interregionally mobile industry is substantial, and this volume is a direct function of the rate of industrial growth. As this rate declines toward zero, the volume of mobile industry becomes progressively smaller. In these conditions, either locational incentives are too small with no results, or, if large enough to have any effect, they merely induce firms to relocate for fiscal benefits without increasing growth. This could lead both to premature abandonment of production facilities in the area of origin and to efficiency losses associated with diversion from an optimal location. Similarly, growth center strategies are even more likely to fail in slowth economies because their initial stimulus is industrial dynamism and the intersectoral linkages around one or more propulsive industries. The concept of a propulsive industry obviously needs reexamination under conditions of slowth.

The first policy option is to accept that regional policies, at least of the place-oriented kind, will not work and to find alternative means of dealing with the equity objectives that are traditionally used to justify regional development policies. This option has two variations. The first is to abandon regional policies, to rely on macro and sectoral policies to maximize GNP, to the extent that slowth constraints permit, and then to redistribute part of the growth benefits from richer to poorer regions. A justification for this approach is that the search for greater economic efficiency and higher production becomes more important than ever under slowth, and efficiency losses are tolerated much less. The strategy clearly accepts the zero-sum-game approach. It is concerned with developing a mechanism for the most equitable distribution of a fixed pie, or at best a slowly growing one. An improved revenue-sharing program might be such a mechanism. According to this strategy, interregional transfer payments arranged through the taxation system are substituted for the regional development expenditures of traditional regional policy programs. The approach has the substantial advantage that it minimizes *net* national government expenditures that will be perpetually sluggish under slowth. On the other hand, a serious drawback is that it probably involves *absolute* income sacrifices by the populations of the richer regions. Thus, interregional conflict may become more serious, even explosive.

The second variant is the substitution of people-oriented policies for place-oriented policies.[9] This also means a clear redistribution strategy, except that the redistribution takes the form of transfers to individuals rather than to local and regional governments as implied by revenue-sharing approaches. People-oriented approaches in a regional policy context cover a variety of measures, which include income maintenance programs and direct taxation reform to reduce poverty regardless of location, welfare payments to immobile populations locked in severely depressed regions, and relocation assistance to migrants from areas with an excess supply of labor to areas where labor markets are closer to equilibrium. The last possibility, recommended by the President's Commission on a National Agenda for the 1980s (the so-called McGill Commission) in the dog days of the Carter administration, created a major controversy in spite of its plausibility and apparent economic soundness. One reason is the argument that migrants to the more prosperous regions would cluster in rapidly growing neighborhoods that already have severe absorption problems. Another reason, heavily stressed in the United States, is that population retention is a dominant policy goal for state and local governments because the formulas for federal expenditure programs (and for political influence as represented by congressional seats) are essentially based on population criteria. In general, the balance among income maintenance, welfare payments, and relocation assistance[10] will depend upon the political and institutional conditions prevailing in a particular country. However, whatever mix is chosen, this approach, by focusing on the needs of individuals implicitly accepts the argument that regional development policies are merely an indirect way of improving their welfare. This argument has merit even under conditions of rapid economic growth when people-oriented and place-oriented policies become *feasible* alternative means to reach the same end. Its strength is reinforced under slowth, however, because the alternative strategy of mainstream regional development policies is almost bound to fail.

A second major policy option does not call for the abandonment of regional policy, but instead makes the case for regional policies that are very different from those pursued in the past. Such a change would again reflect a shift from economic development toward more emphasis on equity and indi-

---

[9]The main rationale for place-oriented policies in the past is that they would be efficient in the long run by promoting sustained economic development. However, if economic development opportunities are very limited and may become more rather than less so in the future, it makes more sense to help people directly.

[10]Relocation assistance is merely one example of measures to increase the income-earning potential of individuals. Education and training programs and other forms of human resource investments are another example. However, their record has been generally poor because of the neglect of demand for labor considerations. In the absence of complementary measures to increase labor demand, they operate largely as an indirect form of relocation assistance (if the trainees subsequently move) or as a more palatable form of welfare payment (if the trainees remain immobile and unemployed).

vidual welfare. For example, a shift of focus from regional economic development policy to regional *social* policy might be highly appropriate under slowth. In many countries, especially developing countries, lagging regions suffer severely from deficiencies in social services (health, education, and general social services) and in social infrastructure and public facilities.[11] Political objections that arise in discussions to transfer income directly from rich to poor regions are more difficult to mobilize where the policy aims at giving priority to backward regions in social service provision on the ground that the prevailing levels of services lag severely behind accepted national standards. Moreover, the design of social sector policies may imply very different regional impacts even if the content of the policy is superficially devoid of spatial considerations. For instance, a policy emphasizing primary education rather than tertiary education and primary health care rather than high-technology curative medical care will discriminate in favor of rural and against highly urbanized regions. The most important attraction of regional social policies is undoubtedly their political acceptability. A policy goal of equalizing social services per capita among regions will (in most cases) absorb substantial resources and require these to be transferred from rich to poor regions,[12] but the goal is probably much more palatable to the residents of prosperous regions than a goal of income equalization.

In the preceding discussion of the potential conflict between industrial and regional policy, negative conclusions were based on analysis of the situation in the United States; thus the topic merits a brief reexamination in the context of slowth conditions. There are two approaches to industrial policy in these conditions. One is to concentrate on the stagnating and declining sectors, by attempting to slow down the decline of older industries; the other is to foster an environment favorable to the spawning and rapid growth of new industries (e.g., the "high-tech strategy"). The first is likely to be more consistent with regional policy because older industries tend to be spatially concentrated in either lagging or potentially lagging regions. The second will probably conflict with regional policy goals in developing countries by encouraging continued development in the primate city and the core region, in developed countries by favoring newer regions rather than older industrial regions. Although the first option may be more attractive from the regional policy prospective, it would be dangerous for the mature industrial economy to adopt it since such a course of action would only hasten its decline relative to newly developing economies.

[11]This generalization is not universally valid. For instance, Firestone (1974) found that regional disparities in social indicators in Canada are much narrower than regional income disparities.
[12]The two main exceptions to this conclusion are where the richer regions have lower per capita services (perhaps because of differential population pressure) and where governments require full cost recovery from users for all services supplied.

On the other hand, whereas the "shoring-up" approach is inadvisable as an overall industrial strategy, this does not rule out the possibility of *some* defensive actions on the regional policy front to help to alleviate problems of industrial structure in lagging regions. For example, it would not be a good idea to use semipermanent public subsidies to keep uncompetitive firms in business or to introduce the frequently recommended policy of charging "exit taxes" to firms that wish to relocate to improve efficiency. On the other hand, there may be reasonably efficient types of public intervention that might be helpful. In the United States, at least, interregional differentials in the growth of firms (hence, output and employment) are largely explained by differentials in the closure rate of establishments (starts are approximately evenly distributed; see Garn and Ledebur, 1982). Local governments, in particular, may be able to slow down closures by various actions at critical phases in a firm's history. Even if these actions have a fiscal cost, they may be justified if the aid is temporary rather than permanent. Of course, such actions should be focused on potentially viable firms that run the risk of bankruptcy because of temporary misfortunes and not on chronically uncompetitive firms that are bound to go out of business sooner or later.

In the probably unusual situation where economic growth is close to zero and interregional differentials in economic performance are substantial *but* interregional cost differentials are small, it may be justified for government to persuade firms to relocate even if no net growth can be expected. However, this special case does not require the retention of a general program of regional locational incentives. Instead, it suggests the desirability of targeting financial assistance to overcome the transaction costs associated with moving, that is, the relocation costs (Ashcroft, 1982).

Another *nationally* justifiable strategy is the deployment of any policies that do not involve heavy public expenditures to attract or retain international industrial investment in lagging regions. Holland's recommendations for "harnessing mesoeconomic power" mentioned above (Holland, 1976) would not be appealing to market-oriented economies, but they may be able to devise an alternative approach based on incentives that, by attracting foreign investment and creating jobs, might create more government revenue than their cost.

Historically, most job decentralization efforts have focused on the manufacturing sector. In current circumstances, this focus is misdirected. Manufacturing is the most serious victim in slowth economies. Moreover, its job-creating potential per unit of investment is much lower than the services sector. In postindustrial society the service sector continues to perform well even under conditions of slowth. The problem here lies in identifying those components of the service sector that are locationally mobile. A substantial proportion of it consists of personal services, commerce, and small-scale business services that are local and remain "dependent" on the formal manufacturing sector. But in most countries the national government remains a major employer, and a considerable proportion of its labor force is engaged in routine functions that can be decentralized. Also, changes in communications technologies provide an unprecedented opportunity for the successful dispersion of quaternary offices.

Because government revenues are likely to be sluggish under conditions of slowth, policies that are economical of government expenditures deserve particular attention. This accounts for the appeal of self-balancing tax-subsidy schemes with which the government, in effect, compulsorily arranges interregional transfer payments through the private sector. For example, cross-subsidy schemes to compensate peripheral regions for specific locational disadvantages (e.g., in transport or energy costs), whereby consumers in rich regions are charged above-cost prices to enable those in lagging regions to be supplied at less than cost, would fall into this category. The most attractive type of tax-subsidy scheme, however, would apply to the industrial sector, either as a whole or in part. Firms in prosperous regions would be taxed in order to subsidize those in lagging regions. This would change interregional production costs, stimulating industrial growth in the latter while discouraging it in the former. Although the policy is a more powerful tool under robust growth conditions, it could also work under slowth. From the point of view of the national economy, the only requirement would be that the growth induced in lagging regions should be at least equal to the growth deterred in more prosperous regions. As previously suggested, there are reasons for believing that this condition may frequently be satisfied.

Given the importance of job creation goals in regional policy, a wage subsidy would seem to be the most appropriate form of subsidy. Glickman (1981) lists several advantages of wage subsidies: they are good substitutes for income-maintenance programs in terms of their impact; they promote the substitution of labor for capital; they can easily be targeted to specific groups; they can attract workers, including those who are discouraged, into the labor force; and they may even have a marginal impact in reducing the inflationary rate via their favorable effect on wage costs. Financing a wage subsidy in peripheral regions by a tax on capital in core regions might be the optimal strategy from the point of view of regional policy and employment goals.[13]

Because some of the preceding arguments imply that the national government is much less effective as the source of regional policy intervention when the aggregate economic growth rate falls, local governments, community organizations, and private sector initiative may step in to fill the void. If it is much more difficult to attract or divert resources from elsewhere, the local development process must be "endogenized." This implies the mobi-

---

[13]Taxing one factor in some locations to subsidize another factor in other locations may result in complex production distortions that are difficult to measure. Intuitively, these distortions are probably quite small.

lization of local resources and their more efficient reallocation to ensure a pattern of development that is less dependent on external economic conditions. This suggests, as discussed above, the relevance of "generative growth," "self-reliant development," and "selective spatial closure" concepts. The underlying assumptions of these strategies are: lagging regions currently operate *inside* rather than on their production possibility frontiers; and, under slowth conditions, the impulses from other regions and abroad are, more likely than not, negative so that the costs of regional closure are much lower than in conditions of rapid growth. Unfortunately, while these self-reliance strategies have a substantial a priori plausibility, there is little practical experience of how they work in practice and what their operational content would be. But they do underline the point that while slowth is a constraint it does not have to be a noose.

Finally, if slowth is closely associated with resource scarcities, especially of energy resources, this offers a new challenge to regional policy. Because these resources are not uniformly distributed but are spatially concentrated in a few regions, their development creates new kinds of interarea equity problems, such as the recent debate in the United States about whether or not state severance taxes should be federalized. Also, resource exploitation creates serious intertemporal problems of development, namely the familiar boom-bust pattern of growth. There is considerable scope for designing regional development policies for resource-rich regions based on optimal rates of exploitation (i.e., orderly development paths that maximize long-run rents and avoid the boom-bust cycle) and promoting high social rates of return (particularly from the perspective of improving local income distribution; resource exploitation is a notoriously regressive form of economic activity).

Implications for the United States

Not all regional policy options are equally applicable in the United States. Indeed, the United States is something of an anomaly among developed countries because it lacks a long history of strong intervention with respect to regional policy. With the partial exception of the 1960s, regional policies have been weak for many reasons: the continued prevalence of an ideology favoring the resolution of economic problems by market forces; constitutional constraints on actions that favor some states and discriminate against others; the pluralism of the political process that assures dilution of programs by giving something for everybody (e.g., the high levels of federal expenditures on regional development in high-income states rather than being heavily concentrated in low-income states); and the reliance on interregional migration as the major mechanism for converging regional (and personal) income disparities.

However, this situation could change in the future. As pointed out in Miernyk (1981), the prospect for interregional income paths in the United States is not that of a stable equilibrium but that of a crossover and subsequent divergence. The extent of Frostbelt–Sunbelt, and energy-poor to energy-rich areal, shifts—while orderly at present—may accelerate. The impacts on the older industrial regions are aggravated because the interregional pressures are coinciding with rapid changes in international competitiveness and capital shifts as well as the changes in international economic conditions (i.e., slowth itself). In these circumstances, especially in view of the political clout retained by the older industrial states, the pressure for regional policy intervention could build to a level never before experienced in the United States. However, if this happens, intervention may be focused on levels of government other than the federal level, in spite of the fact that national governments have been the major promoters of regional policies in almost all countries. The reasons for this view are: the trend against more federal intervention and higher levels of federal spending, which may be more permanent than ephemeral; the above-mentioned constitutional and political obstacles to discriminatory intervention in favor of certain states; the relatively strong states with substantial resources and clear-cut territorial responsibilities and interests; and the existence of some sharp *intra*-state differentials in economic performance. Therefore, measures to avoid plant closures, an important determinant of interregional variations in economic growth rates, are much more likely to be implemented at the state and local than at the federal level.

The regional promotion and economic development policies that are becoming obsolete elsewhere also have little role in the United States if slowth continues. Thus, Miernyk's recommendation that remnants of the apparatus built up to administer regional development programs in the 1960s be finally dismantled is undoubtedly correct. The substitution of people-oriented for place-oriented policies would also seem applicable to the United States. However, the problem with this approach is that the United States has a poor record in redistributing income except as a result of upward mobility and other market forces. For example, welfare payments and unemployment compensation programs in the United States are so much weaker than in Western Europe and other developed countries that they do not offer individuals an effective buffer against the effects of chronic regional stagnation. Given the political obstacles to an expansion of these programs or to introducing redundancy payments legislation of the kind so common in Western Europe, the best bet for aiding low-income target groups in depressed regions may still be expansion of income maintenance programs and reform of direct taxation. For example, the combination of a negative income tax and a flat-rate income tax might be an irresistible attraction to both the Left and the

Right, if only the objections of tax-deduction lobbies could be overcome. Certainly, any solution adopted would have to be compatible with the need to keep tax revenue yields high without expanding net federal government spending.

Given the potential conflicts between industrial policy and regional goals, it would not be advisable for the United States to follow the European tradition of subsidizing declining industries in depressed regions. The pressures of international competition are so strong, and becoming stronger, that the only viable strategy is to continue stimulating an environment in which innovation and new products thrive. This rules out *national* attempts to induce "high-tech" industries to unfavorable locations, though the favored locations do not split on strict Sunbelt/Frostbelt lines (e.g., Massachusetts). Quaternary services are now dispersing into other major office centers, such as San Francisco and Houston, but given the pull of amenity-rich areas for these activities, this dispersion is unlikely to benefit the older industrial regions.

Since migration rates have traditionally been high in the United States, and given the historically strong link between migration and economic opportunity, there may be some scope for the design of relocation assistance policies to improve adjustments in regional labor markets. This idea has been a source of controversy. Two additional points may be mentioned here. First, in spite of rising unemployment, slowth in the last decade has coexisted with surprisingly high rates of employment growth. Although this may not continue, it warns against assuming that slowth automatically implies the lack of employment opportunities. This point is reinforced by the sharp differentials among regions in rates of employment growth. Second, if the phenomena of rising construction costs, high interest rates, the spread of rent control, and sluggish housing markets continue through the 1980s and beyond, housing may become a major constraint on mobility and, even with migration assistance, migration rates may fall to unprecedentedly low levels (see Chapter 4).[14]

The latest concept in United States regional policy discussions is, of course, the enterprise zone. Although it is difficult to be very specific in the absence of operational experience, some generalizations may be offered on the usefulness of the enterprise zone approach under slowth conditions. The tax benefits (i.e., offsets against profits) implied by the enterprise zone strategy are much more effective as an inducement in periods of rapid growth. Furthermore, the approach is essentially a "worst-first" strategy in which enterprise zones are defined in terms of criteria that stress very low incomes and high unemployment (the South Bronx is always used as the textbook example). But worst-first strategies are least likely to be effective in a slowth economy. One of the problems, of course, is that slowth implies a need for

---

[14]Housing is a major constraint on mobility in both Western and Eastern Europe.

more assisted areas, but the greater the number of enterprise zones created the more diluted the impact of each zone. Enterprise zones would work much better as an instrument for dealing with small pockets of stagnation within a rapidly growing economy. Thus, while a zone would fail in the South Bronx one might be successful in some neglected corner of the Dallas–Fort Worth region. The conclusion must be that the enterprise zone approach is not very promising if slowth is going to dominate the future.

Finally, the serious political implications of a slowth economy in which some regions continue to grow, but at the expense of others, need to be underlined. If slowth is closely linked to resource scarcities, these interregional variations in growth rates will not be merely minor, random fluctuations around a mean, but will be permanent, persistent, and wide. The situation is exacerbated in the United States because there are many resource-rich states (Miernyk identifies fourteen energy-surplus states; see Chapter 6), and each individual state has substantial political power and independence. The problems of spatial equity may become more sensitive than ever before, particularly because of the threat of the "haves" becoming the "have-nots." References to "a New Civil War," at least in political if not military terms, may be only a mild exaggeration.

References

Ashcroft, B. 1982. An assessment of regional policies and programs in Western Europe. Paper presented at the Conference on Regional Development Problems and Policies in Eastern and Western Europe, 7–11 June, at Villa Serbellini, Bellagio, Italy.

Ashcroft, B., and J. K. Swales. 1982. Estimating the effects of Government office dispersal. *Regional Science and Urban Economics* 12: 81–98.

Bell, M. E., and P. S. Lande, eds. 1982. *Regional Dimensions of Industrial Policy*. Lexington, Mass.: Lexington Books.

Birch, D. 1979. The Job Generation Process. Report submitted to Economic Development Administration, U.S. Department of Commerce. Cambridge, Mass.: Massachusetts Institute of Technology Program on Neighborhood and Regional Change.

Cameron, G. C. 1979. "The national industrial strategy and regional policy." In *Regional Policy: Past Experiences and New Directions*, edited by D. Maclennan and J. B. Parr, 279–322. Oxford, England: Martin Robertson & Co.

Chenery, H., et al. 1974. *Redistribution with Growth*. London: Oxford University Press.

Courbis, R. 1982. Measuring effects of French regional policy by means of a regional-national model. *Regional Science and Urban Economics* 12: 59–80.

Eckstein, O. 1978. *The Great Recession*. New York: North Holland.

Firestone, O. J. 1974. "Regional economic and social disparity." In *Regional Economic Development*, edited by O. J. Firestone, 205–67. Ottawa: University of Ottawa Press.

Garn, H. A., and L. C. Ledebur. 1982. "Congruencies and conflicts in regional and industrial policies." In *Regional Dimensions of Industrial Policy*, edited by M. E. Bell and P. S. Lande, 47–80. Lexington, Mass.: Lexington Books.

Glickman, N. J. 1981. Emerging urban policies in a slow-growth economy: conservative initiatives and progressive responses. Working Paper 49 in Regional Science and Transportation, University of Pennsylvania, Philadelphia, May.

Glickman, N. J., and E. M. Petras. 1981. International capital and international labor flows: implications for public policy. Working Paper 53 in Regional Science and Transportation, University of Pennsylvania, Philadelphia, August.

Higgins, B. 1973. "Trade-off curves and regional gaps." In *Development and Planning: Essays in Honour of Paul Rosenstein-Rodan*, edited by J. Bhagwati and R. S. Eckaus, 152–77. London: Allen and Unwin.

Holland, S. 1976. *Capital Versus the Regions*. London: Macmillan.

House, P. W., and R. G. Ryan. 1979. *The Future Indefinite: Decision-Making in a Transition Economy*. Lexington, Mass.: Lexington Books.

Hughes, K. 1982. *Corporate Response to Declining Rates of Growth*. Lexington, Mass.: Lexington Books.

Marquand, J. 1980. Measuring the effects and costs of regional incentives. London: Department of Industry, Her Majesty's Government, Government Economic Service Workshop Paper no. 32.

Miernyk, W. H. 1980a. Bioeconomics: international and interregional implications. Paper presented at the First World Regional Science Conference, June, in Cambridge, Massachusetts. (Reprinted as chap. 7 in Miernyk, 1982.)

Miernyk, W. H. 1980b. "Regional shifts in economic base and structure in the United States since 1940." In *Alternatives to Confrontation*, edited by V. L. Arnold, 97–124. Lexington, Mass.: Lexington Books.

Miernyk, W. H. 1980c. Jobs and income. Regional Research Institute, West Virginia University, Reprint Series III, no. 23.

Miernyk, W. H. 1981. Regional policy in a nearly stationary state. Paper presented at the Western Regional Science Association meeting, February, in Newport Beach, California. (Reprinted as chap. 5 in Miernyk, 1982.)

Miernyk, W. H. 1982. *Regional Analysis and Regional Policy*. Cambridge, Mass.: Oelgeschlager, Gunn, and Hain.

Office of the President. 1980. *The Economic Report of the President*. Washington, D.C.: Government Printing Office.

Oltmans, W. L., ed. 1974. *On Growth*. New York: Capricorn Books.

Pickvance, C. G. 1981. "Policies as chameleons: an interpretation of regional policy and office policy in Britain." In *Urbanization and Urban Planning in Capitalist Society*, edited by M. Dear and A. J. Scott, 231–65. London: Methuen.

Renshaw, E. F. 1976. *The End of Progress: Adjusting to a No-Growth Economy*. North Scituate, Mass.: Duxbury Press.

Richardson, H. W. 1973. *Regional Growth Theory*. London: Macmillan.

Richardson, H. W. 1982. "Industrial policy and regional development in less-developed countries." In *Regional Dimensions of Industrial Policy*, edited by M. E. Bell and P. S. Lande, 93–120. Lexington, Mass.: Lexington Books.

Rupferman, M., and M. D. Levi. 1980. *Slowth*. New York: Wiley.

Shefrin, B. M. 1980. *The Future of U.S. Politics in an Age of Economic Limits*. Boulder: Westview Press.

Stöhr, W. B., and D. R. F. Taylor. 1981. *Development from Above or Below? The Dialectics of Regional Planning in Developing Countries*. New York: Wiley.

Thompson, W. F., J. F. Karagonis, and K. D. Wilson. 1981. *Choice over Chance: Economic and Energy Options for the Future*. New York: Praeger.

Thurow, L. C. 1980. *The Zero-Sum Society: Distribution and the Possibilities for Economic Change*. New York: Basic Books.

United Nations Conference on Trade and Development. 1982. *Trade and Development Report 1982*. 3 vol. New York: United Nations.

World Bank. 1982. *World Development Report 1982*. New York: Oxford University Press.

Yergin, D., and M. Hillenbrand, eds. 1982. *Global Insecurity: A Strategy for Energy and Economic Revival*. New York: Houghton and Mifflin.

JONATHAN B. RATNER
TERRENCE W. KINAL

13 A Comparison of Alternative Approaches to Regional Forecasting as Applied to New York State

Economic Prospects for the Northeast reflects a widespread desire to open a window on the future and see if rain or shine lies ahead for our regional economy. A broad-gauge approach to this topic would focus on the fundamental forces shaping private economic actions and government policy in the region. The goals of that approach would be to predict the direction of change, to assess whether the change will be large or small, and to propose policies to foster more desirable change. The typical horizons are medium term, say five years, or long term, ten to twenty years. Many papers in this volume explore the Northeast's prospects using a variant of this general analytical strategy.

Other questions, though, call for a more narrow-gauge approach. Before taking action, decision makers, both public and private, may want their queries answered quantitatively. Often, their horizon is short term—six, twelve, or eighteen months ahead. For example, in preparing budgets, state officials want to know the size of tax revenues in the coming fiscal year. Likewise, state social service agencies require estimates of their case loads for the next budget cycle—and so on.

Both broad-gauge and narrow-gauge approaches involve prediction, yet the term *economic forecasting* is more commonly viewed as a narrow-gauge endeavor. Forecasting can also be distinguished from policy analysis. In the latter, decision makers want to predict the *consequences* of alternative policies or external events—state sales tax increases, higher public utility rates for power, decreases in defense contracts to firms in the state or region.

Econometricians have recently begun using the technique of vector autoregression (VAR) for economic forecasting and have applied it almost exclusively to national macroeconomic data. The papers by Friedman (1981), Sims (1980a and 1980b), Fischer (1981), and Gordon and King (1982) are leading examples. For reasons that will be developed, VAR is not suitable for projecting the consequences of hypothetical changes in government policies. Rather, its use should be limited to forecasting.

This chapter evaluates the use of this relatively new technique for regional economic forecasting. Anderson (1979a) pioneered the use of VAR in a regional context. We build upon his work, but focus on forecasting the economy of a single state—New York. First, the nature and successes of econometric models are described; second, the problems of using econometric models for regional forecasting are identified; third, the key concepts and appeal of a leading alternative—the class of techniques known as time series analysis—are outlined; fourth, the essentials of vector autoregression, which is a specific time series technique designed for multivariate forecasting, are presented; and fifth, a VAR model of the New York State economy is constructed, and its forecasting performance is evaluated.

Structural Econometric Models[1]

REGIONAL DATA: A CONSTRAINT

It should be stressed at the outset that important data problems confront subnational forecasters using virtually *any* prediction method. Three problems stand out:

1. Data for regions are sparser and probably less accurate than for nations.
2. The economic justification for using politically defined boundaries to delimit regions for analysis is often problematic. In cases such as the analysis of labor markets, national boundaries are appropriate because immigration laws "seal" those borders and thus form a well-defined labor market. But because a region like the Northeast or a state like New York is not a closed economy, other rationale for using these boundaries for organizing data must be sought.
3. Even if a consensus on boundaries is reached, the data may not cooperate. For example, a consumer price index for all of New York State is not available, although one for the New York City–northeastern New Jersey metropolitan area and another for the Buffalo metropolitan area are published.

---

[1] Anderson's (1979a) discussion of structural econometric models and their relationship to VAR served as a guide for our own treatment of these topics.

These data limitations may affect the operational feasibility and forecasting accuracy of alternative forecasting methods differently. The forecaster may propose (a method), but the data dispose. This home truth must not be shunted aside when the relative merits of techniques are considered.

NATIONAL ECONOMETRIC MODELS

The methods used to forecast subnational economies have been borrowed from national economic forecasting. The menu of techniques for prediction include: informal judgmental methods, leading indicators, trend extrapolation, structural econometric models, reduced-form econometric models, and advanced methods of time series analysis.[2] Structural econometric models (SEMs) dominate national forecasting; thus it follows that they also loom large in the regional and state forecasting field (examples include Ballard and Glickman [1977]; Duobinis [1981]; Glickman [1971]; Hall and Licari [1974]; Lantham, Lewis, and Landon [1979]; and Rubin and Erickson [1980]). Hence, they are the natural starting point for a discussion of subnational forecasting.[3]

These models are "structural" in the sense that they attempt to capture the structure of the macro economy in a set of relationships that link each variable of interest to its determinants. These relationships, then, are at least implicitly causal or explanatory. Usually the selection of variables as potential determinants to be included is not purely ad hoc, but based upon economic theory. The economic theory of households thus is invoked to generate the structural relationship assumed to govern consumer expenditure. Similarly, the theory of business firms stands behind the structural equations for employment demand and investment expenditures. Note that economic theory is used to isolate which variables affect which, as well as which are to be excluded a priori from each equation. For example, the stock of inventories is assumed to affect business inventory investment but not consumer expenditures. The parameters of the structural equations are crucial because they reflect the magnitude of the responses of a variable of interest to each of its determinants. The "econometric" feature of these models is, of course, that they are estimated from historical data using statistical methods. The set of equations, estimated over a particular sample period, constitutes an empirical

---

[2]Input-output models are not treated in this paper because their primary application is in long-range forecasting and in policy analysis (Harris and Nadji, n.d., pp. 38–39). Reduced-form models are likewise ignored in the text because they have not been used widely in regional forecasting. The best known example of this genre–the St. Louis Federal Reserve monetarist model (Anderson and Carlson, 1970)—describes the United States national economy. Finally, we do not treat export-base or shift-share models because doing so would take us too far afield. See Harris and Nadji (n.d.) for an examination of these and other methods of regional analysis.

[3]For suggested approaches to building regional SEMs and a discussion of the problems encountered, see Klein (1969); Glickman (1977 and 1978); Klein and Glickman (1977); Adams and Glickman (1980); and L'Esperance (1981).

SEM. Standard statistical tests are typically used to weed out explanatory variables with statistically insignificant effects from those sturdier determinants whose effects cannot easily be attributed to chance.

The typical SEM consists of relationships that are interdependent. The level of output depends in part on the wage rate, for example, but the latter is influenced in part by the level of output. If the interdependence or feedback manifests itself during the current time period, then the model is a simultaneous system. If, however, the causal arrow runs one way only during the current time period, then the system is recursive. For example, suppose the wage rate affects output today, but output does not affect the wage rate for three quarters. The typical SEM is simultaneous (although a whole block of equations may also be recursive with respect to at least one other subset of equations in the model).

A further characteristic of most SEMs is that individual equations are often dynamic. Lagged values of explanatory variables and of the dependent variable itself are used to capture inertia in adjustment or expectation formation.

SUCCESSES OF NATIONAL
ECONOMETRIC MODELS

The appeal of SEMs has three sources: first, their causal character dovetails with the predisposition of economists (and perhaps most people in our society) that economic events are explicable, and that economic theory is important in developing such an explanation. Second, SEMs are designed to be used in policy analysis as well as forecasting.[4] It seems natural to try to use the same model for these two purposes. Third, SEMs often have been quite successful as forecasting tools.

The successes of SEMs in national forecasting require some elaboration. Advocates of the econometric approach to forecasting can point to many examples of their value. For example, in a sample of well-regarded forecasters using SEMs, real GNP growth was predicted one year ahead, during the period 1959 to 1976, with an average margin of error of 1 to 1.5 percentage points. The inflation rate was predicted with an average absolute error of about 1.4 percentage points. The forecasts outperformed a naive extrapolation of the previous year's change—though only the real GNP forecasts did so by a wide margin (Zarnowitz, 1978, pp. 315–17). Furthermore, when the record of five major econometric models was studied, over half of the median forecasts of real GNP (for four quarters ahead) were found to be within 0.5 percent of the actual value (McNees, 1979).

But these successes are not the product of a mechanical projection of the

[4]The importance of the policy analysis function of SEMs is stressed by Klein and Young (1981).

econometric models. When making their predictions, forecasters do not rely exclusively on the SEM equations as estimated. Most published forecasts are "managed solutions," in which expert judgment about factors not included in the estimated model are used to modify the equations. These "add factors" generally improve model performance significantly.[5]

Yet, if, as Paul Samuelson is alleged to have remarked, "The secret of the Wharton [econometric] model is that Larry Klein is inside," what is the point of building an SEM for forecasting purposes? One answer is given by Intriligator (1978, p. 528):

> It combines the explicit objective discipline of the formal econometric model and regression estimators with the implicit subjective expertise of individual experts intimately aware of the real world system. The econometric model provides a useful starting place for formulating the forecast, it identifies those factors for which judgmental decisions must be made, and it provides a framework that ensures that the forecast is internally consistent.

Problems with Econometric Models

Sad to say, the state or regional forecaster cannot dine at the enticing econometric model banquet without paying the tab. The price of using SEMs at the subnational level reflects generic problems shared by all structural econometric models regardless of level of analysis, as well as those limitations peculiar to subnational models.

GENERIC PROBLEMS

Structural econometric models are vulnerable to three generic problems: First, the forecasting record of the major national structural econometric models has been uneven (see McNees [1978], Su [1978], and Eckstein and Warburg [1978]). Their successes coexist with substantial variability in accuracy. For example, Zarnowitz (1978, pp. 316–17) observes the performance of the forecasters he studied:

> Real GNP turned down in 1954, 1958, 1970, and 1974, but eight of ten predictions for those years specified continued rises. . . . [E]ven though [turning point errors] occurred in only about 13 percent of the total *number* of forecasts, these errors . . . account for 29 percent of the total absolute error of all real GNP forecasts in our collection . . . [In] quarterly multiperiod forecasting turning points are more frequent and more difficult to predict and errors associated with them are more important.

[5] Yet, as Fair (1971, p. 9) has argued, the use of add factors reduces the value of SEMs for testing economic theories. This in turn weakens the justification for using the same model to forecast and to conduct policy analysis.

This evidence about national SEMs suggests caution about the forecasting prowess of their regional counterparts.[6]

Second, the builders of the big national econometric models of 1970s and early 1980s vintage are trying to defend their efforts against a powerful theoretical challenge. Formulated initially by Lucas (1976) as an extension of "rational expectations" theory, this critique contends that structural relationships do not remain unaffected when policy changes. For example, optimizing households should make their consumption plans in light of their expectation that the government will cut tax rates if a recession occurs. Should this countercyclical tax policy be abandoned, consumers will not respond to a tax cut as they did before. That is, the structural relationship governing the response of consumption to tax parameters will change. If this critique is accepted, say its proponents, then existing structural models cannot be used to analyze the effects of alternative policies (see Gordon [1976], Lucas and Sargent [1978], Sims [1980a], and Malinvaud [1981]). Whether the Lucas critique of policy evaluation using SEMs does revolutionize the foundations of such analysis, as Lucas and Sargent (1978) dramatically maintain, or is more "a cautionary footnote," as their erstwhile convert Sims (1982, p. 108) now believes, is a controversy at the frontier of economic theory.

Third, structural econometric models are usually built to fit historical data. But good within-sample fits do not insure accurate forecasts beyond the sample period (Mayer, 1975). Part of the problem may be that search procedures for better-fitting specifications are ad hoc and are heavily influenced by prior beliefs about the true relationships (Cooley and Leroy, 1981).

PROBLEMS SPECIFIC TO SUBNATIONAL ECONOMETRIC MODELS

Because the regional economic data base is sparser than the national macro data base, the structural approach is harder to apply at the regional or state level. This poses additional problems not found at the national level (Glickman, 1978).

1. The heart of structural modeling involves relating an endogenous variable to a set of independent variables or determinants that are dictated by the relevant economic theory. If key variables are not available, the operational econometric model is an incomplete representation of the relationships explaining variables of interest. Thus, the equations are

---

[6]As McNees (1979, p. 51) remarks, "The record, in sum, is mixed. Examination of variations in forecast accuracy over time reveals instances of outstanding success along with some dismal failures. It is difficult to find a better description in any more sweeping generalization."

pale reflections of the underlying theory. Even when proxy variables can be obtained, they are often crude substitutes for the theoretically appropriate variables. So, theories are frequently fit to a Procrustean bed of state or regional data.[7]

2. Consider this example of misspecification induced by limited data: often, state and regional variables are hypothesized to depend in simple ways on the corresponding national variables.[8] But if intraregional relationships are important as well as this national-regional (or national-state) interaction, the usual approach throws out useful information.

3. Regional and state data are not collected or available with the frequency desired by model builders. Thus, at the subnational level, a model is likely to be annual (an example is the state model developed by the New York State Energy Office). This limits it to annual forecasts or to seasonally decomposed annual forecasts.[9]

EVALUATION OF STRUCTURAL
ECONOMETRIC MODELS

The structural econometric method passes the market test, since policy-makers and business managers continue to pay for SEM forecasts rather than dispensing with organized, formal forecasting entirely. Nevertheless, the forecasts are not received uniformly with huzzahs. In part, this is due to inappropriate standards of evaluation. These may be rooted in failure to understand that forecasts are probabilistic statements (like weather forecasts that predict "a 90 percent probability of rain") or are conditional on policy variables following assumed paths. Or, policymakers (especially elected officials) may want a degree of accuracy which is impossible for any known method to achieve.

Even the most favorable supporter of state and regional econometric forecasting will acknowledge that existing structural models have substantial limitations. First, it is impossible to generalize confidently about the forecasting accuracy of existing subnational econometric models because, as L'Esperance (1981, p. 117) notes, ". . . hardly any forecasting record exists for any regional econometric model." Notably, the study by Brooking and Hake (1980) of forecasting accuracy examines the records of only *four* state

---

[7]An example of this problem is offered ruefully by Thomas, Stekler, and Rutner (1979, p. 3).

[8]Anderson (1979a, p. 4) stresses this point. See also Klein (1969, p. 108), whose "top-down" approach to regional modeling is contrasted by Bolton (1980) to a "bottom-up" strategy, which makes many national variables endogenous in a multiregional system.

[9]Glickman (1971, pp. 23–25) emphasizes important statistical problems that plague regional SEMs estimated on the small samples typical of annual data. See Ratajczak (1974) for more discussion of data limitations as they affect regional SEM construction.

econometric models. Second, limitations on the availability and quality of data are often severe, as previously noted. Hence, even sound structural specifications may emerge in operational form as quite inadequate from the standpoint of economic theory. Third, the construction of structural econometric models is costly, both in dollars and person-hours. The larger the model, the more involved and the more costly it becomes to arrive at equations that reflect the underlying theoretical specification, employ the available variables, and fit the sample data well.

THE ALTERNATIVE OF TIME SERIES ANALYSIS

Users of state and regional econometric forecasts would welcome an alternative forecasting technique with greater forecasting accuracy than existing SEMs. Even if the alternative technique were no more accurate than existing SEMs but were less costly to construct and operate, these users would be interested. At the very least, the alternative method would provide a standard of comparison for an SEM.[10] The leading contender for this role is the set of techniques known as *time series analysis*.

All time series methods rely on statistical regularities in the history of the variable being forecast. Unlike the SEM approach, time series analysis seems devoid of a causal or explanatory framework (like economic theory). The most familiar example of time series analysis is trend extrapolation. Unfortunately, it ignores much information and lacks criteria for assessing the confidence one can place in the extrapolation.

Alternatives to trend extrapolation are illustrated below. *UR* is the unemployment rate, *NR* is the natural (equilibrium) unemployment rate, *d* is the disturbance or error term, *GNP* is the gross national product, *M* is money, *a*, *b*, *c*, and *g* are coefficients, and *t* is time.

Case 1.   Moving Average (MA)

$$UR_t = NR + d_t + a_1 d_{t-1} + a_2 d_{t-2} + \ldots + a_n d_{t-n}$$

Case 2.   Autoregression (AR)

$$UR_t = b_0 + b_1 UR_{t-1} + b_2 UR_{t-2} + \ldots + b_m UR_{t-m} + d_t$$

Case 3.   Autoregressive Moving Average (ARIMA)

$$\Delta UR_t = b_0 + b_1 \Delta UR_{t-1} + b_2 \Delta UR_{t-2} + \ldots + b_m \Delta UR_{t-m} + d_t + a_1 d_{t-1}$$
$$+ a_2 d_{t-2} + \ldots + a_n d_{t-n}$$

[10] For use of ARIMA time series models as a so-called naive method of forecasting in comparison with SEM predictions, see Cooper (1972), Nelson (1972), Behravesh (1976), and Eckstein (1979).

Case 4.   Transfer Function (TF)

$$UR_t = b_0 + b_1 UR_{t-1} + \ldots + b_m UR_{t-m} + d_t + a_1 d_{t-1} + \ldots + a_n d_{t-n}$$
$$+ c_{t-p} GNP_{t-p} + \ldots + c_{t-q} GNP_{t-q}$$

Case 5.   Vector Autoregression (VAR)

$$\begin{bmatrix} UR_t \\ GNP_t \\ M_t \end{bmatrix} = \begin{bmatrix} g_{11} & g_{12} & g_{13} \\ g_{21} & g_{22} & g_{23} \\ g_{31} & g_{32} & g_{33} \end{bmatrix} \begin{bmatrix} UR_{t-1} \\ GNP_{t-1} \\ M_{t-1} \end{bmatrix} + \begin{bmatrix} d_{1,t} \\ d_{2,t} \\ d_{3,t} \end{bmatrix}$$

Case 1 is a moving average model in which a particular economic variable (the unemployment rate) tends toward some equilibrium value (the "natural rate of unemployment"), but at any time deviates from this value because of current and part random disturbances ($d_t \ldots d_{t-n}$), such as government policy, oil price changes, and so forth. In the absence of further shocks, the unemployment rate becomes the natural rate after n periods.

Case 2, the autoregressive model, implies that the variable has a dynamic nature of its own, independent of shocks. Thus, the current value of *UR* can be expressed as a linear combination of past values plus an error term. There is no particular reason why in this model *UR* should reach a steady state.

Case 3, the ARIMA model, in effect combines cases 1 and 2. The statistical procedures capture both the autoregressive influences and any regularities in the residuals. The key to identifying the model is to determine the number of lags of the variables included on the right-hand side of the equation (Box and Jenkins, 1970). These techniques have proved very effective in forecasting time series where the past contains information relevant to the future.

The transfer function model (case 4) incorporates an element of economic theory by hypothesizing that unemployment is also affected by the level of gross national product. To apply the model, therefore, it is necessary to include an additional model to forecast GNP.

These examples show that the more information used to "explain" the behavior of *UR*, the more information must be forecast. Case 1 needs only estimates of *d*, while case 2 needs only forecasts of *UR*. Case 3, on the other hand, needs estimates of both *UR* and *d*, while case 4, in addition, requires forecasts of *GNP*. The choice of model for forecasting depends on the trade-off between improvement in performance from using additional information and the cost of its use.

Case 5 illustrates the vector autoregressive model, which relates the values of a collection (vector) of variables to their past values. Each variable depends not only on its own past values but also on those of other variables in the vector. VAR also draws a distinction between *responding variables*, the variables to be forecast, and *driving variables*, which are not of intrinsic interest to the forecast but are potential prime movers of the responding variables. Thus, in case 5, if $g_{31} = g_{32} = 0$, so that M is independent of UR and GNP, then M is a driving variable. Whereas the length of the lags between responding variables and their past values are chosen on statistical not theoretical economic grounds and the interdependences among responding variables are purely empirical, economic theory may be used to select the most relevant driving variables. Thus the contrast between SEMs as reflecting principles of economic theory and VAR as being atheoretical can be exaggerated.

The likely advantages of the VAR approach over structural econometric modeling involve data, accuracy, and cost.[11] Specifically, the *data requirements* of VAR are less demanding because fewer variables are needed to forecast than to trace out the structural interconnections of an economy. *Accuracy* is likely to be enhanced for two reasons: first, in a regional VAR model, national variables can be built into the model from the start. This allows both national-regional interaction as well as intraregional interaction among variables to appear in the data. Second, and very important, the VAR model automatically generates forecasts of its own driving variables, such as energy prices. In structural econometric models, such variables must be projected separately from the model, using ad hoc or subjective methods. Finally, the *cost* of a VAR model is less than that of an equivalent structural model. This is due to several factors. Smaller data requirements and model size facilitate the estimation and validation of the VAR model. Lower labor and computer costs for model construction are matched by lower operating expenses for generating a forecast.

The VAR method does have some drawbacks. Most important, it is not designed for conventional policy analysis, which is a mission claimed exclusively by SEMs. VAR models are limited in this way because they cannot be interpreted as the reduced forms of explicit, identified structural models. Specifically, even if a VAR model contains government policy variables, they are not embedded in a well-articulated set of relationships (i.e., a structure, which an explicit economic theory implies). The coefficients of a VAR model cannot be unscrambled to reveal the structural coefficients on which they depend. For example, the inclusion of state government spending in a VAR model may be warranted when the aim is to predict retail sales and other state aggregates. Suppose, though, one considers a hypothetical change in state government spending. One cannot be confident about the accuracy of the predicted effects of this change based on manipulating an estimated VAR

---

[11]Litterman (1980, pp. 16–18) reports VAR quarterly forecasts for real GNP growth and inflation that were more accurate than comparable SEM forecasts by Data Resources, Inc. (DRI) and Chase Econometrics. The VAR predictions of unemployment were less accurate than DRI's but more accurate than the Chase forecasts.

model. Although *some* dynamic structural model could be solved to yield a particular VAR model, one does not know *which* structural model that is.

From a specific structural perspective, the relationship between retail sales and government policy in a VAR model may even be spurious. Any reasonable structural model of a state will recognize, for example, that a state must obey a balanced budget constraint. Because the restrictions imposed on a VAR model are derived largely from statistical considerations rather than economic theory, however, such a constraint might be absent from a VAR model. Nonetheless, it might capture the historical association between state retail sales and state government spending quite well, and might produce accurate forecasts. Yet, this hypothetical VAR model should not be used to simulate the effects of a hypothetical change in state government spending, holding tax rates constant. First, a useful VAR forecasting model need not include tax rates a priori. Second, even if tax rates were included, there is no reason to expect them to enter the VAR model as they do in any particular SEM (e.g., in a simple Keynesian income-expenditure model with an income tax function, the marginal tax rate is not an independent variable entering the reduced form additively. Rather, it is one of several parameters that comprise the multiplier term [reduced-form coefficient] in the model). Finally, if the Lucas critique is persuasive, then no existing model—including the VAR— has coefficients that are invariant to changes in policy feedback rules.

A Case Study of VAR Forecasting for New York State

Anderson (1979a) built a small VAR model of the Ninth Federal Reserve District (Minnesota, Montana, North and South Dakota, northwestern Wisconsin, and the upper peninsula of Michigan) using quarterly data. Our case study of VAR for regional forecasting differs from Anderson's by modeling a single state in the Northeast—New York—rather than an amalgam of states and portions of states. In addition, monthly data and a longer sample period are used to increase the number of observations; obviously, the model can be updated and forecasted more frequently because of using monthly data.[12]

The variables included in our model are seasonally unadjusted, except where noted.[13]

Responding variables (all for New York State):

1. Total nonagricultural employment
2. Factory output index

[12]We did not follow Anderson (1979a) in estimating our model by a Bayesian method. Litterman (1979, 1980, and 1982) describes the application of Bayesian estimation to VAR.

[13]Our selection of variables for the model was influenced by Anderson's work as well as by the availability of data.

3. Retail sales (current dollars)
4. Consumer price index (for New York City–northeastern New Jersey only).

Driving variables (all for the United States):

5. Industrial production index (Federal Reserve Board)
6. Personal income (current dollars, seasonally adjusted)
7. Consumer price index, all consumers (seasonally adjusted)
8. Producer price index, fuel and power
9. Three-month Treasury bill yield (secondary market)

All of these series were available for January 1964 through December 1981.

THE VAR MODEL FORECASTS
FOR NEW YORK STATE

The RATS time series package (see Doan and Litterman, 1981) was used to estimate our VAR model of New York State and to make forecasts for twelve periods (months) ahead, using only the information available at the end of the current calendar year.[14]

Predictions for 1980 were generated by supplying to the model data that ended in December 1979. Likewise, predictions for the twelve months of 1981 were based on letting the model employ only the data available as of December 1980. To provide a standard for comparison with the VAR forecasts, results are presented for an ARIMA model and a transfer function (TF) model fitted to the same New York State data (available forecasts from one SEM of New York State are briefly discussed below).

How well did the estimated VAR model for New York State perform? Table 13.1 presents summary statistics that describe the forecast errors made by the three time series models.

The *percent bias* statistic measures the extent of under- or overprediction. The *percent mean absolute error* (%MAE) indicates how large the forecast error was over the twelve forecast periods on average, but does not let an overprediction cancel out an underprediction. The *root mean square percent error* (RMSPE) resembles the percent mean absolute error, but penalizes the larger errors more than proportionately to their size than it does smaller er-

---

[14] Since VAR does not allow for a MA representation, univariate ARIMA models were used to forecast the driving variables. However, the identified models did not have a MA part. Furthermore, a casual comparison of these results with the results from a full VAR model including these driving variables does not reveal any striking differences.

TABLE 13.1

Error Statistics Describing Mechanical Predictions from Three Time Series Models

New York State Economic Indicator	% Bias % Error	ARIMA	Transfer Function (TF)	VAR
		Predictions for 1980		
Retail sales	%Bias*	−2.89	25.42	−0.31
	%MAE†	3.53	25.42	3.83
	RMSPE‡	4.00	27.7	4.6
Nonagricultural employment	%Bias	8.08	−0.88	0.91
	%MAE	9.33	0.88	1.00
	RMSPE	10.1	1.15	1.15
Consumer price index (CPI)	%Bias	44.31	1.44	1.54
	%MAE	54.05	1.44	1.54
	RMSPE	55.7	1.44	1.73
Factory output	%Bias	60.96	13.57	1.11
	%MAE	70.26	13.57	1.79
	RMSPE	76.8	15.6	2.3
		Predictions for 1981		
Retail sales	%Bias	−8.14	−5.32	−6.33
	%MAE	8.14	5.40	6.33
	RMSPE	8.9	7.2	7.2
Nonagricultural employment	%Bias	9.80	0.58	1.16
	%MAE	11.10	0.84	1.16
	RMSPE	11.6	0.9	1.4
Consumer price index (CPI)	%Bias	46.13	−0.39	0.10
	%MAE	58.76	0.65	0.46
	RMSPE	60.3	0.9	0.6
Factory output	%Bias	3.83	10.64	−1.76
	%MAE	4.97	10.64	4.31
	RMSPE	5.5	11.6	5.8

Percent bias measures the extent of under- or overprediction during the forecast period. It is also known as average percent error or mean percent error.

$$\% \text{Bias} = (100) \left(\frac{1}{12}\right) \sum_{t=1}^{12} \frac{(A_t - F_t)}{A_t}$$

The actual value of the variable is denoted by A, the forecasted value by F.

†*Percent mean absolute error* (%MAE) measures the average size of the error, without letting overpredictions cancel out underpredictions.

$$\% \text{MAE} = (100) \left(\frac{1}{12}\right) \sum_{t=1}^{12} \frac{|A_t - F_t|}{A_t}$$

‡*The root mean square percent error* (RMSPE) also measures the typical error, but penalizes large, individual errors more heavily than the %MAE does.

$$\text{RMSPE} = (100) \frac{1}{\sqrt{12}} \sqrt{\sum_{t=1}^{12} \frac{(A_t - F_t)^2}{A_t^2}}$$

rors. These error statistics can be assessed in various ways, each of which is intuitive to some extent (and none of which is rigorously grounded in statistical inference theory). For example, compare the range of percent MAE for the three models:

VAR	1.00 (employment)	3.83 (retail sales)
Transfer Function	0.88 (employment)	25.42 (retail sales)
ARIMA	3.53 (retail sales)	70.26 (factory output)

This comparison suggests several conclusions: first, the VAR model produces the narrowest range of forecast errors, as measured by percent mean absolute error. In that sense, the VAR method is the most accurate of the three methods. Second, for both the VAR and the TF methods, employment is the easiest and retail sales the hardest variable to forecast. The ARIMA model does not follow suit, however. We infer that the extra information concerning other variables that both the VAR and the TF methods use improves predictive accuracy.

To summarize the results in more detail: the VAR forecasts were least biased for 1980 retail sales and factory output and ran a close second for 1980 CPI and 1981 retail sales. The ARIMA method overpredicted factory output and the CPI by large margins, overpredicted employment by a smaller percentage, but ran a reasonably close second in forecasting retail sales. In 1981, the results were much the same except that the best ARIMA prediction was for factory output. The TF model made the least biased forecasts of employment in both years, of the CPI in 1980, and of retail sales in 1981. But it ranked last in forecasting 1980 retail sales and 1981 factory output by substantially overpredicting both. Finally, the rankings of the forecasts by RMSPE are very similar to those arranged by degree of bias.

The preceding comparisons with more familiar and somewhat simpler time series methods are useful in deciding whether vector autoregression is worth the effort. Table 13.1 is innocent, however, of any comparison between VAR and the mainstay of formal subnational forecasting—the structural econometric model. Unfortunately, full comparable forecasts from SEMs of New York State are not available. A rough comparison can be made, however, between our VAR model and a quarterly model of New York State, which was constructed by Data Resources, Inc. and modified by the New York State Division of the Budget (see Burtis). The DRI-Budget Division forecasts of variables made one quarter ahead, from 1980 fourth quarter to 1981 third quarter, displayed a percent bias ranging from a low of 0.2 percent to a high of 2.2 percent. The VAR model forecast its four responding variables over a narrower range for 1980—0.3 percent to 1.5 percent. The range widened in 1981—0.1 percent to 6.3 percent.

Because neither the same variables were being forecast nor the same forecast period was being used, there is no guarantee that this particular SEM and our VAR model faced forecasting tasks of the same degree of difficulty. In one major respect, however, the VAR model was at a disadvantage. The SEM was asked to look only one period ahead, while the VAR had to project twelve periods beyond the most recent data in the sample over which the VAR model was estimated. Since a standard result in econometrics is that expected forecasting accuracy deteriorates with the number of periods being forecast, one anticipates less accuracy for the VAR forecasts, ceteris paribus (Pindyck and Rubinfeld, 1976, pp. 510–11). Nonetheless, despite its handicap, our VAR model worked better in 1980 than did the DRI–Budget Division SEM mentioned above.[15] Specifically, the range of percent mean absolute errors was narrower for the VAR forecasts. The 1981 results for the VAR model, however, cast its mainstream competitor in a more favorable light. Even so, the VAR forecasts for three of the four variables had a bias of less than 2 percent in absolute value.

A recent survey of state SEMs suggests that the standard of forecast accuracy be less than 3 percent error in forecasting four quarters ahead. Brooking and Hake (1980) report that three econometric models of the southeastern states had average errors of 2 to 2.7 percent in forecasting state employment and personal income. This comparison also stacks the deck against the VAR model, but this does not prevent the VAR from standing up well against its competition.[16] (see also L'Esperance, 1981, pp. 114–17).

Anderson's VAR model of the Ninth Federal Reserve District provides a final comparison. Table 13.2 presents the percent mean absolute error encountered in forecasting the years 1972 through 1976. As theory suggests, the forecast accuracy of Anderson's VAR model deteriorates as the forecast horizon is extended. No strong conclusions should be drawn from the comparison of the errors in the Ninth District VAR forecasts and our New York VAR forecasts. Ideally, for each model, one wants to know how intrinsically difficult the data were to forecast. (For example, were there structural breaks, a higher incidence of turning points, etc.?) With that important caveat, note that the twelve-period-ahead forecast of the New York VAR model has a lower percent mean absolute error than does the eight-period-ahead Ninth District forecast.

---

[15] Also, the SEM forecast reflected subjective add-factor modifications of the mechanical predictions generated by the model itself. Burtis (n.d., p. 5) reports that "the subjective add-factoring significantly reduced the error." With only mechanical addfactoring based on serial correlation in recent errors, the range of percent bias statistics for the eighteen variables was 0.8 percent to 10.0 percent. Strictly speaking, it is more appropriate to compare our forecasts with these mechanically adjusted forecasts than with the subjectively adjusted ones reported in the text.

[16] The reason is that the forecast horizon for the VAR model contained more periods.

TABLE 13.2
Percent Mean Absolute Errors of Ninth District VAR Model*

	Forecast Horizon		
Variables	1 Quarter	4 Quarters	8 Quarters
Consumer price index	0.6	1.9	4.5
Civilian labor force	0.7	1.5	3.6
Civilian employment	0.8	1.7	2.4
Personal income	1.4	3.6	5.0
Retail sales	4.8	5.3	7.5

*Quarterly data. *Ex post* forecasts for eight quarters ahead were made each quarter for the period 1972 first quarter to 1976 fourth quarter.
Source: See Anderson (1979a), p. 6.

FROM STATE TO REGIONAL FORECASTING

No conceptual barrier stands in the way of using a vector autoregressive model to forecast the major aggregate economic variables of the Northeast. If Bolton's (1980) typology is followed, two approaches to building a regional model are possible: the first, a "bottom-up" strategy, requires a separate VAR model for each individual state in the region. To make a forecast of the ith variable at the regional level, simply sum the forecasts of that i^{th} variable for each state. The second, a "top-down" strategy, entails estimating a single VAR model on aggregated regional data.

The choice between the two approaches hinges in part on weighing any gains in forecasting accuracy due to disaggregation against the extra costs of estimating, simulating, and updating a set of state models. A wise decision also depends on the extent to which the variables to be included in the model are defined identically across states and, indeed, are available. If these state data sets conform to one another, then each variable can be aggregated across states into a regional variable. In this case, it would be natural initially to build a VAR model for the region following the top-down approach. Moreover, it appears that a VAR model requires relatively few variables in total to generate forecasts of a given number of economic indicators (or responding variables). This feature of VAR models would also favor them over SEMs if the bottom-up strategy were undertaken; state-level VAR models seem to comprise a less arduous enterprise than do state-level SEMs.

Summary and Conclusions

Although state and regional forecasting typically requires a relatively large number of variables, many important variables either are not available in a form that matches the corresponding theoretical construct or are observed too infrequently to be used. This poses particular problems for structural econometric models (SEMs)—the most prevalent formal technique used in short-term forecasting at the subnational level.

The structural econometric approach has had forecasting successes and is appealing as a tool for policy analysis. But these virtues are counterbalanced by forecasting failures and by theoretical doubts about the validity of SEMs as vehicles for policy evaluation.

Time series analysis, which includes techniques such as ARIMA and transfer function modeling, presents a sophisticated alternative to the economist's conventional SEM approach. Where the latter uses economic theory as a prism to focus the light of historical data in ways useful to forecasting, time series analysis makes statistical considerations act as its prism. Forecasts at the national macroeconomic level using ARIMA models have been at least as accurate as SEM forecasts for many important aggregate variables. In addition, time series methods tend to require fewer variables and to be cheaper to build and operate than an SEM.

Vector autoregression (VAR) shares with other time series methods their purely statistical emphasis as well as their virtues regarding data requirements and costs. VAR is distinguished from other time series methods in permitting lagged values of a responding variable, say, Y_1, to affect current Y_1 as well as other responding variables, Y_i, $(i = 2, \ldots, n)$. This dynamic interdependence is augmented by including driving variables in the model to serve as leading indicators; they affect the current values of the responding variables without any feedback. Moreover, the VAR approach determines the categorization of the variables by statistical estimation exclusively.

Our VAR model of New York State predicts four responding variables—employment, retail sales, factory output, and the consumer price index—by lagged values of these responding variables plus lagged values of national economic driving variables. The latter are predicted individually by separate ARIMA equations.

The VAR model made predictions twelve months ahead of 1980 and of 1981 data. When compared with ARIMA and transfer function forecasts, VAR predictions are more accurate. In addition, comparisons with the one available SEM for New York are generally favorable to the VAR approach.

Our exploratory application of VAR supports several claims of its proponents (e.g., Anderson, 1979a, pp. 2, 4, and 5). The data requirements of our VAR model were less demanding than would have been the case for a comparable SEM. Likewise, a VAR model seems to be less expensive to build and operate than does a hypothetical SEM counterpart. Finally, the accuracy of the predictions from our VAR model of New York State indicates that VAR, as a benchmark for structural econometric forecasts and as a forecasting tool in its own right, is a promising approach for state and regional forecasting and warrants further investigation.

References

Adams, F. G., and N. J. Glickman. 1980. *Modeling the Multiregional Economic System*. Lexington, Mass.: Lexington Books.

Anderson, L. C., and K. M. Carlson. 1970. A monetarist model for economic stabilization. *Federal Reserve Bank of St. Louis Monthly Review* 52 (4): 7–25.

Anderson, P. A. 1979a. Help for the regional economic forecaster: vector autoregression. *Federal Reserve Bank of Minneapolis Quarterly Review* 3(3), Summer: 2–7.

Anderson, P. A. 1979b. A test of the exogeneity of national variables in a regional econometric model. Research Department Working Paper 124, Federal Reserve Bank of Minneapolis.

Ballard, K., and N. J. Glickman. 1977. A multiregional econometric forecasting system: A model for the Delaware Valley. *Journal of Regional Science* 17: 161–77.

Behravesh, N. 1976. Forecasting inflation: does the method make a difference? *Federal Reserve Bank of Philadelphia Business Review* September/October: 9–17.

Bolton, R. 1980. Multiregional models: introduction to a symposium. *Journal of Regional Science* 20 (2): 131–42.

Box, G.E.P., and G. M. Jenkins. 1970. *Time Series Analysis: Forecasting and Control*. San Francisco: Holden-Day.

Brooking, C. G., and D. A. Hake. 1980. "The impact of the regional econometric model on the policy formation decision process." In *Modeling the Multiregional Economic System*, edited by F. G. Adams and N. J. Glickman, 223–37. Lexington, Mass.: Lexington Books.

Burtis, D. n.d. The forecast accuracy of the New York State econometric model. New York State Division of the Budget. Mimeo.

Cooley, T. F., and S. F. Leroy. 1981. Identification and estimation of money demand. *American Economic Review* 71: 825–44.

Cooper, R. L. 1972. "The predictive performance of quarterly econometric models of the United States." In *Econometric Models of Cyclical Behavior*, edited by B. G. Hickman. Vol. 2. New York: Columbia University Press.

Doan, T. A., and R. B. Litterman. 1981. *RATS User's Manual*. Version 4.1. Minneapolis, Minn.: VAR Econometrics.

Duobinis, S. F. 1981. An econometric model of the Chicago Standard Metropolitan Statistical Area. *Journal of Regional Science* 21: 293–319.

Eckstein, O. 1979. "Econometric models for forecasting and policy analysis: the present state of the art." Reprinted in *DRI Readings in Macroeconomics*, edited by A. R. Sanderson, 2–18. New York: McGraw-Hill, 1981.

Eckstein, O., and P. M. Warburg. 1978. How have forecasts worked?: discussion. *American Economic Review Proceedings* 68: 320–21.

Fair, R. C. 1971. *A Short Run Forecasting Model of the United States Economy*. Lexington, Mass.: Lexington Books.

Fair, R. C. 1979. An analysis of the accuracy of four macroeconometric models. *Journal of Political Economy* 87: 701–18.

Fischer, S. 1981. Relative shocks, relative price variability, and inflation. *Brookings Papers on Economic Activity* 2: 381–431.

Friedman, B. M. 1981. The roles of money and credit in macroeconomic analysis. Working Paper 831, National Bureau of Economic Research.

Glickman, N. J. 1971. An econometric forecasting model for the Philadelphia region. *Journal of Regional Science* 11: 15–32.

Glickman, N. J. 1977. *Econometric Analysis of Regional Systems*. New York: Academic Press.

Glickman, N. J. 1978. Son of "The specification of regional econometric models." *Papers of the Regional Science Association* 32: 155–77.

Gordon, R. J. 1976. "Can econometric policy evaluations be salvaged—a comment." In *The Phillips Curve and Labor Markets*, edited by K. Brunner and A. Meltzer, 47–61. Vol. 1 of the Carnegie-Rochester Conferences on Public Policy. Amsterdam: North Holland.

Gordon, R. J., and S. R. King. 1982. The output cost of disinflation in traditional and vector autoregressive models. *Brookings Papers on Economic Activty* 1: 205–41.

Granger, C.W.J., and P. Newbold. 1977. *Forecasting Economic Time Series*. New York: Academic Press.

Hall, O. P., and J. A. Licari. 1974. Building small region econometric models: extension of Glickman's structure to Los Angeles. *Journal of Regional Science* 14: 337–53.

Harris, C. C., Jr., and M. Nadji. n.d. Methods of regional and interregional economic analysis. Working Paper No. 82-6.

Intriligator, M. S. 1978. *Econometric Models, Techniques and Applications*. Englewood Cliffs, N.J.: Prentice-Hall, Inc.

Klein, L. R. 1969. The specification of regional econometric models. *Papers of the Regional Science Association* 23: 105–115.

Klein, L. R., and N. J. Glickman. 1977. Econometric model building at the regional level. *Regional Science and Urban Economics* 7: 3–23.

Klein, L. R., and R. M. Young. 1981. *An Introduction to Econometric Models and Econometric Forecasts*. Lexington, Mass.: Lexington Books.

Lantham, W. R., K. A. Lewis, and J. H. Landon. 1979. Regional econometric models: specification and simulation of a quarterly alternative for small regions. *Journal of Regional Science* 19: 1–13.

L'Esperance, W. L. 1981. *The Structure and Control of a State Economy*. London: Pion Ltd.

Litterman, R. B. 1979. Techniques of forecasting using vector autoregression. Research Department Working Paper 115, Federal Reserve Bank of Minneapolis.

Litterman, R. B. 1980. A Bayesian procedure for forecasting with vector autoregressions. Cambridge: MIT. Mimeo.

Litterman, R. B. 1982. A use of index models in macroeconomic forecasting. Research Department Staff Report 78, Federal Reserve Bank of Minneapolis.

Lucas, R. E., Jr. 1976. "Econometric policy evaluation: a critique." In *The Phillips Curve and Labor Markets*, edited by K. Brunner and A. Meltzer, 19–46. Vol. 1

of the Carnegie-Rochester Conferences on Public Policy. Amsterdam: North Holland.

Lucas, R. E., Jr., and T. J. Sargent. 1978. "After Keynesian macroeconomics." In *After the Phillips Curve: Persistence of High Inflation and High Unemployment*, 49–72. Boston: Federal Reserve Bank of Boston.

Malinvaud, E. 1981. Econometrics faced with the needs of macroeconomic policy. *Econometrica* 49: 1363–75.

Mayer, T. 1975. Selecting economic hypotheses by goodness of fit. *Economic Journal* 85: 877–83.

McNees, S. K. 1978. The "rationality" of economic forecasts. *American Economic Review Proceedings* 68: 301–5.

McNees, S. K. 1979. The forecasting record for the 1970s. *New England Economic Review*. (September/October): 33–53.

Nelson, C. R. 1972. The prediction performance of the FRB-MIT-PENN model of the U.S. Economy. *American Economic Review* 62 (5): 902–17.

Pindyck, R. A., and D. L. Rubinfeld. 1976. *Econometric Models and Economic Forecasts*. New York: McGraw-Hill.

Ratajczak, D. 1974. Data limitations and alternative methodology in estimating regional econometric models. *Review of Regional Studies* 4: 51–64.

Rubin, B. M. and R. A. Erickson. 1980. Specification and performance improvements in regional econometric forecasting models: a model for the Milwaukee Metropolitan Area. *Journal of Regional Science* 20: 11–35.

Sargent, T. J. 1979. Estimating vector autoregressions using methods not based on explicit economic theories. *Federal Reserve Bank of Minneapolis Quarterly Review* 3(3). Summer: 8–15.

Sargent, T. J., and C. A. Sims. 1977. "Business cycle modeling without pretending to have too much *a priori* economic theory." In *New Methods in Business Cycle Research: Proceedings from a Conference*. Minneapolis, Minn.: Federal Reserve Bank of Minneapolis.

Sims, C. A. 1972. Money, income, and causality. *American Economic Review* 62 (4): 540–52.

Sims, C. A. 1980a. Macroeconomics and reality. *Econometrica* 48: 1–48.

Sims, C. A. 1980b. Comparison of interwar and postwar business cycles: monetarism reconsidered. *American Economic Review Proceedings* 70: 250–57.

Sims, C. A. 1982. Policy analysis with econometric models. *Brookings Papers on Economic Activity* 1: 107–52.

Su, V. 1978. An error analysis of econometric and noneconometric forecasts. *American Economic Review Proceedings* 68 (2): 306–12.

Thomas, R. W., H. O. Stekler, and J. L. Rutner. 1979. "A model of construction activity in subnational areas." In *An Evaluation of Small-Area Forecasting Models and 1980 Census—Small-Area Statistics Program*. Bureau of the Census. U.S. Department of Commerce. Washington, D.C.: Government Printing Office.

Zarnowitz, V. 1978. On the accuracy and properties of recent macroeconomic forecasts. *American Economic Review Proceedings* 68 (2): 213–319.

About the Contributors

HARRY W. RICHARDSON is Distinguished Professor of Economics, Regional Planning, and Public Policy at the State University of New York at Albany and Professor of Economics at the University of Southern California. He is the author of eighteen books and more than eighty papers. His current research interests are in national urban and regional development policies in developing countries. He has been a consultant for the World Bank, the United Nations, and other international and governmental agencies.

JOSEPH H. TUREK is a Ph.D. candidate and Lecturer in Economics at the State University of New York at Albany. He received his M.P.A. from the Maxwell School of Citizenship and Public Affairs at Syracuse University and has worked in government at the federal, state, and local levels. His research interests include regional growth theory and the analysis of the spatial impacts of public policies.

ROY BAHL is Professor of Economics and Director of the Metropolitan Studies Program in the Maxwell School at Syracuse University. He has served as a consultant to public and private agencies on matters of state and local government finance and is on the board of directors of the New York State Research Authority. He has written widely on matters of state and local government finance and economic development in the Northeast.

BENNETT HARRISON is Associate Professor of Urban Studies and Economics in the Department of Urban Studies and Planning at Massachusetts Institute of Technology, where he teaches political economy, labor economics, and economic development. He works with a number of labor unions and community organizations across the country and writes regularly for both popular and scholarly media. His most recent book, coauthored with Barry Bluestone, is *The Deindustrialization of America* (New York: Basic Books, 1982). With Anna Lee Saxenian, he has recently completed a book on the modern history of the New England economy.

JAMES W. HUGHES is Professor of Urban Planning and Policy Development at the Rutgers University School of Urban and Regional Policy. He received his Ph.D. from Rutgers.

Professors Sternlieb and Hughes have jointly published fifteen books and more than thirty articles. Among them are *Demographic Trends and Economic Reality: Planning and Markets in the '80s*, *The Future of Rental Housing*, *America's Housing: Prospects and Problems*, and *Shopping Centers: U.S.A.*

TERRENCE W. KINAL is Assistant Professor of Economics at the State University of New York at Albany. He received his Ph.D. from the University of Minnesota in 1976 and taught at the College of St. Thomas prior to joining SUNY-Albany in 1980. His teaching and research areas include econometric theory, economic forecasting, and microeconomic theory. He has published papers in *Econometrica* and *Economics Letters*.

WILLIAM H. MIERNYK is Claude Worthington Benedum Professor of Economics and Director of the Regional Research Institute at West Virginia University. He received his Ph.D. from Harvard University, where he was a visiting professor in 1969–70. He is the author of twelve books and a large number of papers on input-output analysis, energy economics, regional development, and other topics in economics. He has served as a consultant to a dozen governmental and research agencies.

JONATHAN B. RATNER is an economist with the United States Government Accounting Office (GAO). His research is in the areas of macroeconomics and labor economics. His recent publications include an examination of the microeconomic foundations of inflation theory. Educated at Harvard University and Yale University, he taught previously at the State University of New York at Albany and Wellesley College.

H. V. SAVITCH is Professor of Urban Affairs and Public Policy at the State University of New York at Purchase. He is the author of *Urban Policy and the Exterior City* (New York: Pergamon Press, 1979) as well as numerous articles on urban politics and national policy. A forthcoming book (co-authored with James Simmie) is entitled *Capital Cities* and examines growth and policy in London, New York, Paris, and Tokyo. Professor Savitch has directed projects dealing with the operations of national and local government.

GEORGE STERNLIEB is founder and Director of the Center for Urban Policy Research at Rutgers University and Professor of Urban Planning and Policy Development. He received his M.B.A. and D.B.A. degrees from the Harvard Business School. As noted under HUGHES, Dr. Sternlieb has copublished many works with his colleague.

BENJAMIN H. STEVENS received his M.C.P. and his Ph.D. in regional planning and economics from the Massachusetts Institute of Technology. He taught in the Department of Regional Science at the University of Pennsylvania from 1956 to 1972, achieving the rank of Professor. Since 1956 he has been Director of the Regional Science Research Institute (RSRI) and co-editor of the *Journal of Regional Science*. Since 1965 he has been President of RSRI. He has numerous publications in professional journals and has co-authored several books. Director of over one hundred research projects, he is currently Senior Research Associate in charge of all research at RSRI. His main areas of research interest are regional economic theory and models and industrial location.

ROGER J. VAUGHAN is a Senior Fellow with the Gallatin Institute in Washington, D.C., conducting research on economic policy. For two years he served as Deputy Director of the Office of Development Planning for New York State. Before that he was an Assistant Vice President with Citibank, N.A., in New York City. He has published several books and articles on tax policy, development finance, and public works. He has a Ph.D. in economics from the University of Chicago.

Name Index

Subject Index

Love and Garbage

By the same author

A Ship Named Hope
My Merry Mornings
My First Loves
A Summer Affair

Ivan Klíma

Love and Garbage

Translated from the Czech by
Ewald Osers

Chatto & Windus
LONDON

Published in 1990 by
Chatto & Windus Ltd
20 Vauxhall Bridge Road
London SW1V 2SA

A CIP catalogue record for this book is available from the British
Library.

ISBN 0 7011 3362 7

Czech title *Láska a Smetí*

Copyright © 1986 Ivan Klíma
Translation copyright © 1990 Ewald Osers

The excerpt from Pushkin's 'The Bronze
Horseman' on page 92 is from the
translation by Oliver Elton
published by Edward Arnold & Co. (1935)

Printed and bound in Great Britain by
Mackays of Chatham PLC, Chatham, Kent

None of the characters in this book — and that includes the narrator — is identical with any living person.

I

The woman in the office told me to go to the locker room: I was to wait there. So I set out across the court to a door which bore the notice LOCKERS. The office was grey and dismal, and so was the courtyard, with a pile of broken bricks and rubble in one corner, several two-wheeled handcarts, a lot of dustbins, and not a touch of greenery anywhere. The locker room seemed to me even more depressing: it was so dirty that, even had I not already known it, I would have guessed that this was a place where people changed who were supposed to look after our cleanliness. The cleanliness of our streets, of course, not the purity of our souls.

I sat down on a seat by the window which looked out on that dismal yard, clutching a small leather case which contained three small sweet buns, a book, and a notebook in which I was in the habit of jotting down anything that occurred to me in connection with what I was writing. Currently I was finishing an essay on Kafka.

There were two other men sitting in the locker room already. One, tall and greying, reminded me of the specialist who many years before had removed my tonsils; the other, a short, stocky man of uncertain age in very dishevelled and dirty trousers scarcely reaching halfway down his calves and with enormous sewn-on pockets rather like misshapen pistol holsters, wore on his head a sea-captain's cap with a peak and a gleaming golden anchor above it. From beneath the peak a pair of eyes the colour of shallow coastal waters were watching me curiously. Those eyes, or rather their glance, seemed somehow familiar. He obviously realised that I was new here and advised me to put my identity card on the table. I did as he said, and as he placed his next to mine I noticed that he did not have a right hand; a black hook protruded from his sleeve.

By now my new workmates were beginning to arrive – the sweepers. A squat young idiot with a nervous facial tic sat down next to me, took out a pair of dirty shaft-boots from a locker, and turned them upside down. From one of them there ran out a quantity of liquid which might just have, but most probably did not, come from a tap. He immediately began to scream at us all in a language of which I was unable to make out a single word.

I am not sure myself what made me decide to try this unattractive occupation. Most probably I thought that I would gain from it an unexpected view of the world. Every so often you feel that unless you look at the world and at people from a new angle your mind will get blunted.

As I was waiting for what would happen next there suddenly came to my mind the scene, fifteen years ago, when I was about to return home from my stay in America and the dean there gave a dinner in my honour. The dean was a mathematician, and wealthy. He owned a stableful of horses and a house in the style of a hunting lodge. I had only met him once before and I didn't really want to go to the dinner: a crowd of strangers tends to depress me. But then, how could I have known anyone properly when I had been teaching at the university for a mere six months? In the event they all turned out to be pleasant to me and full of smiles as Americans are, and with varying degrees of urgency they asked me to explain what on earth possessed me to want to leave their free and wealthy country to return home, to a poor and unfree country, where they'd probably lock me up or send me to Siberia. I tried to be equally pleasant. I conjured up some kind of patriotism, some kind of mission, until I hit on a convincing explanation. I said that back home people knew me. Even if I had to sweep up garbage in the streets I would be for them what I was, what I wanted to be to the exclusion of anything else, a writer, whereas here, even if I could drive around in my little Ford, I would always be just one of those immigrants on whom a

2

great country had taken pity. These were my boastful words. In reality I wanted to return home, to the place where there were people I was fond of, where I was able to speak fluently, to savour the language I loved.

Now I knew that if I was a street-sweeper I would, for the majority of the people, be simply a person who swept the streets, a person hardly noticed. Fortunately I didn't care too much about what I was in the eyes of other people.

At that moment a woman appeared in the cloakroom. She had a good figure, with slim hips in tight-fitting jeans. Her face was suntanned and wrinkled like that of the old Indian women I had seen in the market of Santa Fé. One of them, the oldest and most Indian-looking, had, to my great delight, a notice above her stall, revealing that her Christian name was Venus. This Mrs Venus here did not even sit down; from her handbag she produced a packet of Start cigarettes, and as she lit up I noticed that her hands were shaking. The match went out before the cigarette was alight, and Venus swore at it. Her voice was so drink-sodden, deep and hoarse, and her intonation so perfectly matched her appearance, that the leading ladies of the foremost theatres, who often have to play common women, could have taken lessons from her.

Next came a youngster with a shy, pale and girlish face and a capacious postman's bag over his shoulder, and then a few nondescript elderly men. In the background a short plump man with shrewd features began to change into his working clothes. Like the little idiot next to me he had his own locker. From it he pulled out some khaki overalls.

On the dot of six the woman from the office entered and read out the names of those assigned to cleaning our district of the city that day. First she read out those who were to erect the traffic signs, then the team of three whose job it was to empty the public litter bins. Finally she gave the fat man in the overalls a sheet of paper and announced that the following were detailed for the work party: Zoulová, Pinz, Rada, Štych, and finally she read out my name. At the same time she handed me a sweeper's orange vest. I accepted it, quickly walked round the table and chose the locker nearest the corner. I opened the door, on which *Bui dinh Thi* was written in chalk, took my identity papers, buns, book and notebook from my case, stuffed everything into my pockets and closed the locker again.

We all walked out into the depressing yard, where some garbage trucks had arrived noisily and where two young men were flinging shovels, brooms, scrapers, wheelbarrows, traffic signs and battered dustbins onto a pick-up. It was only a quarter past six in the morning, and already I could feel the stifling expanse of the day stretching out before me.

The man in the overalls, who'd clearly been assigned to us as our foreman, strode over to the gate and four figures stepped out from the bunch of sweepers, including the only woman, the youngster with the girlish face, and the man who reminded me of the ear-nose-and-throat specialist. Also the fellow with the captain's cap. These people seemed as alien to me as the work which I was about to perform with them; nevertheless I walked along, just as they did, at a pace which would have been more appropriate to a funeral cortège. With measured tread we strode through the streets of Nusle in our orange uniforms; all around us people were hurrying to work, but we were in no hurry, we were at work already.

This was not a state of mind in which I found myself often: most of my life I had been in a hurry, obsessed by the thought of what I had to accomplish if I wanted to be a good writer.

I had wanted to become a writer ever since childhood, and authorship for a long time seemed to me the most exalted profession. I believed that a writer should be as wise as a prophet, as pure and rare as a saint, as adroit and fearless as an acrobat on a flying trapeze. Even though I now know that there are no chosen professions, and that what appears to be wisdom, purity, exceptional character, fearlessness and adroitness in one person may seem eccentricity, madness, dullness and uselessness in another, that ancient idea has struck, against my will, in my conscious and subconscious mind, and that is probably why I am afraid to describe myself by the term 'writer'. When I am asked what I do I try to avoid an answer. Besides, who dare say of himself that he is a writer? At best he can say: I've written some books. Now and again I even think that I am unable to define clearly what the subject of my work is, or what is already and what is not yet literature.

Now I was able to enjoy a leisurely walk and the reassuring knowledge that I knew exactly what was expected of me. Slowly we passed the National Committee and the Supreme Court building and arrived at what used to be the Sokol gym hall, where our equipment was already waiting for us: brooms, shovels, scrapers and a handcart whose body was half a dustbin. To show my goodwill I took the biggest shovel.

As a child I had lived on the outskirts of Prague, in a villa which stood next door to a tavern patronised by hauliers. Every day, just before noon, the municipal sweeper would arrive. He'd draw up his cart in the open space where the hauliers had pulled up with their horses, take out his shovel and almost ceremonially sweep up the horse droppings, or any other rubbish, and drop it all into his cart. He would then push his cart up against the wall and make for the bar. I liked him: he wore a peaked cap, though not a sailor's cap, and an upturned moustache in memory of our last emperor. I also liked his occupation, which I thought must surely be one of the most important jobs a man could have, and I believed that street-sweepers therefore enjoyed everyone's respect. In reality this was not so. Those who cleansed the world of garbage or of rats were never shown any respect. A few days ago, when I was reading something about the centre of Prague, where Franz Kafka used to walk, I came across the mention of an Italian stucco worker named Spinelli who, exactly two hundred years ago, in St George's church, had slashed the face, mouth and shoulders of his lover Marianne, the daughter of the royal gardener of the castle of Prague. For that he was gaoled, and taken to the place of execution, but was then reprieved and instead sentenced to clean the streets of Prague for three years. Respect as a rule was shown only to those who cleansed the world of human refuse, to bailiffs, judges and inquisitors.

But I continued to think about sweepers, or rather about their honourable work. When I wrote a short story twenty years ago about the slaughtering of horses – I had actually seen this at a slaughterhouse in Poland – I invented an apocalyptic scene about the incineration of their remains. I tried to get into the Prague incinerator, which as a boy I used to see burning in the distance, reducing everything to one gigantic pile of clinker, but the manager refused to let me inside. He was probably afraid I might wish to uncover some shortcomings in the operation of his crematorium.

Many years later, when I was working as a cleaner at the Krč hospital, I had to cart all the refuse to the big furnace every morning: blood-soaked bandages, gauze full of pus and hair, dirty rags smelling of human excrement, and of course masses of paper, empty tins, broken glass and plastic. I'd shovel everything into the furnace and watch with relief as the rubbish writhed as if in agony, as it melted in the fierce flames, and listen to the cracking and exploding sounds of the glass and to the victorious roar of the fire. On one occasion, I never discovered why, whether the fire was too fierce or, on the contrary, not hot enough, or whether it was the wind, the rubbish did not burn but the draught in the furnace sucked it up and spewed it out from the high chimney-stack, up towards the sky, and I watched with horror and amazement as all my refuse – rags, paper and tatters of bloody bandages – slowly descended to the ground, as it was caught in the branches of the trees, or sailed towards the open windows of the wards. And at that moment the idiots and imbeciles from the Social Welfare Institute, who were responsible for the upkeep of the hospital grounds, came rushing out howling with delight and pointing to a tall silver birch which was draped like a Christmas tree.

It occurred to me that what had just happened was no more than an instructive demonstration of an everyday occurrence. No matter ever vanishes. It can, at most, change its form. Rubbish is immortal, it pervades the air, swells up in water, dissolves, rots, disintegrates, changes into gas, into smoke, into soot, it travels across the world and gradually engulfs it.

We started in Lomnického Street. Our Venus, whose name was

evidently Zoulová, was wielding a broom; she was helped, with a second broom, by the man with the captain's cap who most of the time chewed silently, now and again spitting out some frothy phlegm. They were sweeping the stuff onto my shovel and I would fling all the filthy mess into the dustbin on our handcart. When the dustbin was full we turned it upside down and tipped everything onto the pavement, all the rubbish in one heap; this would later be picked up and removed by the garbage truck. In this way we marked out our progress with those heaps and slowly advanced to Vyšehrad. I looked at the tinted foliage of the trees, they were waving to me from the distance even though no one was waiting for me under them, even though she was no longer waiting for me. I think of her only as 'she'. In my mind I do not give her a name. Names get fingered and worn just like tender words. Sometimes in my mind I called her a soothsayer, because she used to foretell people's futures and she seemed knowing to me. Also she was surrounded by mystery, and made more beautiful by it. When she was christened she was named Daria.

I could not remember if we'd ever been here with each other. Our meetings over the years had blended together, and the years had piled up as in the folksong about the farm labourer. I'd met her as a result of visiting a friend who lived in a caravan; he was training to be a geologist's assistant. My attention was caught by a little sculpture whose fantastic character set it aside from the spartan interior of the caravan. My friend, who until a little while before had been writing art reviews, told me about the woman artist whose world was bounded by dreams, phantoms, passion and tenderness. He assured me that a visit to her studio was a profound experience, and I made a note of her address. One day when I was out looking for a birthday present for my wife I remembered that address.

Her workshop was in a modest-sized vaulted basement in Prague's Little City district. A third of the room was taken up by wooden shelves holding her work.

She received me courteously and we chatted for a while; she even told me about her little girl and asked me what I and my wife did. But

I thought her interest was due to the fact that I had come to her as a customer.

She moved adroitly among her shelves. As she walked there was a movement of eyes and lips on her long skirt, a pattern of brown eyes and bright red lips. Her own eyes were blue and her lips rather pale. What would happen if I embraced her among her shelves? But I knew that I wouldn't.

I bought a bird with a slender neck on which sat a sharp-edged little head with small, impish, human eyes. She wrapped my purchase in tissue paper and saw me to the door. After that we didn't see one another for many months. But on the eve of my forty-seventh birthday she unexpectedly appeared at my front door: she wished to borrow her little sculpture for an exhibition that was to be held in Budapest. I asked her in and introduced her to my wife, who was delighted to make her acquaintance. The three of us sat in my study. Lída, who likes making people happy, said how much she liked her little figurine. We drank tea and talked — about art, about books, about children, about foreign countries we'd visited, about freedom and unfreedom, but nothing in our conversation seemed significant. The only thing I was aware of was the soft voice of the other woman which addressed itself to me with tenderness and expectation. The evening shadows were creeping into the room and it seemed to me that the remaining light was focused on her high forehead, which, oddly enough, resembled my wife's. The strange thing was that the light did not die with the day. It seemed to be emanating from her, from a flame which undoubtedly was burning within her, and I thought that this flame was reaching over towards me and engulfing me with its hot breath.

We had turned a corner and were now moving away from Vyšehrad. I was still using my coalman's shovel to load scraps of paper, plastic cups and squashed matchboxes onto the cart, also the head of a doll, a torn tennis shoe, an empty tube, a smudged letter, as well as — the most numerous items all over the ground — cigarette butts. All that rubbish I shovelled into the dustbin on the cart, and when that was filled to the brim the captain and I got hold of it and together we tipped it out onto the pavement, where the wind, which was stiffening all the time, scattered the rubbish about again, but it didn't really matter: rubbish is indestructible anyway.

When I was growing up every kind of manual work was applauded and celebrated, and the working people were said to be not only endowed with the greatest virtues and wisdom but actually chosen by history to realise man's age-old dreams of paradise – of paradise on this earth.

There were appeals to writers to get closer to the people, to go out among the workers and write about them, to search for new heroes. Those who were willing to do this were promised not only recognition, fame and rewards, but were also allowed to live in a castle which not long before had been the residence of a very noble and wealthy family.

It was the castle that confused me. I didn't know Franz Kafka then, nor therefore his castle, that symbol of isolation and inaccessibility, of the insuperable distance that divides one man from another, but I understood enough to realise that for a writer who wished to be close to the people it was hardly proper to reside in an aristocratic country house.

I was at an age then when a person tries to find some clue, some belief that he might profess in an excessively complex world. Belief in an earthly paradise, to be established by the working class, attracted me. It struck me as eminently reasonable, and I had been brought up in an environment where reason was respected. But even more than finding a faith, I was anxious to get among people, to experience or at least to hear about what was happening.

I really only acted on the first part of the appeal. I volunteered for work in agriculture, on building sites, and in forestry. At that time I was genuinely searching for the dreamed-of figure of the perfect worker, but everything I saw and heard was different from what it should have been according to the tenets of the faith which I was anxious to accept. But what I experienced then helped me to become wiser.

I now remembered those days as I was watching my new mates. I remembered the far-off days of tempting and deceptive hopes, and I realised that there was in me still some latent remnant of my ancient expectations, that I might after all discover something or someone to redeem me.

Nothing happened at that time. Daria left and I went back to my work. I was writing some stories about my boyhood loves and I was flooded by memories of a long-past excitement. As I glanced at the darkest corner of my study, at the armchair she'd been sitting in, that ancient excitement seemed to take shape again.

I went out to a telephone box – the telephone in my flat had been disconnected – and dialled the number she'd given me. I was still feeling an excitement that would be proper at my age only if one accepted that such a state was proper at any age. I enquired how the Budapest show had gone. I said that I often thought of her visit and that I hoped to see her again some time. But I didn't propose anything definite. I returned home and my excitement grew even more.

I had been living in a strange kind of exile for the previous ten years, hemmed in by prohibitions and guarded sometimes by visible, sometimes by invisible, and sometimes only by imagined watchers. I was not allowed to enter into life except as a guest, as a visitor, or as a day-wage labourer in selected jobs. Over those years there grew within me a longing for something to happen, something that would change my life, while at the same time my timidity increased and made me shy away from any kind of change. Thus my home became for me both a refuge and a cage, I wanted to remain in it and yet also to flee from it; to have the certainty that I would not be driven out and also the hope that I'd escape one day. I clung to my children, or at least I needed them more than fathers normally need their children. I similarly needed my wife. The outside world came to me through those nearest and dearest to me, and through them I stepped into that world, from which I'd been excluded.

After they'd all left in the morning I'd sit down at my desk, with stacks of white paper before me, as well as the boundless expanse of the day and the depth of silence. The telephone couldn't ring, and the occasional footsteps that echoed through the building usually alarmed me: I was more likely to have unwelcome than welcome visitors.

I wrote. For hours and days and weeks. Plays I would never see staged and novels which I assumed would never be published in the language in which they were written. I was working, but at the same time I was afraid that the silence which surrounded me would eventually invade me, paralyse my imagination and cloud my senses. I would sit at my desk and be aware of the weight of the ceiling, the weight of the walls and of the things which might overwhelm me at any moment with their indifference.

Thus I would wait for my wife and my children to return. The moment their footfalls on the stairs shattered the silence I could feel tranquillity return to me — not the tranquillity of silence but the tranquillity of life.

I knew of course that the children would very soon grow up and leave home, that the ring of their footsteps was even more temporary than my own temporariness. I talked to them and shared their joys, but I felt them slipping away and I knew that I must not resist that movement if I was not to resist life.

I was also watching my wife seeking her own space to move in, courageously stepping out of that enforced imprisonment, out of the isolation we were thrust into. She had decided that she'd try to understand what the human soul was, penetrate its secret in the hope of finding a way of alleviating its suffering. To me such an enterprise appeared almost too daring, and besides I was always seeing her as she was when I first met her, too childlike and with too little experience of life to master such an undertaking, but neither did I wish to hold her back: everybody sets out in the direction from which he hears at least the hint of a calling.

I too followed my own direction. I was less keen now on what used to attract me, things had ceased to excite me. Until not so long before I had collected old maps and books, and now dust was settling on them. I no longer tried to find out what was happening anywhere, or to discover when the conditions, which could be described as not favouring me, might at last begin to improve. I wanted to know if there was anything beyond those conditions, if there was anything that might raise our lives above pointlessness and oblivion, but I wanted to discover it for myself, not accept anything revealed and given shape by others. I wanted to achieve this not out of some kind of pride but because I realise that the most important things in life are non-communicable, not compressible into words, even though the people who believe they have discovered them always do try to communicate them, even though I myself try to do so. But anyone who believes that he can communicate to others the essence of God, that he has found the right faith for them, that he has finally glimpsed the mystery of existence, is a fool or a fantasist and, more often than not, dangerous.

A few days later she sent me a card to say she would come round to see me, giving the day and the hour, and hoping she'd find me in.

She turned up as promised. Outside the window the autumnal clouds were driving and the room was once again in twilight. I don't know whether a similar glow had issued from me too. A person never sees himself, at best he sees his own light in another person's eyes, and that only at moments of special grace. But maybe she'd seen something after all, because otherwise she wouldn't have wished to meet me again, she wouldn't have voluntarily set out on a pilgrimage which, at moments of anger, she was to proclaim had led her only to pain. I have myself sometimes been amazed that she had come so close to me. At other times I believed that some force of destiny had brought us together, if only for a limited period, and that continually interrupted, just so we should experience the depths into which we could have never ventured on our own.

For the first few weeks we'd walked in the countryside, through forests and in parks. She knew the names of plants, even the most exotic ones, as well as where they came from. And she led me through those places, through the land of the Khmers which, at the time she'd visited it, was still full of happy and carefree people, and along the majestic river Ganges, through the crowds in stifling streets, she even led me through the jungle and into the ashram so I could listen to what a wise guru had to say about the right way to live. She told me about her family, which included industrialists as well as National Revival schoolmasters, a wanderer who settled on the western slopes of the Andes, and a romantic aunt who, when she failed to keep the lover she longed for, decided to starve herself to death. There was also a highly gifted law student who could reel off the whole statute book by heart but who became oversated by the law and turned to philosophy; and who, when he had irrefutably established the vanity of human endeavour, sat down and wrote his philosophical testament, whose conclusion was that happiness was just a dream and that life was a chain of suffering, and directly over that philosophical testament he shot himself through the head, so that the blood pouring from his wound put several final stops under his writings.

Everyone on her father's side of the family, she explained, had a touch of genius, an inflexible will, and clear-sightedness – her father most of all. She often spoke of him to me and, even though I had never seen him, I was reminded of my own father, not only because he was also a graduate engineer but because he too knew no greater happiness than his work, than the calculations in which no one was allowed to disturb him, and because he was strong, healthy and capable of cheerfulness once he decided to set aside that work.

I tried to tell her something about myself too, but I couldn't find anybody among my ancestors who resembled hers. Or rather, I didn't know their life stories. I knew that some of my ancestors had come from far away, but I don't know whether that was two hundred or a thousand years ago. I assume that even then they knew how to read, even if it was a different script from the one I can read now, and that they prayed in a language of which I no longer understand a single word. I don't know what they did for a living. Some of them, my parents still remembered, owned little general stores in the provinces. Both my grandmothers tried to trade in Prague but failed. My grandfathers too came from the country. My father's father had studied chemistry and worked as an engineer in a sugar refinery down in the Hungarian part of the monarchy. There, when my father was only eleven, he fell under a plough drawn by a rope and was seriously injured. At first he was treated by the count's doctor, then they sent him all the way to Prague, but they weren't able to help him there either and he died very young. My mother's father, on the other hand, lived to a ripe old age: he'd been a clerk at the law courts and at the age of eighty he lived to experience the second great war as well as having a yellow star put on him and being forcibly deported to a ghetto. Even of this stocky old man with his grey, slightly tobacco-stained moustache I was unable to report anything remarkable, except possibly that, like his ancestors, he stubbornly believed in the coming of the Messiah, but for him that meant the coming of the socialist revolution. The vision of the promised Eden into which the revolution would lead us all helped him survive the blows of fate: the violent death of his sons and the death of his wife, the loss of his home and of his freedom, his humiliation, hunger and the hardships of imprisonment. More and more often in that unhappy place he would preach to anyone who would listen to him, and more and more often I would be the only listener to remain. He urged me not to believe in a god whom people had invented, whom the masters had fobbed off onto the poor so they should more readily bear their fate. He persuaded me not to believe in a paradise in the beyond nor in some superior justice; when I was free again I should work for an earthly paradise and for human justice. As he grew older his litanies became an unchanging prayer which I knew by heart and to which I no longer had to listen. And then one night I awoke. Everyone else was sleeping, and from the corner of the room where grandfather slept I could hear a strange muttering. I recognised the old man's voice and the plaintive intona-tion of a prayer spoken in the language he still knew but of which I no longer understood anything, a prayer addressed to God. I did not stir and listened with amazement to the voice which seemed to come from a great distance, from some long-past time. That was the first time I realised that the depth of the human soul is unfathomable.

So what could I tell her about my ancestors? I didn't even under-stand their prayers.

Her father would desert his drawing board from time to time and wander about the mountains and climb rockfaces. He would take her with him, and taught her not to be afraid of heights. My father would only wander through the landscape of numbers into which the windings of his machines turned for him. He even took his calculations with him on holiday, and when he was seized by a new idea, which would happen almost continuously, he would virtually forget about the rest of us. When he then found us at the dinner table or outside his window he'd wonder where we'd sprung from. But they forcibly expelled him from his landscape, put him into convict's clothes and locked him up behind electric wires whose windings were all too easily calculable. He concentrated all his willpower and strength on surviving, on surviving with dignity, so that he might once more return to his beloved landscape. Apart from numbers and machines, father, as I understood later, also loved pretty women and socialist visions of a better world. Like every man in love he invested the object of his adoration with excessive and deceptive hopes.

Do you think every love indulges in false hopes? she asked.

I realised that she was asking about us, and I dared not say yes, even though I could see no reason why we should be exceptions.

It was getting on for nine o'clock and our orange procession was moving down Sinkulova Street towards the water tower. The street is cobbled and in the cracks along the kerb clumps of dandelions, plantains and all kinds of weeds had taken root. The youngster with the girlish face was either pulling them out by hand or digging them out with his scraper. Even when he was bending down to the ground his face remained sickly pale.

Under the trees on the pavement some cars were parked. By the wreck of an ancient Volga our party halted. The foreman lifted the bonnet and established with satisfaction that someone had removed the radiator during the week.

A car is also rubbish, a large conglomeration of refuse, and one of them gets in our way at almost every step.

When fifteen years ago I went to see the première of a play of mine in a town not far from Detroit, the president of the Ford company invited me to lunch. As we were sitting on his terrace on the top floor, or more accurately on the roof of the Ford skyscraper, from which there was a view of that hideous huge city through whose streets countless cars were moving, instead of asking about his latest model I wanted to know how he removed all those cars from the world once they'd reached the end of their service. He replied that this was no problem. Anything that was manufactured could vanish without trace, it was merely a technical problem. And he smiled at the thought of a totally empty, cleansed world. After lunch the president lent me his car and his driver. I was taken to the edge of the city, where an incalculable mass of battered and rusty sedans were parked on a vast area. Negroes in brightly-coloured overalls first of all ripped the guts out of the cars with enormous pliers, stripped them of their tyres, windows and seats, and then pushed them into gigantic presses which turned the cars into metal parcels of manageable dimensions. But those metal boxes do not vanish from the world, any more than did the glass, the tyres or the spent oil, even if they were all burned in incinerators, nor did the rivers of petrol that were used on all those necessary and unnecessary journeys disappear. They probably melt down the crushed metal to make iron and new steel for new cars, and thus rubbish is transformed into new rubbish, only slightly increased in quantity. If ever I were to meet that self-assured president again I'd say to him: No, this isn't a mere technical problem. Because the spirit of dead things rises over the earth and over the waters, and its breath forebodes evil.

During the war filth descended upon us: literally and figuratively it engulfed us just like death, and sometimes it was difficult to separate the two. They certainly merged in my mother's mind, death and garbage; she believed that life was tied to cleanliness – literally and figuratively.

The war was over, we were looking forward to living in love and peace, but she was struggling for cleanliness. She wanted to know our thoughts and she was horrified by our boots, our hands and our words. She inspected our library and stripped it of the books which might make our minds unclean, and she bought a large pot in which she boiled our underwear every day. But even so she felt revolted by us and forever sent us back to wash our hands; she would touch other people's possessions and doorknobs only when wearing gloves.

Sometimes at night I'd hear her sighing and lamenting. She was mourning the relatives she'd lost in the war, but she was surely also lamenting the dirtiness of the world she had to live in. In our home, therefore cleanliness and loneliness reigned. Dad hardly ever came home, he'd found a job in Plzeň so he could breathe more freely. When he turned up on Sundays, he'd walk barefoot to his study over a path of newspapers, but even that moment of crossing the hall was enough for it to be filled with a smell in which mother recognised the stench of some unknown trollop. In vain did Dad try to wash it off, in vain did he help to cover the carpet with fresh newspapers.

I was quite prepared for father not to come back one day, for him to remain with that strange malodorous woman of his, and I wouldn't have blamed him for it. But he turned up afresh every weekend, and sometimes he even urged me not to judge mother: she was a good woman, only sick, and not everyone had the strength to come unmarked through what we'd had to endure.

Then they locked Dad up again. The pain inflicted on my mother by others at least partly diverted her from the pain she inflicted upon herself.

A sewage service truck overtook our gang and pulled up a little way in front of us. Its crew exchanged greetings with our foreman and began to examine the nearest drain grating.

'What can they be looking for?' I asked Mrs Venus.

'They're just making sure their sewer isn't all screwed up,' she explained. 'We're not allowed to tip anything into the sewer. One day young Jarda here,' she pointed to the youngster with the girlish face, 'threw some flowers down and just then their inspector came driving past and wanted to fine him fifty crowns on the spot. And all the time they're rolling in it, just like the rat-catchers!'

'Don't talk to me about rat-catchers,' the foreman joined in. 'In Plzeň underneath the slaughterhouse the rats went mad and came up through the sewer gratings at night and ran about the streets like squirrels, squealing. They were desperately looking for a rat-catcher, they were actually ready to give him twenty grand a month, but everyone shied away because it was obvious that if a rabid rat bit you, it'd be curtains! I've a mate in Plzeň, from back in the para corps, and he got annoyed and said: "I'm not going to shit myself for a few mice!" So he got a diving suit and a sheet of asbestos rubber to throw over himself if the rats attacked him.'

'They'd do that?' I expressed surprise.

'Sure they would. I told you they were rabid. You chase after them, but when they've nowhere to escape to they'll turn and fling themselves at you. If that happens you lie down, throw the sheet over you, and they'll run straight over you. So that's what my mate did. Once he was under that sheet nothing could happen to him, but as those rats trampled over him he shat himself from fear.'

'Like it was with them cemeteries on the motorway,' said Mrs Venus. 'When they destroyed them they had to dig up the corpses and they offered a hundred an hour, plus a bottle of rum a day, and even so everybody told them where they could stick it. They had to send in convicts to do the job and of course they paid them bugger-all!' She stopped, stretched, leaned her shovel against a wall and lit a cigarette. 'Corpses ain't no joke, there's poison in them bodies as goes right through your rubber gloves, and once it gets in your blood you snuff it.' She was smoking and seemed to be gazing into the distance, somewhere only she could see. If I had met her years ago I would certainly have repeated her words to myself, I would have been in a hurry to write them down in order to preserve her speech as faithfully as possible. At that time I believed that anything I saw or heard would come in useful for some story. But I have known for a long time now that I am most unlikely ever to find any events other than those I experience myself. A man cannot gain control over someone else's life, and even if he could he would not invent a new story. There are four thousand million people living in the world and every one of them believes that his life is good for at least one story. This thought is enough to make your head spin. If a writer emerged, or better still, was produced, who was obsessed enough to record four thousand million stories, and to then cross out all they had in common, how much do you suppose would be left? Scarcely a sentence from each story, from each human fate, a moment like a drop in the ocean, an unrepeatable experience of apprehension or of a meeting, an instant of insight or pain – but who could identify that drop, who could separate it from the flood of the ocean? And why should new stories have to be invented?

Daria, in tears, once accused me of regarding her as some beetle I had impaled on a pin in order to describe it better. But she was mistaken: in her presence I usually forgot that I sometimes tried to invent stories, and I would watch her so closely only because I wished to understand the language in which she spoke to me when she was with me in silence.

'But I had a great time with them corpses. Got myself a job down there,' Mrs Venus gestured towards the Vyšehrad ramparts, 'on the path lab. That's where they carted all them stiffs what had had their throats cut or been knifed like. Got it through a girlfriend, a dicey job, she said, but with bonus payments, and in the end they gave me bugger-all. Anyway I only did it because of the old boy what gutted them bodies, he was a card and dead keen on stiffs. "Zoulová," he'd say to me, "you've got some arms. I'd love to have a good look at your humerus one day."' And Mrs Venus spread her arms – they really were long and slim.

The sickly smell of decay seemed to engulf me. When I took on the job of a hospital cleaner my colleague could not deny himself the pleasure of taking me to the morgue the very first day in order to show me the corpses on the tables, on the floor and in the refrigerator, and while doing so he was watching me out of the corner of his eye to see if I was turning pale or making for the door. But I was used to dead bodies from childhood, to such quantities of dead bodies that the few solemnly-dressed recent deceased neither frightened me nor turned my insides.

Now I recalled not only that tiled room but principally the wide table, which I saw as clearly as in a dream, and on it lay my father.

My father, in spite of our assuring him of the contrary, was slowly dying, and the malignant disease was gradually destroying him from within, so that he, who had always been so strong and irrepressibly healthy, was now scarcely able to hold a pen in his hand. When I looked at his notes, which were still swarming with numbers and formulae I didn't understand, the figures were so shaky I could hardly read them. Whenever I regarded these figures and formulae, undoubtedly the last of the many my father had worked out and written down in his life, I was gripped by sadness. I knew that to him they meant his life, but from them I could see that father's life was by now shaky, that these figures were getting ready to accompany him on the road to where there are no numbers.

I would have liked to dispel that unhappy vision, but no matter how intently I fixed my eyes on my cart, my father's motionless features remained before me. What is the purpose of a life of suffering? It may teach a man to humbly bow to the inevitable, but he will still be crushed by the approaching death of someone dear to him.

Mrs Venus tossed some rubbish into my cart. 'D'you know how many people he'd had on his table?'

I didn't know, and she said triumphantly: 'Fifty thousand!'

'Nonsense,' came the youngster's voice from behind me. 'You're making it up. That would be several regiments!'

'But that's what it was, Jarda dear. And all of them done in violently!' Mrs Venus laughed as if she had just said something very funny.

Then one day before Christmas we first made love in a tiny attic room with small windows and thick walls under the roof of a baroque building. Facing it was a noble town house with enormous windows on the sills of which sat some freezing pigeons. There was a smell of oil in the room, as well as the faint odour of gas, and though it was midday the room was quite dark. The small windows were moreover partly obstructed by a statue of Saint Stephen the Martyr. The restoration of the statue was nearly complete, but my lover had stopped working on it, she didn't like having her hand controlled by someone else's instructions.

I wanted her to enjoy our love-making. I was thinking of it so much I was trembling with excitement, and she was trembling too. After all, she had a husband at home, and a little girl, but now she curled up in my embrace and let herself be carried to a place from which there would be no return. So I carried her, and at each step I felt her getting heavier until I could scarcely drag her. I was afraid, we were frightened of one another we wanted each other so much. The big surprised bed creaked at every movement and we tried to drown the sound by whispering tender words. We looked each other in the face and I was amazed by the way she was being transformed, she was softening and taking on some ancient, the most ancient, shape. Perhaps it was the forgotten shape of my mother or a recollection of my first visions and dreams of the woman I would love one day.

I got back home late at night and went to bed by my wife's side. She suspected nothing and snuggled up to me. She was still as trusting as a child. When I closed my eyes I realised that sleep wouldn't come to me. In the garden a bird was piping, trains were rushing along in the distance, and out of the darkness before me, like a full moon, there rose the face of the other woman: calm, beautiful, as if it had always been concealed within me, and yet motionless like the faces of her statues. Thus she gazed down on me, suspended in space beyond all things and beyond all time, and I felt something like nostalgia, unease, longing and sadness.

There was a lot of snow that winter. She'd take her little girl to her piano lessons. I'd walk behind them, without the child being aware of me. I'd sink into the freshly fallen snow because I wasn't looking where I was going, I was watching her walking: there was in her walk something of an ill-concealed hurry, or maybe of an eagerness for life. She was holding her little girl's hand and only occasionally did she glance behind. Even at that distance I could feel her love.

At other times we'd set out across the snow-covered fields not far from the city. Below us was an abandoned farmstead and a forest, above us the sky was frosty under a cover of mist. We stopped, she leaned her back against me, I embraced her – a little plump in her winter coat – and at once we were amidst eternity, lifted out of time, lifted from horrors and joys, from the cold and the blowing wind, and she said softly: Is it possible we love each other so much?

At nine o'clock precisely we sat down in the Boženka Tavern. It was a run-of-the-mill place. Nothing enlivened the blackened walls except some slogans and prohibitions. The table-cloths bore the stains of yesterday's food. In the corner stood an abandoned and battered pool table, its green cloth long faded and become grey from cigarette ash and smoke.

The hauliers' tavern of my childhood was full of colour. Not that I went into it all that often, only when Dad sent me out for some beer. Right behind the door a purple pheasant spread its colourful wings, and on the walls were bright pictures of horses and hauliers' carts, the work of some local painter of shop signs and fairground rifle targets. And the landlord wore a neat clean check apron. When he'd drawn the beer for me he'd come round from behind the bar to place the jug securely in my hands. In the tavern of my childhood there was still a spirit of freedom.

I ordered tea for myself while the others, without having to ask, were each served a large beer. The youngster drank mineral water. Venus produced her cigarettes, extended the packet to her neighbour on the other side and then to me. I thanked her and said I didn't smoke.

'Quite a paragon, ain't you?' she said. 'Your wife must be pleased with you.'

'If I hadn't got drunk,' the foreman said, 'I most likely wouldn't have got married at all. Because I had a fair idea that marriage is the end of life.'

I didn't meet Lída until after I'd finished university. There was nothing exceptional about our meeting, it was unaccompanied by any special events or auguries. We just met and found we liked each other. She was only six years younger than me but I felt as if a lifetime lay between us. Her childlike trustfulness and innocence touched me and attracted me.

The first time I invited her to the cinema she was, needless to say, late. I had long been sitting in my seat, reconciled to the fact that she wasn't coming. When I caught sight of her blonde head among the heads of the other latecomers she seemed so beautiful that I doubted that she could be coming towards me.

We went out together for nearly a year, we saw each other almost daily, and throughout that time we never had an argument, it seemed to us that there was nothing that could divide us or alienate us. Most men get drunk on the night before their wedding, but I didn't. Not because of any principle; it simply didn't occur to me. But I lay awake most of that night and I felt depressed.

What depressed me were certainly not doubts about the rightness of my choice, but the knowledge that I'd made a decision once and for all. I suspected that for me the most blissful prospect was not so much having the person I loved permanently by my side as a need, from time to time, to reach out to emptiness, to let longing intensify within me to the point of agony, to alternate the pain of separation with the relief of renewed coming together, the chance of escape and return, of glimpsing before me a will-o'-the-wisp , the hope that the real encounter was still awaiting me.

Man is reluctant to accept that his life has come to a conclusion in that most important respect, that his hopes have been fulfilled. He hesitates to look death in the face, and there is little that comes so close to death as fulfilled love.

For our honeymoon we flew out to the Tatra mountains.

It was the beginning of windy autumnal weather, the larches were turning golden and the meadows were fragrant with ripe grass. We climbed up to the treeline, to where the forests ended, and above us towered the sharp ridges of bare rock. I lay down in the grass, Lída sang to herself. She sang beautifully and I felt as if her singing was filling the entire space from the sky down to the base of the rocks, marking out the space in which I would now forever move.

'You must have been a one, Mr Marek,' Venus said. 'When my old man came home pissed I made him sleep with the horses or in the garage.'

'So when did you have your own wheels?' the foreman asked curiously.

'When we were in Slovakia, of course. Míla got hold of an old Wartburg. When we went off with the kids on our first outing, just past Topolčianky its exhaust snapped and the thing made a row like a bloody tank. He had to knock back a couple of doubles, he was so worked up about it, then he got down under the car so he could at least hold it up with wire, and when he'd finished we drove downhill again, and he'd cut out the engine so it wouldn't make such a row, and we were going faster and faster, the kids had a ball each time he skidded round the bends, but I was screaming at him: "Míla, d'you want us to end up as mincemeat? Have you lost your marbles?" And he said: "Not my marbles, my brakes!"'

I realised that Mrs Venus was relating this story mainly for my benefit, because I was the new boy, so I asked: 'And how did the trip end?'

'He used the engine to brake. He's always managed to tame any mare yet.'

'Except you,' said the foreman. He chuckled and thereby gave the signal for general merriment. The one who enjoyed himself most was the captain, whose vaguely familiar face was still niggling at me. It suggested something, it pointed back to something, only I didn't know what. The youngster with the girlish face scarcely smiled: it suddenly occurred to me that death was hovering over him. I had that sensation from time to time, more often in my childhood. I'd look at somebody and suddenly I'd be scared that the person would soon be gone. I'm not trying to suggest that I have second sight. I've been wrong on numerous occasions. And some people exude the breath of death for years while being alive and well.

It was worst at the fortress, where I spent part of my childhood. All around me walked emaciated old men and women. Sometimes they didn't even walk but just lay in the corridors, between the beams, in the loft, in the heat and in the suffocating stench, and death was continually hovering over them. I was aware of it and I was afraid of it. In the room where I lived I hid a small circular mirror in which I'd look, or else I'd open the window and hold some of the blackout paper behind the glass, and peer if I couldn't see it hovering over me already. But no one sees his own death, or if he does he has no time to report on it.

Where death hovers there also love flourishes – but what could I know about that, being seven at the outbreak of the war?

There were a lot of girls in the fortress ghetto. I talked to them, I passed them and I shouted at them so they should see how I looked down on them. One of them had a name which I later gave to our daughter, and she lived in the room next to ours. I therefore met her more often than the rest, and I also noticed that when we played a ball game called hit-your-opponent and she was the captain of one side she always picked me first. That gave me courage, and whenever we went out to play I'd call on her. She was the same age as myself, and she differed from all the other girls in that she had fair hair, the colour of rye or wheat. We were never alone together, away from the company of our playmates, but I always tried to get as close to her as possible, for instance when we were sitting on the beams of the wooden huts behind the barracks which were our quarters.

We also lent each other the few books we owned, but we dared not go any further, I dared not go any further; and yet everything was suddenly changed, life was moving between different milestones, no longer from morning to evening or from meal to meal, but from meeting to meeting. The fortress ran out of salt, the bread was mouldy and the potatoes black and rotten, but I didn't care; they took grandfather to the camp hospital and we guessed that he'd never come back, but I scarcely took it in. The fortress corridors, always so overcrowded, seemed empty when she walked alongside me, and the tiny space allotted to us grew wide, or rather it was enclosed in itself and thus became infinite.

I owned a few coloured crayons and blank sheets of paper, and I tried in the evening to draw her face from memory. But I didn't succeed. Then it occurred to me that I might compose a poem for her, and I did in fact put together a few verses which, admittedly, dealt more with meteorological phenomena than my feelings, and I took them to her. She said she liked the poem and carved me a little puppet with a smiling face out of conkers. I hung it up on the post of my bunk, right by my head so I could look at it before going to sleep. That was the time of day when I was with her most, because then I was rescuing her from danger. I'd carry her in my arms from the cell into which she'd been thrown naked to be tortured, and which I'd penetrated in disguise to save her. Night after night I thus performed my loyal, heroic deeds until I fell asleep.

In my fantasies I defended her against all evil, but in real life I could not save her. She was assigned to a transport, as were nearly all the occupants of our barracks.

She ran out from the room, which was filled with confusion and tears, where the pitiful remains of the inmates' belongings were being sorted out and packed in a hopeless hurry; she only had a moment, she wanted to be with her mother who was in despair. We knew of a spot in the recess of the ramparts, the slope there was overgrown with grass and shaded by ancient lime trees. It was quieter there than anywhere else in the fortress. That was where we'd most frequently been with the others, but now there was no one else there. We told each other which of our friends had also been listed for deportation and we reassured each other that the war would be over quite soon, that liberation was so near we need not be too much afraid of anything, and then we'd meet again, we'd all of us meet again, we didn't quite know where we'd meet but that didn't seem important. Then we were silent. What was there to talk about at such a moment? We walked round the spot and then she said she had to go back. She stopped for a moment, then suddenly she came close up to me and I felt the touch of her lips on mine. Her breath was on my face and I froze. Then she turned and fled. When I caught up with her she asked me not to come with her any further, we'd said goodbye already.

That afternoon she left. I stood by my window, I was not allowed out. I tried to spot her in the crowd which moved down the street, the crowd over which death was hovering, but I didn't see her. It suddenly occurred to me that she hadn't left, that it wasn't possible that she had vanished, that she was no longer there.

I tore myself away from the window and knocked at the door of the next room, and when there was no answer I opened it. The room which a little while ago had been full of people and voices and things now yawned with emptiness. It seemed to me that I was standing on a rock, on a cliff so high and so steep that the land below me was out of sight. And I was seized by vertigo, I realised that I too was falling, that there was no way out, that it was only a question of time. What seemed solid collapsed in a single instant, and what seemed indissolubly linked to the ground was dissolved.

I escaped from that empty room, lay down on my mattress and closed my eyes. At that moment her face rose above me like the moon and looked down on me from the night sky, serene, remote and inaccessible, and I was engulfed by happiness together with pain and despair.

As all my friends departed I managed to recall their features, and they then floated above me in the darkness, as though they were submerging and rising again from the waters, always unchanged: alive, colourful and close.

When I learned after the war that all those I had been fond of, all those I had known, were dead, gassed like insects and incinerated like refuse, I was gripped by despair. Almost every night I would walk by their sides, entering with them into enclosed spaces. We were all naked, and suddenly we were beginning to choke. I tried to scream but was unable to, and I heard the rattle in the others' throats and I could see their faces turning into grimaces and losing their shape. I awoke in terror, afraid to go to sleep again, and my eyes roamed feverishly through the empty darkness. At that time I slept in the kitchen, near the gas cooker. I'd get up time and again to make sure no gas was escaping. It was clear to me that I had only been spared through some oversight, some omission that might be put right at any moment. In the end I was so crushed by horror and fear that I fell sick. The doctors shook their heads over my disease, unable to understand how a microbe could have got into my heart, but they never thought of the real gateway.

They prescribed bed and absolute quiet. But in that quiet I was able to surround myself with my friends, who had turned into spectres, and spend with them all that slowly passing time, and be drawn into their world, in which time no longer passed at all. I told no one about them but I was with them and they invited me to them, they repeated their invitations so persistently that I understood that I too was to die.

But I was still afraid of death, so much afraid of it I didn't dare to look in the mirror. Thus I spent weeks in immobility, until one day my mother brought me *War and Peace* in three volumes, put them on my bedside table and told me not to pick them up myself, they were too heavy. I really was weak, I could hardly lift one of the volumes although they were just ordinary books. But when my mother handed me a volume I propped it up against my knees and read lying down. And as I read I was gradually transported into a different society. At times it occurred to me that the people I was reading about were also dead by now, that they had to die even if death did not overtake them on the pages of the book. Yet at the same time, though they were dead, they were living. It was then I realised the amazing power of literature and of the human imagination generally: to make the dead live and to stop the living from dying. I was seized by wonder at this miracle, at the strange power of the author, and there began to spring up within me a longing to achieve something similar. That longing took hold of me and began to carry off the faces of my dead.

I asked my mother to buy me some exercise books, and when I was on my own I began to put together my own experiences and to give back their lives to those who were no longer alive. At that moment, as though miraculously, their rigidified, cold and dismal features increasingly began to fade. When the doctor allowed me to get up six months later all the dead faces had dissolved, as though clearing out of my way. I was no longer able to command them, and if anyone had shown me a picture of any of my dead friends I'd have said: I don't know him. But it was not the oblivion of death, nor the oblivion so common in our day when the dead and even some of the living are concealed forever by a blanket of silence, one which even swallows up speech. Instead it was a different kind of remembrance, one which lifted the incinerated from the ashes and tried to raise them up to new life.

So I lived again, and the doctor was pleased at the miracle wrought by some new tablets he'd prescribed for me. But I knew why I was alive. So long as I was able to write I'd be able to live, I'd be free from my spectres. I know that to this day, and I also know that nothing on earth can disappear, that even the picture of a young girl murdered long ago would remain latently somewhere, maybe in my mind, that it would rise from its depths just as her soul rose above the earth and the waters. And it seemed to me, as I was gazing at the face of the woman whom I had now, nearer the end of my life, met, who seemed familiar to me from the depth of my being, that by some miracle the one who had stood at the very beginning had returned, and as after so many years I again saw that motionless, dreamlike, loving face before me at night I was engulfed by a wave of joy mingled with sadness, even though I worked out with some relief that Daria had already been alive for three years when they gassed the other.

'Well, you were shooting downhill,' the foreman turned to Mrs Venus; 'but what would you say if you were whizzing straight up into the air at the same lick?' And he pointed to the ceiling with such a commanding gesture that everybody looked up towards it.

Thirty-five years ago the following had happened to him. He'd been stationed at an airfield near Stříbro in Western Bohemia, and there, as well as the splendid S-199s, they'd inherited a training balloon from the Germans. Anyway, his sergeant had ordered him to get the balloon ready, which meant loading a parachute and ballast bags. The sergeant was giving him a hand himself. But just as they were getting the first sand-filled bag on board the anchor cable got loose and they shot up at such a pace that within a few seconds they were above the clouds. 'I can tell you it was faster than a rocket. We were in shirt-sleeves,' the foreman was getting carried away by his experience, 'because down there it was mid-summer, and suddenly we were at the bloody North Pole. "Comrade sergeant," I said, "Private Marek reporting we're flying, destination unknown, but most probably we'll find ourselves in the shit." He was a fair sort of bloke so he said: "Marek, that was a damn silly order I gave you, to get inside without a parachute. See if you can get out of it alive. I'll manage somehow." And he held out his parachute to me, the only one on board. So I said: "Sergeant, you got a wife and kids, if we're in the shit you'll jump." And he said: "You're a good bloke, Marek, we'll either be in the shit together or we'll both be bloody heroes." By then he had frost on his face!'

'But why didn't you try to let out the gas?' the youngster wondered.

'Imagine we didn't think of that? The bloody valve was frozen up, so we couldn't do nothing.' The foreman went on for a while to describe the terrible conditions at those freezing altitudes before, three hours later, they came down at Lysá.

'Thirty-five years ago,' the man who reminded me of my ear-nose-and-throat specialist joined in, 'I was in a penal camp near Marianská, a short way from the frontier. At that time the Americans were beginning to send over little balloons with leaflets. Some of them came down near us, but anyone picking them up risked being put inside.'

'What did they say?' the youngster wanted to know.

'Nothing worth a stretch inside. Anyway, what do you expect from a piece of paper?'

'Balloons and ships may both have a future, but I wouldn't get into one of your balloons,' the captain brought the conversation back to appropriate bounds. 'Or into a plane. If a ship goes down you've got a chance, but when a plane comes down . . .'

'You don't have to tell me!' the foreman said, offended. 'They were goners all right, there wasn't as much as this left of them.' He flicked a cigarette stub with his finger. 'And if by some miracle one of them got out – well, obviously he was no use for anything, ever again.'

With Daria I was moving above the ground and above the waters; day after day, month after month. Even at night, when distance intervened between us, our dreams or visions were often similar to each other's.

That, she explained to me, was because at night our souls would meet.

You think that the soul can leave a body while it is alive?

She then told me the story of the hundred-year-old sorcerer who disguised his real appearance by means of charms. He lived in a stone house in the middle of the forests which extended all the way to the northern ocean, and he spent his time in solitude. When he got tired of living alone he bewitched a beautiful young girl with his magic charms and tried to make her his wife. But she saw through him and realised his real nature. She was frightened and begged him to let her go: he was an old man, near the end of his days, while she had her whole life before her. The sorcerer replied: I may look old but I shan't die because my soul does not reside in my body. When she wanted to know where his soul resided he explained to her that it was a long way away. Over the mountains, beyond the rivers, there was a lake, and in the middle of it an island, and on the island a temple, a temple without windows and with just one door, and that door could not be opened. Inside a bird was flying around, and unless someone killed it it would never die, and in it was the sorcerer's soul. While the bird was alive he too would live.

The girl had a lover, to whom she sent word of her fate. The young man set out to find the island and the temple. With the help of good spirits he opened the door which couldn't be opened, and caught the bird which could not, of its own, die, and with it he returned to his beloved. She hid them both under the sorcerer's bed and told the young man to squeeze the bird hard. The young man obeyed and the sorcerer immediately felt sick, and as the young man squeezed harder the old man got worse. That was when he began to suspect something, and looked around the room. 'Kill it, kill it!' called the girl. Her lover crushed the bird in his hand and at that moment the sorcerer breathed his last.

I understood that she was telling me this story so I should never forget that her soul was a bird which I held in my fist.

The soul leaves the body after death and enters a different body, an animal or even a tree. That was why she preferred to work with stone or with clay rather than with wood. She could hear a tree

31

groaning when it was cut down. On its journey to a new body the soul could overcome any distance whatever. So why shouldn't it be able to do so during life? After all, it was not corporeal, so there was no force on earth that could fetter or imprison it when a soul wished to escape, rise up or join someone else.

Another time she told me that once in plain daylight she saw a golden ball moving among rosebeds, the blooms were mirrored in the ball and everything was in motion, free and exalted. A little while later, as she was returning home in the evening, or rather at night, she caught sight of me on the other side of the street, leaning against a lamp post; she'd run over to me but I had dissolved before her eyes. Was that a delusion sent her by some evil power or a sign of love?

Everything that happened had to have some superior cause, and she therefore sought for an explanation in the position of the planets. She established that my strongest and lucky star was the sun, which I had in Virgo and in the tenth house, and it was thanks to my sun that I had survived what I had, and thanks to it I would lead my life happily to the point when I had to leave it. I would not step out of my body until I had accomplished my task and performed the work I had to perform. What fate could be happier?

On Twelfth Night we poured melted lead together, and my figure was a woman covering her face and a beast of prey or perhaps a winged Hermes. In the woman she recognised herself, and in the winged creature, me. I was descending to her to carry her off or to bring her a message from heaven.

And why is the woman covering her face?

Probably because she is afraid of me.

She had a pack of fortune-telling cards of the famous Mademoiselle Lenormand and several times told her own and my past, present and future, the immediate as well as the distant future, and surprisingly the cards foretold an encouraging or even a splendid future for me.

I regarded this fortune-telling as a kind of lovers' game, but I said to her that everything was bound to turn out right because I had a charmed life like that man who alone survived the crash of the aircraft which some years ago hit a church tower in Munich, or like that girl who survived an air crash in the Andes and then alone, for several days and nights, tore her way through the jungle until with her last strength she reached some human habitation. It so happens that I met that man not long ago and we got on well together; and although I've never seen that girl we would surely also agree that what crushes others is for us no more than an unimportant trifle.

In reality nothing was a game to her, to her everything was life, every second we spent together was to be filled with love, when we were not together spectres were creeping out on all sides as in the Apocalypse and many-headed serpents were coiling round her legs. She fought back and asked me for help, asked me not to leave her, to remain with her if I loved her, at least for a while. But I was already escaping, in my mind I was hurrying home, chasing the tram that was just leaving to make sure I got home before my wife, who suspected nothing, who smiled or frowned according to her mood and not according to what I did. So we parted, kissed once more at the corner of the street, turned back once more, waved to each other, and I could just see her smile freezing on her loving lips and tears flushing the tenderness out of her eyes.

I'd always been devoted to my work, I'd always fought for every extra minute for my writing. Now I was trimming my writing minute by minute, and these minutes were adding up to hours and days. I was still determined to rebel, to ask for at least one moment's respite. Writing, after all, meant life to me.

She said: What is art compared to life?

When I can't write any more I'll die. But I'll die loving.

Even though my wartime memories were getting dimmer, I kept returning to them. It was as if I had a duty to those whom I'd survived, and had to repay the benevolent forces which had snatched me from the common fate and allowed me to live.

With that burden I entered life. I was barely eighteen when I began to write a play about a revolt in a women's concentration camp, about a desperate decision either to live in freedom or to die. Suffering resulting from a life deprived of freedom seemed to me the most important of all themes to think about and to write about. As then in the fortress town, so now, after the war, I felt that my whole being was clinging to freedom. I was able to quote by heart the thoughts of the captured Pierre Bezukhov on the subject of freedom and suffering, which are so close to each other that even a man in the midst of suffering may find freedom.

I didn't understand Tolstoy, just as I failed to notice that a short distance from my home new camps were being set up, where people again had that final opportunity of seeking freedom in the midst of suffering. I only knew the camps of my childhood. Hitler, Himmler, or the Auschwitz boss Hoess were to me the personification of unparalleled evil; with their deaths I thought it had gone forever from this world.

We walked down the street called V dolinách, which was perfectly clean; we had been preceded by the automatic cleaning machine driven today by Mr Kromholz. It had evidently worked so pains-takingly that it hardly seemed to belong to our age at all, and so we approached the monstrous building they'd set up on the Pankrác plateau. Originally they'd wanted to call it the Palace of Congresses, for that was its proper purpose: to create an appropriately grandiose setting for congresses of all kinds of useful and useless organisations, especially the one which ruled over everything and over everybody, but then they called it, rather absurdly, the Palace of Culture.

'Yeah, they have a different kind of mechanisation here,' said the foreman, having noticed what I was looking at. 'They have tiny little automatic refuse machines running along the corridors, parquet cleaners and floor-polishers – all imported stuff. Only for their use. D'you know how many people they have in there?'

'It's a monstrosity!' the captain spoke up. 'Eats us all out of house and home!'

'Last week,' Mrs Venus cut in, 'some little kid got inside. They thought he'd got lost on Vyšehrad but all the time he was inside there, he'd walked into one of their smaller reception rooms and fell asleep. And when he woke up he kept running round and round the corridors and in the end he got into the boiler-house and by then he was completely lost, wandering around between them coloured pipes and turbines. When they found him in the morning he'd gone completely round the bend.'

Coming up to meet us, in a manner combining clodlike indifference and self-importance, were two policemen. One of them was well-built with a foppish little moustache adorning his pleasant face, while the other seemed to me like a rather tall but sickly fair-haired child with sky-blue eyes. At the sight of them something in me stiffened. Although I hadn't done anything, my experience as an innocent person with members of the police, whether in uniform or not, had not been happy. It didn't occur to me that thanks to my orange vest I was now myself on the borderline of being in uniform.

'Well then, you sweepers,' the more foppish of the two addressed us, 'a bloody mess?'

'Not too bad,' replied the foreman; 'we didn't do the housing estate today – that's where they live like pigs.'

'Ah, but we had some fun and games around here, believe me,' the foppish one put a friendly hand on his shoulder. 'Right next door,' he pointed towards Vyšehrad. 'What with that pervert about, the one who strangles women, some old hag thought he was after her and yelled for help. Some fuss, I can tell you! We combed the whole park, we had five flying squad cars there, all the way from Vršovice HQ, and all we got was one bloke. I could see at once that it wasn't him, because that pervert is no more than twenty and stands 190 tall, and this fellow was getting on for fifty and the size of a garden gnome, but he didn't have as much as a tram ticket on him, so why did we bother?'

'He was some sort of editor,' his colleague added, 'kind of taking exercise after a heart attack.'

'Is it true he's strangled seven women already?' asked Mrs Venus.

'And who told you such rubbish, Missus?' the foppish one said angrily. 'We have two murders reported and four attempted rapes, and that's the lot!'

'And when are you going to nab him?' asked Mrs Venus.

'Don't you worry.' The foppish one stroked his pistol holster. 'We know what to do. We've already established that he's fair and nearly two metres tall, thin, and with blue eyes. So there!' And he looked at his colleague, whom the description fitted surprisingly well. 'If you see a bloke like that . . . Get me?'

'Sure,' the foreman promised.

The foppish one then turned to the captain. 'And what about your trousers,' he joked, 'when will you grow into long ones?'

'In my coffin,' the captain replied. 'I've got them all ready at home.'

The foppish policeman gave a short chuckle, then raised his right hand in the direction of the peak of his service cap. 'All clear then. More eyes we've got the more we see.'

'We'll just have to watch out we don't sweep up your clues,' Mrs Venus said when he'd turned away. 'And for that they get a bigger screw than a miner!'

By twenty past eleven we had finished cleaning up around the Culture Palace. This completed our assignment for the day. We took our equipment back to the former Sokol gym hall, and we now had only one task left: to wait three hours for the end of the working day and then collect our wages. My companions of course had already marked out the tavern they'd go to. I could have gone with them but I didn't feel like it. Going to a tavern once in a while is enough for me.

The first story of Franz Kafka I ever read was one of the few longer prose pieces he'd finished. It told the story of a traveller to whom an officer on some island wants to demonstrate, with love and dedication, his own bizarre execution machine. During the demonstration, however, the machine breaks down and the officer feels so disgraced by this that he places himself on the execution block. The author coolly and matter-of-factly describes the details of that dreadful machine, as though by doing so he can shroud the mystery and the incomprehensible paradox of the recorded event.

I was thunderstruck and fascinated by the seemingly impenetrable mystery of an event which, at the same time, depressed me. But I was able only to comprehend it at its most superficial level. The officer – cruel, pedantic, enthusiastic about his executioner's task – seemed to me like a prophetic vision of the officers I had encountered, a pre-image of Hoess at Auschwitz, and I was amazed that literature could not only bring back to life those who had died but also predict the features of those who were not yet born.

Suddenly I found myself back on Vyšehrad hill. I walked through the park to the cemetery and to the ancient round church, which was surrounded by scaffolding. I'd never been inside the church although I can see it in the distance from the bluff behind our block and I actually own an old engraving of it: *Sacro-Sancta, Regia, et exempta Ecclesia Wissehradensis SS Apostolorum Petri et Pauli ad modum Vaticanae Romanae a Wratislao 1. Bohemiae Rege A.° 1068. aedificata, et prout ante disturbja Hussitica stetit, vere et genujne delineata, et effigiata. A.° 1420. 2. Novembris ab Hussitis destructa, ruinata et devastata.*

The building on the print looked different from the one now before me, and not only because it had been *destructa, ruinata et devastata* by the Hussites, but because the church had been rebuilt several times since the days when my engraving was made, and each time a little for the worse. In our country everything is being forever remade: beliefs, buildings and street names. Sometimes the progress of time is concealed and at others feigned, so long as nothing remains as real and truthful testimony.

As I walked around the little church I noticed that the door was half open. I glanced inside – there was an untidy heap of builders' requisites, scaffolding and buckets, and some of the pews were covered with a tarpaulin. On one side of the altar I caught sight of my companion of the morning, the one who reminded me of the specialist who took out my tonsils. Now without his orange vest he was evidently engaged in meditation.

I preferred not to enter. I didn't want to disturb him, nor to start a conversation with him.

He caught up with me in the park. 'Such nonsense,' he complained; 'the time you mess around waiting for your pay.'

I nodded. He told me his name was Rada. He'd taken note of my name first thing in the morning. He'd shared a room at the Litoměřice seminary with a man of that name forty years ago.

I said that all my relatives had lost their lives during the war, that the only surviving one was my brother who was a good deal younger than me.

He had two younger brothers. The middle one lived in Toronto and the youngest one was a doctor, a radiologist, apparently a good one, but he would have liked to be a traveller, he really came to life only when he saw some foreign scenery. As a matter of fact he was nearly always somewhere abroad, most recently in Kampuchea. 'Would you believe it, he actually learned to speak Khmer. To him it's just a bit of fun, he can learn a language in a few weeks!'

We passed through a brick gateway and approached the areas we'd cleaned that morning. I was glad that my shift was behind me and that I could now walk through the quiet little street onto which, by then, more yellowing leaves had dropped from the adjoining gardens, past the dark eyes of the houses which gazed on me wearily but also contentedly.

Suddenly I froze. In one of the windows I caught sight of a hanged man, his face pressed to the window-pane and his long tongue hanging from his open mouth. From below he was flooded by a blood-red glow.

Mr Rada noticed what I was staring at and said: 'Let's see what our artist has put on show for us today.'

I realised that the figure in the window was only a skilfully got-up dummy. As I looked more closely I saw another head, half female and half dog, its teeth dug into the hanged man's thigh.

'Oh dear,' my companion was not happy. 'He must have got out of bed the wrong side. He usually puts something more entertaining in his window. A little while ago he had some colourful acrobats turning somersaults. I sometimes come here specially to see what he's thought up. My brother, who came along with me once, declared that they're the work of a lunatic.' Mr Rada again returned to the subject of his brother, who seemed to play an important part in his life. 'To him everybody he can't fit into a pattern is a lunatic.

He actually believes that the whole world is crazy, he says the world needs some terrible shaking-up, some great revolution to equalise the differences between the sated and the hungry. We argue a lot. At least until quite recently, when he came back home and told me about such a revolution that even I wouldn't credit it. Right next to a hospital a well full to the rim of murdered people. Corpses everywhere, he just couldn't have imagined it. Maybe he simply saw what any revolution always brings to the people.' Mr Rada stopped and looked about him, but we were alone in the swept street. 'The Apocalypse! That was the word he used, even though he never decided to believe in the Last Judgement and regarded Revelations as, at most, a poetic vision.'

My wife's consulting room was not far from where we were.

Luckily her waiting room was empty. I knocked. After a moment a young nurse put her head round the door, choked back the reproof on the tip of her tongue and asked me to come in.

I saw Lída sitting behind a desk half taken up by a bunch of chrysanthemums. She was examining some sheets of Rorschach blotches.

'You've stopped by to see me? That's nice of you.'

'I was walking past.'

'Are you going straight home?'

'I thought I might look in on Dad first.'

'It's nice of you to have dropped in. Would you like some coffee?'

'No, thank you.' My wife had been offering me coffee for the past twenty-five years; I would have been interested to know if she'd noticed that I don't drink coffee.

The young nurse had disappeared somewhere, I could hear a door shutting quietly. I sat down in the armchair in which normally people would sit with depressions, anxieties, suppressed passions, Oedipus complexes, or even with suicidal tendencies. My feet ached.

'Have you noticed the flowers I got?' she pointed to them.

I said they were beautiful and asked who'd given them to her. Her patients liked her. She was pleasant to them and gave them more time than she was obliged to, and in gratitude they brought her flowers. When was the last time I'd brought her flowers?

I used to give the other woman flowers and repeat to her ad nauseam how much I loved her; she aroused a sense of tenderness in me time and again.

I also felt some tenderness towards my wife, but I was afraid to show it, probably because she might begin to talk about such an emotion and even commend me for it.

She'd got her flowers from a woman patient about whom, as a matter of fact, she was worried. A girl of nearly nineteen, but still unable to come to terms with the fact that her parents had separated. She'd stopped studying, she'd stopped caring for herself, I wouldn't believe how much she'd gone down over the past few weeks.

For a while my wife continued to tell me about the girl whose future was worrying her. My wife always took on the burdens of her patients. She'd try to help them, and she'd torment herself if she failed. Perhaps she was telling me about that girl to make me realise the devastating effect that the break-up of a marriage might have. Certainly situations like this one touched her most closely.

Today the girl had told her about a dream she'd had: at dusk she was walking along a field path when suddenly, ahead of her, she caught sight of a glow. The glow was coming towards her, and she realised that the ground before her was opening and flames were licking up from the depths. She knew she couldn't escape them, but she wasn't afraid, she didn't try to run away, she simply watched the earth opening up before her eyes.

I am looking at my wife, at her vivid features. She is still pretty, there are no lines as yet on her face, or else I don't see them. Whether I like it or not, in my eyes her present appearance blends with that of long ago.

'I'm worried she might do something to herself!'

I stood up and stroked her hair.

'You want to leave already?' She half-opened the door and looked into the waiting room. 'There's no one there, you don't have to go yet. You haven't even told me,' she suddenly realised, 'what it was like there . . . doing that . . .' she was vainly looking for a word for my street-sweeping.

'Tell you about it in the evening.'

'All right, let's have a cosy evening.' She saw me to the door. She said I'd given her pleasure. She's always pleased when she sees me unexpectedly.

I would have liked to say something similar to her, such as that I always revive in her presence, that I feel warm when I'm with her, but I couldn't bring myself to say it.

She went back once more, pulled the biggest flower out of her vase and gave it to me, to take to Dad. It was a full bloom, dark yellow with a touch of amber at the tips of the petals.

She didn't know, she had evidently never noticed, that my father didn't like unnecessary and useless things such as flowers.

I kissed her quickly and we parted.

'And the fourth angel sounded,' I read at home in the Apocalypse, 'and the third part of the sun was smitten, and the third part of the moon and the third part of the stars; so as the third part of them was darkened, and the day shone not for a third part of it, and the night likewise . . . And the fifth angel sounded, and I saw a star fall from heaven unto the earth: and to him was given the key of the bottomless pit. And he opened the bottomless pit; and there arose a smoke out of the pit, as the smoke of a great furnace; and the sun and the air were darkened by reason of the smoke of the pit.' And somewhere else I read: 'And when the thousand years are expired, Satan shall be loosed out of his prison, and shall go out to deceive the nations which are in the four quarters of the earth . . . to gather them together to battle: the number of whom is as the sand of the sea . . . And fire came down from God out of heaven and devoured them. And the devil that deceived them was cast into the lake of fire and brimstone . . . And I saw a great white throne, and him that sat on it, from whose eyes the earth and the heaven fled away; and there was found no place for them.'

Throughout the ages, probably ever since they began to reflect on time, and hence on their own past, men have assumed that at the beginning of everything there had been paradise, where humans had lived happily on earth, where

> *non galeae, non enses erant: sine militis usu*
> *mollia securae peragebant otia gentes . . .*

Yet simultaneously they had prophesied the advent of ruin. It was inescapable, because it would happen by the decision of heaven.

In the evening a French woman journalist unexpectedly turned up at our place. She was young, and she radiated French perfume and self-assurance. She smiled at me with a wide sensuous mouth as if we were old friends. She wanted to know how the struggle for human rights would develop in my country, what was the attitude of my fellow-countrymen to her fellow-countrymen, whether they would welcome them if they arrived as liberators. She was also interested to know whether I regarded war as probable, the peace movement as useful, and socialism as practicable.

Perhaps she really believed that any one of her questions could be answered in a form that would fit into a newspaper column. She questioned me as though I was the representative of some movement, or at least of some common fate. She didn't realise that if I were the representative of anything whatsoever I'd cease to be a writer, I'd only be a spokesman. But then this didn't bother her, she didn't need me as a writer, she wasn't going to read any book of mine anyway.

I recently read an article in an American weekly about how fourteen complete idiots incapable of speech had learned 'jerkish'. That was the name of a language of 225 words, developed in Atlanta for mutual communication between humans and chimpanzees – and there was no doubt, the author of the article believed, that more and more unfortunate creatures would be able to talk to each other in jerkish. It occurred to me immediately that at last a language had been found in which the spirit of our age could speak, and because that language would spread rapidly from pole to pole, to the east and to the west, it would be the language of the future.

I do not understand or make myself understood by those who

recognise only the literature they control themselves and which, because of them, is written in jerkish, and I am afraid that I cannot communicate either with the pretty journalist, even though she assures me that she wishes absolute freedom for me and for my nation just as she wishes it for herseelf and her nation. I am afraid that we speak in languages which have moved too far apart.

As she was leaving she asked, more out of politeness than anything else, what I was working on at the moment. She was surprised to hear that I wanted to write about Kafka. Clearly she believed that people in my position should be writing about something more weighty – about oppression, about prisons, about the lawlessness practised by the state. Anyway, she asked if I was interested in Kafka's work because it was forbidden.

But I am writing about him because I like him. I feel that he is speaking to me directly and personally from a distant past. For the sake of accuracy I added that his work was not forbidden; they were merely trying to remove it, from public libraries and from people's minds.

She wanted to know why they did this to his work in particular. Was it politically so subversive? or was it because Kafka was a Jew?

I think it would be difficult to find, in our century, many writers who were less interested in politics or public affairs than Kafka. There is no mention in his work of war or revolution, or of the ideas which may have helped to bring them about, just as there is nothing in his work which directly points to his Jewishness. The reasons why Kafka's work was suppressed in our country were different. I don't know if they can be simply defined, but I'd say that what was being most objected to in Kafka's personality was his honesty.

The journalist laughed. Who wouldn't laugh at such a reason?

She left before midnight. I hurried to get to bed. I was tired after a day which had started for me at five in the morning.

My wife curled up against me in her sleep, but I was unable to lay my thoughts to rest. A heavy paw law chokingly on my chest.

Long ago, after I'd got well again, I was impatient every evening for the next morning. Night was like an angry dog lying in my way.

Almost as soon as I was awake in the morning I'd walk past all the windows of our flat, which looked out to three points of the compass, to enjoy the distant view clothed in fresh green or white with snow. I enjoyed my work and the people at the newspaper office, I looked forward to seeing them and to those unexpected encounters which might occur. I also always opened my letters full of hope: I was forever expecting some good news, some exciting revelation or some declaration of love. And I looked forward to the books I'd read. I would read at every spare moment: in the tram, in the doctor's waiting room, in the train, and even at mealtimes. I soaked up such a vast number of events and plots that they began to intertwine in my mind and I no longer knew which belonged where. I was enjoying life, and so I rushed from one experience to another, until I became like some obsessive eater who, out of sheer greed for the next course, is unable to savour the one he is eating. I didn't drink or smoke — not from any puritanism but through fear that I might blunt the edge of my perception and thus be deprived of an exciting experience or a possible encounter. I had known ever since my wartime childhood that we are all living on the edge of an abyss, above a black pit into which we must fall one day, but I felt that its jaws were now receding from me and that I was tied to life by a countless number of threads which together formed a firm net on which I was, for the time being, swinging at life's vertiginous height.

But the threads were quietly breaking, some gone rotten with age, some snapped by my own clumsiness, and others severed by other people. Or I might say: by the time we live in.

And so, every now and again when I lie down, I feel that heavy paw on my chest. In the morning, when I wake up, I want to shut my eyes again and sleep on.

Some time ago a classmate of my daughter's came to see me, a youngster who'd already cut his wrists once, and who asked me: Why should a person live?

What could I say to him? We live because that is the law of existence, we live so that we should pass on a message whose significance we cannot quite fathom because it is mysterious and unrevealable. We live because there are a number of encounters ahead of us for the sake of which living is worthwhile. Encounters with people who will emerge when we least expect them, and we shall exchange with them tenderness, wisdom or love. Or else encounters with other creatures whose lives will touch on ours with a single shy glance. Or encounters with a quiet sunny morning . . . What more could I say to him?

Anyway he cut his wrists again one evening, and with his hands bleeding even managed to hang himself on a tree at the northern tip of the Žofín island in the Vltava while his young friends were having a good time in the old dance hall there. My daughter cried bitterly as she told me about it, and in conclusion she said of her dead class-mate: 'But otherwise he was quite normal!'

While I was visiting my father in the afternoon his temperature suddenly began to rise steeply. His teeth were chattering and his eyes grew dim. I soaked a sheet and tried to wrap his emaciated body in the wet cloth, but he resisted, snatched the sheet from my hands and several times shouted: Take it and burn it!

Yes, I replied, I'll take it and burn it.

Father had been imprisoned twice in his life, two different secret police forces had searched our flat – he was probably talking about some letters or papers. But then I asked after all: What is it that I should take and burn?

He looked at me with a lifeless gaze from his greyish blue eyes, which, when I was a child, were still the colour of blue lichen, and said: This fever, of course!

So I took his fever and made a little fire on the parquet floor from newspapers and some old manuscripts of mine which had been lying in a cupboard here uselessly for some thirty years. And as I was burning that fever I could see its face in the flames, it looked like the face of a pale china doll and I was waiting for it to melt or at least to crack up, but it stood up to the fire, only writhing in agony, and I noticed that the doll was crying, amidst the flames tears were glistening on her pale cheeks.

I have been locked up only once in my life. I was ten years old and totally unable to realise the actual state of affairs, the magnitude of the hopelessness we were living in. At first I was even pleased and flattered when strange grown-up women, in whose presence I inevitably spent much time, used to praise me. I would help them carry coal and sweep the military quarters we occupied. I also stoked the iron stove alongside which my mother and I slept. That I enjoyed most. To keep the fire going gave me a sense of importance, the fire seemed to me like some living creature, my own animal that I was looking after. I fed it with whatever came to hand, even though it wasn't much, because in that place there was practically no refuse, not even a scrap of old paper, a newspaper or a piece of worn material.

On one occasion a room-mate, who was only a little older than me, dropped a small porcelain jug. When she cried over it I asked her to let me have the fragments for my fire. Cautiously I threw them into the hot stove and watched what was happening to them. It looked to me as if the fire was really digesting them. The pieces glowed in their own particular way, but when I cleared out the ashes I found the fragments unchanged, perhaps a little sooty but otherwise intact. I fished them out of the ashes, carefully wiped them clean, and some of them I kept. I felt some attachment to them or admiration that they should have survived their fall into the fire and its heat. Maybe they would help me and I would myself one day be dug intact out of the ashes.

My father was then living in the same fortress ghetto, within the same ramparts, but I couldn't see him, a lot of walls and prohibitions divided us. Until one day the door opened and there, unexpectedly, he stood. Grown thin, his hair recently shaved off, wearing a boilersuit, he appeared in that door and his eyes swept the far corners of the dormitory. I cried out and suddenly he saw me and said: Quiet, quiet, I'm only here to repair the wiring. I realised that nobody must see him here and was frightened, but he lifted me in his arms though I was a big boy, pressed me to himself and said softly: My little boy! He who had never cuddled me. And as I looked up at him I saw with amazement that my big, strong and powerful father was crying.

46

The flames had died down. I walked up to my father and touched his forehead. It was cool and moist with sweat. Dad opened his ever-seeing eyes and attempted a smile which was almost guilty. He could smile so tenderly and genuinely that even someone seeing him for the first time could not but realise that here was someone special.

I looked about me. The fever lay in ashes, its china-doll face was dry again, parched and greedy.

I wanted to fall asleep but I could feel the night creeping around me softly, like a cat out hunting, nothing mattering to it except its intended prey. I examined the threads by which life was still tying me to itself, still holding me above the black pit, its jaw so close that sometimes I could make out its smooth edge.

What tied me most firmly to life was my writing: anything I experienced would become images for me. At times they would surround me so completely that I felt I was in a different world, and my stay there filled me with happiness or at least with a sense of relief. Years ago, I persuaded myself that I would be able to communicate these images to someone, that there were even people about who were waiting for them in order to share my joys and sorrows. I did all I could to meet their supposed expectations: I was doing this not from pride or any sense of superiority but because I wanted someone to share my world with me.

Later I realised that in an age where so many were obediently and devotedly embracing the jerkish spirit, if only to avoid having to face the horseman of the Apocalypse, very few people were interested in someone else's images or someone else's words.

I am still writing, putting words and sentences together to make images, events, visions. Often I labour for days over a single paragraph, I cover pages with writing, then throw them away, I keep trying to lend the most complete and the most precise expression to what I have on my mind, to avoid any misunderstanding, to make sure none of those I am addressing should feel cheated. Whenever I finish a book or a play my body rebels and punishes me with pains, and all the time I know that when I send my manuscript to the publishers I'll get a one-sentence reply: We are returning your manuscript because it does not fit into our editorial plans. I then lend it to a few friends, and some who still refuse to submit to the jerkish spirit will probably copy it and lend it to some of their friends. I also send it abroad, provided it doesn't get lost on the way, and it will be published there. So maybe after all – this is the thread I cling to – there may be a handful of people in the world with whom, despite all my irritations, I make contact.

I kept writing through all those years when not a single line bearing my name was allowed to be published in our country, when some of my recent friends would avoid me because they couldn't be sure that meeting me might not cast a shadow on their respectability. I wrote stubbornly, although sometimes the weight of my loneliness lay heavily on me. I'd sit at my table and listen to the silence which was swallowing me up. I could hear nothing but a barely perceptible snapping sound as some of the individual threads broke, and I longed to discover some hope I could attach myself to. That was when she appeared. If we had met at some other time we'd probably have passed each other by, but at just that moment I raced after her like a man drugged, and it took years for me to come to again. At the same time I never stopped conducting a silent argument with her. Even when I longed for her most my words died in my throat the moment she looked at me, whenever the night separated me from her embracing and comforting glance I would compose answers to questions, reproaches, wishes and yearnings which until then I had left unanswered.

And now, as the night lazily stretched its back over me, I was continuing, by force of habit, with the silent letter in which I defended myself and tried to prove that I didn't want to hurt her. Before throwing it into the big box full of unsent letters and wishes I tried once more to visualise what she was doing just then, at least to visualise her room. Who knows if she was even there. I no longer knew how she spent her nights. Maybe she was just returning home, her swift footsteps were closing the circle. If I got up now and ran after her, maybe I could cut the circle open, clutch her to myself, within the confines of that circle forget everything outside it, everything that was, that is, and that would inevitably be. But I knew I wouldn't do it. I'd only get up in the morning to set off for the streets I'd decided to sweep clean. It suddenly occurred to me that this was the reason why I'd found myself in the street with a handcart yesterday morning. I needed to go somewhere in the morning, at least I'd now have a natural objective for a while: set out somewhere, perform whatever kind of activity and listen to whatever kind of talk, just so I don't have to sit amidst the silence listening to the snapping of the threads.

Perhaps, it occurred to me, I was in some new space. I'd entered the place where oblivion was born. Or despair. And also understanding. Or perhaps even love – not as a mirage but as a space for the soul to move in.

II

Four weeks later, again at nine in the morning, we were once more, the same team, sitting in the same tavern as on my first day.

When I'd put on my orange vest then I wasn't sure how often I'd decide to repeat the experience, but to begin with I would come to work at least every other day. I was curious about what parts of Prague my work would take me to, what narrow little streets that otherwise I'd never venture into.

I am fond of my native city, not only of the part through which the tourist crowds stroll, but also of the outskirts, where, among blocks of flats from the Secession period, a few little rural houses have remained standing, either forgotten or, more probably, already sentenced to death in some development plans, where unexpectedly an avenue of ancient poplars has survived or a little wooded hill, or fences bearing appeals and announcements whose bright colours I was aware of but whose texts as a rule I didn't read. More than once, as I pushed my cart with the dustbin I discovered a faded plaque on some familiar and usually dingy wall, a bust, or even a memorial huddling in some recess. These were meant to remind us that here, years ago, was born, lived or died some artist, thinker, scientist or national figure, in other words a spirit of whom it might be presumed that he rose above the rest of us. But more often, in one of those little streets or among the fading gardens, I remembered that here lived someone I knew, an artist, a thinker, a scientist or a national figure, someone who was here no more, someone beyond the hills and beyond the rivers, though mostly not over the river Styx, which would be sad but the common human lot, but someone now a refugee, someone driven out to our common shame. The walls of these houses, needless to say, did not bear plaques or a bust or even a visiting card to remind us that here lived a human spirit that had endeavoured to rise to higher things. I would glance at my companions at those moments, but they suspected nothing, except possibly Mr Rada, if he was one of our party, who might nod his head.

Thus I moved in my orange vest through the little streets and lanes of my native city which was slowly giving up its spirit, my companions at my side as witnesses. We were cleaning the town on which refuse had fallen and soot and ashes and poisoned rain and oblivion. We strode along in our vests like flamingoes, like angels of the dying day, sweeping away all rubbish and refuse, angels beyond life, beyond death, beyond our time, beyond all time, scarcely touched by the jerkish. Our speech resembled our age-old brooms, it came from a long way back and it moved along age-old paths. But behind us others are moving up: already the jerkish sweepers are arriving on their beflagged vehicles, pretending that they are completing the great purge, sweeping away all memories of the past, of anything that was great in the past. And when, with delight, they halt in the space which appears to them to be cleaned up, they'll summon one of their jerkish artists and he'll erect here a monument to oblivion, an effigy of shaft-boots, an overcoat, trousers and a briefcase, and above these an unforgettable face behind which we feel neither spirit nor soul but which, by official decree, will be proclaimed to be the face of an artist, a thinker, a scientist or a national figure.

There has been a slight drizzle since early morning, maybe it isn't even real rain but just condensation of the fog which covers the city with grime and helps to submerge it in oblivion.

On days like this Daria would positively choke and life would seem unbearable to her, her stone or wood incapable of being worked on, and as the droplets fell inexhaustibly from the clouds so the tears began to drip from her eyes, no matter how I tried to console her.

My companions aren't in a good mood either. I hardly recognised Mrs Venus this morning. Her right eye was swollen and below it was a purplish bruise. The captain's face had lost its tan over the past few days and had gone grey. Even the foreman in his freshly laundered and pressed overalls walked along in silence.

I ordered some hot tea and the captain, instead of his usual beer, ordered a grog. 'Tell me, who gave you that monocle?' he turned to Mrs Venus.

'A different bloke from what you are,' she snapped. 'One like you I'd have torn apart before he even raised his hand!'

Mrs Venus liked to make out how tough she was, but in reality she was good-natured, and she'd paid the price for it all her life. There were many men she'd loved, or at least lived with, but they'd all left her, or else she'd run away from them. She'd raised three sons, even though she probably hadn't had much time for raising them. When she was young, the order of the day was that women must devote themselves to more important duties than looking after their children. Now she lived on her own. Her flat, as I understood it, was reached by an open upstairs passage; the term flat meant a single room with a cooker. Her eldest son, who was a steelworker in Vítkovice, had given her a television set on which she could follow our jerkish programmes in colour. So for those evenings when she preferred home to the company at the bar, she had a reliable companion. Besides, at the far end of the passage lived, or rather slowly died, a lonely widower who'd been incapacitated by a stroke some years back, and now and then she'd go and clean up for him and bake him a cake – so he shouldn't be left alone like an abandoned dog.

'Yeah, maybe if two other blokes were holding me down,' the captain growled.

Normally there was nothing eccentric about his speech. Mostly he'd conceal the oddity of his thoughts. He wasn't a real captain, he'd merely worked in the shipyards before he lost his hand. But his real interest was not ships but inventions. That's what he softly told me on the second day we were sweeping alongside each other: he'd think up machines which would improve people's lives. Unfortunately, he'd so far not met with any understanding. Wherever he turned with his inventions, there were blinkered people behind desks, instructed to block real progress and prosperity. He offered to demonstrate some of his inventions to me.

I hadn't been mistaken when I'd felt his face seemed familiar to me.

It was when I was still working in newspapers. One day the editor received a letter from an inventor who'd had his idea turned down. He had devised a way of utilising waste materials, especially soot, for the removal of the Arctic and Antarctic ice caps. The editor passed the letter on to me for answering. I wrote that in this matter we were unable to help him. A few days later, however, the writer turned up at the editorial office. He was quite a pleasant and amusing fellow. I couldn't see anything odd in his appearance, anything that might make me doubt his sincerity. He merely had a deeper tan than would be usual for that time of the year, but he told me he'd just returned from the shores of Africa. Out there, even at night-time when he couldn't sleep because of the heat, he had reflected on the curious and dangerous imbalance of the planet. In some places it would offer warmth and in others humidity, and elsewhere nothing but sand or ice. During those nights he'd thought a lot about abolishing that imbalance, but his head buzzed with more crazy ideas than were found in the Academy. In the end, however, he'd discovered the fundamental mistake which nature and mankind had committed. They'd come to dislike black! Was there anything in nature that was truly black? And mankind, with the possible exception of the Chinese, regarded black as the colour of mourning. Yet black was in fact the colour which combined most completely with the basic life force, that is with warmth, whereas white, allegedly the colour of innocence, the colour of wedding dresses, repulsed heat; it was the colour of snow and of most of the poisons. Those immense white areas had to be removed from the surface of the earth, and life would then establish itself where deserts had been before, and warmth would invade the areas which until now had been frosty. It had taken him a long time to discover the right means and the right method. The means was a mixture he'd invented, a solution of soot in seven solvents and three catalysts, and the method was the melting of the polar ice. As soon as the ice caps were sprayed with his mixture they'd lose their deadly whiteness, they'd begin to soak up heat and to melt.

I realised of course that I was talking either to a madman or to a joker with a magnificent, elaborate joke. Or he might be both. A crazy inventor pulling his own leg. But I found his exposition so entertaining that I continued to listen to his vision of the world of the future, when oranges and rice would be cultivated beyond the Arctic and Antarctic circles, while in our country there would be two harvests, and breadfruit trees and date palms would thrive.

I heard him out to the end but I told him I didn't have the time to go along with him then to see how his machine for the spraying of the mixture worked. He shrugged and left, and as a farewell gift handed me a few colour photographs which showed an array of strangely shaped objects arranged on the grass. I have no technical memory, so I'm unable after all these years to recall their shapes, and the photographs were lost when I was forced to leave the paper.

A few days later he turned up again. Had I noticed that there'd been a fresh fall of snow? He'd borrowed his neighbour's car solely for the purpose of convincingly demonstrating his equipment to me. Once I'd seen it I'd realise its revolutionary significance and would maybe write an article about it after all.

The elderly Tatra car took us all the way to Kralupy. There, on the outskirts, immediately behind the railway crossing, we stopped. It was a small house, and evidently a bachelor establishment. On the wall facing the front door hung a framed photograph of a white-haired man: unless I was mistaken it was a picture of Edison, and below it in large letters the inventor's statement: 'My work is the work of peace!' A desk below the window was covered with cartridge paper with drawings on it and with some rolled-up plans; on the shelves stood several skilfully-made model ships. I hurriedly drank a cup of coffee and then we went out by the back door into his yard.

I noticed that the snow which had fallen that morning had none of the usual deathly whiteness about it, but was dirty grey. My guide didn't even look about him but hurried to a shed behind the house, opened its wide double door, and wheeled out his machinery. Unlike the house itself this was an object of impressive appearance. It reminded me of an ancient fire engine: all brass and gleaming metal parts. It might equally well have been a perfect artefact for some exhibition of op art. The long hose was fitted with a nozzle.

He wheeled the assembly into the garden, uncoiled the hose and began to pump some handles. A smelly mist issued from the nozzle. I watched the mist settling on the snow, but that dirty snow, instead of getting blacker, seemed to be getting lighter. No doubt there was some chemical reaction between the artificial mist and that chemical mess that had dropped from the sky. Thus we found ourselves in the middle of a near-white island while all around lay black clods of snow. I didn't say anything, and he too was silent. In his eyes I saw neither disappointment nor the joy of a perfectly played practical joke. After a while he stopped pumping, coiled up the hose, and wheeled his shining equipment back into the shed. I seized on the moment when he was inside and quickly walked along the railway line to the station. As I walked through the black snow I thought to myself that even if that man was crazy, he was no crazier than the rest of humanity which, in its eagerness for comfort, was spraying the world with a black mist in the belief that this was the direct road to the Garden of Eden.

It would have been embarrassing if he'd recognised me too, but he didn't seem to remember me. He had been too obsessed with his own mission at the time to take note of the face of someone who served him, at best, as an intermediary.

I promised him I'd come and look at his inventions as soon as I had some time, and he did not press me any further.

'For all you know your Harry may have been with me,' Mrs Venus said. Her face seemed even more swollen than in the morning and she was gazing at us with her right eye like an owl. 'He's not like you, he doesn't only go in for machines!'

'He can do better than you, you old hag!' The captain took a swig of grog, pulled out his pipe and filled it with his good hand.

Last Monday it rained even harder than today. We had to stop work before time was up, and as we were only a short distance from where the captain lived this seemed a suitable moment for a visit.

He led me to a house which looked even more dilapidated than the one where, years ago, he had demonstrated his equipment to me. He unlocked the door and hung up his captain's cap on a rusty nail behind it. The walls of the hall were damp and hadn't been painted for a long time; everywhere lay heaps of dusty objects and scattered pieces of clothing. The room's appearance and dimensions suggested a ship's cabin. Over his bunk hung various drawings, mostly of windmills. Nowhere did I see anything that suggested our first encounter. Perhaps I was the victim of some fixed idea and the captain had nothing in common with that young man years ago. No doubt the number of unsuccessful inventors in the world was increasing like that of unsuccessful poets.

He opened the bottom drawer and took out some folders of plans. He'd lately concerned himself with the most effective way of using wind power. He unrolled the first sheet and I saw a dreamlike ship whose deck was taken up by turrets carrying windmill sails, five turrets in all. He showed me further drawings, among them a windmill bus and a flying windmill, all these craft driven by wind. The drawings were meticulously done, the individual parts all bearing letters and numbers: the drive assembly, the transmission gears and the blades of the propellers. Other drawings had landscapes dotted with wooden turrets towering picturesquely above the tops of the trees.

It struck me that the captain was not so much a madman, not so much a joker, as a poet at heart. What else could a real poet do when he realised that crowds of jerkish wordmongers and image-mongers had already flooded the world with their rubbish? What else could he do in the face of the monstrous palatial blocks choking the earth but build his windmills which rise up silently and leave behind neither noise nor smell?

I asked him how much time he spent on his inventing. He said not so much now. He was usually too tired. At one time his head used to buzz with so many ideas that there weren't enough days and nights to put them down. Then he'd got married. He'd thought his wife would support him in his endeavours, but what woman could work up an enthusiasm for something that brought her no practical advantage? She'd begun to nag him, she even threw out his drawings and models. Finally, when their son was three, she'd run off. The captain spat towards the corner of his cabin and opened a cupboard which was full of strange objects. He'd wanted to go back to his old drawings but he'd suddenly discovered that there were stones rattling in his head. He was going downhill. One day, when he was cutting a sheet of metal with a welding torch, he'd handled it so awkwardly that the cut strip fell and crushed his hand. They had to amputate it at the wrist. So he'd been transferred to storekeeping. There, now and again, some idea would come to him. He hadn't heard from his ex-wife for many years, but she'd not had a good time either. The fellow she'd run off with beat her, he knew that from his son. Maybe she'd come back some day. He wouldn't drive her out, she'd find her bed all ready. He pointed to the upper part of the bunk, and it was only then that I noticed that the check bedcover had a thick layer of dust on it.

'How old is your son now?' it occurred to me to ask.

He looked at me in astonishment, and Mrs Venus answered for him: 'Why, Harry's off doing his military service now.'

In the dim saloon bar it was getting darker still and the raindrops were beating noisily against the windowpanes. But this was nothing compared to the drops which would beat a tattoo on the roof of the attic studio, where on days like this it got so dark we became invisible to one another, so we could find each other only with our hands and our lips and our bodies. Then, all of a sudden, she'd be overcome by tears, and as we were saying goodbye, as she was kissing me with moist lips in the doorway of the building, she begged me not to be angry with her, that it was only those clouds which had so depressed her, and she promised she'd write me a letter.

I've always wanted to get a letter from which I could see that I was being loved, and indeed she sent me one written on a rainy evening, or maybe late at night when the wind had dispersed the clouds.

> My darling, my dearest, at this moment I'd leave everything, I wouldn't take anything with me, and if you said: Come! I'd go wherever you commanded. I realise that one pays for this, but this is right because one should pay for it. But even if I were to die, even if I were to go out of my mind, which to me seems worse still, I'd go . . .

I was alarmed by these promises and resolutions, but at the same time I was flooded with a happiness, like the warmth of sunbathing.

She also wrote to me that she loved me to the point of feeling anguish and pain, that she experienced a terrible pain because I was not with her at this moment, just now when everything that was good in her was crying out to me.

That's how she called me to her, and I knew that I had always longed for just such a woman. It gave me so much happiness that the reality of her pain and despair did not impinge on me. Or else I was too old to share her hopes without fear. Was I afraid we would end up like all those whose longing dies away and who can then scarcely bear to lie down by the side of each other night after night? Or was I not so much afraid as simply unable to brush my wife out of my life, my wife of whom I was still fond and who, after all, was supposed to belong to me to the end of my or her days?

How can a man win love if he can't make up his mind? But how can a man still believe in love if he has no compassion?

The foreman finished his second beer and unbuttoned himself. I realised that he was not so much worried by the change in atmospheric pressure as by the fact that he might lose his bonus. He ordered a third beer and announced that he'd made up his mind: he'd finally teach that Franta a lesson!

Franta is that young idiot with the tic in his face, the one I don't understand a word of when he speaks. To my amazement he is also a foreman, he even drives a car and it looks as if he is checking on our work, not by official authority but so he can grass on us. Everyone hates him. Whether because he's a cripple or because he's a grass I can't judge.

Mrs Venus told me that he'd recently had an operation. They'd taken his manhood from him. Franta did indeed have big breasts and his incomprehensible talk was in a falsetto. Last week, the foreman was now telling us angrily, that cripple had grassed on him, that he'd gone to have a beer when he'd claimed he was seeing the doctor. 'I saw that shit at the final stop of the number 19 yesterday, in that bloody refuse truck of his, so I grabbed him by his collar and dragged him out on the pavement and said to him: "You'll kneel down right here and ask my pardon, you swine, or else bring a pot along to collect up the bits of your bloody mug!" He had to get down into the mud and repeat after me: "Mister Marek, I apologise to you, I'll never say a word about you again." "Mister," I made him say to me, because to him, and to him alone, I'm no Comrade'!

The foreman is an ex-NCO, certainly no fool, and with a memory I envy him. Not only does he remember a mass of stories and sayings, but he also knows the names of all the streets in our district, and that's several hundred. He is as expert about the names and closing times of all the taverns as he is about street-cleaning technology. And they put him on an equal footing with that cripple.

'You should have made him stand a round of beer,' the captain remarked. 'He'd remember that all right, having to dip into his own pocket.'

'I wouldn't accept one from him,' Mrs Venus said. 'I'd sooner stick to water.'

'He's a poor wretch,' Mr Rada cut in from the next table. 'What do you want from him?'

'That one?' the foreman became heated. 'He's a cunning little bastard, he knows very well that if they cut my bonus his will go up. Who d'you suppose grassed on us last month, the day we had that downpour, when we left out Lomnického?'

'He's a poor wretch all the same,' I joined in.

'You didn't know him,' Mrs Venus said, her swollen eye flickering between Mr Rada and me, 'before they did that operation on him. By the time he got down to work it would be midday, and out in the street the moment he'd catch sight of a skirt he'd whip out that thing of his!'

'Creatures like him should be done in at birth.' The foreman knew no pity.

'How could they do that?' I objected.

'And why not? You only bugger about with them all your life, and there's no time left for normal people. Aren't I right?' the foreman turned to the others. 'And a decent bloke's got to work till he croaks.'

'And who'd decide who is normal?'

'Leave it to the doctors; they can tell pretty well nowadays. Let me tell you,' the foreman decided to cut short the discussion on euthanasia, 'that if that damned pervert grasses once more on any one of us, I'll catch hold of the bastard and kick him all the way down to the Botič stream and there I'll hold his bloody mug under the water till he sees reason'.

Two and a half thousand years ago it is believed that the Greeks in Asia Minor, whenever their community was threatened by the plague or some other disaster, picked a cripple or otherwise deformed person, led him to the place of sacrifice, gave him a handful of dried figs, a loaf of wheat-flour bread and cheese, then struck him seven times on his genitals with a scourge, and to the accompaniment of a flute burnt him to death.

It was another rainy day, but at the beginning of spring. On the window-sill of the noble town house opposite two drenched pigeons were huddling together, and we were also huddling together, exhausted from love-making. I was beginning to get up because I wanted to get home, where my wife and children were expecting me, my unsuspecting and deceived family and my neglected, abandoned work. By now she knew that cautious movement which was the beginning of my moving away from her, but she didn't, as usual, say: Don't go yet! She just started to cry.

I asked what was wrong, but she only sobbed and pushed me away from her. It had been getting too much for her, she no longer had the strength for those perpetual goodbyes, for that coming together and breaking apart, she wasn't cut out to be a two-man woman, she couldn't bear the deception, the pretence sickened her, she wanted to live according to her conscience, she wanted to be with the one she loved.

'But surely we're almost continually together.'

How could I say something so outrageous when every night I was in bed with another woman?

'But that is my wife!'

How did I dare say this to her? She was shaking with sobs. She'd never wanted to live like that, what had I made of her? A whore who wasn't even entitled to see me when she felt depressed but who had to come running the moment I felt like it, whenever I could find the time for her.

I didn't say anything, I was so taken aback by her grief and anger, and she screamed that I should say something, why didn't I defend myself, why didn't I try to convince her that she was mistaken, why didn't I tell her that I loved her, that I cared for her?

Then we made love again, night descended on the palace outside our window, the drenched pigeons had disappeared. She wanted to hear again and again that I loved her. I kept repeating it with a strange kind of obsessiveness. We made love with the same obsessiveness, and she whispered to me that we had been predestined for each other, that we were resisting our fate in vain, that I was resisting in vain when I longed for her so much.

And I didn't say anything. I embraced her, I melted into her, and I tried to dispel the unease which was growing within me.

But I didn't want to live like that permanently. A lie clings to one's soul and to the world one moves in, as well as to the people one lives with. When I got home I told my wife about the other woman.

It was getting on for ten o'clock, the time when we normally left our hospitable tavern. The foreman, who was a great one for precision, looked closely at his watch: 'One more beer,' he decided, 'and then we're off, even if it's pissing like from a fireman's hose.' And to comfort us he related how exactly thirty years ago it had rained just like this all through the summer. He was encamped down beyond Kvilda, at the back of beyond. Luckily he managed on the second day to pick up a pretty dark-haired girl from accounts at the timberyard. He'd stopped at her office in the morning, and within half an hour he'd done all the calculations for her that she'd have spent the whole day on, so that they could get down to the real business.

The foreman was a good raconteur, and the standard of his story-telling rose with the interest of his listeners. In me he found an attentive listener, for which he rewarded me not only by addressing me more often than the rest but also, as a sign of his favour, by occasionally giving me the better and more profitable jobs. His most grateful listener, however, was the youngster, either because at his age he was the most eager to hear other people's stories or because fate had prevented him from experiencing most of the things the foreman recounted.

I knew by then that he hadn't been sickly from childhood. As soon as he'd finished school he'd let himself be lured by favourable terms into a chemical plant, where they offered him a flat within a year and special danger pay straight away. That danger pay was not just a lure. He'd hardly been at the plant five months when an incident occurred, which is the term used in the jerkish press for an event which costs the health and even the lives of an appreciable number of workers. There'd been an escape of poison gas. Two women died instantly and the young man was discharged from hospital after six months and pensioned off. His liver and kidneys were damaged, and he'd better forget about women altogether. Nevertheless he'd taken a liking to a tram driver called Dana, admittedly the divorced mother of two girls and his senior by ten years, or maybe it was just because of that that he thought he had a chance. Apparently he'd been courting her for a year and he'd been cleaning the city's streets for that period in order to earn a little extra money so he wouldn't come to her as a pauper.

The rain thirty years ago had been an obstacle to the foreman's intentions until he remembered that a little beyond the airfield there was a rusty old Messerschmitt which had been wrecked during the war. Its innards had of course been torn out, but if you pulled the canopy shut and put a rug on the floor it was almost a hotel. First time they did it the dark-haired girl had hardly taken her skirt off when she let out a terrible shriek because a snake was creeping out from one of the holes in the instrument panel. There was a whole nest of vipers there, and the foreman had to get rid of them all and stuff up the holes with tow before he could get to the most delicious hole of all. 'Let me tell you,' the foreman concluded, 'one thing I've learnt in my life more than once: a bed isn't everything!'

It was nearly a quarter past ten and it was still raining outside. Listening to other people's tales, whatever they are, I sometimes feel like a debtor, like an eternal dinner guest who never offers any invitations himself, but usually I cannot bring myself to demand the attention of others.

A few years ago my wife's sister was moving to another flat. She asked if I would help her. The woman who'd let her have her one-room flat was quite mad, she'd piled it high with junk she'd picked up at rubbish dumps, but she was anxious about it and wouldn't let the removal men touch it, and so she didn't know how to move her things out.

How many things can you get into a room? I thought my sister-in-law was exaggerating. I took the word rubbish heap figuratively. I promised to move the lady's things bit by bit in my car. Even outside her door I felt a strange odour wafting from inside. The instant she let me in the smell of rot and mildew hit me violently. The woman, however, was neat and clean, the hand she held out to me was scoured white. She showed me in. I walked a narrow path between crates, boxes and masses of parcels until I reached the window and asked if I might open it. A wave of fresh air full of smoke and exhaust fumes rushed inside, but the atmosphere of decay which persisted here was not to be drowned. Then I helped the woman finish her packing. We tied up children's copy books and stacked them in a crate together with burnt-out lightbulbs and an unmatching pair of sandals without straps, bits of worn-out cork tiles and armless dolls, old envelopes, the shells of radios, rusty saucepans, a broken chandelier and a glass marble. The woman had clearly spent her life collecting and storing other people's rubbish, which possibly gave her a sense of hope or security. For five whole days I drove to and fro. She thanked me and promised me eternal salvation for my trouble, a salvation I'd soon experience because the time was nigh when mankind would assemble for judgement in the place called Armageddon. I felt like asking her why in that case she was keeping all those things, but there was no sense in putting this question to a crazy woman when I might just as well ask anyone else or myself.

As I was carrying downstairs what must have been the fiftieth package at least I couldn't resist the temptation to untie the string and to tip the contents into the nearest dustbin. I covered it up with some empty paper cups and kitchen waste from the bin next to it, and drove off with the rest of the junk to my sister-in-law's flat.

About an hour later I returned for the next load, but I had to wait a long time for her to let me in. She was standing in the door as if hesitating whether to admit me. 'You, you . . .' she said to me. 'And I trusted you!'

'What a hope,' the foreman spoke up, 'Let me tell you, I've

learned this more than once in my life: you won't get any thanks from a woman!'

Wisps of fog were drifting outside, rising from the pavements and the sodden lawns. In the telephone box outside the tavern a girl was smiling prettily down the instrument at someone.

I too used to smile. I thought that I was really seeing the woman I loved and that I could touch with my eyes what she was seeing just then. She told me: outside my window a raven is freezing on a branch, he's telling me something but I can't hear him. I was freezing as much as that raven. I had to breathe on the glass to see out. On a rime-covered tree there actually sat a raven. What could he say? Nevermore, nevermore. I thought I understood him: we'd never find anyone to love so much again.

The girl stepped out of the phone box. My companions were still lazily hanging about the tavern door. I lifted the receiver. I hesitated for a moment, but I so needed to hear a familiar voice that I dialled. Lída said she was pleased to hear me and wanted to know where I was calling from, what I had just been doing and if I wasn't cold. She was looking forward to my coming home. I would have liked to say something nice to her, to my wife, to address her tenderly as I used to: Lída darling, or at least Lída dear, at least ask her what she was doing, what she was thinking about, but I was unable to say anything other than that I'd come straight home after visiting Dad at the hospital.

I remained in the box for a moment. My garish vest was brilliantly reflected in the glass. I fished in my pocket for a coin. That other number so vehemently forced itself on my mind that I repeated it in a whisper.

I stopped fishing for that coin. I watched my companions marching slowly uphill to the little park where we'd left our tools in a small shed. Mrs Venus caught sight of me and waved.

Some other time, my love, but I'm not silent because I'm not thinking of you, it's just that I have nothing new to say to you.

And you think that this silence, the way we live now, is good?

I don't know if it's good, but I don't know anything better.

You don't know anything better? Just look at yourself, the stuff you're wearing, this masquerade? Have you gone in for repentance or what?

No, it's perfectly honest work. I can think while I'm doing it.

You can think, can you? How nice for you. And what about me? Are you at all interested in what's happening to me? How I've been feeling? After all those years I haven't even merited a single phone call from you.

We had a lot of phone calls with each other. At least a thousand!

Don't count them up. I don't want to hear numbers. Anyway, that was before. Afterwards you didn't ring even once.

We'd said everything to each other. We were exhausted from those conversations. What else was there to say to each other?

You're asking me? You might at least tell me whether the whole thing meant anything to you.

You know very well what you meant to me.

I don't know anything after the way you behaved. I always thought . . .

What did you think?

Never mind. I didn't want to believe it. After all you'd told me when we were together, how could I believe that you'd chase me away like some . . .

Please don't cry!

Tell me at least, did you love me at all?

You know I did.

I don't know anything. How am I to know?

An old woman was approaching the box. Perhaps she didn't even want to telephone, but to be on the safe side I opened the directory and pretended to look for a number.

If you'd loved me you wouldn't have behaved the way you did!

I was crazy about you.

Don't be evasive. I asked you if you'd ever loved me. If you're capable of loving anyone.

Don't torture me!

Me torturing you? Me you? Tell me, my love, what have you

done to me? At least explain to me what was good about it.

I just couldn't carry on like that. Forgive me, but I couldn't go on living like that!

And me, how am I to live? You never thought what would happen to me, did you? How can you be silent like this, it isn't human! Surely you must say something to me, do something. You must do something about us!

At one time I used to write plays. The characters were forever talking, but their words went past each other, their remarks slid past one another like the slippery bodies of fish, without making contact. Did I write that way because I believed we could step out of our loneliness? Or because I needed to find a way of avoiding answers? Where words miss each other, where humans miss each other, real conflict may arise. Or did I suspect that a man cannot successfully defend himself in the eyes of another, and when he is talking he's doing so only to drown the silence which spreads around him? To conceal from himself the reality of life, a reality which, at best, he perceives only at exceptional moments of awareness?

The man who had alone survived the crash of the aircraft which hit a church tower in Munich was working as a newspaper editor in Belgrade. I was curious to meet a person who had risen from the ashes, but his sister had just died of cancer and he asked me to postpone our meeting for a few days. When I called on him later his other sister was gravely ill with the same disease. 'The doctors are giving her no more than two months,' he said to me; 'they told me this morning. You know what is odd? I went out into the street and I didn't hear anything. There were trams and cars moving about and people talking, but I didn't hear any of it. There was the same sudden quiet then, after the crash.'

I caught up with my companions. The youngster passed me my shovel, which he had carried for me on his handcart, and Mrs Venus said: 'Bet that wasn't your wife you've just phoned.'

Right by the kerb I noticed a dead mouse. I picked it up on my shovel and flung it on the rest of the rubbish.

My wife was amazed by what I told her. She couldn't believe that I'd lied to her for so long. Now she wanted to hear details. Any kind of truth was preferable to silence. I was to tell her where she'd gone wrong and how she could put it right.

I poured out all my complaints and self-exculpating explanations, but after a while we were merely rehearsing who did the shopping, who the cooking, the laundry, the washing up and the floors, until I was horrified by the poverty of my own speech. I fell silent, but my wife wanted to hear something about the other woman and I, suddenly freed by my newly-discovered openness, began to praise the qualities and talents of my lover, to describe the uniqueness of what we were experiencing. But as I was forcing all this into words I transformed the experiences which had been mine only, and which had seemed inimitable and unique, into something common, categorisable and conventionally melodramatic. Yet I was unable to stop talking, and my wife listened to me with such involvement, such readiness to understand me and maybe even advise me that I fell victim to the foolish idea that she might even share some of my feelings. But she was merely hoping that if only she received my confession and listened to me attentively she might transform my words on how we had drifted apart into the first act of a mutual drawing together. She would confront the urgent attraction of the other woman with her own patient understanding.

When – suddenly not too convinced that this was what I truly and urgently desired – I suggested that I might leave home, at least for a time, she said that if I wished to leave her and the children she wouldn't stand in my way, but if after a while I decided to return home she couldn't guarantee that they would be able to have me back. I was far from considering what I would wish to do after a while, but I thought I could see in her eyes so much regret and disappointment, and anguish at the thought of impending loneliness, that I did not repeat my suggestion.

We didn't go to bed until the early hours. I couldn't have slept for more than a few minutes because daybreak had not yet come, but when I woke up there were muted sobs by my side.

She was crying, sobbing steadily and persistently, her mouth buried in her pillow so she shouldn't wake me.

I would have liked to caress her or say something kind to her, to comfort her as I always did when something depressed her, but this time it was me who'd crushed her. Unless I changed my decision I had become the one person who couldn't comfort her. I suddenly realised that the position I found myself in frightened me rather than gave me a sense of liberation.

In the morning I was awakened by a crash, by the sound of splintering.

I found my wife in the hall: by her feet were fragments which I recognised as those of the only piece of sculpture we'd ever had in our home. The angular bird's head was shattered and its human eyes had rolled God knows where.

For an instant we were both silent, then my wife said: 'I'm sorry. I had to do something.'

And I, in a sudden flush of compassion, without reflecting that the previous day I'd been determined to do the opposite, promised her that I wouldn't leave her. We had had our children together, and surely we'd once linked our lives together till death did us part.

Shortly afterwards we went to see our daughter's art teacher. He was exhibiting his paintings in a small-town gallery. We walked round the pictures, which somehow all seemed to express the loneliness of men, and I tried to suppress my nostalgia. In the evening some visitors arrived. They were nearly all painters and they talked a lot about art, which reminded me of the other woman. They took their observations seriously, and seemed to me to be genuinely seeking a meaning behind their activity, but to me all talk seemed unnecessary at that moment, it was no more than a substitute for life, for movement, for passion. I fled the company and went down to the riverbank. My wife found me there and wanted to know if I was sad, if I felt nostalgic. My wife, that voluntary healer, promised me that things would be good between us, we'd start another life, and I'd be happy in it. She wanted to know what I was planning to write and to hear what was on my mind that instant, she talked about sincerity and about life in truth. I was listening to her and I felt as if something was snapping inside me, as if every word was a blow which cut something in two. I was surprised she couldn't hear the blows herself, but simultaneously it seemed to me that the despair was fading from her voice. I had always hoped that she would feel comfortable with me, that life's hardships would not weigh her down too much – her relief gave me at least some satisfaction.

The street was still wet but the air had been cleansed, and as we stepped out of the shade of the residential blocks we even felt the rays of the autumn sun which somehow dispelled our gloomy mood of the morning. The youngster was whistling a Gershwin tune and Mr Rada all of a sudden showed me a slim little book on the cover of which was a street-sweeping truck and a broom, while its title to my surprise promised a critical essay on the personality cult. 'Do you know it?'

I'd never seen the book before in my life.

'An interesting reflection on how we used to deify ourselves and physical matter.' He opened the book and read aloud: 'Here lies the root of the cult, here is that proton pseudon: that the miserable, mortal, ephemeral human ego declares of itself: *Ich bin ich. Das Ich ist schlechthin gesetzt.* I am the finest flower of the materialist God!' He shut the little book again and I caught another glimpse of its cover. On the sweeping truck, as I now noticed, lay a big human head.

'And what are we really?' I asked Mr Rada, and at that instant I understood the connection between the cover picture and what I'd just heard.

The youngster was still whistling that familiar tune and I felt irritated at not being able to think of the words that went with it.

'It's 'The Man I Love', of course,' he told me, delighted at my display of interest and my acquaintance with the composer, and immediately he sang to me the four-beat tune: 'Some day he'll come along, the man I love.' He asked: 'You like Gershwin?'

I told him that thirty years ago a black opera company had

come to Prague with *Porgy and Bess*; it had been the first visit for a long time of any company from the other side of our artificially divided world. Getting tickets required a miracle, but I'd been lucky.

The memory took me away from the swept street. Not that I could recall anything of the performance which had then delighted me, but I could see before me the little street in the suburbs of Detroit, where a lot of black children were shouting on the sidewalk and a white-haired black man sat in a wheelchair in front of a dingy low house. Someone was playing a trumpet, or more likely had put on a record with Louis Armstrong or somebody, there was rubbish everywhere, bits of paper, advertising leaflets and Coca-cola cans, and in the hot air hung a smell of onions, slops and human bodies.

I was seized by nostalgia for that country. Suddenly I was seeing myself in my orange vest pushing that miserable handcart. Of course I needn't have worn that particular vest, but they made me wear some garishly coloured jacket to make sure everyone recognised me from afar and gave me a wide berth. This was now happening to me, even though, having been put into a colour-marked jacket in childhood, I longed for nothing more than to get rid of the mark of disinheritance.

'We used to play him a lot,' the youngster said. When he saw my surprise he explained: 'We had a jazz band, you know, before I got my liver all buggered up.'

The captain rolled up the sleeves of his grubby pullover. 'I may have something useful for your garden,' he said to the foreman.

'So long as it isn't that greenfly spray of yours,' the foreman was alarmed. 'Made my greenflies scamper about like squirrels and screwed up my roses proper.'

'We used to play Duke Ellington, Irving Berlin, Jerome Kern, or Scott Joplin ragtime,' the youngster said enthusiastically, 'but we liked George Gershwin best, and he also came across best because people had heard his stuff before.'

'And now you don't play at all?'

'Not a hope. Couldn't blow now. Know what impressed me most? That he'd never had any special schooling, and look at the music he wrote!'

'Did you write any yourself?' I asked.

'We all did. We just had jam sessions and something or other would come out of them.'

From one of his enormous pockets the captain produced a piece of collapsed rubber fitted to a small bellows. He squeezed the bellows a few times and the rubber swelled up into a small balloon.

Now balloons were something the foreman was interested in.

'What kind of bird-brained contraption is this then?' he asked, leaning his broad shovel against the wall of a house. He couldn't know how appropriately he'd described the device, for it was actually intended, as we were informed, for scaring birds away. The balloon with the bellows also included, on one side, sails like a windmill's and, on the other, a whistle. The windmill, by means of the bellows, would blow up the balloon, and once the air pressure in it exceeded a certain limit a valve would open and the whistle would emit a short but powerful blast, which would scare away any flying intruder.

Using his hook the captain pulled from a pocket an object reminiscent of a small organ pipe and with his sound fingers he screwed it into a thread at the end of the balloon.

We were all intently watching his antics, but the expected blast did not materialise: there was only the hiss of escaping air.

'How is this superior to an ordinary rattle?' the foreman asked doubtfully.

'Hasn't it occurred to you that a rattle goes all the time and the little bastards get used to it?' The captain once more began to squeeze his bellows and we, now all leaning on our tools, were watching the balloon filling up.

'And if there's no wind?' the foreman asked with interest.

At that moment there was a brief sound of bursting, rather like a distant shot, and what had just been a balloon was no more.

'You know, they let us rehearse at the works club twice a week,' the youngster reminisced, 'but we could stay there as long as we needed to. Sometimes we'd fool around till the early hours of the morning, just stretching out on the tables for a moment if we felt like a rest.'

'Weren't they waiting for you at home?' I asked in surprise.

'At home? But I didn't live at home!'

'If there's no wind,' the captain replied to the foreman, 'it works by electricity.'

'If you felt like it and could spare the time,' the youngster suddenly remembered, 'the boys are playing in Radlice this Sunday.' He fished about in his wallet and pulled out two tickets. 'Maybe you'd like them.'

I objected that he'd got the tickets for himself, and while we were sweeping up the leaves and conkers which had dropped from a huge horse-chestnut tree he explained to me how to get there.

I sometimes feel nostalgic for America. Even in my dreams I wander among the skyscrapers or drive along highways through endless landscapes, always full of expectation. Yet nearly every one of these dreams ends sadly: I'd stayed on in that country, beyond the sea, I'd never return home again, to the place where I was born and where people, or at least some of them, speak my native language.

They've put me in a vest in which I feel restricted. I could take it off, or even with a fine gesture chuck it away and go somewhere where they won't force one upon me, but I know that I won't because by doing so I'd also be chucking away my home.

Franz Kafka was certainly the most remarkable writer who ever lived and worked in Bohemia. He used to curse Prague and his homeland, but he couldn't bring himself to leave, he couldn't make up his mind to tear himself away from them. His seemingly dreamlike plots unroll in an environment which appears to have little connection with any real place. In reality his native city provided him with more than just a backdrop for his plots. It pervaded him with its multiplicity of voices, its nostalgia, its twilight, its weakness. It was the place where the spirit could soar up to any heights, but it was also the place where there was in the atmosphere a barely perceptible smell of decay, which more particularly affected the spirit.

Kafka spoke perfect Czech, perhaps just a trifle stiffly, but he wrote in German. But he was not a German, he was a Jew.

Not a single Czech literary historian has ever found in himself enough generosity, courage or affability to range him among the Czech authors.

Kafka's stories appeared in German periodicals and were published in Leipzig, so far as they appeared at all. Because this genius had such serious doubts about his writings that he preferred not to publish them; he even requested that everything he had written be destroyed after his death.

The sense of exclusion and loneliness which repeatedly emerges from his prose writings certainly stemmed from his disposition, from the circumstances of his life. In fact he shared it with many of his contemporaries. But Prague greatly intensified it. He longed to escape from it, just as he longed to escape from his old-bachelor loneliness. He failed to do so. He was unable to liberate himself except by his writing.

If he had succeeded in liberating himself in any other way he'd probably have lived longer, and somewhere else, but he wouldn't have written anything.

Home had become a cage for me. I needed to break out, but whenever I went out while my wife was at home I could see fear in her eyes. She never voiced it, suspicion was not part of her nature, she was trying to trust me as she'd done before, as she trusted strangers, but her eyes would follow me wherever I moved. When I returned she'd run out to meet me, pleased that I was back home again and welcoming me tenderly. And she, who'd never been too concerned about how I spent my time, what I was thinking about, what I ate, would ask if I wasn't hungry, and during supper she'd shyly reflect on where we might go together so we should enjoy ourselves, and she'd agree in advance with whatever I suggested.

She'd never been like this before, she'd known how to pursue her own interests and have her own way, but now, humbled and humiliated, she was trying to live up to her idea of my idea of a good and loving wife, and her gaucherie both shamed and touched me.

She was clever, and determined too. She'd graduated from two universities, from the second, moreover, at an age when most people are content to embellish their old achievements, and in her new field too she'd earned recognition. She moved more freely in the world of ideas and theorems than among people. In dealing with people she lacked intimacy. And yet she wished she had it, she needed it in her profession, which required her to gain her patients' confidence. I noticed her trying desperately to achieve what others had received as a gift. I knew that she wanted people to be fond of her. She is happy whenever others appreciate her good qualities or her ability, and she hastens to repay them for it by deeds, or at least by words so eager that she embarrasses them. I'd wanted to help her not to feel isolated among people, and now I had brutally pushed her back into the corner from which she'd tried to escape.

Of course she had a lot of acquaintances and colleagues who respected her, but she had few real friends. The children were growing up and the day when they'd be leaving us was approaching. If I were to leave her as well, who would look after her as she moved towards her advancing years, who would walk by her side?

But could I still do it?

We are lying next to each other, we embrace. She wants to know if it was good for me; behind that question I suspect a multitude of suppressed and anxious questions and I ask her not to ask me anything. She says that she loves me, we'll be happy together yet, and she falls asleep, exhausted, whereas I am sinking into a strange void between dream and wakefulness. I am fighting against sleep, against the state when I shan't be able to drive away the voice which begins to speak to me.

At one time it was my wife who spoke to me. She'd wait for me at street corners in dream towns, she'd miraculously appear in a moving train, she'd seek me out in desert landscapes, she'd find me in strange houses and in the midst of crowds. By some miracle we'd jointly discover forgotten box rooms, or a ready-made bed in a deserted corridor, or a hidden spot in a garden or a forest, and there we'd whisper tender words and verses to one another, there we'd embrace, and in my dream, as usually happens, we'd make love more passionately and completely than in reality.

Then she began to disappear from my dreams and other women appeared in them, but in their embraces I felt treacherous and unclean, and when I woke up I was relieved to find my wife lying by my side. Sometimes a different dream would recur repeatedly. I was aware of my age, of my approaching old age, and I realised that I'd remained alone in my life, that I'd failed to find a woman with whom I'd beget children, and that depressed me.

What speaks to a man in his dream is the secret or suppressed voice of his soul. This dream, I tried to explain to myself, echoed the memory of the time when I was growing up and when I was afraid I'd never succeed in finding a woman's love. But had I understood my soul's voice correctly?

At other times I'd dream that I was waiting under my plane tree and I knew that people might come from different directions. I wouldn't therefore remain alone. Simultaneously I was afraid that the two women I was waiting for might meet. True, they both belonged to me, but they certainly did not belong to each other. Usually it was my lover who arrived first. I'd hurriedly lead her away, then we'd stray through ever more deserted regions, looking for a place where we could be together quietly. But each time someone would turn up and watch us intently. Now and then, however, we'd find some place of refuge, we'd make love in strange and inhospitable surroundings, snatched out of the world around us, the way it can only happen in a dream, intoxicated with each other, but just as the instant of greatest pleasure was approaching my wife would suddenly appear through some hidden or forgotten door and I'd try in vain to hide the other woman under a blanket that was too short. My wife would stand in the door, staring at me with desperation in her eyes. She didn't reproach me, she didn't scream, she just stared.

At the last house, just where the slope of Vyšehrad hill begins to drop steeply, our foreman glanced up at the closed windows and reassured himself with satisfaction that there was no sign of life behind them. 'They're all in jug!' he informed us. Then he told us the name of the owner of the place and that the fellow had worked in long-distance haulage and had smuggled precious metals. When they'd nabbed him they'd found two kilograms of gold and half a million dollars in cash at his place.

'Half a million?' the youngster squealed. 'You're exaggerating!'

'I got it rock-bottom reliably from a mate in the Criminal Branch,' the foreman said, offended. 'They found three and a half tons of silver alone. From all over the place, from Poland to Vienna. And everything for dollars.'

'Wish you'd told me about him sooner!' The youngster was leaning on his scraper, red with excitement. 'My doctor was saying ... Fact is, in Switzerland they've got some drug, dearer than Legalon even. If I had that, the doctor says, I might get my liver right again.'

'And why,' Mrs Venus asked, 'can't they get it for you at the centre?'

'The doctor said I'd have to be at least a National Artist.'

'That's how it is,' the foreman agreed; 'those who're entitled to Sanops treatment can get any kind of pills; if they swallow them they can stuff themselves and booze at their receptions as long as they like. But people like us don't stand a chance. I can tell you from personal experience: if you're an ordinary person no one gives a monkey's fart for you! Mortally ill? Well then, die! At least they save money on you!'

'I only thought,' the youngster said, 'if I'd really known sooner ...'

'What then?' the foreman snapped. 'A crook like that would have shown you his arse!'

78

Our days passed relentlessly. Sometimes I'd ring Daria and we'd talk until the freezing cold drove me out of the telephone box, or we'd walk in the Šárka hills, climbing up the dusty slopes together, and she'd urge me to tell her what was going to happen to our lives, and she'd complain that I'd treacherously abandoned her.

Then she phoned one day and asked me to come to the studio at once. Her voice sounded so urgent that I was alarmed.

Come in quickly, she welcomed me, I've been waiting for you. She told me she'd had a dream, a dream like a vision about the two of us, and she realised that we belonged to each other, that it was fate, and that there was no point in resisting it.

When we embraced, when we embraced again, I didn't think of what would happen, of what I'd do, of what I'd say, where I'd return to or where we'd go together; I was only conscious of her proximity, of the bliss of her proximity.

I returned to lies once more. There is nothing by which a person can justify a lie. It corrodes the soul just as much as indifference or hate. There are many ways of destroying one's soul.

Night after night I lay awake for hours on end, reflecting on how to save myself. If I did fall asleep I'd wake up after a few hours and at once I'd hear that fine sand which was corroding me internally. In desperation I composed defence pleas and explanations, but I never uttered them, knowing full well that I had no defence. Man doesn't live to defend himself, there are moments when he has to act or at least to admit his helplessness and keep quiet.

For action I lacked the necessary hardness or blindness, and I also lacked the requisite self-love. I know that to remain with one's past partner when one has come to like another person is considered weakness or even a betrayal of ourselves and the person we now love.

We remove discarded articles to a dump, and these dumps grow sky-high. And so do the dumps of discarded people who, as they grow old, are no longer visited by those dear to them, or by anyone except perhaps others who have themselves been discarded. They still try to conjure up a smile and to fan some hope inside them, but in reality they already exude the musty smell of being discarded.

And you'd discard me like that? Daria would ask. At other times she'd say: It's their own fault. Everyone is responsible for his fate and also for his own downfall, no one else can save him.

By writing, Kafka not only escaped his torments, but only thus was he able to live at all. In his notes, letters and diaries we find that he never tried to put into words what he thought of literature. People normally express themselves about the world around them, but for Kafka literature was not external, not something that he could explore or separate from himself. Writing to him was prayer – this is one of the few statements he ever made about what literature meant to him. He switched the question to another sphere: what was prayer? What did it mean to him, who had so little faith in any revealed or generally accepted God? Most probably it was a way of personal and sincere confession of anything on a person's mind. We turn to someone whose existence and hence also whose language we can scarcely surmise. Perhaps just that is the essence or the meaning of writing: we speak about our most personal concerns in a language which turns equally to human beings as to someone who is above us and who, in some echo or reflection, also resides within us. If a person does not glimpse or hear within himself something that surpasses him, that has cosmic depth, then language will not make him respond anyway. Literature is not intended for him. Such a definition has the advantage of including both the author and the reader. Literature without those who receive it is nonsensical anyway, as would be a world where no other language was heard than jerkish, where language could no longer make anyone respond, not even someone above human beings.

The winter was barely over when I developed some strange illness. My lips, tongue, palate and the entire inside of my mouth were covered by sore blisters, so that I couldn't swallow anything without pain. I was feverish, I lay in a silence not penetrated by a voice all day long. My wife came home in the evening, she was kind to me, cooked me some porridge and told me about a seminar she'd attended and where they'd commended her paper.

On the third day I got up, dressed and set out to the telephone box. It was a clear and mild morning, and through the deserted street wafted the fragrance of spring flowerbeds.

I got through to my lover.

You're ill? she asked in surprise. I was afraid you'd made a clean breast of everything again and you weren't allowed to see me any more.

She wanted to know how much my mouth hurt, what I did all day when I couldn't do anything, if I was thinking of her. As for her, she'd received a commission, at least she'd be able to complete it undisturbed. She had such a chunk of stone at her studio she couldn't even move it, that stone was almost like me, except that with the stone a girlfriend could give her a hand. She went on for a while to talk about her rocky burden, i.e. about me. Suddenly she was afraid I might catch cold in the box, promised to write me a letter and ordered me back to bed.

Her voice was coming to me softly from a distance, her lips settled lightly on my aching mouth, her tongue was touching my sick tongue, and I was shaken by shivers. I wanted to be with her, to watch her hammering into her heavy stone, to let myself be lulled to sleep by those sounds, to wake up and find her close to me.

Two days later a small package was delivered. On top of it was a letter and a bag of herbs she'd dried herself. Camomile, horehound and silverweed, our heads in the dry grass, we were lying in a meadow and making love. I was to brew it all up together and gargle with it, but, even more important, I should find peace within myself, so my soul could be in harmony with my body. Although illnesses were seated in the body they really came from the soul, which writhed in spasms unless one learned to listen to it and enclose and restrain it by one's actions.

I read the letter all the way through, and only then freed a little figure from a protective wrapping of rags. She'd made it for me, two naked bodies leaning against a tree. A man and a woman, Adam and Eve, Eve not ashamed of her nakedness and not offering Adam the fruit of the tree of knowledge. The serpent was also missing. It wasn't Adam and Eve, it was the two of us in the Garden of Eden which our love had unlocked for us.

When I was well again she explained to me: I have seven bodies, and the person who, even only once, gets through to the innermost one, will trap me and I'll belong to him totally and always.

I asked: What does that innermost body look like?

You're right, that isn't a body any longer, that's the last shell of the soul. It's thin and transparent.

In this way she wanted to tell me about the fragility of that shell. So what is it like inside?

When I was fourteen the first atomic bomb was dropped on the earth. Some time later I read the book of a Hiroshima doctor who'd experienced the explosion: factually and dispassionately he described the destruction which had befallen the city and its people, but understandably enough he didn't mention any souls. But I was pondering then about what happened to the human soul at the epicentre of an atomic explosion. Even if the soul was non-corpuscular, even if it was only space enveloped by matter, even if it was of an entirely different nature, could it really survive that heat? Who could visualise a soul at the centre of the sun or some other star?

You're always racking your brain with pointless questions. What's the use of it?

Tell me at least what you think happens to a soul which cannot stand the pressure of the world around it and bursts or shatters into fragments which no one can ever bring together again?

Don't worry, it doesn't perish. Maybe a new soul springs from each fragment, like a tree from a seed. Or else all the fragments combine together again in another time, in another life, coming together like droplets in a fog. Better ask what you should do so the souls around you don't perish.

I'm asking that one too.

Better still, don't ask any more questions. Try to be a little less clever. Be with me now and don't think of anything at all!

She told me about the Kampucheans, who struck her as a happy people. They danced, sang and didn't worry about the future. They knew that God was near, but they didn't ponder about him. And look at the things they managed to create even in ancient times! That art, those buildings, those sculptures!

A pity, she regretted, you weren't there with me. But one day we'll go there together.

I don't know how we can go anywhere; it's ten years since they took my passport away.

Don't be so practical!

Even if I'm not, the men at the frontier will be.

Apply for a passport then. Surely we must go somewhere together someday. There should be a sea there and warmth, so we can stay together all the time.

I'll apply for a passport so we can travel to Kampuchea together, where the people are happy and carefree, where we'd be so far away that no voice other than hers would reach me.

No voice reaches me anyway.

All around me fog is spreading, what is left of the world loses its outlines. Now and then the fog curtain tears and we catch a glimpse of the landscape bathed in a reddish evening light, in a heavy rain the surface under the windows of the little hotel is ruffled and across the street gleams a plump baroque turret, from a fresco washed pale by time an interceding Holy Virgin is smiling at us, maybe we shan't be altogether damned, the beeches are donning fresh greenery before our eyes, they turn golden, and red, a leaf floats downwards and we sink down with it, we're lying in the grass, we're lying in the moss and in the sand, above our heads flocks of migratory birds are flying, as well as clouds and time, only time stops still for an instant in repeated cries; and we light the gas stove because it is cold in the room, we move the bed right up against its hot body, in our brief intervals we tell one another about the days when we didn't know each other, about yesterday, about meetings and dreams, we fry bits of meat on the only pan, we eat together at the low table, we drink red wine, while the snowflakes swirl outside the window. In the room there is a fragrance of clay, paint and her breath. In the evening we go out to the little park on Kampa island, we still can't tear ourselves away from each other, we kiss on the swept path under the bare trees. A little old woman with the head of a crow, as if modelled by her fingers, croaks at us: That's a fine thing, that's a fine thing! Adding something about our age and we should be ashamed!

And all the time I have my work, there are people in the world whom until quite recently I wanted to see, our daughter Beta wants to draw my portrait, our son Peter has invited me to a concert, but I have no time.

Beta experiences her first love, she is experiencing her second love, a drug addict who adores Pink Floyd and sniffs toluene. My wife is alarmed and asks me to intervene somehow. I talk with my daughter until late at night, she understands everything, she agrees with me, she'll soon find another love, but I still have the same one, so am I also an addict? I inhale that mist, my blood absorbs those intoxicating droplets which dull my reason and willpower. I see nothing before me or around me, I see only her, I live only for the present moment. Am I to rejoice at the gift that's been granted to me or am I to despair at my weakness, at being unable to resist the passion which is corroding me?

I can't make up my mind, I can't renounce my passion, nor can I draw the consequences from it. I cannot depart altogether nor arrive altogether, I am unable to live in truth. I've hedged myself in with excuses, I'm having every sentence I utter examined by a guard dog. I've accommodated a whole pack of them within me. I pick my way between them, their barking at times deafens me and their soundless footfall frightens me in my dreams. One of these days one of them will approach me from behind and sink his fangs in my throat and I shan't even cry out, I'll remain mute forever, as I deserve to be.

How long can I stand it, how long can it last?

Till death, my darling!

You really believe that?

Or till I leave you because you never make up your mind to do anything. She starts crying. She is crying because I cannot make up my mind, because I am too circumspect, because I put principles above love, because I am shuttered against life like a stone, even more shuttered because a stone can be worked, a stone can be turned into a shape, she is crying because I am harder than if I were made of stone, I'm playing a cruel game with her and I torture her as I have never tortured anyone before, she is crying because I am good, because I stay with her as no one before managed to, she is crying because everything in her life is turning into suffering.

I know that she has surrendered herself to my mercy, and I am terrified by the thought that I might disappoint her.

The spring sun is shining on the little terrace under the wooden steps, from the washing line comes the smell of nappies and over the wall of the house opposite we can see the monastery roof with its ornament of a maple-wood halo.

Daria is sitting alongside me in a freshly-ironed white blouse and a chocolate-coloured velvet skirt, she's dressed up because this evening we're going to a concert. She seems to me so beautiful, so precious, as if I'd gone back forty years or so and gazed in adoration at my mother. Except we're getting up, climbing a few steps, and she is stepping out of her clothes and her exalted untouchability and stepping into my embrace, and I feel as if the thin walls of my veins are bursting from the barely tolerable surge of delight.

We're lying next to each other in the descending night. Somewhere out of sight beyond the palace and the river the musicians are getting ready for a Beethoven concerto.

What would you like most of all?

I know what I am expected to reply but I ask: Now or altogether?

Now and altogether, if there's any difference.

To stay here with you, I answer, to stay with you now.

And altogether?

I'd like to know what happens to the soul.

You'd really like to know that?

I embrace her. She presses herself against me and whispers: You always want to know so much, my darling, do you always have to find out something or other?

It was you who asked.

Be glad that there are things which can't be known – only surmised.

She holds me so tight I groan. What do you surmise?

Don't worry, the soul doesn't perish, somehow it lives on.

In another body?

Why in a body at all? I see your soul as a pillar. It looks stony but it's made of fire and wind. And it towers so high that from down on the ground you can't see the top of it. And up there it is smiling.

That pillar?

Your soul, darling. Because you have a smile inside you, even if you think you've only got grief, and that's why I feel good with you. Then she asks: Have you applied for a passport?

In the woods liverwort and anemones are out again, no one but us ever goes there. She makes love to me in a way that blots out my reason. She wants to know: Don't you feel good with me?

I do feel good with you. I've never known anything like it before.

But you're not entirely with me. And she asks: How can you live like that?

Like what?

So incompletely, so divided.

She is waiting for a sign that I've made up my mind at last, but there is no sign. She asks: Are you going away with me somewhere in the summer?

How can I arrange things so that I can go away with her? What lie can I invent? I am gripped by cold fear.

Are you capable of doing anything for me at all?

I'll apply for a passport but I am tired. Worn down by love-making and by love and by reproaches, by longing and by my own indecision, worn down by my ceaseless escapes.

I can scarcely believe it, I am given a passport, the wild roses are beginning to bloom. Far and wide, no one lies down under them. The petals are soundlessly floating down on our naked bodies and bees are buzzing above us. She asks: Are you also feeling happy, darling?

I am feeling happy with her, and she whispers: Are you going away with me to the sea in the summer?

It has been calculated that if all those murdered in Kampuchea were stacked up on a pyre with a one-hundred-metre base that pyre would be taller than the country's highest mountain.

I have found another remark by Kafka on the mission of literature: What we need, he wrote, are books which strike us like the most painful misfortune, like the death of someone we loved more than ourselves, books which would make us feel that we've been driven out into the forest far from another human being, like suicide. A book must be an axe for the frozen sea within us.

With his honesty Kafka could write only about what he had himself experienced. He recorded his lonely road into the depths. He descended as far as anyone could descend, and down there came the end, the end of his road and of his writings. He was unable to sever himself from his father, nor did he bring himself to complete adult love – that was his abyss. At its bottom he saw a person he loved, and as he descended that person's image drew closer and at the same time began to disappear in the dark, and when he was close enough to reach out with his hand he had no breath left and was engulfed by unconsciousness.

His abyss, however, is like the abyss into which we all descend or into which, at least, we gaze with curiosity or fear. We can see in it a reflection of our own destinies, of ourselves endeavouring in vain to reach adulthood, in vain reaching out to another being and to the one who is above us. Except that I don't know if we are still capable of gazing into any depth, whether we are not so pampered or so spoiled that we can no longer recognise honesty when we see it and stand before it in admiration, whether instead we are not trying to diminish it, to question it and to adapt it to our own ideas. Honesty then becomes for us an inability to live or even a source of mental disorder, courage becomes pitiable weakness. That, at any rate, is what I read about Kafka. Only a weak person, one incapable of living according to our ideas and demands, seems acceptable and comprehensible to us. Indeed, we pity him for his loneliness, his vulnerability or his sick body. For the way he suffered, for being, compared to us, unhappy. We do not even perceive what that painful descent into the depths brings. The lonely diver sees in one instant what most of us who pity him don't see in a whole lifetime.

The highest mountain in Kampuchea is in the Kardamon range not far from Phnom Penh and is called Ka-kup. It is covered in primeval forest and is 1744 metres high. Our aircraft struck the treetops and crashed into the undergrowth. We managed to jump out of the split fuselage before it caught fire. We tore our way through the dense vegetation and she was looking for a spot where we could lie down safe from snakes and scorpions. But whenever she found one, whenever she found a cleared spot it was full of dead bodies.

I said: We'll have to find another country for just the two of us to be together.

Just then two soldiers with red tabs on their muddy uniforms emerged from the jungle and one of them said in a language which surprisingly we understood very well: Better find another world.

The two soldiers burst into shrill Khmer laughter, they laughed till they shook, and then they began to shoot at us. At the last moment I realised that in a world where four thousand million people lived, most of them starving, what did anyone care about us two?

By midday we were at the end of our stint. 'Took us a bit longer today,' the foreman said, looking up at the sky which was once more hidden by clouds composed of steam and sulphur dioxide. 'Let me tell you, there are months when I have people coming and going like in a taproom, everybody just out for quick money, and the streets like a pigsty. Everything has to have its – you know. But you lot, hats off! They've noticed it even at the office. The other day they went through my whole district without finding a single fault. Only that bloody castrated bastard's running us down wherever he can.'

We were walking along in a disorderly column – on one side residential blocks, on the other a little park with massive maples and lime trees, from whose tops every gust of wind brought down a shower of tired leaves. The youngster stopped and looked into the park, perhaps walking up the slight hill had tired him or else he'd caught sight of someone he knew on the gravel path, or else he needed to let his eyes linger on something at least a little way above the ground:

> And it may happen to a sweeper
> as he waves
> his dirty broom
> about without a hope
> among the dusty ruins
> of a wasteful colonial exhibition
> that he halts amazed
> before a remarkable statue
> of dried leaves and blooms . . .

These verses suddenly came to my mind – as well as the voice of the man who'd spoken them.

'There's money to be made in other places too,' Mrs Venus said. 'I know a fellow got into a gang what collects the mess in trucks in Slivenec. After all, they shift it from there by the cartload!'

'Don't tell me that,' the foreman got excited. 'You wouldn't stand a chance there, it's the private preserve of the Demeter gang and nobody can winkle that lot out, not even the public prosecutor.'

In the crowded bar at the bottom of the street we were lucky enough to find room at a table from which a gang of bricklayers from a nearby building site was just getting up. Our foreman jerked his head towards them: 'My girl's been waiting for a flat for seven years, and she was told at the co-op she'd have to wait at least another seven years. So when I see those pissed malingerers I feel like kicking their teeth in. And who knocked you about like this?' he turned to Mrs Venus. 'Don't you tell me you slipped on the stairs!'

'But I did,' said Venus in a voice I still admired. 'Now and again my legs give way under me.'

'If I was you, Zoulová, I wouldn't stand for it. you go to the centre,' the foreman advised her, 'get them to confirm it and then go and report it as grievous bodily harm. They'll throw the book at him, so much he'll never be able to pay up in full.'

'But it was my brother-in-law!' Mrs Venus objected.

'Which one?'

'The one from Ostrava, of course, the brother of my Joe what died a couple of years ago. Always turns up at my place like this. Once a year.'

'Still working down the mines?' the foreman wanted to know.

'That's what it was all about,' Venus explained; 'he's just as stupid as Joe was. His lungs are all shot to hell, full of coal dust. And the same doctor, that murderer what did my Joe in, told him he couldn't send him to a disabled home, they wouldn't authorise that, and if he wrote down what the matter really was with him they'd put him on surface jobs where he'd be cleaning lamps for bugger-all, and then he could whistle for his pension. Exactly how that murderer chatted up my Joe. In another year, he promised him, we'll put you straight into a disabled centre, that's what that shit promised him when the poor bugger couldn't even walk up a few steps. Six months later he couldn't care a monkey's whether he was declared disabled or not. I told my brother-in-law: Vince, look at what happened to Joe. Are you stupid or what? What bloody use is money to you when you're pushing up the daisies? That made him angry. So I said to him: You're all alike, you men, brave enough to hit a woman all right, but when it comes to standing up to the deputy you'd sooner shit yourself!'

'Men aren't all alike,' the foreman protested.

'Don't tell me that! How long were you in the army?'

'Twenty-five years.' There was a ring of pride in the foreman's voice.

'And how often were you in action?'

'No one to fight,' the foreman said dryly.

'Who told you that?'

'A soldier fights when he's ordered to,' he told her. 'If there's no order he can do bugger-all.'

'Women would fight even without an order,' Venus snapped. 'Why d'you think they won't give women weapons? And what are you grinning about?' she turned on me. 'No doubt you were a real Ho Chi Minh!'

'Now watch your tongue, Zoulová!' the foreman admonished her. 'You know that I've always stood by you people. There'll soon be an opportunity for you to realise it.' We all of us knew that the post of radio dispatcher was soon falling vacant at the office and that the foreman was firmly counting on getting it. 'You'll get tired of wielding that broom one day.'

'So what,' Mrs Venus snapped. 'I can just see you letting me drive a carriage with golden wheels!'

I noticed that the captain was enjoying the argument.

The crazy inventor had called on me once more at the newspaper office. That was when foreign soldiers were trampling through Prague. He sat down on a chair. The recent events had led him to concern himself once again with his soot solution. He'd changed the proportions of his seven solvents and added two catalysts. Now he was certain of the result. The ice would turn to water, to whole oceans of water. Did I understand the consequences? Did I realise which countries would be flooded if the ocean levels rose?

My first thought was The Netherlands, but he produced from his pocket a map of Europe on which he'd carefully cross-hatched the territory which would disappear under the sea. True, parts of The Netherlands and the Jutland peninsula would be affected, but worst affected of all would be the lowlands in the east, complete with all their gigantic cities.

I conjured up a vision of only the head of the Bronze Horseman showing above the waves, and even that was slowly disappearing:

> 'Here cut' – so Nature gives command –
> your window through on Europe; stand
> firm-footed by the sea, unchanging!'
> Ay, ships of every flag shall come
> by waters they had never swum
> and we shall revel, freely ranging.

'Do you understand now?' he asked, folding his hands as if in prayer.

> A siege! The wicked waves, attacking
> climb thief-like through the windows; backing
> the boats stern-foremost, smite the glass,
> trays with their soaking wrappage pass;
> and timbers, roofs, and huts all shattered,
> the wares of thrifty traders scattered,
> and the pale beggars' chattels small,
> bridges swept off beneath the squall,
> coffins from sodden graveyards – all
> swim in the streets!

I understood. His mind may have been disturbed, but there burned within him the flame which the rest of us, from cunning or from common-sense, were stifling.

I had always hoped that life's flame would burn pure within me. To live and at the same time have darkness within one, to live and exhale death, what point would there be in that?

But what kind of flame had there been burning within me these past few years? I couldn't answer my question, I'd lost my judgement. Everything that had surrounded me in the past, everything that had been significant and had filled me with joy or sorrow, had gone flat and like a strip of faded material now drifted at my feet.

In the evenings my son would play to himself the songs of his favourite singers. The words of these songs persistently and vehemently protested against the unhappy state of our society. He was clinging to protest, which was one-sided, as though he wanted subconsciously to make up for the one-sided way in which I had turned my back on any injustices which might keep me from my private region of bliss.

My daughter was now often coming home late, smelling of wine and cigarette smoke and talking cynically about love. Was she not finding the love she was seeking because I had found it, or, on the contrary, because she was seeking it where I remained blind?

My wife went regularly to her psychoanalyst. She too was descending into her depths, looking about herself there, confident that she was accompanied by the light of a wise guide, and she arrived at unexpected conclusions about herself and about me, about her relationship with her mother and about my relationship with mine. Her findings would have provoked me to argue with her if I'd been able to take them in.

She was now devoting a lot of time to self-education. She'd long surpassed me with her knowledge of the hidden mysteries of the soul and the motivations of human passions and emotions. She was developing an interest in ancient myths, she studied books on the customs and ceremonies of savages whose native countries she'd never seen and most probably never would see, and she tried to convince me that what people, including we two, were lacking, was ritual. For years we hadn't courted one another much, and as a result a mundane element had invaded our relationship. She asked me if she might read part of her study on sacrifice and self-sacrifice to me, and I told her I'd be glad to listen to it. I lay down on the couch, my head next to the armchair she was sitting in, and tried to listen to her attentively, but I was overcome by fatigue and the sense of the words drifted away. Now and again I looked up at her, at my wife, with whom I'd lived and not lived for nearly twenty-five years. I was aware of her keen involvement and I tried to catch the meaning of at least some of the sentences. At one point she looked up from her paper and asked anxiously if she wasn't boring me, and I replied hastily: No, the problem of sacrificial lambs interested me – if only because of my own childhood experiences – as did the sacrificial rites of the Ndembas and the Indian Khonds, although I was amazed by the amount of brutality or sadism that was hidden beneath human nature. She seemed satisfied and continued with her reading, her fingers having first tenderly touched my head. I was suddenly conscious of her closeness and I felt depressed by not being able to give her my full concentration and to stay with her. I felt guilty for my inattention. It was a childish sense of guilt: my mother was bending down over me lovingly while I, in order to conceal my feelings, pretended not to notice, pretended to be asleep. I felt tenderness towards her and also regret that I'd let her talk for so long, that I'd let her address me for so long while I wasn't listening. I would have liked to embrace her and tell her everything that was troubling me: Forgive me and stay with me like this always! And to call on myself: Stay with her, after all she's your wife. And on my soul: Come to rest! And to ask the other woman: Let me go without anger and without a sense of wrong. And aloud I said: You really did a good job there. And she smiled at me with her old girlish smile. Time again moved on.

'I once got on a ship that was skippered by a woman,' the captain reminisced. 'In the Baltic it was.'

'What was her name?' the foreman wanted to know.

'The woman's? I don't know. The ship's name was the *Dolphin*, she belonged to the fishing combine. We had put her engine through sea trials after a general overhaul, so we took her out without cargo, only about six fellows, that woman and myself.

'She was the only woman with six fellows aboard?' the foreman asked, hoping for a story of erotic entanglements. But the captain had other things to relate. They'd left Warnemünde on a northerly course, then they'd turned east by thirty degrees because otherwise they would have soon found themselves in the Danish port of Gedner. There was a north-westerly blowing and it was raining, visibility was down to about 300 metres. After an hour or so they spotted something floating in the sea. It seemed incredible, fifteen miles off shore, but it was two people, a man and a woman on rubber mattresses, both of them only in swimsuits.

'Carried out by the wind?' asked the youngster.

'I just told you the wind was onshore. They wanted to skidaddle to Denmark. They'd got through the cordon at night, the foul weather helped them. Otherwise they'd have got nabbed inshore.' Whenever he left the realm of his poetry the captain was logical and matter-of-fact. 'And they'd have made it to Denmark all right, if they hadn't run into us.

'As soon as they spotted the ship they paddled away from us like people possessed, but the woman captain ordered the boat to be lowered and had them brought aboard. The poor wretches were frozen stiff, but even so they begged to be left in the water, all they needed now was half a day, but the old woman decided she had to hand them over.'

'What happened to them?' I asked.

'How should I know?' the captain replied. 'If I was those people I'd build myself a boat that no one could keep up with. Except that that sort haven't got a clue about engineering. They just try to swim across: backstroke, breaststroke. And they're never seen again, unless the sea throws them up on the beach, all gnawed.' The captain pushed his cap back and took a swig. No doubt among his designs there was the blueprint of a small submarine driven by compressed air or a propane-butane bottle.

'Well, we none of us have a written guarantee for our lives,' the foreman remarked in an attempt to regain the centre of the stage.

'I wonder they even try it,' the youngster sounded surprised, 'when they must know it's useless.'

'Because they're idiots,' the foreman again intervened: 'Everyone thinks he can make it. Stupid!'

'Maybe they're not the only stupid ones!'

'Who then?' The foreman seemed surprised at my remark.

'If they were allowed to board a ship they wouldn't try that kind of thing.'

'Can't have just anyone boarding a ship and sailing wherever he pleases, can we now?' he turned to the others. 'When I saw they weren't going to let me out I'd sit tight on my arse and wait.'

By a miracle we got a little room with a two-tier bunk in a small brick house at the spot where the neck of the Dar peninsula was narrowest. From the little garden, where blackcurrants were ripening, you could see the surface of the inland sea, above its surface coloured masts and sails, above them seagulls, and above them the sky which, for most of the days we stayed in this normally rainy area, was cloudlessly blue; on the other side, immediately beyond the road, was a gently rising field of wheat. If you climbed up to the nearby ridge you could see the sea proper. We took a brightly-coloured bus to a stop called Three Oaks and walked down a sandy path to the beach, which was as spotlessly clean as everything else here. There we rammed into the ground a few sticks we'd collected which had been leached out and bleached by the sea. On them we spread a piece of yellow material, which was soon covered by small metallically shiny black beetles. We buried a bottle of lemonade, spread a blanket on the sand and lay down on it. Thus we lay there hours, in immobility and mutual proximity. I had never before been able to stay by the water for even a few hours, I was frightened by the void of laziness. I could not be totally lazy, just as I could not love totally or surrender to work totally, though this last perhaps more than the rest. I always had to escape from the reach of the black pit which I invariably saw before me as soon as I was quietly relaxing anywhere, but here I saw only the sea, only the sky, only her loving features. Time here was slowed down. Sometimes during its retarded flow I read Kierkegaard or the story of Adrian Leverkühn as the ageing Thomas Mann had invented it and was telling it at the same slow and leisurely pace. Sometimes I read to her aloud and she listened with the concentration of a person who did everything she did in life with total completeness. But when, in that sun-scorched wasteland, where countless naked bodies were indulging in total inactivity, I read to her that action and decision in our – that is Kierkegaard's – age was just as rare as the intoxication with danger felt by someone swimming in shallow water, the rule that a man stands or falls with his action no longer applies. I observed in her concentration an almost excessively attentive and enthusiastic agreement, and I realised that these sentences I was reading told against me, that I was merely continuing her silent, ceaseless and scarcely disguised evidence for the prosecution. We argued about the philosopher's theses, pretending that we were not talking about ourselves or about our conflict. We argued until the moment when I shook the sand grains out of my book and put it back in my bag. Then we just lay, our naked bodies touching each other, and gazed on the white crests of the waves which managed to touch each other without causing each other pleasure and pain. Not until evening did we get up, climb the sand dune along the line of dustbins towering there, metallic, among the flowering wild roses, and return to the road.

The evenings were long northern evenings. When we'd eaten we went back down to the beach, which by then was deserted. She sat down cross-legged on a rock, gazing at the seemingly cooling sun, while I looked at the dark surface of the water, noticing the menacing cordon of ships on the distant horizon, a cordon designed to block even here the freest and most unfettered area of water, and I also looked at her sitting there statue-like, perceiving how in the silence of the sea, in this marine solitude, she was receding, changing into an unfamiliar being that lived in inaccessible regions, and I couldn't decide if I was feeling sadness or relief. I was still able to cut loose from her, and at that moment I was seized with longing for my wife. I wanted her to be here with me, for her to sit here with me on that rock.

We also borrowed bikes and set out early in the morning, not along the road but along sandy paths, along the footpaths which intertwined on the narrow ridge which rises above the sea.

The waves roar and the wind howls, we stop to embrace, to sit down and look across to the distant shores. Then we continue in a westerly direction and our bikes sink so deep into the sand that we have to carry them. Before us lies a dark green expanse of heather, we turn into it; the soil here is black, our path is blocked by an ever thicker tangle of roots, the air is full of whining mosquitoes, our little path has almost disappeared, we don't know where we are, whether to turn back or go on, path or no path. Our bikes are useless now, we wheel them along, I try to discover the way ahead while she sees the shapes of spirits in the twisting branches and hears the whispering of the dead in the sighing of the wind, the last breaths of suicides and the vain shouts of the drowning, there is a wizard crouching in the undergrowth whose body lacks a soul, and over the treetops the carrion crows circle, soundless and dark. We circumvent pools from which gas bubbles rise up and eventually reach the road. Now she is riding in front of me, her hair, which would be almost grey by now if she didn't give it a blonde rinse, shines around her head. We are approaching Bad Müritz, where half a century ago our fellow countryman, my beloved author, the unsuccessful lover Franz Kafka, was preparing for his fall into the black pit, where his brittle soul concurred with his sick lungs that they would give up the exhausting struggle.

We are riding through the streets from which they haven't yet driven out the *fin de siècle* spirit as they have done so thoroughly from our native city, thirstily we drink beer at a pavement stall, hungrily we sit down at a battered table in a shabby café. We sit opposite each other, far from our near and dear ones, in a strange café in a strange town, we eat cakes, we are silent, we look at one another, and I can see in her eyes a devotion I didn't believe I'd ever find anywhere, I can feel it invading me deeply, pervading me, settling into every cell of my body. I don't know how or when I'll end my struggle, but at that moment my soul is still capable of rising up, of making one last flight to where it belongs, to the place of its longings, to the regions of blissful paralysis from the proximity of a loved being; after that it will fly out to this battered and by now deserted little table, for a last time briefly smile with sudden relief, and then accept its fate.

Later we stand in the cathedral of Güstrow before Barlach's rising angel. I can see my lover going rigid, rising up to those exalted shapes, moving away from me into heights which I cannot conceive, which my vision cannot reach, where only angels and perhaps the souls of great artists reside. I move away, unnoticed, and sit down in a pew in a corner of the cathedral and wait for her to come back to me.

Nach der Rede des Führers am Tage der Deutschen Kunst in München haben die zuständigen Stellen nunmehr beschlossen, das von dem Bildhauer Ernst Barlach im Jahre 1926 geschaffene Ehrenmal für die Gefallenen des Weltkriegs aus dem Dom in Güstrow entfernen zu lassen. Die Abnahme wird in den nächsten Tagen erfolgen. Das Ehrenmal soll einen schwebenden Engel darstellen und war schon seit langem ein Gegenstand heftigster Angriffe.

(Following the Führer's speech on the Day of German Art in Munich the appropriate authorities have now decided to remove from the cathedral in Güstrow the memorial created by the sculptor Ernst Barlach in 1926 for the fallen of the World War. The removal will take place during the next few days. The memorial, designed to represent a hovering angel, has long been the object of fierce attacks.)

When eventually she returns to me she has tears in her eyes.

Do you think you could manage an angel like that?

I don't know. I'm probably not sufficiently obsessed – by stone or by wood.

I don't ask her what she is possessed by, I know. But I also suspect that there is a burning ambition in her, at the price of exhaustion if need be, to ensure that those who view her work go rigid.

The next day she walks down to the edge of the beach, where the sand has soaked up the seawater, and her fingers, used to creating shapes out of shapeless matter, there create a sand relief of a creature resembling a winged centaur rather than an angel. That creature has my features, except that perhaps it smiles more in all directions. Small groups of sunbathers gather around her and with admiration watch her work taking shape, but she pretends not to notice them, she only wants to know if I like her sand sculpture.

I like it and it's like me, I answer, in order to amuse her with my pun. My only regret is that this strange creature with my face will not survive the next tide.

What does it matter? Tomorrow, if we feel like it, we'll make something different. At least we aren't burdening the world with another creation. This is something we are both aware of: that the world is groaning, choking with a multitude of creations, that it is buried by objects and strangled by ideas which all pretend to be necessary, useful or beautiful and therefore lay claim to perpetual endurance.

We don't need either objects or creations, we don't even need ideas, for us it is enough to have one another.

We are together while the day ascends, while the night descends, we are so totally together that it saps all our strength, that the fire consumes us, that the heat consumes her till I am alarmed: suppose we are buried in ashes from which we won't rise again?

I have never been as close to anyone, I have never known a person capable of being so close to me, capable of such passion, of such intensity.

Maybe both of us have been gathering strength all our lives for just this moment, for just this meeting, maybe we have gravitated here in our dreams, to this small room, to this coastal spot, where water, sand and sky blend into each other, where time trickles softly and cleanly, this is where unconsciously we have wanted to come at moments of loneliness.

Were you often alone?

But she doesn't know, she knows nothing beyond what just *is*. And when our bodies are finally exhausted, when only a few last moments are left of the northern summer's night, when I am about to climb down to my bunk, she begs me not to go yet, to stay with her at least here, and so I persevere in immobility, even though I now long to be alone, so many days of absolute proximity have exhausted me and I am longing for a moment of isolation; in the midst of a strange world into which I was snatched I now long for the undemanding routine of home. But have I got a home left? After all, I'm breaking it up myself. My daughter has left, she is a mother now, and my son is leaving very soon. And as for my wife, even if she smiles at me sweetly, where is she really at home? What is left of our love?

My yearning is growing within me, a nonsensical regret because it is backward-facing, a regret that my life, against which I want to rebel just now, is running away.

The other woman is lying by my side. She's asleep. Her breath has gone quieter, her spirit has calmed down. I try to make out her features, I bend down over her, I do not kiss her, I just look at her, at a remote creature whom, despite everything, I have not managed to absorb fully into myself, to accept fully. I climb quietly down and lie on the lower bunk, I gaze into the blackness before me. Outside a tomcat is noisily complaining and the wind is driving a thunderstorm before it. I get up and open the window wide, on the dark sky a soundless flash of lightning now and then lights up the huge plane tree in the garden.

And suddenly I see her – my wife. The lightning illuminates her, she is sitting on a bench, waiting for me. We are walking down a little path in the park, I am pushing a pram whose wheels keep coming off but we haven't got the money to buy a new one, I am pushing it along the Prokop valley, now I can even hear her voice, my wife is singing to the children and to herself, I return home from the editorial office, I can hear the singing from the staircase, I unlock the door, she and the children are rushing up to greet me, they want to know what I've brought them.

A nonsensical yearning directed backwards, but what am I to do? There remain in me, rooted, countless days and nights together, from which time has gradually eroded everything that was not solid, leaving behind boulders on an autumnal field, boulders which can't be rolled away, even if I walk around them I can't get rid of them, I only have to turn my head and I see them: towering there like immovable milestones, they regard me like some monstrous stony eyes of the night, motionless, they wait for me to give up everything. I take a few more steps but I can feel their stony stare on my back, my legs are growing heavy, and I come to a halt. I am not going back and I am not going forward, I am standing in a void, I am standing between two fields, at the meeting point of two calls which intersect each other, I am nailed to the cross, how can I move?

And the other woman, the one I've come here with, the one I followed from weakness, from longing, from loneliness, from mental confusion, from passion, from prodigality, from the hope that I might forget my mortality for a while, now complains about my immobility, she curses it and my wife, instead of cursing me.

So here I stand, she is asleep behind me while I am listening to my wife's singing. What is she singing? As usual I cannot make out the words, but words are not essential in a song. I am waiting by the window for my wife to look up and see me. But she doesn't see me. Suddenly I am conscious that between us lie mountains and rivers, life and death, betrayal and lies, years of unfulfilled longing and vain hopes. I see my wife beginning to tremble like an image on the surface of water when the first raindrop strikes it, in a sudden surge of longing I reach out towards the window to hold her, to save her, to draw her to me from that distance, but it is in vain, the rain is getting heavier, and I become aware of the other woman looking at me from behind. What are you doing, dearest, why aren't you asleep?

I'm just shutting the window, I answer, it's beginning to rain.

I got up from the table simultaneously with Mr Rada. No sooner were we out in the street than he could no longer restrain himself from telling me what, clearly, he'd wanted to keep from the others. 'I got back from Svatá Hora yesterday. Have you heard about it?'

The fact that there had been a great pilgrimage and rally of believers had been mentioned even in our jerkish press, probably to enable the rally of believers to be portrayed as a peace festival.

'It was fantastic', he said joyfully. Evidently he'd brought back from there the little book from which he'd read a passage to me that afternoon, or at least a taste or enthusiasm for reading from it, if necessary in the street.

We usually went together to draw our pay. I told him what paper I used to work on. I didn't mention the books I'd written. He in turn confessed to me that all his life he'd had to do something other than what he wished to do. Although he'd studied to be a priest he'd worked as a miner, a boilerman, a storeman, a stage-hand and even a lorry driver. Now, in order to help his mother, he was making some extra money by street-sweeping. What he liked about the job was that it was outdoor work, often indeed among gardens, he was a countryman. He also had a sense of doing something useful. In a city filthy with refuse people might at best find a place to sleep and store their belongings, but never one to establish a home and experience the thrill of belonging to the place, to their neighbours, to God. Today's people were like nomads, he complained, they moved from one home to another, carrying their little household gods with them. They didn't establish ties either with their surroundings or with people, often they didn't even take their children out into the country. They either killed them while still in the womb or they abandoned them in their chase after pleasure. And how were those children going to live when they had known no home? They'd develop into real Huns, they'd move through the world and turn it upside down.

But he didn't complain about his own fate. He spoke without bitterness about what had happened to him.

'There were at least thirty thousand of us there, mostly young people.' He sounded pleased, as if he'd quite forgotten his own gloomy prophecies.

At night they had sat in front of the church and in the surrounding meadows, passing the time in prayer and singing.

Holy Wenceslas, prince of the Czech realm – the hymn imploring the patron saint not to let his progeny perish – had been sung three times. If I'd heard what the hymn sounded like under the open sky perhaps I too after all would look forward to better days.

We were advancing down the narrow little street which runs round the park by the ramparts. Mr Rada was engrossed by what he was telling me but I couldn't resist looking up curiously to the window which the artist had turned into his showroom. The hanged man had long disappeared, there had since been a three-legged swan and later a fountain which instead of water spewed dirty sand or ash, letting it rain down on a female head whose plaster features seemed pretty, and down whose cheeks it slid like solidified tears. Now the head and the cloud of ash were gone, there was a manikin sitting on a little horse, made up, as was his steed, of plastic items evidently picked up from a rubbish heap: old containers, motor oil and spray cans, hideous toys for infants and coloured fragments of handbasins and jugs. His open mouth was a red butter-dish, in one of his eyes was a poisonously green pot of paper paste, Koh-i-noor brand, and in the other the dark-haired head of a doll. At first glance it seemed that the horseman was smiling, a mere toy, a present-day Don Quixote riding out into the world in armour, but then I noticed the rider was showing his light polystyrene teeth and I could make out some bare bones. This was not the noble though confused knight but rather the fourth horseman of the Apocalypse, as seen by Dürer. 'And behold a pale horse; and his name that sat on him was Death, and Hell followed with him,' the horseman with the head of the mouth of hell of Breughel's 'Dulle Griet'.

What kind of head, I wondered, had that unknown artist? Why and for whom was he staging these exhibitions in a little street into which hardly anyone ever strayed? Why was death so often on his mind?

'These young people,' Mr Rada continued enthusiastically, 'have realised that they've had distorted values imposed on them. From childhood they've had it drilled into them that hate and struggle are the levers of history. That there is no superior being above man! And they came to pray and to listen to the tidings about Him who is above us and who, despite everything, looks down on us with love.' It was possible, he concluded, that by the grace of God a period of rebirth was beginning, a new Christian age.

He communicated his joy to me and supposed that I would fully share it with him. It is certainly encouraging to hear that people are not content with the jerkish notion of happiness. But it occurred to me, even while he was reading to me about how man strayed off his path by deifying himself, that man can behave arrogantly not only by deifying his own ego and proclaiming himself as the finest flower of matter and life, but equally when he proudly believes that he has correctly comprehended the incomprehensible or uttered the unutterable, or when he thinks up infallible dogmas and with his intellect, which wants to believe, reaches out into regions before which he should lower his eyes and stand in silence. We might debate for a long time about when that fatal shift occurred (if it occurred) which gave rise to the arrogant spirit of our age, and also about how far we must go back to put matters right, but what point would there be in such an argument when there is no rerturn anyway, either in the individual's life or in that of humanity?

'What about your brother?' it occurred to me to ask. 'Was he there with you?'

'Him?' he made a dismissive gesture. 'It might cost him his career!' His own words struck him as too harsh, for he added: 'He might perhaps just walk along in some Buddhist procession.'

Dad had been in hospital for a week. Lately, even before he was laid so low by fever, he'd complain that he couldn't sleep at night. I wanted to know why and he didn't tell me, he made some excuse about some undefined burning pain, an elusive ache. But I suspected that he was suffering from anxiety. His intellect, which all his life had been concerned with quantifiable matter, knew of course that nothing vanished completely from this world, but he also knew that nothing kept its shape and appearance forever, that in this eternal and continuous motion of matter every being must perish just as every machine, even the most perfect, just as the worlds and the galaxies. Dad's intellect realised that everything was subject to that law, so why should the human soul alone be exempt from it? Because the Creator breathed life into it? But surely He too, if he existed at all, was subject to that law. But what sense would there be in a God whose existence and likeness were subject to the same laws as everything else, a God who'd be subject to time?

Dad was standing on the frontier which his intellect was able to visualise, the chilling nocturnal fear of the black pit was crushing him – and I was unable to help him. My dear father, how can I help you, how can I shield you from fear of your downfall? I wasn't even able to burn your fever. I am only your son, I was not given the power to liberate you from darkness, or to liberate anyone.

Dad is lying in a white ward which smells of doctoring and of the sweat of the dying. They have temporarily kept his fever down with antibiotics and they have dulled his fear by antidepressants. They'd given him the middle bed of three. On his left lay a hallucinating fat man who'd been irradiated at night by unknown invaders with hooded faces, on his right a wizened old man, punctured all over by hypodermics, was dying.

Dad was sitting up and welcomed me with a smile. I fed him, then I took out a razor from his bedside table and offered to shave him. He nodded. Lately he'd hardly spoken at all. Maybe he didn't have the strength, or else he didn't know what to tell me. He'd never talked to me about personal matters, nor had he ever spoken about anything abstract. In his businesslike world there was no room for speculations which led too far from firm ground. So what was he to talk to me about now that the firm ground itself was receding from him? And what was I to talk to him about?

The dying man on his right emerged for an instant from his unconscious condition and whispered something with a moan.

'Poor fellow,' Dad said, 'he's all in.'

I helped my father to get up. I took his arm and he moved out into the corridor with small shuffling steps. I should have liked to say something nice and encouraging to him, something meaningful.

'I have those dreams nowadays,' he confessed to me. 'They proclaimed a beet-picking drive, and Stalin was personally in charge. I had to join, and I was afraid he'd notice how badly I was working.'

During the Stalin period they had, with the deliberate intention of hitting him where it would hurt most, found him guilty of bad work.

I might have told him that I'd always admired his ability to concentrate on his work, that I knew what outstanding results he'd achieved, but it would have sounded like empty phrases from a premature funeral oration. He knew better than anyone what he had achieved, and he also knew what I thought of his work.

We were approaching the end of the corridor – everything was spotlessly washed and polished, almost as it used to be in our home. We were on our own, although in the distance we could see a young nurse hurrying from one door to another. Only a few days earlier Dad had been irritated by the nurses, who'd seemed to him disobliging. Now he wasn't complaining. He sat down on a chair by an open window, his grey-streaked hair was stuck together by sweat. He looked out through the window, where the birches were shedding their yellow leaves in the gusts of wind, but he was probably unaware of them, he'd just witnessed an explosion at a cosmic height and he was alarmed. 'It's stupid,' he said softly, 'to play about with it. Any piece of machinery will malfunction some time. If they don't stop it it'll be the end. You ought to tell them!'

'Me?'

'You ought to tell them.' Dad was still looking out of the window, but he was silent again. A plane roared past overhead, it moved on, it didn't crash.

Had he perhaps just uttered the most important thing he'd

intended to say to me? Or did he merely wish to confess a further disappointment of his – that not even the technology in which he'd believed so much would lead man into the Garden of Bliss but would, more probably, incinerate him and his earth.

I helped him get up and we returned to his ward. I sat him up in his bed, straightened his blanket and told him how well he'd walked. I should have asked him, while there was time, if there was anything else he wanted to tell me, anything he hadn't told me so far, some instruction, advice or message. Was he perhaps leaving a grave behind somewhere that I should visit for him? But Dad was certainly not thinking of graves, he regarded it as nonsensical to waste time on the dead, and he wouldn't venture to give me any advice. He'd been wrong with so many of his expectations, and he had nothing left to pass on to me.

Maybe I should have been saying to him that, if anything, I was finding some hope in his disappointments, because he'd been misled only by a self-assured intellect which thought it knew everything and which refused to leave any room for the inexplicable, that is for God, eternity or redemption. Would he even understand me, could he still hear me?

I noticed that his chin had dropped on his chest and that he had slipped down on his side. I slackened the screw behind his bedhead and brought the bed down into the horizontal position. Dad didn't wake up as I laid him down, he didn't even open his eyes when I stroked his forehead.

The Buddhist idea of paradise differs from ours.

Man enters the paradisal state by attaining nirvana; nirvana frees him from the bonds of existence and from earthly relationships, it interrupts the cycle of life, death and rebirth. In nirvana there is no suffering, nor thought, nor even awareness of one's own ego. Nirvana may be attained in one's lifetime, but basically it is a state of non-being, or at least non-awareness. Such a state may precede death and also birth. In the concept of nirvana man, in a manner of speaking, recalls the state preceding birth, the state of earliest infancy.

When I got home a young man was waiting for me who, by coincidence, had just arrived from a town near Svatá Hora. About two years ago I'd given a reading of some of my short stories to a few friends of his at his place. Since then he'd turned up occasionally for a chat about literature. He was always well-groomed, his fair hair looked as if it had just been waved with curling tongs and in his grey eyes there was some painful anxiety as if he'd taken on more of life's burdens and responsibilities than he could bear. He was interested in Kierkegaard, Kafka and Joyce, as well as in the cinema and in art. In one of the stories I'd read that evening there was a mention of Hegedušić; after I'd finished he told me that there was a short film available in our country about him. I was surprised to find a young man, who worked in the mines near Svatá Hora, being interested in a Yugoslav painter. He'd now arrived suspiciously soon after the famous pilgrimage, but he made no mention of it, which reassured me. He'd come to get my advice about his future. He'd decided he wouldn't stay in the mines any longer. He'd find some unskilled job and would try to study aesthetics, art history or literature by correspondence. The work he was doing, he explained to me, made no sense. The people among whom he moved disgusted him. If only he knew what people he'd have to move among if he succeeded in getting where he wanted to go! But I don't like imposing my dislikes on others. I merely dug out some recent article by a leading jerkish official who'd been appointed to a university chair to ensure the oblivion of all literature.

From that article I read him just a few introductory sentences on communism, which had become the highest form of freedom of the individual and the human race, and in consequence provided the writer with an unprecedented scope, whereas in the USA, that bastion of unfreedom, the greatest artists, such as Charlie Chaplin, had to escape.

My visitor smiled. He considers it more acceptable to have to listen, voluntarily and for no pay, to jerkish babbling than to destroy and pollute the landscape for good pay, to mine the ore from which others would produce an explosive device capable of turning everything into flames.

What stands at the beginning and what at the end? The word or fire, babbling or explosion?

Speaking of explosions, my visitor was reminded that in his little town some unknown persons recently blew up the monument of the 'workers' president'. The president had died more than thirty years ago, at a time when my visitor was still in a state of innocence. All he knew about that remarkable man was that he brought upon us all that 'highest form of freedom of the individual and the human race', and also that, in its name, he had masses of innocent people liquidated, including his own friends and comrades. My visitor wanted to hear how I felt about the destruction of monuments. It is my impression that people don't take any notice of monuments, especially the new ones, or if they do there is nothing about those statues that could impress them. After all, what appeal can one expect of shaft-boots, overcoats, trousers and briefcases, with on the top, accounting for less than one-sixth of the whole, a face behind which we detect neither spirit nor soul? What I mind about the monuments of officially proclaimed giants is that they are ugly and mean, in other words that they disfigure their surroundings. But then it would be difficult to imagine different ones, considering whom they have to represent and given the abilities of the artists from whom these statues are commissioned for a fat fee. Besides, there are so many things disfiguring this world! If we were to destroy them all, where should we stop? To destroy is always easier than to create, and that is why so many people are ready to demonstrate against what they reject. But what would they say if one asked them what they wanted instead?

The young man nodded. He hoped his studies would help him find what to aim for himself. He apologised briefly for having kept me up so late and vanished into the night.

The Buddhists also have their own vision of the apocalypse. Once all our good deeds, love or renunciation no longer offset our sins, the equilibrium between good and evil in the universe is upset. Then snakes, crocodiles, dragons and many-headed monsters will emerge from all the openings in the earth and from the waters, breathing fire and devouring mankind. This will restore the disturbed equilibrium, and harmony of silence and nothingness will reign once more.

Night and silence and nothingness. In the sleeping city distant people and near ones, friends and strangers are all swallowed up by darkness. Where in all this darkness have we lost our God?

Kafka too could not see through that darkness, he did not believe, or at least not in the way most people believe. But it was not his intellect that stopped him from believing. It was, if anything, his honesty. He could not accept anything that came from outside, no order and no dogma, no ideas or findings of others, if they did not match his own experience and internal attunement.

The questioning intellect normally penetrates into the depths of the individual, the world and the universe until it encounters the boundary beyond which mystery begins. There it either stops or else rushes on, failing to realise, or reluctant to realise, that it calls out its questions into the void.

In his questioning Kafka stopped at the very first step, at himself, because even here he'd entered an impenetrable depth. In a world in which the intellect predominates more and more, the intellect which believes that it knows everything about the world and even more about itself, Kafka rediscovered the mysterious: that was everything to him, for that he lived. If God represents to us the supreme mystery, then we can say that man, who possesses the gift of seeing mystery even where others do not suspect it, can at least open the door to that supreme mystery.

Unexpectedly the telephone rang. I ran out to the hall, lifted the receiver and identified myself, but there was silence at the other end. It was listening to me, silently. I replaced the receiver and lifted it again. The silence had gone, the dialling tone was buzzing.

That was you?

You aren't angry, are you, darling? Were you asleep? I'm here on my own. I was lying in bed, reading, and suddenly I thought this was nonsense: to lie here and read about another person's life. I'm sad. Aren't you?

Just now?

Just now . . . And altogether. I do something and then it hits me: why am I doing it, and for whom? Now I'm lying here, everything is quiet, but why should I be lying here? I don't need any rest when tomorrow I won't be alive anyway. You assured me that you were happy when you were with me, that you'd never experienced anything so complete. Was that a lie then?

Surely you'd have known if I'd told you a lie at that moment.

So why don't you come? Tell me what has changed, in what way have I changed that you don't even ring me? What wrong did I do to you?

You didn't do me any wrong, but we just couldn't go on. Neither me nor you. It was impossible to carry on that divided life.

And like this one can live? Don't tell me you're living. Tell me, you really believe you're living?

Surely living doesn't only mean making love.

It doesn't? I always thought it meant just that to you. So what, in your opinion, does have any meaning? Eating and sleeping? To botch up some important work, some great piece of art?

What I am trying to say is that one can't indulge in love at any price. Like at the expense of others.

You think that's what we were doing?

You don't think so?

You are asking me? You who were always ready to sacrifice me? As if I wasn't a human being at all, as if only she was one. Why don't you say something? You're angry now. Wait, wait a moment, surely you admit that you've always decided against me.

I didn't decide against you, I wasn't free to decide for you.

That didn't worry you in some respects.

It worried me precisely in the respect you're talking about.

You're making excuses, you've always only made excuses. You know very well that you never gave me a chance.

A chance of what? Weren't we together enough?

You were never only with me. Not even a week. Not even a day! You were never with me except secretly. Even by the sea . . .

Don't cry!

And I believed you. I thought you loved me and would find some way for us to remain together. At least for a time.

I did love you. But there was no way round. Surely people aren't things which you can move to another place when they seem to have served their purpose. I could only either remain here or join you.

You're so noble about other people. But you calmly moved me as far away as possible when I'd served my purpose. Wait, wait, tell me one more thing: are you happy at least? Don't you regret anything? Why aren't you saying anything? If you've no regrets about me don't you at least have any about yourself?

You think I should have regrets about myself?

Surely it's sad if a person has loved somebody and then loses him.

I know, but a person can lose something worse.

What is there that's worse for a person to lose?

Perhaps his soul.

Your soul? You lost your soul with me? You shouldn't have said that! What do you know about the soul? You're just a pack of excuses!

III

◆

The morning rises from the autumnal mists and the sky slowly turns blue. On the far bank of the river, ever since dawn, there has been a rapid procession of cars escaping for the weekend from the polluted city. Over breakfast I'd read a poem in the paper by the leading author writing in jerkish:

> *Chain of Hands*
>
> Who knows who knows
> where beauty is born
> where happiness seeks us
> why love trusts us
>
> People people
> maybe that day is dawning
> when children may play
> everywhere is white peace
>
> People people
> let's be ever vigilant
> they who sow the wind
> must reap the storm
>
> People people
> we're but a chain of hands
> we're but the music of dreams
> we're but the beauty of deeds

For this poem of sixty-nine words, including the title, the author needed a mere thirty-seven jerkish terms and no idea at all, no feeling or image. The substantives – beauty, happiness, love, peace, people, children – are of course interchangeable, the sense or nonsense of the rambling remains unchanged. The obligatory call for hatred of the unworthy and for love of the worthy strikes one by its clichés, even if one allows for the limited scope of the jerkish language. It's almost as if the author was afraid that among the chimpanzees there might after all be one individual who would not understand him.

Anyone strong enough to read the poem attentively will realise that for a jerkish poet even a vocabulary of 225 words is needlessly large.

On the far side of the river – you have only to cross the bridge – are rocks and woods. We used to go for walks there with the children, now someone said they'd established some huge depôt there. My wife agrees that we should set out in that direction, she is happy that we're going on an excursion.

Under the bridge gypsies are playing football, the beds of a nursery patch look like an oriental carpet. My wife is walking ahead, with an energetic step. Her fears have left her, hope has returned to her, hope of a life that can be lived in harmony and love. And I still feel relief at her proximity, relief unblemished by pretence or lies, I am conscious of the lightness of the new day, upon which I am entering full of expectation.

One reason why I like walking in the country is probably that I was never able to do so in my childhood. The first thing I ever wrote in my life – I was eleven at the time and had been in the Terezín fortress ghetto for over a year – was not about love or suffering or my personal fate, but about landscape:

> As we climb up the steep slope of Petřín Hill we feel increasingly like birds rising into the air. And then, at one instant, we turn round. We see before us such a multitude of Little City roofs that we catch our breath and regret that we are not really birds and so can never alight on those roofs or see their secrets from close up . . .

At that time I didn't know yet what I was doing, I had no idea how many books had been written by then, how many minds had spoken in them. I wrote because I was dying from a yearning for freedom, and freedom for me then meant stepping out of my prison, walking through the streets of my native city; I wrote to fortify my hope that outside the fortress walls the world still existed, a world which had seemed to exist then only in dreams and visions.

I still believe that literature has something in common with hope, with a free life outside the fortress walls which, often unnoticed by us, surround us, with which moreover we surround ourselves. I am not greatly attracted to books whose authors merely portray the hopelessness of our existence, despairing of man, of our conditions, despairing over poverty and riches, over the finiteness of life and the transience of feelings. A writer who doesn't know anything else had better keep silent.

Kafka was desperate in nearly every situation of his life, and yet he was always looking for hope. When it seemed out of reach he'd put his manuscript aside and not return to it again.

Man goes through the landscape, seeking hope and waiting for a miracle, waiting for someone to answer his questions. Some monk, pilgrim, enlightened Buddha, prophet or at least a talking bird, to tell him if he's really been endowed with a soul, whose existence would not be cut short even by death, of what matter that soul was woven, what there was above man, what order, what creature or being, in what kind of big bang time had its origin and where it was heading; man passes through the landscape, waiting for an encounter, or at least for a sign, without knowing its nature.

My wife stops, she is waiting for me. I catch up with her, I embrace her. She goes rigid in my embrace, I can feel her trembling.

When I'd met her years ago I was tormented by my loneliness, and I was happy that someone was interested in me. She was very young then, she probably didn't understand what I was feeling, or how impatiently I would wait for her, she was regularly late for our dates.

I'd stand on the edge of the little park not far from where she lived, in the shadow of a magnificent plane tree, or in winter under its bare branches, watching the hands of the street clock. Time and again I worried that she wouldn't come, that something had happened to her, that we'd missed one another or that one of us had made a mistake about the time. When eventually she arrived I was so happy she'd come I couldn't bring myself to be angry with her.

No matter where we'd set out for, we felt good. It seemed to me that we were jointly looking for the same signs. For her everything changed into images, as happens to children, savages or the elect among the poets, and I felt buoyed up by her side.

To this day I can feel the joy which pervaded her, her pleasure at everything we met and saw: a little flower whose name she didn't know, or the roof of the distant estate building, or the little feather lost by a bird of prey, and most of all our being close together. And it struck me that our actions, wherever they might seem to aim, were in fact aimed at just this point, at the close proximity of a person who might become a companion. At the bottom of all our hopes lies a yearning for encounter.

Daria was convinced that we belonged together, that we'd merely not known about one another, or that the right time had not yet come for us to meet in the way we'd now met. And she found this belief confirmed in the stars, in her cards, in the prophecies of an old clairvoyant whom she'd sought out on one occasion when, after all, she was overcome by doubts.

She pressed me: Why do you tell lies at home? You're only wronging me, your wife and yourself. She reminded me of Buddha's words. Apparently he said: No one's deed is lost, it comes back to him! I understand those words, I also understand her. She asks me: Why don't you come all the way to me, why do you resist so? Surely no one else can love you as I do.

Suppose we loved one another just because we do have to part all the time and then find each other anew?

She went to Greece with her husband. She was so far away that her voice came to me only as a soft whisper at night, from the region of the stars, her tenderness too was fading over that distance, and I felt easier. As though I were returning from some beautiful exile, descending from mountain heights where I'd felt happy but uneasy. How could I go back to the home that I had needlessly and wilfully left?

I went on holiday with my wife, on the way we stopped at a campsite managed by our son.

We sit together and eat porridge out of billycans, it smells faintly of burnt wood, and in the evening we sing at the campfire. Lída's voice carries above everybody else's, there's tranquillity in it, it drives out everything alien and evil that still clings to my soul. It's raining, the fire is smoking, we huddle under a single rubber coat, we touch as if embracing, and it seems to me that my lies have disappeared somewhere without trace and I'll never return to them. And I wish time would not march on, that it would delay the return of my lover whom, surely, I can't betray either, I can't just chase her away. And somewhere deep down within me something is stirring, and amidst the raindrops I can hear her rapid footsteps, I can see her emerging from the dark and hurrying down the stony path among the olives, among the fig trees, among the umbrella pines, I can see her alone, even though I know that she is not alone. In my mind, however, she lives separated from all other people, with the possible exception of the swarthy villager who pours her wine. From that great distance there comes to me the muted roar of the Minotaur. I duck under the onrush of longing. In how many days will she come back to me, if she comes back to me at all?

The days have now gone, it is only two hours' journey now, no frontier to cross, I could embrace her, provided she comes back to me.

The thought of it pushes everything else out of my mind. I walk down a path and she is coming towards me, we run towards each other, again and again we run towards each other in daylight and in darkness. At night she slips into my bed, we make love like people possessed. She moans and caresses me, I whisper tender words in her ear.

119

One day I'll pretend I'm meeting some friends, I'll get into the car and drive off. I don't know with whom I'll find her, or if I'll find her at all, I don't know if I'll make up my mind to knock at the door I've never stood before, the door I know only from her account. I'll arrive at the village which is so remote it hasn't even got a church, I'll leave the car under a tall lime tree and set out at random towards where I suspect her temporary place to be.

And there she is, coming towards me, real and alive, tanned by the southern sun, I know her from afar by her rapid life-hungry step. She recognises me, she raises her hand in greeting but we do not run towards each other, we walk towards each other, and she asks in surprise: You've come to see me, darling? We don't kiss, and she says: I've brought you a stone from Mount Olympus. And she opens her eyes wide, she embraces me with her eyes till I sigh at the thought of ecstasy to come.

We'd walked through the patch of woodland outside the city, there were even mushrooms and chanterelles growing by the footpath, and through the branches we could see the blue sky.

My wife wanted to know whether street-sweeping wasn't depressing me too much.

It certainly would depress me if I had to do it for the rest of my life.

What about the people who actually do it for years on end?

I don't know what to tell her about them. After all, street-sweeping isn't all that different from lots of other jobs which all have one thing in common: they are not inspiring. Sweepers pass their time just like other people, by talking, by reminiscing about better moments in their lives. Maybe they talk in order to rise above what they are doing, but more probably they just talk to make the time pass more pleasantly.

Didn't they look to me somehow marked, outcast or humiliated? But my wife is asking these questions only so she can tell me about her experiences with her patients, whom circumstances had picked on as sacrificial lambs: as a result they were marked for the rest of their lives, most of them had had their self-assurance broken and their mental health had been affected.

I asked her if something like that must inevitably occur, and my wife said it did. In this manner people satisfied their innate need to find a sacrificial lamb onto whom they'd transfer their own guilt. Sacrifices to superior powers were age-old, indeed they used to be performed with solemn rituals, and for their victims men chose those whom their society considered the best or the purest.

The ritual of sacrifice no longer existed today – disregarding the symbolical sacrifice of the body of Christ. What had persisted, however, was the need for sacrifice. People now sought their sacrificial victims in their own midst, and mostly they chose the ones who were the weakest and most vulnerable. They no longer spilled their blood, they merely destroyed their souls. The most frequent victims were the children.

Yesterday, as we were moving down the street of the housing estate, the dustbins were overflowing and everywhere on the pavement and in the road rubbish was blowing about. In front of one of the refuse dumpsters was a large red puddle. It might have been human or animal blood, if it was blood at all. On the surface of the puddle dust and dirt had formed an uneven scum in which some bits of greasy paper had been trapped. Mrs Venus turned away. I thought her Red-Indian face had gone yellow. 'Ugh, can't look at that. Different thing at the path lab, but here in the street . . .' she said as we were sweeping the rubbish in the roadway into a little heap. 'That's how I found her – my little Annie.'

She told me that before she'd had her three sons she'd had a daughter. Doing her shopping one day she'd left her in the pram outside. She'd already paid for her purchases when there were shrieks outside, then something crashed into the wall and the glass in the shop window was shattered. She rushed out, there was an overturned lorry, two adults lying there, blood everywhere, and nothing left of the pram. 'I was beside myself then, I'd have killed that drunken pig behind the wheel if they'd let me. But they rushed up from all sides and held me until the doctor who came with the ambulance gave me a jab of something.'

At that time she was still working at the stud in Topolčianky.

And just a few days after her little girl was killed it so happened that her favourite mare Edith, a chestnut with white socks, fell at a fence and broke her right foreleg just at the fetlock. The vet insisted that she'd never race again, in fact she wouldn't even walk again, and he wanted to put her down. She ran straight to the manager of the stud and begged him to let her look after the filly. The manager knew what she'd just gone through and took pity on her. After that she spent every free moment with Edith. She made splints for her, mixed saltpetre with water parsnip and nasturtium leaves and alternated these applications with an ointment which the vet, in the end, gave her. With that filly she could talk just as she'd talked to her little girl, the animal understood her. At night, when Mrs Venus woke up and saw her little girl all bloody and mangled on that pavement, she'd run to the stable; her filly was never asleep, just as if she knew she'd come to see her. After six months she was riding Edith, they even allowed her to enter her for their local steeplechase and she rode her herself. As she was waiting at the start she forgot for the first time what had happened to her.

'And did you win?' I asked.

'Some hope! We were doing all right as far as the third fence. But I was so excited I got a belly-ache, and then I couldn't control Edith any more, she just ran as she pleased. We finished last, by ten lengths, but we finished.'

As we walked on through the deserted little wood there was more and more rubbish on the ground, and not only on the ground – even the branches of the trees were festooned with translucent tatters of plastic. At every gust of the wind they emitted a rustling sound and with the sound came the smell of rotting, mould and mildew.

Where is there any untouched nature left? The road up Mount Olympus, Daria had told me, led through rubbish, and even the way up Fujiyama, which she'd also climbed, was lined with garbage. On Mount Everest, just below its summit, lay drums, abandoned tents and plastic containers. Even a crashed helicopter is said to be rusting there.

122

My dear Lída is mistaken when she thinks that sweepers must feel ostracised or humiliated. They might, on the contrary, if they cared about such things, regard themselves as the salt of the earth, as healers of a world in danger of choking.

I asked if it was possible to help those who had already borne the brunt of ostracism. My wife, thankful for a question that was seeking for hope, replied that the best chance was psychotherapy. This might help to uncover the causes of their rejection by others and shift their sense of being wronged from their subconscious to their conscious minds.

The main theme of my wife's life is finding hope for other people. The pain of others hurts her personally, she suffers with every rejected person, she tries to alleviate his lot, to help him see into his own soul and to discover there what he wouldn't discover otherwise. If she feels she is succeeding she is happy, she knows she isn't living in vain.

If my life has been assigned any main theme by fate, it is probably the theme of freedom.

How can you write about freedom when you're unable to act freely, Daria objects. By which she means that I am unable to leave my wife.

I don't know why leaving someone should be a freer action than staying with them.

All right then, why didn't I stay with that dreadful woman who battened on other people's misfortunes, and leave her alone.

Perhaps my theme ought to be not so much the search for freedom as the search for action. Or maybe resolution, or determination, or ruthlessness? I'll write a novel about a hero who sweeps aside anyone standing in the way of his happiness or satisfaction. He'll go on sweeping everybody aside until somebody sweeps him aside. Maybe, if he is sufficiently determined, vicious, resolute, ruthless and at the same time circumspect his turn will not come at all: only death will sweep him aside.

A few days ago an aircraft crashed not far from the Irish coast with 325 people aboard. The plane didn't strike a church tower or a mountain veiled in mist, but a time bomb exploded in it. Not a single passenger survived. Among the victims were eighty children. Floating in the water – wrote the journalists, knowing that people in their secure armchairs love reading moving or harrowing details – were dolls and other toys.

Heroes impose themselves. They'd placed a bomb aboard the plane and they were not only resolute and ruthless, but were no doubt also fighting for someone's freedom.

A lot of people talk about freedom, those who deny it to others most loudly. The concentration camps of my childhood even had a slogan about freedom inscribed over their gates.

But I continue to believe that an action can be free only if it is inspired by humanity, only if it is aware of a higher judge. It cannot be linked to acts of arbitrariness, hatred or violence, nor indeed to personal selfish interest.

The amount of freedom is not increasing in our age, even though it may sometimes seem to be. All that increases is the needless movement of things, words, garbage and violence. And because nothing can vanish from the face of the planet, the fruits of our activity do not liberate us but bury us.

They even held an international conference about the Apocalypse. Scientists have calculated that if less than half of the existing atomic warheads exploded, a firestorm would sweep over the continents and the oceans, igniting anything inflammable on earth. The air would be filled with poisonous vapours, including lethal cyanides from certain plastic materials which we ourselves have manufactured. The heat would destroy not only all living things on the surface of the planet but also the seeds in the ground. The fire would be followed by darkness. For a week after the explosions the air would be filled with two hundred million tons of black smoke, and these clouds would block out 95 per cent of the light that used to reach the earth. If any plants had remained unburnt, they would die in the months-long darkness. During the darkness a prolonged arctic winter would begin, turning the water on the planet's surface into ice and thus destroying what remnants of life might have survived in the waters.

Between Crete and Rhodes lies the little island of Karpathos, and on it stands the small town of Olimbos. A tiny church and a few dozen houses climbing in terraces up an almost bare mountain flank. The stone houses have flat roofs and huddle together in narrow streets. Here one still finds women in dresses as black as their hair, and there is something age-old in the swarthy faces of the men. Even the silence and the sounds are age-old. This is where we'll go, the two of us together, it came to her in a flash, and as she was climbing the steep little street to the church she knew for certain that she'd be coming back here, and that I would come with her. Maybe we shall stay there and grow old. She'll lead me through ruins, among the remains of temples, she'll lead me through little villages whose names I instantly forget and whose names even she possibly doesn't know. I inhale the scent of rosemary, tamarisk and lavender, the fragrance of the hot, sun-parched soil, I hear the chirping of the cicadas and the braying of the donkeys and the pealing of bells, wedding bells overhead, and together we are conscious of what others are not conscious of: the spirit of our breath and the breath of our spirits.

I know that she is visualising her future life and that she includes me in it, that she imagines the travels we'll undertake together, as well as her old age by my side, just as if we now really belonged together forever, as if there were no longer other people alongside us. Perhaps it doesn't even occur to her that we are wronging anyone, she is convinced that our love justifies everything. Or is she just more genuine than me, does she want to accept the consequences of having decided to love me?

I love her too, I try to dispel my uneasiness, my anxiety to escape from her visions, I want to be with her. At least for a day, at least for some fraction of time.

And so we loved each other with all our strength and passion, out of uneasiness and out of loneliness, out of love, out of longing and out of despair. The fragments of time piled up into weeks, into further months. The winds blew, storms passed over, snow fell, her daughter was growing up, my son began studying management science, he was increasingly interested in programmes for the management of the world in which he had to live, a downpour drove us into an abandoned basement where we held each other as tight as if we'd just met after a long separation, we waded through the tinted leaves in the park where the ravens in the tops of the tulip trees again called out their Nevermore to us. Her husband fell ill so that she had virtually no time for me, but she wrote me long letters in which she embraced and caressed and cursed me: Life without you is almost like death! My son celebrated his twentieth birthday, he was told to choose a present that was useful and would also give him pleasure, and after some reflection he asked for a Geiger-counter. My wife noticed that I was taciturn, I looked drawn, and she asked me whether I didn't sometimes feel nostalgic for that other woman. She suggested that I should ask her round some time, and then left for an indoctrination course, and I was able to stay with my lover day and night.

Next spring, she says, something decisive is at last going to happen.

Why next spring?

After twelve years Jupiter would enter the house of life for her.

And indeed in early spring a gallery owner in Geneva expressed interest in her work and offered to stage an exhibition for her.

I'd come to her attic studio as usual, and as soon as I'd opened the door I could see that something out of the ordinary had happened: cupboards and packing cases on which the soot from the little chimney-flue had settled for years now stood open; wherever I looked I saw mountains of her creations and monsters, succubi, witches, little demons, shameless displayers of their sex as well as angelic creatures without any sex, men-jackals, and ordinary drunks from a Little City tavern. Most of them I saw for the first time.

She kissed me, cleared a chair for me, told me her news, and wrung her hands in lamentation: she didn't know what to do. For a while we continued to unpack some of her earlier work from crates. She placed each on a modelling stand, inspected it carefully for a few minutes, like an archaeologist who'd just unearthed an unexpectedly large fragment, and then put it down with the rest. She didn't know if she was justified in dredging up and exhibiting such ancient work. She pointed to the head of an old woman: she'd made that while still at school. It was her father's mother, she'd lived to the age of ninety. With her left eye she was winking while with the other one she was smiling.

I recognise the forehead, which is as high as her own, and the smile too is familiar. And that bronze youngster hanging his head, in which there is an opening for a long-stemmed flower, was a fellow student who'd committed suicide, she'd told me about him. At that time she'd wanted to make portraits of all the members of her family she knew anything about. Many of them were still in her basement workshop, she'd probably leave them there. Then she says: That gallery owner is inviting me to the private view and you're coming with me.

How can I go to Switzerland?

I don't know how, she says, but I do know that you'll see my exhibition.

As I get up to leave she neither holds me back nor sees me out, she wants to get on with her work.

I see her every other day, that's what she wants. I always find her at work, and nearly always I am welcomed by a new arrival from the realm of her imagination. He'd gaze at me out of stone or clay eyes, and in his gaze I'd recognise a familiar passion. My lover goes on working for a little longer, while I fry up something simple for lunch, then she puts down her tools, takes off her stained smock and washes her hands. Now she doesn't want to think of work any more, only, just before we embrace, she has to tell me what she's been thinking about, who she'd had a beer with last night, what they'd told her at the agency this morning, the one that is supposed to negotiate her exhibition, and finally she must tell me her dream. Her day is so rich that she will never enter the kingdom of heaven.

I admire her. I'm sure I'd be spending weeks before the stand without finishing more than one or two things.

How can you be so sure?

Because I know how long it takes me to think up a sentence before it more or less satisfies me.

That's because you're tense, she explains to me. You try to master everything by your intellect and your strength. You don't know how to submit to life.

She doesn't force herself to do anything. What she needs most is a sense that she is free. If she doesn't feel like work she'll go out with a girlfriend and they'll get drunk, or else she comes here, she sits down, she doesn't want anything, she isn't driven anywhere by her thoughts or her imagination, she just gazes as if she were gazing at the clear sky, into pure water, into emptiness. She realises that nothing need happen, and that's also all right by her. Or else some shape suddenly appears before her, a face, a likeness, maybe just a coloured blotch which may take on form or else dissolve. She can't tell where they come from, these shapes don't seem to come from within her, she feels she's only a mediator. She then executes whatever she has to, and she feels good while doing it. She doesn't reflect on what it will turn into. That, she feels, is not her concern but the concern of whoever put that vision into her. If I could write like that, without torturing myself beforehand about the outcome, without seeing some mission before me, I'd also feel good.

But I can't work the way she does, I'm different.

You don't know what you're like, she says with assurance.

And who does?

I do, because I love you.

So what am I like?

You're more passionate than rational.

I don't know whether I am passionate. I know that she is. Her passion will destroy us both one day.

Next time I found her in tears amidst fragments of clay. The stand was empty.

What happened?

Nothing. What should have happened? Better leave again, I'm out of sorts today!

Has anybody hurt you?

Everybody's hurting me, but that's not the point.

So what is?

How could I ask? Didn't I understand, couldn't I see? All we were doing was pointless, nothing but a self-important and vain playing at art. Nothing but desperate caricaturing and endless repetition of what had already been repeated a thousand times. And if she'd now and then managed to catch something more, to realise some higher clue, who'd detect it, who'd notice it? Why did she have to choose this particular occupation, such a useless, joyless and exhausting drudgery? She hated all art! She didn't want to exhibit anywhere, she didn't want to show anyone her fumblings. There was no sense in it!

What about Barlach's angel?

Yes, Barlach's angel – but they'd had it removed, hadn't they? He survived only because angels are immortal. She's laughing through her tears. If you'd sit for me I'd make you a pair of wings and maybe you'd be immortal too.

I'll sit for you.

Better lie down with me!

We embrace and she forgets all her sorrow. She looks forward to our love-making on the shores of Lake Geneva.

Three days later the organisation, or rather agency whose task it is to organise, in other words authorise, exhibitions abroad informed her that it would not handle her exhibition.

I want to know why she's been refused but she only shrugs.

I suspect that it might have been because of me.

It's possible, darling, they're envious of me because I have you, they know that nobody loves them so much.

However, we composed a letter of protest, which she'd send to the Ministry of Culture. She then went out to see her fortune-teller friend to discover what the cards had to say about the chances of her appeal. Told that they weren't too good, she decided to hold an exhibition in Kutná Hora instead of Geneva.

We were still walking in the direction where I expected the

depôt to be. The trees all round were more and more heavily festooned with tattered pieces of plastic. At the base of the miserable little tree-trunks dirty crumpled bags were tumbling about, and whenever there was a gust of wind the yellowed pages of some jerkish newspaper rose up from the ground like monstrous emaciated birds and weakly flapped their mutilated wings.

Franz Kafka became a sacrificial victim by his own decision. It does not seem as if those around him were as anxious to sacrifice him as he was himself. Time and again he recorded the state of mind experienced by the victim. With few exceptions the victim resists, and even thinks up elaborate means of self-defence, but his tragic end, which we surmise beforehand, is predetermined from the outset and is therefore unalterable. In this respect Kafka certainly anticipated the fate of the Jews in our age of upheaval. His youngest sister met her end in a gas chamber. That is where he would probably have met his end too if he hadn't been lucky enough to die young.

Jewish authors, such as Kafka's contemporary Werfel, or later Bellow and Heller, keep returning to the theme of the sacrificial lamb with an obsession that is possibly subconscious and possibly prophetic. The theme of the victim of sacrifice and the person staging sacrifices, of an increasingly random victim and of the victimiser prepared to drag to the altar of his god any number of human beings, if not indeed the whole of mankind, is increasingly becoming the theme of the present-day world, of a mankind that once believed in an earthly paradise and in the beneficial effect of revolutions in leading it there.

At last we emerged from the forest. Before us, behind a high wire fence, we saw a mountain with many ridges, crevices and humps. Its slopes glistened here and there as the fragments of plastic reflected the sun's rays. Along its long crest a yellow bulldozer was moving, its scoop pushing a multicoloured mass before it. From one side a road led up to the mountain. Access, however, was barred by a red-and-white striped barrier. Just then an orange dumpster came hurtling out of the forest, an invisible guard raised the barrier, and the vehicle entered the enclosure. As it slowly climbed up the slope of the artificial mountain some fat crows rose up from both sides of the path, beating their massive wings. On the crest the garbage truck stopped, its body bright in the sunlight. Then it began to evacuate its entrails. No sooner had it begun to move off than a group of little figures rushed out from some invisible hiding place. I counted thirteen of them – if Daria had been here she'd have said an unlucky number! – men, women and children. The grown-ups had rakes in their hands, and pitchforks and poles fitted with hooks, or else they were pushing discarded prams. They all pounced on the fresh rubbish and began to dig around in it as if in a race; they flung items from one pile onto another, a few items they picked out and put aside for themselves, and others, which were evidently still useful for something or other, i.e. for sale, they flung straight into handcarts or prams.

I was reminded of the woman whose things I'd moved. She had a dead soul, she believed in Armageddon, and she took delight in things she'd saved from the dustbins. She probably used them to fill the emptiness that had remained within her after her soul had died. Here she'd be in her element. She wouldn't have sold any of the items she found here, she'd have piled them into a heap which would have grown ever higher and wider. She'd have laboured till she dropped, not until nightfall would she have sat down by the base of her own mountain and anxiously rested in its shelter for a while. Like Sisyphus, that woman would never have completed her work, not only because the supply of new garbage will never stop, but also because an inner emptiness cannot be filled even with all the objects in the world.

We soon became aware that nothing that was happening before us was happening without a plan, and that all the running around and exploratory digging was directed by a massive bald-headed fatty in a black suit. Unlike all the rest, he never once bent down to pick up anything, but merely strolled about as their supervisor.

And just then his name came to me and I surprised Lída with the information that, to the best of my knowledge, that fellow was called Demeter, and that he'd had to pay a good deal of money for the right to mine the treasures in this mountain, though I didn't know to whom. Now and again the searchers might dig up a pewter plate, an antique coffee grinder, a discarded television set, or a banknote thrown out by mistake.

When the Kampuchean victim-makers, known as the Khmer Rouge, occupied Phnom Penh they broke into the abandoned bank buildings, burst open the safes, carried out armfuls of banknotes and flung them out of the windows – not only rials but also American dollars, Swiss francs and Japanese yen, the banknotes of every country in the world sailed out of the windows, but none of those who were still alive in the city dared pick any of them up. The coloured pieces of printed paper were gently scattered by the wind. They rose into the air alongside scraps of newspaper, torn posters, blank picture postcards and the petals of orchids, then they settled by the kerbs or in the middle of the streets which nobody came to sweep. The rubbish gradually rotted, unless the monsoon rains washed it away and the waters of the Mekong carried it down to the sea.

What Kafka was longing for most in his life was probably a human encounter. At the same time it represented for him a mysterious abyss whose bottom seemed to him unfathomable. But he lived at a period which, more than anything else, began to exalt revolution. Anything that was revolutionary in art, as much as in the social order, seemed worthy of admiration or at least of interest.

For that reason, too, we look in his sentences and images for a revolutionary message. But when I read his letters to the two women he loved, or at least tried to love, for whom he yearned and of whom he was afraid, I realised that if I did the same I had no hope of understanding him.

His first love lasted for more than five years. He invited her to him, he drove her away again, he implored her not to leave him unless she wished to destroy him, and he implored her to leave him or they would destroy one another. He got engaged to her and immediately afterwards he fled from her. When she kept silent and failed to answer his letters he lamented his fate and begged for a single word of favour. Encounter, coming close together with a woman he loved was for him a chance of fulfilling his life, a chance he persistently missed. The struggle he was waging with himself totally consumed and exhausted him.

Could a person as honest as that write about anything other than what was shaking his whole being, what occupied him day and night? About anything other than the struggle he was waging, even though that struggle, by comparison to the revolutionary events in the world, was less than trivial?

Although he mostly speaks of himself and although his heroes are, even in their names, avowedly himself, he yet concealed the true nature of his struggles. He was not only shy, he was so much an artist that he expressed everything he experienced in images. The torturing machine, which slowly murders the sentenced man, was invented by him at the very moment when, after a bitter inner struggle, he decided to get engaged after all. A few weeks later, when he broke off his engagement, treacherously as he himself felt, he conceived the trial in which the tribunal judges the accused for an offence that is not clear to the reader and has, for the most part, been interpreted as metaphysical guilt, as a metaphor of original sin.

Even in a revolutionary period there were undoubtedly other writers whose works, without our feeling obliged to search them for hidden messages about the meaning of existence, were full of images and metaphors. But in Kafka's work there is something more than just a cleverly invented image, something that moves us and grips us, something that lures us fatally on like a sheer drop.

Daria's exhibition was being set up in three reasonably sized rooms of a Gothic house. The exhibition – including twenty drawings – comprised seventy-three items. She could easily have shown a few items more or less, but that number seemed to her the most suitable. 1973 was the year her daughter was born.

For almost two weeks we packed and heaved crates with figures and paintings. Our faces and hair were covered with a layer of wood-shaving dust.

You're so kind to me, she said, brushing the dust off her jeans and embracing me. And I'm not devoting myself to you at all. Have a glass of wine at least!

She promised to make it all up to me. We'd travel somewhere that I'd like, there wouldn't have to be any water there, she knew that I didn't care for water, she'd come to the mountains with me.

I wasn't anxious to go either to the water or to the mountains, I didn't need a rest, I'd much rather work undisturbed. But I behaved like a good boy, I didn't raise any objections, I unpacked the sculptures we'd brought along, I helped to nail pedestals together and hang cords from the ceiling, I adjusted the lights, and in the evening I drove her back home as fast as I could.

My wife, it seemed to me, still had no suspicion of how I was spending most of my time. Or didn't she want to suspect? The day before the opening of the exhibition she was leaving for an ethological conference and wanted to know if I minded being left on my own for so long.

I didn't betray my relief at her going away just then. I assured her I could look after myself.

If I wished, she suggested, I might come along with her. I was sure to find the people at the conference interesting. For a while she told me earnestly about people who kept snakes or exotic butterflies, about experts on owls, marmosets and white stags. She wanted to provide some diversion for me, some experiences I wouldn't have in my solitude, and when I declined her offer I felt guilty. I was about to repay her offer of help with betrayal.

It was her husband who drove my lover out to the private view of her exhibition. He'd finally emerged from the darkness. I suggested to her that I stay at home that day, I'd seen her work anyway. But she didn't want me to leave her at such a moment. I had to overcome a cowardly wish to avoid what would be an awkward encounter, to make the excuse of being ill, or of the car being out of action. There are plenty of excuses a man can invent, but I didn't wish to lie, at least not to her, so I went.

I knew her husband only from photographs, but I instantly identified his tall athletic figure. The room was crowded by then and I don't know if he noticed me too. He was talking to a bald-headed, wizened old man, almost certainly her father, whom I hadn't met either. I didn't know any of the people in the room, I belonged solely to her, to her who was severed from all ties and relationships. I felt so much out of place that it depressed me.

She came over to me almost instantaneously. Unfamiliar, almost strange in a long poppy-crimson dress. Even her features seemed strange to me, the little lines which I'd so often touched with my lips were skilfully covered by a layer of cream and powder. She kissed me, as no doubt she'd kissed other guests as well, and whispered that she loved me. Then she asked me if I wanted to meet her husband. She declared herself as belonging to me in front of everybody — 'My lover' — and I suddenly wasn't sure whether I was pleased about it or not.

After all, why shouldn't I shake hands with you? her husband said to me and gave me a slightly injured smile. Although I'm not exactly short, he was a head taller than me, and also ten years younger. At first glance he was one of those men women run after of their own accord. He said that Daria had worked pretty hard these past few weeks, they'd scarcely seen her at home, and he shrugged as if to say: And on top of everything there's you and that's really a bit much. But instead he said he'd read my new novel, and this would have been the right moment for me to shrug but he gave me his injured smile again and walked away. I hung about near the door but lacked the courage to make a getaway. I had a feeling that they were all furtively watching me, for the moment I had become one of the exhibits. I might have a little card by my feet: Banned but active in another field. Or: The lover presented. Or simply: That's him!

In the last room Daria's sister, whom I had likewise never seen before, was setting out canapés from cartons on a little table and pouring wine into paper cups. I took a canapé but I declined the wine because I was driving back that evening.

I'm sorry about that, she said.

An elderly man whom I knew from somewhere took a drink and said that it was years since he'd seen anything so free and so liberating. He was looking at the sister but I was sure he was talking to me.

That's what she's like, her sister agreed. When she was small she'd run away from home and play truant from school.

Her husband was approaching and I beat a hasty retreat. I was unable not to take notice of him, even though, to my own surprise, I looked upon him without jealousy, as if it were no concern of mine that she lay down by his side night after night. I only felt a little embarrassment, shame and perhaps even guilt. That man had never wronged me, whereas I had for several years now secretly and insidiously worked my way into his life.

She guessed my mood and hurried over to comfort me. Her husband was leaving now, he'd be taking the rest of her family with him, the whole circus would be over in a little while, there'd only be a few friends left whom she hadn't seen for years and whom she'd like to invite for a glass of wine, also the representatives of the gallery, they'd promised to buy one or two of her things, but that too would soon be over and then there'd be just the two of us.

I asked if there was anything I could do, but there wasn't, her sister had already gone to reserve two tables. I would have liked to tell her how pleased I was that the exhibition had been a success but I was somehow paralysed and she'd run off before I could pull myself together.

Her husband was still not leaving, maybe he needed to demonstrate his satisfaction. I could hear his loud, good-natured, jolly laugh. He might stroll over at any moment, slap me on the back and tell me that in spite of my gaucherie I seemed quite amusing, he'd expected worse. Indeed, he felt some sympathy with me. On top of all my problems I'd landed myself with his wife! Perhaps we should finally settle this business.

I thought I was choking in that close and stuffy space.

Outside I was surprised by the bright lights. I didn't know the small town; although we'd spent a lot of time here during the past few days we'd had no time for a walk. Now I chose a narrow street which ran steeply downhill. Somewhere in the neighbourhood there was obviously a fair: the wind carried snatches of round-about music to me and I was meeting children with coloured balloons, hooters and large puffs of candy-floss.

I used to love fairs, the sideshows of conjurers, fire-eaters and tightrope walkers, but I couldn't recall when I'd last been to one. Over the last few years I'd neglected all my interests except one, all my friends, all my near and dear ones, everybody except one. Most of all I'd neglected my work.

I wasn't satisfied with the way I was spending my life, but I couldn't blame anyone for it except myself. I'd come to the end of the little street and below me lay a wide open space. Above the merry-go-round shone a wreath of deceptive but alluring lights and the circus tent was decorated with red and blue pennants. Gigantic white swans made a pretence of noble flight.

For a moment I stopped at my slightly elevated vantage point and watched the crowd milling below me. I longed to mix with it, not to have to worry about anybody, not to think of anything, of my guilt or my lies, even of my love, not to step into anyone else's life, not to belong to anyone, to move freely and unrecognised in the crowd, to catch snatches of conversation and human faces, to dream up incidents which I would shape according to my will, to have before me something other than perpetual escapes and guilty returns.

My wife maintains that I am unable to forget my wartime experiences. They, she says, are preventing me from getting close to another person: I know I would suffer when I lost that person too, but I cannot believe that I would not lose them. I remain alone, even though I am seemingly by her side. Clearly I would remain alone by anybody's side.

I ought to be getting back, I wouldn't like to spoil my lover's day of success with my moodiness. But I went on to a shooting gallery and asked the dolled-up beauty there for an air rifle. I scored enough to win a little bear on an elastic string and a parrot made of colourful rags and feathers. As I accepted my fairground trophies it struck me that they were more appropriate to me than those exalted soaring sculptures which I'd just left behind.

One of the rubbish searchers had just caught a red flag with his hook. With a great effort he extricated it from underneath the mass of ashes and other filth, rolled it round his pole, and when he'd got it out eventually waved his wife over and together they unrolled the rag. When they'd opened it out in the wind we could see that it was really a red flag which was now flying above the mountain of garbage.

The Khmer Rouge did not fill the void in their souls with objects or with the money they so despised. They understood that the void in the soul cannot be filled even by all the objects in the world, and that was why they tried to fill that void by human sacrifices. But the emptiness of the soul cannot be filled by anything, not even if the whole of mankind were driven to the sacrificial block: the emptiness would continue, terrifying and insatiable.

Everything on earth is gradually transformed into rubbish, into refuse, which must then, in one way or another, be removed from the earth – except that nothing can be removed from it. Some time ago our jerkish newspapers reported that some Czech inventor had invented a machine for the destruction of old – that is, useless – banknotes, securities and secret documents. Abroad, the article claimed, banknotes were destroyed in crushing mills the height of a two-storey building. The compressed waste mass, however, was so dense that each kilogram of it had to be doused with half a litre of petrol before it would burn; in contrast, the Czech invention did not exceed the dimensions of a medium-sized machine tool. This splendid machine, quite possibly the invention of none other than our captain, produced a shredded mass which could then be fed by pipes into the boiler of a central heating system: thus not only was petrol saved but also a lot of precious hard coal.

Methods and machines for the efficient and economical removal of uncomfortable people from this world have of course been known for a long time.

I watched the items on the carts piling up. Although I couldn't make out any details at that distance, I suspected that they were old boots and pots, bottles and dolls rather like the ones which had floated on the sea off the Irish coast, and certainly also sacks and old blankets. Where are the days when the poor from the hovels on the outskirts of our cities didn't even have a sack to call their own, to cover their nakedness? They are behind us and they are before us.

The light breeze rose again and this time it carried to us not only the stench of the garbage but also snatches of hoarse conversation and of delighted childish shrieks. If Breughel or Hieronymus Bosch were alive now they would surely have sat here and drawn this scene. They might have added a few little figures at various points among that plastic mass, or they might have heightened the mountain so that its peak touched the heavens, and at its foot they might have placed a happy treasure seeker, a woman, a never satiated mad Margareta. What would they have called the picture? 'The Dance of Death' or, on the contrary, 'Earthly Paradise'? 'Armageddon' or just 'Dulle Griet'?

It struck me that any second now a new orange vehicle might arrive and tip out a load of skulls and bones. At just that moment those at the top of the heap were dragging out an old feather mattress and as they were trying to free it from the stranglehold of the rest of the rubbish its cover burst, and because a somewhat stronger gust of wind had just sprung up the feathers began to rise, and along with light scraps of paper and plastic and fine particles of ash began to circle in the air. The dancers underneath almost disappeared in the snowstorm, and I felt a sudden chill. Anxiously I looked at the sky to make sure the megaton cloud was not already sailing over from somewhere, but the sky still seemed clear and clean, though a chill was falling from it that made me shiver.

The Apocalypse can take different forms. The least dramatic, at first sight, is the one in which man perishes under an avalanche of useless objects, emptied words, and excessive activity. Man becomes a volcano which imperceptibly sucks up the heat from below the ground until, in an instant, it trembles and buries itself.

139

The sweepers in their orange vests go on sweeping, sweeping silently and without interest, while their brothers the dustmen cart off what has been swept into piles and thrown away. They pile those useless objects into heaps which swell, spread and disintegrate, like yeast they rise skywards, like a cancerous tumour they invade their surroundings, human habitations, so that we find it difficult to distinguish between what are still objects of our life and what are objects of our death.

Of all the garbage that swamps us and threatens us by its breath of decay, the most dangerous are the masses of discarded ideas. They tumble about us, they slide down the slopes of our lives. The souls they touch begin to wither and soon no one sees them alive again.

But those without souls do not vanish from the earth either. Their processions move through the world and subconsciously try to reshape it in their own image. They fill the streets, the squares, the stadiums and the department stores. When they burst into cheers over a winning goal, a successful pop song or a revolution it seems as if that roar would go on forever, but it is followed at once by the deathly silence of emptiness and oblivion.

They flee from that silence and seek something that would redeem it, a sacrifice they might cast on the altar of whatever demon they happen to be venerating. Now and then they'll fire a gun at random, or place a time bomb, or inject some narcotic into their veins, they'll do anything to survive that dead period before the tremor of the volcano, before the lava fills the void. The void within them.

We read Kafka's prose and we stumble over the incomprehensible. Not only are the images he employs often obscure, but they also seem to deliberately display a multitude of heterogeneous and disparate objects. We read his strictly logical narration, which often suggests a precise official memorandum, and suddenly we come across a detail or a statement which appears to have drifted in from another world, from another plot, and we are confused. In the story about the execution machine, for instance, why do some ladies' gloves suddenly appear and, without obvious reason, pass from the condemned man to the executioner and back? Why does the judge in *The Trial* hold a debt book instead of the trial papers? Why does the official in *The Castle* receive the surveyor K. in bed? What is the meaning of his absurd paean in praise of bureaucratic work? The author leads us through a savannah where, in addition to the antelopes and lions we would expect, polar bears and kangaroos are also roaming about as a matter of course.

Surely a writer as logical, as precise and as honest as Kafka must have meant something with his paradoxes, must have intended some hidden communication, must have wanted to create his own myth, his own legend about the world, some great, revolutionary message which perhaps he only surmised and was therefore unable to express clearly; he only adumbrated it, and it is up to us to decipher it and give it precise shape.

I don't know how many clever people fell into that error, for that mystery-cracking delusion, but they were numerous. I myself am convinced that Kafka did not conceal anything deliberately, that he did not construe or invent any revolutionary messages. He didn't even concern himself with them. Like most authors, like most people, he had his theme: his torments, and these imposed themselves on anything he did, thought or wrote.

His torment, however, seemed a personal thing to him, and with his shyness he sought a way of communicating it and simultaneously concealing it. Yet it was so personal that it was not enough for him to express it only in hidden form, only in metaphor; time and again he was prompted to make an open confession of the experiences which touched on the essence of his being. As if he were relating an event twice. First, at the level of imagery, he develops his bizarre and mysterious trial, he describes the execution machine, or records each separate step in the surveyor's desperate effort to get into the castle, and secondly he assembles the fragments of real experiences and events. He writes everything on translucent sheets of paper or on glass and places them one over the other. Some things supplement each other, some

141

things cover each other, some things find themselves in such surprising company that he must surely have been blissfully amazed himself. Behold, he no longer lies fatally exhausted and impotent in bed with his lover who offers him her redeeming and merciful proximity, but he finds himself, as a mortally weary surveyor, in bed with the castle official, and that man offers him his liberating bureaucratic mercy.

This must have been how that strange, mysterious world of Kafka's arose, that labyrinth in which we so easily lose our way and from which we then seek ever more complicated and elaborate ways out. A labyrinth which allures and frightens us.

We didn't go to Switzerland, we didn't even go to Kutná Hora again. The exhibition was over, and all that was left to us was the attic studio, where the view of the window of the palace opposite was still blocked by the statue of Saint Stephen the Martyr. We'd meet, sit by the low table, drink wine and talk in that strange state of enchantment which stems from the knowledge that everything we do and experience takes on new meaning and importance the moment we impart it to the person we love. In the past we loved one another with longing and with an insatiability which seemed to me unchangeable, even though she was seized by impatience now and again. Something's got to change, surely we can't spend our entire lives in such immobility, in such hopeless repetition of the same actions, we don't want to end up as two clowns who are happy if in their old age they can be walk-ons in an amateur circus performance. A bitterness has crept into her conversation. She is angry about people who don't know how to live, she rails against artists who are betraying their mission, she curses all men who are treacherous and cowardly and unable to pursue anything in their lives to its conclusion. Most frequently she is angry with my wife.

We are lying by each other's side. It is evening, an autumnal rainy twilight, we are reluctant to tear ourselves away from one another, to get up and flee into discomfort. I kiss her, once more I embrace her. She presses herself to me: suppose we both stayed here until morning?

She's testing me, and I keep silent.

Anyway, she can't understand how I can live with that person. She'd heard some things about her, about what she does to her patients, that had made her quite sick.

I don't wish to end the day with a quarrel, but nevertheless I ask what she'd heard and from whom. But she refuses to give me any details. She'd spoken to somebody who knew my wife well. He'd said that it was criminal to treat people like that.

I try to discover if this is about some drugs my wife has prescribed.

We're still lying beside one another, but she is so angry she hardly seems to know where she is. Why bring up drugs? She knew nothing about drugs. Perhaps a perverted doctor would also prescribe perverted drugs, but had my wife never told me about that revolting, humiliating play-acting those poor wretches had to go in for? How she compelled them to vomit up their intimate secrets, how she dug about in their beds? Did I really not understand that that woman was a pervert? She's unable to live for herself, unable to love, to look after a family, keep an eye on her own husband, and so she's gone in for professional do-goodery. In reality, and in this she was no different from all other do-gooders, she merely got a kick out of the suffering of others, she merely latched on to the lives of those who still managed to have real emotions and were therefore suffering. And, like a leech, she pretended to be helping them. Or did I think that a woman who for ten years or whatever couldn't tell that her husband had someone on the side, that he was living with her only out of pity, could discover anything about the souls of others?

I tell her it isn't like that at all, but she starts shouting at me that I shouldn't stand up for that person. She doesn't know why, on top of everything that I'm doing to her, she should bother about my wife's mission. She'd merely like to know if I was really so blind that I couldn't see that everything those psychologists, psychiatrists and similar psychopaths were doing was perverted, the arrogance of miserable individuals and spiritual cripples who're telling themselves that they are better than the rest?

Was she still talking about my wife?

We could leave my wife alone now, she didn't want to waste another second of her time on her. But she begs me to think about what she's told me, if only for the sake of my writing. I was unlikely to produce anything while by the side of a person who made a living out of dissecting the souls of others, as if they were rats in a laboratory, ripping out all their secrets and then trampling on them.

She has a fit of the shivers, she is transformed before my eyes. Her face which a moment earlier had seemed gentle and loving is now that of a stranger, and it frightens me.

I ought to silence her, somehow douse that flame of hate in her, or flee from it before it singes me too, but how can I flee when that flame is burning because of me?

At last I embrace her to soothe her and she curls up in my arms, she moans in ecstasy, everything drops away from her, the tenderness returns to her features: Do you at least understand that I love you, that I love you more than anything in the world, that I mean you well?

If I don't do something we'll both fall into the fire from which there will be no escape.

My darling, she insists, why won't you realise that we're made for each other? Tell me, are you happy with me?

I tell her that I am happy with her but I am aware of a tension within me, an unbearable tension pressing on my lungs so I can hardly breathe.

I walk home through the wet streets, as usual at a brisk pace. Always escaping – from whom and to whom? A place with an unmade bed and unswept floors, a place I spend so little time in that dust settles even on my desktop, my home is falling apart and I with it.

My wife enters. I feel I am in a different sphere, where no corrosive flames are flickering.

My wife is neither arrogant nor conceited, nor does she long to take possession of other people's secrets. If anything she is

144

childishly trusting. She believes hopefully in the perfectibility of things and of people, and her belief has so much determined strength in it that it can perhaps encourage also those who are on the verge of despair.

I walk up to her and embrace her. At that moment my tension vanishes, I can breathe freely.

It's nice to have you home, she says. I've been looking forward to this.

The method of effectively and economically removing human garbage from this world, in a businesslike and precise manner, in the spirit of our revolutionary age, its ideas and aims, is described in his autobiography by that super-sweeper and sacrifice master of Auschwitz, Hoess.

> The Jews earmarked for liquidation were led away to the crematoria as quietly as possible – the men in one group, the women in another... When the Jews had undressed they stepped into the gas chamber, which was equipped with showers and water pipes, so that they assumed they were entering a bath-house. First the women and children went in, and after them the men... Now and again it would happen that the women, while undressing, suddenly issued bone-chilling shrieks, they would tear their hair and act like persons demented. In that case they were led out quickly and killed by a bullet in the nape of the neck... I saw one woman trying to push her children out as they were locking the chamber, shouting amidst tears: 'At least let my dear children live!'

> The doors were swiftly screwed down and the waiting disinfecters immediately injected cyclon through openings in the roofs. It flowed down to the floor through special tubes, forming the gas instantaneously. Through a little window in the door it was possible to see how those standing nearest to these tubes fell down dead immediately. Nearly a third of the victims died instantly. Others began to push, to shout and to gasp for air. But soon the shouting turned to choking and after a few minutes they were all on the floor. No more than twenty minutes later all movement had ceased.

Hoess was a victim-maker with a burnt-out soul. He was

therefore exchangeable and replaceable, and has indeed been exchanged and replaced a great many times.

The figure of the victim maker with a burnt-out soul belongs, more than any other, to the drama of the world in a revolutionary age. To the drama in which the person who in his actions perfectly embodies emptiness and vanity, cruelty and a moral void, is granted the right to regard all those who differ from him as garbage to be swept away, garbage of which he cleanses the world.

It belongs to the drama of a world which permits the activity of victim-producing sweepers cleansing it. Of Armenians, of kulaks, of gypsies, of counter-revolutionaries, of intellectuals, of Jews, of Ibos, of Kampucheans, of priests, of blacks, of lunatics, of Hindus, of the rich, of Muslims, of the poor, of prisoners-of-war. One day, perhaps not too far away, they will cleanse it of people altogether. Their brooms are becoming ever more efficient. The Apocalypse – that is, the cleansing of the world of human beings and of life altogether – is increasingly becoming a mere technical problem.

Hoess factually describes the flames which licked up to the sky twenty-four hours a day and roasted the corpses of his victims. Those flames were so high and so bright that the anti-aircraft command lodged a complaint, and the smoke was so dense and the stench so strong that the population in the whole neighbour-hood began to panic. These reasons, he records, led to the rapid design and construction of crematoria. They built two, each with five huge furnaces, and together these were capable of incinerating two thousand murdered units, but that was not enough, so they set up another two incinerators, but even that was not enough. The largest number of persons gassed and incinerated ever achieved in one day, he records, was just under ten thousand.

That was how it was done, and looking at it purely from the technical point of view, it was a very primitive procedure. However, the human spirit has not been idle in this revolutionary age: the flames which the cleaners have at their disposal today are capable of simultaneously incinerating any number of people in their own homes.

Yet nothing has ever disappeared from this world or will disappear. The souls of the murdered, the souls of all those sacrificed, of all those burnt alive, gassed, frozen to death, shot dead, beaten to death with pickaxes, blown to smithereens, hanged or starved to death, of all the betrayed and of those torn from their mothers' wombs are rising above the land and the oceans and are filling space with their lamentations.

At first I was alarmed at my attempt to knock the great creator down from heaven to earth. But I don't believe that this can be done. Our heavens, after all, are linked to our earth. Anyone who pretends that he knows other heavens, more exalted ones, has lost contact with people. How can anyone unable to relate to the person he loves expect to relate to those he does not love? Kafka realised this, and to stand by the side of the woman he loved meant to him standing by the side of people, becoming one of them, participating in their order. In his honesty he also realised what a difficult and exhausting task he'd set himself. That drawing close to another being, accepting another being as well as another order meant the surrender of freedom. He wrote about how he was failing to attain his objective and how in doing so he was hurting and betraying the woman he loved, and that thereby he'd committed a crime.

A lawyer by training, he wrote about one single case. He himself prepared the evidence for his own prosecution, he defended himself passionately, and mercilessly found himself guilty.

He never abandoned his theme, but by living it through himself, completely and truthfully, he managed to embrace both the heights and the depths of life. We are not therefore in error if we look for them and find them in his writings.

From below the mountain another flock of crows started up, darkening the sky and making the air vibrate with the beat of their wings. The birds alighted around the treasure-hunters who'd by then finished their work. But it didn't seem that the two groups took any notice of one another.

One of the men looked down towards us and called out

something I couldn't make out. Immediately the others also started shouting at us. I could see my wife was beginning to be afraid. 'What are they shouting?'

I couldn't make it out. Most probably they were offering to start trading with us.

'Do you want to go over to them?'

She was prepared to go over to them with me, even though she was afraid of them. She'd been trying, at least over the past few years, to indulge my wishes and even my eccentric ideas. She raised no objections to my having been an orange-clad street-sweeper for several months now, although she must have wondered uneasily whether some ulterior motive, or at least a wish to escape from home, was not perhaps concealed behind my occupation. Sometimes when I got back home I felt a note of uncertainty in her question of how I was. Suppose she suspected me of doing something different from what I said I was doing? She had plenty of reasons to distrust me, but neither now nor in the past had she dared ask me straight out. She regarded distrust as something unworthy, something that soiled whoever let it enter their minds.

I realised how often I'd betrayed her confidence in the past. I felt a shaming sense of guilt as well as a need to compensate for it somehow. For a start I said that it was a lovely day, that we'd done well to get out into the country. It sounded a little paradoxical, standing as we were below the mountain of garbage.

Back home our daughter and little grand-daughter were waiting for us. Our son, too, sat down to dinner with us. He'd long been trying to find a place of his own and as always he had a multitude of carefully worked-out plans which, he hoped, would lead him to his objective, whereas our daughter, as always, was giving no thought to her future. There were times when she felt that everything, absolutely everything, still lay ahead of her, while at other times she felt that everything, absolutely everything, lay behind her, that there was nothing left to her but to live out her days — as tolerably as possible. For the most part, however, she gave herself joyfully to the moment. After dinner she wanted to draw me. She cut some large sheets out of wrapping paper, pinned one of them to a stiff folder, and made me sit in an armchair for a long time.

From the kitchen came the clatter of plates, there was the muted sound of my son's tape recorder, and my grand-daughter could be heard through the wall delightedly recounting some feeble-minded incident she'd seen on our jerkish television. I asked if I might close my eyes and my daughter, having warned me that this would make me look like my own deathmask, agreed. At least I wouldn't fidget.

From outside came the smell of the sea and a wave licked up the sandy beach.

Hold on a little longer!

Her fingers were moving swiftly in the sand. How I love those beautiful fingers which so often touch me with tenderness and which, moreover, know how to turn shapelessness into shape.

I don't know if this is my likeness, I'm never sure of my own shape. I have an animal body and the wings of a swan, but I look happy.

Because you are happy, she explains. Or aren't you happy with me?

Aren't you afraid that the water will carry me away at night?

That's why I've given you wings, so you can fly away. You have wings so you can be free, so you can go wherever you please. By this she meant: so I could get to her at any time. But the water washed me away, complete with wings, and did not carry me to her, the water has its age-old pattern and rarely departs from it.

The charcoal swishes across the paper, the tape now sounds louder, my son's left the door of his room open. The year before we'd visited him in the provincial town where he was then doing his military service; we'd set out on Saturday morning, we'd decided to put up at a hotel and return on Sunday evening, but Lída had a headache and left early on her own, and I stayed on at the hotel alone. On Sunday morning the bus took me to the barracks where our son was waiting for us at the gates. I thought that he looked quite good in uniform, even though I'm not too fond of uniforms.

He asked me where I'd like to go, but I left it to him to decide: he knew his way around here better than me.

So he took me up some hill where Těsnohlídek was reported to have walked, along a cemetery wall with slender yews standing upright behind it, and down a farm track. The weather was cool and windy, around the birches by the track blew small leaves like flakes of coloured snow.

My son spoke about his experiences in the army, then he shyly mentioned that his girlfriend had visited him here too, and hastily returned to military matters. We were in no hurry with our conversation, we had the whole day before us. I couldn't recall when we had last spent a whole day together, if indeed I ever found that much time in the course of a single day. It seemed to me that my son was suddenly emerging from the dark or returning from a great distance. I'd spent time with so many people, I'd spent days and weeks with my lover, while my son was a fleeting figure in the evening or in the morning or at Sunday lunches. Of course he sat in the room sometimes, along with other guests, listening silently or perhaps coming over for a few words with me – most often about political events or about his classes, never about his personal worries or hopes, and as a rule I'd sit down at my desk after a while and thereby dismiss him. He'd also invite me to listen to protest songs which he'd recorded and which he was sure would interest me, and I'd either decline or else soon doze off while listening to them.

I knew that he had identified with my destiny to such an extent that, even though he'd studied engineering, he was closely – indeed more closely than I – following the fate of literature, at least in the part of the world we lived in, and he'd think up plans for making banned works known to the public, and took delight in any indication, however slight, of a turn for the better.

I regretted that for so long, for whole years on end, I'd never managed to find more time and interest for what made up his life. I now questioned him about his friends, about his girl, and about what he thought about the future. I could see that my interest pleased him, and it occurred to me that he might feel as lonely as I had at his age.

I decided to invite him out for a special meal, but when we got to the tavern all they had was cheap salami, bread and onions. At least I ordered some wine. Our conversation was leaping from one event to another, the most essential things we continued to carry locked up within us. It is difficult to voice the feelings a father and son have for each other. My father had also been unable to do it, we'd never talked about anything too personal. What we did talk about provided no opportunity for him to show any emotions whatever. I knew that he was childishly proud of what he regarded as my literary successes. But he never commented on what I had written.

My bus was leaving in the evening. Peter was sorry I had to go so soon, he was off duty until midnight. I asked him what he would do with the rest of the evening. He said he'd go to the cinema or else return to the barracks and listen to the radio or read. I gave him a little spending money, and because it was getting chilly I got on the bus.

My son stood motionless outside, waiting. I noticed that the frosty wind was bending over even the trunks of sturdy saplings, but my son was still waiting. He looked up at the little window behind which he saw my face, he stood there in a strange uniform, cast into a strange world, and waited faithfully for us to move off. Then, because the bus circled the square, he ran over to the other side so that I caught sight of him once more, standing on the stone surround of the fountain, close to the roadway, waving.

Then I was alone. The bus hurtled through the dark of the forest and I closed my eyes, but even in that double darkness I could see the figure of my son carved out of the stony greyness of strange houses, I could see him standing there, separated from me by impervious material, but at least waving to me. At that moment I was gripped with unease at my own doings, at my double life, from which loyalty had disappeared, to be replaced by pretence and betrayal.

My son was an adult now, and if I left home it shouldn't have any fatal effect on him. At least that's what is accepted nowadays. A child remains the child of his parents, just as his parents remain his parents, even though their paths may divide. Surely parents are entitled to their own emotions, to their own lives, at least when their children have grown up. But is it conceivable that my departure for good would not strike a blow to his notions of loyalty, his faith in the fellow-feeling of his nearest and dearest, his concept of home?

'You may wriggle now,' my daughter said. She was looking quizzically at her production.

'Did it come out as a deathmask?' I wanted to know.

'Somehow it isn't you at all,' she complained, and held the sheet out to me.

'I don't know. How can I know what I look like when my eyes are closed?'

But for a deathmask there was still too much life in my features.

Dad had never been ill in his life. A year ago he started losing weight and stopped enjoying his food. Then they found a malignant tumour in his colon and decided to operate at once. I took him to hospital the day before his operation. I sought out the surgeon and tried to explain to him that although Dad was nearly eighty his mental faculties hadn't been affected by age, and his students still came to him for help when they were stumped by some complicated problem.

The surgeon was short and plump. In his white coat and cap he looked more like a chef than a medical man. He listened to me politely, as he must have listened to many similar persuasive speeches, he accepted my envelope with money, and assured me that he'd do anything in his power, I might get in touch with him the following day, about lunchtime.

Lída thought that I should stay at the hospital during the operation. Dad would feel that I was close by, and that would be reassuring for him and would perhaps make waiting easier for me.

I drove over to the hospital first thing in the morning. I was in time to see Dad on the trolley, as he was waiting in the corridor outside the theatre. From the distance it seemed to me that he was smiling and very slightly raising a hand to acknowledge he'd seen me.

Then I sat down a little way beyond reception, in a dim corridor where orderlies were ceaselessly wheeling trolleys to and fro, and new patients were walking past. There was so much bustle there that I couldn't concentrate on my father.

An hour later I was informed that the operation had not yet begun.

I phoned my wife to tell her I was staying on at the hospital, and she tried to reassure me, I shouldn't worry, the operation was sure to be successful, Dad had a strong constitution – he'd even survived the death march just before the end of the war.

I also rang my lover, just to hear her voice, to tell her where I was, and that most probably there wouldn't be time for me to come and see her.

Only a short while later I caught sight of her, passing through reception with her rapid step. She kissed me. She brought me a gingerbread angel she'd baked for Saint Nicholas's, and a twig with yellow witch-hazel flowers. She'd managed to just break it off from somewhere.

The waiting room had emptied after lunchtime and we sat down on a bench. She took my hand in hers and said: He'll be all right, I can feel it. His time hasn't come yet.

Then we were silent. I seemed to see a white corridor before me, I couldn't see all the way down to its end, and a trolley was moving along it. Dad was lying on it, white and unconscious and moving away from me. What does a man feel, what does a man think, when he is firmly convinced that there is no other life than the one that's just then threatening to slip away from him? What hopes does he have at his age? His own fear got a fierce hold on me. I got up and went to ask if the operation was finished but I was told that it wasn't, I had to be patient.

I returned to the waiting room. I could see my lover in the

distance, but she was taking no notice of me, she sat there as if turned into stone, as if removed from her own body. When I walked over to her she looked up at last and it seemed to me that I could see pain in her features. It's all right now, she said. It looked bad, but it's all right now, they're sewing him up now.

She took my hand and led me along the corridor to the exit. Outside large autumnal snowflakes were falling; they lay on the ground only briefly and then melted. We went into the little park behind the hospital, and she was talking to me softly. She said that man spent only an insignificant portion of time in this life, in the shape we know him. What is important is that he should spend it well and fully, because that would decide which way he went on. I was unable to concentrate properly on what she was saying, instead I just took in the timbre of her voice, her comforting, loving presence.

I had told her many times that I loved her, that I was very fond of her. Now I didn't tell her anything, but that moment entered into me forever: the bedraggled park with a few rain-wet trees, her proximity, her voice, and her hand which was pressing mine.

And if we are ever to be so far apart that we can no longer reach out to each other, that our voices are seemingly lost in the distance, and this will undoubtedly happen, she is now so firmly embedded in me that if ever she groans in pain or fear I shall hear her, no matter where I am at the time. And if I'm alive I shall go to her to repay her for at least this pressure of her hand.

We returned to the hospital. The surgeon received me. The tumour had been a bad one, and neglected, but it was out now. My father was now sleeping.

I spotted the youngster the moment we entered the hall. He was standing below the stage and talking to one of the musicians. He was wearing jeans and a pullover with a Norwegian pattern. Perhaps it was the artificial light but he seemed to me even paler, more drawn, more sick than usual. I introduced him to Lída. She said she was glad to meet him, I'd told her a lot about him. She was also looking forward to the concert, it was good of him to have thought of us.

The youngster unexpectedly blushed and hurriedly rattled off the names of the composers and the compositions we were about to hear, he also told us the names of the clarinettist and the drummer, and we went off to look for our seats.

'Isn't he very sick?' my wife asked as we sat down.

I told her what I knew about his illness and also that there was possibly a drug available abroad that might help him, but that it was too expensive for it to be prescribed.

'And couldn't you get it for him?' she asked in surprise.

The music began. I am a bad listener, I can't concentrate even on the spoken word let alone on music. Lída, on the other hand, responds to tones with her whole being. I could see the music entering into her and arousing in her a pleasurable astonishment, taking her out of the not-too hospitable tavern's dance hall.

I too could hear at least the echoes of primordial rhythms and glimpse the reflections of tribal fires around which half-naked dancers of both sexes were whirling.

When the first missionaries in Africa saw those painted and masked savages prancing round their fire they thought they had just glimpsed something akin to a ritual from hell. In reality, of course, what they saw were the last remnants of paradise. Those dancers may have been troubled by evil spirits, hunger or drought, but they were not weighed down by any sinful past or a retributory judgement in the future; the vision of the Apocalypse did not rise before them. They were still in the childhood of mankind.

I have never set foot on the black continent, but when I had some time to spare in St Louis, where I'd been invited for the opening night of a play of mine, I got on a tourist excursion steamer down the Mississippi, and there was a black band playing on board. A colourful company was celebrating something, I don't know if it was a wedding, the birth of an heir or somebody's saint's day, or the fact that a manned spacecraft was then on the way to the moon which their not-too-distant ancestors may have revered as a deity, but I could feel that close to them, and under the influence of their music, I was slipping into another, more carefree and less knowing age.

This mood persisted even the following day when, at the home of the producer who, like me, was a native of Prague, we watched the television screen in the evening and I saw those strange bulky figures bouncing with light steps about the wasteland of the moon, while from the street came delighted cheers; I thought then that man, as the newspapers put it, had really got closer to heaven. It seemed to me that mankind was entering upon a new era full of promise. Not until some time later did I realise that the opposite was the case: mankind had reached out into the regions of eternal cold and had finally moved away from the place where the Garden of Eden was once situated.

During the interval the youngster came over to us, and because my wife knows more about music than I do I let them talk to each other while I went to the bar to get ourselves something to drink.

When I got back towards the end of the intermission the youngster was about to leave for his place just below the stage. My wife took a glass of juice, took a sip, and before the musicians started up again told me what she'd learned from the youngster about his life; needless to say, she'd learned more in those few minutes than I had in several weeks. His father, it appeared, had left his mother before he was even born, and because the mother was a little odd he grew up in children's homes. His mother was now dead and his only relative was a stepbrother with whom he didn't get on. She'd guess that the youngster was a sensitive boy but, because of his circumstances, had never completely grown up, almost certainly also because in his life he hadn't yet met a man with whom he wished to identify. I ought to bear this in mind, maybe he'd attach himself to me.

I couldn't think why the youngster should want to attach himself to me of all people, but I promised to watch out.

The master of ceremonies announced the next composition, a Gershwin medley. The musicians started up. At one point the clarinettist on the stage made use of a brief pause, held his instruments out towards the audience, motioned to someone, and a moment later we saw the youngster jumping up onto the stage and taking the clarinet.

'Surely that's him,' Lída said in surprise. She doesn't see too well at a distance and moreover she has a poor memory for faces.

From his borrowed instrument the youngster conjured up the glissando which opens the first theme of the 'Rhapsody in Blue'. I could see his pasty face turn red, either with excitement or with the effort.

My wife went off to the mountains for a week's skiing with our daughter and grand-daughter, but I didn't want to leave Dad for so long and therefore stayed behind at home. Only on one day did I go out into the country with my lover. She led me to some sandstone rocks where an anonymous sculptor had over the decades carved out statues of saints, knights and the Czech kings, as well as a lion which towered massively on a rocky ledge. We climbed up narrow icy chimneys and descended on steeply-cut steps. Half-hidden by the fir trunks and raspberry thickets we discovered ever new sculptures. I could see that she was touched and also amazed by the intensity of the creative will of some unknown person who, either not caring for an audience or, on the contrary, full of confidence in his own work, had imposed his visions on these lonely rocks.

I was curious whether it would amuse her to create a similar gallery for herself.

She said she preferred gardens, parks, the sea, and wide open spaces. And she preferred ordinary people to saints.

And whom did she regard as ordinary people?

Everybody else. Saintliness had been invented by those who were afraid of life and real emotions. That's why they elevated ecstatic rapture to something we should look up to, to something we should regard as a model.

And if she was given the kind of space she wanted, a garden by the seashore, what would she adorn it with?

She was taken aback by my question. She hadn't thought about it. Certainly with nothing that might give a person a sense of his own poverty, inadequacy or sinfulness.

We found a room for the night in a small hotel; it was built before the war and its tall windows reached almost down to the floor.

Of course there's something sacred in everyone, she added. She wasn't thinking of that contrived ecstasy, that baroque gesture, but of something untouchable and unportrayable, the human soul. At moments of enlightenment a person could catch a glimpse of it within himself, he could see his own face as others couldn't see it. If she were given a garden she'd like to fill it with such shapes that those who came to look at them might see themselves, the way they saw themselves at such an illuminated instant.

What shapes would they be?

The most natural ones. As in that Prévert poem:

> And it may happen to a sweeper
> as he waves
> his dirty broom
> about without a hope
> among the dusty ruins
> of a wasteful colonial exhibition
> that he halts amazed
> before a remarkable statue
> of dried leaves and blooms
> representing we believe
> dreams
> crimes celebrations lightning
> and laughter and again longing
> trees and birds
> also the moon and love and sun and death . . .

All of a sudden she burst into tears.

I asked her to tell me what she was crying about.

Nothing, nothing, she sobbed. There wouldn't be any point in talking about it anyway. She'd merely been reminded of death.

Not by that poem, but earlier on, among the rocks. She attempted a smile: even though the fortune teller had told her she'd live to be eighty-seven, and the lifeline on my palm was also long, one day it must come, and then we wouldn't be meeting any more, no matter where our souls moved, no matter what fate awaited them.

I embraced her as if trying to carry her in my arms over that river of oblivion which would indubitably divide us for all time. Simultaneously we were looking at the window beyond which lay the rocky hills. In a kind of ecstasy we pressed ourselves to each other, and we also observed that from an invisible sky snow was now falling. You belong to me, regardless, she whispered as she fell asleep. You really want to stay with me only.

And I said nothing, even though that evening I wanted to be with her, to stay with her, to shield her from the icy waters whose roar I'd managed to hear myself at a moment of total silence. But who'd stay with my wife, who'd embrace her in the silence which would enfold her? To whom would she turn when fear gripped her?

The other woman, who cursed me again and again, was now asleep. She was here with me, I could still touch her, still hold her tight, but instead I was in full flight, fleeing backwards, in a hopeless desire to return I was wandering blindly through landscapes which were ever more parched, where life had ceased, where not a single human being was to be seen, until it dawned on me that I was not blundering about any roads back, but going forward in time, and that any moment now I'd catch sight of that river. But I stopped, I was still able to stop. And at that moment I understood that it wouldn't be a river that divided us, but myself. And if I were the man she wanted me to be, the man I wanted to be myself, I'd now wake her and tell her that I was leaving: God bless you, my dearest, there's no other way, I can't decide otherwise, much as I love you, you most loving of women. But I didn't do it. From that moment onward, therefore, I was no longer just lying to my wife, I was also lying to her and to myself, every time that I left home to see her, that I embraced her, that I moaned with pleasure.

And I condemned myself to silence. At the moment when she turned to me full of trust and love, and also at the moment when she overwhelmed me with reproaches, when she asked me for an answer, for pity or at least for hope – all I could do was keep silent. I condemned myself to silence, which gradually turned into a river, into the river we were both getting closer to, but which has now spread within me so that I can no longer hear it outside.

The youngster finished his part and handed the clarinet back to its owner. Somebody clapped, my wife clapped too, the youngster bowed awkwardly; when he jumped down from the stage his face was back to its usual pallor.

The concert was over. The people around us were pushing towards the exit. It had got cold outside, and a brilliant full moon stood in the cloudless sky.

To us, who'd stayed behind on earth, the astronaut Aldrin said then:

I'd like to take this opportunity to ask every person listening in, whoever and wherever they may be, to pause for a moment and contemplate the events of the past few hours, and to give thanks in his or her way!

IV

◆

Autumn is well advanced, the streets are full of dry leaves which add to our work, from the houses fly tired unenthusiastic flags, public buildings are displaying streamers with jerkish slogans which would undoubtedly please any chimpanzees that might happen along. Luckily we don't have to pick up any of this colourful textile rubbish: flags and slogans are put up and taken down by special motorised squads.

A little way short of the beflagged Palace of Culture we met our now familiar uniformed pair. The foppish one looked a little wilted, he'd probably come on duty after a heavy night; his companion seemed unchanged.

'Bloody mess, isn't it?' the fop addressed us, pointing vaguely ahead.

'People are pigs,' the foreman agreed. 'Hey, what about the murderer?' he remembered. 'Got him yet?'

'Signed, sealed and delivered,' the fop said casually; 'the lads did a good job.'

'Name of George,' his companion explained.

'George who?' the foreman asked curiously.

'Would you believe it, he was a juvenile,' the fop yawned. 'Introduced himself to a girl he wanted to strangle as George from Kladno. But he made a mistake there; she got away from him.'

'Told her he was a mining apprentice,' the fair one added.

'Yeah. Our lads chased up all the Georges who were mining apprentices, though they realised it might have been a trick.'

'That's right,' our youngster sounded pleased. 'And was it?'

'Course it wasn't. The man was simple! Know how many women he raped? Go on, you tell him,' he encouraged his companion.

'Sixteen!'

'And they identified him beyond any doubt.'

'And he was a mining apprentice?' the foreman voiced his astonishment.

'I'm telling you he was simple. Fellow like that commits one murder, and then has to go on. Things ain't what they used to be – mining being an honourable job!' The fop yawned broadly. 'Still no pantaloons?' he turned to the captain.

'After my death!' the captain snapped. But maybe I misheard him and he really said: 'Save your breath!'

The fop didn't even laugh this time. He nodded to his companion and the two continued down the road.

Mrs Venus pushed her shovel into my hand and grabbed the cart. With her free hand she immediately produced a cigarette and lit it. Her eyes were wet with tears. As we were tipping the rubbish into the cart I asked if anything had happened to her.

She looked at me as if deciding what lay hidden behind my inquiry: 'Happened? Why should anything've happened to me? Only the old gent died.'

It took me a while to work out whom she was talking about. 'The one on your passage?'

'Well, he was eighty, so he died!' She flicked her fag-end into the dustbin on the handcart and lit another. To change the subject away from death she pointed to the palace: 'They say they found a gypsy buried in the concrete there!'

'You're telling me,' the foreman was angry; 'I've got a chum working in the garages there. Last month they came along with pneumatic drills and started to knock down the wall. And d'you know who they were looking for? That woman singer from the National Theatre, the one who went missing eight years ago.'

'Did they find her?' I ask.

'They found bugger-all. Their drills all got screwed up!'

'It's a monstrosity,' the captain gave the palace its proper description. 'They can drive a million people inside, they switch the radiation on and they've turned them into a million sheep!' At the thought of it he spat mightily. 'One day someone will set fire to it,' he added prophetically, 'and good luck to him!'

At that moment a suspicion grew inside me about the direction of his latest dreams.

Winter that year was severe. The sky remained blue and cold, the frozen snow crunched underfoot and the air stank so revoltingly that one regretted not being a fish. I went to see Dad nearly every day, he was picking up rapidly. He was once more working on his calculator. Don't you go thinking that I'm written off, he said to me, and immersed himself in his world of numbers, where he felt most at home, and was pleased at the thought of the many machines he would design yet. Sometimes, however, he'd put on his fur-lined coat and go out with me to walk down the chilly ugly street. The fate of the world had not ceased to interest him. He confided his fears and disappointments to me. It grieved him that socialism had not brought freedom to the people and that technology had not lightened their drudgery but was instead threatening them with annihilation. We stopped at the dairy. Here Dad thawed out and was rejuvenated because the pretty girl behind the counter smiled at him pleasantly, asked him how he was getting on and assured him that he was looking wonderful. Dad at any rate still believes that women are good creatures. Sympathetic and worthy of attention and love. He'd have gone on chatting to the dairy girl, but I was in a hurry to get to my own good creature.

We'd had to abandon the attic studio with its view of the palace opposite, and we now met in her basement workshop, where – long, long ago – I'd first set eyes on her. From outside the window came the continuous footsteps of strangers passing by and from the corners came a smell of mildew and mould. On the stone floor stood a storage heater. It was only seven years younger than me and just as stubborn, sometimes it worked and at others, for unfathomable reasons, it didn't switch itself on at night at all. Fortunately the thick medieval walls stopped the place from freezing up completely.

She is waiting for me. She hasn't even taken off her coat but her lips are hot. Again she presses herself to the tepid metal shell of the heater and I hurry to make some tea while she tells me her news. Listening to her I feel that the incidents I look for in vain are all homing in on her, all her encounters seem to have a special and higher meaning, something essential to tell her, to open, at least in part, a view into the infinite spaces of other people's inner lives.

As she speaks I watch a little cloud of her living breath rising from her mouth. The room is in semi-darkness which obliterates even those little lines which I would probably not have seen anyway with my long-sighted eyes. She seems to me tenderly and soulfully beautiful. I know that I still love her and I suspect that she must love me too if she's staying with me in this inhospitable and cold basement.

She notices my glance and presses herself against me – together we slip into the icy bed. But her body is warm, we cling to each other, ecstasy blots out the outside world, at this moment it doesn't matter where we are, we are in the seclusion of our love and we know that there isn't a palace in the world whose solitude we would exchange for this place of joint occupation.

Her slight body ceaseless rears against mine, she trembles with delight, her eyes grow misty. Devoutly she begs me not to leave her, again and again she wants me, she knows no respite in love-making any more than in her work, any more than in anything she undertakes, she sweeps me along like a vortex, she rouses in me a strength I never suspected I had. My head spins, I am in ecstasy, I am on earth solely for this moment, for this action.

Yet even so the moment must come when we are exhausted, when the chill that's seeping from the floor and the walls gets between us, enters her eyes. I know that she's asking herself how long I intend to make love to her without giving her any hope, without finding a solution which would bring her out of her icy loneliness. But she only asks what I'm going to do tonight.

I say that I will work, even though I know that my answer will seem unsatisfactory to her if I don't decide to stay with her. I want to know what she'll be doing.

Why should I care? I wasn't going to stay with her anyway, after all, there was my wife waiting for me at home, I have to be with her, act the part of the faithful loving husband, create an atmosphere of home. Yes, of course, I also had to work, make money so I could keep the lady, my wife, in appropriate style. Also I mustn't forget to buy something for dinner so she needn't put herself out, and bring her a little present so she should know what a fine model husband she has. All she wants to know now is why she should plunge with me into this sacchariney sticky filthy mess of ours? She curses the moment when I crossed her path. Why didn't I say something, why didn't I at least speak up in my defence?

I reached out for my cold shirt and she screamed that I should push off, that I should get back as fast as possible to that sacred cow of mine who has ruined her life. She'll still try to save herself, to dig herself out of the shit I have dragged her into.

Outside, darkness had fallen, and its icy maw swallowed us up instantly. The snow had turned grey and seemed to collapse under our feet. We got to the metro station and she asked: When shall I see you?

As always, Hope was looking down on us from her stone plinth with her invariably gentle, even warm, smile.

Tomorrow I have to take Dad to the doctor. How about the day after?

She took hold of both my hands: I really won't see you all day tomorrow?

Shortly before nine — we were just getting ready to put our tools into the dustbin recess by the supermarket and to make for the tavern, as was appropriate at that time of day — a garbage truck pulled up alongside us and out jumped Franta, the little idiot. His forage cap at a rakish angle, a red kerchief round his neck, he treated us all to a smile. The foreman walked up towards him but Franta, before saying anything, produced a packet of Benson & Hedges from his pocket, holding it out first to Mrs Venus, then to the foreman and then, one by one, to the rest of us. Only then did he take the foreman aside and talk to him for a while. I could clearly hear him uttering some barely articulated screeches in his castrato's falsetto.

'Coo, wasn't he ponged up,' Mrs Venus hardly restrained herself the moment Franta had driven off in the direction of the Pankrác prison. 'Must have done a chemist's somewhere. And a tobacconist's too,' she added, remembering the golden pack.

'I don't like it!' The foreman was staring after the vanished garbage truck as if expecting some message from that direction.

I wanted to know what he didn't like, but he didn't like anything: neither the cigarette, nor the kerchief, nor the unexpected visit.

'Did he say anything to you?' I wanted to know.

'What can he say? D'you think he can talk?' The foreman retrieved his shovel from the recess. 'That shit's getting ready for some hanky-panky. We'd better not go anywhere, we'll have our beer on the hoof!'

The youngster set out to get some beer from the supermarket and I joined him, I said I'd get a snack for myself. Mrs Venus asked us to get her her favourite cigarettes, while the captain wanted a box of matches.

'I'm somehow half-croaked,' the youngster was all hunched up as if shaken by the shivers. 'But last night, have you heard?'

There'd been a real New Orleans band performing in Prague, hardly anyone knew about it, it wasn't a public performance, but he'd managed to get in. 'You should have heard them! The pianist they had, a real second Scott Joplin, and the stuff they played! At the end they asked us if we'd like to jam with them. Think of it, them and us!' The youngster's cheeks were flushed with excitement. He stopped at the entrance to the supermarket and demonstrated how one of his friends had strummed on a dolly-board. 'I couldn't stop myself and tried to blow a little, but I had a sick turn. Surely this must stop some time, don't you think?'

I said I was sure it would, he just had to be patient.

'I can join the boys whenever I like,' he said. 'We were a happy crew. You saw for yourself how they let me play the solo in the Gershwin.'

'You played superbly.'

'You really can't play it otherwise. I imagine that when he composed it he was thinking of something noble, something . . .' he was vainly searching for a word, 'it should actually sound like music from heaven.'

Our daughter told my wife and me about a dream she'd had. She was walking in the forest with her husband when they heard strange soft music. They stepped out onto a clearing and there they saw a tall naked Negro blowing a golden trumpet. The trumpet was so bright it illuminated the whole clearing, filled it with so much light that objects were losing their shadows. Suddenly from all sides brilliantly coloured birds came flying in, perhaps they were humming birds, also parrots and birds of paradise, she'd never seen such birds in the flesh. But her husband noticed that there was a swing hanging between some branches. He sat her on it and then disappeared somewhere. But the swing began to swing on its own accord, the music was still there, a kind of music she'd never heard before. She looked about, trying to discover where it came from, but couldn't see a single musician. It was then that she realised that the music was coming straight out of the ground, that the stones were humming and the trees singing like some gigantic violin. In the clearing stood some naked people, among whom she also recognised us, and on the shoulders, the heads and the extended fingers of everyone those magnificent brightly coloured birds were perching. She was naked too, but she didn't feel ashamed because she was still quite small. At that moment one of the coloured birds approached and sat on her hand. Its plumage had colours she'd never seen before. She was also aware of a delicious perfume she'd never smelled before, and it was then she understood that she was in paradise.

'And what seemed to you most beautiful in that dream?' my wife wanted to know.

Our daughter thought for a moment and then said: 'That I was a little girl again.'

Daria attributed my loneliness and reluctance to attach myself to anyone to the stars. I am a saturnian person, my Saturn is in fact retrograde and capricornian, there was a smell of bones coming straight out of it. Love alone could liberate me from my loneliness: real love, embracing my whole being. That was the kind of love she was offering me, to save me. She offered me her proximity, such sharing that I became alarmed. Man is afraid to attain what he longs for, just as subconsciously he longs for what he is afraid of. We are afraid we might lose the person we love. To avoid losing that person we drive him or her away.

She wanted us, at least once in a while, to be together for a few days. At least some movement, some change to that immobility, she lamented. Just one evening when we didn't have to say goodbye! But I resisted so I shouldn't have to invent more lies at home – I'd find that distasteful to the point of being sickened.

And to keep silent about what you're doing doesn't make you sick? Such craven weakness, such hypocrisy. What kind of life are you living! It's all so miserable and vile!

I couldn't think of an excuse. I tried to placate her with presents.

I don't want you to buy me. I want you to love me!

I do love her, but I can't go on like this. I'd like to find some conciliation – with her and with all those I am fond of, but I can't muster the courage to reveal the truth to all of them. And she keeps urging me more and more often: When will you finally make up your mind? Have you no pity at all?

For whom?

For yourself. For me! How can you treat me like this? She cries.

Her husband has gone away. She has remained behind for a week, entirely on her own. One day she'll be entirely alone with only her stones, they are more merciful than me. What kind of life had I made for her? she cries. Well then, so lie for my sake if you can't speak the truth for my sake!

At home I say that I'm off to visit a friend whose daughter is getting married.

A good idea, my wife says, you're always at home on your own, at least it'll make a change for you. And she begins to wonder what present I should take along for my friend's daughter. And she'll bake me a guggelhupf cake for the journey.

But there'll be plenty of food at the wedding! And we kiss goodbye. It's shameful. How can I treat her like this!

We arrived at a chalet in the foothills. In the small wood-panelled hall tropical plants are growing and lianas climbing, even though spring has not yet come outside, a black terrier is lying lazily and devotedly by the feet of the woman guarding the door. I stiffen as I show her my identity card, which proves me guilty, but the receptionist cares little about other people's infidelities, she has her own worries and my lover inspires confidence in her. Indeed the two women chat together as if they'd known one another for years, while the terrier on the floor regards me without interest as I wait in this strange hall like a faithful unfaithful dog.

Our room looks out on the lake. For a while we gaze at the deserted water, then we embrace. She wants to know if I like it here, if I'm glad to be here with her. I assure her that I do and that I am. At our moments of ecstasy we whisper to each other, as we have done for years, that we love one another.

Before supper we set out for a walk. We stroll round the lake and continue through the woods until we find ourselves on a wide piece of flat ground in the midst of which, as in a dream, stands an extensive wooden construction: a pattern of roofs, turrets, silos and metal hoppers. Probably a stone-crushing mill or a building for the shredding of old banknotes, securities and secret documents, all brought here by the lorries which are now parked in the deserted yard. We don't see a living soul anywhere, only a few rooks cawing from beneath a tall wooden tower. For a while we stand waiting, in case a face appears in one of the windows, or somebody yells at us to get out of here. She is also anxiously looking about in case some vision appears from somewhere in the darkness, but nothing happens, except for the wind making a half-open door creak now and then. We step through that door. In the vestibule, where everything is covered with a layer of grey dust, towers the metallic bulk of some machinery. The huge motionless wheels glisten greasily in the twilight. We climb some rusting iron stairs, up to a boarded platform above the machinery. Through a narrow window we can see the woods and beyond them part of the lake, now darkening in the fading light. Across the sky float drink-sodden faces with reddish noses. Through the cracks in the walls or in the roof rustles the wind. Do you still love me at all? she asks. She takes off her coat and her soft leather skirt and lays them down on the blackened boards, we make love on the platform of the abandoned mill.

The dusk is obliterating her features. I see her now as I saw her when we first met. I feel as though I were returning to those days, or rather as though I was outside any definite time. With her I am outside anything, and that emptiness bewitches me. I am tossed by the waves, I rise up in my net so high that I can see absolutely nothing from it.

The floorboards are creaking, the wind is rattling some loose corrugated iron, but these sounds merely heighten the silence in here, the absolute isolation. I say tender words to her and she replies to me. Then we just lie by each other in the darkness. I am conscious of the familiar scent of her body and the smell of stone and timber, and suddenly it hits me that I know this enclosure, that I've been here before. I feel the icy touch of fear, even though I have probably only been reminded of the wooden huts in the fortress ghetto of my childhood, or perhaps of the wooden floors of the barracks to which I was forcibly confined, and where death reigned. At just this moment I have to think of death!

My uneasiness won't go, we make love again, I clutch her to myself in the darkness of this seclusion, in my own ecstasy, I press myself to her, grateful that she is here with me, that she has climbed up with me to this spot which is more suggestive of some elevated hell, where the bones of sinners are ground to dust, than a place intended for love-making.

Out of the blue she asks: Do you also make love with your wife?

Her question snatches me back into the present.

I don't want you to sleep with another woman, I want you to be with me alone! She draws away from me. Do you hear what I'm saying?

I hear her. What am I to say? How can I chase away her question, how can I chase her away, she who's lying next to me, when she wants nothing but that I accept the consequences of the fact that I am embracing her, that I've been embracing her for quite a few years now, that I call her to me and that I hasten to her whenever she calls. The meanness of my situation and my behaviour overwhelms me and stifles all the words within me.

She pushes me away, gets up hurriedly, dusts down her skirt and dresses. For a while she rummages in her bag, then strikes a match and runs down the creaking stairs. Tell me, who do you think you are? she asks when we are back in our room. You think I have to take everything from you, you think I couldn't find another man like you? Maybe she really couldn't find another man who'd treat her the way I do, she adds, who'd treat her like a slut from the streets.

I never ask her how she lives with her husband, but now I say that, after all, she isn't living on her own either.

What did I mean by that? The fact that she had a husband suited me very well. If she were on her own I'd have dumped her long ago, I'd be afraid for my splendid marriage.

A few weeks ago we were at the cinema together. In the interval she noticed that in the row in front of us sat her husband with a strange woman. From that moment onwards I could see that she couldn't keep her eyes on the screen. When the film was over she kissed me hurriedly, I mustn't mind her leaving me now, and she ran off after those two. The following day we met as usual. Her eyes were swollen from crying and from lack of sleep. Her husband, she explained to me, had consistently denied the existence of that woman, now at last she'd caught him. They'd been awake all night, she said things to him he'd probably never forget, she'd reminded him of what he'd be without her. In the end she'd given him a choice: either he stayed with her alone, or else he could pack his things and leave. He'd promised to stay with her.

I was afraid she might have had to make a similar promise. But she had not accepted any talk about herself and me: that was totally different. After all, she'd never denied or concealed my existence.

I am disgusting, she now screams at me, first I get her into such a humiliating and shaming situation, she'd never thought this kind of thing could happen to her, and now I have the effrontery to reproach her with it.

She starts to sob.

How long have I now been listening to her passionate accusations which are seemingly flawless but which apply one yardstick to herself and another to everyone else, so that no one had a hope of defending himself?

She changes her clothes and attends to her eyes. She'll have a drink somewhere but she doesn't want me to come with her.

She wants me to persuade her to stay with me or to let me go with her. She loves me, she merely demands that I should decide for her, she is afraid that otherwise she might lose me. In order not to lose me she's going out. She slams the door behind her.

On the other bed, near enough for me to touch it, lies her open suitcase. Immediately next to it lies her leather skirt, the stone dust is still clinging to it.

The Garden of Eden, as a learned rabbi described it two thousand years ago, has two gates adorned with rubies. At each of them stand sixty thousand comforters. The joyful features of each one of them shines like the light in the firmament. When a just and faithful person approaches they will take off his clothes, in which he'd risen from the grave, and clothe him in eight robes of clouds of glory, on his head they will place two crowns, one of precious stones and pearls, the other of gold from Parvaim, into his hands they will place eight twigs of myrtle, and they will say to him: Go forth and eat your nourishment in joy!

Each person, according to the honour he deserves, has his chamber, from which flow four springs: one of milk, one of wine, one of balsam, and one of honey. Sixty angels hover over each just and faithful person. They repeat to him: Go forth and eat honey in joy, for thou hast devoted thyself to the Torah, which is like unto honey, and drink wine, for thou has devoted thyself to the Torah, which is like unto wine.

For the just there is no more night, night-time is transformed for them into three periods of wakefulness. During the first the just becomes a child and enters among children and delights with them in childish games. In the second he becomes a young man, he enters among young men and delights in their games. In the third he becomes an old man, he enters among old men and delights in their games. In the midst of the Garden of Eden grows the Tree of Life, its branches reach out over the whole garden and provide five hundred thousand kinds of fruit – all different in appearance and taste.

The just and faithful are divided into seven classes and in their midst the Holy Everlasting, blessed be his name, explains to them the Writ, where it is said: I shall choose from all the land the faithful, so they can dwell with me.

When I awoke in the morning I realised that I was alone in the room. Her skirt and suitcase had disappeared. It was odd I didn't wake up when she packed her things, I am a rather light sleeper.

I went down to the hall where the talkative receptionist was watering the plants.

The lady had been in a hurry to catch the morning train, she told me. She asked how long I intended to stay. But I had no reason to stay on at all. I went back up to my room and began to pack my things. I realised that my predominating sensation was relief.

We have been expelled from paradise, but paradise was not

destroyed, Kafka wrote. And he added: In a sense, the expulsion from paradise was a blessing, because if we hadn't been driven out paradise itself would have had to be destroyed.

The vision of paradise persists within us, and with it also the vision of togetherness. For in paradise there is no such thing as isolation, man lives there in the company of angels and in the proximity of God. In paradise we shall be ranged in a higher and eternal order, which eludes us on earth, where we are cast, where we are outcast.

We long for paradise and we long to escape from loneliness.

We attempt to do so by seeking a great love, or else we blunder from one person to another in the hope that someone will at last take notice of us, will long to meet us or at least to talk to us. Some write poetry for this reason, or go on protest marches, cheer some figure, make friends with the heroes of television serials, believe in gods or in revolutionary comradeship, turn into informers to ensure they are sympathetically received at least at some police department, or they strangle someone. Even murder is an encounter between one man and another.

Out of his isolation man can be liberated not only by love but also by hate. Hate is mistakenly regarded as the opposite of love, whereas in reality it stands alongside love and the opposite of both of them is loneliness. We often believe that we are tied to someone by love, and meanwhile we're only tied to them by hate, which we prefer to loneliness.

Hate will remain with us so long as we do not accept that loneliness is our only possible, or indeed necessary, fate.

When we got back the others had gone on a little way with their equipment, up to the seats on which, while it was improper to sit down while on duty, one could comfortably put down the bottles of beer.

The foreman smoked and talked a lot. He promised better jobs to all of us, provided of course he managed to gain influence in the organisation. He'd send us to clean at the building sites, where, admittedly, you may get a damn tough job but you can earn more.

I could move up into his place, he'd fix that. He'd make some significant changes without delay. He'd try to introduce some light mechanisation, he'd also make sure they drove us straight to our workplace. This would save a lot of time, we'd make more money, our earnings would really go up. That's what he'd do, whereas those in charge of street cleaning now didn't give a monkey's, all they were interested in were their own bonuses, and they relied on perverts walking about all ponged up like hard-currency tarts.

The foreman was getting more and more agitated, and less assured. He stopped talking only when he took a swig from his bottle or when he looked in the direction of the prison, from where, it seemed, he was expecting the insidious attack.

He wouldn't like us to think he was afraid of anything, he knew what was what, and he'd been in a few tight spots in his life. Had he ever told us how, years ago, when they first introduced the supersonic MIG-19s, it happened that a machine, almost as soon as it had taken off, sucked in a pigeon or some other bird, and instantly plunged down again. It was piloted by his chum, Lojza Havrda. He should have ejected straight away, stands to reason, but because it was a brand-new plane he didn't want to abandon it. Naturally he was way off the runway, and as he tried to brake his MIG he took along with him anything that stood in his way: bushes, empty drums, and the mock planes outside the hangar. Worst of all, he was headed straight for the new quarters. They were just having their midday break when someone yelled: Get the hell out! He'd looked out of the window and saw the eight-ton giant, fully tanked up, tearing straight towards them. No one quite knew what was happening, they leapt out of the back windows. He alone stayed behind and watched Lojza wrestling with that kite. It was like a dream, but a few yards from the men's quarters he braked it to a halt. Now of course he should have got out of the crate as quickly as possible, but not Lojza! And he, the foreman, had wasted no time then, jumped out of the window and raced up to the plane. Found Lojza in the cockpit, all bloody, unable to move by himself. He got him out of the harness and carried him down on his back. Not till he'd dragged his mate to the crew quarters did it occur to him that the whole caboodle could have blown up, and them with it.

'And did it?' I asked.

The foreman hesitated, as if he couldn't remember, then he shook his head. 'The fire crew drove up and sprayed it with foam.'

'D'you know that he gave me a picture?' Mrs Venus said to me.

'Who?' I didn't understand.

'My old gent, of course. About a month ago. A big picture he had over his bed.'

'Oil?'

'Virgin with the infant Jesus. Said to me: "You take this picture, dear lady, I can't see it any longer anyway."'

The beer was finished. The youngster picked up the empties and put them into his big bag; he'd take them back to the supermarket. He was walking slowly, as if the uphill journey exhausted him.

I too found it difficult to breathe. A blanket was spreading over the city, and smoke and fog were billowing right down into the streets.

I thought we wouldn't see each other in a hurry, that she'd also made a decision for me. She hadn't just left the chalet in the foothills, but she'd left me as well, she'd been wise to withdraw from me. Even though the dawning day would now and again greet me with dead eyes, I still felt a sense of relief.

For nearly a month we both remained silent, then I phoned her to ask how she was.

She'd been in bed for the best part of a week, she informed me, she couldn't even move, she felt so sick. Her voice was full of pain, reproach, but also tenderness. I suddenly realised that I'd been waiting for that voice all that time. I was still close to her, so close she could move me with a few words.

Why did you wait so long before you rang? she asked. You were offended? I was able to offend you after all you've done to me?

This is a way of telling me she still loves me, she's waiting for me. An hour later I give her a purple gerbera and kiss her. Her lips are dry.

She'd gone to the country when she didn't hear from me, she'd planted some trees, she'd obviously injured her back, for three days she'd lain motionless in her cottage, alone.

She limps over to the bed and I fill a vase with water.

A neighbour had found her and called for an ambulance, at the hospital they'd given her a jab so she could at least manage the bus ride. And I hadn't even phoned her. You could really forget me so soon? she asks.

I know I won't forget her as long as I live, but for her the inevitable question is: What good does it do to lie somewhere all alone?

You've never considered staying with me altogether?

She's testing my resolution, my devotion, she forgets that I couldn't very well stay with her even if I wanted to. After all, she's got her husband. Maybe she's prepared to drop him, but I've never asked her to do that, I've never wanted that kind of arrangement.

How could I possibly not consider it?

But what good is that to her?

What good is it to her that I have spent nights reflecting on how I would, how we would, live – what use is it to her when nothing has actually changed, when I'm not really with her, when I see her only in secret?

I go out to the supermarket and then cook lunch for us.

You're so good to me, she says. When you have time! When you can fit me in.

I want to wash up, but she asks me to leave everything and come to her. She's lying down. I hold her hand. She looks at me, her eyes, as always, draw me into depths where there isn't room for anything else, for anything except her.

She asks what I've been doing all this time.

I tell her about Dad, about my son, I try to explain what I've been writing about, but she wants to know if I've thought of her, if I thought of her every day.

She'd left me in the middle of the night and she'd left me on my own in a strange hotel, and then for a few more weeks, so I should feel the hopelessness of living without her. I'm beginning to understand that she left me in order to push me, at long last, into making a decision.

She asks: How can you live like this? How can you believe that you'll write anything when all the time you're living a lie?

She regards me with anxious love. She's hoping I will at last find the strength to live truthfully. That is, to stay with her according to the command of my heart. She believes that she understands me. She's been appealing to me for so long to abandon my unworthy life of lies, and it hasn't occurred to her that by doing so she is appealing to me to leave her. She is right, I must make up my mind to do it.

On the little table by the bed lie a few books. I pick up the one on top – short stories by Borges. I read her one of them. It is about a young man who is crucified for an illicit love affair.

The plot sounds outrageous to our ears, we've got used to the notion that there is no such thing as illicit love, or, more accurately, that all's fair in love.

She listens to me attentively. I ask her if she wants me to read another story.

Better still, come to me!

She isn't thinking about her painful back, she presses herself to me and moans with pleasure: My darling, I love you so much, and you torture me! Why do you keep hurting me when you know that you'll never feel so good with anyone else, that no one will ever love you as I do?

I embrace her once more and then I have to hurry, her husband will be home shortly.

Will you come again tomorrow?

Her gentle fingers, her lips, her eyes: No one will ever love you as I do! No one will make love to you as I do! Why won't you admit to yourself that you belong to me? Let's go away somewhere together. We'll make love till we die! Why do you resist when you know it's bound to happen? Surely it couldn't be so perfect if there was anything bad about it.

She looks at me, I look at her face. She's changed over the years, there is less tenderness and enchantment in her now, and there is more tiredness, or even bitterness. She has aged. Over the last few years she has aged at my side, in my arms, in her vain waiting, in bad dreams and in fits of crying. In sleepless nights more little lines have appeared in her face, and I have only been able to kiss them away temporarily.

I was aware of a surge of regret or even pity, and promised to come the next day without fail.

We were approaching the metro station. We watched the crowds of people who, out of a need to be transported as quickly as possible from one place to another, were voluntarily descending into an inhospitable underworld. Around the stations there is always an increase in litter, the grass is almost invisible under a multitude of bits of paper and rubbish, of course we don't sweep the grass, even if it is totally covered with rubbish. I noticed the youngster falling behind, then stopping completely, leaning against a street lamp and turning motionless.

I walked back to him. His pallid face had turned even whiter, and there were droplets of sweat on his forehead.

'Are you all right?' I asked.

He looked at me without answering. In his right hand he was still holding the scraper, his left hand was pressing below his stomach.

'Does it hurt there?'

'It's nothing. It catches me there now and then.'

'Shouldn't you see your doctor?'

He said that mostly it passes by itself.

But it didn't look to me as if his pain was passing. I offered to accompany him to the doctor. The foreman let us go without objections. 'If you finish in time, you know where to find us!'

It didn't take us more than twenty minutes to get to the hospital, but even so it seemed a long time to me. On the bus I made the youngster sit in the seat for disabled passengers. He was silent. From his postman's bag he produced a dirty, army-khaki handerchief and wiped his forehead with it. Who does his laundry? I knew nothing about him, I could not picture the place where he slept.

We got off in front of the hospital. I suggested he leant on me but he shook his head. He gritted his teeth but didn't complain.

The young nurse with whom we checked in was angry that we had no kind of personal papers with us, but in the end accepted the information the youngster gave her and sent us to the waiting room with its depressing atmosphere of silence and greyness. We sat down on a peeling bench. The sweat was trickling down his cheeks.

'Probably got over-excited last night. At that concert.'

'Not at all, that was quite fantastic.' After a while he added: 'I've always wanted to play in a decent band, but at the children's home we had a director . . . well, he didn't think music was a proper career, we each had to learn something proper, like working a pneumatic grinder or cutting out soles – he was a qualified shoemaker.'

He took off his orange vest and put it on the seat beside him. 'I never told the boys what I'm doing now. I mean this business.'

'Do you have to do it?'

'They've cut back my pension – any convict on costume jewellery gets more!' He turned white as the pain gripped him.

I am sure that at his age I'd have felt humiliated by having to be a street-sweeper. It would humiliate me even now if I had no other choice and if I had to be a regular sweeper like him.

All of a sudden it came to me how little in fact I had in common with what I pretended to be. What does my fate really have in common with the fate of those with whom I work? What was a desperate choice to the youngster was to me, at best, a rather grim game, which tested my perseverence, of which I was actually proud, and which moreover afforded entertaining and unexpected insights. I felt ashamed. I too took off my sweeper's vest, rolled it up beside me and decided never again to put it on.

He mopped his face again.

'Aren't you thirsty?' it occured to me to ask.

'I wouldn't mind a drink, that's a fact.'

I went off in search of a glass.

Ten years ago I worked in the next block. I'd come in three times a week, and put on white trousers and a white jacket, on which as a rule at least one button was missing, but I never became a genuine hospital orderly.

When does a person genuinely become what he otherwise only pretends to be? Most probably when he finds himself in a spot from which he cannot or doesn't want to escape, the place of his torture. Genuineness is always associated with torture because it closes all doors of escape, because it leads a person to the edge of the precipice into which he can crash at any moment.

The nurse in reception lent me a jam jar and herself filled it with water. But when I returned to the waiting room the youngster was already in the consulting room.

I sat down and put the glass of water on the chair next to me.

Even a person who manages to lie his way through his whole life cannot escape that one moment of truth, the moment from which there is no escape, from which he cannot lie or buy his way out.

I recalled the day when I was sitting in another, similar, hospital waiting room. If I phoned you now, would you come again?

You're waiting at the hospital again? Has anything happened to your dad?'

He's not well, but now I'm here with someone else. We were sweeping together and he was taken ill in the street.

And you've taken him to hospital. You see what a good person you are? You haven't changed at all over the years.

He was really in need of help. His liver's all gone. I've written abroad for some drug but so far it hasn't arrived.

I've often been ill. So ill I thought it was the end.

I didn't know.

How could you have known? You'd have had to phone me, at least. But of course you had no time left for that while you were comforting the sick. Must be a great feeling to help others.

Especially the poor and needy. That was your wife's idea, about that drug?

I'm sorry you were ill.

No need for you to grieve. I was very ill, but you're probably worse if you've taken up good deeds. What are you trying to make yourself believe about yourself? Doesn't it seem a little cheap to lie your way out of everything?

I'm not lying my way out of anything. You can't simply judge me from your own viewpoint.

So how am I to judge you? Do you remember sometimes what you used to say to me when we were together? I thought it also meant something to you, something real, something one can't just walk away from. And now you're trying to exchange me for a few good deeds! Why don't you say something? Hasn't it occurred to you at all that you've betrayed me?

Kafka endeavoured to be honest in his writing, in his profession and in his love. At the same time he realised, or at least suspected, that a person who wants to live honestly chooses torture and renunciation, a monastic life devoted to a single God, and sacrifices everything for it. He could not, at the same time, be an honest writer and an honest lover, let alone husband, even though he longed to be both. For a very brief instant he was deluded into believing that he could manage both, and that was when he wrote most of his works. Every time, however, he saw through the illusion, he froze up, and stopped motionless in torment. He'd then either lay his manuscript aside and never return to it, or sever all his ties and ask his lovers to leave him.

Some of Kafka's biographers – delighted by his paradox – assert that the great writer was also an outstanding insurance clerk. I don't believe it. At least, he didn't come up to his own expectations as a clerk, just as he didn't as a lover.

Fools – with whom our revolutionary and non-monastic age abounds – believe they can combine anything with anything else, have a little of everything, take a small step back and still create something, experience something complete. These fools reassure each other, they even reward each other with decorations which are just as dishonest as they are themselves.

I too have behaved foolishly in my life in order to relieve my own torture. I have been unable either to love honestly or to walk away or to devote myself entirely to my work. Perhaps I have wasted everything I've ever longed for in life, and on top of it I have betrayed the people I wanted to love.

At last the youngster appeared in the door. 'Have you been waiting for me with that water all this time?' He'd had an injection and the doctor had ordered two days' rest. I offered to see him home, but he declined. If I didn't mind, he'd like to sit down for a little while, after which we might rejoin the others.

'When I was a little boy,' he reminisced, 'my grannie would sometimes wait for me at the school. She'd always take me to the fast-food buffet, the Dukla in Libeň, a little way beyond the Sokol gym if you know the neighbourhood. She'd have a beer and I'd get an ice-cream. And if she had another one, I got another one too, she was fair all right. And how she could play the accordion!' The youngster sighed. I preferred not to ask what had happened to her, it seemed to me that everything connected with him would be touched by tragedy.

Outside, a fine rain had begun to fall. The youngster put on his orange vest but I, faithful to the vow I'd just taken, carried mine rolled up under my arm.

Everything in life tends towards an end, and anyone rebelling against that end merely acts foolishly. The only question is what the end actually means, what change it makes in a world from which nothing can disappear, not a speck of dust, not a single surge of compassion or tenderness, not a single act of hatred or betrayal.

I had to leave for the mountains, on doctor's orders, and my lover also needed a break. Her work was tiring her out, she complained of being permanently exhausted. To work her material, often hammering into stone for hours on end, was enough to wear out even a strong man, but I knew that she had a different kind of weariness in mind. She reproaches me for her having to remain in the border region between love and betrayal, between meeting and partings, in a space which, she claims, I have set out for her and where strength is quickly consumed, exhausted by hopeless yearnings and pointless rebellion.

We could go somewhere together. I know that she wants to be with me completely just once in a while. I mention the possibility to her. She agrees, and a moment later I wonder if I really want that joint trip, if I wouldn't have preferred to remain on my own. And suppose my wife offers to come with me? I am alarmed at the mere thought. What excuses, what lies would I invent? I am terrified like a habitual criminal who knows that he's bound to be caught in the end.

But my wife suggests nothing of the kind, she doesn't suspect me. She says a stay in the mountains will do me good. Everybody needs a change of scene from time to time. She'll visit Dad for me, I'm not to worry about him, he's doing well now anyway.

I know that my wife is immersed in her own world, which, as happens in work which brings one face to face with the sorrow and suffering produced by sick minds, is unlike the real world. In it no one wishes to hurt anyone else, evil appears in it only as suppressed, unawakened or misdirected good, and betrayal is as incomprehensible as murder.

Who does she see in me when she lies down by my side, when she nestles up against me and whispers that she feels good with me? What justifies her reasserted and ever newly betrayed trust? Or does she believe that one day I will, after all, prove myself worthy of that trust?

My lover observes my embarrassment: Do you actually want me to come with you?

I don't answer quickly enough, I don't say yes convincingly enough, my uncertainty can be read in my eyes, and she cries. She suspected that I'd be scared at the last moment, she knows me now, I've lost the notion of freedom, I no longer have any self-respect, I've become a slave to the mirage of my despicable marriage, I can no longer manage without my yoke and now I'm trying to impose it on her. What am I trying to do to her, how dare I treat her like this, humiliate her like this.

I try to placate her, but she's crying more and more, she's shaken by sobs, she can't be comforted. This is the end, the absolute end, she'll never go anywhere with me again, she never wants to see me again!

I am conscious of relief and, simultaneously, of regret.

Once more she looks up at me, her beautiful eyes, which always lured me into the depths, have turned bloodshot, as though the sun had just set in them. I kiss her swollen, now ugly, eyes, also her hands which have so often embraced me, which have so tenderly touched me: I don't understand why she is crying, I do want her to come along with me, I'm begging her to.

She'll think it over, I should phone her from there.

And here I am, alone, in the Lower Tatra. I walk through meadows fragrant with warmth. Above me, on the mountainsides, snow is still lying. At dinner I talk to an elderly doctor about yoga, he tells me about the remarkable properties of medicinal herbs. I walk along forest paths and enjoy the silence all round me, I recover in that solitude, even though I know it is short-lived, as is the relief I am feeling; the rack to which I have tied myself is waiting, it is within me.

I gaze at the distant peaks. Mist rises above the lowlands. I look back to where the waves roll, where the surf roars, washing away my likeness moulded in sand, she bathes in abandoned rock-pools, the soil is black, the path is barred by an ever thicker tangle of roots, carrion crows fly darkly over the tree-tops. I walk with her among the rocks until we find ourselves in the middle of a snow-covered expanse of flat ground, I embrace her: is it possible we love each other so much?

Nights descend, prison nights, nights as long as life, her face is above me, my wife is beside me, I am alone with my love, with my betrayal. She bends down to me at night, she calls me to herself, she calls me to herself forever: We'll go away together, darling, we'll be happy. And I actually set out towards her, I run through cold streets, streets deserted and devoid of people, empty in a way not even the deepest night could make them, I drag myself through the streets of the dead ice-bound city and an uneasiness rises up in me, suddenly I hear a voice within me, from the very bottom of my being, asking: What have you done? Halfway I stop in my flight and return to where I've come from, to the side of my wife. I act this way night after night, until suddenly I realise that I don't want to leave, that I no longer want to walk through this dead city, at least not for the moment. I say: For the moment, and eventually I am overcome by the relief of sleep.

She too is reconciled, for the moment, to having waited in vain, but after a while she starts asking again why I haven't come, what has been happening to me? Didn't I love her, weren't we blissfully happy when we're together, so why couldn't I make up my mind? She seeks an explanation, she puts forward factual and plausible reasons for my behaviour and instantly rejects them, she's angry with me, she cries, she's in despair at my immobility, my obstinacy, my insensitivity and my philistinism. She assures me that there was no decision to make: I wouldn't be leaving my wife now, I'd left her long ago, and I was only a burden to her. And the children were grown-up now, they'd remain my children wherever I was. I listen to her in silence, I do not argue with her. The voice which holds me back time and again isn't, after all, a reason; it can't even be broken down into reasons, it is above reasoning. Is it possible, I wonder, that she does not hear a similar voice within her, a voice of doubt if not of warning?

Not even now, here amidst the mountains with no one urging me to do anything, can I break that voice down into separate reasons: into love for my wife or my children, or regret, or a sense of duty. But I know that if I hadn't obeyed it I'd feel even worse than I do anyway.

Perhaps there is within us still, above everything else, some ancient law, a law beyond logic, that forbids us to abandon those near and dear to us. We are dimly aware of it but we pretend not to know about it, that it has long ceased to be valid and that we may therefore disregard it. And we dismiss the voice within us as foolish and reactionary, preventing us from tasting something of the bliss of paradise while we are still in this life.

We break the ancient laws which echo within us and we believe that we may do so with impunity. Surely man, on his road to greater freedom, on his road to his dreamed-of heaven, should be permitted everything. We are all, each for himself and all together, pursuing the notion of earthly bliss and, in doing so, are piling guilt upon ourselves, even though we refuse to admit it. But what bliss can a man attain with a soul weighed down by guilt? His only way out is to kill the soul within him, and join the crowd of those who roam the world in search of something to fill the void which yawns within them after their soul is dead. Man is no longer conscious of the connection between the way he lives his own life and the fate of the world, which he laments, of which he is afraid, because he suspects that together with the world he is entering the age of the Apocalypse.

The mist from the valley below me is rising and has almost reached me. I know that I must change my way of life, which piles guilt upon me, but I'm not leading it on my own. I feel fettered from all sides, I've let myself be chained to the rockface without having brought fire to anyone.

What was there left in my favour? What could I claim in my defence? What order, what honesty, what loyalty?

Suddenly from the mists a familiar figure emerges. I stiffen. From the mists her heavenly eyes look on me: You could give me up?

There is no reason that could stand up in her eyes. I might at best make some excuses, beg her to understand, beg for forgiveness or for punishment, but there's no point in any of this, none of it will bring her relief.

I phoned her as I'd promised. She said she'd join me for ten days, she was looking forward to it. She added: We'll have a lovely farewell holiday. But I didn't believe that she meant it.

We found our companions in place – that is, in the tavern. The first to catch sight of us was the captain. He touched two fingers to his cap.

I joined him and noticed that the beermat before him already bore four marks.

'I'm celebrating!' he explained.

He didn't look to me like a man celebrating, more like a man drowning his sorrows. Nevertheless I asked: 'Has one of your inventions been accepted?'

'Haven't I told you? They've found the *Titanic*!' He gave a short laugh and spat on the floor.

'The *Titanic*?'

'With everything she had on board. Only the people have gone.'

'That a fact? So what happened to them?' The youngster was no longer in pain and was therefore able to show interest in the pain or death of others.

'Probably jumped overboard,' the captain explained casually. 'No one stays on a ship that's going down. Everybody thinks he'll save himself somehow.'

The foreman, evidently still preoccupied with the morning visit, decided to find out how things really stood; he'd ring the office. For a while he searched in his pockets, then he borrowed two one-crown pieces from Mr Rada and with a demonstratively self-assured gait made for the telephone.

'That really must have been terrible, finding yourself in the water like that,' the youngster reflected, 'and nothing solid anywhere.'

'That's life,' said the captain. 'One moment you're sailing, everyone saying Sir to you, and in your head maybe a whole academy of science, and suddenly you're in the water. You go down – finish!'

The waiter brought more beer, and before the captain he also placed a tot of rum.

The captain took a sip: 'And all your ideas, windmills, encyclopedias, end of the ice age– everything goes down with you.'

He got up and unsteadily walked over to the battered billiards table. From the sleeve of his black leather jacket projected his even blacker metal hook. With this he adroitly picked up a cue and played a shot.

I watched the ball moving precisely in the desired direction.

'Do you know that I've written to her?' he said to me when he got back to the table.

'To whom?'

'To Mary. Asking if she wanted to come back.'

'And did you get a reply?'

'Came back yesterday. Addressee unknown. So she's unknown now!'

'Probably moved away.'

'Person's here one moment, gone the next. All going to the bottom!' The captain turned away from his glass; he muttered something to himself and softly uttered some figures. Perhaps some new and revolutionary invention, or the number of days he'd spent on his own. Or the number of tricks he'd scored in the round of cards he'd just finished. There was sadness in his features, maybe in his poetic mind some clear vision, perhaps his last one, was just then fading and disintegrating. Again I experienced a sense of shame at sitting there studying him. High time for me to get up and get away from all that street-sweeping. I looked around at the others, as if expecting that they'd read my thoughts, but they were all engrossed in their own troubles.

From the billiards table they were calling the captain again. For a moment he pretended not to hear them, then he rose, firmly gripped his chair, then the back of my chair, then he held on to the table and, moving along the wall, made it to the billiards. He picked up a cue with his hook and concentrated for a moment before imparting the right speed to his ball. I watched the red ball move over the green baize, passing the other balls without coming anywhere near them.

'You'd better not drink any more,' I said to him when he got back.

He turned his clouded eyes on me. 'And why not?' His question reminded me of my daughter's classmate who'd put an end to his own life at the northern tip of Žofín island years ago.

By then the foreman was returning from the telephone. His face purple, as if he were near a stroke, he sat down heavily, picked up his glass, raised it to his lips and put it down again. 'Well folks, we've got a new dispatcher!'

'Would it be you?' Mrs Venus guessed.

'Don't try to be funny with me, Zoulová, I'm not in the mood!' He fell silent to give us time to go on guessing, then he announced: 'It's that fucking bastard!'

'Franta? But he's an idiot,' Mrs Venus expressed surprise.

'That's just why,' Mr Rada explained while the captain began to laugh, laughing softly and contentedly, as if something about that piece of news gave him particular pleasure. Maybe at that moment he gained a clearer understanding of that radiation which turns us all into sheep.

The foreman finally swallowed his first gulp of beer, then drained his glass, and finally announced: 'If they think I'll let that shit make out my work schedule for me they've got another think coming! This is the end of my work for his organisation!'

'Don't take on so,' Mrs Venus tried to comfort him. 'He isn't going to pong up his office for long! He'll grass on them too, and he'll be kicked upstairs again!'

They were calling the captain again from the billiards, but he had difficulty getting up, he turned towards the corner of the room, waved his hand and sat down again.

'No,' said the foreman, 'I've had it!'

'It's getting cold now anyway,' the youngster piped up. 'I think that's what was behind my funny turn.' This was evidently his way of announcing that he too intended to leave. I ought to join them as well, but I was still too much of a stranger to think it appropriate to emphasise my departure. As I got up a moment later I merely said to the foreman; 'All the best, I'm sure we'll meet again.' But he got to his feet, ceremoniously shook hands with me, addressed me by my name, and said: 'Thank you for your work!'

It was a long time since any superior of mine had thanked me for my work.

Mr Rada joined me as usual. 'You see, the things they'll fight over!'

He seemed dejected today. To cheer him up I enquired about his brother, whether he was about to go off to any foreign parts again.

'Don't talk to me about him,' he said. 'it's all I can think about anyway. Just imagine, he's joined the Party! So they can make him a chief surgeon. Would you believe it? A man who speaks twelve languages, and after all he's seen in the world, after what he himself told me not so long ago!'

I suggested that perhaps it was a good thing that just such men should be chief surgeons. It wasn't his fault that the post required a Party card.

'A man isn't responsible for the situation into which he is born,' he proclaimed, 'but he is responsible for his decisions and actions. When my mother heard about it she nearly had a stroke. Have you any idea what she's already been through in her life because of those people? And I . . . I used to be proud of him, I thought that the Lord had endowed him with special grace . . . even if he didn't acknowledge it, even if he acted as if he didn't acknowledge Him . . . I believed that one day he'd see the truth.'

In his depression he began to reminisce about the years he'd spent in the forced labour camp. Among the prisoners there'd been so many unforgettable characters, who, even in those conditions, were aiming at higher things. Some of them had there, in the camp, received the sacrament of baptism, he himself had secretly baptised a few of them. Thinking back to those days it was clear to him that, in spite of all he'd been through, God's love had not abandoned mankind. He believed, for just that reason, that he'd spent the best or at least the most meaningful years of his life there.

We'd reached the little street where our unknown artist lived and exhibited. I looked up curiously to his window, but this time it contained no artefact; instead a live person, presumably the artist himself, was standing in the window-frame, clad only in a narrow strip of sack-cloth. On his head was a fool's cap with little bells, on top of this cap he'd placed a laurel wreath, and in his right hand he held a large bell-shaped blossom, I'd say of deadly nightshade.

Thus he stood, motionless, his forehead almost pressed to the glass, as if awaiting our arrival. I was surprised to find that he was still young, his hair, where it peeped out from beneath his fool's cap, was dark and his skin was swarthy. We looked at him and he looked at us without giving any sign of seeing us, of taking any notice of us.

'Well really!' Mr Rada was outraged. 'That's a bit much!'

But I was aware of sympathy for the unknown young man who offered himself up to our gaze, who had no hesitation in exhibiting his misery, longings and hope. Hope of what? Of fame, of being understood, or at least of getting somebody to stop, look, and see. Standing there with my orange fool's vest – in what way did I differ from him? In my misery, my longings, or perhaps in my hope?

So I waited for my lover at the small railway station in the foothills. All round me half-drunk gypsies were noisily conversing. A total stranger, smelling of dirt and liquor, invited me to have a drink with him.

I escaped to the very end of the platform and stood waiting there for the train.

Was I waiting for it with hope or with fear, out of longing or out of a sense of duty? What was there left for me to wait for, what to hope for?

At the most for some conditional postponement that would briefly prolong our torment and our bliss.

The train pulled in, I caught sight of her getting off the last carriage, a bulging rucksack on her back. She saw me, waved to me, and even at that distance I could see that she'd come in love.

I was suddenly flooded with gratitude; undeservedly rewarded, I embraced her.

It was getting dark. The station had emptied, and the lights of some train were approaching in the distance.

I wished it would be a special train, a train just for the two of us. We'd board it, we'd draw the curtains across the windows, we'd lock the door, the train would move off, speed along through the day and the night, over bridges and through valleys, it would carry us beyond seven frontiers, away from our past lives, it would take us into the ancient garden where one might live without sin.

Along the track clanked a tanker train, filling the air with the stench of crude oil. I picked up her pack and we walked out of the station.

That evening I phoned my wife from the hotel where we'd taken a room. In her voice too I was aware of love and of her pleasure at hearing me. She told me she'd been invited to an ethological conference somewhere near where I was staying. No, not just yet, in a week's time, but we might meet then, that would be nice, I must be feeling rather blue being on my own for so long, besides, we'd been to the place she was going to before, surely I remembered, on our honeymoon . . .

I was in a panic. I wasn't sure. How could I tell, a week from now. And she too seemed taken aback; of course, she said, if it didn't suit me I needn't come to see her. She just thought that I might like to, but she didn't want to push me or make things difficult for me.

I promised to phone her to let her know, and hung up.

I was finally trapped. My mind, trained on those lines, was still concocting excuses, but I suspected that I wouldn't escape this time, nor did I wish to.

Why hadn't she asked straight out? Why hadn't she objected? The strange humility of her voice still rang in my ears. I was seized by a sense of sadness and regret, I also felt tenderness towards my wife who wanted to comfort me in my pretended solitude, who promised me from afar that we'd walk up among the rocks, where so long ago we'd felt happy, where we'd started our life together. If I were here on my own I'd go to her at once and tell her that, in spite of everything I'd done, I'd never stopped being fond of her and that I didn't want to leave her. If I were here on my own I wouldn't have had to put her off, I'd be glad to have her come.

I couldn't bear to stay indoors. The moon was shining on the flank of the mountain and a hostile wind blew down its slopes. My lover wanted to know what I was doing. But I felt ambushed by my own emotions – I felt unable to assure her that I longed to remain with her.

She faced me on the narrow footpath: But you invited me here! I beg you, maybe this is the last time I'll beg you for anything, that you should at least behave like . . . at least like a decent host!

The wind was blowing her hair into her face. Now she really looked like a witch, like a sorceress who'd emerged from some depth of the mountains.

But I'll pack my things and leave this instant if that's what you want!

There was no need for her to leave immediately. We could stay here a whole week, just three days less than we'd intended.

You want to bargain with me? Amidst the silent noctural landscape she screamed at me: I was a coward, a liar and a hypocrite. A trader in emotions. A dealer with no feelings. At least not for her. How could I be so cruel to her, so shameless?

She was right.

I took her by the hand and led her further along the path below the mountain. In the dusk we stumbled over projecting roots and stones. I tried to talk as if nothing had happened. We're here together, after all those months we're together at last.

The following day we left for another place in the mountains.

I felt humiliated by the knowledge that I was fleeing, fleeing belatedly, at a moment when I no longer wished to flee from anywhere or from anybody. Except from myself.

Spring was exceptionally beautiful that year. The meadows turned purple with wild crocus and clumps of coltsfoot sprang up along the paths. But we climbed to higher altitudes, we were climbing side by side for the last time, we waded through drifts of hardened snow, clambered over great rocks, watched the flight of the eagle and the leaps of the chamois, and when we returned to the twilight of the mountain chalet we made love just as we'd been making love over the years whenever we met.

Then she fell asleep, exhausted, while I lay motionless on the bed, listening to the soft drip of water outside and gazing through the window at the fantastic mass of the mountain glistening in the moonlight, wondering what I'd do when I got back home, how I would live, even if I could live, but my thoughts stumbled at the first step over the huge boulder that lay in my path.

Then I listened to her quiet breath, and remorse overcame me: What have I brought you to, my pet, where have you followed me, where have we set out together, we stride across snowy wastes, the night is deep and frosty, the silence of the universe is engulfing us. You wanted to save me, I wanted to be with you at all your difficult moments, I probably didn't love you as I should have, I was unable, I was unwilling, to love you more. I am still very fond of you, you've grown painfully into me. If I were stronger, if I were wiser, wise enough to know everything essential about myself, I would have driven you away as soon as you'd come close to me because I would have known that I would not remain with you the way you wanted me to, how happy I would have been if I'd remained alone, because I wouldn't then have met a woman I longed for so much. I didn't decide to drive you away. I wasn't wise enough, and I was moreover afraid of your pain and of my own, I was afraid of a life in which you weren't present; I believed that with you my life would be full of hope, that I'd found another safety net to spread out between myself and nothingness.

The mountain tops were beginning to emerge from the darkness and the sky above them was turning pale. The mountain rose straight up, it towered, virtually eternal, into a sky that was even more eternal, while we mortals , here only for a single winking of the divine eye, have, in our longing to fill our lives, in our longing for ecstasy, filled our brief moment with suffering.

On the tenth day we returned home, each to our own home. We said goodbye, we kissed once more, and she hoped I'd be strong and not do anything against her.

But I am not strong, at least not in the way she meant. I don't wish to demonstrate my strength towards the woman who had for so many years shared both good and bad with me. I go back, in my mind I turn over some sentences asking for forgiveness. I long for forgiveness and conciliation. Suddenly I am conscious of really returning this time. After a long journey, the start of which was almost out of sight now, I was coming home.

What a fool I am, my wife laments, to have trusted you again.

She is standing there facing me, dropping her eyes. She doesn't know what to do, what to say. She says she's decided to move out, she's looking for somewhere to live.

I ask her not to do anything silly.

The silliest thing I ever did was to trust you again.

She wants me at least to explain how I could do what I did, while I assured her that I never stopped loving her.

I loved the other woman too!

You see how embarrassing it is! There's no sense in it any more. How could you deceive me so?

I keep silent. I have no answer other than that it just happened like that. But I won't deceive you again!

Supposing you do mean what you say, how will you prove it to me?

I don't know how I can prove anything – I'll stay with you.

That's what you tell me now, but what will you tell her?

I'll tell her the same thing.

Very well. We'll go and see her and you can tell her straight away. I want to be present.

No, I can't do that.

Why not? Why can't you tell her in front of me, if you really want to tell her?

I am silent. I am trapped.

You see, you wanted to deceive me again.

I didn't want to deceive you.

You expect me to believe you?

There's nothing I can say. I can't promise or swear.

'I'm an idiot, how could I have been such an idiot! Even if I wanted to believe you I can't any longer.

Again she asks to go and see the other woman. I can say

whatever I like to her, but maybe at such a moment I would be speaking the truth.

At the moment, however, it isn't the truth I'm afraid of. I simply know that I cannot part from the woman I've been in love with for so long, with whom I'd made love without witnesses and with whom I'd forgotten my loneliness – I cannot part from her in a theatrical scene in front of an appreciative audience.

I'll tell her on my own. Or I'll write her a letter.

And why should I believe that you'll do that?

I shrug.

Night. My wife is sobbing in the next room. She's waiting for me to come to her. I'll tell her I'm sorry for everything that's happened, that I've realised that I can only be happy with her. And I'll tell the other woman to her face so that she too will hear it, so that everyone who knows about us should know that we love one another.

But I can't do anything of the kind, I can't even say any more than I've said already.

I can see myself, I see myself from a great height. Not yet stooping but greying at the temples, I'm standing at the corner, in the familiar spot with a single tree against which I can lean. The clock at the corner has stopped. I wait and wait, no one comes, I wait for her, at least, to show up, but she is not coming.

I kneel down on the ground and press my forehead against the tree-trunk. I can't manage to cry. I embrace the trunk, I hold it frantically as though someone might wish to tear me away from it. I'd whisper her name, but I can't. I notice that the clock has moved, but I know that this is the only movement – no one will ever come again.

So what are you waiting for? What do you want? What do you feel? What are you longing for?

The following day I wrote her a letter. I won't return to a life of lies. I won't leave my wife, and I can't live by her side and torment her by informing her that I also love another woman, even if she herself were able to live like that. I also wrote that what we had together will be with me all my life. I would have liked to add something tender, such as that there might be a time when I would come to her at some difficult moment, though differently from the way she'd imagined, also that what we had together couldn't have been devoid of some meaning, that some part of it might cast a light into our future lives, that I would never hide that light in myself – but I felt that all words were pointless and in vain, that I was perhaps improperly comforting myself and her.

After two days I posted the letter. As the flap of the postbox dropped back I was conscious of the familiar old vertigo getting hold of me.

I knew that I'd never see her or hear her voice again. But from time to time, in the middle of the night I would start up from my sleep and with my fingertips touch her high forehead, and feel a strange distant pain enter into me, and then a soft snapping sound. My net was tearing, I had no idea how many threads were still left, but there couldn't be many.

I should have liked to know if the man in the window experienced anything similar, whether he felt a sudden sense of relief from this unexpected meeting. I thought that he might step out of his frame, open the window and perhaps ask us in, or at least wave to us with his flower, but this would probably have disturbed something delicate and mysterious that was extending between us, between me and him, he would have crossed that invisible, barely perceptible boundary that divides art from mere tomfoolery, so that I was actually glad to see him remain motionless.

'They don't know what to think of next,' was Mr Rada's judgement on what he'd just seen.

His remark seemed unfair to me. Before beginning to judge and condemn one another, people should do more to understand one another.

We got back to the office. I thought that perhaps that little idiot Franta might already be inside, but it was the same woman as always. She accepted my vest from me, returned my ID card, and handed out my final pay to me.

'You're right,' Mr Rada said to me in parting, 'we're not here to judge others.' But I was sure he was thinking of his brother rather than of the strange artist.

I followed him with my eyes. He stopped at the bus stop. He was a tall, well-built man, with just a slight stoop, as if he were carrying a load on his back. Even if he took on his burden for others he possibly took it on needlessly. Who can see into the soul of another person, even the one closest to him, even his own son or his brother who was like a son?

I might still have caught up with him, but just then the bus came along and he got on. I probably wouldn't see him again, nor would I meet his brother, unless I found myself in his care.

It occurred to me that I might spend the banknote I'd just earned, my last swept-up fifty crowns, in some festive way, and so I walked down into Nusle, where there are lots of shops.

In a little market they were selling flowers. My daily wage was just sufficient for five chrysanthemums. I chose three butter-yellow ones and two amber ones, colours my wife was fond of. At home I put the bunch in a vase and placed it on her table. I picked up the shopping bag with my lunch, which she had prepared for me in the morning, and set out to visit Dad at the hospital.

He opened his eyes, saw me, slightly moved his lips in an attempted smile, and closed his eyes again. He'd hardly spoken these past few days, either it tired him out too much or else he didn't think anything was sufficiently important for him to utter aloud. The last time he spoke to me he recalled that my mother used to reproach him for devoting too little attention to me, for not looking after my upbringing enough. But surely you didn't expect any sermons? he asked. And I said hurriedly that he'd always been a model to me, the way he lived and, above all, the way he worked. After all, I stayed with you lot, Dad said. His eyes misted up with tears. I understood that hidden behind these few words was some long-past difficult decision, perhaps even a sacrifice.

I unscrewed the stopper of the thermos flask and put a little custard on a spoon. Without opening his eyes Dad swallowed a few mouthfuls. Then he said: I had a fall today and couldn't get up. And the sister, the pretty one, shouted at me to get up at once, she wasn't going to lift me up. Dad fell silent for a long time. I thought he'd dropped off. Suddenly he opened his eyes: Tell me, how can a woman be so wicked?

As I tidied his things in his bedside table I noticed his little notebook. Day after day he'd entered in it, in an increasingly shaky hand, his temperature and the medication he took. The last entry was three days old and I couldn't make out the numbers. My throat was constricted by pity. I stroked Dad's forehead and left the ward. Outside I didn't make for the main gate but walked down a narrow path to the back entrance. The path wound between overgrown lawns, past the morgue. Immediately behind the morgue was a huge heap of broken bricks, rusty cans and shattered infusion bottles, also a rusting old electric motor, maybe one of those for which Dad had calculated the design. He'd spent whole days and evenings calculating motors. When I visited him I'd be afraid to disturb him in his work. And so we hurriedly covered what news there was in the world, and in our lives, but about the most important thing, about our sojourn here, we talked very little.

Round the bend in the path appeared an orderly, pushing the metal cart into which the dead were placed. I used to push that cart too. I gave him a wide berth, but I couldn't get rid of the thought that he was making for that refuse heap in order to tip out his load there.

What, when it comes to it, is man?

V

The alarm went off at six o'clock, my wife and my son had to get up to go to work. I ought to get up too. Dad died two days ago and I should go and see his pupils at the Academy and get one of those he was fond of to speak at his funeral. And yesterday afternoon I received a package with the drug I'd written off for some time ago for that youngster Štycha, I ought to give it to him as soon as possible. I hadn't written off for any drug for Dad, there was probably no such thing.

By now it was too late to catch my mates in the changing room anyway. If I had any time left, I'd find them at the tavern during their mid-morning break.

On the final day of Dad's life Peter and I left for the hospital first thing in the morning. It was a Sunday and there were only two nurses on duty in the department. One of them told me that 'it could happen' at any moment.

Dad was lying in his bed, his lips slightly open, breathing heavily. The pauses between breaths seemed to me incredibly long. His eyes were firmly shut. He hadn't eaten or drunk anything for two days, his veins were so torn with punctures that they couldn't feed him artificially any more. I tried to give him a spoonful of sweetened tea but at first he was unable to swallow it. When he finally managed it I could see that it had taken all his strength, and that another drop might make him choke. The last drop of hope had dried up, vanished in the dust. All I could do was to mop Dad's lips and tongue with a piece of moistened cotton-wool.

Then I sat down by his bed and took his hand, as he used to take mine when I was a little boy and he was taking me for a walk. My grown-up son was standing in the door, crying.

Then suddenly Dad breathed out, but he didn't breathe in again. I could see the terrible effort of his lungs, as they strained to catch another breath, his faced closed up in a grimace of such pain that it went right through me. What kind of son was I if I couldn't even give him a tiny puff of breath?

I got up and in my mind begged: Lord, receive his soul, you know how good it was! Then I walked out in the corridor, deserted on a Sunday, and all around there were walls, and one more wall, quite thin, transparent but nonetheless impermeable, was slipping between that moment and everything that preceded it.

In the room next door my son was listening to the news. Life – and hence also death – went on. In Colombia, on the very day my father died, a volcano erupted. The red-hot lava melted the snow and ice in the neighbourhood of the crater. The water together with the ash produced a flow of mud which rushed downhill into the valley, where it engulfed human habitations. It was estimated that twenty thousand people remained buried under the mudslide.

My wife bent over me and kissed me goodbye. She whispered that I should sleep on, she'd get home early.

I couldn't fall asleep again. When I closed my eyes Dad's face returned to me in its final pain-distorted shape, and his chopped breath came to me from all corners.

A bell rang again, this time the front door.

Early morning visits fill me with foreboding. But standing at the door was only the fair-haired young man from Svatá Hora, and in his features there was even more painful anxiety than usual. It was obvious that something serious had happened, or else he wouldn't have called at this hour.

He asked me to come with him, he wanted to talk to me outside. In the street he informed me that he and his friends had been pulled in for questioning. In his case the interrogation had gone on

202

for half a day and had touched on my reading two years before, my stories, my opinions, as well as the opinions of other authors who'd refused to write in jerkish language in the society that was accomplishing 'the greatest freedom of man and the human race'. They also asked him why and how often he visited me, and several times in this context they mentioned the destroyed monument.

Life – and hence also death – went on.

I tried to calm him. Surely they wouldn't accuse either him or me of blowing up a monument. They merely liked bracketing these two offences – the reading of short stories written in a language comprehensive only to humans, and the destruction of a statue of an officially-proclaimed giant. Even they must realise that the latter was more criminal than the former.

But the young man was in the depths of despair. This was the first time he'd been interrogated and had experienced the stubbornly uncompromising and suspicious jerkish spirit. I've been aware of it for years, recording how under its influence living voices were falling silent and language was being lost. It pervades everything, it gets into the water and into the air, it mingles with our blood. Mothers give birth to shrunken cripples and the landscape to dead trees, birds drop in mid-flight and children's bodies are afflicted by malignant tumours.

He was walking beside me, afraid. He'd already handed in his notice at work, he'd found a job as projectionist in a cinema, and he was hoping to be accepted as a correspondence student of jerkish literature. True, he'd learn there that Charlie Chaplin left the United States, that bastion of unfreedom, but he'd have a little time left over to read books and reflect. But suppose they didn't accept him now. He wanted to know where he'd find a safety net for himself when the one they'd assigned to him as well as the one offered to him at the department store were so large-meshed that a person fell through at once. Of course, everybody should weave his own net, he knew that. But if they burst in, if they stole into his home and tore it up for him? Fight them or begin to weave a finer mesh from scratch? How often could a person start from scratch?

I don't know how to reassure him. Words always seem abstract and impotent compared to action. But what scope for action was left to us? Blow up monuments in the dead of night, so they can erect them anew and, to be on the safe side, surround them with hidden cameras? Oppose their vindictive and base actions by vindictiveness and baseness of one's own? What could we create, who would we help by that? Often our only action is the way we shape our own lives. Fortunately this is more essential to the state of the world than it would seem at first glance.

I apologise for the banality of my thoughts, but when he leaves me he is smiling. He'd wanted to hear something like that. If they didn't accept him as a student he'd find something else.

Only nine o'clock. If I hurried I might be able to catch the youngster in the Božena tavern, hand over the drug, and then go and find a funeral speaker.

The tavern was still half-empty at this early hour, and I didn't have to search through a crowd: my former companions, apart from the youngster and the captain, were sitting at the table next to the bar. Enthroned at the head of the table, to my surprise, was our foreman, moreover in new overalls.

I entered unobserved and managed to overhear the foreman earnestly recounting how someone was a real show-off, always nose-dived right to the ground and pulled out only when all those who were merely standing and staring had plastered their trousers.

'And what are you doing here?' Mrs Venus had spotted me. 'Come to help us?'

The foreman turned his head irritably, he didn't like anyone spoiling his heroic episodes. I produced the medicine from my pocket and asked about the youngster; did anyone know where I might find him.

'This ain't no kindergarten,' the foreman informed me. 'If he comes, he's here, if he don't, he ain't. We haven't seen him,' he turned to Mrs Venus as his witness, 'for at least a week.'

'This ain't no weather for him, you remember that sick turn he had. Maybe they'll give you his address at the office,' Mrs Venus said. 'Bound to have it there. Why don't you sit down?'

I ordered tea with rum.

'Maybe you don't know yet,' Mrs Venus continued, 'that they've locked our Mr Pinz up in the loony bin?'

Obviously I hadn't heard about what had happened to the captain.

'Wanted to set fire to the place he was living in. Scraped off the heads of matches, tried to make a bomb from them. Had it all ready, God knows what he'd intended it for. But then that Mary of his turned up, just looked in after all them years, and when he asked her if she'd stay with him she told him he was a nut and she'd sooner string herself up. So he decided to set that bomb off outside his own door.'

'The stupidity of it,' the foreman said in disgust; 'scraping off two hundred thousand match-heads, stuffing them into a metal soda siphon, and then using it on a building like that! But if I was you I wouldn't put my nose in that office, there's another idiot sitting there!' And he returned to his airfield, where his friend didn't manage to pull out of a spin that time and rammed himself with his MIG so deep into the ground that when they'd put out the fire and cut the wreckage up with a blow-torch they were left with a hole big enough for twenty blokes to hide in.

When the rescue teams arrived in the area of the volcanic disaster they found, in addition to the thousands of dead, a few who'd survived on the roofs of houses or in tree-tops, and also some who were stuck in the mud and couldn't get out by themselves. Of one little girl only the head was showing. Below the surface her legs were firmly clutched by her drowned aunt. The rescuers spent many hours trying to free the girl, and themselves got stuck in the mud in the attempt. All that time a reporter with a television camera was filming them, so he could bring the fate of the little girl closer to those who were contentedly or perhaps sympathetically bored in their own nets and wanted to be witnesses. After sixty hours the little girl's sufferings were over and the tired reporter was able to return to his television net. By the time they'd cut the clip they needed from the recorded shots, the little girl's soul had already risen and was lamenting above the dark waters and the mud, above the red-hot crater of the volcano, and also above a million TV screens which were flickering all over the world in order to show the vain struggle of the rescuers and the touching death of the little girl, who'd never rise from the ashes but who became famous for those few exciting seconds. And who heard the calling of her soul, who was shaken by her sobs? Who at least pictured her features at the moment when her lungs were vainly trying to catch that last breath of air?

Our forefathers were still able to experience the misfortunes as well as the endeavours and joys of others, because their gaze was confined to horizons they could encompass. We attempt to feel the misfortunes and the endeavours of the whole world, but in reality we experience nothing. We have grown old and dull.

We are growing old as individuals, but mankind too is growing old. A child can still be reached by the world – but at the same time he knows nothing about it, he suspects nothing of guilt or sin. He has before him a space that seems as infinite as time, as his own time. A child almost lives in paradise. Sometimes I wonder why my own childhood, which surely ended in a difficult and even terrifying manner, should arouse nostalgia in me. But that is just a longing for a state of innocence.

The beginnings of the human race were obviously also beset with difficulties, but man continued in a state of innocence. Adam hadn't yet tasted of the fruit of the tree of good and evil, he did not think about dying, he had before him a space that seemed as infinite as time, as his own time.

But as mankind grew older it began to perceive the dimensions of the world and of time, of its own finiteness, and hence also its exclusion from a state of bliss. Man moved away from paradise, and hence also from Him who'd led him into it. It occurred to him that he had to commit something as irrevocable as death. So he took up his guilt, his sin, and with it strode towards his end. But the vision of paradise persisted in him, the vision, that is, of the state prior to guilt, the state prior to sin, when time and space had seemed infinite or else were moving in an eternal cycle. Man realised that only if he returned to that state could he attain real happiness. He suspected that he couldn't attain any of this in his human time and space, but only in a different space and time, in a dimension in which God reigns. Man dreamed of returning, after his death, to God's garden or of fusing with the universe or of returning to the creator in a different shape. He surmised that at least his soul would get close to God.

But over the years, as the human race grew older and memories became confused, man exchanged the idea of blissful innocence for that of happiness through pleasure. Ageing man confused the soul with the body and believed he could enter paradise in his lifetime. As soon as he succumbed to the old man's error of believing he could return to the state of childlike innocence he actually entered the age of foolishness and totally succumbed to it in his senile childishness. Man thinks he's building paradise by inventing motor-cars, aircraft, plastics, nuclear power stations or underwater tunnels, whereas in reality he is ever more speedily moving towards his own end, in reality he invents and brings about the Apocalypse. Mankind has grown old but it has not become wise, or else it has passed the age of wisdom and entered the age of senility.

'In case you don't get his address there,' Mrs Venus returned to the youngster, 'you could try that Dana of his. He might be there.' And she described for me the house where the woman Dana lived. I've no idea how she knew. The house was in the Little Quarter.

The tea with rum had warmed me through nicely and I was now able to set out for the office. My way led me through the familiar little street of family homes, and when I got to the artist's window I gazed in amazement on a vest which, suspended from a cord, shone brilliantly with its orange colour. Set out behind it into the depths of the room were the stems and stalks of exotic plants. They had been arranged by the artist's hand to suggest human figures. As I stared into the window I could make out individual likenesses, familiar facial features. A woman with a jockey cap on her head undoubtedly represented Mrs Venus, still without her

207

Red-Indian wrinkles, but already with a sorrowful expression around her mouth. At the same time, however, there was something joyous in her attitude, in the gestures of her hands. Perhaps the artist had caught her just at the moment when she was about to mount the filly she'd nursed back to health. A moment later I identified a sculptural likeness of the foreman, carrying a wounded airman out of an imaginary aircraft and, in doing so, very nearly soaring up himself on the wings of his bravery. I also recognised the captain, his stocky, as yet unbowed figure looked good in a naval uniform. Perhaps, after all, there was in him both the eccentric inventor and a great prankster. But at the beginning of his actions probably stood a childlike dream, a mirage of distant voyages. Mr Rada, on the other hand, stood there in ugly brown convict's garb and was pouring water from a billy-can onto the head of another convict. His face was frozen at the instant of sudden inner illumination, at the touch of bliss. At that moment I heard the notes of Gershwin's rhapsody. In the youngster's expression there was so much concentration in his own playing and so much happiness that he seemed transformed. His clarinet was intended to suggest not so much a musical instrument as a conjurer's wand which caused rocks to part and transported humans into the realm of their own dreams.

I realised then that all these faces were, in their likeness, both real and unreal. They seemed younger and more attractive, as though nothing of the working of time or life had marked them. At the same time I understood that this exhibition had been prepared by a different artist, by a woman artist. The sculptor here had only let her use his exhibition window and she, surmising the direction of my walking, had set out for me her park, a garden where a person might see his own likeness as he himself wished it to appear at moments of grace. Maybe she had done this to remind me of her, or to demonstrate to me her loving and generous vision of what art should represent of life.

I was still looking for myself among the sculptures, but I didn't see my own face: there was only a tall pillar, as if hewn from stone, but I couldn't see its top through the window. I remembered, and I wondered if it might have a smile at the top. But I knew that I wouldn't find a smile – I'd have to be at peace with myself first.

The figures were now slowly beginning to dissolve before my eyes, and I was surprised to find myself in the grip of nostalgia. A person may think that the fate of people who are sufficiently remote does not touch him. Yet all of a sudden he will catch sight of them in an unexpected situation, will recognise their unsuspected likeness to him, whether it be beautiful or terrible, and he realises that not only have they touched him, but they have actually entered into him. This is what happens so long as life isn't totally extinct in a person. My father, in a dying flash of consciousness, suffered from the thought that a strange woman could be more wicked than he'd thought possible.

Coming along the opposite pavement was the uniformed patrol. The foppish one, however, was accompanied this time by a policeman I hadn't seen before. I was prepared to pass them without acknowledging them when the fop suddenly changed direction and made straight for me.

I stiffened, as always. Why had my presence in the world annoyed them this time?

The fop carelessly raised his hand to his cap. 'Day off today?' he asked.

'Sort of,' I answered evasively.

'What about the one in the high-water trousers then?'

I said I'd heard the captain had been taken to psychiatry.

'What else could we do, we didn't really want to,' the fop explained. 'We said to him, stop this nonsense, grandad, in the middle of the night. But instead of pissing off he lit that bottle of his. Would have killed him if we hadn't nabbed him, his fuse was only one metre!' he added with professional outrage. 'Anyway, they'll let him go, everybody'll testify that he's screwy, that he walked about in those ridiculous trousers even in the snow – I ask you!' He turned to his companion, but he had walked on out of earshot. 'But d'you know that he put on long trousers that evening, real baggy ones, perfect pantaloons, and a tie as well!' The fop shrugged his shoulders in amazement and raised two fingers to his cap. 'He was touched all right', he said, tapping his forehead, and walked away.

Sitting behind the desk at the office really was the little idiot, and he didn't know the youngster's address, or more correctly refused to know it – he might have had to get up from his chair and look up some file. A smile spread over his fleshy lips – the self-assured smile of a man who had been given power. Power over those who swept up garbage, and hence also over the garbage itself, and hence over the world of things. He explained something to me in his jerkish language but I didn't understand, we lacked an interpreter.

No matter, I thought to myself in an upsurge of spite, I'll find the youngster without him! I got on a tram which took me to the Little Quarter.

The spot which Mrs Venus had described was well known to me. It was on the other side of the place at the windows of which I used to look from the little attic I'd visited so often.

I'd frequently had to walk round the building but I'd never taken any notice of it. The walls were thick and the staircase dark. I thought I sniffed the familiar smell of gas.

I was lucky at least that the youngster's lady friend had a split shift and was therefore at home at this hour. She asked me into the hall. I didn't know if she was on her own, all other sounds were drowned by a noisy military band, and from somewhere came the rattle of a washing machine.

'But he's not here,' she informed me when I'd explained who I was looking for. She was a bulky, powerful woman of mature years. I couldn't picture her in the youngster's embrace. 'And he won't come again,' she declared.

I said I'd got him the drug he'd been waiting for. Perhaps I could leave it with her for when he dropped in.

'But he won't be dropping in,' she said with the finality one uses in talking about the dead. 'I told him not to come again.'

210

I asked her where I could find him.

'I've no idea where he could be, he never said where he came from.' Suddenly she remembered: 'Didn't he play somewhere? Maybe those musicians of his could tell you.'

I thanked her. I'd got to the door when she added: 'He was such a poor little thing, if you ever met him. He'd sit down and just look. Couldn't even eat anything proper, and as for drink only juice. Once he came in from somewhere, all wet through, I made him a grog, he didn't tell me he wasn't allowed to, and he nearly died on me.'

The youngster had gone and the waters had closed over him. I didn't know what to do with his medicine. Maybe the woman who used to sit in the office might help, might at least remember the name of the street or the town he'd come from. But I was in no mood to search for her. I began to suspect that by the time I tracked down the youngster the medicine might have become superfluous.

I left the house. It was midday, the low sun lit up the side of the palace, on the window ledge the pigeons were warming themselves as in the past. They were probably different pigeons, but who can tell them apart?

It suddenly occurred to me that I had nowhere to go, no one to see. Except that I had to arrange for a funeral oration. They'd be having their midday break at the Academy, and what then, what afterwards? Here I was with a medicine I had no use for, all round me people were hurrying whom I had no use for either. My net was suddenly swinging, a few threads snapped, and below me I saw darkness.

My daughter told me about her dream of the end of the world. She was walking through a landscape with her husband, it seemed a vast expanse, bordered only by the horizon. It was clear day. Suddenly the light began to turn yellow, until it was sulphurous, and at that moment the left part of the horizon began to move towards the right part, and as the two parts approached one another the light faded, it was getting dark, and the earth started

211

trembling. The two of them lay down side by side, closed their eyes and began to pray: Shema Yisrael Adonai elohenu Adonai ekhad. When they opened their eyes again she saw above her the entire universe and in it our sun with its planets, including our earth and the moon. Whoever had seen this, she realised, could no longer be alive. She also realised that no life was left on earth. The horizons collided, the land masses burst and the waters flooded everything. Just then she noticed that among the planets a large fiery-red sharp-edged gambler's die was orbiting, and also revolving, so she could watch the white dots on its sides, and she wondered who had cast the die, whether it had been the humans themselves or the Eternal Holy One, blessed be his name!

I walked round the palace and entered the little square. I walked over the familiar uneven pavement and pushed the heavy door open. In the hallway I was surrounded by a familiar smell. I climbed the wooden stairs. Waving on a line were nappies, the nappies of some new child. Anyway, I never even saw the child, I had no eyes for her. But the roof of the monastery rose up as before, in so far as it is possible to say that anything can be the same at two different moments in time, and I climbed on towards the attic. The door was adorned on the outside by a poster which used to be there, but the smell of oil and gas still came through all the cracks. The name by the bell-push meant nothing to me.

I didn't ring. There was no point in it. Even if I'd been able to ring a bell into the past, and she really appeared at the door, what would I say to her? I didn't have a single sentence prepared, not a single new sentence.

In front of the building stood a small group of tourists, gazing with appropriate interest at the wall of the palace. What can they see there, what can they feel? These walls do not speak to them, they don't remind them of a single breath, of a single cry or a shed tear. After all, I had something that they didn't.

Slowly I drifted along the little streets, roughly by the same route that my beloved Franz Kafka would take to the Castle.

What used to fascinate me most about literature at one time

was that fantasy knows no frontiers, that it is as infinite as the universe into which we may fall. I used to think that this was what fascinated and attracted me in Kafka. For him a human would be transformed into an animal and an animal into a human, dream seemed to be reality for him and, simultaneously, reality was a dream. From his books there spoke a mystery which excited me.

Later I was to understand that there is nothing more mysterious, nothing more fantastic, than life itself. Whoever exalts himself above it, whoever isn't content with horrors already reached and passions already experienced, must sooner or later reveal himself as a false diver who, out of fear of what he might discover in the depths, descends no further than into a solidly built basement.

Kafka, too, did not portray anything but the reality of his own life. He presented himself as an animal, or he lay down on his bed in his cleverly constructed murdering machine to punish himself for his guilt. He felt guilty about his inability to love, or at least to love the way he wanted to. He was unable to love his father or to come together with a woman. He knew that in his longing for honesty he resembled a flier and his life a flight under an infinite sky, where a flier is always lonely and longs in vain for human contact. The longer he flies the more his soul is weighed down by guilt and forced down towards the ground. The flier can jettison his soul and continue his flight without it – or crash. He crashed, but for a moment at least he managed to rise from the ashes in order, second by second, movement by movement, to describe his fall.

Like everyone who hangs on for a moment above the abyss, or who has risen from the ashes and realises how tenuous his net is, Kafka was purged of anger and hate just as his language was of superfluous words. Kafka's soul was pure, marked only by one passion: a longing for human contact, for understanding. Kafka never spoke about literature, such talk seemed to him superfluous and too self-evident. Literature to him was principally a meeting place, space where a person encountered not events, not the products of fantasy, not wisdom of God, but human beings. The author is already standing on the edge of the black hole, yet he still longs to look into another's eyes in truth and in love, to speak to him in a language which his fall has cleansed of all hatreds and superfluous words.

Anyone longing to become a writer, for even a few moments of his life, will vainly weave fantastic events unless he has experienced that fall during which he doesn't know where or whether it will come to an end, and unless his longing for human contact awakens in him the strength to rise, purged, from the ashes.

A tension was growing in me, tearing up my thoughts. I needed to do something – to talk, to shout, to cry, to write something, at least to chalk up on the wall the names of those I shall never see again.

I was passing a baker's shop from which the smell of sweet rolls wafted out. These rolls were baked only at this bakery, a little way from the stone bridge, a little way from our palace. The last time I was in there to buy some was the day before I started street-sweeping. Then, as I entered the bakery, I was racked by longing, I was afraid that the time when I was granted the grace of human contact was coming to an end, and I saw only the edge of the precipice before me. My greatest fear was that I had dragged her to that abyss with me.

I walked on to the end of the bridge and leaned against the stone parapet. Below me, above a little ornamental balcony, was the picture of the Virgin Mary which was said to have been carried here on the waves of a great flood. By my side stood Brokoff's Turk, with his many-buttoned doublet and with a dog guarding his Christian prisoners, above him the three founders of the Order of the Holy Trinity. Observe, darling, how most of the life is in the dog and in the Turk; animals and heathens have no prescribed gestures, they're alive, they aren't saints. Saintliness doesn't belong to life, it was invented by various cripples who were unable, or afraid, to live and therefore wanted to torture those who knew how to live.

The sun was bright on the roofs of the houses and the almost

214

bare branches of the horse-chestnuts cast a filigree of shadows on the ground. From the bridge came the discontinuous click of footfalls. I thought I could even hear the hum of the weir.

I tore myself away from the parapet. Time was moving on and I had to find a funeral speaker. I cast one last glance down into the neighbourhood where we had sometimes walked together to the nearby park, and just then I saw her. I couldn't, from my height, make out her face clearly, but I recognised her hurried, life-hungry way of walking. I looked after her, I followed her with my eyes as she passed under the arch of the bridge. I could have let her lose herself again in the distance from which she'd appeared, but I ran down the stairs, caught up with her and uttered her name.

She stopped. For a while she stared at me as if I were an apparition. 'Where have you sprung from?' she asked, the blood rushing into her face.

I tried to explain that I'd got a drug for someone but that that person had vanished from the surface of the earth, in fact not even his former woman friend knew where I might find him.

'Yes,' she agreed, 'one instant a person's here, and the next instant it's as if he'd never existed!' She looked at me. How many reproaches did she have prepared for this moment? Or was she, on the contrary, about to persuade me that I'd made a mistake, that I'd betrayed myself?

'What about your Dad?' she asked instead. 'I prayed for him,' she said when I told her, and simultaneously her eyes embraced and gently kissed me.

That day came back to me. She was sitting with me in the hospital waiting room, then we walked out, snow was falling. Suddenly I felt the touch of time, the time on the far side of the thin wall, she came to me then, the person I loved, the person I loved as much as I knew how to. I used to wait for her impatiently and patiently, with longing and with fear, I waited for her with anxiety and with hope.

I quickly asked about her daughter and about her work.

Just like me, she said, I was more interested in her work than in her. But she wasn't doing anything at the moment. She'd discovered the joys of laziness. Sometimes she'd read the cards for friends or she'd botch up some figure from her dreams. Some of them still bore my likeness.

We walked along the little streets where we used to walk so often, and as always she talked to me as we walked. In the summer she'd made the acquaintance of an old woman herbalist and had got a lot of recipes from her. For days on end she'd collected and dried herbs – besides, what was she to do with her time when I hadn't been in touch even once? If I was ever in pain or if my soul felt heavy I might phone her: she could mix me a tisane – I obviously wasn't interested in anything else.

We stopped at the edge of the park. I still had to find a funeral speaker. 'You've never ceased to exist for me!'

She could have asked, as she'd done before, what good that was to her, or what use, or she could have complained about the sorrow I'd caused her, about how I'd hurt her. But she didn't wish to torment me at that moment. She only said: 'That's good!' And she added: 'Maybe our souls will meet somewhere. We'll meet in some future life. Provided you don't find an excuse at the last moment.' We briefly embraced and kissed goodbye, and she walked away at her hurried pace.

I couldn't move. I didn't even tell her that I'd never intended to hurt her, nor did I ask her if she understood that I hadn't done anything against her, that it was just that I was unable to return to her in this halfway manner, to be a little and to not be a little, I can only honestly be or honestly not be – like herself.

She stopped at the corner. She looked back, and when she saw me at the spot where she'd left me her hand rose up like the wing of a featherless little bird and from the distance touched my forehead.

At last I moved.

On the path that went to the bank of the Čertovka stream a few figures were busying themselves in their familiar orange vests. With slow, seemingly weary movements, the movements I knew so well, they were sweeping the withered leaves into small heaps.

Down there we stood and kissed in a long embrace.

A fine thing! A fine thing!

It occurred to me that I put on that orange vest for a time because I was longing for a cleansing. Man longs for a cleansing but instead he starts cleaning up his surroundings. But until man cleanses himself he's wasting his time cleaning up the world around him.

In the middle of the swept path lay the brownish lobed leaf of a horse-chestnut. Perhaps they'd overlooked it or perhaps it had just sailed down from above. I picked it up and for a while studied its wrinkled veins. The leaf trembled in my fingers as if it were alive.

I was still full of that unexpected meeting.

People search for images of paradise and cannot find anything other than objects from this world.

But paradise cannot be fixed in an image, for paradise is the state of meeting. With God, and also with humans. What matters, of course, is that the meeting should take place in cleanliness.

Paradise is, above all else, the state in which the soul feels clean.

September 1983–July 1986